Perspectives on Sexuality

The Lovers by René Magritte.

Perspectives on Sexuality

A Literary Collection

James L. Malfetti
Teacher's College, Columbia University

Elizabeth M. Eidlitz

HOLT, RINEHART AND WINSTON, INC.
New York Chicago San Francisco Atlanta Dallas Montreal Toronto

Acknowledgments

For the materials copyrighted by authors, publishers, and agents, the editors are indebted to the following:

AMERICA   for Robert O. Johann, S. J., in *America* 113 (1965):404. Reprinted by permission of America • for "The New Morality" by Thomas A. Wassmer in *America* (February 10, 1968) © *America*, National Catholic Weekly, New York, N.Y. 10019 • for "Modern Morals in a Muddle" by Richard A. McCormick in *America* (July 30, 1966) © *America*, National Catholic Weekly, New York, N.Y. 10019.

AMERICAN MERCURY   for "Chastity on the Campus," in *American Mercury*, 1938, Vol. 44, pp. 175–180. Reprinted by permission of American Mercury.

ASSOCIATION PRESS   for *Love and the Facts of Life* by Evelyn Duvall. Reprinted by permission of Association Press • for "A Moral Philosophy of Sex," by Joseph Fletcher, in *Sex and Religion Today*, edited by Simon Doniger. © Association Press, 1953. Used by permission.

BALLANTINE BOOKS, INC.   for "Girl Walking" by Charles G. Bell from *New Poems by American Poets*, No. 2, edited by Rolfe Humphries. Copyright © 1957 by Ballantine Books, Inc. Reprinted by permission of Ballantine Books, Inc.

BARTON MUSIC CORP.   for "Love and Marriage" by Sammy Cahn and James Van Heusen. Reprinted by permission of Barton Music Corp.

RODERICK G. BATES   for "They Laugh" by Ricky Bates, an unpublished poem. Reprinted by permission of Roderick G. Bates.

PAUL BLACKBURN   for "The Once-Over," © copyright Paul Blackburn, 1960. Reprinted by permission of Paul Blackburn.

GEOFFREY BLES LTD.   for *The Pilgrim's Regress* by C. S. Lewis. Reprinted by permission of Geoffrey Bles Ltd.

CURTIS BROWN LTD.   for excerpt from "Conduct and Work" by Donald Hall. Reprinted by permission of Curtis Brown, Ltd. Copyright © 1955 by Donald Hall • for "Eros" in *The Four Loves* by C. S. Lewis. Reprinted in Canada by permission of Curtis Brown, Ltd. • for 'The Symposium" by Plato. From *Ion, and Four Other Dialogues*. Reprinted in Canada by permission of Curtis Brown, Ltd., London.

JONATHAN CAPE LTD.   for *Too Late the Phalarope* by Alan Paton. Reprinted by permission of Jonathan Cape Ltd., publishers • for *In the Orchard* by Muriel Stuart. Reprinted by permission of the Estate of Muriel Stuart and Jonathan Cape Ltd., publishers.

CHAPPELL & CO., INC.   for "I Cain't Say No" (from *Oklahoma*). Copyright © 1943 by Williamson Music, Inc. Used by permission of Williamson Music, Inc. • for "I Enjoy Being a Girl" (from *Flower Drum Song*). Copyright © 1958 by Richard Rodgers and Oscar Hammerstein, II. Used by permission of Williamson Music, Inc. • for "Much More" (from *The Fantasticks*). Copyright © 1960 & 1963 by Tom Jones and Harvey Schmidt. Used by permission of Chappell & Co., Inc.

CHILD STUDY ASSOCIATION OF AMERICA, INC.   for excerpts from *Sex Education and the New Morality*. Copyright © 1967 by the Child Study Association of America, Inc.

COLLINS-KNOWLTON-WING, INC.   for *Real Women* by Robert Graves. Reprinted by permission of Collins-Knowlton-Wing, Inc. Copyright © 1962, 1963, 1964, 1965 by Robert Graves • for *Woman and Tree* by Robert Graves. Reprinted by permission of Collins-Knowlton-Wing, Inc. Copyright © 1958 by Robert Graves.

WILLIAM DICKEY   for "Resolving Doubts" by William Dickey, *Saturday Review*, March 10, 1962. Reprinted by permission of William Dickey.

DODD, MEAD & COMPANY, INC.   for *Through the First Gate* by John Craig Stewart. Reprinted by permission of Dodd, Mead & Company, Inc.

DOUBLEDAY & COMPANY, INC.   from *Marlene Dietrich's ABC*, Copyright © 1961, 1962 by Marlene Dietrich. Reprinted by permission of Doubleday & Company, Inc. • from *Anne Frank, The Diary of a Young Girl*. Copyright 1952 by Otto H. Frank. Reprinted by permission of Doubleday & Company, Inc., and Vallentine, Mitchell & Co., on behalf of Otto Frank • for "The Female of the Species," Copyright 1911 by Rudyard Kipling. From *Rudyard Kipling's Verse* • for "Ars Poetica," by X. J. Kennedy. Copyright 1961 by X. J. Kennedy. From the book *Nude Descending a Staircase*. Reprinted by permission of Doubleday & Company, Inc. • from *Of Human Bondage* by W. Somerset Maugham. Copyright 1915 by Doubleday & Company, Inc. Used by permission of the publisher • for "The Gift of the Magi" by O. Henry. From *The Four Million* by O. Henry. Reprinted by permission of Doubleday & Company, Inc.

• "Part of Plenty," by Bernard Spencer. Copyright 1946 by Bernard Spencer. From the book *Aegean Islands* by Bernard Spencer. Reprinted by permission of Doubleday & Company, Inc. • from *Marjorie Morningstar*. Copyright © 1955 by Herman Wouk. Reprinted by permission of Doubleday & Company, Inc., and Herman Wouk.

E. P. DUTTON & CO., INC.   for "The Symposium" by Plato. From the book *Ion, and Four Other Dialogues* by Plato. Everyman's Library Edition • from the book *Sex before Twenty* by Helen F. Southard. Copyright, ©, 1967 by Helen F. Southard. Reprinted by permission of E. P. Dutton & Co., Inc.

NORMA MILLAY ELLIS   from Sonnet XXVI ("Love Is Not Blind") by Edna St. Vincent Millay. *Collected Poems*, Harper & Row. Copyright 1923, 1951 by Edna St. Vincent Millay and Norma Millay Ellis • for Sonnet XXIX ("Pity Me Not") and "Recuerdo" by Edna St. Vincent Millay. From *Collected Poems*, Harper & Row. Copyright 1917, 1922, 1923, 1944, 1950, 1951 by Edna St. Vincent Millay and Norma Millay Ellis.

ANN ELMO AGENCY, INC.   for *Death of a Hero* by Richard Aldington. Reprinted by permission of Ann Elmo Agency, Inc. • for "Philander Musing" by Judson Jerome. By permission of Judson Jerome and The Ann Elmo Agency, Inc. Copyright © 1959 by Harper's Magazine, Inc. Reprinted from the March 1959 issue of Harper's Magazine by permission of the author.

ENCOUNTER   for "Das Liebesleben" by Thom Gunn, *Encounter*, March 1961. Reprinted by permission of Encounter and Thom Gunn.

ESQUIRE, INC.   for "Snowfall in Childhood" by Ben Hecht. Reprinted by permission of Esquire Magazine. © 1934 (renewed 1962) by Esquire, Inc.

FABER AND FABER LIMITED   for an extract from "Are You There?" and "That Night When Joy Began" by W. H. Auden. Reprinted in Canada by permission of Faber and Faber Ltd. from *Collected Poems 1927–1957* • for "Carnal Knowledge" by Thom Gunn. Reprinted by permission of Faber and Faber Ltd. from *Fighting Terms* by Thom Gunn • for "Circe" and "Trilogy for X" by Louis MacNeice. Reprinted in Canada by permission of Faber and Faber Ltd. from *The Collected Poems of Louis MacNeice*.

IRVING FINEMAN   for "Spelling Lesson" by Irving Fineman. Reprinted by permission of Irving Fineman.

FRANK MUSIC CORP. AND RINIMER CORPORATION   for "The Sadder-But-Wiser Girl for Me" by Meredith Willson. © 1957 Frank Music Corp. and Rinimer Corporation. Used by permission.

ELAINE GREENE LTD.   for "Difficulty with a Bouquet" by William Sansom from *The Stories of William Sansom* published by The Hogarth Press, London, © William Sansom 1963. Reprinted in Canada by permission of William Sansom through his agents, Elaine Greene Ltd.

GROVE PRESS, INC.   for "The One-Night Stand: An Approach to the Bridge" by Paul Blackburn. from *The Cities* by Paul Blackburn. Reprinted by permission of Grove Press, Inc. Copyright © 1967 by Paul Blackburn.

HARCOURT BRACE JOVANOVICH, INC.   for extract from "because it's" by E. E. Cummings, © 1963 by Marion Morehouse Cummings. Excerpted from "because it's" in 73 POEMS by E. E. Cummings by permission of Harcourt Brace Jovanovich, Inc. • for "if everything happens that can't be done" by E. E. Cummings. Copyright, 1944, by E. E. Cummings. Reprinted from his volume *Poems 1923–1954* by permission of Harcourt Brace Jovanovich, Inc. • for "i like my body when it is with your" and "when i have thought of you somewhat too" by E. E. Cummings. Copyright, 1925, by E. E. Cummings. Reprinted from his volume *Poems 1923–1954* by permission of Harcourt Brace Jovanovich, Inc. • for "may i feel said he" by E. E. Cummings. Copyright, 1935, by E. E. Cummings; copyright, 1963, by Marion Morehouse Cummings. Reprinted from *Poems 1923–1954* by E. E. Cummings by permission of Harcourt Brace Jovanovich, Inc. • for "somewhere i have never travelled" by E. E. Cummings. Copyright, 1931, 1959, by E. E. Cummings. Reprinted from his volume *Poems 1923–1954* by permission of Harcourt Brace Jovanovich, Inc. • for "Sex Education" by Dorothy Canfield Fisher. Copyright, 1945, by Dorothy Canfield Fisher. Reprinted from her volume *A Harvest of Stories* by permission of Harcourt Brace Jovanovich, Inc. • excerpted from "Eros" in *The Four Loves* by C. S. Lewis, © 1960 by Helen Joy Lewis. Reprinted by permission of Harcourt Brace Jovanovich Inc. • for *The Steep Ascent* by Anne Morrow Lindbergh. Reprinted by permission of Harcourt Brace Jovanovich, Inc. • for "The Downward Path to Wisdom" by Katherine Anne Porter. Copyright, 1939, 1967, by Katherine Anne Porter. Reprinted from her volume *The Leaning Tower and Other Stories* by permission of Harcourt Brace Jovanovich, Inc. • for *The Little Prince (Le Petit Prince)* by Antoine de Saint-Exupery. Reprinted by permission of Harcourt Brace Jovanovich, Inc. • for "Honey and Salt," "Kisses, Can You Come Back Like Ghosts?" and "One Parting," by Carl Sandburg. © 1963 by Carl Sandburg. Reprinted from his volume *Honey and Salt* by permission of Harcourt Brace Jovanovich, Inc. • for "Solo for Saturday Night Guitar" by Carl Sandburg. © 1958 by Carl Sandburg. Reprinted from his volume *Honey and Salt* by permission of Harcourt Brace Jovanovich, Inc.

HARPER & ROW, PUBLISHERS   for "Is Love and Art?" and abridgment of "The Theory of Love" by Erich Fromm. From *The Art of Loving* by Erich Fromm. Copyright © 1956 by Erich Fromm. Reprinted by permission of Harper & Row, Publishers • from pp. 100–104, 175–176 (hardbound edition) *A High Wind in Jamaica* by Richard Hughes. Copyright 1928, 1929 by Richard Hughes; renewed 1956, 1957 by Richard Hughes. Reprinted by permission of Harper & Row, Publishers • for *Do What You Will* by Aldous Huxley. Reprinted by permission of Harper & Row, Publishers • for *Love and Marriage* by F. Alexander Magoun. Reprinted by permission of Harper & Row, Publishers • from pp. 397–398 *A Tree Grows in Brooklyn* by Betty Smith. Copyright 1943, 1947 by Betty Smith. Reprinted by permission of Harper & Row, Publishers • abridged from pp. 12–14, 57–59, 162–164, *Seventeen* by Booth Tarkington. Copyright 1915, 1916 by the Metropolitan Magazine Company; renewed 1943, 1944 by Booth Tarkington. Reprinted by permission of Harper & Row, Publishers • from pp. 137–138 in *The Meaning of Persons* by Paul Tournier. Copyright © 1957 by Paul Tournier. Reprinted by permission of Harper & Row, Publishers, and SCM Press Ltd., London.

HART PUBLISHING COMPANY, INC. for "Sex Attitudes" by A. S. Neill. from *Summerhill: A Radical Approach to Child Rearing* by A. S. Neill, copyright 1960 Hart Publishing Company, New York.

HARVARD UNIVERSITY PRESS for *i: Six Nonlectures* by E. E. Cummings. Reprinted by permission of Harvard University Press.

HILL AND WANG, INC. for "Slowly, Slowly" by Mark Van Doren. From *Collected and New Poems: 1924–1963* by Mark Van Doren. Copyright © 1963 by Mark Van Doren. Reprinted by permission of Hill and Wang, Inc.

HOLT, RINEHART AND WINSTON, INC. from *The Bent Twig* by Dorothy Canfield. Copyright 1915 by Holt, Rinehart and Winston, Inc. Copyright 1943 by Dorothy Canfield Fisher. Reprinted by permission of Holt, Rinehart and Winston, Inc. • for "The Greatest Thing in the World" by Henry Drummond from *Treasures of the Kingdom*. Reprinted by permission of Holt, Rinehart and Winston, Inc. • for "Home Burial" by Robert Frost from *Complete Poems of Robert Frost*. Copyright 1931, 1939 by Holt, Rinehart and Winston, Inc. Copyright © 1958 by Robert Frost. Copyright © 1967 by Lesley Frost Ballantine. Reprinted by permission of Holt, Rinehart and Winston, Inc. • for "Look Not in My Eyes, for Fear" and "Oh, When I Was in Love with You" by A. E. Housman. From "A Shropshire Lad"—Authorized Edition—from *The Collected Poems of A. E. Housman*. Copyright 1939, 1940, © 1959 by Holt, Rinehart and Winston, Inc. Copyright © 1967, 1968 by Robert E. Symons. Reprinted by permission of Holt, Rinehart and Winston, Inc. • from "The Woman on the Stair" from *Public Speech* by Archibald MacLeish. Copyright 1936, © 1964 by Archibald MacLeish. Reprinted by permission of Holt, Rinehart and Winston, Inc. • from *Jean-Christophe* by Romain Rolland. Translated by Gilbert Cannan. Copyright 1910, 1911, 1913, 1938, 1939, 1941 by Holt, Rinehart and Winston, Inc. Reprinted by permission of Holt, Rinehart and Winston, Inc., and William Heinemann, Ltd.

HOUGHTON MIFFLIN COMPANY for "Winter Term" from *The Touching Hand* by Sallie Bingham. Copyright © 1967 by Sallie Bingham. Reprinted by permission of the publisher, Houghton Mifflin Company. This article originally appeared in *Mademoiselle* Magazine, copyright © 1958 by Sallie Bingham • for "Merrymakers" by Walter Clemons from *The Poison Tree and Other Stories*. Copyright © 1959 by Walter Clemons, Jr. Reprinted by permission of the publisher, Houghton Mifflin Company • for "A Decade" and "Apology" by Amy Lowell. From *The Complete Poetical Works of Amy Lowell*. Reprinted by permission of Houghton Mifflin Company • for *The Heart is a Lonely Hunter* by Carson McCullers. Copyright 1940 by Carson McCullers. Reprinted by permission of the publisher, Houghton Mifflin Company • for *The Member of the Wedding* by Carson McCullers. Reprinted by permission of Houghton Mifflin Company • for *The Happy Marriage* by Archibald MacLeish. Reprinted by permission of Houghton Mifflin Company.

THE HUMANIST The article "Searching for the Roots of Moral [Judgments] Decisions" by Lester A. Kirkendall first appeared in *The Humanist*, January/February 1967, and is reprinted by permission.

INTERNATIONAL FAMOUS AGENCY, INC. for "First Love and Other Sorrows" by Harold Brodkey, originally published in The New Yorker. Reprinted by permission of Harold Brodkey c/o International Famous Agency. Copyright © 1957 by Harold Brodkey • for *The City of Trembling Leaves* by Walter Van Tilburg Clark. Reprinted by permission of International Famous Agency. Copyright © 1945 by Walter Van Tilburg Clark.

LEA AND FEBIGER for "Some Observations on Sexual Morality" by Warren R. Johnson.

LAURIE LEE for "What Love Must Be" by Laurie Lee. Reprinted by permission of Laurie Lee.

LITTLE, BROWN AND COMPANY Copyright 1930, 1958 by Rudolf Besier, from *The Barretts of Wimpole Street* by Rudolf Besier, by permission of Little, Brown and Co. • for "The Figures on the Frieze" by Alastair Reid. Copyright © 1963 by Alastair Reid, originally appeared in The New Yorker. From *Passwords* by Alastair Reid, by permission of Atlantic-Little, Brown and Co. • for "Difficulty with a Bouquet" by William Sansom. Copyright © 1963 by William Sansom. From *The Stories of William Sansom* by William Sansom, by permission of Atlantic-Little, Brown and Co.

THE MACMILLAN COMPANY reprinted with permission of The Macmillan Company from *Manchild in the Promised Land* by Claude Brown. Copyright © by Claude Brown, 1965 • reprinted with permission of The Macmillan Company from *Love and Orgasm* by Alexander Lowen, M.D. Copyright © by Alexander Lowen, M.D., 1965 • for "Wax" by Winfield Townley Scott. Reprinted with permission of The Macmillan Company from *Scrimshaw* by Winfield Townley Scott. Copyright © by Winfield Townley Scott, 1959.

NICHOLAS MOORE for "Fred Apollus at Fava's" by Nicholas Moore, of Trinity College, Cambridge, England. Reprinted by permission of Nicholas Moore.

HOWARD MOSS for "Rain" by Howard Moss, as appeared in *A Swimmer in the Air* published by Charles Scribner's Sons, 1957, copyright Howard Moss. Reprinted by permission of Howard Moss.

THE NATION for "A Problem in Morals" by Howard Moss, as appeared in *The Nation*, June 1, 1957. Reprinted by permission of The Nation.

NEW DIRECTIONS PUBLISHING CORPORATION for "That Sensual Phosphorescence" (Poem 26), "See It Was Like This When" (Poem 9), and "We Squat upon the Beach of Love" (Poem 24) by Lawrence Ferlinghetti. Lawrence Ferlinghetti, *A Coney Island of the Mind*. Copyright © 1957 by Lawrence Ferlinghetti. Reprinted by permission of New Directions Publishing Corporation. • for "The Wife" by Denise Levertov. Denise Levertov, *With Eyes at the Back of Our Heads*. Copyright © 1959 by Denise Levertov Goodman. Reprinted by permission of New Directions Publishing Corporation • for "Twenty-third Street Runs into Heaven" and "As We Are So Wonderfully Done with Each Other" by Kenneth Patchen. Kenneth Patchen, *Collected Poems*. Copyright 1939, 1942 by New Directions Publishing Corporation. Reprinted by permission of New Directions Publishing Corporation • for "Homage to Sextus Propertius," by Ezra Pound. Ezra Pound, *Personae*. Copyright 1926 by Ezra Pound. Reprinted by permission of New Directions Publishing Corporation • for "The Advantages of Learning" by Kenneth Rexroth. Kenneth Rexroth,

Collected Shorter Poems. Copyright 1944 by New Directions Publishing Corporation. Reprinted by permission of New Directions Publishing Corporation • for "Escapist's Song" by Theodore Spencer. Theodore Spencer, *The Paradox in the Circle.* Copyright 1941 New Directions. Reprinted by permission of New Directions Publishing Corporation.

THE NEW YORK TIMES for "Death Wish," © 1967 by The New York Times Company. Reprinted by permission • for "Little Brother Comes to America" by Barbara W. Wyden. © 1967 by The New York Times Company. Reprinted by permission.

THE NEW YORKER MAGAZINE, INC. for "Gather" by Michael Dennis Browne. Reprinted by permission; © 1969 The New Yorker Magazine, Inc.

W. W. NORTON & COMPANY, INC. reprinted from *Identity, Youth and Crisis* by Erik H. Erikson. By permission of W. W. Norton & Company, Inc. Copyright © 1968 by W. W. Norton & Company, Inc.

OXFORD UNIVERSITY PRESS, INC. for "Circe" and "Trilogy for X" by Louis MacNeice. From *The Collected Poems of Louis MacNeice,* edited by E. R. Dodds. Copyright © The Estate of Louis MacNeice 1966. Reprinted by permission of Oxford University Press, Inc.

PENGUIN BOOKS LTD. for *Logic and Sexual Morality* by John Wilson. Reprinted by permission of Penguin Books Ltd.

PHI DELTA KAPPA PUBLICATIONS for "The Pill" by Ashley Montagu, *Phi Delta Kappan,* May 1968. Reprinted by permission of Phi Delta Kappa Publications.

PLAYBOY for excerpts from "The Playboy Philosophy" by Hugh M. Hefner (*Playboy,* Vol. 10, No. 5, May 1963) used by special permission; copyright © 1963 by HMH Publishing Co. Inc.

LAURENCE POLLINGER LIMITED for Llewelyn Powys, *The Glory of Life,* published by The Bodley Head Limited. Acknowledgment is given to Malcolm Elwin the Literary Executor and biographer of Llewelyn Powys.

PRENTICE-HALL, INC. for *The Sex Game* by Jessie Bernard. Reprinted by permission of Prentice-Hall, Inc.

RANDOM HOUSE, INC. ALFRED A. KNOPF, INC. for "That Night When Joy Began" by W. H. Auden. Copyright 1937 and renewed 1965 by W. H. Auden • for an extract from "Are You There" by W. H. Auden. Copyright 1941 and renewed 1969 by W. H. Auden. Reprinted from *Collected Shorter Poems 1927–1957* by W. H. Auden. By permission of Random House, Inc. • for "Entry August 29" and "Entry November 12" by Walter Benton. From *This Is My Beloved* by Walter Benton. Copyright 1943 by Alfred A. Knopf, Inc. Reprinted by permission of the publisher • from *The Well of Days* by Ivan Bunin. Published 1934 by Alfred A. Knopf, Inc. Reprinted by permission of the publisher • for *Studies in the Psychology of Sex* by Havelock Ellis. Reprinted by permission of Random House, Inc. • from *Growing Up Absurd,* by Paul Goodman. Copyright © 1960 by Paul Goodman. Reprinted by permission of Random House, Inc. • from *A Raisin in the Sun,* by Lorraine Hansberry. Copyright © 1958, 1959 by Robert Nemiroff as Executor of the Estate of Lorraine Hansberry. Reprinted by permission of Random House, Inc. • for "Double-Sunrise" and "Oyster Bed" by Anne Morrow Lindbergh. Exercepts from *Gift from the Sea,* by Anne Morrow Lindbergh. Copyright © 1965 by Anne Morrow Lindbergh. Reprinted by permission of Pantheon Books, A Division of Random House, Inc. • for "Psyche with the Candle" and "The Rape of the Swan" by Archibald MacLeish. Copyright 1948 by Archibald MacLeish. Reprinted from *Actfive and Other Poems,* by Archibald MacLeish, by permission of Random House, Inc. • for "When in My Arms" by Alexander Pushkin. Copyright 1936 and renewed 1964 by Random House, Inc. Reprinted from *The Poems, Prose and Plays of Alexander Pushkin,* ed. by Avrahm Yarmolinsky, by permission of the publisher • from *The Nature of Love: Plato to Luther,* by Irving Singer. Copyright © 1966 by Irving Singer. Reprinted by permission of Random House, Inc. • for "The Confirmation" by Karl Shapiro. Copyright 1942 by Karl Shapiro. Reprinted from *Selected Poems,* by Karl Shapiro, by permission of Random House, Inc. • for "A Lodging for the Night" by Elinor Wylie. From *Last Poems of Elinor Wylie,* Copyright 1943 by Alfred A. Knopf, Inc. Reprinted by permission of Alfred A. Knopf, Inc. • for "I Hereby Swear" (Sonnet XVI) by Elinor Wylie. Copyright 1929 by Alred A. Knopf, Inc. and renewed 1957 by Edwina C. Rubenstein. Reprinted from *Collected Poems,* by Elinor Wylie, by permission of the publisher • from *Portnoy's Complaint,* by Philip Roth. Copyright © 1967, 1968, 1969, by Philip Roth. Reprinted by permission of Random House, Inc. • from *Rabbit, Run,* by John Updike. Copyright © 1960 by John Updike. Reprinted by permission of Alfred A. Knopf, Inc.

VIRGINIA RICE "Parma Violets" and "The Dawn of Hate" from *Things as They Are* by Paul Horgan. Reprinted by permission of Virginia Rice. Copyright © 1951, 1963, © 1964 by Paul Horgan.

THE RYERSON PRESS for "The Collector" by Raymond Souster. Reprinted from *The Colour of the Times* by Raymond Souster, by permission of The Ryerson Press, Toronto.

JOHN C. SAMUELSON for "a stream of consciousness" by John C. Samuelson. This poem first appeared in *The Sextant* (June 1969), a publication of Belmont Hill School, Belmont, Mass.

WILLIAM SAROYAN for *Romance* by William Saroyan. Reprinted with the permission of William Saroyan.

SATURDAY REVIEW, INC. for "Plaque for a Brass Bed" by Charles Philbrick, *Saturday Review,* November 9, 1968. Copyright 1968 Saturday Review, Inc. Reprinted by permission of Charles Philbrick and Saturday Review, Inc.

VERNON SCANNELL for "Act of Love" by Vernon Scannell. Reprinted by permission of Vernon Scannell.

JOHN SCHAFFNER for *The Book of True Love* by Jean Ruiz, translated by Hubert Creekmore and published by Random House, Inc. Reprinted by permission of John Schaffner, Literary Agent.

CHARLES SCRIBNER'S SONS reprinted with the permission of Charles Scribner's Sons from *A Night of Watching,* pages 13–20, by Elliott Arnold. Copyright © 1967 Elliott Arnold • "The Crisis" and "A Marriage" (Copyright © 1961 Robert Creeley) are reprinted with the permission of Charles Scribner's Sons from *For Love* by Robert Creeley. Copyright © 1962 Robert Creeley • for *Candelabra: Selected*

Preface

M EMBERS of each generation must work out their own sexual destinies. Young persons should be free to choose appropriately, and for their own good reasons, among the sexual alternatives available to them. When "sex problems" first attracted the professional interest of the present editors, there was a noticeable shortage of reliable material about sexual development and behavior. There is no such shortage today. Now the young person's task is to extract what is personally valid and relevant from a mass of information, to separate myth from meaning, and to construct a reality that he can support intellectually and emotionally. *Perspectives on Sexuality* is directed toward that end.

The primary objective of this book of readings, therefore, is to widen the perspectives from which sex and decisions relating to it may be viewed. The many facets of sexuality portrayed in this book encourage examination of one's personal attitudes and behavior as well as those of the characters and societies represented.

Selections have been drawn from a wide range of sources including novels, short stories, plays, poems, essays, songs, advertisements, graphics, and scholarly articles. They are relevant to the questions asked by young—and even not so young—people about sexual behavior. Their concrete, dramatic details of universal human experience are depicted in the context of daily living, and explode with implications about the emotional spectrum recognized by poets, playwrights, and novelists who suggest rather than state, illustrate rather than tell.

No selection pretends to be comprehensive or absolutely definitive, yet each adds a dimension to the central concern of sexuality and aims to provoke reflection, dialogue, and questioning. While the contents of this book are premised and oriented to choices of sex standards, they are further and deliberately intended to strengthen an awareness of man's power not only to create conflicts about sex but also to resolve them.

The more than 200 selections included have been grouped into five parts: "I," "They," "You-I," "We," and "Night-Lights." Discussion questions, which follow each selection in the first four parts, include frequent cross-references to minimize the arbitrary dividing line between the parts. The related questions also utilize the methods of comparison and contrast to clarify and expand the reader's point of view. All selections in "Night-Lights" have been cited in questions connected with previous selections, thus weaving in related perspectives to provide opportunities for re-encounter from several vantage points.

Although most of the selections reflect at least some degree of literary quality, they were chosen for other reasons: their relevance to the questions young persons ask; their readability; their emotional appeal to young persons; their discussion potential; and the possibility of broadening perspectives, and thus for their contribution toward helping man to understand himself and others, assuming that "human improvement is from within outwards."

The first four parts parallel human psychosexual development:

1. "I"   deals with physical development from birth through puberty and the seeking of self-gratification through others. The discussion questions accompanying the selections review the reproductive facts, for both male and female, and consider sexual self-awareness. Most of the selections depict adolescents. The final two readings, however, viewing the limitations of an "I"-orientation as an end in itself rather than a means, show that intense sexual preoccupation is not restricted to youth.

2. "They"   presents conditioning forces in the environment encountered by the growing individual: peers, parents, public prejudice, the press, as well as views of poets, professors, and philosophers. The part exhibits a range of conflicting attitudes, thus encouraging the individual to crystallize and identify his own.

3. "You–I"   shows how sexual acts and relationships can convey a wide gamut of intentions and messages, presenting sex as a purely playful activity, a way to have babies, an expression of hostility, a duty, an outlet from tension, a protection against alienation, a form of "togetherness," a punishment, a reward, an act of rebellion, a form of self-aggrandizement, a deceit and exploitation.

4. "We"   includes selections depicting respect for individuality and its contribution to maximum mutual satisfaction. "We" deals with discovery of the "we" of "me." Without experiencing a loss of identity, each partner here has found—whether in or out of marriage—the meaning of "we" being "wonderful one times one." Stressed in this section are: the building of attitudes and feelings that might sustain a human being in the contemporary world; the examination of words such as "like," "cherish," and "affection" as descriptions of one's genuine human feeling in relation to other persons; the relationship, if any, between love and sex in human intercourse—the ability to put sex in the context of a touch-embrace, not a touch-and-go relationship; and the fact that not one meaning of love is true and valid for all, but rather many meanings, each one of which can and must be explored for its own truth and validity.

5. **"Night-Lights"** comprises selections that have been correlated with one or more readings elsewhere in the book, but which can be looked at singly as well. Many of them not only show more than one perspective or reinforce some of the ideas presented in the **"They"** section, but also supply answers to questions asked by young adults during the development of this manuscript.

These selections, like the others, were chosen in line with Galsworthy's sentiment, which introduces this final section:

> . . . if it were not for the physical side of love we should none of us be here, and the least sophisticated of us knows intuitively . . . much about it. . . . But the atmosphere and psychology of passion are other matters, and the trackless maze in which the average reader wanders where his feelings are concerned is none the worse for a night-light or two.

J. L. M.
E. M. E.

Editors' Notes

W E recommend that the "I," "They," "You-I," and "We" parts, as well as the selections within each part, be read in sequence. The discussion questions following each selection sometimes refer to situations and characters in selections that have preceded it. The exceptions are selections from "**Night-Lights.**" When discussion questions refer ahead to a selection from this part, the reader should interrupt the sequence to follow the comparison or contrast.

There are no "right" or "wrong" answers to the discussion questions. They are more nearly stimuli; the answers they provoke might be more accurately termed responses. The questions are sometimes ambiguously phrased and open-ended. Material in one question may suggest possible answers to another. The important thing is the process by which you arrive thoughtfully at your own conclusions, discovering why they are valid for you. Convictions, if they are to hold up—and to hold you up—are formulated by knowing why and where and with what you agree or disagree and by choosing among alternatives. Usually convictions are strengthened, not threatened, by exposure to opposing views.

Since the questions call for opinions, nothing about them can be scored. They arc deliberately comprehensive and their arrangement is somewhat arbitrary; you should feel no obligation to deal with all of them, or to follow them in order. The discussion questions which immediately follow a selection relate specifically to it. Those under the heading "Related Questions" are cross-references to the situations and characters of other selections, and suggest connections for comparing perspectives. The critical connections, however, are the ones you make yourself.

A reader on his own can work out reactions to questions posed here. Or he may profit from the give-and-take of honest controversy—in bull sessions with peers, in family discussions, in religious fellowship groups, or in classrooms. We have faith in the ability of young people—if they are forthrightly presented with the feelings as well as the facts of life, if they are allowed and encouraged to assess openly the attitudes surrounding them—to make honest, responsible, individually meaningful decisions, the only kind which can joyfully sustain them.

Although some selections, or the discussion questions following them, have "built-in" materials which may enlarge one's objective knowledge, the editors assume that the reader has a fairly broad information base and knows how to go about filling in any factual gaps which the text may reveal to him. The selections give priority to feelings, interpersonal relations, and values as they relate to sexual behavior and to love.

It is neither possible nor desirable to agree with each of the perspectives presented in the selections. Deliberately, a wide range of actions and viewpoints has been included. Bawdy limericks, for example, are included not to be "daring," but because they speak candidly as well as metrically or raunchily about aspects of sex that are long overdue for a good airing. And however lofty they may seem by tonal contrast, the creative products of poets, professors, and philosophers are still articulated from their own sexual identities.

We hope that the reader will identify, not only with the characters who share his situation, but with those who make real for him situations that might be his. Because the characters are likely to enact their feelings rather than to state their conclusions, the reader can appreciate their situations emotionally and intellectually; he is involved in the dramatic process as a witness to the scene, rather than having to settle for a second-hand account.

Nevertheless, some of the readings may leave you puzzled, distressed, or bored. Some may strike close, even too close, to home. Some may seem, for this moment—but not perhaps for the next—irrelevant to your concerns. Some may appear difficult to understand, others too obvious. Some may seem so dull they hardly justify skimming, others worth several re-readings.

At the very least, however, the selections illustrate points of view large enough for a variety of tastes and needs. Likemindedness can be reassuring, but it can be dangerous as well when people attribute their own views to others, thus misinterpreting or misunderstanding them.

To derive maximum value from this book keep in mind the advice of Atticus Finch to his daughter in Harper Lee's *To Kill a Mockingbird:* "You never really understand a person until you consider things from his point of view—until you climb into his skin and walk around in it." By changing perspective, you learn that there is a reason for almost everything and a value in it for someone—even for you.

Contents

TOWARD A DEFINITION OF MORALITY

TOWARD A DEFINITION OF MARRIAGE

YOU-I / interrelationships   359

I and you

xx

Contents

Perspectives on Sexuality

"I"

EMERGENCE OF THE SELF

The focus of this first section is on the "I"—an observing center of awareness and of volition—viewed at critical stages of the individual's physiological and psycho-sexual development.

Early selections, such as the photograph of birth and the art work of primary school children, call for discussion of the facts and myths of human birth, understanding of human reproduction, and the nature of the parent-child relationship. To other manifestations of the sexuality which begins at birth, *Parma Violets* adds the illustration of an early form of love "that creates only a self."

Emily, in *A High Wind in Jamaica,* and Anne, in *The Diary of a Young Girl,* present female perspectives on such bodily changes as menstruation and breast development, just as George in *Through the First Gate,* Portnoy in *Portnoy's Complaint,* K. B. in *Manchild in the Promised Land,* and the youth in *The Confirmation* present a variety of attitudes toward comparable changes in the male, preoccupation with masturbation, and the size of the genitals.

Yet more important than the separation of superstition from truth in physiological areas are the psychological implications surrounding them: concepts of masculinity and virility, the need for making exaggerated sexual claims, curiosities and concealments, the meanings of words, and, above all, evidence from sexual awareness and responsiveness of the differences between masculinity and femininity which would seem to refute Montaigne's claim that "both male and female are cast in one same mould; instruction and custom excepted, there is no great difference between them" [1].*

Physical self-awareness, with its special sexual pressures during this period of intensified emotional and instinctive drives, is accompanied by psychological

*The bracketed numbers correspond to the source numbers of each excerpt, which are to be found in the "**Notes,**" p. 595 ff.

3

self-awareness, self-appraisal, and at least some effort to locate one's self in the surrounding world. Questions like "Who am I?," explored by Emily in *A High Wind in Jamaica,* give rise to others: Where do I belong? What do I believe in? What is my value to others and theirs to me? What are my powers? How can and should I use them? Toward what ends? And why?

4

**"I"
emergence of the
self**

Role playing in adolescent love as an attempt to define one's identity can be seen through the clouded lenses of Joan in *Joan and Peter* or through the rose-colored glasses of Willie Baxter in *Seventeen.* But the romantic excesses of those like the sixteen-year-old girl in *The Fantasticks* who sings *Much More* and Theodore in *The Bulpington of Blup* "whose chosen ideas of love [are] after the sublimated fashion of the Troubadors" more frequently give way to nightmarish torments. The powerful and perplexing influence of heightened sexual awareness—particularly for the male—can be vicariously endured with Aldington's hero, with Young Lonigan, Stephen Daedalus, the student in *Death Wish,* or Jean-Christophe. Some "I"-oriented solutions to conflicts between physical desires and social codes—aggravated by veiled and distorted sex information, adolescent secrecy, cultural and religious pressures, and cumulative guilt—are masturbation and prostitution.

Interpretations and uses of feminine sexuality are illustrated by the subjects of *The Once-Over* and *Girl Walking;* Susie in *I Enjoy Being a Girl* explains her concept of being a strictly "female female" and some of the problems it engenders, a view illumined from Graves' perspective on *Real Women,* a suggested correlative reading in the last section, "Night-Lights" (p. 556).

The Advantages of Learning and *The Collector,* unlike the other readings in this section, deal neither with children nor with adolescents. The male and female in these poems are chronologically adults, yet their emotional adolescence, like their painful, lonely, self-centered and unproductive lives, testify to the unhealthy dangers of a prolonged "I"-orientation that becomes an end in itself rather than a natural stage of healthy adolescent growth toward emotional and sexual maturity.

Early Sexual Consciousness

"The Universe Resounds with the Joyful Cry I Am."
ALEXANDER SCRIABIN

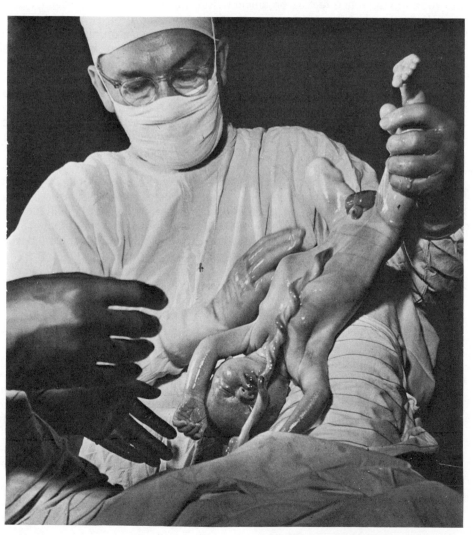

Photo by Wayne Miller. Reprinted with permission of Magnum Photos, Inc.

The sex of an individual is determined long before birth. In fact, sex is fixed at the instant of conception, when the father's sperm cell and the mother's egg cell unite.

In every sperm and egg cell there are twenty-three microscopically small bodies called chromosomes which constitute the principal working machinery of heredity, including the determination of sex. All egg cells have similar "sex" chromosomes called X; half of the sperm cells have one small sex chromosome called Y and the other half have an X chromosome similar to that of the egg cell. If a sperm cell with a Y chromosome fertilizes an egg cell, the individual created is male (XY); otherwise, it is female (XX).

From fertilization on, sexual characteristics develop, but it takes some time before differences become apparent. The external genitals are identical in the two sexes during the early stages of life within the mother. Not until well along in the third month after conception do small projections on the outer surface of the developing body begin to undergo changes that make it possible to distinguish between the male and female organism before birth.

By the end of the seventh month after conception the sex glands of the male, called the testes, descend into the pouch called the scrotum, and the female sex glands called the ovaries take their position in the lower abdomen. At that time all the principal details of the male and female organs are complete. From then until birth, change in sex organs is limited to growth and refinement.

When the male is born (see the photograph), he has in his testes all the material out of which billions of sperm will eventually be produced. Generally, however, it is not until he is between thirteen to fifteen years old that sperm production begins. The female is born with many thousands of eggs in her ovaries, yet only 300 to 400 of these will be available for fertilization—one egg about every twenty-eight days from approximately the thirteenth to the forty-fifth year.

But, before the male and female reach puberty and are biologically capable of creating children, many influences will have shaped their readiness for and attitudes toward each other and toward sexual expression. Some of the influences on males have biological roots in the sex chromosome of the male. Other influences on both sexes have roots in family and other social attitudes toward sexual expression and the role of men and women.

The event so poignantly captured in the photograph can be viewed from a variety of perspectives.

For a poet like William Wordsworth, "our birth is but a sleep and a forgetting."

For a new father, birth can be a clear sign that he is a man, and has a new sense of family responsibility, an heir.

For a mother, birth can bring a sense of fulfillment—the climax to nine months of unseen development during which a fertilized egg divides as it travels down the fallopian tube, burrows into the uterine wall, develops (a five-week-old embryo is about one-third of an inch long) and grows large and strong enough to move headfirst into the pelvis in preparation for delivery, all organs sufficiently mature to maintain life independent of the mother's body.

For an obstetrician, birth is the moment when the protruding head can be guided through the mother's birth canal, enabling the rest of the body to pass through; a point at which the physician holds the infant upside down, slapping it to facilitate drainage of mucus from mouth and throat; and a time when the umbilical cord connecting the newborn to the placenta in the uterine wall can be tied off and cut, thus literally disconnecting the attachment to the mother. Although his ears remain pressed flat against his head, and his eyes focus poorly, and in fact, the human baby is more helpless at birth than any other animal, he is symbolically free to begin a life of his own.

For a philosopher, birth raises questions concerning the nature of existence: Does life begin at conception? At delivery? Why? Are oriental cultures more realistic than occidental ones in reckoning a child's age from conception rather than from the date of delivery? Is the title of Geraldine Lux Flanagan's book on earliest human development, *The First Nine Months of Life,* an accurate description of this period in which the fetus "breathes" oxygen in the fluid of the amniotic sac, and "nourishes" himself with food substances from the mother's blood, and "excretes" wastes into the mother's system?

For a psychologist, birth initiates sexual life as well as fundamental learning patterns, which recent Harvard studies have found to be well set before the age of three. Although it is still erroneously believed by some that the sexual instinct is absent in childhood and first appears in puberty, sexual responses in four- or five-month-old babies of both sexes do occur. Authorities today acknowledge that children possess the capacity to experience sexual sensations and emotions and to learn attitudes and behavior patterns with respect to sex.

To understand human sexual behavior fully we must recognize and accept the essential sexuality of all ages from birth to death. Sex is not merely what we do, but what we are. Human sexuality is interrelated with thinking, feeling, doing, and, above all, with the formulation of a system of values. It is clear now that the emotion of love and the sexual impulse do not appear suddenly in adolescence or adulthood. These human characteristics, like personality, begin to develop at birth and continue developing throughout one's life; psychosexual identity is a cumulative process. The human organism begins to feel the influence of his heredity and his environment from the very utterance of the joyful cry which signifies "I am!"

Children's Drawings

The art work of children affords a perspective from which the event of birth may be viewed. Children's knowledge of the conditions of their birth reflects what they have learned about themselves from all sources with which they have had contact.

The eighteen reproductions selected here were drawn by school children in the first three primary grades. They were asked to paint their answers to the question, "Where was I before I was born?" or "What did I look like before I was born?" Explanatory notes made by each artist appear as captions.

"Where was I before I was born?"

(A) Before I was born I think I was a seed. And after I was born my father was at a ball game. And in the middle of the game my father came to the hospital and I was there.

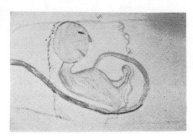

(B) This is a tube to feed the baby. The baby is inside the mother's body.

(C) You were born in the hospital in the baby section. Because your mother was operated on and they found you in her stomach.

(D) Before I was born I was in my mother's stomek. I was born on May 5, 1957, my big brother was born on Nov. 27, 1955. This picture tells about the baby head comes out first, if the feet come first in India They would kill the baby.

(E) I was born in a baby carriage.

(F) When I was a baby I went to Babyland, and my mom had to be took to the hospital in Babyland. And we took them in a hospital and then I came out with my mother in a balloon.

(G) I was in my mommy before I was born.

(H) The baby is drinking milk from a cord before it is born.

(I) Where I was born. I was born in heaven. God created me. When I was born, I went through three stages and I became my real form.

8

(J) The baby. I am the third to the oldest in the family. Mom told me the nurse called me peaches and cream. I don't believe it. I don't think I'm very cute. The part I don't like is my freckles.

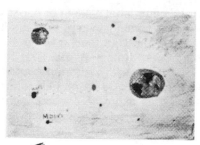

(K) Where I was before I was born. Before I was born I was up in the sky, up on a planet far away from Earth every time when a baby was born a stork would come and take the Baby to the hospital.

(L) My mother is having me. She is on her way to the hospital and the doctor is going to help her get me out.

(M) This is my mother. She had to stay in bed. The egg is inside her.

(N) Where I think I was before I was born in heaven up in the clouds. Then God brought me down in my mom's stomach. And I grew up.

(O) I was born in a glass case. I cried all the time. All babies are born in glass cases.

(P) This is my mommy before the operation. When she was having Scott I could feel the baby kicking inside Mommy.

(Q) This is the little egg that's inside my mother's body. This is me inside the egg.

(R) I was born in the Holy Cross hospital on the third floor. My picture shows it. The window with the red on it was my mom's.

Would you expect the sex of a primary school child to be apparent from a drawing on this topic? Would one sex perhaps have more accurate knowledge than the other? Why? Would use of detail or shapes be clues to the child's sex? Would word choice or attitude toward the subject, as suggested by the captions, signify masculinity or femininity?

As an experiment, label a sheet of paper with the letters A through R. Examine the children's paintings. Then, after the corresponding letter, write "male" or "female" according to your feeling about the probable sex of each artist. (Answers are given in the "**Notes**," p. 595.)

Try this experiment with your friends and family. Do results vary? Are older people any more successful at correct identification than younger ones?

What conclusions might be drawn concerning differences among primary school males and primary school females toward the event of birth?

Very early in life a child develops gender identity by choosing a sex with which to identify. While this identity is certainly influenced by the child's own external genitalia, it is largely social, and influenced by perceptions and conceptualizations of the roles of males and females. The child usually models his gender identity on his parents or parent figures and the behavior they exhibit.

Views of Mother, Father, and Self

(A)

(B)

(C)

(D)

(E)

(F)

(G)

(H)

(I)

(K)

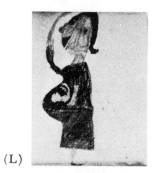

(L)

(J)

What message is communicated by each of the twelve drawings?

What does each drawing reveal of sexuality that begins at birth?

What does each drawing indicate about both the child's knowledge of the world and his attitude toward life, as his individual past experience seems to have influenced him?

For example, what anatomical sexual confusion does Child D show in her drawing of "Mummy"? What might account for such errors?

How might you guess that B was drawn by a boy whose mother often left him alone in the house at night?

What seems to be G's concept of himself?

How does A see the parental relationship?

Why might children tend to draw clothed rather than naked figures?

Despite the existence of realistic photographs like that on p. 5, children—and even adults—hold many misconceptions concerning human birth. What are some of these faulty notions?

What are the most frequent sources of misinformation?

Why do some parents persist in telling the myth about the stork, or the one about babies being found under cabbages? Why are children not given the truth instead?

Drawings A, C, E, F, H, I, K, and L on pp. 10–11 depict some aspect of birth. To what extent is each drawing accurate? What fallacies can you locate?

Can you remember some of the stories which you or your friends first heard about the birth of babies? How did you find out the truth?

If a five- to eight-year-old whom you liked and knew well were seriously to ask you "Where do babies come from?" what would you answer? Would you try to laugh off the question? Tell the child to ask somebody else? Spin one of the old tales? Tell the truth? If so, how much of it? What words might you use to help a child grasp abstract ideas or terms which have no concrete applications for him?

How much of your attitude about discussing sex would be contagious? What would the child "catch"?

How might each of these drawings be captioned by an eight-year-old?

What captions would you write if the descriptive phrases were to show the point of view of your own age group?

What are the chief differences in the two perspectives?

RELATED QUESTIONS

One fifteen-year-old author (see "Night-Lights," p. 583) argues that birthdays should celebrate conception rather than delivery. Would you agree? Why? What reasons does John Samuelson give? How would you complete the speculation raised at the end of his poem, *A Stream of Consciousness*, which provoked the "oh hell"?

One fictional portrait of the developing "I" is found in the following excerpt from *Parma Violets,* a chapter in *Things as They Are*
by Paul Horgan. This selection deals with the concept of childhood
sexuality and describes what Horgan terms "a child's love that
creates only a self."

Parma Violets
PAUL HORGAN

When children love, they do not give, they only receive. It is a love
that creates only a self. The aching desire to give, to create life beyond the self,
calls boy into man. Gratified, this love creates an analogue of heaven on earth.
Denied or betrayed, it sets forth the terms of hell in the very stuff of life, unless
it can be resolved by sanctity.

During the first World War, imprisoned as I was in the last year of childhood, I knew intuitions of what people meant when they spoke of love.

At that time, the most frequent and beloved visitor at our house in Dor-
chester was a lady I called Aunt Bunch. I had given her this name because so very
often she wore a bunch of Parma violets, now pinned to her grey fur coat, now to
an ermine muff she carried, or again at her waist in the style of the period. She
was not a real aunt. The title was merely a possessive courtesy.

I loved her with tyranny and excitement. I believed her to exist for me
alone, and I behaved accordingly. When she came to see us, I rudely interposed
myself between her and all other persons and relationships, until general laughter
resulted, and I was returned to the childhood which I was ready to lose—which,
in fact, I had forgotten.

There lay the key to my worship. She treated me not like a youngster in
black ribbed cotton stockings, itchy knee breeches, a jacket whose sleeves never
seemed long enough, and a starched collar, but like a young man to whom she
could send silent messages confident that they would be received and understood, no matter what the world might hear her say or see her do in ostensible
propriety.

She was I now think in her early thirties. Her hair was so blonde as to seem
silvery. She wore it loosely in a maddening way—I wanted to put my hands into
it and make it all fall down, heavily sliding like gold and silver treasure whose
surrender would mean everything that I could not precisely imagine. Her eyes
were violet-blue, which must have accounted for her bunches of violets, and the
effect she knew they made. Dark lashes shadowed her gaze in which great liquid
purities shone forth right into your heart. Her mouth fascinated me. The lips were
full, yet ever so delicate in their scrolling, and when she smiled, they flattened
slightly against her white teeth. Her cheeks always looked warm, but felt cool,
as I knew.

I knew, because our ardent relationship included embraces. She would
come in from a winter day with snowflakes on her furs, her violets, her lashes,
her veil, and let me climb against her until we both hurt. She would kiss me, put
her cheek on mine, press me in her arms a few times, and I smelt snow, and vio-

lets, and felt the exquisite tickle of melting snowflakes between our faces. Her face was always softly glowing as though in the light of a rose-shaded lamp. If she ever looked archly and humorously just over my head at other adults I never saw her do it.

She belonged to me. How could I doubt it? She always called me "My dear," as she might call a man, and in that winter we became acknowledged as a cunning joke, "lovers," with quotation marks, and many an eyebrow went up, and voice went down, and pang went deep, at the spectacle we made, and the living reference we were to all that was meant by love, and suffered, and revered, in its name.

My own part in this passion explains itself if enough years are allowed to ensue. But for her part—why did she come to take me out driving in the afternoons, after school, in her electric car? The cushions were grey, there were always violets in the little crystal vases flanking the curved plate glass of the front window, and we were alone together as the batteries hummed us along, and the elegant bell rang at street crossings. We rode for the most part in ecstatic silence through the park, watching for swans on the lake, and if we saw one, our excitement made us hold one another. Sometimes she let me steer the electric. To do so, I had to crowd near to her, and lean upon her lap, the better to manage the long black bar which made the wheels point this way or that. I would steer, she would control the speed by a shorter bar above the other, and we would spin on our way with joy.

"Poor dear, she has no children, and he is like a son to her"—this was one explanation I overheard. It meant nothing to me. What did it matter why, so long as she would put her head down to mine, and leave it there in dreaming silence and contentment? Or hold my hand and play with my fingers, one after another, slowly and broodingly, while flooding me with the daytime moonlight of her eyes? I believed that she never looked at anyone else that way. How could she, what could it possibly mean to anyone else, when she was mine entirely?

Sometimes on our drives she would take me to Huyler's for a chocolate soda, or again to her house in the park for cocoa with whipped cream. If we were early enough, I preferred her house, where we could be so intimate and private about nothing, but if we were late, I was unwilling to go there because we might then encounter her husband, "Uncle" Dylan.

My reluctance to meet him there had nothing to do with guilt over my love for his wife. I simply preferred to meet him at my house because as a visitor there he always brought me some sort of present. For this I despised him even as I greedily reached for his pockets. He was a rich man, much older than Aunt Bunch. . . .

"Now, Richard," he would say to me, one greedy creature virtuously reproving another, "let us not be so sure we have a present today. Why should we have? What have we done to earn it? Do we think others are made of money? Presents cost something, my boy. Do you ever think of your poor old Uncle Dylan except when he has something for you?"

Such an attitude made me shudder for him, as he looked over to his wife to see if she smiled upon his humor, blinking both his dry scratchy eyes at her, and as he then besought my parents to witness his openness of heart, forcing them to deprecate his latest gift, and to swear that I would not be allowed to accept another single thing after this time. . . . I never considered him an odd choice as a husband for Aunt Bunch. He simply *was* her husband, and that ended the matter. As such, he belonged to my world, as she belonged, and I could not possibly imagine any disturbance of its order. So long as they remained fixed, any relationships were accepted. If a new one should appear, the quicker it were absorbed and fixed, the better. Only, let it be added to what existed, without changing anything.

In that season of so much love, when the heavy winter brought snow that would stay for weeks, and the warmth and light of our house made a twilight joy after the steely cold out of doors during the day, a familiar friend returned to us as somebody new. He was my father's business associate. . . . Many months ago he had joined the Army, and was now a captain of artillery on leave before receiving new orders, which everybody knew meant going overseas to France to fight the Hun in World War I.

Now he came to see us in his uniform. . . . Captain Jarvis McNeill seemed like an entirely new individual, with no relation to the occasional visitor of the same name before the war. He was unmarried and so appeared at parties mostly as a stray, to fill in. Now home on leave, he took to coming to our house late in the day, when the curtains were drawn, a fire was rippling in the fireplace, and other friends dropped in and out without announcement. Sometimes such little gatherings would turn into supper parties, people would stay, and the animation and conviviality of my parents would have happy expression. Almost always, late in such an evening, the piano would sound, and then Captain Jarvis McNeill would sing. . . .

I always knew when Captain Jarvis McNeill arrived. I would know it by the sound of his boots in the entrance hall. . . .

When I heard him below, I held my breath the better to overhear messages from life beyond me. His speaking voice had heavy grain and carried through the rooms. I listened to hear if it grew louder in my direction. Then I would hear the heavy trot of his big body coming up the stairs. He was coming to see me in my room—a real captain, a soldier who fired cannons, who had a sword, and wore boots and spurs, and would himself hang the Kaiser, and was a hero.

One of the qualities of heroes may be their instinct for true worship amid all the false. Captain Jarvis McNeill repaid mine with serious and simple appreciation, which took the form of getting down on the floor of my room where my imaginative possessions were marshalled, and playing there, as I played, so long as the company downstairs would let him. He filled the room with his presence in every way, including the way he brought the spicy, sharp aromas of a barbershop with him—the clean, adventurous smell of a man who has been combed, spanked and shined to his most presentable state, for private and urgent purposes. His cheeks got hotter like mine as he bent down to the miniature tasks of imagination with my large relief model of battlefields in France, set with leaden soldiery and wooden artillery. His collar choked him, his big legs were in the way but splendid with boots and spurs, and he made the double magic of seeing with my eyes and making me see with his.

"Do you have a sword?" I asked.

"Yes. Would you like me to bring it?"

"Yes."

He brought it next time, and let me have it for several days. It lay by me in bed, sheathed and shining. My belly hung heavy in me at the glories that leaped out of the scabbard with that blade. Only in secret did I strap the big sword to my belt, for I was now old enough to know that it would look ridiculous to anyone else. I gave it up with a scowl of indifference that fooled nobody when Captain Jarvis McNeill said to me on our floor one evening that he had to pack a lot of stuff to be shipped, and he supposed his officer's sword had better go too.

"But when I come back you can have it again," he said, and put his big hand like a heavy helmet on my head and roughed me once or twice. That promise was enough for me. To whom else was he offering his beautiful acid-etched sword with its gold sabre-knot and its tinkling scabbard? He was a great captain, a hero, and my friend, and he came to my house almost daily to see me, to crawl with much humorous breathing and difficulty of scale among the delicate litter of my parapets and trenches, my tanks and ambulances and field hospitals. To see me. He was mine to love and to own, through whom I could extend myself into a heroic life as a soldier.

He would stay so long in my playroom that almost invariably others would come upstairs to inquire: and standing in the doorway they would smile and chatter at the sight of the handsome young officer and the hot-faced boy both intent upon war games. At such moments I realized that the grown-up world was about to win all over again. Aunt Bunch usually was one of those who came to see. The sight of her, waiting for me to admit to bedtime, changed, dropped, my spirits, I knew not why. Dimly I did not want her and Captain Jarvis McNeill with me together. I wanted them with me each separately. More, I wanted them never to be together at all, lest each might forget me. How complicated that fidelity, and that betrayal.

At last with comfortable sighs of change, the Captain would rise and put himself in order for his return downstairs with the company. Aunt Bunch would let him go, as she lingered to assuage the endless disappointments of day's end. Invisibly the tendrils of scent from Parma violets sought me out and wrapped me round; and when she left me to go below where unimaginably trivial events were gathering purpose for the adults, I was proved again in love, and the terms I imagined for it were unquestioned, and I felt choked with well-being, rich emotion, and a swelling conviction that nothing would ever change that I loved.

For a boy at the shore of boyhood's farewell, those were passionate loves— Aunt Bunch and Captain Jarvis McNeill; and that was a passionate if scornful loyalty—Uncle Dylan. The issue was not whether I was a small monster of sensibility, but whether the power of love is ever really contained within conventions, no matter how desperately appearances may be preserved.

We take our parents for granted till we have lost them.

"Richard, Richard," they would say, fondly shaking their heads at each other over my infatuations, recognizing how fixed was my view of life, and how innocent it was of any other values but my fierce, joyful, tyrannical ones which seemed to me eternal, and to them dangerous. They saw everything, even to what must be coming, though not in what event it might come. They tried to rob me painfully but healthily of the possessions of my heart.

"You must not make yourself a nuisance when Jarvis comes, Richard, after all, there are others who want to see him."

"He comes to see me."

"Ah, my darling boy."

"Well, he does too, he told me so."

"Yes, of course, of course," in hurried agreement, as though to conceal from me after all a truth best left with my elders. Or again,

"You will be a young man before long, and you will look for a pretty girl your own age to love."

"I love Aunt Bunch."

"Now, yes. But she is already married. And her age!"

"I thought you loved her too."

"We do, we do, my boy."

"And I thought you loved me."

"Ah, Richard, as if you did not know."

And I hated my father and mother for their good sense which then seemed to me so evil and so hard.

Our household liked to combine music and society. There was a dinner party before a concert to be given by an illustrious American singer. . . . The party was to consist of my father and mother, Uncle Dylan and Aunt Bunch, Captain Jarvis McNeill and Monsignor Tremaine, who was very musical and had no prejudice against good company outside the rectory. . . .

It was snowing when the guests arrived. I looked out the window and saw their cars—Uncle Dylan's big limousine with its cabin lighted and his chauffeur standing by the door; Monsignor Tremaine's old touring car with its cracked side curtains up. I counted. Someone was missing. Captain Jarvis McNeill had not arrived with the others. By prearrangement I was permitted to stay downstairs until I had toured the party to say good evening and display my dancing school manners—jerked handshake, ducked bow.

"My. How we have grown, all of a sudden. And are we still a very good young fellow?"

"Yes, M'nsignor."

A pair of shining, hard, old brown eyes like horse-chestnuts polished in spring seemed to knock at my heart, sounding its formless guilt. *What have we here: a boy who is already feeling certain things? Does he know their true and holy purpose? Does he have to think too much about them? Does he have to lose them in troubling dreams? Ah: how hard it is to inherit feeling before there is knowledge. Ah: does knowledge really help? Let us trust in the mercy of God. God bless you, Richard.* Then the beloved old pastor laughed genially over his power to enter into the secrets of man, and let me go on to Uncle Dylan.

"Well, Richard? And why do you look at me like that? As if I had something for you tonight! Well, sir, let me tell you, you have another think coming."

How disgusting, this arch attempt to torture me, and draw the attention of all to the act of material generosity about to appear, as inevitable, hoped-for and boring as the magician's dry silk flag out of the glass of water.

"All right, Uncle Dylan, excuse me, then,"—and I made as if to pass on.

"He what? Look at him. I never knew such a boy, so impatient, can't he take a little joke from an old man?—All right, try the lefthand pocket."

My father revealed the shame and irritation of us all, though he kept smiling and silent above his tall evening collar and wide white bow tie.

"—No?" exclaimed Uncle Dylan blinking his sandy eyes, "not there? Nothing? How peculiar. Then try the other side!"

So I found a small leather case ("Well, go on, go on, Richard, open it, let us all see what it is, I've even forgotten since I bought it for you") containing a shiny brass telescope, so beautiful it shamed me for all my sins of opinion. I wanted so much to own it that I handed it back to Uncle Dylan.

"What? The ungrateful. No, really, it is for you."

Unable to resolve my feelings, I stood looking at the floor with my hands behind my back. Aunt Bunch saved me. She came forward and knelt down to me as if we were quite alone. By doing this she made me taller than herself. She put her white arms around me and drew my face down to hers. We both shut our eyes: audible smiles once again in the room at the spectacle of the "lovers." Her hair shone like waves under sunset light. She wore a heavy shining dress of some pale color that showed much of her bosom and back and all her arms bare. Violets were held to her breast by a great spray of diamonds in a pin. In a moment she gave me a pat, and said, "There!", and made me release her as she lightly took the telescope from Uncle Dylan and gave it back to me. I kept it. Was there anyone else in the world for whom she had so much love, which she would show so proudly? . . .

"And now," said my mother, . . . "you may say good night, Richard, and go up to your tray, and to bed."

"But I want to wait and see the Captain."

"He will not be here for quite some time," she said. "He telephoned. He is delayed. If you are not sleeping when he comes, he may run up to see you for a moment. Now good night, darling."

I hurried through my supper tray, changed to my pajamas, carried the tray to the head of the back stairs as was the custom, and then on my belly went to the head of the carpeted front stairs to watch and to listen. I saw them all downstairs when they crossed the hall to the dining room to sit down under the many shaded candles above the table. I strained to hear every car out in the street making its grinding song on snow with tire chains, thinking every car would bring Captain Jarvis McNeill. When the company was through dinner and returning to the drawing room for coffee, I picked out one then another with my new telescope from the distance of the flight of stairs. There, glowing in midair, rimmed faintly with pale blue and yellow optical magic, were those familiar faces, brought near and separate in a new kind of ownership.

A brief halt between dining room and drawing room took place for an important question.

"But what shall I do if he does not come?" asked Uncle Dylan, taking out his wallet and carefully spreading his six box seat tickets like a hand of cards. "I have all the tickets."

"I cannot understand," said my mother. "He did not think he would be this late."

"He must have a thousand things to do," said Aunt Bunch, "getting ready for his orders, and of course he cannot talk about them.—There is no reason," she added with persuasive sweetness, "for anybody who does not have to to miss the concert. Here," she said, leaning forward with grace and swiftly taking the tickets from Uncle Dylan, "leave me two, and since we are the hosts at the box party, I will wait for Jarvis here a little while, and bring him if he comes; and if he does not come soon, I will follow alone. There!" she finished, giving four tickets back to Uncle Dylan, and shutting two into her bag of solid gold mesh, as Uncle Dylan always called it.

. . . They all vanished into the other room for coffee.

Soon my mother came to say goodnight. I was discovered virtuously in bed. . . . She kissed me, idly told me to be good and go right to sleep, and then asked me if I did not love my new telescope.

"Yes," I replied.

"Yes, Richard, then love what you have, *and can have,* and not what you do not have. Good night, my darling," she said in a whisper, leaving me baffled and somehow reduced in spirit.

I listened intently until the sounds of departure were all done. From the kitchen dimly came the after-dinner work, and unaccustomed rumbles of conversation as Aunt Bunch's chauffeur talked with Anna and the caterer, who would soon be done with his work, and would head for the streetcar tracks two blocks away leading downtown. I listened for sounds from the drawing room where Aunt Bunch must be. I heard nothing. Planning to go down and see, I fell asleep.

How much later I didn't know, but it felt much later, I awoke to the icy sizzle and clank of tire chains slowing down and stopping in the caked snow out in the street. Then I heard boots on the porch, and the door open and shut as someone let Captain Jarvis McNeill in, and then the stamp in the vestibule to loosen the snow from his spur chains.

He was here at last and my pulse began to rip along. I leaped from my bed, turned on my light, and went over my toys rapidly. The regular ones were ready. In a moment he would come up to see me, to settle down on the floor, as usual, to create and enter in the world where he and I, and only we, were heroes. Leaving the light on for encouragement, I went to my door to wait for him.

But he did not come.

I listened.

Where was he? I heard nothing from below, not even the soft but penetrating diapason of his heavy Irish voice that could enter the fabric of our house and make it vibrate in response.

I turned to my toys that waited with me. Was it possible that he had forgotten my old castle with its real drawbridge, and rows of leaden archers on the battlements, and in the great hall a double throne with a king and queen under a canopy? I had outgrown these things, but surely he had not, who had known them for only a few months! . . .

The silence took on so great a strangeness that a hint of panic came with it.

I could not wait any longer. I took my telescope and went swiftly down the carpeted stairs. He was there, somewhere, for I had heard him come in. And then everything became clear to me. I'd been a fool. It was plain that Captain Jarvis McNeill was enjoying a game with me. He was hiding somewhere in the big front room, waiting for me, even as I had waited for him. The happy hunter came alive in me. I went down to my belly and crawled silently from the hall into the drawing room with my telescope ready. Coming around the forest-like obstruction of a green velvet chair with heavy wooden arms and legs (moss and rock), I carefully put my glass to my eye and slowly swept the softly-lighted far end of the room to find him.

Familiar details came into view—a picture on the wall, flowers on a table, books, a lamp—as I ranged from left to right, toward the great sofa that stood across the last corner of the room. Everything was colored softly and as though by a brush, and as still as the dead.

As still as the dead until into my telescope glided life and motion, and I saw the gloss of dark hair turning and turning and ruddy cheeks above pale cheeks and the heavy massed treasure of golden waves of hair, and pure piercing bolts of light from pale violet eyes that opened and closed, gazed away, and again near, away, and near, with such intensity of expression that it could have meant the extreme of suffering or of joy, or of both, and there came the restricted but mortal leverage of arms holding and closing and enclosing, and all in stillness that with such vision was not quite silence, for little sounds of breath, and lips, and thrust weight traveled to me and told the same that the telescope told, and at the same time, and with the same shattering power.

My world fell.

I knew sharply and deeply that what was mine was no longer mine. Aunt Bunch was mine in just my way no more. Captain Jarvis McNeill was lost to me in the arms of love. Even Uncle Dylan suffered breaking change in the discovery, for he was Aunt Bunch's, and thus mine, though with scorn, in the old order of the world which was now broken.

But he came to see me, Captain Jarvis McNeill? And yes—I knew now that every time Aunt Bunch was there too, as it "happened." I was torn with rage and betrayal.

And this evening? When he was late, who arranged everything, to wait for him, in her great beauty so enhanced by hope and hopelessness? What were the warnings of my parents, and how general were they, and how particular?

I understood nothing, really, except that I was overwhelmingly robbed, and of what, even, I was not then very sure. But the two lost people in my round lens were alone and far away. I must make them crash with me, or I must vanish into thin air.

"No!" I cried out, and lurched to my feet, and threw my telescope at the wall where it broke some picture glass. I turned over the big chair where I had played my hunter's game of hide and seek. So I declared myself.

The more-than-kiss broke apart and the real lovers stared at me with vacant faces.

"Oh—dear," said Aunt Bunch softly and slowly, with solemn sweetness and pity that made a thickness come to my throat until I began to fear the emotions I had made between us all.

Captain Jarvis McNeill roughly pulled himself together and then made for me with his hands outstretched as though to choke me.

"—Than a sneak," he whispered loudly, having said in his mind that there was nothing worse.

"Hush, Jarvis," said Aunt Bunch quietly, knowing what I felt. She was settling her hair, her gown.

"Yes, I'm sorry," he said, and knelt down before me to be reasonable and winning, and tried to take me kindly; but I kicked and flailed at him, shocked by the scared look in his face, a look I was mature enough to know since fear of exposure was childhood's one explicit emotion. In a gesture he tried to recover me, but I pushed at him and ran upstairs to my room, turned off the light and, trampling my battlefield in France which had lost its point, forever, went into my bed with my hands over my ears and my mouth open. I was full of chagrin at the fall of man.

Presently in the ringing darkness of my misery with my ears covered and my eyes squeezed shut, I inhaled a waft of that cool, moist fragrance that always meant Aunt Bunch. The scent of Parma violets would always seem to me the odor of purity itself, and yet just as intimately and powerfully, and at the very same time, that of profane love.

She knelt by my bed and put her quiet hand on my hot neck. She said nothing but waited for me to speak if I must. Soon I was trying to rebuild my follies.

"You will stay here with me, alone?" I whispered urgently.

But she refused to be false to what we all now knew.

"Nonsense, my dear," she said gently, "you are going to sleep, and we are going to the concert."

"But—but—" but I could not think of what crowded in me to want. I clung to her and like any betrayed lover begged for lies with my touches. She would not tell them, even with caresses, any more. She held me and I began to die into sleep, suffering for the last time from the confusion called childhood.

The last I remember as I fell asleep, bitter with spent woe under her touch, was the sound of her voice. It returns to me a lifetime later whenever I meet the fragrance of her little flowers, saying the only thing to say in pity and certainty that made me ache even as it promised of life all I did not yet know, "Some day . . . some day. . . ."

How do Richard's feelings for Aunt Bunch bear out the accepted concept of childhood sexuality? What might the author mean in characterizing a child's love as one that "creates only a self"?

The sight of [Aunt Bunch], waiting for me to admit to bedtime, changed, dropped, my spirits, I knew not why. Dimly I did not want her and Captain Jarvis McNeill with me together. I wanted them with me each separately. More, I wanted them never to be together at all, lest each might forget me.

How does the above passage warrant using the following adjectives to describe Richard's "love": jealous, possessive, intense, exclusive, passionate, tyrannical, exciting, immature? Which of these labels refer to elements often considered destructive to a relationship? Why?

I was proved again in love, and the terms I imagined for it were unquestioned, and I felt choked with well-being, rich emotion, and a swelling conviction that nothing would ever change that I loved.

What is dangerously unrealistic about Richard's point of view?

Richard's parents consider his love for Aunt Bunch an infatuation. In what sense do they seem to be using the term? Would they agree with the common definition of infatuated: inspired with a foolish or extravagant love or admiration?

Does Richard fully misinterpret Aunt Bunch's role? In what ways might Aunt

Bunch be fulfilling through Richard her own emotional needs for "sex" and "love"?

What contrasts do you find between "the spectacle of the lovers" (Aunt Bunch and Richard) and the "real lovers" (Aunt Bunch and Captain McNeill)? Are there similarities?

What are the connotations of "real lovers" and "spectacle of the lovers"? Does the contrast in meaning explain Richard's sense of "rage and betrayal" when he makes his telescopic discovery?

Parents are said to love their children, and children to love their parents. What are some of the signs of this love? In what ways are they similar to and different from signs of love in later relationships with other people?

Richard's age is unstated, but initially he is described "imprisoned in the last year of childhood," and finally as "suffering for the last time from the confusion called childhood." Do you think the author considers "the last year of childhood" as a chronological and/or psychological period?

The words "love" and "sex" are variously used, and the distinction between the two terms, if it exists, is often an arbitrary one. Considering the situation presented here, what elements of Richard's feeling for Aunt Bunch would you consider "sexual"? What elements might be termed "love"?

While Richard of **Parma Violets** is figuratively imprisoned in childhood, Emily Bas-Thornton, one of a group of children captured by pirates in the novel **A High Wind in Jamaica,** actually is a prisoner aboard a pirate ship. But, like Aunt Bunch's youngest "lover," Emily, too, is on "the innocent voyage"* into experience.

The first excerpt from this novel by Richard Hughes describes Emily's awakening from naïveté during a shipboard event of considerable importance when at age eleven she "suddenly realized who she was." The moment constitutes her first awareness and acceptance of herself as a unique physical being.

The second excerpt, occurring later in the story when Emily is flying home after rescue from the pirate ship, deals with the concept of childhood sexuality from a female's perspective as Emily further develops her initial recognition of self.

A High Wind in Jamaica
RICHARD HUGHES

And then an event did occur, to Emily, of considerable importance. She suddenly realised who she was.

There is little reason that one can see why it should not have happened to her five years earlier, or even five later; and none, why it should have come that particular afternoon.

She had been playing houses in a nook right in the bows, behind the windlass (on which she had hung a devil's-claw as a door-knocker); and tiring of it

*This is sometimes used as an alternate title of the book.

was walking rather aimlessly aft, thinking vaguely about some bees and a fairy queen, when it suddenly flashed into her mind that she was *she*.

She stopped dead, and began looking over all of her person which came within the range of her eyes. She could not see much, except a fore-shortened view of the front of her frock, and her hands when she lifted them for inspection; but it was enough for her to form a rough idea of the little body she suddenly realised to be hers.

She began to laugh, rather mockingly, "Well!" she thought, in effect. "Fancy *you*, of all people, going and getting caught like this!—You can't get out of it now, not for a very long time: you'll have to go through with being a child, and growing up, and getting old, before you'll be quit of this mad prank!"

Determined to avoid any interruption of this highly important occasion, she began to climb the ratlines, on her way to her favourite perch at the masthead. Each time she moved an arm or a leg in this simple action, however, it struck her with fresh amazement to find them obeying her so readily. Memory told her, of course, that they had always done so before: but before, she had never realised how surprising this was.

Once settled on her perch, she began examining the skin of her hands with the utmost care: for it was *hers*. She slipped a shoulder out of the top of her frock; and having peeped in to make sure she really was continuous under her clothes, she shrugged it up to touch her cheek. The contact of her face and the warm bare hollow of her shoulder gave her a comfortable thrill, as if it was the caress of some kind friend. But whether the feeling came to her through her cheek or her shoulder, which was the caresser and which the caressed, that no analysis could tell her.

Once fully convinced of this astonishing fact, that she was now Emily Bas-Thornton (why she inserted the "now" she did not know, for she certainly imagined no transmigrational nonsense of having been anyone else before), she began seriously to reckon its implications.

First, what agency had so ordered it that out of all the people in the world who she might have been, she was this particular one, this Emily; born in such-and-such a year out of all the years in Time, and encased in this particular rather pleasing little casket of flesh? Had she chosen herself, or had God done it?

At this, another consideration: who was God? She had heard a terrible lot about Him, always: but the question of His identity had been left vague, as much taken for granted as her own. Wasn't she perhaps God, herself? Was it that she was trying to remember? However, the more she tried, the more it eluded her. (How absurd, to disremember such an important point as whether one was God or not!) So she let it slide: perhaps it would come back to her later.

Secondly, why had all this not occurred to her before? She had been alive for over ten years, now, and it had never once entered her head. . . . She felt like a man who suddenly remembers at eleven o'clock at night, sitting in his own arm-chair, that he had accepted an invitation to go out to dinner that night. There is no reason for him to remember it now: but there seems equally little why he should not have remembered it in time to keep his engagement. How could he have sat there all the evening, without being disturbed by the slightest misgiving? How could Emily have gone on being Emily for ten years without once noticing this apparently obvious fact?

It must not be supposed that she argued it all out in this ordered, but rather longwinded fashion. Each consideration came to her in a momentary flash, quite innocent of words; and in between her mind lazed along, either thinking of nothing or returning to her bees and the fairy queen. If one added up the total of her periods of conscious thought, it would probably reach something between four and five seconds; nearer five, perhaps; but it was spread out over the best part of an hour.

Well then, granted she was Emily, what were the consequences, besides enclosure in that particular little body (which now began on its own account to be aware of a sort of unlocated itch, most probably somewhere on the right thigh), and lodgement behind a particular pair of eyes?

It implied a whole series of circumstances. In the first place, there was her family, a number of brothers and sisters from whom, before, she had never entirely dissociated herself; but now she got such a sudden feeling of being a discrete person that they seemed as separate from her as the ship itself. However, willy-nilly she was almost as tied to them as she was to her body. And then there was this voyage, this ship, this mast round which she had wound her legs. She began to examine it with almost as vivid an illumination as she had studied the skin of her hands. And when she came down from the mast, what would she find at the bottom? . . . The whole fabric of a daily life which up to now she had accepted as it came, . . . now seemed vaguely disquieting. What was going to happen? Were there disasters running about loose, disasters which her rash marriage to the body of Emily Thornton made her vulnerable to?

A sudden terror struck her: did anyone know? (Know, I mean, that she was someone in particular, Emily—perhaps even God—not just any little girl.) She could not tell why, but the idea terrified her. It would be bad enough if they should discover she was a particular person—but if they should discover she was God! At all costs she must hide *that* from them.—But suppose they knew already, had simply been hiding it from her (as guardians might from an infant king)? In that case, as in the other, the only thing to do was to continue to behave as if she did not know, and so outwit them.

But if she was God, why . . . should she hide it? She never really asked herself why: but instinct prompted her strongly of the necessity. Of course, there was the element of doubt (suppose she had made a mistake, and the miracle missed fire): but more largely it was the feeling that she would be able to deal with the situation so much better when she was a little older. Once she had declared herself there would be no turning back; it was much better to keep her godhead up her sleeve, for the present.

Grown-ups embark on a life of deception with considerable misgiving, and generally fail. But not so children. A child can hide the most appalling secret without the least effort, and is practically secure against detection. Parents, finding that they see through their child in so many places the child does not know of, seldom realise that, if there is some point the child really gives his mind to hiding, their chances are nil.

So Emily had no misgivings when she determined to preserve her secret, and needed have none.

•   •   •   •   •

. . . When the kind stewardess bent over her to kiss her she caught tight hold of her, and buried her face in the warm, soft, yielding flesh, as if to sink herself in it. . . .

When the stewardess stood up again, Emily feasted her eyes on her, eyes grown large and warm and mysterious. The woman's enormous, swelling bosom fascinated her. Forlornly, she began to pinch her own thin little chest. Was it conceivable she would herself ever grow breasts like that—beautiful, mountainous breasts, that had to be cased in a sort of cornucopia? Or even firm little apples.

Thank God she had not been born a boy! She was overtaken with a sudden revulsion against the whole sex of them. From the tips of her fingers to the tips of her toes she felt female: one with that exasperating, idiotic secret communion: initiate of the γυναικειον.

What answers does Emily give to the all-important question "Who am I"? To what chain of questions does Emily's answer to "Who am I?" give rise? Why does the realization that she is "someone in particular" strike Emily with a "sudden terror"?

Do you agree with the author that "grown-ups embark on a life of deception and generally fail," whereas "a child can hide the most appalling secret without the least effort" and be practically secure against detection? Can you recall situations from your own experience that support the author's observation? If his comment is valid, why is it so, since adults are supposedly wiser, more experienced, and more sophisticated than children?

Although we may expect the really significant moments in life to present themselves dramatically, more often we are surprised to find that they occur quietly, even unexpectedly, without our recognizing their importance until they have passed. Yet, from the new perspective they bring about, we may find, as Emily did, that "the whole fabric of a daily life" is altered. From your own experience can you isolate some landmark on your innocent voyage from childhood? A moment so significant that afterward you knew that you could never again feel quite the same way as you had before?

If you are a female, can you remember ever wishing you were a male? When? What advantages do you see in being a male rather than a female?

If you are a male, did you ever wish you were a female? Why? What advantages do you think females have?

Emily says that "from the tips of her fingers to the tips of her toes she felt female." Is this the same as being "feminine"? Womanly"? "Sexy"?

While Emily in **A High Wind in Jamaica** was captive on a pirate ship after her Jamaican home was wrecked by hurricane, Anne Frank in **The Diary of a Young Girl** was confined to the Secret Annexe of an office building in Amsterdam, Holland, to avoid capture by the Nazis during World War II. The young Jewish girl is in hiding with her mother, her father, her sister, Margot, and the Van Daan family. (Anne's relationship with Peter Van Daan is considered in the **"They"** section, see p. 133.)

For Emily the real world seemed far away; for Anne the real world is frighteningly close. Yet there are similarities in the self-awareness discovered by each girl, even though it "suddenly flashed into Emily's mind while she was playing house in a nook of the ship's bows" and Anne thoroughly analyzed hers as she recorded in her diary, which was published after she died in a Nazi concentration camp.

The Diary of a Young Girl

ANNE FRANK

Wednesday, 5 January, 1944

. . . Yesterday I read an article about blushing. . . . This article might have been addressed to me personally. Although I don't blush very easily, the other things in it certainly all fit me. . . . that a girl in the years of puberty becomes quiet within and begins to think about the wonders that are happening to her body.

I experience that, too, and that is why I get the feeling lately of being embarrassed about Margot, Mummy, and Daddy. Funnily enough, Margot, who is much more shy than I am, isn't at all embarrassed.

I think what is happening to me is so wonderful, and not only what can be seen on my body, but all that is taking place inside. I never discuss myself or any of these things with anybody; that is why I have to talk to myself about them.

Each time I have a period—and that has only been three times—I have the feeling that in spite of all the pain, unpleasantness, and nastiness, I have a sweet secret, and that is why, although it is nothing but a nuisance to me in a way, I always long for the time that I shall feel that secret within me again.

[The article explains how] girls of this age don't feel quite certain of themselves, and discover that they themselves are individuals with ideas, thoughts, and habits. After I came here, when I was just fourteen, I began to think about myself sooner than most girls, and to know that I am a "person." Sometimes, when I lie in bed at night, I have a terrible desire to feel my breasts and to listen to the quiet rhythmic beat of my heart.

I already had these kinds of feelings subconsciously before I came here, because I remember that once when I slept with a girl friend I had a strong desire to kiss her, and that I did do so. I could not help being terribly inquisitive over her body, for she had always kept it hidden from me. I asked her whether, as a proof of our friendship, we should feel one another's breasts, but she refused. I go into ecstasies every time I see the naked figure of a woman, such as Venus, for example. It strikes me as so wonderful and exquisite that I have difficulty in stopping the tears rolling down my cheeks.

If only I had a girl friend!

At puberty the production of sex hormones increases markedly, and thus body sensitivity, sexual awareness, and sensitivity in general are heightened. Individuals respond with intense awareness to all changes; they are often given to hours of self-analysis and frequently plagued by acute self-consciousness. To what extent does Anne Frank seem to bear out these characteristics?

Why does Anne feel embarrassed about her sister, her mother, and her father?

Do you consider Anne's diary entry typical of a fourteen-and-one-half-year-old girl? Why or why not? How much are Anne's adolescent concerns affected by time and place, and the conditions which both of these factors created?

Do both boys and girls keep diaries? What sorts of information do they contain? What purpose do they serve? What needs might they satisfy?

What might Anne mean in terming her menstrual period "having a sweet secret"? Why then is menstruation so often called "getting the curse" or "being unwell"?

RELATED QUESTIONS

Both *A High Wind in Jamaica* and *The Diary of a Young Girl* show something of the conscious recognition: I am a person! Beyond the similar realizations shared by Emily and Anne what are the differences? Would the three-and-one-half-year discrepancy in their ages account for them? Would environmental circumstances explain them?

Both Emily and Anne feel a need for secrecy: Emily is "determined to preserve her secret"; Anne confides only to her diary—"I never discuss myself or any of these things with anybody; that is why I have to talk to myself about them." What lies behind this unwillingness to share new feelings with others? Is it as true of boys as it is of girls?

Emily has a sense of marvelous possibilities—even God-like powers at work; Anne writes "what is happening to me is so wonderful. . . . I go into ecstasies. . . . I have difficulty in stopping the tears rolling down my cheeks." Is Anne overly emotional? Does Emily have delusions of grandeur? Why are both girls' feelings so extreme? How are they affected by the emotional and instinctive drives at puberty which are part of the impetus toward psychological maturity?

If Emily's and Anne's growing self-awareness has more to do with the unmeasurable quality of experience than with measurable quantities (like age and physical stature), what kinds of emotional settings would you think might be best for helping a child attain responsible maturity? Consider ways in which adults (parents, other relatives, teachers, even strangers) might behave if they wanted to help in this constructive process. What sort of behaviors might they avoid?

All words are symbols. They have denotative meanings, that is, their dictionary definitions. But words also have connotative meanings, or certain overtones of meaning, which suggest something beyond what is expressed. Words gain their power from our attitudes toward them, the emotions with which we invest them, and the contexts in which they appear. Students who would think nothing of ordering chicken breasts in a strange grocery store may feel awkward in front of a familiar teacher and class reading a line "pillowed upon my fair love's ripening breast" from Keats' sonnet "Bright Star." Although "night" and "evening" are denotative synonyms, one translator of a Russian novel changed the heroine's character by saying that she appeared at a party in her *night*gown, instead of *evening* dress. A math teacher assigning problem sixty-nine for discussion might have to contend with muffled giggles from embarrassed students for whom the denotatively harmless number is emotionally charged with sexual overtones of connotative significance.

Emily describes the stewardess' "enormous, swelling bosom" which fascinated her; she buries her "face in the warm, soft yielding flesh, as if to sink herself in it. . . ." Anne, on the other hand, felt terribly inquisitive about the body of a modest girl friend. Anne wanted to feel her own breasts and those of her friend,

Sexual Intercour...

and she went into ecstasies upon seeing the naked figure of Venus. Do the word "bosom" and the word "breast" have a different connotation for you? Would there be any change in the interpretation of the passages if Anne Frank had used the word "bosom" and the stewardess' description read "enormous, swelling breasts"?

In what order would you expect the following human characteristics to develop:

____Aesthetic appreciation of the female form.
____Need for the security symbolized by the mother's breast.
____Curiosity about and attraction toward members of the same sex.
____Desire to explore one's own body.

Which of the above characteristics are true of Emily? Of Anne? Which girl's stage of development then is the more mature?

How does the following explanation clarify Anne's behavior with her girl friend:

When we examine other species of mammals, we find homosexual activity, sometimes to the point of ejaculation, in all of the animals in captivity. It is rare, however, for individual mammals to show an exclusive pattern of homosexual behavior. The majority have both heterosexual and homosexual activity, but heterosexual behavior predominates. Thus homosexual activity is "natural" in the sense that it occurs commonly in nature [a]. Instead of asking, "Why do human beings engage in homosexual behavior?" it is more meaningful to ask, "Why doesn't everyone engage in homosexual behavior?" inasmuch as it is part of our mammalian heritage. [2]

Comment on the following interpretations: "Anne Frank may be a very smart kid, but she sure is a queer. She'll probably turn into a lesbian when she grows up. As for Emily, she's sort of emotionally retarded. By eleven, you'd think she'd have outgrown baby feelings like hers, wouldn't you?"

Biological maturation is signalled by the appearance of secondary sex characteristics in early adolescence. For girls like Anne Frank in **The Diary of a Young Girl** and Emily Thornton of **A High Wind in Jamaica,** menstruation, breast development, and pubic hair growth become sources of paramount interest and possible concern. For boys, deepening voice, growth of beard, and the enlargement of penis and testes become sources of singular interest, pride, or concern.

If the male's testes do not descend into the scrotum by puberty, his later sperm-producing ability will be affected by the body's higher temperature. To avoid this impairment, when a boy is eight or nine years old glandular injections can be administered or an operation can be performed to assist the descent of the testes into the scrotum.

The facts of such cases as well as the terrors, doubts, and fantasies that may be generated by this occurrence are described by Philip Roth in the following excerpt from **Portnoy's Complaint.**

The Jewish Blues
PHILIP ROTH

Sometime during my ninth year one of my testicles apparently decided it had had enough of life down in the scrotum and began to make its way north. At the beginning I could feel it bobbing uncertainly just at the rim of the pelvis—and then, as though its moment of indecision had passed, entering the cavity of my body, like a survivor being dragged up out of the sea and over the hull of a lifeboat. And there it nestled, secure at last behind the fortress of my bones, leaving its foolhardy mate to chance it alone in that boy's world of football cleats and picket fences, sticks and stones and pocketknives, all those dangers that drove my mother wild with foreboding, and about which I was warned and warned and warned. And warned again. And again.

And again.

So my left testicle took up residence in the vicinity of the inguinal canal. By pressing a finger in the crease between my groin and my thigh, I could still, in the early weeks of its disappearance, feel the curve of its jellied roundness; but then came nights of terror, when I searched my guts in vain, searched all the way up to my rib cage—alas, the voyager had struck off for regions uncharted and unknown. Where was it gone to! How high and how far before the journey would come to an end! Would I one day open my mouth to speak in class, only to discover my left nut out on the end of my tongue? In school we chanted, along with our teacher, *I am the Captain of my fate, I am the Master of my soul,* and meanwhile, within my own body, an anarchic insurrection had been launched by one of my privates—which I was helpless to put down!

For some six months, until its absence was observed by the family doctor during my annual physical examination, I pondered my mystery, more than once wondering—for there was no possibility that did not enter my head, *none*—if the testicle could have taken a dive backwards toward the bowel and there be-gun to convert itself into just such an egg as I had observed my mother yank in a moist yellow cluster from the dark interior of a chicken whose guts she was emp-tying into the garbage. What if breasts began to grow on me, too? What if my penis went dry and brittle, and one day, while I was urinating, snapped off in my hand? Was I being transformed into a girl? Or worse, into a boy such as I under-stood (from the playground grapevine) that Robert Ripley of *Believe It or Not* would pay "a reward" of a hundred thousand dollars for? Believe it or not, there is a nine-year-old boy in New Jersey who is a boy in every way, *except he can have babies.*

Who gets the reward? Me, or the person who turns me in?

Doctor Izzie rolled the scrotal sac between his fingers as though it were the material of a suit he was considering buying, and then told my father that I would have to be given a series of male hormone shots. One of my testicles had never fully descended—unusual, not unheard of . . . But if the shots don't work, asks my father in alarm. What then—! Here I am sent out into the waiting room to look at a magazine.

The shots work. I am spared the knife.

––––––––––

Portnoy's case, as Dr. Izzie announced, is "unusual," but "not unheard of," and with two known methods of remedy, not a major physical concern. How is it a source of major psychological concern to young Portnoy?

What does he imagine may happen next?

What is his most agonizing fear which threatens his very 'I'-ness?

RELATED QUESTIONS

Like Anne Frank in **The Diary of a Young Girl** (p. 26) and Emily in **A High Wind in Jamaica** (p. 24), Portnoy keeps his discovery secret, pondering his "mys-tery," and the horrors which might accrue to it, "for some six months, until its ab-sence was observed by the family doctor" during a routine annual physical exami-nation.

Why didn't Portnoy seek some reassurance or enlightenment? Were his rea-sons for silence probably the same as Anne's and Emily's?

In the Garden of Eden lay Adam,
Complacently stroking his madam,
And loud was his mirth
For on all of the earth
There were only two balls—and he had 'em.

Emily may worry that her own "thin little chest" will never develop "firm little apples" much less "beautiful, mountainous breasts" that have to be cased "in a sort of cornucopia." Yet, advertisements and displays of brassieres should reassure her that considerable variation in the shape and fullness of the bust is normal, and that even breast fashions change. Women traditionally desire the type of breasts that are in vogue at any particular time: A California firm offers an exerciser, a course of instruction for bustline development, and endorsements from happy women who report three-inch gains in just eight weeks; a New York manufacturer of foundation garments offers a 'minimizer' bra with special controlling cups and floating wire inner construction to meet "small-on-top" demands. Meanwhile some women go braless to observe the fashion.

As to his physical development, a male may not be able to disguise his endowments. Padded "cod pieces" or jock straps, unlike bras, are not widely advertised. If males listen to the world's message as Robert transmits it in the following excerpt from *Through the First Gate* by John Stewart, they may detect a note of admiration in comments like "Lordy, ain't George hung though?" Unless, like Adam in the bawdy limerick, he is the only male on earth, a person may easily acquire the popular misconception that the larger the penis, the more masculine and virile the male.

Through the First Gate

JOHN STEWART

. . . George came back across the catwalk. . . . As he walked his body swung back and forth with the swaying of the catwalk, and that private part of him, which seemed already fully grown to manhood as if it had sapped the meat and strength from his long-boned thin body, swayed like a length of heavy rope.

Robert pointed at him. "Lordy, ain't George hung though? No wonder he's so skinny carrying that thing around all the time."

"Hell, he ain't but fifteen. I'd hate to see him when he's twenty," Andrew said.

"If any of these gals see him on that catwalk, he won't live that long," Spunky Davis said. Spunky was the freckle faced, cotton headed one, the one who for some strange reason had become noted as a sheik. They grinned knowingly.

"You tell em Spunky," Robert said.

Douglas said nothing; he looked on indifferently and smiled occasionally. George, sensing that he was the center of attraction, whooped and did a caper on the catwalk. . . . They were amused. As he danced, that better part of him performed various gyrations which threw them all into uproarious laughter. Then he lost his footing and slipped.

Why is the notion untrue that the larger the penis, the more masculine and virile and desirable the male? On what does virility actually depend? Is masculinity the same as virility?

Why do you think that at puberty both males and females become extremely interested in each others' physiological changes?

Which do you think more apt to arouse sexual desire: seeing an attractive member of the opposite sex completely naked; or seeing that same person covered by clothing that reveals nothing, but hints at a great deal (for example, miniskirts, tight-fitting trousers, bikinis, and satin-smooth swim shorts)? Would you expect the masculine and feminine viewpoint to coincide in answering this question? Why, or why not?

RELATED QUESTIONS

Why might girls in the company of other girls be likely to behave like Anne Frank's friend—always keeping her body hidden—while boys in the company of other boys not only might willingly parade naked, but also whoop, caper, and dance like George?

Physical Sexuality

Masturbation, or self-stimulation of the genital organs for erotic arousal, is a common form of sexual outlet. Authorities agree that masturbation does no physical harm but some caution against carrying it to excess. The excess they speak of is psychological, for masturbation can become a substitute for other outlets to relieve tensions and anxieties that are not in the main sexually derived—for example, concern over one's schoolwork, rejection by peers, and uncertainties about self-worth.

Even those who know a great deal about masturbation may still be troubled by it as a habit. Most problems which develop from masturbation are due not to ignorance but to a deep conviction that masturbation is wrong or harmful. Often, even though people have assured themselves intellectually of the acceptability and normality of masturbation as a sexual outlet, they worry about it nevertheless.

It is usual and normal to find children of both sexes fingering their genitals in the very early years, and stimulating them deliberately from the age of six to eight. For the small child, genital stimulation can be as pleasurable and exciting as any other play activity. It is one way the child discovers the pleasure potential that his own body offers. By bringing gratification through the genitals, masturbation actually predisposes the individual toward sexual maturity. The concentration of erotic gratification in the genitals is desirable in all respects and nothing should be done to interfere.

It is unusual, however, for a child to develop a realistic emotional attitude toward masturbation because adults tend to confuse the sexual activity of children, which is really erotic play, with adult genital activity. Adults impose an entirely different perspective on masturbation as a result.

Thus the same parents who joyfully call in the neighbors to witness their infant's discovery of a nose, or fingers, or toes, display no such enthusiasm when that baby discovers his genitals and derives noticeable pleasurable sensations from them.

The same small boy who is taught to hold his penis to urinate may feel his hands slapped if he is found fingering his penis in bed, not to mention in public. The same small girl who is encouraged to play on her rocking horse, in the process of which she may discover the pleasures of clitoral stimulation, may be punished at bedtime if discovered at genital exploration.

Hoping to discourage or eliminate masturbation, adults have threatened children with old wives' tales and superstitions attributing to masturbation a host of consequent disasters ranging from pimples to insanity.

Thus half-understood fears, guilts, and conflicts continue to torment individuals, who continue to note society's condemnation of masturbation, and who continue to practice this form of sexual self-gratification for a variety of reasons: biological, psychological, and, ironically, even social.

The next two selections, one a scene excerpted from Claude **33**

Brown's *Manchild in the Promised Land* involving a group of young-sters sent by courts to Wiltwyck School for problem boys, the other a poem, *The Confirmation,* by Karl Shapiro, deal with the male's confirmation of his sexuality. Yet the writers present masturbation from quite different perspectives: the first is devoid of symbolism and focuses on the act; the second is almost devoid of the act in terms of the symbolism. Brown, a prose writer, uses the first person, re-creates the scene as a participant in it, and employs "locker-room language," the idiom of the boys. Shapiro, a poet, commenting on the scene, sanctifies it through the use of religious images.

Manchild in the Promised Land
CLAUDE BROWN

. . . K. B. must have been real shy when he came to Wiltwyck, because he used to beg me to tell him about the girls I knew. Late at night when I was sleepy and tired of lying all day and half the night, I would listen to K. B. tell me about Linda. For the six months that my bed was next to K. B.'s, I went to sleep hearing about Linda. After a week of hearing about Linda, I had to meet her just to see if she was as fine as K. B. said she was. K. B. said she was real dark-skinned, had long hair, wore lipstick, had "titties, little ones, but tits just the same," had a pretty face, and was real fresh. K. B. said he had done it to her one time up on the roof, and he used to tell me about it so much and in so many different ways that it had to be a lie.

Most of the time, K. B. couldn't think about anything but girls, and anybody who could tell him a good lie about girls could get him to do things. Sometimes when I wanted K. B. to help me steal something, I would have to promise to tell him about a real pretty, real fresh girl. K. B. was always trying to jerk off, and he said he shot one time; but I didn't see it, so I didn't believe it. But about a year after K. B. and I had moved to Aggrey House, I heard K. B. come tearing down the stairs yelling as loud as he could. It was around one in the morning. He woke up everybody in the first-floor dormitory. I was awake and wondering what was going on, when K. B. came running into the dormitory with his dick in his hand and yelling, "Claude, I did it! I did it!" When he reached my bed and yelled out, "Man, I shot," all the beds in the dormitory started jumping, and everybody crowded around my bed with flashlights before K. B. stopped yelling.

Some guys just said things like "Wow" or "Oh, shit," but Rickets said, "Man, that's the real stuff."

Horse said, "Man, that ain't nothin' but dog water."

K. B. said, "That ain't no dog water, man, 'cause it's slimy."

Horse, who was always talking about facts, said, "Man, that can't be scum, 'cause scum is white."

Knowing that scum was white, most of the guys said that Horse was right and that it was just dog water. I said that dog water was more than he ever made. Horse went heading for the bathroom saying he was going to show me what the real stuff looked like. Everybody followed Horse and watched and cheered him on while he tried for the real stuff. Horse only made dog water, just like K. B., but nobody paid much attention—everybody was trying to jerk off that night. It was a matter of life or death. After what seemed like hours of trying and wearing out my arm, I shot for the first time in my life. A lot of other guys did it for the first time too, but some cats just got tired arms.

The author of **Manchild in the Promised Land** describes the boys' group efforts to masturbate and ejaculate "the real stuff" as a matter of life or death. Why?

Would you call the boys' needs social? Biological? Psychological? Something else? Why?

Do you find the vocabulary used in the passage offensive? Why, or why not?

Why are these boys so open with each other about masturbation and so free in their speech? Do you think girls are as candid with each other in discussing their sexual development?

When K. B. runs into the dormitory holding his penis and announcing that he "did it," group opinion is at first divided: Horse, somewhat skeptical, terms K. B.'s ejaculation mere "dog water." Rickets, like K. B., noting that it is "slimy," considers it "scum," and thus genuine. The presence of semen in the ejaculatory fluid, thickening it and making it whitish, would establish it as the "real stuff" in the eyes of the Wiltwyck boys. But even if their ejaculations contained semen, would virility and masculinity be established?

Does the fact that a girl menstruates indicate her readiness to bear children?

What determines male potency and a female's ability to conceive?

The narrator is skeptical of K. B.'s claims to have had intercourse with Linda: "K. B. said he had done it to her one time up on the roof, and he used to tell me about it so much and in so many different ways that it had to be a lie." Do you suspect that K. B.'s sexual claims are more likely fantasy than fact?

Would you agree that among "boys, to boast of actual or invented prowess is acceptable, but to speak soberly of a love affair or a sexual problem in order to be understood is strictly taboo; it is more acceptable among girls." [3] If so, why should this be?

RELATED QUESTIONS

What similarities and differences do you see between the first paragraph of **Manchild in the Promised Land** about K. B.'s sexual claims and the following description of sixteen-year-old Rodney Harrington in **Peyton Place** (p. 400):

> . . . the only thing that Rodney had learned while away at school was that all boys of good family had sexual intercourse with girls before reaching prep school age, and those who had not were either fairies or material for the priesthood. Rodney had learned quickly and by the time he had been at New Hampton for less than a year he could outtalk the best of them. According to Rodney, he had deflowered no less than nine maidens in his own home town before reaching the age of fifteen, and he had almost been shot twice by the irate husband with whose wife he had carried on a passionate affair for six months.

What motivates boys to fabricate tales of sexual conquests in a culture which presumably frowns on premarital and extramarital sexual relations? Do boys talk in these terms to girls, or only to other boys? Why? Do girls behave similarly?

In "De Profundis," Dorothy Parker asks:

Oh, is it, then, Utopian
To hope that I may meet a man
Who'll not relate, in accents suave,
The tales of girls he used to have? [4]

How would you answer her question? Does boasting about sexual conquests—major or minor, real or imagined—stop at maturity? When is maturity?
What light does Fred Apollus in the poem *Fred Apollus at Fava's* by Nicholas Moore (see **"Night-Lights,"** p. 577) shed on this problem?

The Confirmation

KARL SHAPIRO

When mothers weep and fathers richly proud
Worship on Sunday morning their tall son
And girls in white like angels in a play
   Tiptoe between the potted palms
   And all the crimson windows pray,
     The preacher bound in black
Opens his hands like pages of a book
   And holds the black and crimson law
     For every boy to look.

Last night between the chapters of a dream,
The photograph still sinning in the drawer,
The boy awoke; the moon shone in the yard
   On hairy hollyhocks erect
   And buds of roses pink and hard
     And on the solid wall
A square of light like movies fell to pose
   An actress naked in the night
     As hollyhock and rose.

And to confirm his sex, breathless and white
With benediction self-bestowed he knelt
Oh tightly married to his childish grip,
   And unction smooth as holy-oil
   Fell from the vessel's level lip
     Upon the altar-cloth;
Like Easter boys the blood sang in his head
   And all night long the tallow beads
     Like tears dried in the bed.

Come from the church, you parents and you girls,
And walk with kisses and with happy jokes

Beside this man. Be doubly proud, you priest,
    Once for his passion in the rose,
    Once for his body self-released;
      And speak aloud of her
Who in the perfect consciousness of joy
    Stood naked in the electric light
      And woke the hidden boy.

The poem depicts a boy (who apparently has a suggestive photograph of an actress in his desk or bureau drawer) waking at night in the middle of a dream, seeing the hollyhocks and roses by moonlight and a combination of light and shadow on the wall. What meanings and associations does the boy seem to attach to these elements? How does his imagination combine them in reality and in fantasy to bring him to the point where he achieves sexual release?

If the poet were describing a nocturnal emission, what changes would he have to make in the poem?

"Confirmation," by definition, is an act or process of confirming or proving, as: a Christian rite admitting a baptized person to full church privileges; a ceremony confirming Jewish youths in their ancestral faith. How, in a figurative sense, has the poet made parts of this definition relevant to the sexual experience he describes?

RELATED QUESTIONS

Contrast the vocabulary used by the authors of **The Confirmation** and **Manchild in the Promised Land.** What phrases are parallel? How do their different connotations affect your attitude toward the scene depicted?

What other circumstances in **The Confirmation** and **Manchild in the Promised Land** create differences of mood?

Montaigne, in one of his essays, comments on sex:

On the one side nature urgeth us unto it: having thereunto combined, yea fastened, the most noble, the most profitable, and the most sensually pleasing, of all her functions: and on the other suffereth us to accuse, to condemn and to shun it, as insolent, as dishonest, and as lewder to blush at it, and allow, yea and to commend abstinence. Are not we most brutish, to term that work beastly which begets, and which maketh us? [5]

What relevance has Montaigne's passage for **The Confirmation?** How might Shapiro answer Montaigne's final question?

If the conflict between physical desire and social codes is severe, the conflict and confusion confronting the individual whose sex information is half-veiled, inaccurate, distorted, or rooted in superstition can be equally unbearable.

The sufferer's state of mind is portrayed through the following interior monologue of an adolescent whose fragmented thoughts blend what he hears and feels in this excerpt from Richard Aldington's **Death of a Hero,** a novel about Victorian hypocrisy.

Death of a Hero

RICHARD ALDINGTON

One part of the mystery was called SMUT. If you were smutty you went mad and had to go into a lunatic asylum. Or you "contracted a loathsome disease" and your nose fell off.

The pomps and vanities of this wicked world, and all the sinful lusts of the flesh. So it was wicked, like being smutty, to feel happy when you looked at things and read Keats? Perhaps you went mad that way too and your eyes fell out?

"That's what makes them lay eggs," said the little girl, swinging her long golden hair and laughing, as the cock leaped on a hen.

O dreadful, O wicked little girl, you're talking smut to me. You'll go mad, I shall go mad, our noses will drop off. O please don't talk like that, please, please.

From fornication and all other deadly sins. . . . What is fornication? Have I committed fornication? Is that the holy word for smut? Why don't they tell us what it means, why is it "the foulest thing a decent man can commit"? When that thing happened in the night it must have been fornication; I shall go mad and my nose will drop off.

Hymn Number. . . . A few more years shall roll.

How wicked I must be.

Are there two religions? A few more years shall roll, in ten years half you boys will be dead. Smut, nose dropping off, fornication and all the other deadly sins. Oh, wash me in Thy Precious Blood, and take my sins away. Blood, Smut. And then the other—a draught of vintage that has been cooled a long age in the deep-delved earth, tasting of Flora and the country green, dance and Provençal song, and sunburned mirth? Listening to the sound of the wind as you fell asleep; watching the blue butterflies and the Small Coppers hovering and settling on the great scented lavender bush; taking off your clothes and letting your body slide into a cool deep clear rock-pool, while the grey kittiwakes clamoured round the sun-white cliffs and the scent of sea-weeds and salt water filled you; watching the sun go down and trying to write something of what it made you feel, like Keats; getting up very early in the morning and riding out along the white empty lanes on your bicycle; wanting to be alone and think about things and feeling strange and happy and ecstatic—was that another religion? Or was that all Smut and Sin? Best not speak of it, best keep it all hidden. I can't help it, if it is Smut and Sin. Is "Romeo and Juliet" smut? It's in the same book where you do parsing and analysis out of "King John." Seize on the white wonder of dear Juliet's hand and steal immortal blessing from her lips. . . .

What creates the suffering which the character in *Death of a Hero* endures?

How would you suggest relieving his misery?

Why do you suppose the early sexual myth-makers chose lunacy, or the falling off of one's nose, or the falling out of one's eyes as suitable punishments for "deadly sins"?

What is "smut"?

Is fornication the "holy word" for smut? Are there others?

RELATED QUESTIONS

Which of the following do you think the character in *Death of a Hero* would call "smutty": Richard of *Parma Violets* (p. 13)? Anne Frank as she reveals herself in *The Diary of a Young Girl* (p. 26)? The Wiltwyck boys of *Manchild in the Promised Land* (p. 34)? The adolescent in *The Confirmation* (p. 36)? How many would you consider smutty? Why?

"Ode to a Nightingale," the nineteenth-century Romantic English poem by John Keats contains the reference to "a draught of vintage that has been cooled a long age in the deep-delved earth, tasting of Flora and the country green, dance and Provencal song, and sunburned mirth" [6]. Why does the character in *Death of a Hero* find the contrast of Keats' poem "another religion"?

Romantic Sexuality

William Sylvanus Baxter, affectionately termed "Silly Billy" in Booth Tarkington's novel *Seventeen,* is an adolescent in the throes of his first love affair.

Unlike the character in *Death of a Hero,* William is not pre-occupied with smut or sin, partly because, like the poet Keats, he is a romantic, "marked by the imaginative or emotional appeal of the heroic, adventurous, remote, mysterious or idealized."

In the first excerpt from *Seventeen* which follows, William has just met Lola Pratt, the creature upon whom he lavishes his attention.

In the second excerpt, he has encountered opposition: a rival for Miss Pratt's affections, named George Crooper.

Seventeen
BOOTH TARKINGTON

"Oh eyes!" he whispered, softly, in that cool privacy and shelter from the world. "Oh, eyes of blue!"

The mirror of a dressing-table sent him the reflection of his own eyes, which also were blue; and he gazed upon them and upon the rest of his image the while he ate his bread-and-butter and apple sauce and sugar. Thus, watching himself eat, he continued to stare dreamily at the mirror until the bread-and-butter and apple sauce and sugar had disappeared, whereupon he rose and approached the dressing-table to study himself at greater advantage.

He assumed as repulsive an expression as he could command, at the same time making the kingly gesture of one who repels unwelcome attentions; and it is beyond doubt that he was thus acting a little scene of indifference. Other symbolic dramas followed, though an invisible observer might have been puzzled for a key to some of them. One, however, would have proved easily intelligible: his expression having altered to a look of pity and contrition, he turned from the mirror, and, walking slowly to a chair across the room, used his right hand in a peculiar manner, seeming to stroke the air at a point about ten inches above the back of the chair. "There, there, little girl," he said in a low, gentle voice. "I didn't know you cared!"

Then, with a rather abrupt dismissal of this theme, he returned to the mirror and, after a questioning scrutiny, nodded solemnly, forming with his lips the words, "The real thing—the real thing at last!" He meant that, after many imitations had imposed upon him, Love—the real thing—had come to him in the end. And as he turned away he murmured, "And even her name—unknown!"

This evidently was a thought that continued to occupy him, for he walked up and down the room, frowning; but suddenly his brow cleared and his eye lit with purpose. Seating himself at a small writing-table by the window, he proceeded to express his personality—though with considerable labor—in something which he did not doubt to be a poem.

Three-quarters of an hour having sufficed for its completion, including "rewriting and polish," he solemnly signed it, and then read it several times in a state of hushed astonishment. He had never dreamed that he could do anything like this:

MILADY

I do not know her name
Though it would be the same
Where roses bloom at twilight
And the lark takes his flight
It would be the same anywhere
Where music sounds in air
I was never introduced to the lady
So I could not call her Lass or Sadie
So I will call her Milady
By the sands of the sea
She always will be
Just Milady to me.

WILLIAM SYLVANUS BAXTER, Esq., July 14

It is impossible to say how many times he might have read the poem over, always with increasing amazement at his new-found powers, had he not been interrupted. . . .

•   •   •   •   •

Here, in the shade of a great walnut-tree which sheltered the little building, he gave way—not to tears, certainly, but to faint murmurings and little heavings under impulses as ancient as young love itself. It is to be supposed that William considered his condition a lonely one, but if all the seventeen-year-olds who have known such half-hours could have shown themselves to him then, he would have fled from the mere horror of billions. Alas! he considered his sufferings a new invention in the world, and there was now inspired in his breast a monologue so eloquently bitter that it might deserve some such title as A Passion Beside the Smoke-house. During the little time that William spent in this sequestration he passed through phases of emotion which would have kept an older man busy for weeks and left him wrecked at the end of them.

William's final mood was one of beautiful resignation with a kick in it; that is, he nobly gave her up to George and added irresistibly that George was a big, fat lummox! Painting pictures, such as the billions of other young sufferers before him have painted, William saw himself a sad, gentle old bachelor at the family fireside, sometimes making the sacrifice of his reputation so that *she* and the children might never know the truth about George; and he gave himself the solace of a fierce scene or two with George: "Remember, it is for them, not you—you *thing!*"

After this human little reaction he passed to a higher field of romance. He would die for George—and then she would bring the little boy she had named William to the lonely headstone— Suddenly William saw himself in his true and fitting character—Sydney Carton! He had lately read *A Tale of Two Cities*, immediately re-reading until, as he would have said, he "knew it by heart"; and even at the time he had seen resemblances between himself and the appealing figure of Carton. Now that the sympathy between them was perfected by Miss

Pratt's preference for another, William decided to mount the scaffold in place of George Crooper. The scene became actual to him, and, setting one foot upon a tin milk-pail which some one had carelessly left beside the smoke-house, he lifted his eyes to the pitiless blue sky and unconsciously assumed the familiar attitude of Carton on the steps of the guillotine. He spoke aloud those great last words:

"It is a far, far better thing that I do, than I have ever done; it is a far, far better rest that I go to ——"

————————

What are some of the signs of William Baxter's romanticism?

On what basis can the scenes from **Seventeen** be viewed as perspectives on the "I"-orientation, even though the existence of Lola Pratt might indicate grouping the excerpts with "**You-I**"-relationships?

On what does William base his rather questionable conclusion that "after many imitations had imposed upon him, Love—the real thing—had come to him in the end"? Why might one tend to disagree with him?

What "tests" would you apply to determine whether or not you were really in love?

One writer on the subject of love proposes the following six criteria:

1. Love is outgoing: It is other-centered. The one in love is more concerned about his sweetheart than about his own selfish interests. He does anything he can to make his beloved happy. He actively promotes and encourages whatever will be best for the one he loves. He cares more about the relationship he enjoys with her than about his own pride.
2. Real love releases energy: Some feelings inactivate one. At times we are so entangled emotionally that we cannot do anything. Our work falls off. We cannot study. We do not want to eat, or do anything. If this continues, the chances are that it is not real love.

    Love that lasts is creative. It releases a great deal of energy for work. When a boy really loves a girl, he is eager to accomplish and achieve . . . .
3. Love wants to share: Love is best known by the desire to share. When you are in love you want to share a great deal with your lover. You want to share your thoughts. You cannot ever get enough of talking through the things that interest you. You want to share your feelings and your attitudes about things. Lovers do not lack for anything to talk about, for both of them have been saving up the choice anecdotes of every hour of the day to share with the other. Everything that happens is of interest when it happens to be someone you care about. It is this sharingness that keeps love from becoming boring and dull.
4. Love is a We-feeling: You are in love to the extent to which you think and feel and talk and plan in terms of We instead of I. The person who is only partly in love still thinks in terms of himself and his interests and plans. . . .
5. You must like as well as love: For love to last it must have a solid foundation of genuine liking. You must be able to respect and admire your loved one if you expect to love him or her for a very long. If you cannot enjoy each other as two whole persons, whatever your feelings for each other they cannot last. . . .
6. Time is the surest test: When in doubt about love feelings, time will tell. The love that lasts is the love that does last. When a summer's romance is over before autumn, it obviously is not the real thing. When a mad infatuation does not survive the first difference of opinion, it quite certainly is not true love. When love feelings come along for a person who is not

for you, they cannot persist permanently without keeping you both out of bounds. But when love continues around the calendar, through troubles and trials as well as joys, it may well be the kind that will go on through the years.

There used to be a saying that fitted this principle nicely. It went, "Never marry a man until you have summered and wintered with him." More important than the seasons are the emotional climates that you weather together. When you have seen each other through all sorts of situations that have called forth a variety of feelings and you still love each other, it may well be the real thing. If you have experienced together a wide gamut of emotions—sympathy, anger, resentment, sorrow, fear, hatred, as well as love—so that you know deep down inside how each of you feels under these conditions, then you can be said to know your loved one enough to expect the relationship to endure.

There is no quick and easy trick for testing love that will work reliably. Young people will continue to pull daisy petals and cross out letters in each other's names, seek fortunetellers, read tea leaves, and play all the other games that are such fun. But when it comes down to deciding seriously whether we are really in love or not, we turn to more reliable evidences such as those we have been discussing.

Lasting love is too precious to confuse with any of its dazzling substitutes. That does not mean that we should avoid anything but the real thing. Far from it. But it does mean that when all the fooling around is over, and we want to settle down to a lifetime of loving someone with whom we can be deeply and truly in love forever, we should stop playing games and take the longer, surer tests. [7]

From so brief a sampling of William's behavior in "love" it would be unfair to pass final judgment on him. But applying these tests as far as is possible, what seem to you to be William's chances of a lasting love with Milady?

How might you add to, subtract from, or modify these six tests of love? For example, must true love have durability? Have not some of the greatest loves of a lifetime been actually of very short duration?

If one "must like as well as love," contemplated marriage poses the question, "Can I like or tolerate this person endlessly?" Would trial marriages be an effective means of trying to find the answer to the question?

Do you find William's reaction to the girl's preference for another suitor pathetic? Tense? Touching? Silly? Laughable? Universal? Noble? Something else?

William sees resemblances between himself and the appealing figure of Sydney Carton from Dickens' *A Tale of Two Cities* who took Charles Darnay's place and went to the guillotine so that Lucie Manette, the girl whom both men loved, might be happy. Why does Sidney Carton appeal to William? Where do you feel the resemblances between the two might end? Why?

"The lover's criterion is: I want you to be happy—but with me" [8]: Yet here, William's "beautiful resignation" permits him to give up his girl to George—for her sake. What clues does the author establish to let readers know that William is not so self-sacrificing and unselfish as he appears?

What might have been some of those "phases of emotion" which William passed through before reaching his "final mood . . . one of beautiful resignation with a kick in it"?

Whether on the small scale of a few moments' distraction during Latin class or on the large scale of Walter Mitty, everyone has tasted the richness of a fantasy life. William, one foot on a tin milkpail, which his imagination easily transforms into a scaffold, is part of a longstanding tradition which includes Cinderella's dreams of the ball; Elmer Dowd's companion rabbit, Harvey; the six-year-old dressed up in her mother's hat and shoes; the punished ten-year-old imagining his parents' grief when he dies next week; or the adolescent who tries on a series of facial expressions before the mirror while rehearsing a projected conversation with her next date. What purpose does such role-playing serve?

Although he considers his condition a lonely one, why is William actually painting pictures such as billions of other sufferers before him have sketched in their imaginations?

The author's comment that William "gave way—not to tears, certainly," is in keeping with the popular notion in Western cultures that males should not cry. The converse seems equally true: in critical moments the female often gives way to tears. Is the emotional impact from the same experience essentially different for the male and the female? Do you think there is anything morally wrong with crying by either sex?

Consider both excerpts from **Seventeen** in the light of the following comment:

> . . . young people, to keep themselves together . . . temporarily over-identify with . . . heroes . . . to the point of an apparently complete loss of individuality. Yet in this stage not even "falling in love" is entirely, or even primarily, a sexual matter. To a considerable extent adolescent love is an attempt to arrive at a definition of one's identity by projecting one's diffused self-image on another and by seeing it thus reflected and gradually clarified. This is why so much of young love is conversation. [9]

The novel **Seventeen** was written in 1916, before the atomic bomb, television, moon landings, "the Pill," widespread teenage use of drugs, liquor, or cars. And while its portrait of adolescence is still valid, the novel seems dated because the pace of contemporary life makes the behavior of William, a seventeen-year-old ready for college, incredible. If the author were to ask you to retitle his novel, what age would you suggest be put on the cover today?

RELATED QUESTIONS

What element of at least implied concern to other characters in the "I" section seems to be no part of William Sylvanus Baxter's problem? Does its omission seem logical or plausible to you?

What elements of Richard's relationship with Aunt Bunch in **Parma Violets** (p. 13) are also apparent in William's feelings for Milady? What modifications have these elements undergone by virtue of the fact that William is a teenager and Richard only a child?

Theodore Bulpington, a fifteen-year-old in the following excerpt from H. G. Wells' **The Bulpington of Blup,** suffers from a combination of elements experienced by adolescents. Like William Sylvanus Baxter of **Seventeen,** Theodore has been rejected by his sweetheart, Margaret Broxted, in favor of another, and resorts to fantasy to satisfy his unfulfilled desires and to compensate for his feelings of inferiority by imagining a "second self," The Bulpington of Blup. But like the central character in **Death of a Hero,** Theodore suffers from the "powerful and perplexing influence" of heightened sexual awareness which makes his dreamland border on nightmare.

The Bulpington of Blup

H. G. WELLS

The four years of adolescence that followed Theodore's first meeting with Margaret Broxted were years of incessant discovery and complication for the teeming grey matter which was the material substance both of Theodore and of that second self of his, the Bulpington of Blup. Strange things, affecting both of them, were being thrust upon that incessant brain by the body it directed; new ferments and stimulants came, whispers on incitement, to its stirring cells. These whispers asked: What are you doing? What are you going to do? What are your plans about life? What do you think you are? There is strange business to be done. Get on with it all. Time is short for life.

The whispers were so subtle that Theodore's mind was only plainly aware of the evasive, reluctant, perplexed answers, the confusing impulses, they evoked. He did not perceive that he was changing; he realized only that he was growing up and learning new things about the world, masses of things about this world and about himself; some of them extraordinarily distressing and unpalatable.

Sex was becoming a more powerful and perplexing influence. It was no longer simply lovely and romantic. It was entangling itself with unclean and repellent processes in life. Bodily forms and animal movements that had once been merely mystically attractive and beautiful were now becoming infected with intimations and gestures of urgency. Some profoundly obscene business was afoot in the universe amidst its engaging patterns and appearances. The apprehension of that urgent sustaining activity became more and more pervasive. The lines and contours of life converged upon disconcerting issues.

At fifteen Theodore had a great store of bookish and romantic knowledge and a belated ignorance and innocence. Francolin and Bletts came along to hint and tell, with flushed cheeks and a furtive defiance in their manner, of remarkable discoveries. And Theodore told nobody of certain discoveries his own body was forcing upon him. His chosen ideas of love were after the sublimated fashion of the Troubadours. There was at last an ecstasy, a physical ecstasy. He had found out something of the nature of that for himself during his bedtime reveries on the verge of dreamland. But his wilful and waking life recoiled from too exacting a scrutiny of that close and thrilling embrace. The secrets of the adults about him, he knew, were heavy stuff, and Francolin abounded in the gross particulars.

The tension on Francolin's mind relieved itself in facetiousness. Dawning adolescence had turned the world upside down for him and filled him with laughter at the trick. He saw everything as it were from the pedestal upward, all "bums" and "bubs" and bellies. He developed an unsuspected gift for drawing, seeking to adorn his environment with formidable reminders of the great secret. His vocabulary was increased by a virile sexual terminology. He would not, if he could, have anything to hide.

There was less indecent uproar about Bletts, but a more direct and personal intentness. A quiet covetousness had come into his eyes. There had been something with the "slavey" at home, and he was for accosting girls and wandering off with them to quiet places. A large part of his leisure was devoted to prowling to that end. He sought Theodore's company for his prowling, because hunter and quarry, amidst the mysteries of petting and flirting, work best in confidential couples. The couples pair off for their researches, in silence on the male side and with a disposition to giggle . . . on the female. Bletts said things about servants and work-girls and girl visitors to the seaside, gross things, that put Theodore into a state of great uneasiness. Theodore felt such things should not be said of any girl, that they smeared a sort of nastiness across all femininity, but they haunted his imagination afterwards and he was never able and decisive enough about it to stem the flow of Blett's magnetized preoccupation.

Amidst such influences as these, in the atmosphere created by a Christian civilization that, for better or worse, had substituted rigid restriction, concealment and shame for the grotesque initiations and terror-haunted taboos of pagan peoples, Theodore grew towards sexual maturity. There was a steady resistance in him to this self-induction into sexual life. For some time, therefore, more and more of their common grey matter was diverted from the material existence of Theodore to the purposes of his partner, the Bulpington of Blup and the life of reverie. The Bulpington of Blup had no use for the squalid adventures of Bletts; and Francolin approached him only distantly as a court jester under reproof. The Bulpington of Blup was the sublimating genius. He went through the air with ease while Theodore stumbled in the mire. He vanished whenever Theodore wallowed. Blup was still a high upstanding place, but now it was coming into more rational relations with prevalent and established things.

The Delphic Sibyl, who was sometimes altogether herself and sometimes more or less Margaret Broxted, remained the ruling heroine of his adolescent reveries. He and she went about side by side, they had great adventures and she was lost and rescued, they embraced and kissed, but everything between them was always very clean and splendid. Only once or twice on the very borderland of dreaming did that bodily ecstasy occur, and then it was very indistinct and confusing because suddenly it seemed that the Sibyl was someone else—who vanished. And the strange and forcible dreams that were now assailing him had only the remotest connexion or no connexion at all with his world of fantasy.

This dreamland was becoming now more and more obscured by a monstrous sexual life of its own. Dreadful old witches, young women with absurdly opulent contours who exaggerated every distinctly feminine trait, caressing animal monsters, sphinxes, mermaids, strange creatures, and yet labelled, as it were, so that they were identified with, rather than resembled, persons he knew, chased and seduced this sub-Theodore in a warm and weedy underworld, overwhelmed him in soft rotundities, lured him into a false intimacy and found him helplessly responsive to startling embraces.

A dismayed youth would sit up rubbing the cobwebs of sleep from his eyes, and slip out of bed to sponge off a sense of clammy uncleanness with cold water.

Theodore did not "perceive that he was changing; he realized only that he was growing up and learning new things about the world, masses of things about this world and about himself; some of them extraordinarily distressing and unpalatable." What sorts of experiences or feelings lead to the realization of growing up?

What might some of the "masses of things about this world and about himself" be? Why are some of them "extraordinarily distressing and unpalatable"?

Do you think males are more tormented by the "powerful and perplexing
influence" of heightened sexual awareness than females? What physiological and
psychological differences in this respect exist between the male and female?

What does it mean that Theodore's "chosen ideas of love were after the sublimated fashion of the Troubadours"? What is sublimation? What purpose does it
serve? How might it explain Theodore's fantasy of "the Bulpington of Blup, the
sublimating genius"?

What does "there was at last an ecstasy, a physical ecstasy" mean?

Theodore tells "nobody of certain discoveries his own body was forcing
upon him." Yet he suspects that "the secrets of the adults about him were heavy
stuff." Why does he not talk to an adult instead of listening to Francolin and Bletts
who "came along to and hint and tell, with flushed cheeks and a furtive defiance
in their manner, of remarkable discoveries . . . [and] the gross particulars"?

How might the dismay of Theodore and others who find "dreamland . . .
becoming more and more obscured by a monstrous sexual life of its own" be prevented or relieved?

RELATED QUESTIONS

For Theodore, sex "was no longer simply lovely and romantic." For which
characters in selections you have already read is sex still simply lovely and romantic? How?

Is Theodore's physical ecstasy, discovered during his "bedtime reveries
on the verge of dreamland," similar to the experience of the youth in Shapiro's
poem, *The Confirmation* (p. 36)?

What light is shed on certain sexual attitudes and on adolescent concealments like those of Theodore in *The Bulpington of Blup,* Emily in *A High Wind in
Jamaica* (p. 22), Anne in *The Diary of a Young Girl* (p. 26), and the boy in *Death of
a Hero* (p. 38) by the comment that "in the atmosphere created by a Christian civilization that, for better or worse, had substituted rigid restriction, concealment
and shame for the grotesque initiations and terror-haunted taboos of pagan
peoples, Theodore grew towards sexual maturity"? In your judgment, is this
atmosphere for the better? Or for the worse?

What are some of the "grotesque initiations" and "terror-haunted taboos"
of pagan peoples?

Why might the character in *Death of a Hero* (p. 38) consider Theodore and
his friends, Francolin and Bletts, "smutty"?

What parallels do you find between the experiences and sexual attitudes of
adolescents portrayed in the "I" section and those apparent in the poem *Wax* by
Winfield Townley Scott (see "**Night-Lights,**" p. 588) in which a group of girls and
boys discover a dildo?

The Self in Conflict

Males can be proud and delighted to have an attractive sister, yet there are occasions when an attractive female can cause her brother acute personal distress. In the following excerpt from *Young Lonigan,* a study of adolescence by James T. Farrell, young Lonigan is alarmed and frightened by "dirty thoughts that rushed to his head like hot blood" when his sister Frances comes into his room and stirs up what he fears may signal incestuous feelings.

Young Lonigan

JAMES T. FARRELL

Frances came in. She wore a thin nightgown. He could almost see right through it. He tried to keep looking away, but he had to turn his head back to look at her. She stood before him, and didn't seem to know that he was looking at her. She seemed kind of queer; he thought maybe she was sick.

"Do you like Lucy?"

"Oh, a little," he said.

He was excited, and couldn't talk much, because he didn't want her to notice it.

"Do you like to kiss girls?"

"Not so much," he said.

"You did tonight."

"It was all in the game."

"Helen must like Weary."

"I hate her."

"I don't like her either, but . . . . do you think they did anything in the post office?"

"What do you mean?" he asked.

She wasn't going to pump him and get anything out of him.

She seemed to be looking at him, awful queer, all right.

"You know. Do you think they did anything that was fun . . . or that the sisters wouldn't want them to do . . . or that's bad?"

"I don't know."

Dirty thoughts rushed to his head like hot blood. He told himself he was a bastard because . . . she was his sister.

"I don't know," he said, confused.

"You think maybe they did something bad, and it was fun?"

He shrugged his shoulders and looked out the window so she couldn't see his face.

"I feel funny," she said.

He hadn't better say anything to her, because she'd snitch and give him away.

"I want to do something . . . They're all in bed. Let's us play leap frog, you know that game that boys play where one bends down, and the others jump over him?" she said.

"We'll make too much noise."

"Do you really think that Weary and Helen did anything that might be fun?" she asked.

She got up, and walked nervously around the room. She plunked down on the piano stool, and part of her leg showed.

He looked out the window. He looked back. They sat. She fidgeted and couldn't sit still. She got up and ran out of the room. He sat there. He must be a bastard . . . she was his sister.

He looked out the window. He wondered what it was like; he was getting old enough to find out.

He got up. He looked at himself in the mirror. He shadow-boxed, and thought of Lucy. He thought of Fran. He squinted at himself in the mirror.

He turned the light out and started down the hallway. Fran called him. She was lying in bed without the sheets over her.

"It's hot here. Awful hot. Please put the window up higher."

"It's as high as it'll go."

"I thought it wasn't."

He looked at Fran. He couldn't help it.

"And please get some real cold water."

He got the water. It wasn't cold enough. She asked him to let the water run more. He did. He handed the water to her. As she rose to drink, she bumped her small breast against him.

She drank the water. He started out of the room. She called him to get her handkerchief.

"I'm not at all tired," she said.

He left, thinking what a bastard he must be.

He went to the bathroom.

Kneeling down at his bedside, he tried to make a perfect act of contrition to wash his soul from sin.

He heard the wind, and was afraid that God might punish him, make him die in the night. He had found out he was old enough, but . . . his soul was black with sin. He lay in bed worried, suffering, and he tossed into a slow, troubled sleep.

———————

Beginning with her entrance in a transparently thin nightgown, there are at least seven ways in which Frances contributes to her brother's sexual arousal. What are they?

Do you consider Frances' behavior innocent or deliberate? If you believe Frances is unaware of what she is doing and insensitive to the effects she produces, what ought she to learn about the nature of sexual arousal in the male?

If you think that Frances' actions are conscious designs to tease Lonigan, what might be her possible motives for attempting to arouse him sexually?

Whom do you hold more responsible for sexual situations that go "too far": the male or the female? Why?

What parallels do you see between Frances of *Young Lonigan* and Aunt Bunch of *Parma Violets* (p. 13)?

In James Joyce's semiautobiographical *A Portrait of the Artist as a Young Man,* the needs of Stephen Daedalus, a sixteen-year-old student in an Irish Jesuit school, are no longer satisfied by romantic fantasies and role playing, although in earlier moods of soft languor he identified with the hero of *The Count of Monte Cristo,* imagining trysts and holy encounters with a female and the speech he would make to her in a moonlit garden after years of estrangement and adventure.

In the following excerpt dealing with sexual and spiritual conflict, Stephen tries to contend with the "wasting fires of lust" which "sprang up again" when "his blood [was] in revolt" by seeking whorehouses through a "maze of narrow and dirty streets" in Dublin.

A Portrait of the Artist as a Young Man

JAMES JOYCE

He saw clearly . . . his own futile isolation. He had not gone one step nearer the lives he had sought to approach nor bridged the restless shame and rancour that had divided him from mother and brother and sister. He felt that he was hardly of the one blood with them but stood to them rather in the mystical kinship of fosterage, foster child and foster brother.

He turned to appease the fierce longings of his heart before which everything else was idle and alien. He cared little that he was in mortal sin, that his life had grown to be a tissue of subterfuge and falsehood. Beside the savage desire within him to realise the enormities which he brooded on nothing was sacred. He bore cynically with the shameful details of his secret riots in which he exulted to defile with patience whatever image had attracted his eyes. By day and by night he moved among distorted images of the outer world. A figure that had seemed to him by day demure and innocent came towards him by night through the winding darkness of sleep, her face transfigured by a lecherous cunning, her eyes bright with brutish joy. Only the morning pained him with its dim memory of dark orgiastic riot, its keen and humiliating sense of transgression.

. . . He wanted to sin with another of his kind, to force another being to sin with him and to exult with her in sin. He felt some dark presence moving irresistibly upon him from the darkness, a presence subtle and murmurous as a flood filling him wholly with itself . . . . He stretched out his arms in the street to hold fast the frail swooning form that eluded him and incited him: and the cry that he had strangled for so long in his throat issued from his lips. It broke from him like a wail of despair from a hell of sufferers and died in a wail of furious entreaty, a cry for an iniquitous abandonment, a cry which was but the echo of an obscene scrawl which he had read on the oozing wall of a urinal.

He had wandered into a maze of narrow and dirty streets . . . . Women and girls dressed in long vivid gowns traversed the street from house to house. They were leisurely and perfumed. A trembling seized him and his eyes grew dim. The yellow gasflames arose before his troubled vision against the vapoury sky, burning as if before an altar. Before the doors and in the lighted halls groups were gathered arrayed as for some rite. He was in another world: he had awakened from a slumber of centuries.

He stood still in the middle of the roadway, his heart clamouring against his bosom in a tumult. A young woman dressed in a long pink gown laid her hand on his arm to detain him and gazed into his face. She said gaily:

—Good night, Willie dear!

Her room was warm and lightsome. A huge doll sat with her legs apart in the copious easychair beside the bed. He tried to bid his tongue speak that he might seem at ease, watching her as she undid her gown, noting the proud conscious movements of her perfumed head.

As he stood silent in the middle of the room she came over to him and embraced him gaily and gravely. Her round arms held him firmly to her and he, seeing her face lifted to him in serious calm and feeling the warm calm rise and fall of her breast, all but burst into hysterical weeping. Tears of joy and relief shone in his delighted eyes and his lips parted though they would not speak.

She passed her tinkling hand through his hair, calling him a little rascal.

—Give me a kiss, she said.

His lips would not bend to kiss her. He wanted to be held firmly in her arms, to be caressed slowly, slowly, slowly. In her arms he felt that he had suddenly become strong and fearless and sure of himself. But his lips would not bend to kiss her.

With a sudden movement she bowed his head and joined her lips to his and he read the meaning of her movements in her frank uplifted eyes. It was too much for him. He closed his eyes, surrendering himself to her, body and mind, conscious of nothing in the world but the dark pressure of her softly parting lips. They pressed upon his brain as upon his lips as though they were the vehicle of a vague speech; and between them he felt an unknown and timid pressure, darker than the swoon of sin, softer than sound or odour.

The swift December dusk had come tumbling clownishly after its dull day and as he stared through the dull square of the window of the schoolroom he felt his belly crave for its food. He hoped there would be stew for dinner, turnips and carrots and bruised potatoes and fat mutton pieces to be ladled out in thick peppered flourfattened sauce. Stuff it into you, his belly counselled him.

It would be a gloomy secret night. After early night-fall the yellow lamps would light up, here and there, the squalid quarter of the brothels. He would follow a devious course up and down the streets, circling always nearer and nearer in a tremor of fear and joy, until his feet led him suddenly round a dark corner. The whores would be just coming out of their houses making ready for the night, yawning lazily after their sleep and settling the hairpins in their clusters of hair. He would pass by them calmly waiting for a sudden movement of his own will or a sudden call to his sinloving soul from their soft perfumed flesh. Yet as he prowled in quest of that call, his senses, stultified only by his desire, would note keenly all that wounded or shamed them; his eyes, a ring of porter froth on a clothless table or a photograph of two soldiers standing to attention on a gaudy playbill; his ears, the drawling jargon of greeting:

—Hello, Bertie, any good in your mind?

—Is that you, pigeon?

—Number ten. Fresh Nelly is waiting on you.

—Good night, husband! Coming in to have a short time?

The equation on the page of his scribbler began to spread out a widening tail, eyed and starred like a peacock's; and, when the eyes and stars of its indices had been eliminated, began slowly to fold itself together again . . . .

The dull light fell more faintly upon the page whereon another equation began to unfold itself slowly and to spread abroad its widening tail. It was his own soul going forth to experience, unfolding itself sin by sin, spreading abroad the balefire of its burning stars and folding back upon itself, fading slowly, quenching its own lights and fires. They were quenched: and the cold darkness filled chaos.

A cold lucid indifference reigned in his soul. At his first violent sin he had felt a wave of vitality pass out of him and had feared to find his body or his soul maimed by the excess. Instead the vital wave had carried him on its bosom out of himself and back again when it receded: and no part of body or soul had been maimed, but a dark peace had been established between them. The chaos in which his ardour extinguished itself was a cold indifferent knowledge of himself. He had sinned mortally not once but many times and he knew that, while he stood in danger of eternal damnation for the first sin alone, by every succeeding sin he multiplied his guilt and his punishment. His days and works and thoughts could make no atonement for him, the fountains of sanctifying grace having ceased to refresh his soul. At most, by an alms given to a beggar whose blessing he fled from, he might hope wearily to win for himself some measure of actual grace. Devotion had gone by the board. What did it avail to pray when he knew that his soul lusted after its own destruction? A certain pride, a certain awe, withheld him from offering to God even one prayer at night though he knew it was in God's power to take away his life while he slept and hurl his soul hellward ere he could beg for mercy. His pride in his own sin, his loveless awe of God, told him that his offence was too grievous to be atoned for in whole or in part by a false homage to the Allseeing and Allknowing.

. . . Towards others he felt neither shame nor fear. On Sunday mornings as he passed the church door he glanced coldly at the worshippers who stood bareheaded, four deep, outside the church, morally present at the mass which they could neither see nor hear. Their dull piety and the sickly smell of the cheap hairoil with which they had anointed their heads repelled him from the altar they prayed at. He stooped to the evil of hypocrisy with others, sceptical of their innocence which he could cajole so easily.

On the wall of his bedroom hung an illuminated scroll, the certificate of his prefecture in the college of the sodality of the Blessed Virgin Mary. On Saturday mornings when the sodality met in the chapel to recite the little office his place was a cushioned kneelingdesk at the right of the altar from which he led his wing of boys through the responses. The falsehood of his position did not pain him . . . .

It was strange too that he found an arid pleasure in following up to the end the rigid lines of the doctrines of the church and penetrating into obscure silences only to hear and feel the more deeply his own condemnation. The sentence of Saint James which says that he who offends against one commandment becomes guilty of all had seemed to him first a swollen phrase until he had begun to grope in the darkness of his own state. From the evil seed of lust all other deadly sins had sprung forth: pride in himself and contempt of others, covetousness in using money for the purchase of unlawful pleasures, envy of those whose vices he could not reach to and calumnious murmuring against the pious, gluttonous enjoyment of food, the dull glowering anger amid which he brooded upon his longing, the swamp of spiritual and bodily sloth in which his whole being had sunk.

The rector did not ask for a catechism to hear the lesson from. He clasped his hands on the desk and said:

—The retreat will begin on Wednesday afternoon in honour of Saint Francis Xavier whose feast day is Saturday. The retreat will go on from Wednesday to Friday. On Friday confession will be heard all the afternoon after beads. If any boys have special confessors perhaps it will be better for them not to change. Mass will be on Saturday morning at nine o'clock and general communion for the whole college. . . .

He ceased to shake his clasped hands and, resting them against his forehead, looked right and left of them keenly at his listeners out of his dark stern eyes.

In the silence their dark fire kindled the dusk into a tawny glow. Stephen's heart had withered up like a flower of the desert that feels the simoom coming from afar.

He went up to his room after dinner in order to be alone with his soul: and at every step his soul seemed to sigh: at every step his soul mounted with his feet, sighing in the ascent, through a region of viscid gloom.

He halted on the landing before the door and then, grasping the porcelain knob, opened the door quickly. He waited in fear, his soul pining within him, praying silently that death might not touch his brow as he passed over the threshold, that the fiends that inhabit darkness might not be given power over him. He waited still at the threshold as at the entrance to some dark cave. . . .

Murmuring faces waited and watched; murmurous voices filled the dark shell of the cave. He feared intensely in spirit and in flesh but, raising his head bravely, he strode into the room firmly. A doorway, a room, the same room, same window. He told himself calmly that those words had absolutely no sense which had seemed to rise murmurously from the dark. He told himself that it was simply his room with the door open.

He closed the door and, walking swiftly to the bed, knelt beside it and covered his face with his hands. His hands were cold and damp and his limbs ached with chill. Bodily unrest and chill and weariness beset him, routing his thoughts. Why was he kneeling there like a child saying his evening prayers? To be alone with his soul, to examine his conscience, to meet his sins face to face, to recall their times and manners and circumstances, to weep over them. He could not weep. He could not summon them to his memory. He felt only an ache of soul and body, his whole being, memory, will, understanding, flesh, benumbed and weary.

That was the work of devils, to scatter his thoughts and overcloud his conscience, assailing him at the gates of the cowardly and sincorrupted flesh: and, praying God timidly to forgive him his weakness, he crawled up on to the bed and, wrapping the blankets closely about him, covered his face again with his hands. He had sinned. He had sinned so deeply against heaven and before God that he was not worthy to be called God's child.

Could it be that he, Stephen Dedalus, had done those things? His conscience sighed in answer. Yes, he had done them, secretly, filthily, time after time and, hardened in sinful impenitence, he had dared to wear the mask of holiness before the tabernacle itself while his soul within was a living mass of corruption. How came it that God had not struck him dead? The leprous company of his sins closed about him, breathing upon him, bending over him from all sides. He strove to forget them in an act of prayer, huddling his limbs closer together and binding down his eyelids: but the senses of his soul would not be bound and, though his eyes were shut fast, he saw the places where he had sinned and, though his ears were tightly covered, he heard. He desired with all his will not to hear nor see. He desired till his frame shook under the strain of his desire and until the senses of his soul closed. They closed for an instant and then opened. He saw.

A field of stiff weeds and thistles and tufted nettlebunches. Thick among the tufts of rank stiff growth lay battered canisters and clots and coils of solid excrement. A faint marshlight struggling upwards from all the ordure through the bristling greygreen weeds. An evil smell, faint and foul as the light, curled upwards sluggishly out of the canisters and from the stale crusted dung.

Creatures were in the field; one, three, six: creatures were moving in the field, hither and thither. Goatish creatures with human faces, horny browed, lightly bearded and grey as indiarubber. The malice of evil glittered in their hard eyes, as they moved hither and thither, trailing their long tails behind them. A rictus of cruel malignity lit up greyly their old bony faces. One was clasping about his ribs a torn flannel waistcoat, another complained monotonously as his beard stuck in the tufted weeds. Soft language issued from their spittleless lips as they swished in slow circles round and round the field, winding hither and thither through the weeds, dragging their long tails amid the rattling canisters. They moved in slow circles, circling closer and closer to enclose, to enclose, soft language issuing from their lips, their long swishing tails besmeared with stale shite, thrusting upwards their terrific faces . . .

Help!

He flung the blankets from him madly to free his face and neck. That was his hell. God had allowed him to see the hell reserved for his sins: stinking, bestial, malignant, a hell of lecherous goatish fiends. For him! For him!

He sprang from the bed, the reeking odour pouring down his throat, clog- ging and revolting his entrails. Air! The air of heaven! He stumbled towards the window, groaning and almost fainting with sickness. At the washstand a convul- sion seized him within; and, clasping his cold forehead wildly, he vomited pro- fusely in agony.

When the fit had spent itself he walked weakly to the window and lifting the sash, sat in a corner of the embrasure and leaned his elbow upon the sill. The rain had drawn off; and amid the moving vapours from point to point of light the city was spinning about herself a soft cocoon of yellowish haze. . . .

His eyes were dimmed with tears and, looking humbly up to heaven, he wept for the innocence he had lost.

When evening had fallen he left the house and the first touch of the damp dark air and the noise of the door as it closed behind him made ache again his conscience, lulled by prayer and tears. Confess! Confess! It was not enough to lull the conscience with a tear and a prayer. He had to kneel before the minister of the Holy Ghost and tell over his hidden sins truly and repentantly. Before he heard again the footboard of the housedoor trail over the threshold as it opened to let him in, before he saw again the table in the kitchen set for supper he would have knelt and confessed. It was quite simple.

The ache of conscience ceased and he walked onward swiftly through the dark streets. There were so many flagstones on the footpath of that street and so many streets in that city and so many cities in the world. Yet eternity had no end. He was in mortal sin. Even once was a mortal sin. It could happen in an instant. But how so quickly? By seeing or by thinking of seeing. The eyes see the thing, without having wished first to see. Then in an instant it happens. But does that part of the body understand or what? The serpent, the most subtle beast of the field. It must understand when it desires in one instant and then prolongs its own desire instant after instant, sinfully. It feels and understands and desires. What a horrible thing! Who made it to be like that, a bestial part of the body able to un- derstand bestially and desire bestially? Was that then he or an inhuman thing moved by a lower soul? His soul sickened at the thought of a torpid snaky life feeding itself out of the tender marrow of his life and fattening upon the slime of lust. O why was that so? O Why?

He cowered in the shadow of the thought, abasing himself in the awe of God Who had made all things and all men. Madness. Who could think such a thought? And, cowering in darkness and abject, he prayed mutely to his angel guardian to drive away with his sword the demon that was whispering to his brain.

. . . An old woman was about to cross the street, an oilcan in her hand. He bent down and asked her was there a chapel near.

—A chapel, sir? Yes, sir. Church Street chapel.

—Church?

She lifted the can to her other hand and directed him: and, as she held out her reeking withered right hand under its fringe of shawl, he bent lower towards her, saddened and soothed by her voice.

—Thank you.

—You are quite welcome, sir.

The candles on the high altar had been extinguished but the fragrance of incense still floated down the dim nave. . . .

He bowed his head upon his hands, bidding his heart be meek and humble that he might be like those who knelt beside him and his prayer as acceptable as theirs. He prayed beside them but it was hard. His soul was foul with sin and he dared not ask forgiveness with the simple trust of those whom Jesus, in the mysterious ways of God, had called first to His side, the carpenters, the fishermen, poor and simple people following a lowly trade, handling and shaping the wood of trees, mending their nets with patience.

A tall figure came down the aisle and the penitents stirred: and, at the last moment glancing up swiftly, he saw a long grey beard and the brown habit of a capuchin. The priest entered the box and was hidden. Two penitents rose and entered the confessional at either side. The wooden slide was drawn back and the faint murmur of a voice troubled the silence.

His blood began to murmur in his veins, murmuring like a sinful city summoned from its sleep to hear its doom. Little flakes of fire fell and powdery ashes fell softly, alighting on the houses of men. They stirred, waking from sleep, troubled by the heated air.

The slide was shot back. The penitent emerged from the side of the box. The farther side was drawn. A woman entered quietly and deftly where the first penitent had knelt. The faint murmur began again.

He could still leave the chapel. He could stand up, put one foot before the other and walk out softly and then run, run, run swiftly through the dark streets. He could still escape from the shame. Had it been any terrible crime but that one sin! Had it been murder! Little fiery flakes fell and touched him at all points, shameful thoughts, shameful words, shameful acts. Shame covered him wholly like fine glowing ashes falling continually. To say it in words! His soul, stifling and helpless, would cease to be.

The slide was shot back. A penitent emerged from the farther side of the box. The near slide was drawn. A penitent entered where the other penitent had come out. A soft whispering noise floated in vaporous cloudlets out of the box. It was the woman: soft whispering cloudlets, soft whispering vapour, whispering and vanishing.

He beat his breast with his fist humbly, secretly under cover of the wooden armrest. He would be at one with others and with God. He would love his neighbour. He would love God Who had made and loved him. He would kneel and pray with others and be happy. God would look down on him and on them and would love them all.

The slide was shot to suddenly. The penitent came out. He was next. He stood up in terror and walked blindly into the box.

At last it had come. He knelt in the silent gloom and raised his eyes to the white crucifix suspended above him. God could see that he was sorry. He would tell all his sins. His confession would be long, long. Everybody in the chapel would know then what a sinner he had been. Let them know. It was true. But God had promised to forgive him if he was sorry. He was sorry. He clasped his hands and raised them towards the white form, praying with his darkened eyes, praying with all his trembling body, swaying his head to and fro like a lost creature, praying with whimpering lips.

—Sorry! Sorry! O sorry!

The slide clicked back and his heart bounded in his breast. The face of an old priest was at the grating, averted from him, leaning upon a hand. He made the sign of the cross and prayed of the priest to bless him for he had sinned. Then, bowing his head, he repeated the *Confiteor* in fright. At the words *my most grievous fault* he ceased, breathless.

—How long is it since your last confession, my child?

—A long time, father.

—A month, my child?

—Longer, father.

—Three months, my child?

—Longer, father.

—Six months?

—Eight months, father.

He had begun. The priest asked:

—And what do you remember since that time?

He began to confess his sins: masses missed, prayers not said, lies.

—Anything else, my child?

Sins of anger, envy of others, gluttony, vanity, disobedience.

—Anything else, my child?

There was no help. He murmured:

—I . . . committed sins of impurity, father.

The priest did not turn his head.

—With yourself, my child?

—And . . . with others.

—With women, my child?

—Yes, father.

—Were they married women, my child?

He did not know. His sins trickled from his lips, one by one, trickled in shameful drops from his soul festering and oozing like a sore, a squalid stream of vice. The last sins oozed forth, sluggish, filthy. There was no more to tell. He bowed his head, overcome.

The priest was silent. Then he asked:

—How old are you, my child?

—Sixteen, father.

The priest passed his hand several times over his face. Then, resting his forehead against his hand, he leaned towards the grating and, with eyes still averted, spoke slowly. His voice was weary and old.

—You are very young, my child, he said, and let me implore of you to give up that sin. It is a terrible sin. It kills the body and it kills the soul. It is the cause of many crimes and misfortunes. Give it up, my child, for God's sake. It is dishonourable and unmanly. You cannot know where that wretched habit will lead you or where it will come against you. As long as you commit that sin, my poor child, you will never be worth one farthing to God. Pray to our mother Mary to help you. She will help you, my child. Pray to Our Blessed Lady when that sin comes into your mind. I am sure you will do that, will you not? You repent of all those sins. I am sure you do. And you will promise God now that by His holy grace you will never offend Him any more by that wicked sin. You will make that solemn promise to God, will you not?

—Yes, father.

The old and weary voice fell like sweet rain upon his quaking parching heart. How sweet and sad!

—Do so, my poor child. The devil has led you astray. Drive him back to hell when he tempts you to dishonour your body in that way—the foul spirit who hates Our Lord. Promise God now that you will give up that sin, that wretched wretched sin.

Blinded by his tears and by the light of God's mercifulness he bent his head and heard the grave words of absolution spoken and saw the priest's hand raised above him in token of forgiveness.

—God bless you, my child. Pray for me.

He knelt to say his penance, praying in a corner of the dark nave: and his prayers ascended to heaven from his purified heart like perfume streaming upwards from a heart of white rose.

The muddy streets were gay. He strode homeward, conscious of an invisible grace pervading and making light his limbs. In spite of all he had done it. He had confessed and God had pardoned him. His soul was made fair and holy once more, holy and happy.

It would be beautiful to die if God so willed. It was beautiful to live in grace a life of peace and virtue and forbearance with others.

He sat by the fire in the kitchen, not daring to speak for happiness. Till that moment he had not known how beautiful and peaceful life could be. The green square of paper pinned round the lamp cast down a tender shade. On the dresser was a plate of sausages and white pudding and on the shelf there were eggs. They would be for the breakfast in the morning after the communion in the college chapel. White pudding and eggs and sausages and cups of tea. How simple and beautiful was life after all! And life lay all before him.

What does Stephen mean that "he wanted to sin with another of his kind, to force another being to sin with him and to exult with her in sin"?

How can the connotations of "exultation," meaning filled with extreme joy or jubilance, be reconciled with Stephen's shame, his "keen and humiliating sense of transgression"?

Was it chance timing that drove Stephen to a prostitute? The fact that he had "wandered into a maze of narrow and dirty streets" in Dublin's "red light" district? Was it the crescendoing pressure of the "dark presence subtle and murmurous as a flood filling him wholly with itself"?

Did Stephen think that a sexual experience with a whore might combat his sense of futile isolation?

Would you agree that "no matter what the norms have been, repressive or stimulating, male sexuality seems to have its own laws"? [10]

Re-examine the description of Stephen's relationship with the prostitute:

As he stood silent in the middle of the room she came over to him and embraced him gaily and gravely. Her round arms held him firmly to her, and he, seeing her face lifted to him in serious calm and feeling the warm calm rise and fall of her breast, all but burst into hysterical weeping. Tears of joy and relief shone in his delighted eyes and his lips parted though they would not speak.

She passed her tinkling hand through his hair, calling him a little rascal.

—Give me a kiss, she said.

His lips would not bend to kiss her. He wanted to be held firmly in her arms, to be caressed slowly, slowly, slowly. In her arms he felt that he had suddenly become strong and fearless and sure of himself. But his lips would not bend to kiss her.

With a sudden movement she bowed his head and joined her lips to his and he read the meaning of her movements in her frank uplifted eyes. It was too much for him. He closed his eyes, surrendering himself to her, body and mind, conscious of nothing in the world but the dark pressure of her softly parting lips.

Why is the prostitute the aggressor? Why doesn't Stephen kiss the prostitute, even after she asks him?

Do you feel the experience was a satisfactory one for Stephen?

By what set of values or ethical standards did Stephen make his decision to seek a prostitute? What is the yardstick for measuring human behavior? Is the ruler of "right" and "wrong" the same in every case where it is applied?

Would sexual relations with a girl his own age whom he knew and liked be preferable?

If abstinence is desirable, how is Stephen to control, if not deny, "the savage desire within him to realise the enormities which he brooded on"?

In evaluating Stephen's sexual behavior, how important are such considerations as the fact that he is sixteen, male rather than female, and repeating his sexual indulgences with prostitutes rather than having a single experience?

Could the tormented individual pictured in **A Portrait of the Artist** be a girl? Why, or why not?

After Stephen's initial experience with the prostitute, "his first violent sin,"

he had felt a wave of vitality pass out of him and had feared to find his body or his soul maimed by the excess. Instead the vital wave had carried him on its bosom out of itself and back again when it receded: and no part of body or soul had been maimed, but a dark peace had been established between them.

What does "a dark peace" connote? What changes in Stephen's mood and/or behavior would you expect it to make?

If Stephen knows that "he had sinned mortally not once but many times, and . . . that, while he stood in danger of eternal damnation for the first sin alone, by every succeeding sin he multiplied his guilt and punishment," why does "a cold lucid indifference" reign in his soul?

Why does he feel "neither shame nor fear" toward others?

Does the fact that Stephen does not resign his position as a student religious leader make him a hypocrite?

Does the fact that the "falsehood of his position did not pain him" indicate that Stephen really feels no guilt?

When does the "ache of conscience" penetrate Stephen's benumbed state?

Brooding on his "mortal sin," which "could happen in an instant," when "eyes see the thing, without having wished first to see," Stephen raises a chain of questions:

> Does that part of the body understand or what?
> Who made . . . a bestial part of the body able to understand bestially and desire bestially?
> Was that then he or an inhuman thing moved by a lower soul?

How would you answer his questions?

Although equally preoccupied sexually, individuals depicted in previous selections do not experience sexual intercourse. Since this excerpt from *A Portrait of the Artist as a Young Man* deals with Stephen's overt relations with whores, on what basis can it be classified in the "**I**" category as well as the "**You-I**"? In what sense does Stephen's relationship with the prostitute constitute no more than masturbation and temporary gratification of the most primary needs?

To what extent do his religious convictions both help and hinder Stephen in his sexual crisis?

If the sexual appetite may be paralleled: Does every meal we eat have to be sanctified? Can we never eat alone without being unhealthy? Can we eat only with people we love? With people we love only in a certain way? Can eating be good in and of itself without there being a need to sublimate it with all kinds of other meanings, to gild the lily?

RELATED QUESTIONS

Do you find any similarities between Stephen's needs and attitude toward the prostitute and those of Emily toward the stewardess in *A High Wind in Jamaica* (p. 24)?

How do Stephen's guilt feelings compare or contrast with those of Theodore in *The Bulpington of Blup* (p. 45); young Lonigan in terms of Frances (p. 48); and the youth in *Death of a Hero* (p. 38)?

In *The Bulpington of Blup:*

Dreadful old witches, young women with absurdly opulent contours who exaggerated every distinctly feminine trait, caressing animal monsters, sphinxes, mermaids, strange creatures, and yet labelled, as it were, so that they were identified with, rather than resembled, persons he knew, chased and seduced this sub-Theodore in a warm and weedy underworld, overwhelmed him in soft rotundities, lured him into a false intimacy and found him helplessly responsive to startling embraces, . . .

Stephen Daedalus in *A Portrait of the Artist:*

By day and by night . . . moved among distorted images of the outer world. A figure that had seemed to him by day demure and innocent came towards him by night through the winding darkness of sleep, her face transfigured by a lecherous cunning, her eyes bright with brutish joy.

What parallels do you see between the sexual restlessness and preoccupations of both boys? In what ways are the images of their dreams similar? Different? What realities might account for the fantastic distortions in each case?

"Excess" appears to be a critical modifier in terms of adolescent sexuality: Daydreams like those of **The Bulpington of Blup** are not, in themselves, unhealthy, but because Theodore's fantasies continue with "*excessive* frequency," reality seems always to fall short of his expectations. Comments on masturbation caution against its "psychologically *excessive*" use as an outlet for general rather than specifically sexual tensions. Stephen, in **A Portrait of the Artist as a Young Man,** fears to find his body or his soul maimed by the *excess* sexual indulgence. In areas of sexual behavior, what would you consider some of the criteria for "excessive"?

The two-year-old views his feces with pride and pleasure, but he is trained in our culture to suppress his delight and to flush his creation down a toilet. The five-year-old learns from society's frowns that in public he cannot always scratch where he itches. By the same token, many of the physical-sexual competitions in which boys like George, Andrew, Spunky Davis, and Robert of **Through the First Gate** or K. B., Claude, Rickets, and Horse of **Manchild in the Promised Land** participate; much of the dismay of the youth in **Death of a Hero,** Theodore in **The Bulpington of Blup,** young Lonigan, Stephen Daedalus, and the Abraham Lincoln High School student cited in the following newspaper account **Death Wish,** is engendered by social and moral values—"good," "bad," "right," "wrong"—which society stamps on sexual behavior.

Death Wish
THE NEW YORK TIMES

Last week, an English teacher at Abraham Lincoln High School in Brooklyn marked what he thought was a routine set of compositions on students' personal reminiscences. One student who had recently transferred from a Jewish parochial school tried to catch the flavor of the difference between public school instruction and teaching by the clergy. He concluded his paper:

The rabbis also repeated dozens of times that if we did certain things, we would get coras, which is the Hebrew word meaning death or years off your life. One of these things was thinking about sex. I think if I got years off my life for thinking about sex, I would be dead by now.

———————————

It has been said that many people would never have been in love if they had not heard love talked about [11]. Certainly "our attitudes cannot be separated from the ideas to which we are born and through which we express ourselves" [12]. Do your religious convictions in any way determine your behavior in sexual areas?

A contemporary theologian says:

The Christian churches must shoulder much of the blame for the confusion, ignorance, and unhealthy guilt associations which surround sex in Western culture. In the Old Testament and in Judaism generally, sexuality has been honored as a part of the divinely ordered nature of human beings, although the law and the prophets and rabbis steadily held the view that sex is a purposive or *instrumental* value, a means to procreation rather than an end in itself; sex for its own sake was always scorned. But there have been, beginning in the primitive church, many puritanical Christians, both Catholic and Protestant, who have treated sexuality as something inherently evil. . . .

The general assumption has been that only by suppressing instinctual demands can "goodness" be achieved. [13]

Assuming the statements to be valid, what reasons do you think churches might give in defense of their attitude toward sex and sexuality?

Do you think that adults who give advice on sexual behavior today still operate on the "general assumption . . . that only by suppressing instinctual demands can 'goodness' be achieved"? Do you believe in the theory?

. . . the religious sanctions of obedience and loyalty to God are weakening. . . . The old religious threat of hell is gone, as a negative sanction. And now what? With the loss or weakening of religious sanctions, and the disappearance of prudential sanctions under the new technology of sex, the only motivating force to turn to, to buttress our sexual ideals, is the positive one of love rather than the negative one of fear. . . . When people have stuck to ideals out of fear of what will happen when they cheat, they are helpless when that crutch is gone. Fear as a motive *is* a crutch, a sign of weakness and not of strength. . . .

Religious faith is not needed to tell us *what* is good, but it *is* needed to make us *want* it enough to do it. [14]

What do you think is meant by a positive motivating force of love? Might it mean that our sex standards will have to find a foundation in loyalty and devotion to some loved one—human or divine?

What examples are there of high commitment relationships, based on devotion rather than dread?

In terms of the Jewish boy's problems in *Death Wish,* what is the significance of the comment that "religious faith is not needed to tell us *what* is good, but it *is* needed to make us *want* it enough to do it"?

RELATED QUESTIONS

How does the comment on religious faith apply to the dilemma of Stephen Daedalus in *A Portrait of the Artist as a Young Man* (p. 50)?

Review the scene in which the youth in *Death of a Hero* cries "O Wash me in Thy Precious Blood," (p. 38); the scene in which young Lonigan tries to "make a perfect act of contrition to wash his soul from sin," (p. 49); and the scene in which Stephen feels he has "sinned so deeply . . . that he is not worthy to be called God's child" (p. 54). Do such situations attest to a culturally ingrained sense of guilt from fears of having violated the ethical precepts of church and community? Or to something else?

The psychologist, Erik Erikson, noted that throughout childhood,

. . . tentative crystallizations of identity take place which make the individual feel and believe . . . as if he approximately knew who he was —only to find that such self-certainty ever again falls prey to the discontinuities of development itself. . . . Such discontinuities can, at any time, amount to a crisis and demand a decisive and strategic repatterning of action. . . .

The adolescent, during the final stage of his identity formation, is apt to suffer more deeply than he ever did before or ever will again from a confusion of roles . . . [rendering him] defenseless against the sudden impact of previously latent malignant disturbances. . . .

It is not always easy to recall that in spite of the similarity of adolescent "symptoms" and episodes to neurotic and psychotic symptoms and episodes, adolescence is not an affliction but a normative crisis, i.e., a normal phase of increased conflict characterized by a seeming fluctuation in ego strength as well as by a high growth potential. [15]

Among the fictional characters portrayed during the final stage of identity formation is Jean-Christophe, a European musical genius. The following excerpt, dealing with inner aspects of his adolescent life, is part of Romain Rolland's ten-volume biographical novel, *Jean-Christophe.*

Jean-Christophe
ROMAIN ROLLAND

Christophe was conscious of extreme weariness and great uneasiness. He was for no reason worn out; his head was heavy, his eyes, his ears, all his senses were dumb and throbbing. He could not give his attention to anything. His mind leaped from one subject to another, and was in a fever that sucked him dry. The perpetual fluttering of images in his mind made him giddy. At first he attributed it to fatigue and the enervation of the first days of spring. But spring passed and his sickness grew only worse.

It was what the poets who only touch lightly on things call the unease of adolescence, the trouble of the cherubim, the waking of the desire of love in the young body and soul. As if the fearful crisis of all a man's being, breaking up, dying, and coming to full rebirth, as if the cataclysm in which everything, faith, thought, action, all life, seems like to be blotted out, and then to be new-forged in the convulsions of sorrow and joy, can be reduced to terms of a child's folly!

All his body and soul were in a ferment. He watched them, having no strength to struggle, with a mixture of curiosity and disgust. He did not understand what was happening in himself. His whole being was disintegrated. He spent days together in absolute torpor. Work was torture to him. At night he slept heavily and in snatches, dreaming monstrously, with gusts of desire; the soul of a beast was racing madly in him. Burning, bathed in sweat, he watched himself in horror; he tried to break free of the crazy and unclean thoughts that possessed him, and he wondered if he were going mad.

The day gave him no shelter from his brutish thoughts. In the depths of his soul he felt that he was slipping down and down; there was no stay to clutch at; no barrier to keep back chaos. All his defenses, all his citadels, with the quadruple rampart that hemmed him in so proudly—his God, his art, his pride, his moral faith, all was crumbling away, falling piece by piece from him. He saw himself naked, bound, lying unable to move, like a corpse on which vermin swarm. He had spasms of revolt: where was his will, of which he was so proud? He called to it in vain: it was like the efforts that one makes in sleep, knowing that one is dreaming, and trying to awake. Then one succeeds only in falling from one dream to another like a lump of lead, and in being more and more choked by the suffocation of the soul in bondage. At least he found that it was less painful not to struggle. He decided not to do so, with fatalistic apathy and despair.

The even tenor of his life seemed to be broken up. Now he slipped down a subterranean crevasse and was like to disappear; now he bounded up again with a violent jerk. The chain of his days was snapped. In the midst of the even plain of the hours great gaping holes would open to engulf his soul. Christophe looked on at the spectacle as though it did not concern him. Everybody, everybody,—and himself—were strange to him. He went about his business, did his work, automatically: it seemed to him that the machinery of his life might stop at any moment: the wheels were out of gear. At dinner with his mother and the others, in the orchestra with the musicians and the audience, suddenly there would be a void and an emptiness in his brain: he would look stupidly at the grinning faces about him: and he could not understand. He would ask himself:

"What is there between these creatures and . . . ?"

He dared not even say:

". . . and me."

For he knew not whether he existed. He would speak and his voice would seem to issue from another body. He would move, and he saw his movements from afar, from above—from the top of a tower. He would pass his hand over his face, and his eyes would wander. He was often near doing crazy things.

It was especially when he was most in public that he had to keep guard on himself. For example, on the evenings when he went to the Palace or was playing in public. Then he would suddenly be seized by a terrific desire to make a face, or say something outrageous, to pull the Grand Duke's nose, or to make a running kick at one of the ladies. One whole evening while he was conducting the orchestra, he struggled against an insensate desire to undress himself in public: and he was haunted by the idea from the moment when he tried to check it: he had to exert all his strength not to give way to it. When he issued from the brute struggle he was dripping with sweat and his mind was blank. He was really mad. It was enough for him to think that he must not do a thing for it to fasten on him with the maddening tenacity of a fixed idea.

So his life was spent in a series of unbridled outbreaks and of endless falls into emptiness. A furious wind in the desert. Whence came this wind? From what abyss came these desires that wrenched his body and mind? He was like a bow stretched to breaking point by a strong hand,—to what end unknown? —which then springs back like a piece of dead wood. Of what force was he the prey? He dared not probe for it. He felt that he was beaten, humiliated, and he would not face his defeat. He was weary and broken in spirit. He understood now the people whom formerly he had despised: those who will not seek awkward truth. In the empty hours, when he remembered that time was passing, his work neglected, the future lost, he was frozen with terror. But there was no reaction: and his cowardice found excuses in desperate affirmation of the void in which he lived: he took a bitter delight in abandoning himself to it like a wreck on the waters. What was the good of fighting? There was nothing beautiful, nor good: neither God, nor life, nor being of any sort. In the street as he walked, suddenly the earth would sink away from him: there was neither ground, nor air, nor light, nor himself: there was nothing. He would fall, his head would drag him down, face forwards: he could hardly hold himself up; he was on the point of collapse. He thought he was going to die, suddenly, struck down. He thought he was dead. . . .

Christophe was growing a new skin. Christophe was growing a new soul. And seeing the worn out and rotten soul of his childhood falling away he never dreamed that he was taking on a new one, young and stronger. As through life we change our bodies, so also do we change our souls: and the metamorphosis does not always take place slowly over many days; there are times of crisis when the whole is suddenly renewed. The adult changes his soul. The old soul that is cast off dies. In those hours of anguish we think that all is at an end. And the whole thing begins again. A life dies. Another life has already come into being.

How does **Jean-Christophe** illustrate Erikson's point that in adolescence "self-certainty ever again falls prey to the discontinuities of development itself [which] can, at any time, amount to a crisis"?

What evidence does Jean-Christophe give that this normal phase of increased conflict in adolescence can be a psychological state with physical symptoms?

Jean-Christophe's frightening desire to do "crazy things," his irrational pressures, so perverse that "it was enough for him to think that he must not do a thing for it to fasten on him with the maddening tenacity of a fixed idea," would alone justify the fear of madness which haunts adolescents unnecessarily. What other feelings during the "identity crisis" make the comment that "it is not always easy to recall that . . . adolescence is not an affliction but . . . a normal phase of increased conflict" seem to be an understatement?

Life is a series of deaths and rebirths. As the author of **Jean-Christophe** points out, even "the adult changes his soul." Whatever the nature of these metamorphoses and whenever in the life cycle they occur, it is as typical of age as it is of youth that in those hours of anguish we think that all is at an end. What kind of honest reassurance might be given to a teenager who confides: "I don't think anyone has ever felt the way I do—sort of taken over by demons. If I'm not going crazy, then I must be really over-sexed. Maybe even a sex maniac or something."

RELATED QUESTIONS

In "what the poets who only touch lightly on things call the unease of adolescence," Jean-Christophe, Stephen Daedalus in **A Portrait of the Artist as a Young Man** (p. 50), and Theodore in **The Bulpington of Blup** (p. 45), seem defenseless against such "previously latent malignant disturbances" as physically exhausting, bestial nightmares; a deep sense of isolation and alienation from others, including one's family; feelings of futility ranging from rock-bottom resignation to cynical despair; and total self-doubt. What other symptoms or previously latent disturbances would you add to the list?

The main characters in the long-run, off-Broadway musical *The Fantasticks* are a boy, a girl, two fathers, and a wall.

The sixteen-year-old girl, Luisa, claims that everyday something happens to her. She is given to hugging herself until her arms turn blue, and closing her eyes and crying until she can taste her tears. She loves to taste her tears.

Additionally, her fantasies reach to swimming in a cold, clear blue stream; loosening her hair until it billows to the floor; wearing a golden gown to town to have her fortune told; dancing until 2 A.M., or dawn, or indefinitely if the band could stand it.

Before her youth and chances disappear, Luisa would like to do all the things she has dreamed about but never done.

She reveals her adolescent wishes and her concept of the feminine role in the following excerpt from one of the songs she sings, *Much More.*

Much More (*from* The Fantasticks)

HARVEY SCHMIDT and TOM JONES

I am special . . .
Please, God, please don't let me be normal . . .

I'd like to be not evil but a little worldly-wise,
To be the kind of girl designed to be kissed upon the eyes . . .

I'd like to take a week or two and never do a chore, . . .
Perhaps I'm bad or wild or mad with lots of dreams in store,

But I want much more than sweeping up, Much more. . . .

How "much more" than the routine household chores which constitute part of the female role does Luisa want?

What are the connotations of hugging yourself, swimming in a clear cold blue stream, tasting your tears, wearing a golden gown, having your fortune told, loosening your hair so that it billowed to the ground, being kissed upon the eyes, and feeling—like Eliza in *My Fair Lady*—that you could have danced all night?

In what sense do you think this sixteen-year-old girl means "Please, God, please don't let me be normal"?

Do you think Luisa's attitude is typical of sixteen-year-old girls?

RELATED QUESTIONS

What similarities and differences are there between the fantasies of Luisa in *Much More* and those of William Sylvanus Baxter in *Seventeen* (p. 40)?

Can any significant conclusions be drawn about the general nature of male and female daydreaming?

Like Jean-Christophe, Joan, in the following excerpt from *Joan and Peter* by H. G. Wells, is described in that "normative crisis" of adolescence. She, too, finds that self-certainty—in her case "that happiness, that perfect assurance, that intense appreciation of the beauty in things"—has fallen "prey to the discontinuities of development itself." From a female perspective, Joan views this familiar period of "stormy, indistinct desires and fears."

67

the self in conflict

Joan and Peter

H. G. WELLS

Joan had long since lost that happiness, that perfect assurance, that intense appreciation of the beauty in things which had come to her with early adolescence. She was troubled and perplexed in all her ways. She was full now of stormy, indistinct desires and fears, and a gnawing, indefinite impatience. . . . She had a horror of marriage lurking in her composition; every one around her spoke of it as an entire abandonment of freedom. . . . And who could one marry? She could not conceive herself marrying any of these boys she met, living somewhere cooped up in a little house. . . . She had no object in life, no star by which to steer, and she was full of the fever of life.

All her being, in her destitution of any other aim that had the slightest hold upon her imagination, was crying out for a lover.

It was a lover she wanted, not a husband; her mind made the clearest distinction between the two. He would come and unrest would cease and beauty would return. Her lover haunted all her life, an invisible yet almost present person. She could not imagine his face nor his form, he was the blankest of beings, and yet she was so sure she knew him that if she were to see him away down a street or across a crowded room, instantly, she believed, she would recognize him. And until he came life was a torment of suspense. Life was all wrong and discordant, so wrong and discordant that at times she could have hated her lover for keeping her waiting so wretchedly.

And she had to go on as though this suspense was nothing. She had to disregard this vast impatience of her being. And the best way to do that, it seemed to her, was to hurry from one employment to another, never to be alone, never without some occupation, some excitement. Her break with Peter had an extraordinary effect of release in her mind. Hitherto, whatever her resentment had been she had admitted in practice his claim to exact a certain discretion from her; his opinion had been, in spite of her resentment, a standard for her. Now she had no standard at all—unless it was a rebellious purpose to spite him. On Joan's personal conduct the thought of Oswald, oddly enough, had scarcely any influence at all. She adored him as one might a political or historical hero; she wanted to stand well in his sight, but the idea of him did not pursue her into the details of her behavior at all. He seemed preoccupied with ideas and unobservant. She had never had any struggle with him; he had never made her do anything.

. . . Joan had had a very few flirtations; the extremest thing upon her conscience was Bunny Cuspard's kiss. She had the natural shilly-shally of a girl; she was strongly moved to all sorts of flirtings and experimentings with love, and very adventurous and curious in these matters; and also she had a system of inhibitions, pride, hesitation, fastidiousness, and something beyond these things, a sense of some ultimate value that might easily be lost, that held her back. Rebelling against Peter had somehow also set her rebelling against these restraints. Why shouldn't she know this and that? Why shouldn't she try this and that? Why, for instance, was she always "shutting up" Adela whenever she began to discourse in her peculiar way upon the great theme? Just a timid prude she had been, but now—.

And all this about undesirable people and unseemly places, all this picking and choosing as though the world was mud; what nonsense it was! She could take care of herself surely!

She began deliberately to feel her way through all her friendships to see whether this thing, passion, lurked in any of them. It was an interesting exercise of her wits to try over a youth like Troop, for example; to lure him on by a touch of flattery, a betrayal of warmth in her interest, to reciprocal advances. At first Troop wasn't in the least in love with her, but she succeeded in suggesting to him that he was. But the passion in him released an unsuspected fund of egotistical discourse; he developed a disposition to explain himself and his mental operations in a large, flattering way both by word of mouth and by letter. Even when he was roused to a sense of her as lovable, he did not become really interested in her but only in his love for her. He arrived at one stride at the same unanalytical acceptance of her as of his God and the Church and the King and his parents and all the rest of the Anglican system of things. She was his girl—"the kid." He really wasn't interested in those other things any more than he was in her; once he had given her her role in relation to him his attention returned to himself. The honour, integrity, and perfection of Troop were the consuming occupations of his mind. This was an edifying thing to discover, but not an entertaining thing to pursue; and after a time Joan set herself to avoid, miss, and escape from Troop on every possible occasion. But Troop prided himself upon his persistence. He took to writing her immense, ill-spelt, manly letters, with sentences beginning: "You understand me very little if—." It was clear he was hers only until some simpler, purer, more receptive and acquisitive girl swam into his ken.

Wilmington, on the other hand, was a silent covetous lover. Joan could make him go white, but she could not make him talk. She was a little afraid of him and quite sure of him. But he was not the sort of young man one can play with, and she marvelled greatly that any one could desire her so much and amuse her so little. Bunny Cuspard was a more animated subject for experiment, and you could play with him a lot. He danced impudently. He could pat Joan's shoulder, press her hand, slip his arm round her waist and bring his warm face almost to a kissing contact as though it was all nothing. Did these approaches warm her blood? Did she warm his? Anyhow it didn't matter, and it wasn't anything.

Then there was Graham Prothero, a very good-looking friend of Peter's, whom she had met while skating. He had a lively eye, and jumped after a meeting or so straight into Joan's dreams, where he was still more lively and good-looking. She wished she knew more certainly whether she had got into his dreams.

Meanwhile Joan's curiosity had not spared Jelalludin. She had had him discoursing on the beauties of Indian love, and spinning for her imagination a warm moonlight vision of still temples reflected in water tanks, of silvery water shining between great lily leaves, of music like the throbbing of a nerve, of brown bodies garlanded with flowers. There had been a loan of Rabindranath Tagore's love poems. And once he had sent her some flowers.

Any of these youths she could make her definite lover she knew, by an act of self-adaptation and just a little reciprocal giving. Only she had no will to do that. She felt she must not will anything of the sort. The thing must come to her; it must take possession of her. Sometimes, indeed, she had the oddest fancy that perhaps suddenly one of these young men would become transfigured; would cease to be his clumsy, ineffective self, and change right into that wonderful, that compelling being who was to set all things right. There were moments when it seemed about to happen. And then the illusion passed, and she saw clearly that it was just old Bunny or just staccato Mir Jelalludin.

In Huntley, Joan found something more intriguing than this pursuit of the easy and the innocent. Huntley talked with a skilful impudence that made a bold choice of topics seem the most natural in the world. He presented himself as a leader in a great emancipation of women. They were to be freed from "the bond-age of sex." The phrase awakened a warm response in Joan, who was finding sex a yoke about her imagination. Sex, Huntley declared, should be as incidental in a woman's life as it was in a man's. But before that could happen the world must free its mind from the "superstition of chastity," from the idea that by one single step a woman passed from the recognizable into the impossible category. We made no such distinction in the case of men; an artist or a business man was not suddenly thrust out of the social system by a sexual incident. A woman was either Mrs. or Miss; a gross publication of elemental facts that were surely her private affair. No one asked whether a man had found his lover. Why should one proclaim it in the case of a woman by a conspicuous change of her name? Here, and not in any matter of votes or economics was the real feminine grievance. His indignation was contagious. It marched with all Joan's accumulated prejudice against marriage, and all her growing resentment at the way in which emotional unrest was distracting and perplexing her will and spoiling her work at Cambridge. But when Huntley went on to suggest that the path of freedom lay in the heroic abandonment of the "fetish of chastity," Joan was sensible of a certain lagging of spirit. A complex of instincts that conspired to adumbrate that unseen, unknown, and yet tyrannous lover, who would not leave her in peace and yet would not reveal himself, stood between her and the extremities of Huntley's logic.

There were moments when he seemed to be pretending to fill that oppressive void; moments when he seemed only to be hinting at himself as a possible instrument of freedom. Joan listened to him gravely enough so long as he theorized; when he came to personal things she treated him with the same experimental and indecisive encouragement that she dealt out to her undergraduate friends. Huntley's earlier pose of an intellectual friend was attractive and flattering; then he began to betray passion, as it were, unwittingly. At a fancy dress dance at Chelsea—and he danced almost as well as Joan—he became moody. He was handsome that night in black velvet and silver that betrayed much natural grace; Joan was a nondescript in black and red, with short skirts and red beads about her pretty neck. "Joan," he said suddenly, "you're getting hold of me. You're disturbing me." He seemed to soliloquize. "I've not felt like this before." Then very flatteringly and reproachfully, "You're so damned intelligent, Joan. And you dance—as though God made you to make me happy." He got her out into an open passage that led from the big studio in which they had been dancing, to a yard dimly lit by Chinese lanterns, and at the dark turn of the passage kissed her more suddenly and violently than she had ever been kissed before. He kissed her lips and held her until she struggled out of his arms. Up to that moment Joan had been playing with him, half attracted and half shamming; then once more came the black panic that had seized her with Bunny and Adela.

She did not know whether she liked him now or hated him. She felt strange and excited. She made him go back with her into the studio. "I've got to dance with Ralph Winterbaum," she said.

"Say you're not offended," he pleaded.

She gave him no answer. She did not know the answer. She wanted to get away and think. He perceived her confused excitement and did not want to give her time to think. She found Winterbaum and danced with him, and all the time, with her nerves on fire, she was watching Huntley, and he was watching her. Then she became aware of Peter regarding her coldly, over the plump shoulder of a fashion-plate artist. She went to him as soon as the dance was over.

"Peter," she said, "I want to go home."

He surveyed her. She was flushed and ruffled, and his eyes and mouth hardened.

"It's early."

"I want to go home."

"Right. You're a bit of a responsibility, Joan."

"Don't, then," she said shortly, and turned round to greet Huntley as though nothing had happened between them.

But she kept in the light and the crowd, and there was a constraint between them. "I want to talk to you more," he said, "and when we can talk without someone standing on one's toes all the time and listening hard. I wish you'd come to my flat and have tea with me one day. It's still and cosy, and I could tell you all sorts of things—things I can't tell you here."

Joan's dread of any appearance of timid virtue was overwhelming. And she was now blind with rage at Peter—why, she would have been at a loss to say. She wanted to behave outrageously with Huntley. But in Peter's sight. This struck her as an altogether too extensive invitation.

"I've never noticed much restraint in your conversation," she said.

"It's the interruptions I don't like," he said.

"You get me no ice, you get me no lemonade," she complained abruptly.

"That's what my dear Aunt Adelaide used to call changing the subject."

"It's the cry of outraged nature."

"But I saw you having an ice—not half an hour ago."

"Not the ice I wanted," said Joan.

"Distracting Joan! I suppose I must get you that ice. But about the tea?"

"I *hate* tea," said Joan, with a force of decision that for a time disposed of his project.

Just for a moment he hovered with his eye on her, weighing just what that decision amounted to, and in that moment she decided that he wasn't handsome, that there was a something *unsound* about his profile, that he was pressing her foolishly. And anyhow, none of it really mattered. He was nothing really. She had been a fool to go into that dark passage, she ought to have known her man better; Huntley had been amusing hitherto and now the thing had got into a new phase that wouldn't, she felt, be amusing at all; after this he would pester. She hated being kissed. And Peter was a beast. Peter was a hateful beast. . . .

Joan and Peter went home in the same taxi—in a grim silence. Yet neither of them could have told what it was that kept them hostile and silent.

The author says that Joan "had the natural shilly-shally of a girl; she was strongly moved to all sorts of flirtings and experimentings with love, and very adventurous and curious in these matters." Would you agree that showing hesitation, or lack of decisiveness or resolution is a female trait? If vacillation or shilly-shallying is equally natural to the male, does the characteristic take a less obvious form?

Do you believe that females flirt and experiment with love more than males? Why, or why not?

Who chases whom? Is the male the hunter or the hunted? The manipulator or the manipulated? What is the evidence in **Joan and Peter?**

Part of the adolescent male's unrest may derive from the cultural pressure he feels to be a man. In his absorption in the physical self, masculinity is perhaps the male's deepest concern. To what extent do cultural expectations of the female appear to cause Joan some uneasiness?

If you were Joan, would you be most interested in Peter, Oswald, Bunny Cuspard, Troop, Wilmington, Graham Prothero, Jelalludin, or Huntley? Why? Which one appeals to you least? Why? Is there any respect in which all of them seem to be unsatisfactory choices? If so, what element(s) which you consider important would be missing from the relationship? What undesirable factors in the relationship would you want to eliminate?

Joan "began deliberately to feel her way through all her friendships to see whether this thing, passion, lurked in any of them." Among the many definitions of passion are: the state or capacity of being acted on by external agents or forces; the emotions as distinguished from reason; violent, intense, or overmastering feeling; emotion that is deeply stirring or ungovernable; an outbreak of anger; ardent affection: Love; a strong liking for or devotion to some activity, object, or concept; sexual desire. Which of the definitions seem most relevant to Joan's test?

From her efforts to see whether "passion lurked in any of them," what conclusions might Joan reach? Why?

It has been observed that

> . . . Adolescent sexual attitudes and behavior at first have little similarity to those of a mature relationship between a man and a woman. Sexual feelings as well as the newly-won physical maturity are often felt as alien, and not as integrated components of the self. Frequently the sexual drive is used as an instrument to relieve some of the conflicts of adolescence, for example, as an assertion of masculinity or femininity . . . for girls it may provide an outlet for defiant self-assertion and hostility. . . . The adolescent's feelings of loneliness and depression may be temporarily relieved by the illusion of love. . . . [16]

How does Joan's conduct—particularly her fantasies and her relationship with Peter—illustrate this description of an immature sexual attitude?

How does Joan's stage of development further bear out that "although sexuality can be exploited in the service of more infantile needs, it already has in it the seed of what will become an expression of a deep and intimate bond between a man and woman" [17]?

RELATED QUESTIONS

In what ways does Joan remind you of Jean-Christophe (p. 63) or of Stephen Daedalus in *A Portrait of the Artist as a Young Man* (p. 50)? In what ways are the symptoms of her identity crisis different from theirs? Do you think the differences arise from the fact that she is a female, or simply from the fact that she is Joan?

Does the introductory comment to *Jean-Christophe* (p. 62) apply equally to males like Jean-Christophe and to females like Joan?

The Power of Sex

Suzie, who's "strictly a female female" in *Flower Drum Song,* details some sources of her enjoyment of her feminine sexuality in the following song, *I Enjoy Being a Girl.*

Her pleasure in brand new hairdos, curled eyelashes, frilly clothes, her curvy silhouette and free, girlish gait, are only a few of the reasons she sings, "I'm a girl and by me that's only great."

I Enjoy Being a Girl (*from* Flower Drum Song)

RICHARD RODGERS and
OSCAR HAMMERSTEIN

I flip when a fella sends me flowers,
I drool over dresses made of lace,
I talk on the telephone for hours,
With a pound and a half of cream upon my face.

If someone with eyes that smoulder
Says he loves every silken curl,
That falls on my ivory shoulder,
I enjoy being a girl.

When I hear a complimentary whistle
That greets my bikini by the sea,
I turn and I glower and I bristle,
But I'm happy to know the whistle's meant for me.

I'm strictly a female female,
And my future I hope will be
In the home of a brave and free male who'll
Enjoy being a guy having a girl like me.

What is Suzie's concept of being a "female female"? Is it a learned attitude? Is it the same as being "feminine"? "Womanly"? "Matronly"? "Ladylike"?

Does Suzie's concept of being a "female female" leave anything to be desired? In what sense might it be considered superficial?

If Suzie is happy to know that the complimentary whistle that greets her bikini by the sea is meant for her, why does she "turn" and "glower" and "bristle"? **73**

In what other situations involving members of opposite sexes do we learn to act contrary to our feelings?

What function(s) do social, and often hypocritical, conventions serve?

If we can all translate the signs, even when they are contradictory, what is the purpose of such game-playing?

Is Suzie looking for a complimentary or a complementary partner? Why might one be more desirable than the other in terms of a lifelong relationship?

What might Suzie mean by a "brave and free" male? How might her ideal demonstrate his bravery? Would "free" male more likely connote unmarried, and hence eligible; or liberal, and hence unconventional?

One sex educator believes:

We don't know what it means to be a woman today. I don't think we have really explored the new dimensions of womanhood . . . where woman has within her own hands for the most part the choice of whether or not she is going to have a child, the opportunity to be aggressive about dating, and to be extremely aggressive in the relationship—which was not woman's role at the turn of the century. [18]

What do you think a woman's role should be?

RELATED QUESTIONS

What light does Robert Graves' essay *Real Women* (see "**Night-Lights**," p. 556) shed on the question of what it means to be a woman and what her role should be?

Does Suzie of *I Enjoy Being a Girl* have anything in common with Luisa of *Much More* (p. 66)? With Joan of *Joan and Peter* (p. 67)?

The Once-Over
PAUL BLACKBURN

The tanned blonde
     in the green print sack
in the center of the subway car
       standing
though there are seats
      has had it from
1 teen-age hood
1 lesbian
1 envious housewife
4 men over fifty
(& myself), in short
the contents of this half of the car

         Our notations are:
long legs, long waist, high breasts (no bra), long
neck, the model slump
       the handbag drape and how the skirt

cuts in under a very handsome
                    set of cheeks
'stirring dull roots with spring rain' sayeth the preacher

Only a stolid young man
with a blue business suit and the New York *Times*
does not know he is being assaulted

So.
She has us and we her
all the way to downtown Brooklyn
Over the tunnel and through the bridge
                    to DeKalb Avenue we go

all very chummy

She stares at the number over the door
and gives no sign
                    yet the sign is on her

How does the notion that sex is not merely what we do, but what we are,
apply to the tanned blonde in **The Once-Over?**
Is the blonde strictly a "female female"? Why, or why not?

She stares at the number over the door
and gives no sign
Yet the sign is on her. . . .

What is the "sign" that is on her?
If the girl gives no sign and does not even look at the other passengers, why
does the poet charge her with assault?
How does she attack all but the "stolid young man with a blue business suit
and *The New York Times*"?
Is hers what might be termed passive aggression, that is, an apparently violent attempt or a willful offer with force or violence to do hurt to another without
the actual doing of the hurt threatened?
Is the blonde an animate form of erotic advertising? How does she manage
to activate sexual interest at a sly and prurient level of secrecy?
The poet, pointing out that the blonde stands in the center of the subway
car although there are vacant seats, seems to imply that her actions, like her appearance, are deliberate. If so, what might be her motive?
It has been said that clothes, as a language, are almost as conventionalized
as verbal language:

The habit of the nun [says] "no sex here" . . . The way the clothes are worn
helps to interpret them and to translate them into signals. The swiveling hips
or the mincing gait can revise the message of any kind of clothes. . . .
Most men refuse to believe, or cannot believe, that the nubile young
woman, luscious in her tennis shorts or bikini, is not deliberately signaling
a come-on. But the signal is not necessarily the one the men pick up. She

may be asking for admiration; the man hopes she is asking for him. Her body keeps signaling: I am a desirable woman. The men who see her reply, Don't be so damn provocative about it unless you want us to make something of it. The clothes . . . seem to signal clear and loud, Take Me! The girl may actually mean nothing more than, Admire me. [19]

What message is the tanned blonde trying to communicate?

RELATED QUESTIONS

What does Suzie in *I Enjoy Being a Girl* (p. 73) intend her clothing signals and cosmetic signs to convey?

Girl Walking

CHARLES G. BELL

Here comes a girl so damned shapely
Loungers stop breathing. Conceive how subtly
She works those hips. She is all sex; she knows it.
Lace shows the bubs; she is proud of notice;
Head high, back arched, long braids, wide crupper,
She walks like dancing, calls the gods to tup her.

Her mother goes before, as broad as tall,
A moving hill of flesh, a breeding sack,
Swollen with stoking of all appetites.
She stirs her buttocks too, but not to our delight.

Sweet amorous girl, how can you stroll
With such impulsive beauty, admired by all,
Your destiny waddling before you down the road?

What does the judgment mean that the girl walking is "all sex"? What evidence does the poet provide that "she knows it"?

What is her "destiny" in the last line?

How would you answer the question put to the "sweet amorous girl," " . . . how can you stroll/With such impulsive beauty, admired by all,/Your destiny waddling before you down the road?" What is "impulsive beauty"?

Why does the poet choose unflattering animal imagery usually associated with cattle to describe the girl and her mother, for example, "a breeding sack," "crupper," "tup"?

RELATED QUESTIONS

According to the author of *Girl Walking,* why would the housewife's envy in *The Once-Over* (p. 74) be unnecessary?

What similarities are there between the girl walking and the tanned blonde in *The Once-Over*?

Does "she is all sex" apply to Suzie in *I Enjoy Being a Girl* (p. 73)? To Luisa who wants *Much More* (p. 66)? To Frances of *Young Lonigan* (p. 48)?

Do you think the authors of *Girl Walking* and *The Once-Over* have exaggerated the ease with which the male can become sexually interested or aroused?

Rudyard Kipling, in this excerpt from "The Female of the Species," asserts that the female is "more deadly than the male":

. . . The female of the species is more deadly than the male.
Man, a bear in most relations—worm and savage otherwise,—
  Man propounds negotiations, Man accepts the compromise.
Very rarely will he squarely push the logic of a fact
  To its ultimate conclusion in unmitigated act.
Fear, or foolishness, impels him, ere he lay the wicked low,
  To concede some form of trial even to his fiercest foe.
Mirth obscene diverts his anger—Doubt and Pity oft perplex
  Him in dealing with an issue—to the scandal of The Sex!
But the woman that God gave him, every fibre of her frame
  Proves her launched for one sole issue, armed and engined for the same,
And to serve that single issue, lest the generations fail,
  The female of the species must be deadlier than the male. . . .

And man knows it! Knows, moreover, that the woman that God gave him
  Must command but may not govern—shall enthral but not enslave him
And *she* knows, because She warns him, and Her instincts never fail,
  That the Female of Her Species is more deadly than the Male. [20]

What is the "one sole issue" for which the female is "armed and engined"? How "deadly" are the females of the human species encountered in selections you have read in this section?

Do you approve of Kipling's concept of the female? Is Kipling's assessment of the male a valid one?

The Advantages of Learning

MARTIAL

Translated from the Latin by Kenneth Rexroth

I am a man with no ambitions
And few friends, wholly incapable
Of making a living, growing no
Younger, fugitive from some just doom.
Lonely, ill-clothed, what does it matter?
At midnight I make myself a jug
Of hot white wine and cardamom seeds.
In a torn grey robe and old beret,
I sit in the cold writing poems,
Drawing nudes on the crooked margins,
Copulating with sixteen year old
Nymphomaniacs of my imagination.

Carving initials on trees, drawing naked figures or sex organs in notebook margins, scrawling obscenities such as Stephen Daedalus "read on the oozing wall of a urinal" seem a universal, natural part of the process of growing into maturity. What needs are thereby fulfilled? When are they outgrown? Why?

Many problems with which the adolescent is preoccupied

... have to be settled within the youngster himself, for he has as yet no arena in which to act out his aspirations, his ideals and his ambitions. Of necessity he must resort to reflection and fantasy. This is the age ... of daydreams and imagination. [21]

And some individuals who, chronologically speaking, would be termed adults, are, emotionally speaking, still adolescents. In what ways does the man in *The Advantages of Learning* demonstrate less than average maturity?

Why is he a man of no ambitions?

Why are his sexual fantasies insufficient?

Do you think he might be more satisfied if he had intercourse with *real* sixteen-year-old nymphomaniacs? Might he be less lonely? More ambitious? Why, or why not?

The Collector
RAYMOND SOUSTER

What she collects is men
As a bee honey, leaving out
The sublety of that swift winger. There's little
In the way her eyes look into theirs (O take me)
Her body arches forward (possess me *now*).

At her age (other women say)
It's ridiculous: but how much envy
Mixes with fact? They will say: none,
But we know better, watching their faces. Still, admit
What she collects, finally, is pain.

"At her age (other woman say)/ It's ridiculous"; what is ridiculous about the situation? Why?

What do you think her age might be? Why?

What stark reality is implied in the final lines: "Still, admit/ What she collects, finally, is pain"? What sort of pain?

Although the other women deny it, the poet believes that they really envy "the collector." Would you agree with him?

How important is it that a female, whatever her age, be capable of attracting men? What are the implications of the number of commercially available hormone creams and beauty preparations, and the fact that women tend to suppress, if not lie about, their age?

What is the sexual philosophy of "the collector"?

One writer on the subject of sex controls contends that they are necessary

... to keep an individual from being exploited. There are predatory boys and men who make a game of seeing how far they can go with their female companions. Some girls demand more response than a fellow may feel is appropriate. To protect oneself from "the wolf" of either sex, a boy or girl or a man or woman finds sex controls necessary in many a potentially exploitive situation. . . .

. . . Since most of us have built-in standards that are a part of us, we must restrain our behavior to fit our sense of what is right as we have learned it, in order to live at peace with ourselves.

. . . Sex and love belong together. This is why a boy's relationship with a prostitute or a pick-up, and a girl's giving in to the demands of a casual date, are so unrewarding. Sex without love satisfies only the animal passions and violates the essentially human qualities of a person—the ability to feel with and to care for another human being. The habitually promiscuous individual is usually a lonely soul, deprived of the lasting affections that give meaning to life. The more he chases the more lost he feels in an aloneness that no physical intercourse can assuage. [22]

How does the perspective on sex controls clarify the last line of *The Collector?*

The street morality is based on the adage "all things are better if they are fun." And as a popular, well-educated, church-going girl who stands high in her school and community put it: "If you have sex, you both will have a lot of fun. Sex is an active sport, more enjoyable than tennis or bowling" [23].

In the street morality, "considerations of mature values and regard for others give way to an emphasis on momentary excitement and gratification. . . . the relations between the sexes are devoid of any give and take, with males and females being temptations and threats to one another" [24]. What arguments might be developed in a debate on street morality versus personal morality of self-restraint?

RELATED QUESTIONS

How do parts of the remarks on sex controls specifically apply to other fictional characters in this "I" section, particularly Stephen Daedalus of *A Portrait of the Artist as a Young Man* (p. 50) and the old man in *The Advantages of Learning* (p. 77)?

Sir Philip Sidney, in his sixteenth-century sonnet "Thou Blind-Man's Mark," describes sexual desire or lust as a "fool's self-chosen snare," "fond fancy's scum," a "web of will, whose end is never wrought," and admits that he has "too dearly bought,/ with price of mangled mind, thy worthless ware." Although Sidney speaks from a masculine perspective, what evidence—fictional or otherwise—supports the idea that relationships like "the collector's," based merely on gratification of sexual appetite, are temporary and unsatisfying?

"To the baby the world is himself and he is it. . . . He is omnipotent and controls the world" [25]. His grasp of the universe that he knows extends possessively from the central "I" to "my mummy," "my daddy," "my cookie," and "my toy." "During childhood he learns differently," and in most adolescents "the drive toward [sexual maturity] is ultimately strong enough to master the more infantile tendency to self-love" [26].

From readings in this section and from your own observations and experience, what is your concept of an "I"-orientation? What are some of its signs?

While the "I"-orientation is a natural transitional stage of adolescence, what are some of the consequences for adults who never outgrow it and who thus never become emotionally mature?

What is required to be emotionally adult? One psychiatrist lists "the acceptance of responsibility as a counterpoise to privilege; the capacity for giving and receiving love; the ability to tolerate a delay in getting satisfaction" [27]. Would you agree with these? Would you add to the criteria?

How would you interpret your criteria for emotional maturity in terms of sexual issues and decisions in a culture where simultaneously "there is pressure toward full sexual expression and there is pressure against it" [28] and where the ultimate solution to the double-bind must rest with the individual?

"They"

AWARENESS OF OTHERS

Prepared by students at Ramsey High School, Ramsey, N.J.

The counterplayers of the "selves" are the "others," various conditioning forces in the environment which the "I" must encounter and with which the "I" compares himself, for better or worse.

Whether his image seems favorably reflected or shamefully distorted by his encounter with others, the growing individual must view himself in the cultural mirror of the mass media; must be influenced by expository views of professors, metaphoric insights of poets, and abstract theories of philosophers. The individual absorbs the knowledge and attitudes of his peers, his parents, and the prevailing public. As Tennyson noted in "Ulysses," "I am a part of all that I have met."

Communicated directly or indirectly, knowledge serves as the medium through which the individual comes to an actualization of himself as a person in terms of freedom and responsibility. This realizing experience occurs within a milieu of other persons who are coming, or who have come, to an actualization of themselves in these same terms.

Thus the "**They**" forces cover a range of conflicting attitudes. As visual or verbal stimuli, these attitudes can force the thinking individual to define his own convictions, principles, and standards. At the very least, these attitudes provide the public faces to be aped, and they contribute to the individual's repertoire of behavior. At the other extreme, "**They**" forces can pressure the individual into absolute rebellion or rejection of society's attitudes.

As the self-oriented "I" moves into the wider area of the "**They**", he may flounder initially among his peers and with his parents. The acute self-consciousness, self-torment, awkwardness and embarrassment of early social contacts with the opposite sex are viewed from the perspective of the sophisticated Anna who awakens the sexual interest of a thirteen-year-old in *Snowfall in Childhood;* from the perspective of an adolescent group playing sex games in *The City of Trembling Leaves;* from the perspective of a fifteen-year-old male in *Merrymakers* **83** who is conditioned by social conventions insured by the "iron mothers" who run monthly dances; and from the perspective of a sixteen-year-old male in *First Love and Other Sorrows* whose self-doubts are aggravated by a subtle and not atypical combination of pressures from his peers and family.

The generation gap, as manifested in attempts to communicate about sex and love, apparently widens when Mr. Frank's efforts at sex education in *The Diary of a Young Girl* threaten Anne's growing self-reliance, insight, and relationship with Peter; and apparently shrinks in *The Bent Twig* and *A Tree Grows in Brooklyn* where children like Sylvia and Francie searching for sexual values find mothers both honest and approachable. And the generation gap becomes irrelevant for those able to follow Mama's advice and concept of love in *A Raisin in the Sun.*

The closeness of love and hate in the emotional spectrum, as well as Horgan's generalization that "we are subject to what we are taught to hate," becomes apparent through multiple examples of adults interpreting for children: in learned attitudes toward exhibitionists in *Dawn of Hate;* toward one's body in *The Downward Path to Wisdom;* and toward homosexuality in *Hands,* where a man suffers as a target of public prejudice.

The general social attitude toward sex and sexuality—contradictory practice in a tangle of incompatible and inconsistent standards—is stated in the excerpt from *Playboy's* editorial, revealed in the public reception of *Little Brother,* and exhibited in multifaceted advertisements that may justify the expectations of the anonymous creator of the limerick about the bather. Sex does sell in America, as evidenced by the button fad and "Personals," from a sexually aware newspaper. Sex is also exploited incongruously or irrationally to maximize sales in a culture that seems to value the shadow because the reality is forbidden, as conveyed by *Avant-Garde* magazine.

Toward a clarification of the major confusion between love and sex—graphically symbolized in the photograph from *Newsweek*—poets, philosophers, and professors make distinctions between feelings of the heart and feelings of the glands. Their views, often overlapping, converge on the nature of mature love: it is variously described as being not a surrender of the body without the heart, but as "the heart joined to the genitals" in Lowen's terms, so that it becomes not "an instinctual drive which obeys the pleasure principle in a broad responsiveness to the opposite sex, but a conscious psychological experience which restrains sexual tension for a loved person." To Lowen's contention in *Sex and Love* and *Love and Sex* from *Love and Orgasm,* Gunn in *Das Liebesleben* adds, "If love were sex, and without any other element, then sex would be love, which I know it isn't." C. S. Lewis in *Eros* shows how Need-pleasure is transformed into the "most Appreciative of all pleasures" when the Beloved is wanted for herself rather than for the sensory pleasure she can give; Singer in *Appraisal and Bestowal* equates interest in the Beloved as a person rather than as a commodity with the bestowed value created by love.

Fromm in *The Art of Loving* and Lee in *What Love Must Be* concur about the need to preserve individual integrity and identity in the act of will and commitment which entails care, responsibility, respect, knowledge, judgment, and promise, not merely "passion at its first blush," the characteristic of the "simple accident" described by Stevenson in *On Falling in Love,* and by Lindbergh in *Double-Sunrise.*

In *Revolution in Sexual Ethics,* Shinn explores sexuality as the expression of selfhood, noting six hallmarks of our culture's search for the meaning of sexuality: confusion, liberation, commercialization, mechanization, trivialization, and realization. Shinn's comments on mechanization are further explained by Trilling in excerpts from his reaction piece, "The Kinsey Report," which analyzes the classic sex study.

Lindbergh writes in **Double-Sunrise** that "validity need have no relation to time, to duration, to continuity," while Shakespeare claims in **Sonnet 116** that "love is not love which alters when it alteration finds." Shakespeare insists that love is blind while Millay argues that love is not blind. Reik, as quoted by Lowen, maintains that there is "straight sex" while Lowen holds that there is no sex without love. The contradictions and paradoxes point to MacLeish's view in **Psyche with the Candle** that love is indeed "the most difficult mystery/Asking from every young one answers." And perhaps it is only the poet, characterizing the protean feeling by metaphor, who is able to state: "There is no answer other to this mystery."

Some of the issues inherent in discussions of morality revolve about definitions of the term. As Quentin asks in **After the Fall,** "What the hell is moral? What does that really mean?" Or as *Playboy* editor Hugh Hefner queries, "Whose foot is to be the measure?" Additional problems ensue from the fact that many, like Ado Annie in **I Cain't Say No,** seem unable to make practice correspond to theory. The readings toward a definition of morality run the gamut from moral absolutism to moral relativism. They present both the fear ethic that plagued **The Young Lady Named Wilde** and the love ethic that guides decision-making in Fletcher's **Situation Ethics.** Acknowledging that there is no longer a sexual morality universally acceptable in contemporary society, Warren Johnson outlines three honest, responsible, but more or less incompatible moral positions prevalent today in **Some Observations on Sexual Morality.**

In the broad sense of the term, Kirkendall in **Searching for the Roots of Moral Judgments** pinpoints the essence of morality in the quality of interrelationships which create trust and appreciation. In applying the term moral to sexual behavior, Evelyn Havens in **I Thought I Was Modern** argues for virginity before marriage. An anonymous coed, on the other hand, presents a case for sexual relations outside marriage in **Chastity on the Campus.**

Sex Attitudes examines the sex taboo which Neill considers the root evil in the suppression of children. He traces hatred and fear of sex to unnecessary conditioning in infancy, just as Powys in **Glory of Life** attributes more "slow, malign torturings of the human spirit" to sexual restraints than to sexual indulgences. Shinn views morality from a biblical perspective in **Faithful Love,** examining Genesis as an expression of the belief that sexuality is a "gift from God and the basis of a profound human relationship."

Plato's **Symposium,** like Fletcher's **Situation Ethics,** distinguishes among motives relevant to sexual decisions, while **The New Morality** and **Modern Morals in a Muddle** critically probe some problems and pitfalls of making hard ethical choices from the situational perspective.

The final selections from **The Scarlet Letter** make explicit several moral viewpoints through images of "right" and "wrong" concerning a single case in Puritan New England and give the reader a chance to question, agree, refute, or modify as he tries to match theory with practice and to build his own ethical construct.

The relationship of love to marriage is as implicit in each of the readings toward a definition of marriage as is the agreement of all authors with Van Duyn's notion that it is "to make a fill, not find a land." Dietrich's perspective yields advice for the female strategist whose antennae must be sensitive in **Married Love;** Lindbergh focuses on the middle years of marriage in **Oyster Bed;** Miller, in **Forsaking All Others,** considers marriage "not as a state, but a unique emotion, potent and unalterable."

Peers and Parents

Snowfall in Childhood

BEN HECHT

I got out of bed to see what had happened in the night. I was thirteen years old. I had fallen asleep watching the snow falling through the half-frosted window.

But though the snow had promised to keep falling for a long time, perhaps three or four days, on opening my eyes I was full of doubts. Snowstorms usually ended too soon.

While getting out of bed I remembered how, as I was nearly asleep, the night outside the frosted window had seemed to burst into a white jungle. I had dreamed of streets and houses buried in snow.

I hurried barefooted to the window. It was scribbled with a thick frost and I couldn't see through it. The room was cold and through the open window came the fresh smell of snow like the moist nose of an animal resting on the ledge and breathing into the room.

I knew from the smell and the darkness of the window that snow was still falling. I melted a peephole on the glass with my palms. I saw that this time the snow had not fooled me. There it was, still coming down white and silent and too thick for the wind to move, and the streets and houses were almost as I had dreamed. I watched, shivering and happy. Then I dressed, pulling on my clothes as if the house were on fire. I was finished with breakfast and out in the storm two hours before school time.

The world had changed. All the houses, fences, and barren trees had new shapes. Everything was round and white and unfamiliar.

I set out through the new streets on a voyage of discovery. The unknown surrounded me. Through the thick falling snow, the trees, houses and fences looked like ghost shapes that had floated down out of the sky during the night. The morning was without light, but the snowfall hung and swayed like a marvelous lantern over the streets. The snowbanks, already over my head in places, glowed mysteriously.

I was pleased with this new world. It seemed to belong to me more than that other world which lay hidden.

I headed for the school, jumping like a clumsy rabbit in and out of snow-banks. It seemed wrong to spoil the smooth outlines of these snowdrifts and I hoped that nobody else would pass this way after me. In that case the thick falling snow would soon restore the damage. Reassured by this hope I continued on my devastations like some wanton explorer. I began to feel that no one would dare the dangers of my wake. Then, as I became more aware of the noble proportions of this snowstorm I stopped worrying altogether about the marring of this new and glowing world. Other snows had melted and been shoveled away, but this snow would never disappear. The sun would never shine again and the little Wisconsin town through which I plunged and tumbled to school on this dark storm-filled morning was from now on an arctic land full of danger and adventure.

When eventually, encased in snow, I arrived at the school, I found scores of white-covered figures already there. The girls had taken shelter inside, but the boys stayed in the storm. They jumped in and out of the snowdrifts and tumbled through the deep unbroken white fields in front of the school.

Muffled cries filled the streets. Someone had discovered how far-away our voices sounded in the snowfall and this started the screaming. We screamed for ten minutes, delighted with the fact that our voices no longer carried and that the snowstorm had made us nearly dumb.

Tired with two hours of such plunging and rolling, I joined a number of boys who like myself had been busy since dawn and who now stood for the last few minutes before the school bell with half-frozen faces staring at the heavily falling snow as if it were some game they couldn't bear to leave.

When we were finally seated in our grade room we continued to watch the snowstorm through the windows. The morning had grown darker as we had all hoped it would and it was necessary to turn on the electric lights in the room. This was almost as thrilling as the pale storm still floating outside the windows.

In this yellow light the school seemed to disappear and in its place a picnic spread around us. The teachers themselves seemed to change. Their eyes kept turning toward the windows and they kept looking at us behind our desks as if we were strangers. We grew excited and even the sound of our lessons—the sentences out of geography and arithmetic books—made us tremble.

Passing through the halls during recess we whispered to one another about the snowstorm, guessing at how deep the snowdrifts must be by this time. We looked nervously at our teachers who stood in the classroom doorways stiff and far removed from our secret whispers about the snow.

I felt sorry for these teachers, particularly for the one who had taught me several years ago when I was in the Fifth Grade. I saw her as I walked by the opened door of her room. She was younger then the other teachers, with two dark braids coiled around her head, a white starched shirtwaist and soft dark eyes that had always looked kindly at me when I was younger. I saw her now sitting behind her large desk looking over the heads of her class out of the window and paying no attention to the whispers and giggles of her pupils.

As for my own teacher, a tall, thin woman with a man's face, by afternoon I had become so happy I could no longer hear what she was saying. I sat looking at the large clock over her head. My feeling on the way to school that it would never be light again and that the snowstorm would keep on forever had increased so that it was something I now knew rather than hoped. My eagerness to get out into the world of wind, gloom, and perpetual snow, kept lifting me out of my seat.

At three o'clock we rushed into the storm. Our screams died as we reached the school entrance. What we saw silenced us. Under the dark sky the street lay piled in an unbroken bank of snow. And above it the snowfall still hung in a thick and moving cloud. Nothing was visible but snow. Everything else had disappeared. Even the sky was gone.

I saw the teachers come out and look around them, frowning. The children of the lower grades stood chattering and frightened near the teachers. I waited until the teacher with the two black braids saw me and then, paying no attention to her warning, spoken in a gentle voice, I plunged into the storm. I felt brave but slightly regretful that Miss Wheeler could no longer see me as I pushed into the head-high piles of snow and vanished fearlessly into the storm. But I was certain that she was still thinking of me and worrying about my safety. This thought added excitement to the snowstorm.

After an hour I found myself alone. My legs were tired with jumping and my face burned. It had grown darker and the friendliness seemed to have gone out of the storm. The wind bit with a sharper edge and I turned toward my home.

I arrived at the house that now looked like a snow drift and ploughed my way up to its front door. My heart was beating violently. I stopped to take a last look at the storm. It was hard to leave it. But for the first time in my life an adult logic instructed me. There would be even more snow tomorrow. And in this wind and snow-filled gloom and even in the marvelously buried street, there was something now unplayful.

I entered the house calling for something to eat, but as soon as I had taken my coat off and shaken myself clean, I was at the window again. The way this storm was keeping on was hard to believe.

At the table I was too excited to eat. I trembled and was unable to hear what was being said around me. In this room I could feel the night outside and the storm still blowing on my face. It seemed as if I were still in the street. My eyes kept seeing snow and my nose breathing it. The room and the people in it became far away. I left the table, taking a slice of bread and butter with me, and ran upstairs to my own room.

There were a lot of things to do, such as making my leather boots more waterproof by rubbing lard on them, putting my stamp collection in order, sharpening a deer's-foot knife I had recently acquired, winding tape on my new hockey stick, or reading one of the half dozen new books I had bought with my last birthday money. But none of these activities or even redrawing the plans for the iceboat on which I was working was possible. I sat in a chair near the window unable to think. The pale storm in the night seemed to spin like a top and, keeping the window frost melted with my palms, I sat and watched it snowing for an hour. Then, becoming sleepy, I went to bed. I thought drowsily of how happy Miss Wheeler would be to see me alive on Monday after the way I had rushed into the storm.

There was no seeing through my window when I awoke. The furnace never got going until after seven and before that hour on a winter's morning the house creaked with cold and the windows were sheeted thick with ice. But I knew as I dressed that the snowfall was over. There was too much wind blowing outside and the breath that come in from the snow-banked window ledge was no longer as fresh as it had been.

It was still dark. The bleak and gusty dawn lay over the snow like a guttering candle. The sky had finished with its snowing but now the wind sent the snowbanks ballooning into the air and the roof tops burst into little snowstorms.

I went outside and explored for ten minutes. When I came back into the house I needed no warning against going out to play. My skin was almost frozen and the wind was too strong to stand up in. I settled down as a prisoner in front of the fireplace after breakfast, lying on my stomach and turning the pages of a familiar oversized edition of Dante's "Inferno." It was full of Doré's nightmarish pictures.

The house bustled with cooking and cleaning. But these were the dim activities of grown-ups. I felt alone and took care of the fire to keep it from going out and leaving me to freeze to death. I carried logs all morning from the cellar and lay perspiring and half-scorched on the hearthstone. Every half-hour I went to the window to have a look at the enemy. The sight of the whirling snowbanks and the sound of the brutal wind as it hit against the houses sent me back to the fireplace to scorch myself anew.

In this way I spent the day until late afternoon. It grew dark early. The snow turned leaden. The wind stopped. The dead storm lay in the street and as far as I could see from the window there were no inhabitants in the world. The dark snow was empty. I shivered and went back to the fireplace.

A half-hour later our door bell rang. Company had arrived for supper. They were the Joneses, who lived in the town of Corliss some eight miles away. They had brought their daughter Anna.

The lights went on in the house. Baked and dizzy with the fire's heat, I joined the two families in the larger parlor. They were talking excitedly about the damage done by the storm. Accounts of store windows blown in, roofs blown off, signs blown down, and wagons abandoned in the drifts, were exchanged and I listened happily. Later when the talk turned to duller topics I became aware of Anna.

She was sitting in a corner watching me. She was a blondish girl two years older than I was and she went to high school. I had known her for a long time but had never liked her because she was too calm, never laughing or running, but always looking at people with a sad smile or just a stare as if she had something important on her mind. But now that she was watching me that way I felt suddenly interested in her. I wondered what she could be thinking of me and what made her smile in that half-sad way at me.

I sat next to her at the table and after looking at her several times out of the side of my eyes and catching her eyes doing the same thing, my heart started beating faster. I lost interest in eating. I wanted to be alone with her so we could sit and look at each other without the others noticing.

After supper the two families let us go to the hall upstairs, where I kept most of my possessions, without asking us any questions. I found a deck of cards and a cribbage board for a table. Underneath the lapboard our knees touched.

She played cribbage better than I and smiled at me as I kept losing. But I was only half aware of the game. I kept looking at her, unable to talk, and the light pressure of her knees began to make me feel weak. Her face seemed to become brighter and more beautiful as we played. A mist appeared around her eyes and her smile became so close, as if it were moving swiftly toward me, that I began to tremble. I felt ashamed of being so tongue-tied and red-faced, but with a half-frightened blissful indifference to everything—even Anna—I kept on playing.

We hardly spoke. I grew too nervous to follow the game and I wanted to stop. But I thought if we stopped we could no longer sit this way with our knees touching. At moments when Anna withdrew her touch I trembled and waited as if I were hanging from somewhere. When finally her knees returned to their place against mine, I caught my breath and frowned at the cards as if I were completely taken up with them.

As the hour passed, my face began to feel swollen and lopsided and it seemed to me my features had grown ugly beyond words. I tried to distract Anna's attention from this phenomenon by twisting my mouth, screwing up my eyes and making popping noises with my cheeks as we played. But a new fear arrived to uncenter my attention. I became afraid now that Anna would notice her knees were touching mine and move them away. I began at once pretending a deeper excitement in the game, complaining against my bad luck and denouncing her for cheating. I was determined to keep her interested in the game at any cost, believing that her interest in what we were doing made her unaware of her knees touching mine.

Finally Anna said she was tired of the game. She pushed the cribbage board away. I waited, holding my breath, for her to realize where her knees were and to move them away. I tried not to look at her but I was so frightened of this happening that I found myself staring at her. She seemed to be paying no attention to me. She was leaning back in her chair and her eyes were half closed. Her face was unsmiling and I felt she was thinking of something. This startled me. My throat filled with questions but I was so afraid of breaking this hidden embrace of our knees under the lapboard that I said nothing.

The mist seemed to have spread from her eyes to her hair and over the rest of her face. Wherever I looked this same glow rested around her. I noticed then that her hand was lying on the lapboard. I thought desperately of touching it but there was something disillusioning in this thought. I watched her fingers begin to tap gently on the board as if she were playing the piano. There was something strange about her hand as if it did not belong to the way her knees were touching mine or to the mist that rose from her eyes.

The minutes passed in silence and then Anna's mother called her from downstairs.

"I guess they're going home," I said and Anna nodded. She pressed closer against me but in my confusion I couldn't figure out whether this was the accidental result of her starting to get out of her chair or on purpose.

"Why don't you ride out with us?" she said. She leaned over the lapboard toward me. "We've got the wagon sleigh and there's plenty of room."

Before I could answer she had stood up. My knees felt suddenly cold. I slid the lapboard to the floor, ashamed and sad. Anna, without looking back at me, had gone down the stairs. I kept myself from running after her. I was sure she was laughing at me and that she was saying to herself, "He's a big fool. He's a big fool."

The Joneses were ready to leave when I came into the parlor. Anna's mother smiled at me.

"Why don't you come and visit us over Sunday?" she said. "There's even more snow in Corliss than here."

"More snow than you can shake a stick at," said another member of the Jones family. They all laughed and while they were laughing my mother hustled me off for my wraps. I was to drive away with the Jones family in the sleigh drawn by the two strong horses that stood in front of our house.

I pulled on my leather boots, sweater, and overcoat while the goodbyes were being made. I kept trying to catch Anna's attention, but she was apparently unaware that I was in the room. This made me sad, and slowly my eagerness to go to Corliss left me. I wanted instead to go up to my room and slam the door forever on all the Joneses. Anna's gayety, the way she said goodbye over and over again and laughed and kissed all the members of my family as if nothing had happened to her, as if she hadn't sat with her eyes closed pressing against my knees in the hallway upstairs, made me almost ill. I felt abandoned and forgotten.

Finally I stood muffled and capped and scowling as my family offered some final instructions for my behavior. I heard nothing of what was said but turned over and over in my mind what I was going to do on the ride and after we got to Corliss. Chiefly I was going to ignore Anna, neither speak to her nor show her by a single look that I knew she was alive.

At this point Anna, having said goodbye to everybody several times, seized my arm unexpectedly and whispered against my ear.

"Come, hurry," she said. "We want to get a good place."

Without a word I rushed out of the house, slipping down the snowcaked steps and tumbling headlong into a snowdrift. I scrambled after Anna into the wagon sleigh. It was a low-sided farm wagon placed on wide, heavy wooden runners and piled with warm hay and horse blankets. There was room for only one on the seat. The rest of the Joneses, seven including me, would have to lie in the hay covered by the robes.

Anna was already in the wagon half-buried in the hay, a blanket over her. She gave me excited orders to brush the snow from my clothes, to cover myself well and not to get out and run alongside the horses when we were going up hill.

"It doesn't help any," she said. "They can pull just the same if you stay in here. And besides I don't want you to."

The rest of the Joneses came out and crowded into the wagon around us. Anna's father took his place on the driver's seat, assuring my mother, who had come out with a shawl over her head, that there was no danger because the State plow had cleared the road even to way beyond Corliss. I heard my mother ask where I was. Mrs. Jones answered that I was buried somewhere in the hay and Anna whispered close to me not to answer or say anything. I obeyed her.

The sleigh started off. I heard the horses thumping in the snow and the harness bells falling into a steady jingling. Lying on my back I looked into the night. Stars filled the sky and a white glare hung over the house tops. The street was silent. I could no longer see the snowcovered houses with their lighted windows. My nose filled with the fresh smell of snow and the barn smells of hay and horse blankets, I lay listening to the different sounds—the harness bells and the snow crunching under the runners.

The stillness of this winter's night was as intense as the storm that had raged for three days. I felt all the wind and snow there was had blown themselves out forever and that the night as far as the highest star had been emptied by the storm. This emptiness as I lay looking into it was like being hypnotized. It was something to run out into, to fly up into, as the snowfall had been. I began to want to see further and the star-filled sky that had seemed so vast a few minutes ago now didn't seem vast enough.

I had almost forgotten about Anna when I felt a now familiar warmth press against me. She had moved closer as if joggled by the sleigh. I held my breath waiting for her to order me to move away and give her room but she was silent.

My hand at my side touched her fingers. Now I forgot the sky and the great sprinkle of stars that seemed like a thin, far-away snowfall that had stopped moving. The night, the glare of snow, the jingling harness bells died away; only my fingers were alive. When I had looked at her hand tapping gently on the lapboard, it had seemed strange and the thought of touching it somehow disillusioning. But now under the horse blankets, hidden in the hay, this hand seemed more breathing and mysterious and familiar than anything about her. I lay unable to move closer to it, our fingertips barely touching. I grew dizzy wishing to reach her hand but I felt as powerless to move toward it as to fly.

The minutes passed. Two of the Joneses started singing. The thump of the horses, the jingling of the sleighbells, and the crunching of the snow under the runners seemed part of this soft singing. I too wished to sing, to stand up suddenly in this sweeping-along sleigh and bellow at the silent night.

Then the fingers for which I had been wishing until I was dizzy, seemed to start walking under the horse blankets, seemed to be running toward me in the warm hay. They came as far as my hand, closed around it, and I felt the throb of their tips against my palm. The night turned into a dream. I opened my eyes to the wide sprinkle of stars and a mist seemed to have come over them. The snow-covered hills over which we were gliding sparkled behind a mist and suddenly the night into which I was looking lost its hours. It stretched away without time as if it were not something that was passing like our sleigh over the snow, but a star-filled winter's night that would never change and never move.

Lying beside Anna, her hand in mine, with the sleigh now flying in a whirl of snow down the white hill, I thought this night would never end.

At thirteen, the narrator says of his fifth-grade teacher, who always "looked kindly" at him when he was younger:

> I waited until [she] saw me and then, paying no attention to her warning, spoken in a gentle voice, I plunged into the storm. . . . But I was certain that she was still thinking of me and worrying about my safety. This thought added excitement to the snowstorm. . . . becoming sleepy, I went to bed. I thought drowsily of how happy Miss Wheeler would be to see me alive on Monday after the way I rushed into the storm.

How is his feeling for Miss Wheeler still a child's love, one that "creates only a self"? An "I"—orientation?

Anna Jones initiates the narrator's sexual awakening. Sexual excitement is recognizable because certain physical signs appear. As one sex educator notes:

> Because of the differences between boys and girls in the way they are made and the ways in which they have been brought up, the boy usually experiences the first symptoms of sexual expression. His face may become flushed. Usually his breathing becomes rapid, his pulse is fast, and his heart starts to pound. Changes in his sex organs are obvious. The girl as well as the boy may find that hands perspire freely under sexual stimulation. Girls tend to experience an all-over relaxation. [1]

Which of these physical signs of sexual arousal are depicted in **Snowfall in Child-**

hood? What further signs could the author of this story have added to the list? Are there still more signals of which the aroused one is fully conscious, although they are not discernible to others?

In his innocence, the narrator believes that Anna's interest in their cribbage game made her unaware that their knees were touching. Later, he says, she "pressed closer against me but in my confusion I couldn't figure out whether this was the accidental result of her starting to get out of her chair or on purpose." Finally, he determines childishly to punish Anna by ignoring her, because when he had tried to catch her attention she was "apparently unaware" that he was in the room. Why would so sophisticated a fifteen-year-old high school girl be interested in so naïve a thirteen-year-old boy? Do you think she is really interested in him?

When the narrator noticed Anna's hand lying on the lapboard he "thought desperately of touching it but there was something disillusioning in this thought." In the sleigh, after his hand at his side touched her fingers, he recalls that when he

> . . . had looked at her hand tapping gently on the lapboard, it had seemed strange and the thought of touching it somehow disillusioning. But now under the horse blankets, hidden in the hay, this hand seemed more breathing and mysterious and familiar than anything about her. . . . I grew dizzy wishing to reach her hand. . . .

How would you account for the change in his attitude? Why in one case is the thought "disillusioning," and in the other "dizzy-making"?

Is "under-cover" experimental love-making a way of evading responsibility? Of pretending that sexual overtures are accidental? Of heightening emotional intoxication? Is it similar to a dress that reveals nothing but hints at a great deal? The ambiguous remark? The interested glance? Flickering candlelight rather than midmorning daylight?

Why is adolescence described as a period of acute self-consciousness?

By his choice of title and his many descriptions of the weather, the author puts considerable emphasis on the snowfall. How do the timing and the effects of the snowfall condition the narrator's mood, contributing to his readiness to feel "suddenly interested" in a girl he had known "for a long time," and intensify his feelings, particularly at the end of the story?

How does the environment function symbolically as well as literally in the story? Note the narrator's early comments:

> The world had changed. All the houses, fences, and barren trees had new shapes. Everything was round and white and unfamiliar.
>
> I set out through these new streets on a voyage of discovery. The unknown surrounded me. . . . The snowbanks, already over my head in places, glowed mysteriously.
>
> I was pleased with this new world. It seemed to belong to me more than that other world which lay hidden.

What are the parallels between the internal and external world of the narrator? Are they maintained throughout the story until finally "the snow-covered hills over which we were gliding sparkled behind a mist"?

Young people name their peers as the major source of sex information [2]. A broad sex education, however, imparts more than the facts of life and dirty jokes about them; it provides knowledge of the feelings and attitudes toward sexuality. Although there is only a two-year age difference between them, how does Anna serve as voluntary tutor in the most basic elements of an education for sexuality? How does the narrator serve as her obedient student?

RELATED QUESTIONS

Which of the so-called "deadly" females portrayed in the "I" section does Anna Jones most nearly resemble? Why?

Although the narrator in **Snowfall in Childhood** is older than Richard of **Parma Violets** (p. 13), what characteristics of Richard's feeling for Aunt Bunch also stamp the narrator's feeling for Miss Wheeler?

The "hidden embrace" of their knees under the lapboard, so thrilling to the narrator of **Snowfall in Childhood,** is only one form of minor sexual experimentation and acting out of roles.

A varyingly sophisticated group of peers, as well as one person like Anna, may be part of the "**They**" forces which pressure individuals. In the following excerpt from Walter Van Tilburg Clark's novel **The City of Trembling Leaves,** boy-girl sex games like post office and spin-the-bottle supply the setting wherein males and females may have brief encounters strictly according to rule, exempting players from having to take initiative or responsibility in a sexual episode, but affording the shy an opportunity to engage in sex play on a chance, game-like basis.

The City of Trembling Leaves
WALTER VAN TILBURG CLARK

After supper, Billy led them all into the living room. "Let's play something," he said.

"What?"

"I know," one of the girls said. "Drop the handkerchief."

There was groaning. She . . . was questioned about her age and mentality.

"Charades," another girl said, and there was more groaning.

There was some hope about musical chairs, but Billy said they couldn't play that because of the new floor, and anyway there was no piano and the new phonograph hadn't come yet.

There was more groaning about Teakettle.

"Oh, let's play something that's some fun," Billy said. "I'll tell you what. Let's play spin-the-bottle."

Tim didn't know what spin-the-bottle was, except that it was probably a boy-girl game and embarrassing, because several of the boys whooped and laughed, and the girl with the big mouth suddenly clutched him by the arm, as if to save herself from falling into a paroxysm of laughter, and when she got barely enough breath, squealed, "He *would* want to play that."

Tim saw that Rachel also either didn't know the game, or was afraid of it.

She was standing like a soldier by herself at the other end of the couch, trying to smile and look as if she understood. There was a row of many, small, red-and-yellow plaid buttons down the front of her velvet jacket. They bound the jacket closely over her sharp, small breasts, and he could see how quickly she was breathing.

Some of the boys were pushing the couch out of the way against the fire-place. Tim helped to roll the rug and put it against the wall. Billy stood out in the middle of the shining floor with an empty pop bottle in his hand.

"O.K., here we go," he yelled. "Everybody get in a big ring. First a boy, then a girl, all the way round like that."

He came over and dragged Rachel into the ring, and then went back out in the middle. "O.K.," he said again. "No moving. You gotta stay right where you are."

He laid the bottle down on its side, and spun it between his thumb and finger. The bottle twinkled rapidly, glittered as it slowed down, and finally lay still and gleaming, with its neck pointing at a boy. There was lamentation, as if this were a disappointment.

"Be a fish," Billy told him.

The boy lay down full length on the floor, and vaguely imitated some sort of a swimming creature. He was mildly applauded and heavily insulted.

"You spin now," Billy told him.

The game went on. The modest purpose of its first stage was to inflict upon the person chosen by the bottle a physical maneuver entailing some in-dignity. The transition period began when the dark boy called Sheik, who wore a college-cut suit and a red necktie, was told to go around the circle and bow to each girl and kiss her hand. There were fake protests from the girls and cheers from the boys. One boy yelled, "That ain't nothin' for you, is it, Sheik?" When Sheik went around the circle the girls giggled, and posed haughtily, like movie countesses. Rachel became red and then white, and Sheik had to reach for her hand. When he kissed it, she had a spasm of laughter.

After that all the penalties were of the same sort, and everyone watched the spinning bottle intently, and sometimes a victim would try to change his place when he saw that the bottle might pick him. Timmy had to get down on his knees before each girl, and touch his forehead to her right hand, as in token fealty. When he finished this labor he was sweating, although it wasn't hot in the room, for the door and the windows were open, so that the night breathed in, and pale moths came and quivered upon the screens or drummed against them. He believed that the only hand he could still feel on his forehead was Rachel's, which was small and cold. He felt that probably there was a sacred mark left by her fingers, their imprint shining like a light.

It was Rachel who ended spin-the-bottle before its possibilities were fully explored. When the bottle picked her, the ringmaster ordered her to go around the circle and kiss each boy on both cheeks. Rachel stood like the soldier. The fields of her soul were given over to battle. Some of the boys offered loud advice. One of them cried that he would take two in the middle instead of one on each side, and everybody laughed explosively, and then stopped laughing suddenly, and only giggled. They all felt their personal futures involved in the battle Rachel was fighting.

Rachel was very red. She made quick little gasping laughs, and looked quickly at different girls, but when she wasn't laughing her lower lip trembled. Her hands were pulling at each other in front of her. She still didn't say anything. The circle broke up, and she was besieged. She began to shake her head. She was bombarded by arguments, ridicule and doubts of her innocence. She kept shaking her head and trying hard to laugh, but getting further and further from really laughing. Tim was a prisoner watching his own destroyed. Even Billy's powers were weakened by internal dissension. His desire to remain the champion of the liberals was checked by the threat to his personal privilege.

The siege was lifted by accident. One of the boys, intending only to add his bit to the popular pressure, yelled, "I know what's the trouble with her. She wants to play post-office, so we can't see her, don't you, Rachy?" But the suggestion turned a common desire, and at once pressure groups began to form to make it a real plan. A few extremists continued the personal fight though. They agreed to post-office, but worked up a chant, "Rachy has to go first, Rachy has to go first."

Rachel dumbly opposed this action also, and finally the chant died because she could hardly keep herself from crying. The debate shifted to method. One faction insisted that the choice should be personal, and the other that the names should be drawn. Feeling the swing of opinion, Billy voiced the majority preference.

"We'll draw," he yelled. "Then it won't be just one fellow getting all our mail or something." He was cheered, and also accused of fearing to risk himself in open contest. He began to give orders.

"Everybody write his name on a slip of paper," he yelled. He went into a side room and came back with several sheets of paper and a fistful of pencils. While he was folding the sheets together and tearing them into strips, he was assailed as having had the whole thing plotted out beforehand. Tim signed like an illiterate putting his name to a contract before a lawyer he mistrusted. He didn't know how post-office was played either, except that it must be an advance over spin-the-bottle because there was secrecy connected with it. Billy collected all the boys' names in one hat, and the girls' in another.

"First one I pick is post-master," he announced.

There was silence as he drew a slip from the girls' hat.

"Pauline Chester," he announced.

There was an uproar. The bosomy girl in whom Tim's elbow had been buried at supper stepped forth.

"Where do I go?" she asked, when it was quiet.

"The study is the post-office," Billy announced. "You go on in," he said to Pauline. "Then I'll hold the hat in for you."

"No lights," somebody cried.

"No lights," everybody shouted.

"No fakes, either," somebody else shouted. "You have to really kiss. Anybody that won't really kiss has to kiss everybody." This rule was adopted by acclaim, although there were a few skeptics who wanted to know how it was going to be enforced when they couldn't see what was going on. "If they're both a-scared, how do we know what they did?"

This simple game did not grow dull. There was an outburst as each name was read. There was an intense quiet during each interval in which Billy held the hat, and the hand from the dark room reached out and chose a name. There was a fleeting expression of dread or doubt, but also the room was electrical with particular hopes. On a few faces was the blanched agony of the card players in the Suicide Club. As each post-master emerged, he was hailed, belittled and cross-examined. The girls all attempted to appear unmoved by this public prominence. The boys, assuming the license of the double standard, came out in different ways. Some looked knowing and remained silent. Some expressed glee. One skinny youth, blond and freckled, whose pants were too short, came out with his hands clasped before him, his face raised in praise of the Lord who gave such bliss, and his knees sagging and wavering. This interpretation was popular, and was played frequently, with variations. The most successful imitator was practically original. He came out on his hands and knees, rolled over, and expired in jerking agony.

Even though the game was turned over to Fortune, the spear of personal implication was felt often. There was loud booing when one girl chanced to pick the name of a boy who spent most of his time with her anyway. There was laughter and satire when a notoriously unilateral affair attained the secret climax. Loud suggestions for deliberate manipulation were made to Billy, and he pretended to act upon them. Billy himself was called, and somebody else took over the hat. If the door opened too soon, the deed was questioned. If it remained closed a long time, protest, scandalized accusation, and expressions of envy rose into a storm.

Tim kept looking back at Rachel. The davenport had been turned around, and she was sitting on one arm of it. She laughed everytime everybody laughed, but never said anything. Tim understood that she was practicing the art of disappearing into the background. He was saying a good many things himself, but they all arose from that same desire to appear inconspicuous, and most of them were just poor imitations of previous successes. Each time it was a girl's hand working around the door, his breath and his pulse were suspended. He took as a sweet if brief reprieve each period during which a boy held office. It was in these moments that he made his few really witty comments which could be quoted. Only one hope, and that half dread, remained constant in him. The numerical chances of entering the study with Rachel were small. Still, he kept thinking how it would be, and each time the chance came up that it might be, suddenly the inside diplomatic preliminaries appeared insurmountable, and a desert without water would begin to expand between his chair and the door of the study.

There were several repeats, one boy being called so often that there were accusations of fixing, and still Rachel wasn't called, and neither was Tim. Tim allowed himself guardedly to begin to hope both ways. He began to look at Rachel even more often, hoping to establish a union by means of their isolation, but she would accept no ally.

The skinny boy who had first swooned was acting as panderer. The dark boy with the red necktie was in the study. The dark hand held up the slip, and the skinny boy took it. He read solemnly, "Rachel Wells."

When the skinny boy said "Rachel" Tim's breath stopped as if it had been his own name. He didn't even hear as far as Wells.

"About time," somebody shouted.

"Do a good job on her, Sheik."

"One ain't enough, Sheik. Take one for all of us."

"Two, you mean," somebody amended.

This became a chorus. "Two for each of us, Sheik."

Finally Rachel got up and walked across to the study door quickly, smiling hard and with her arms straight down. She was cheered and hooted. At the door she stood and waited. She was speaking. Everybody became quiet. She was making a last desperate appeal to Pander.

"I don't have to pick one too, do I?"

She received a great many replies, among which Pander's was lost. It required another moment to quell her own rebellion, and then she entered. The skinny boy put his finger to his lip and his ear to the door. There was silence outside. There was also silence inside. The skinny boy straightened up, shrugging his shoulders and spreading his hands.

The boy called Sheik chose to be non-committal when he came out, and so far as the public was concerned Rachel remained a figure of mystery, as inviolate as upon her entrance. Her hand chose and the skinny boy intoned, "Tim Hazard."

This was also greeted as overdue, and Tim received a good many suggestions. The desert between his chair and the door swelled and sank under him. He entered the difficult portal, and it was closed behind him. He was standing in absolute darkness. He also felt that many-eared silence outside. He waited. Since she was already there, and had seen him come in, Rachel should make the overture. He didn't even know where she was in there. He couldn't even remember what shape the room was, or where the furniture was. He stood very still, except for the roaring in his brain, and listened. Rachel finally made the overture.

"Well," she whispered hard, "don't take all night. I don't want to be in here all night with any boy."

It was impossible to tell from the whisper how angry or tearful or merely matter-of-fact and in a hurry she was.

"Where are you?" he whispered.

This became at once, to him, a question of great significance. The dark study took on the dimensions of a dead planet in eternal night, and across its vast wastes, its tundras and glaciers and cold and whispering seas, he ran and swam and climbed frantically, in quest of a tiny, solitary, lost, perhaps dying, Rachel.

"Here," Rachel whispered.

"Where?"

"Right here," she whispered angrily, "behind the door."

It was shocking that she was so close. Even their whispering had not told him she was so close. He moved only one step, with his hand out, and touched her. He was shivering with expectation, dread and ignorance. It was the velvet jacket he had touched. He was terribly ashamed and bewildered. He didn't know what part of the velvet jacket he had touched. She didn't say anything, or move to help him.

"Is that you?" he asked. The word "you" in his mind began with a capital and from its letters arose tongues of oriflamme.

"It's my sleeve," she whispered.

He ventured to close his hand.

"Hurry up, will you?" she whispered sharply.

He felt that this was an accusation of timidity. He put his other arm around her waist. She was rigid and trembling. It was impossible to pass this barrier of fear. He was the hunter paralyzed by the eyes of the deer that has turned.

The tittering began outside. It had seemed to Tim that the laws of time were revoked. Now they returned in force, at once, and even retroactively. Probably he had been in this darkness with Rachel for a hundred years, and they would never dare to come out. The comments began in the living room.

"Hurry up, will you?" Rachel said again, almost out loud this time. He felt a paroxysm, as of a breath of wind through the aspen, pass down the little body in his arm.

He stammered when he whispered, "You don't really want me to kiss you really, do you?"

"I don't care what you do," she whispered, "only for goodness' sakes do something, will you?"

Tim was bewildered by a great tenderness. He was trembling more than she was. He had no pride and wanted only to do what she wished.

The comments outside had become a clamor.

Suddenly she was pushing him off and whispering, "Let go of me, will you? Let go of me."

She got him loose from her, and scurried past him, and he heard the door knob rattle as she found it, and then saw her in the beam of light as she opened the door quickly. She controlled herself enough to go out slowly, but her face must have given something away about which he wasn't sure himself, because she was met by a sudden outburst of laughter and cries.

Tim started to follow her out, and this brought on another burst of laughter.

"Oh, no, you don't" the skinny boy said, and pushed him back in. Tim remembered that he was supposed to pick a name also.

"What's the matter, Tim? Want more?" somebody called.

Another answered him. "Go on. I bet they didn't even kiss. I bet it was a fake. They just stayed in there to make us think it was something."

Everybody began to ask Rachel if had been just a fake.

Tim reached into the hat in the opening of the doorway, and then the slip was taken from him.

After a moment the skinny boy announced, "Pauline Chester."

The bosomy girl, the girl like cushions or a woman, came in. The door closed. There was nothing religious about this encounter, but there was no delay either. There was nothing said. Tim reached out to let know where he was. She took his hand and worked up along his arm and closed on him. He tried to stimulate cooperation, but that probably wouldn't have mattered anyway. It was a long and suffocating kiss. For one minute he forgot Rachel, but not because of any change of heart.

What reasons might explain Rachel's opposition to the after-supper games?
When the bottle points to Rachel and the ringmaster orders her to kiss each

boy around the circle, "Rachel stood like the soldier. The fields of her soul were given over to battle." What is Rachel's conflict? What are the opposing forces in this battle? What might happen if Rachel simply refused to play? If she burst into tears? If she walked out and went home? Why did Rachel have a "spasm of laughter" when Sheik kissed her hand? Did she find it funny?

What is the nature of Tim's feeling for Rachel? How strong is it? When neither Rachel nor Tim were called, why did the latter allow himself "guardedly to begin to hope both ways"? Why is Tim so awkward, fearful, and fumbling when he enters the darkness with Rachel? Why is Tim compared with "the hunter paralyzed by the eyes of the deer that has turned"?

Although Tim interprets Rachel's "hurry up, will you?" as "an accusation of timidity," and asserts his masculinity by putting his other arm around her waist, Tim seems to resist the rewards of the game. Is he bothered by the tittering outside? Afraid Rachel will make a fool of him? Not attracted to Rachel physically? Doubtful of his masculinity? Genuinely concerned for Rachel's welfare?

Is Tim's sexuality already showing signs that it will become an expression of a deep and intimate bond between a man and a woman? How does Tim reveal his feeling of great tenderness? Why is he bewildered by it? Would you agree or disagree that "tenderness is greater proof of love than the most passionate of vows" [3]? What does the author mean when he says "Tim had no pride"?

What effects has Tim's experience with Rachel on his encounter with Pauline Chester? From your knowledge of Rachel, how would you expect her to feel while Tim was behind the closed door with Pauline?

Do boy-girl games teach the players anything of the difference between sex as an exercise and sex as an expression of affection?

It is generally acknowledged that females mature socially at an earlier age than males, possibly because of earlier physical maturation. What is meant by "social maturity"? Do the girls portrayed in the scene from *The City of Trembling Leaves* seem to you more mature socially than the boys?

A "board of iron mothers" who run the monthly Merrymakers Club dances constitute another pressure group among "**They**" forces. The fifteen-year-old in Walter Clemons' short story *Merrymakers* must try to reconcile these forces with conflicting pressures from contemporaries.

Merrymakers

WALTER CLEMONS

During the intermission we washed down gravelly oatmeal cookies with pineapple punch. Somebody figured out what oatmeal cookies are good for and lobbed one at a pal across the dancefloor. Back it came, spinning through the air. Squeals. War broke out, but the chaperons crushed it. The orchestra lurched into a fox trot, net skirts rustled, chairs scraped, and boys in their first tuxedos, fifty faces blank with doom, rose and launched their partners.

Every month we came to these Merrymakers' Club dances upstairs in the old Junior League building. We were fifteen years old; there was no out. A board of iron mothers ran the club, and a week before each dance, if you hadn't asked a date yet, you were apt to come home from school in the afternoon to find a telephone number to call. At the other end of the wire a mother was waiting, with news that some sad tall girl or bouncy pill hadn't been asked yet, and a suggestion. So if you knew what was good for you, you asked a popular girl a month ahead, sent a carnation corsage trimmed with net the color of her dress, and box-stepped under the balloons without reasoning why, until another Merrymakers' evening was done. Our merrymaking was a thick gruel, stirred slowly clockwise to music by the mothers.

Someone tapped me on the shoulder. I said politely, "Thank you, Kitty," and smiled down into a grotto of tiny white teeth. Impartial as a lighthouse, she turned her smile to the partner who replaced me, and I started for the edge of the dancefloor. You had to be careful, for if you so much as brushed against one of the toiling couples they would split like a dry pod, the boy would make for the punch table without a blush of shame or a backward look, and you would find yourself dancing. I tiptoed around Hallie Beth Bosley as if she were a bomb and made it to the wall where Edwina Moore had been standing since the music began, thin and unhappy, with a worthless dance card dangling from her wrist. I said, "Would you care to dance, Edwina?"

"Oh, yes, thank you." She cast a farewell look around the room. "I was supposed to have this dance with Jack, but he chickened out." Then she gave it up and put her cool hand in mine and I led her out on the floor. Edwina didn't dance cheek to cheek like the popular girls and that made it awkward because we kept looking each other in the eye and having to say things. I said, "It's an awfully good dance, isn't it?"

"Yes, it is," Edwina said hopelessly. "The orchestra's good, isn't it?"

"Yes, it is." We danced on, uttering little pale sentences. I asked whom she'd come with and was sorry I'd brought it up. Her cousin. A put-up job, obviously.

"JoAnne looks pretty tonight," Edwina said.

Not knowing whether to say, "Thank you," or "Yes, she does," or to attempt a flight of fancy like, "Not as pretty as you," I kept my mouth shut. JoAnne was the girl I'd brought to the dance and whose silver identification bracelet I wore on my left wrist.

I was in my usual condition of misery. I really only wanted to dance with the prettiest girls, like JoAnne, but then I would see some poor thing marooned and feel bad and go ask her instead. But it was shallow kindness, for no sooner had I done it than I would be chewing the inside of my mouth and wondering if I was going to be stuck. The shiftings of half-hearted do-unto-others and flighty panic gave me sweating palms I kept wiping on the hip of my tux.

I danced with Edwina until my left hand was moist beyond social acceptability. I couldn't jerk it away, and clearly nobody was going to cut in. I said, "Gee, it's hot in here. Let's go on the porch and sit a while, why don't we?"

We made our way among the couples, me wiping my hand, and stepped out on the long second-story veranda, overlooking a patio planted with banana and palm trees. Edwina sat down and I brought two Dixie cups of water from the cooler. These we drank in deep silence, and then Edwina slowly crushed her cup and tore it in small pieces. Meanwhile I stared. Her straight yellow hair was brushed severely back, and under the lights along the wall her high curved forehead gleamed as gently as pearl. Her face was centered high up, in her forehead and gray eyes; her serious thin mouth I hardly looked at. I was always riotously and guiltily thinking about kissing people, for lack of conversational topics, and my impulse was to kiss Edwina on her clear, vulnerable-looking forehead. Now that I looked at her, for the first time really, I was puzzled why Edwina wasn't pretty. Her hair was pretty, her skin was, her—

I suddenly saw her lips finish a sentence I hadn't heard a word of. "What'd you say, Edwina?"

"I just said, you were looking at me so funny. Is there something on my face?" She lifted a thin hand, with bitten nails, and touched her cheek.

"Oh, no, I was just—I mean, I was thinking you look—pretty," I said, whereupon Edwina blanched, and my remark fell between us like a new-laid egg. In an effort to bury it I opened my mouth and loosed a second horror. "And that's an awfully nice dress you have on." We both stared aghast at the dress, which I observed dimly was green. Then, utterly undone, we sprang up from our chairs, bits of Dixie cup falling softly to the floor, and fled back to the dance-floor.

As we stepped through the french doors JoAnne whirled past in the grip of a handsome, dangerous boy a year older than me, who rode a motorcycle, and my heart went up in flames like a ball of crumpled paper. I hardly noticed that Edwina had stopped dead by my side. I turned and saw her stricken face and said, "What's the matter, Edwina?"

She said, "You were awfully nice to dance with me, but I don't want you to be stuck with me—" She began to back away.

"What're you talking about, what're you talking about?" I cried distractedly.

"Please, don't feel responsible. I'm used to it. I'll go comb my hair a while, that's what I always do."

I caught her wrist. I could see JoAnne not far away, laughing with her partner, and I was scared Edwina was about to cry, she was all pink. I said, nearly in tears myself, "What are you talking about, stuck? I like to dance with you, Edwina, honestly. Please don't talk like that, please don't."

Some time later, when one of the partners on Edwina's dance card had appeared and I was at large again, I hunted up a buddy who was playing odd-or-even for nickels in the stagline. "Hey, Stan, do me a favor?" He looked wary, and when I said, "Go dance with Edwina Moore," he dropped his nickel in alarm.

"Are you crazy?" said Stan. "What I want to dance with her and be stuck the whole rest of the night for?"

"You won't be. I'll send somebody."

"But she's a head taller'n me and she's so serious and everything. In fact, she hates me. Man, have mercy."

"Come on, she's nice."

In sheer uneasiness he began to look around the room and snap his fingers in time to the music. Then he looked back at me more considerately. "What's the trouble? You bring her?"

"No, I just feel bad about her. Come on, five minutes, for pete sake."

Stan closed his eyes and nodded glumly. "But if you leave me with her, I swear—"

"I won't, go on."

"Where've you *been?*" said JoAnne when I got back to her half an hour later, haggard.

I swallowed. "Well, you know Edwina Moore, how I was dancing with her for a long time?"

"And now you're mad for her and it's all over between us."

"Uh-huh, she's so much prettier'n you," I said wittily and was rewarded with a snuggle. "Listen, JoAnne. There I was, dancing with her, and all of a sudden she said I didn't have to be stuck with her and she'd go comb her hair and thanked me and all." JoAnne groaned. "But I hadn't done anything wrong, JoAnne. I was nice, really. And I thought that was so nice of her, not to just hang on like old Hallie Beth does and talk you to pieces, it made me feel for her, and so when somebody finally cut in on me I decided to go hunt up guys to dance with her, you know, try to make her have a better time."

"And what happened?"

"Well, I got Stan. Then I got Bob to follow him. But then I got in hot water, because when I was trying to talk Horace Ackney into going—what a stinking rat, that Horace Ackney, he wanted a quarter—Edwina looked right over where I was, and I got scared if Horace went, she'd catch on I put him up to it, so there wasn't anything to do but go back and cut in on Bob myself, he was rolling his eyes around. So there I was, big as life, dancing with her again, and it looked so fishy, bouncing back when I'd just got through dancing with her, I had to have some excuse, and what I said was, 'Edwina, I forgot to ask you when I was dancing with you before, would you go to next month's Merrymakers' with me?'"

"But you're supposed to be taking me."

I was totally unhappy. "I know, JoAnne. But there'll be hundreds of guys asking you, and it's just for this once."

"I just don't understand it," JoAnne said.

"Boy, me either! I just couldn't get over it, what she said. I wanted to do something to kind of make up for things. She never acts happy."

JoAnne nodded and said softly, "Well, with her parents the way they are."

"What way?"

"Oh, they don't get along. I don't know exactly. I've heard my parents talk."

"Are you mad, JoAnne—what I did?"

"No, I'm not mad. What did Edwina say?"

"When I asked her? Not much. She just said, 'Yes, thank you, I'd like to,' and then she piped down and not another word. She didn't seem real delighted or anything."

Yes, thank you, I'd like to. Then, I supposed, if you were Edwina Moore, you fell silent because you just didn't know how to talk to a green boy you'd known distantly all your life. He came bungling up and asked you to a dance a month ahead; probably no one had ever done that before. What should you have done? Make big eyes or say something cute or at least, at the very least, dance cheek to cheek like other girls? Instead, you took the news inside, having been by yourself too much to change and be anything besides alone at a dance. It must be pretty terrible, I imagined, to stand unasked on the outskirts of the grins and music; you probably thought about being twenty-five years old and miraculously beautiful—and unhurt.

The dance ended while you were combing away at your hair in the powder room. Your cousin Jerry, I was fairly sure, held your velvet coat with a cousin's apathy just too high for you to get your arms into the sleeves. At your front door he grunted and shuffled away down the front walk before you'd even got the key out of your mother's beaded bag.

Other girls, maybe, rushed upstairs to sit at the foot of their parents' beds and chat about the dance. Your parents were social, beautiful people; I had seen them at wedding receptions. You would probably feel like a discredit to them, stiff and shy and sorry-looking. Though they probably didn't always look so handsome; sometimes they stopped talking when you came into the room, the skin on their faces shrunken with anger. You would have learned by now not to look, just get out of the room, not think about things you couldn't do anything about. Anyway, you wouldn't go tell about the dance.

As Jerry's car started off in the dark outside, you climbed the stairs. You sat down at the cool mirror in your bedroom and blurred your eyes to see yourself at twenty-five. At the dance your face burned, your skinny arm on your partner's shoulder felt light and outlandish, as if you had fever. Now you would be calmer; you could feel almost as if the dance had never taken place. Now nobody could touch you. I was sure it would never occur to you a boy was lying awake thinking about you.

A month later, Edwina and I sat on straight chairs at one end of the dance-floor. Hallie Beth Bosley in vibrating yards and yards of hot red taffeta bore down on us, fists full of oatmeal cookies. "May we sit down next to youall?" she said, sitting down. She had Horace Ackney with her, a peaked boy with thick glasses behind which his eyes rolled whitely, like those of a terrified horse. Hallie Beth bounced around on her chair, establishing herself, and began to bolt down oatmeal cookies in some hazard of biting her hand off at the wrist. "Idn't it a divine dance? Don't you just love it?" she inquired thickly out of a full mouth. We said it was a very good dance. Horace Ackney declared he didn't think it was as good as the dance before last, though better than last month's, and we batted that around for a while.

"I love your hair that new way," Hallie Beth said to Edwina.

"Thank you, Hallie Beth."

"I mean it. I think it's super. You must be with someone pretty special tonight." She gave me a brassy smile. Die, Hallie Beth, shrivel up and immediately die, I said with my eyeballs. Where Edwina was looking, I couldn't imagine. Hallie Beth prodded Horace, causing him to spill a few drops of punch. "Listen, y'all. Horace has made up this divine new word. Tell them, Horace."

We all looked at Horace, who waited for perfect silence and then said in a hollow tone, *"Repetuous."* We recoiled as if to give him air.

"I just love it," Hallie Beth said. "You see, it's sort of a combination of 'repetitious' and 'impetuous.'"

We pondered. "What do you do with it?" I asked.

"Oh, *everything!*" Hallie Beth cried. "*You* know. Like you might say, uh, 'a repetuous old houn' dog.' Idn't that right, Horace."

"Well," said Horace fastidiously. "Something like that." I couldn't stand this Horace. I was a bookworm too, and concealed it in public like nose-picking. Then I would look at Ackney and tremble to realize I was more like him than I was like the football heroes I tagged around with and aped; I hated poor Horace therefore.

Our little conversation ran out of gas. It was always happening. We scrutinized our punch cups. My social instinct inflamed me even to consider building sentences around "repetuous," but it didn't come to that, for the music started and I danced Edwina away. I said full of hope, "Are you having a good time?"

"Oh, yes," said Edwina. Her cheeks were pink; she was nearly pretty. "Are you?"

"Oh, yes," I said extravagantly.

As we revolved, my mind churned. I wanted everything to be nice, everybody football captains and May Queens in a world turning smoothly. When any surface cracked, I felt threatened. Tell me parents didn't love each other, show me somebody like Edwina in pain, and I wanted to plaster over the trouble. The squeamish with their gentle fingers are as cruel as the woodenhearted; they only look kinder: I wasn't able to admit to myself how much I wished I'd never seen Edwina.

At home, I'd been cross-examined at the dinner table when the news came out that I wasn't taking JoAnne to this dance. JoAnne's father and mother were bridge cronies of my parents; naturally they were interested. "You and JoAnne had a squabble, eh?" No, Dad, no, for pete sake. Well, who was I taking then? It seemed to me parents had no respect for a son's private life. I answered sullenly. So; Ned and Caroline Moore's daughter. My parents exchanged a silence. "Well, I always sorta *liked* Ned Moore," my father said in an in-spite-of-everything tone. My mother moved in, ominously neutral, with "I saw Caroline in the A & P last week." The air was heavy with opinions unspoken. "Oh, now, Caroline's all right," my father said, with more warmth than he'd *liked* Mr. Moore, and plainly disagreeing with whatever way my mother saw Mrs. Moore in the grocery. Why wouldn't parents come out and *say*? I peered back and forth. "Um," my mother concluded the duet on a diminished seventh.

Tonight I had been shown into a warm library. There were sets of Thackeray and Gibbon; a line of Heritage Press books caught my eye; my fingers itched to take them down and feel the creamy laid paper and florid bindings. But I made urbane conversation with Mr. Moore. I thought he was the most handsome man I'd ever seen; he was lean and gray, furnished with a glass of brandy and a garnet satin smoking jacket. This was the way to live, it seemed to me. I bet myself the Moores ate dinner by candlelight and spoke intricate sentences in soft voices, entirely unlike our slapdash suppers after which my father snoozed on the living room couch in sock feet and cigar ash. Could such people be unhappy? My eyes grew big as Mr. Moore went to a decanter on a silver tray beside his armchair and poured a few inches of brown liquid into a snifter like his own. I'd never been offered it before, but I knew about brandy from novels; I even knew from *Before the Fact* that you could murder a man by encouraging him to drink a whole bottle of it, and I mentioned that to Mr. Moore. "You're quite safe," he said coolly. I accepted the glass and fondled it like a man of the world. I had a notion that after the fondling routine you imbibed brandy through your nostrils; I smelled around the rim of my glass, wondering how in the world, meanwhile eyeing Mr. Moore, who simply tossed his off. I did that too and coughed. Mortification. "It's turning some cooler out," I remarked. "I seem to be catching a cold." I fetched up a couple of frightening fake coughs and added, "This brandy really hits the spot."

When I was through coughing, Mr. Moore asked after my parents. I said they were just fine. "Did your mother ever tell you I was one of her beaux in college?" I said politely, no, she sure hadn't. "Oh, yes. Yes. Lots of water under the bridge since then." I looked at him more closely. He poured himself another brandy and held the decanter toward me with raised eyebrows. I shook my head, a little uneasy. "Oh, yes. Yes," he said again. "Well, we marry and lose track. I sometimes sit and think, what if I'd married your mother? She was one of the prettiest girls of 'em all, did you know that?"

I whispered, "No, sir," incredulous. Our conversation was beginning to seem pretty unsuitable to me.

"And now," he said darkly. "And now, Martha's son is taking my little girl to a dance." My nostrils were stinging, my head swam. Since from across the room it looked as if Mr. Moore's eyes were moist with tears, I didn't think I ought to bring it up about my mother's name being Margaret. We heard rustling on the stairs, and I jumped up when Edwina and her mother came into the room. I didn't miss the glance tipped with curare which Mrs. Moore darted first at my glass and then at her husband, before her teeth smiled and she extended her hand to me. In a daze, I helped Edwina into her velvet coat and promised to have her home early.

I hadn't ever entertained the idea before of parents having been anybody before they were married. Now, as I danced with Mr. Moore's voice in my ears, the lawn on which my own home stood seemed to tremble and crack. I tried to think it out. Suppose Mr. Moore had married my mother? Then my father would be wandering off I couldn't imagine where, married to—? Then who would I be, or would I at all? And what if my parents' *parents* had never got together? I seemed to exist by the shakiest chance, and if the planks of the dancefloor had split apart just then, I felt no sure ground underneath. We could plunge through, and then down, down, and go out like matches dropped in the dark.

I entered the Paul Jones, where the girls hand-in-hand moved in an inner circle facing an outer ring of boys passing the opposite way. To me, it was a drifting of specters. The music broke, the circles stopped, I stepped up to my partner. JoAnne's fingers brought me back to life. "I thought you weren't going to dance with me at all," she said. "What's the matter?"

"Nothing. I've just been—Which dance is this?"

"Ninth, silly. The dance is almost over." She pressed my hand. "Tell me what's the matter."

I said, "Listen, JoAnne, what does it mean when you feel like you could just fade out and not be anybody? Do you ever feel like that? I feel like if somebody stuck a knife in somebody next to me, that would hurt, but if they stuck me, there wouldn't be anybody there. What is that, feeling like anybody except me? I wish it would stop."

JoAnne solved that poser very simply. She said, "I don't know, honey. They're playing Our Song," and glancing around to check the chaperons she kissed me deftly on the neck. We silently pressed our faces together; she smelled of sweet powder and Ivory soap. As we turned in reverent circles, the orchestra slowly poured "Squeeze Me but Please Don't Tease Me" over us.

I looked down at my fingers laced in JoAnne's and found something new to worry about, more concrete this time. I was afraid she might look at my left wrist and misunderstand. But she didn't notice. The music stopped, and we separated in happy agony. The trumpets blasted a fanfare announcing the last dance, and Horace Ackney who must have been maneuvering Edwina near me dumped her at my side and fled. JoAnne was charming to Edwina; she envied Edwina's dress, she said. She looked around for her partner and thanked me impersonally for our dance, as if the orchestra had been playing any old song. She went quickly away. How pretty she was, what secrecy, what resources of rich tact and sureness! If JoAnne wore my identification bracelet, I felt, I probably existed.

It was the custom at the Merrymakers' to turn the lights out for the last dance while we wallowed in warm darkness to "Goodnight, Sweetheart." It was a boon to the tongue-tied like me. "Do you?" a girl would murmur.

"Do I what?"

"You know."

"Oh. Sure."

"Well, say it."

"I." Swallow. "Love you." I could never, in bright light.

With Edwina, no message to whisper and no agreement of touch, I felt only discomfort. She applied her forehead to my cheek, the first time she had danced like that; we clung together and waded in. We fitted badly; she was tall for me and I had to crick my neck. Clasped couples near us mumbled. I felt I should say something to break the silence of our embarrassed bodies, but I didn't like to boom in her ear, "It's been an awfully good dance, hasn't it," we'd covered that.

We danced on. I began to perspire. I could feel my cheek dampening her smooth forehead, but I hadn't the courage to remove it. I clung to her and Edwina too tightened her grip; cringing intimately, we suffered the grief of being jolted by another couple and feeling our mutual skin slip softly, with a slight wet noise. After a shift of position I found myself with my nose in Edwina's hair; when I inhaled, a wisp of it entered my left nostril; when I breathed out, it fluttered free, but next time it came to stay. The saxophones groaned on about the sorrow of parting. I held my breath and went through the rudiments of the fox trot like a man faintly performing the Australian crawl on his way to the bottom, my mind taken up with wondering which would come first, my sneeze or the end of the music. They were simultaneous, as it turned out. The song stopped, I exploded, the lights flashed on, and everybody began to tear down the balloons.

"I had an awfully nice time," Edwina said. We faced each other across a black-topped table in a sandwich shop, finishing our waffles and milk. Edwina leaned her elbows on the table and then, mortified, corrected them to her sides.

"Look, put your elbows all over the table if you want to," I said recklessly. "I won't tell."

Edwina looked as if I'd hit her, and I was scared myself. Evidently I looked even more shocked than she did, for I saw her peep out from behind her own embarrassment at mine. With a heartbreaking smile, she leaned forward and propped her thin arms on the table. It was a proud moment for me, the first time in my life I ever said the right thing. Edwina looked straight at me and said, "I hate dances. I get sick in the ladies' room. I've never told anyone that before."

"You mean—*really* sick?"

"Really sick," she said.

We sat and thought it over. I wanted to tell her how proud I was that she should have told me this secret; I would have liked to say, too, that I thought she looked pretty now, and that she wouldn't always be shy and unpopular. But I was no hero. I just looked at her, and our glances began to waver. Slowly, inexorably, coach back into pumpkin, ball gown to rags, we faded back into torment. We looked down at the table and blinked and suffered.

Then I reached with my left hand for the check which lay on top of the napkin dispenser. As I did, my black sleeve slid back from my wrist, and Edwina made a little sound. I looked at her and saw her stare at my bare wrist and then up at me. She blurted out, "But I didn't know you and JoAnne were broken up. I thought you and JoAnne—"

"Edwina, I—" As before, I felt I couldn't stand the sight of her pain, I must say anything to make it stop, but I couldn't speak.

She blushed dark red. "It's none of my business. I didn't mean to say anything. It was just the surprise . . ." She ducked her head and began to fight into the sleeves of her coat. I jumped up to help her and then scampered away to the cashier's desk.

In my father's car I turned on the radio and drove the few blocks to Edwina's house with such attention to the music and not having a wreck that "There's my driveway," Edwina said. "You missed my driveway." I turned in and came to a stop on the gravel. I began to breathe quickly. Without looking at Edwina, I jumped out and ran around to her door. She rustled out beside me.

There was a bald light shining in the porte-cochere at the side of the house. At the door Edwina turned to me to say something. I opened my mouth to speak, but instead, having no idea I was going to do any such thing, I veered across the gaping distance between Edwina's face and mine. Our eyes closed, our mouths met.

Edwina was standing on tiptoe. As we kissed, she breathed out and sank back on her heels; my lips smeared upward and bumped against the end of her nose. My eyes popped open in bright, dolly surprise and stared into two equally amazed ones careering away from mine. We backed apart and stood in a pool of embarrassment, under the gloating porch light. Such was Edwina's first, I guess, kiss.

There was one thing I had to say quickly: "Edwina, about the bracelet. JoAnne and me—I mean, I just thought it would be more polite to take it off for this evening." But I didn't say it. If I'd started talking I would have stood there apologizing all night; and I couldn't see any use in saying, "I meant to be nice," when underneath I felt chicken and cruel. I didn't want to be saddled with Edwina. I wanted her not to be unhappy, I wanted her to think I was nice. But I wanted out, I needed to be seen with a popular girl.

Edwina hunted in her bag for her key, and when she'd found it she said in her wan, formal way: "You were awfully nice to ask me to the dance, I had a nice time. Thank you."

She stepped inside the screen door. June bugs, big ugly brown things, thumped and clutched at the screen. I couldn't see Edwina clearly, behind the door in shadow. I said, "Thank you, Edwina. I had a nice time too," and ran away down the dark driveway, scalded.

"Merrymakers" may seem a rather ironic description of the participants in these monthly evenings. What value, however, did such experiences provide? What could be learned about oneself? About members of the opposite sex? About adults? About social conventions? Could you discover these things just as well under different social circumstances—ones of your own, less formal, choosing?

How do males try to handle their awkwardness and embarrassment in first painful social contacts with females? How do girls try to cope with similar feelings of unease?

Edwina Moore handles her discomfort by being terribly honest. She admits to a boy:

> I was supposed to have this dance with Jack, but he chickened out. . . . You were awfully nice to dance with me, but I don't want you to be stuck with me——. . . . Please, don't feel responsible. I'm used to it. I'll go comb my hair a while, that's what I always do. . . . I hate dances. I get sick in the ladies' room. I've never told anyone that before.

What is your reaction to Edwina's confessions? Do you think she says these things to make the listener feel sorry for her? To make him feel special as the sole recipient of her confidence? Because she doesn't know what else to do?

Do you admire Edwina for her candor? Cringe with embarrassment and chagrin for her? Think that she will be the butt of boys' locker-room jokes? Admire her skillfully calculated technique? What is the effect of Edwina's statements on the narrator of **Merrymakers?** Would you expect all males to react as he does?

The narrator admits, "I really only wanted to dance with the prettiest girls. . . . I needed to be seen with a popular girl." Why do most boys this age have such a need and desire? What qualities in girls, which will later be of great importance in choosing a wife, do males minimize—if not overlook—at this stage? Why?

Do girls attach similar importance to being seen with a popular and good-looking fellow? What other attributes, such as athletic ability, might they look for? What qualities, which will later seem of great importance in selecting a husband, seem of less consequence to girls at this point? Why?

Consider the implications of the following statements:

> I really only wanted to dance with the prettiest girls, . . . [with] resources of rich tact and sureness . . . like JoAnne, but then I would see some poor thing marooned and feel bad and go ask her instead. But it was shallow kindness, for no sooner had I done it than I would be chewing the inside of my mouth and wondering if I was going to be stuck. . . . I wanted everything to be nice . . . in a world turning smoothly. When any surface cracked, I felt threatened. . . . and I wanted to plaster over the trouble. . . . I couldn't see any use in saying, "I meant to be nice," when underneath I felt chicken and cruel. I didn't want to be saddled with Edwina. I wanted her not to be unhappy, I wanted her to think I was nice. But I wanted out, I needed to be seen with a popular girl.

How much of the narrator's effort seems to be a product of genuine kindness and feeling for others? How much is "shallow kindness and . . . the shiftings of half-hearted do-unto-others"? Do you consider the narrator more idealistic than realistic, or more realistic than idealistic? Why?

In his "kindnesses" to Edwina do you think he was doing the right thing for the right reasons? The right thing for the wrong reasons? The wrong thing for the right reasons? The wrong thing for the wrong reasons? On what standards are you basing your judgments about "right" and "wrong"?

What similarities exist between the expressions of nervousness shown by the Merrymakers and those of characters in *The City of Trembling Leaves* (p. 94)? Are the causes in each case also similar?

Which of the two boys seems the more mature: the narrator of *Merrymakers* or Tim Hazard in *The City of Trembling Leaves?* (p. 94)? Which of the two seems the more honest with himself?

> It was the custom at the Merrymakers' to turn the lights out for the last dance while we wallowed in warm darkness to "Goodnight, Sweetheart." It was a boon to the tongue-tied like me. "Do you?" a girl would murmur.
> "Do I what?"
> "You know."
> "Oh. Sure."
> "Well, say it."
> "I." Swallow. "Love you." I could never, in bright light.

How does darkness in *Merrymakers, Snowfall in Childhood* (p. 86), and *The City of Trembling Leaves* serve as a catalyst to romance? What are some other environmental conditions that may intensify romantic moods? Do they enable the expression of deepest emotions, or do they foster the expression of sentiments not genuinely felt? Why?

The narrator says,

> "Listen, JoAnne, what does it mean when you feel like you could just fade out and not be anybody? . . . I feel like if somebody stuck a knife in somebody next to me, that would hurt, but if they stuck me, there wouldn't be anybody there. What is that, feeling like anybody except me?"

How would you and the author of *Jean-Christophe* (p. 63) answer the narrator's question?

Which of the fictional characters you have encountered so far would understand, from direct experience, the feelings that the narrator of *Merrymakers* is talking about? Why?

Preoccupation with masculinity and handling of sexual drives are key contributors to the agony of boys like K.B. in *Manchild in the Promised Land,* Theodore Bulpington, Stephen Daedalus, Jean-Christophe, the teenager in *Death of a Hero,* young Lonigan, and a sixteen-year-old in the following short story.

One of the characters in it, Coach Mackyz, aware of the value attached to "being a man," spurs boys on in track by yelling, "Faster! Whatsa matter—you all a bunch of girls!" The narrator's mother, providing an incentive for greater neatness, points out, "I'm sure girls don't like boys with fuzz on their chin."

Through a subtle, not atypical combination of pressures from peers and parent and sister, the self-doubts of the central character in *First Love and Other Sorrows* by Harold Brodkey are amplified.

First Love and Other Sorrows
HAROLD BRODKEY

Toward the end of March, in St. Louis, slush fills the gutters, and dirty snow lies heaped alongside porch steps, and everything seems to be suffocating in the embrace of a season that lasts too long. Radiators hiss mournfully, no one manages to be patient, the wind draws tears from your eyes, the clouds are filled with sadness. Women with scarves around their heads and their feet encased in fur-lined boots pick their way carefully over patches of melting ice. It seems that winter will last forever, that this is the decision of nature and nothing can be done about it.

At the age when I was always being warned by my mother not to get overheated, spring began on that evening when I was first allowed to go outside after dinner and play kick-the-can. The ground would be moist, I'd manage to get muddy in spite of what seemed to me extreme precautions, my mother would call me home in the darkness, and when she saw me she would ask, "What *have* you done to yourself?" "Nothing," I'd say hopefully. But by the time I was sixteen, the moment when the year passed into spring, like so many other things, was less clear. In March and early April, track began, but indoors; mid-term exams came and went; the buds appeared on the maples, staining all their branches red; but it was still winter, and I found myself having feelings in class that were like long petitions for spring and all its works. And then one evening I was sitting at my desk doing my trigonometry and I heard my sister coming home from her office; I heard her high heels tapping on the sidewalk, and realized that, for the first time since fall, all the windows in the house were open. My sister was coming up the front walk. I looked down through a web of budding tree branches and called out to her that it was spring, by God. She shrugged—she was very handsome and she didn't approve of me—and then she started up the front steps and vanished under the roof of the porch.

I ran downstairs. "The bus was crowded tonight," my sister said, hanging up her coat. "I could hardly breathe. This is such a warm dress."

"You need a new spring dress," my mother said, her face lighting up. She was sitting in the living room with the evening paper on her lap.

She and my sister spread the newspaper on the dining-room table to look at the ads.

"We'll just have to settle for sandwiches tonight," my mother said to me. My father was dead, and my mother pretended that now all the cooking was done for my masculine benefit. "Look! That suit's awfully smart!" she cried, peering at the paper. "Montaldo's always has such nice suits." She sighed and went out to the kitchen, leaving the swinging door open so she could talk to my sister. "Ninety dollars isn't too much for a good suit, do you think?"

"No," my sister said. "I don't think it's too much. But I don't really want a suit this spring. I'd much rather have a sort of sky-blue dress—with a round neck that shows my shoulders a little bit. I don't look good in suits. I'm not old enough." She was twenty-two. "My face is too round," she added, in a low voice.

My mother said, "You're not too young for a suit." She also meant my sister was not too young to get married.

	111
	peers and parents

My sister looked at me and said, "Mother, do you think he shaves often enough? How often *do* you shave?"

"Every three days," I said, flushing up my neck and cheeks.

"Well, try it every other day."

"Yes, try to be neater," my mother said. "I'm sure girls don't like boys with fuzz on their chin."

"I think he's too proud of his beard to shave it," my sister said, and giggled.

"I feel sorry for the man who marries you," I said. "Because everybody thinks you're sweet and you're not."

She smiled pityingly at me, and then she looked down over the newspaper again.

Until I was four, we lived in a large white frame house overlooking the Mississippi River, south of St. Louis. This house had, among other riches, a porte-cochere, an iron deer on the lawn, and a pond with goldfish swimming in it. Once, I asked my mother why we had left that earlier house, and she said, "We lost our money—that's why. Your father was a very trusting man," she said. "He was always getting swindled."

She was not a mercenary woman, nor was she mean about money—except in spells that didn't come often—but she believed that what we lost with the money was much of our dignity and much of our happiness. She did not want to see life in a grain of sand; she wanted to see it from the shores of the Riviera, wearing a white sharkskin dress.

I will never forget her astonishment when she took us—she was dressed in her best furs, as a gesture, I suppose—to see the house that was to be our home from then on and I told her I liked it. It had nine rooms, a stained-glass window in the hall, and neighbors all up and down the block. She detested that house.

As she grew older, she changed, she grew less imperious. She put her hair into a roll, wore dark-colored clothes, said often, "I'm not a young woman any more," and began to take pride in being practical. But she remained determined; she had seen a world we didn't remember too clearly, and she wanted us to make our way back to it. "I had it all," she said once to my sister. "I was good-looking. We were rich. You have no idea what it was like. If I had died when I was thirty, I would have died completely happy. . . . "

But being practical did not come easy to her. She was not practical in her bones, and every spring brings back the memory of my mother peering nearsightedly, with surprise, at the tulip shoots in her flower border. And it brings back her look of distraught efficiency during spring housecleaning. "You'd better clear your closet shelves tonight," she would warn me, "because tomorrow Tillie and I are going in there with a vacuum cleaner, and we'll throw out everything we find." Year after year, I would run upstairs to save my treasures—even when I was sixteen and on the verge of a great embarkation, the nature of which I could not even begin to guess. My treasures consisted of my postcard collection— twenty-five hundred cards in all, arranged alphabetically by states of the Union and countries of the world (the wonder was that *I* lived in St. Louis)—an old baseball glove, my leaf collection, two obscene comic books I had won in a poker game at a Boy Scout jamboree, my marble collection, the thirty-five pages of secret thoughts written out in longhand. All these had to be taken out to the garage and hidden among the tools until the frenzy of cleaning was over and I could smuggle them back upstairs.

After supper, as the season grew warmer, my mother and sister and I would sit on the screened porch in the rear of the house, marooned among the shadows and the new leaves and the odor of insect spray, the light from our lamps sticking to the trees like bits of yellow paper. Usually the radio was on, and my mother, a book on her lap, her face abstracted (she was usually bored; her life was moved mainly by the burning urge to rise once more along the thin edge of social distinction), would listen to the comedians and laugh. When the phone rang, she would get up and go into the house with long strides, and if the call was for my sister, my mother would call her to the phone in a voice mottled with triumph.

Sometimes in the evening my mother would wash my sister's hair. My sister would sit in front of the basin in Mother's bathroom, a towel around her shoulders, smiling. From my room across the hall I would hear my sister chattering about the men she knew—the ones she dated, the ones she wanted to date, the ones she wouldn't touch with a ten-foot pole. My mother would interrupt with accounts of her own cleverness, her sorties and successes when young, sometimes laughingly, but sometimes gloomily, because she regretted a lot of things. Then she and my sister would label my sister's suitors: one or two had family, one had money, one—a poor boy—had a brilliant future, and there were a few docile, sweet ones who were simply fillers, who represented the additional number of dates that raised my sister to the rank of a very popular girl.

In these conversations, my mother would often bring up matters of propriety. Late dates were improper, flirting with boys other than one's date, breaking dates. Then, too, she would try to instruct my sister in other matters, which had to do with keeping passion in its place and so preventing embarrassment for the boy and disaster for the girl. My sister would grow irritated. "I don't know why you talk like that—I behave very well," she would tell my mother. "Better than the other girls I know." Her irritation would please my mother, who would smile and say that only good-looking girls could afford to be good, and then they would both laugh.

I used to wonder why my mother didn't take my sister's success for granted. My sister was lovely, she had plenty of dates, the phone rang incessantly. Where was the danger? Why did she always lecture my sister?

Once, my mother said my sister ought not to dance with too many boys or she would frighten off the more serious ones. My sister was getting dressed for the spring dance at the country club. Arrogant and slender, she glistened like a water nymph, among her froth of bottles and jars and filmy clothes. She became furious; she screamed that she *liked* to dance. I closed the door to my room, but I could still hear the two of them. "Don't be so foolish," my mother kept saying, over and over again. "Please don't be foolish. . . . " Then my sister, on the verge of tears, said she just wanted to have a good time. My sister's date arrived, and I went downstairs to let him in, and by the time I came back upstairs, the two of them were laughing. My mother said she was just trying to be helpful; after all, my sister was impractical and her looks wouldn't last forever. My sister, as she opened the door of her room, said, under her breath, "They'll last a lot longer yet."

I'll never forget the wild rustling of her voluminous white skirt as she came down the hallway toward me. Her face was strangely still, as if seen by moonlight. Her hair was smooth and shining, her hands bent outward at the wrist, as if they were flowers. "How beautiful you look!" I cried. My sister smiled and then solemnly turned all the way around, and her huge skirt rose and fell like a splash of surf. She was so beautiful I could hardly bear it. I hugged her, and she laughed.

Later that night I asked my mother why she got so distraught. Wasn't my sister popular enough? My mother was sitting in the kitchen, in an old, faded yellow housecoat, drinking a glass of warm milk. "You don't know anything about it," she said, with such sadness that I rose from the table and fled to my room.

"I know what I'm saying!" my mother would cry when she argued with my sister. "You must listen to me. People talk. . . . You don't know who you'll meet on a date; it's good to accept even if you don't like the boy. . . . Girls have to be very careful. You're thoughtless. Don't you think in fifty years I've learned what makes the world go around? Now, listen to me. I know what I'm saying. . . ." But my sister's face was so radiant, her charm was so intense, she pushed her blond hair back from her face with a gesture so quick, so certain, so arrogant and filled with vanity, that no one, I thought, could doubt that whatever she did would be right.

I wanted to be arrogant, too. I didn't want to wear glasses and be one of the humorless, heavy-handed boys my sister despised. I was on her side as much as she'd let me be. She was the elder, and she often grew impatient with me. I didn't seem to understand all the things involved in being on her side.

Night after night I saw her come home from work tired—she had a secretarial job in a hospital and she hated it—and two hours later she would descend the stairs, to greet her date, her face alight with seriousness or with a large, bright smile, depending on her mood or on where her escort was taking her that evening. A concert or an art movie made her serious; one of the hotel supper clubs brought the smile to her face. She would trip down the stairs in her high heels, a light, flimsy coat thrown over one arm, one hand clutching a purse and gloves, her other hand on the banister. In the queer yellow light of the hall chandelier, her necklace or her earrings would shine dully, and sometimes, especially if she was all dressed up, in a black dress, say, with a low neck, because they were going out to a supper club, there would be an air, in spite of her gaiety, of the captive about her. It was part of her intense charm. In her voluminous white skirt, she went to the spring dance at the country club and brought back to my mother the news that she had captured the interest of Sonny Bruster, the oldest son of M. F. Bruster, a banker and a very rich man—more than interest, it turned out, because he started calling my sister up almost every day at work and taking her our almost every night. My mother was on the phone much of the afternoon explaining to her friends that my sister wasn't engaged. It was criminal the way some people gossiped, she said. My sister had only gone out with the boy ten or twelve times. They were just getting to know each other. Then my mother began to *receive* calls; someone had heard from a friend of Mrs. Bruster's that Mrs. Bruster had said her son was very serious about my sister, who was a very charming, very pretty girl, of good family. . . . My mother rubbed her hands with glee. She borrowed money from her brothers, and every week my sister had new clothes.

My sister would come home from work and run upstairs to change. Sonny would be due at seven, to take her out to dinner. My sister would kick her shoes off, struggle out of her dress, and dash around the upstairs in her slip.

"Mother, I can't find my earrings."

"Which earrings, dear?"

"The little pearls—the little tiny pearl ones that I got two Easters ago, to go with my black . . ."

My sister was delighted with herself. She loved being talked about, being envied.

"Mother, do you know what Ceil Johnson said to me today? She said that Beryl Feringhaus—you know, the real-estate people—was heartbroken because she thought Sonny Bruster was going to get engaged to her." My sister giggled. Her long hair was tangled, and my mother yanked a comb through it.

"Maybe you ought to cut your hair," my mother said, trying to hide her own excitement and to stay practical. During this period, my mother was living in the imminence of wealth. Whenever she stopped what she was doing and looked up, her face would be bright with visions.

That spring when I was sixteen, more than anything else in the world I wanted to be a success when I grew up. I did not know there was any other way of being lovable. My best friend was a boy named Preston, who already had a heavy beard. He was shy, and unfortunate in his dealings with other people, and he wanted to be a physicist. He had very little imagination, and he pitied anyone who did have it. "You and the word 'beautiful'!" he would say disdainfully, holding his nose and imitating my voice. "Tell me—what does 'beautiful' mean?"

"It's something you want," I would say.

"You're an aesthete," Preston would say. "I'm a scientist. That's the difference."

He and I used to call each other almost every night and have long, profound talks on the telephone.

On a date, Preston would sit beside his girl and stolidly eye her. Occasionally, toward the end of the evening, he would begin to breathe heavily, and he would make a few labored, daring jokes. He might catch the girl's hand and stare at her with inflamed and wistful eyes, or he might mutter incoherent compliments. Girls liked him, and escaped easily from his clumsy longing. They slipped their hands from his grasp and asked him to call them up again, but after a few dates with a girl Preston would say disgustedly, "All she does is talk. She's frigid or something. . . ." But the truth was, he was afraid of hurting them, of doing something wrong to them, and he never really courted them at all.

At school, Preston and I had afternoon study hall together. Study hall was in the library, which was filled with the breathing of a hundred and fifty students, and with the dim, half-fainting breezes of high spring, and with books: it was the crossroads of the world. Preston and I would sign out separately, and meet in the lavatory. There we would lean up against the stalls and talk. Preston was full of thoughts; he was tormented by all his ideas. "Do you know what relativity means?" he would ask me. "Do you realize how it affects every little detail of everyday life?" Or it might be Spinoza that moved him: "Eighteenth-century, but by God *there* was a rational man." I would pace up and down, half listening, half daydreaming, wishing *my* name would appear on Preston's list of people who had elements of greatness.

Or we talked about our problems. "I'm not popular," I would say. "I'm too gloomy."

"Why is that, do you think?" Preston would ask.

"I don't know," I would say. "I'm a virgin. That has a lot to do with every-thing."

"Listen," Preston said one day, "you may not be popular but you're likable. Your trouble is you're a snob." He walked up and down the white-tiled floor, mimicking me. He slouched, and cast his eyes down, and jutted his chin out, and pulled a foolish, serious look over his face.

"Is that me? I cried, heartbroken.

"Well, almost," Preston said.

Or, leaning on the window sill, sticking our heads out into the golden after-noon air and watching a girl's gym class doing archery under the trees, we talked about sex.

"It starts in the infant," Preston said. "And it lasts forever."

"Saints escape it," I said mournfully.

"The hell they do," Preston said. The girls beneath us on the hillside drew their bows. Their thin green gym suits fluttered against their bodies. "Aren't they nice?" Preston asked longingly. "Aren't they wonderful?"

After school, Preston and I went out for track. The outdoor track was a cinder oval surrounding the football field. A steep, grassy hill led up to the en-trance of the school locker room. "Run up that hill every night boys," the coach pleaded—Old Mackyz, with his paunch and his iron-gray wavy hair—at the end of the practice period. "Run, boys, because when you're abso-lootly exhausted, that's when you got to give *more*. It's the *more*, boys, that makes champions." And then he'd stand there humble, and touched by his own speech.

During our warmup sessions, we used to jogtrot the length of the field and back again, keeping our knees high. The grand inutility of this movement filled me with something like exaltation; and on every side of me, in irregular lines, my fellow-males jogged, keeping their knees high. What happiness!

"The turf's too springy," Preston would mumble. "Bad for the muscles." Preston was a miler. He was thickset and without natural grace; Mackyz said he had no talent, but he ran doggedly, and he became a good miler. I ran the 440. I was tall and thin, and even Mackyz said I ought to be good at it, but I wasn't. Mackyz said I didn't have the spirit. "All you smart boys are alike," he said. "You haven't got the *heart* for it. You always hold back. You're all a bunch of goldbricks." I tried to cure my maimed enthusiasm. As I ran, Mackyz would bawl desperately, "Hit the ground harder. Hit with your toes! Spring, boy! SPRING! Don't coddle yourself, for Christ's sake. . . . " After the race, I'd throw myself down on a knoll near the finish line, under a sycamore tree, where the track man-ager dug a new hole every day for us to puke in. Three or four others would join me, and we'd lie there wearily, our chests burning, too weak to move.

Among my other problems was that I was reduced nearly to a state of tears over my own looks whenever I looked at a boy named Joel Bush. Joel was so incredibly good-looking that none of the boys could quite bear the fact of his existence; his looks weren't particularly masculine or clean-cut, and he wasn't a fine figure of a boy—he was merely beautiful. He looked like a statue that had been rubbed with honey and warm wax, to get a golden tone, and he carried at all times, in the neatness of his features and the secret proportions of his face and body that made him so handsome in that particular way, the threat of seduction. Displease me, he seemed to say, and I'll get you. I'll make you fall in love with me and I'll turn you into a donkey. Everyone either avoided him or gave in to him; teachers refused to catch him cheating, boys never teased him, and no one ever told him off. One day I saw him saying goodbye to a girl after school, and as he left her to join me, walking toward the locker room, he said to her, "Meet you here at five-thirty." Track wasn't over until six, and I could tell that he had no intention of meeting her, and yet, when he asked me about some experiments we had done in physics, instead of treating him like someone who had just behaved like a heel, I told him everything I knew.

He never joined us under the sycamore tree, and he ran effortlessly. He would pass the finish line, his chest heaving under his sweat-stained track shirt, and climb into the stands and sit in the sunlight. I was watching him, one afternoon, as he sat there wiping his face and turning his head from side to side. At one moment it was all silver except for the charred hollows of his eyes, and the next it was young and perfect, the head we all recognized as his.

Mackyz saw him and called out to him to put his sweatshirt on before he caught a cold. As he slipped the sweatshirt on, Joel shouted, "Aw, go fry your head!" Mackyz laughed good-naturedly.

Sprinkled here and there on the football field were boys lifting their arms high and then sweeping them down to touch their toes, or lying on their backs and bicycling their legs in the air. I got up and walked toward them, to do a little jogtrotting and high-knee prancing. I looked at Joel. "I'm cooling off," he said to me. I walked on, and just then a flock of crows wheeled up behind the oak tree on the hill and filled the sky with their vibrant motion. Everyone—even Preston—paused and looked up. The birds rose in a half circle and then glided, scythe-like, with wings outspread, on a down current of air until they were only twenty feet or so above the ground; then they flapped their wings with a noise like sheets being shaken out, and soared aloft, dragging their shadows up the stepped concrete geometry of the stands, past Joel's handsome, rigid figure, off into the sky.

"Whaddya know about that?" Mackyz said. "Biggest flock of crows I ever saw."

"Why didn't you get your gun and shoot a couple?" Joel called out. Everyone turned. "Then you'd have some crow handy whenever you had to eat some," Joel said.

"Take a lap," Mackyz bawled, his leathery face turning red up to the roots of his iron-gray hair.

"He was only kidding," I said, appalled at Mackyz's hurt.

Mackyz looked at me and scowled, "You can take a lap too, and don't talk so much."

I took off my sweatshirt and dropped it on the grass and set off around the track. As soon as I started running, the world changed. The bodies sprawled out across the green of the football field were parts of a scene remembered, not one real at this moment. The whole secret of effort is to keep on, I told myself. Not for the world would I have stopped then, and yet nothing—not even if I had been turned handsome as a reward for finishing—could have made up for the curious pain of the effort.

About halfway around the track, Joel caught up to me, and then he slowed down and ran alongside. "Mackyz isn't watching," he said. "Let's sneak up the hill." I looked and saw that Mackyz was lining up the team for high-jump practice. Joel sailed up over the crest of the hill, and I followed him.

"He's getting senile," Joel said, dropping to a sitting position, sighting over the crest of the hill at Mackyz, and then lying down. "Come on, jerk, lie down. You want Mackyz to see you?"

I was uneasy; this sort of fooling was all right for Joel, because he "made the effort," but if Mackyz caught me, he'd kick me off the team. I pointed this out to Joel.

"Aw, Mackyz takes everything too seriously. That's his problem," Joel said. "He's always up in the air about something. I don't see why he makes so much fuss. You ever notice how old men make a big fuss over everything?"

"Mackyz' not so old."

"All right, you ever notice how *middle-aged* men make a big fuss over everything?" A few seconds later, he said casually, his gaze resting on the underside of the leaves of the oak tree, "I got laid last night."

"No kidding?" I said.

He spread his fingers over his face, no doubt to see them turn orange in the sunlight, as children do. "Yeah," he said.

From the football field came the sounds of high-jump practice starting. Mackyz was shouting, "Now, start with your left foot—one, two, three—take off! TAKE OFF, GODDAMN IT! Spread your Goddamned legs, spread 'em. You won't get ruptured. There's sand to catch you, for Christ's sake." The jumper's footsteps made a series of thuds, there was a pause, and then the sound of the landing in the sand. Lifting my head, I could see the line of boys waiting to jump, the lead boy breaking into a run, leaping from the ground, and spreading his arms in athletic entreaty.

"It was disappointing," Joel said.

"How?" I asked.

"It's nothing very special."

I was aroused by this exposé. "You mean the books——"

"It's not like that at all." He turned sullenly and scrabbled with his fingers in the dirt. "It's like masturbation, kind of with bells."

"Maybe the girl didn't know how to do it."

"She was a grown woman!"

"Yeah, but—"

"She was a fully grown woman! She knew what she was doing!"

"Oh," I said. Then, after a minute, "Look, would you mind telling me what you said to her? If I ever had a chance, I wouldn't know what to say. I . . . ."

"I don't remember," Joel said. "We just looked at each other, and then she got all tearful, and she told me to take my clothes off."

We lay there a moment, in the late afternoon sunshine, and then I said we'd better be getting back. We walked around behind the hill, and waited until Mackyz wasn't looking before we sprinted out into the track.

The jumping went on for fifteen or twenty minutes more; then Mackyz raised his arms in a gesture of benediction. "All right, you squirts—all out on the track for a fast lap. And that includes you, goldbrick," he said to me, wagging his finger.

All the boys straightened up and started toward the track. The sun's light poured in long low rays over the roof of the school. Jostling and joking, we started to run. "Faster!" Mackyz yelled. "Faster! Whatsa matter—you all a bunch of girls! Faster! For Christ's sake, faster!"

Since Preston, in his dogged effort to become a good miler, ran three laps to everyone else's one, he was usually the last in the locker room. He would come in, worn out and breathing heavily; sometimes he even had to hold himself up with one hand on his locker while he undressed. Everyone else would long since have showered and would be almost ready to leave. They might make one or two remarks about Preston's running his legs to stumps or trying to kill himself for Mackyz's sake. Preston would smile numbly while he tried to get his breath back, and somehow, I was always surprised by how little attention was paid to Preston, how cut off and how alone he was.

More often than not, Joel would be showing off in the locker room—walking around on his hands, singing dirty songs, or engaged in some argument or other. Preston would go into the shower. I would talk to Joel, dressing slowly, because I usually waited for Preston. By the time I was all dressed, the locker room would be empty and Preston would still be towelling himself off. Then, instead of hurrying to put his clothes on, he would run his hand over his chest, to curl the few limp hairs. "Oh come on!" I would say, disgustedly.

"Hold your horses," he would say, with his maddening physicist's serenity. "Just you hold your horses."

It took him half an hour to get dressed. He'd stand in front of the mirror and flex his muscles endlessly and admire the line his pectorals made across his broad rib cage, and he always left his shirt until last, even until after he had combed his hair. I found his vanity confusing; he was far from handsome, with his heavy mouth and bushy eyebrows and thick, sloping shoulders, but he loved his reflection and he'd turn and gaze at himself in the mirror from all sorts of angles while he buttoned his shirt. He hated Joel. "There's a guy who'll never amount to much," Preston would say. "He's chicken. And he's not very smart. I don't see why you want him to like you—except that you're a sucker. You let your eyes run away with your judgment." I put up with all this because I wanted Preston to walk me part way home. It seemed shameful somehow to have to walk home alone.

Finally, he would finish, and we would emerge from the now deserted school into the dying afternoon. As we walked, Preston harangued me about my lack of standards and judgment. The hunger I had for holding school office and for being well thought of he dismissed as a streak of lousy bourgeois cowardice. I agreed with him (I didn't like myself anyway); but what was to be done about it? "We might run away," Preston said, squinting up at the sky. "Hitchhike. Work in factories. Go to a whorehouse. . . . " I leaned against a tree trunk, and Preston stood with one foot on the curb and one foot in the street, and we lobbed pebbles back and forth. "We're doomed," Preston said. "Doom" was one of his favorite words, along with "culture," "kinetic," and "the Absolute." "We come from a dying culture," he said.

"I suppose you're right," I said. "It certainly looks that way." But then I cheered up. "After all, it's not as if we were insane or anything."

"It wouldn't show yet," Preston said gloomily. "It's still in the latent stage. It'll come out later. You'll see. After all, you're still living at home, and you've got your half-assed charm——"

I broke in; I'd never had a compliment from him before.

"I didn't say you were charming," he said. "I said you have a half-assed charm. You behave well in public. That's all I meant."

At the corner where we separated, Preston stood a moment or two. "It's hopeless," he said.

"God, do you really think so?" I asked.

"That's my honest opinion," he said.

He turned toward his house. I jogged a block or two, and then felt my stomach muscles. When I came to a maple with a low, straight branch, I ran and jumped up and swung from the branch, while a big green diesel bus rolled ponderously past, all its windows filled with tired faces that looked out at the street going by and at me hanging from the branch and smiling. I was doomed, but I was very likely charming.

I ran in the front door of my house and called out, "Mother! Mother!"

"What is it?" she answered. She was sitting on the screened porch, and I could see a little plume of cigarette smoke in the doorway. There was the faint mutter of a radio news program turned on low.

"Nothing," I said. "I'm home, that's all."

At the dinner table, I would try to disguise myself by slouching in my chair and thinking about my homework, but my mother and my sister always recognized me. "How was track today?" my sister would ask in a slightly amused way.

"Fine," I would say in a low voice.

My mother and my sister would exchange glances. I must have seemed comic to them, stilted, and slightly absurd, like all males.

Almost every evening, Sonny Bruster used to drive up to our house in his yellow convertible. The large car would glide to a stop at the curb, and Sonny would glance quickly at himself in the rear-view mirror, running his hand over his hair. Then he'd climb out and brush his pants off, too occupied with his own shyness to notice the children playing on the block. But they would stop what they were doing and watch him.

I would wait for him at the front door and let him in and lead him into the living room. I walked ahead of Sonny because I had noticed that he could not keep himself from looking up the stairs as we passed through the hallway, as if to conjure up my sister then and there with the intensity of his longing, and I hated to see him do this. I would sit in the high-backed yellow chair, and Sonny would settle himself on the couch and ask me about track, or if I'd picked a college yet. "You ought to think carefully about college," he would say. "I think Princeton is more civilized than Yale." His gentle, well-bred voice was carefully inexpressive. In his manner there was a touch of stiffness to remind you, and himself, that he was rich and if some disrespect was intended for him he wouldn't necessarily put up with it. But I liked him. He treated me with great politeness, and I liked the idea of his being my brother-in-law, and I sometimes thought of the benefits that would fall to me if my sister married him.

Then my sister would appear at the head of the stairs, dressed to go out, and Sonny would leap to his feet. "Are you ready?" he'd cry, as if he had never dared hope she would be. My sister would hand him her coat, and with elaborate care he'd hold it for her. It would be perhaps eight o'clock or a little after. The street lamps would be on, but looking pallid because it wasn't quite dark. Usually, Sonny would open the car door for my sister, but sometimes, with a quick maneuver, she would forestall him; she would hurry the last few steps, open the door, and slip inside before he could lift his hand.

Sonny was not the first rich boy who had loved my sister; he was the fourth or fifth. And in the other cases there had been scenes between my mother and sister in which my mother extolled the boy's eligibility and my sister argued that she was too young to marry and didn't want to stop having a good time yet. Each time she had won, and each time the boy had been sent packing, while my mother looked heartbroken and said my sister was throwing her chances away.

With Sonny, the same thing seemed about to happen. My sister missed going out with a lot of boys instead of with just one. She complained once or twice that Sonny was jealous and spoiled. There were times when she seemed to like him very much, but there were other times when she would greet him blankly in the evening when she came downstairs, and he would be apologetic and fearful, and I could see that her disapproval was the thing he feared most in the world.

My mother didn't seem to notice, or if she did, she hid her feelings. Then one night I was sitting in my room doing my homework and I heard my mother and sister come upstairs. They went into my sister's room.

"I think Sonny's becoming very serious," my mother said.

"Sonny's so short," I heard my sister say. "He's not really interesting, either, Mother."

"He seems to be very fond of you," my mother said.

"He's no fun," my sister said. "Mother, be careful! You're brushing too hard! You're hurting me!"

I stopped trying to work, and listened.

"Sonny's a very intelligent boy," my mother said. "He comes from a good family."

"I don't care," my sister said. "I don't want to waste myself on him."

"Waste yourself?" My mother laughed derisively. I got up and went to the door of my sister's room. My sister was sitting at her dressing table, her hair shining like glass and her eyes closed. My mother was walking back and forth, gesturing with the hairbrush. "He's the one who's throwing himself away," she said. "Who do you think we are, anyway? We're nobodies."

"I'm pretty!" my sister objected angrily.

My mother shrugged. "The woods are full of pretty girls. What's more, they're full of pretty, rich girls. Now, Sonny's a very *nice* boy —— "

"Leave me alone!" My sister pulled her hair up from her shoulders and held it in a soft mop on the top of her head. "Sonny's a jerk! A jerk!"

"He's nice-looking!" my mother cried.

"Oh, what do *you* know about it?" my sister cried. "You're old, for God's sake!"

The air vibrated. My sister rose and looked at my mother, horrified at what she had said. She took her hands from her hair, and it fell tumbling to her shoulders, dry and pale and soft. "I don't care," she said suddenly, and brushed past me, and fled into the bathroom and locked the door. There was no further sound from her. The only trace of her in the house at that moment was the faint odor in her room of the flowery perfume she used that spring.

"Oh, she's so foolish," my mother said, and I saw that she was crying. "She doesn't know what she's doing. . . . Why is she so foolish?" Then she put the hairbrush down and raised her hands to her cheeks and began to pinch them.

I went back to my room and closed the door.

When I came out again, an hour later, my mother was in bed reading a magazine; she looked as if she had been wounded in a dozen places. My sister sat in her room, in front of the mirror. Her hair streamed down the back of her neck and lay in touching, defenseless little curls on the towel she had over her shoulders. She was studying her reflection thoughtfully. (Are flowers vain? Are trees? Are they consumed with vanity during those days when they are in bloom?) She raised her finger and pressed it against her lower lip to see, I think, if she would be prettier if her lip, instead of being so smooth, had a slight break in the center as some girls' did.

Shortly after this, my mother, who was neither stupid nor cruel, suggested that my sister stop seeing Sonny for a while. "Until you make up your mind," she said. "Otherwise you might break his heart, you know. Tell him you need some time to think. He'll understand. He'll think you're grown-up and responsible."

Sonny vanished from our house. In the evenings now, after dinner, the three of us would sit on the screened porch. My sister would look up eagerly when the phone rang, but the calls were never for her. None of her old boy friends knew she had stopped dating Sonny, and after a while, when the phone rang, she would compose her face and pretend she wasn't interested, or she would say irritably, "Who can that be?" She began to answer the phone herself (she never had before, because it wasn't good for a girl to seem too eager) and she would look sadly at herself in the hall mirror while she said, "Yes, Preston, he's here." She tried to read. She'd skim a few pages and then put the book down and gaze out through the screens at the night and the patches of light on the trees. She would listen with my mother to the comedians on the radio and laugh vaguely when my mother laughed. She picked on me. "Your posture's no good," she'd say. Or "Where do you learn your manners? Mother, he behaves like a zoot-suiter or something." Another time, she said, "If I don't make a good marriage, you'll be in trouble. You're too lazy to do anything on your own." She grew more and more restless. Toying with her necklace, she broke the string, and the beads rolled all over the floor, and there was something frantic in the way she went about retrieving the small rolling bits of glitter. It occurred to me that she didn't know what she was doing; she was not really as sure of everything as she seemed. It was a painfully difficult thought to arrive at, and it clung to me. Why hadn't I realized it before? Also, she sort of hated me, it seemed to me. I had never noticed that before, either. How could I have been so wrong, I wondered. Knowing how wrong I had been about this, I felt that no idea I had ever held was safe. For instance, we were not necessarily a happy family, with the most wonderful destinies waiting for my sister and me. We might make mistakes and choose wrong. Unhappiness was real. It was even likely. . . . How tired I became of studying my sister's face. I got so I would do anything to keep from joining the two women on the porch.

After three weeks of this, Sonny returned. I was never told whether he came of his own accord or whether he was summoned; but one night the yellow convertible drove up in front of our house and he was back. Now when my mother would watch my sister and Sonny getting into Sonny's car in the evenings, she would turn away from the window smiling. "I think your sister has found a boy she can respect," she would say, or "They'll be very happy together," or some such hopeful observation, which I could see no basis for, but which my mother believed with all the years and memories at her disposal, with all the weight of her past and her love for my sister. And I would go and call Preston.

I used to lie under the dining-room table, sheltered and private like that, looking up at the way the pieces of mahogany were joined together, while we talked. I could cup the telephone to my ear with my shoulder and hold my textbook up in the air, over my head, as we went over physics, which was a hard subject for me. "Preston," I asked one night, "what in God's name makes a siphon work?" They did work—everyone knew that—and I groaned as I asked it. Preston explained the theory to me, and I frowned, breathed heavily through my nose, squinted at the incomprehensible diagrams in the book, and thought of sex, of the dignity of man, of the wonders of the mind, as he talked. Every few minutes, he asked "Do you see" and I would sigh. It was spring, and there was meaning all around me, if only I were free—free of school, free of my mother, free of duties and inhibitions—if only I were mounted on a horse. . . . Where was the world? Not here, not near me, not under the dining room table. . . . "Not quite," I'd say, untruthfully, afraid that I might discourage him. "But I almost get it. Just tell me once more." And on and on he went, while I frowned, breathed hard, and squinted. And then it happened! "I see!" I cried. "I see! I see!" It was air pressure! How in the world had I failed to visualize air pressure? I could see it now. I would never again not see it; it was there in my mind, solid and indestructible, a whitish column sitting on the water. "God damn but science is wonderful!" I said, and heaved my physics book into the living room. "Really wonderful!"

"It's natural law," Preston said reprovingly. "Don't get emotion mixed up with it."

One evening when my sister and Sonny didn't have a date to go out, my mother tapped lightly on my foot, which protruded from under the dining-room table. "I have a feeling Sonny may call," she whispered. I told Preston I had to hang up, and crawled out from beneath the table. "I have a feeling that they're getting to the point," my mother said. "Your sister's nervous."

I put the phone back on the telephone table. "But, Mother—" I said, and the phone rang.

"Sh-h-h," she said.

The phone rang three times. My sister, on the extension upstairs, said, "Hello. . . . Oh, Sonny. . . ."

My mother looked at me and smiled. Then she pulled at my sleeve until I bent my head down, and she whispered in my ear, "They'll be so happy. . . ." She went into the hall, to the foot of the stairs. "Tell him he can come over," she whispered passionately.

"Sure," my sister was saying on the phone. "I'd like that. . . . If you want. . . . Sure. . . ."

My mother went on listening, her face tilted to one side, the light falling on her aging face, and then she began to pantomime the answers my sister ought to be making—sweet yesses, dignified noes, and little bursts of alluring laughter.

I plunged down the hall and out the screen door. The street lamps were on, and there was a moon. I could hear the children: "I see Digger. One-two-three, you're caught, Digger. . . ." Two blocks away, the clock on the Presbyterian church was striking the hour. Just then a little girl left her hiding place in our hedge and ran shrieking for the tree trunk that was home-free base: "I'm home safe! I'm home safe! Everybody free!" All the prisoners, who had been sitting disconsolately on the bumpers of Mr. Karmgut's Oldsmobile, jumped up with joyful cries and scattered abruptly in the darkness.

I lifted my face—that exasperating factor, my face—and stared entranced at the night, at the waving tops of the trees, and the branches blowing back and forth, and the round moon embedded in the night sky, turning the nearby streamers of cloud into mother-of-pearl. It was all very rare and eternal-seeming. What a dreadful unhappiness I felt.

I walked along the curb, balancing with my arms outspread. Leaves hung over the sidewalk. The air was filled with their rustling, and they caught the light of the street lamps. I looked into the lighted houses. There was Mrs. Kearns, tucked girlishly into a corner of the living-room couch, reading a book. Next door, through the leaves of a tall plant, I saw the Lewises all standing in the middle of the floor. When I reached the corner, I put one arm around the post that held the street sign, and leaned there, above the sewer grating, where my friends and I had lost perhaps a hundred tennis balls, over the years. In numberless dusks, we had abandoned our games of catch and handball and gathered around the grating and stared into it at our ball, floating down in the darkness.

The Cullens' porch light was on, in the next block, and I saw Mr. and Mrs. Cullen getting into their car. Eleanor Cullen was in my class at school, and she had been dating Joel. Her parents were going out, and that meant she'd be home alone—if she was home. She might have gone to the library, I thought as the car started up; or to a sorority meeting. While I stood there looking at the Cullens' house, the porch light went off. A minute later, out of breath from running, I stood on the dark porch and rang the doorbell. There was no light on in the front hall, but the front door was open, and I could hear someone coming. It was Eleanor. "Who is it?" she asked.

"Me," I said. "Are you busy? Would you like to come out for a little while and talk?"

She drifted closer to the screen door and pressed her nose against it. She looked pale without make-up.

"Sure," she said. "I'll have to go put my shoes on. I'm not in a good mood or anything."

"That's all right," I said. "Neither am I. I just want to talk to somebody."

While I waited for Eleanor to come out, Mattie Seaton appeared, striding along the sidewalk. He was on the track team. "Hey, Mattie," I called out to him.

"Hi," he said.

"What's new?"

"Nothing much," he said. "You got your trig done?"

"No, not yet."

"You going with *her?*" he asked, pointing to the house.

"Naw," I said.

"Well, I got to get my homework done," he said.

"See you later," I called after him. I knew where he was going: Nancy Ellis's house, two blocks down.

"Who was that?" Eleanor asked. She stepped out on the porch. She had combed her hair and put on lipstick.

"Mattie Seaton," I said.

"He's pinned to Nancy," Eleanor said. "He likes her a lot. . . . " She sat down in a white metal chair. I sat on the porch railing, facing her. She fumbled in her pocket and pulled out a pack of cigarettes. "You want a cigarette?" she asked.

"No. I'm in training."

We looked at each other, and then she looked away, and I looked down at my shoes. I sat there liking her more and more.

"How come you're in a bad mood?" I asked her.

"Me? Oh, I don't know. How did you know I was in a bad mood?"

"You told me." I could barely make out her face and the dull color of her hands in the darkness.

"You know, I think I'm not basically a happy person," Eleanor said suddenly. "I always thought I was. . . . People expect you to be, especially if you're a girl."

"It doesn't surprise *me,*" I said.

A breeze set all the leaves in motion again. "It's going to rain," I said.

Eleanor stood up, smoothing her yellow skirt, and threw her cigarette off the porch; the glowing tip landed on the grass. She realized I was staring at her. She lifted her hand and pressed it against her hair. "You may have noticed I look unusually plain tonight," she said. She leaned over the porch railing beside me, supporting herself on her hands. "I was trying to do my geometry," she said in a low voice. "I couldn't do it. I felt stupid," she said. "So I cried. That's why I look so awful."

"I think you look all right," I said. "I think you look fine." I leaned forward and laid my cheek on her shoulder. Then I sat up quickly, flushing. "I don't like to hear you being so dissatisfied with yourself," I mumbled. "You could undermine your self-confidence that way."

Eleanor straightened and faced me, in the moonlight. "You're beautiful," I burst out longingly. "I never noticed before. But you are."

"Wait," Eleanor said. Tears gathered in her eyes. "Don't like me yet. I have to tell you something first. It's about Joel."

"You don't have to tell me," I said. "I know you're going with him. I understand."

"Listen to me!" she said impatiently, stamping her foot. "I'm *not* going with him. He——" She suddenly pressed her hands against her eyes. "Oh, it's awful!" she cried.

A little shudder of interest passed through me. "O.K.," I said. "But I don't care if you don't tell me."

"I want to!" she cried. "I'm just a little embarrassed. I'll be all right in a minute——

"We went out Sunday night . . ." she began after a few seconds. They had gone to Medart's, in Clayton, for a hamburger. Joel had talked her into drinking a bottle of beer, and it had made her so drowsy that she had put her head on the back of the seat and closed her eyes. "What kind of car does Joel have?" I asked.

"A Buick," Eleanor said, surprised at my question.

"I see," I said. I pictured the dashboard of a Buick, and Joel's handsome face, and then, daringly, I added Eleanor's hand, with its bitten fingernails, holding Joel's hand. I was only half listening, because I felt the preliminary stirrings of an envy so deep, it would make me miserable for weeks. I looked up at the sky over my shoulder; clouds had blotted out the moon, and everything had got darker. From the next block, in the sudden stillness, I heard the children shouting, uttering their Babylonian cries as they played kick-the-can. Their voices were growing tired and fretful.

"And then I felt his hand on my——" Eleanor, half-drowned in shadow was showing me, on her breast, where Joel had touched her.

"Is that all?" I said, suddenly smiling. Now I would not have to die of envy. "That's nothing!"

"I—I slapped his face!" She exclaimed. Her lip trembled. "Oh, I didn't mean —I sort of wanted—Oh, it's all so terrible!" she burst out. She ran down the front steps and onto the lawn, and leaned against the trunk of an oak tree. I followed her. The pre-storm stillness filled the sky, the air between the trees, the dark spaces among the shrubbery. "Oh, God!" Eleanor cried. "How I hate everything!"

My heart was pounding, and I didn't know why. I hadn't known I could feel like this—that I could pause on the edge of such feeling, which lay stretched like an enormous meadow all in shadow inside me. It seemed to me a miracle that human beings could be so elaborate. "Listen, Eleanor," I said, "you're all right! I've *always* liked you." I swallowed and moved closer to her; there were two moist streaks running down her face. I raised my arm and, with the sleeve of my shirt, I wiped away her tears. "I think you're wonderful! I think you're really something!"

"You look down on me," she said. "I know you do. I can tell."

"How can I, Eleanor. How *can* I?" I cried. "I'm nobody. I've been damaged by my heredity."

"You, too!" she exclaimed happily. "Oh, that's what's wrong with me!"

A sudden hiss swept through the air and then the first raindrops struck the street. "Quick!" Eleanor cried, and we ran up on her porch. Two bursts of lightning lit up the dark sky, and the rain streamed down. I held Eleanor's hand, and we stood watching the rain. "It's a real thundershower," she said.

"Do you feel bad because we only started being friends tonight? I mean, do you feel you're on the rebound and settling on the second-best?" I asked. There was a long silence and all around it was the sound of the rain.

"I don't think so," Eleanor said at last. "How about you?"

I raised my eyebrows and said, "Oh, no, it doesn't bother me at all."

"That's good," she said.

We were standing very close to one another. We talked industriously. "I don't like geometry," Eleanor said. "I don't see what use it is. It's supposed to train your mind, but I don't believe it. . . ."

I took my glasses off. "Eleanor——" I said. I kissed her, passionately, and then I turned away, pounding my fists on top of each other. "Excuse me," I whispered hoarsely. That kiss had lasted a long time, and I thought I would die.

Eleanor was watching the long, slanting lines of rain falling just outside the porch, gray in the darkness; she was breathing very rapidly. "You know what?" she said. "I could make you scrambled eggs. I'm a good cook." I leaned my head against the brick wall of the house and said I'd like some.

In the kitchen, she put on an apron and bustled about, rattling pans and silverware, and talking in spurts. "I think a girl should know how to cook, don't you?" she let me break the eggs into a bowl—three eggs, which I cracked with a flourish. "Oh, you're good at it," she said, and began to beat them with a fork while I sat on the kitchen table and watched her. "Did you know most eggs *aren't* baby chickens?" she asked me. She passed so close to me on her way to the stove that, because her cheeks were flushed and her eyes bright, I couldn't help leaning forward and kissing her. She turned pink and hurried to the stove. I sat on the kitchen table, swinging my legs and smiling to myself. Suddenly we heard a noise just outside the back door. I leaped off the table and took up a polite position by the sink. Eleanor froze. But no one opened the door; no one appeared.

"Maybe it was a branch falling," I said.

Eleanor nodded. Then she made a face and looked down at her hands. "I don't know why we got so nervous. We aren't doing anything wrong."

"It's the way they look at you," I said.

"Yes, that's it," she said. "You know, I think my parents are ashamed of me. But someday I'll show them. I'll do something wonderful, and they'll be amazed." She went back to the stove.

"When are your parents coming home?" I asked.

"They went to a double feature. They can't possibly be out before eleven."

"They might walk out on it," I said.

"Oh no!" Eleanor said. "Not if they pay for it . . ."

We ate our scrambled eggs and washed the dishes, and watched the rain from the dining-room windows without turning the light on. We kissed for a while, and then we both grew restless and uncomfortable. Her lips were swollen, and she went into the kitchen, and I heard her running the water; when she returned, her hair was combed and she had put on fresh lipstick. "I don't like being in the house," she said, and led me out on the porch. We stood with our arms around each other. The rain was slackening. "Good-bye, rain," Eleanor said sadly. It was as if we were watching a curtain slowly being lifted from around the house. The trees gleamed wetly near the street lamps.

When I started home, the rain had stopped. Water dripped on the leaves of the trees. Little plumes of mist hung over the wet macadam of the street. I walked very gently in order not to disturb anything.

I didn't want to run into anybody, and so I went home the back way, through the alley. At the entrance to the alley there was a tall cast-iron pseudo-Victorian lamppost, with an urn-shaped head and panes of frosted glass; the milky light it shed trickled part way down the alley, illuminating a few curiously still garage fronts and, here and there, the wet leaves of the bushes and vines that bordered the back yards and spilled in such profusion over the fences, hiding the ashpits and making the alley so pretty a place in spring. When I was younger, I had climbed on those ashpits, those brick squares nearly smothered under the intricacies of growing things, and I had searched in the debris for old, broken mirrors, discarded scarves with fringes, bits of torn decorated wrapping paper, and such treasures. But now I drifted down the alley, walking absently on the wet asphalt. I was having a sort of daydream where I was lying with my head on Eleanor's shoulder—which was bare—and I could hear the slow, even sound of her breathing as I began to fall asleep. I was now in the darkest part of the alley, the very center where no light reached, and in my daydream I turned over and kissed Eleanor's hands, her throat—and then I broke into a sprint down the alley, slipping and sliding on the puddles and wet places. I came out the other end of the alley and stood underneath the lamppost. I was breathing with difficulty.

Across the street from me, two women stood, one on the sidewalk, the other on the front steps of a house, hugging her arms. "It's not a bad pain," the woman on the sidewalk said, "but it persists."

"My dear, my dear," said the other. "Don't take any chances—not at our age . . ."

And a couple, a boy and a girl, were walking up the street, coming home from the Tivoli Theatre. The girl was slouching in order not to seem taller than the boy, who was very short and who sprang up and down on the balls of his feet as he walked.

I picked a spray of lilac and smelled it, but then I didn't know what to do with it—I didn't want to throw it away—and finally I put it in my pants pocket.

I vaulted our back fence and landed in our back yard, frightening a cat, who leaped out of the hedge and ran in zigzags across the dark lawn. It startled me so much I felt weak. I tucked my shirt in carefully and smoothed my hair. Suddenly, I looked down at my fingertips; they were blurred in the darkness and moist from the lilac, and I swept them to my mouth and kissed them.

The kitchen was dark. There was no sound in the house, no sound at all, and a tremor passed through me. I turned the kitchen light on and hurriedly examined myself for marks of what had happened to me. I peered at my shirt, my pants. I rubbed my face with both hands. Then I turned the light off and slipped into the dining room, which was dark, too, and so was the hallway. The porch light was on. I ran up the front stairs and stopped short at the top; there was a light on in my mother's room. She was sitting up in bed, with pillows at her back, a magazine across her lap, and a pad of paper on the magazine.

"Hello," I said.

I expected her to bawl me out for being late, but she just looked at me solemnly for a moment, and then she said, "Sonny proposed to your sister."

Because I hadn't had a chance to wash my face, I raised one hand and held it over my cheek and chin, to hide whatever traces of lipstick there might be.

She said, "They're going to be married in June. They went over to the Brusters' to get the ring. He proposed practically the first thing when he came. They were both so—they were *both* so *happy!*" she said. "They make such a lovely couple. . . . Oh, if you could have seen them."

She was in a very emotional state.

I started to back out the door.

"Where are you going?" my mother asked.

"To bed," I said, surprised. "I'm in training——"

"Oh, you ought to wait up for your sister."

"I'll leave her a note," I said.

I went to my room and took the white lilac out of my pocket and put it on my desk. I wrote, "I heard the news and think it's swell. Congratulations. Wake me up when you come in." I stuck the note in the mirror of her dressing table. Then I went back to my room and got undressed. Usually I slept raw, but I decided I'd better wear pajamas if my sister was going to come in and wake me up. I don't know how much later it was that I heard a noise and sat bolt upright in bed. I had been asleep. My sister was standing in the door of my room. She was wearing a blue dress that had little white buttons all the way down the front and she had white gloves on. "Are you awake?" she whispered.

"Yes," I said. "Where's Mother?"

"Downstairs," my sister said, coming into the room. "Sending telegrams. Do you want to see my ring?" She took her gloves off.

I turned the bedside-table lamp on, and she held her hand out. The ring was gold, and there was an emerald and four diamonds around it.

"It was his grandmother's," my sister said. I nodded. "It's not what I——" she said, and sat down on the edge of the bed, and forgot to finish her sentence. "Tell me," she said, "do you think he's really rich?" Then she turned a sad gaze on me, through her lashes. "Do you want to know something awful? I don't like my ring. . . ."

"Are you unhappy?" I asked.

"No, just upset. It's scary getting married. You have no idea. I kept getting chills all evening. I may get pneumonia. Do you have a cigarette?"

I said I'd get her one downstairs.

"No, there's some in my room," she said. "I'll get them. You know, Sonny and I talked about you. We're going to send you to college and everything. We planned it all out tonight." She played with her gloves for a while, and then she said, looking at the toes of her shoes, "I'm scared. What if Sonny's not good at business?" She turned to me. "You know what I mean? He's so young. . . ."

"You don't have to marry him," I said. "After all, you're——"

"You don't understand," my sister said hurriedly, warding off advice she didn't want. "You're too young yet." She laughed. "You know what he said to me?"

Just then, my mother called out from the bottom of the stairs, "Listen, how does this sound to you? 'Dear Greta——' It's a night letter, and we get a lot of words, and I thought Greta would like it better if I started that way. Greta's so touchy, you know. Can you hear me?"

"I have to go," my sister whispered. She looked at me, and then suddenly she leaned over and kissed me on the forehead. "Go to sleep," she said. "Have nice dreams." She got up and went out into the hall.

"'——Dodie got engaged tonight,'" my mother read. "Is 'got engaged' the right way to say it?"

"Became engaged," my sister said, in a distant voice.

I put on my bathrobe and slippers and went out into the hall. My sister was leaning over the banister, talking to my mother at the bottom of the stairs about the night letter. I slipped past her and down the back stairs and into the kitchen. I found a cold chicken in the icebox, put the platter on the kitchen table, and tore off a leg and began to eat.

The door to the back stairs swung open, and my sister appeared. "I'm hungry, too," she said. "I don't know why." She drifted over to the table, and bent over the chicken. "I guess emotion makes people hungry."

My mother pushed open the swinging door, from the dining-room side. "There you are," she said. She looked flustered. "I'll have to think some more, and then I'll write the whole thing over," she said to my sister. To me she said, "Are you *eating* at this time of night?"

My sister said that she was hungry, too.

"There's some soup," my mother said. "Why don't I heat it up." And suddenly her eyes filled with tears, and all at once we fell to kissing one another—to embracing and smiling and making cheerful predictions about one another—there in the white, brightly lighted kitchen. We had known each other for so long, and there were so many things that we all three remembered. . . . Our smiles, our approving glances, wandered from face to face. There was a feeling of politeness in the air. We were behaving the way we would in railway stations, at my sister's wedding, at the birth of her first child, at my graduation from college. This was the first of our reunions.

Our self-image is conditioned by what we perceive to be our affect on others; we judge our worth by our reflection from the mirrors of those around us. Consider how the narrator characterizes himself in the following statements:

> That spring when I was sixteen, more than anything else in the world I wanted to be a success when I grew up. I did not know there was any other way of being lovable.

> I'm not popular . . . I'm too gloomy. . . . I'm a virgin. That has a lot to do with everything.

> Among my other problems was that I was reduced nearly to a state of tears over my own looks. . . .

> The hunger I had for holding school office and for being well thought of . . . I agreed . . . [was] a streak of lousy bourgeois cowardice . . . (I didn't like myself anyway); but what was to be done about it?

> I was doomed, but I was very likely charming.

> I felt that no idea I had ever held was safe.

> I lifted my face—that exasperating factor, my face. . . . What a dreadful unhappiness I felt.

> I felt the preliminary stirrings of an envy so deep it would make me miserable for weeks.

> "I'm nobody. I've been damaged by my heredity."

In what ways do Preston and Joel Bush contribute to the narrator's discontent and feelings of inferiority, as evidenced in his self-portrait?

In what ways have his sister's and mother's values influenced his self-image and his ambitions?

Preston, with his "maddening physicist's serenity" and "confusing vanity," mimicks the narrator, calls him a "snob" and a "sucker," acknowledges his "half-assed charm," but labels his situation "hopeless." Why, then, is Preston the narrator's best friend?

Why does Preston hate Joel? Why does he call him "chicken" and "not very smart"?

Preston claims that sex "starts in the infant and lasts forever." To the narrator's mournful modification that "saints escape it," Preston responds "the hell they do." Preston is a "scientist." To what data might he point for confirmation of his notion about infantile sexuality?

Casually initiating the subject, Joel Bush announces: "I got laid last night." He further volunteers that his experience with a fully grown woman who "knew what she was doing" was "disappointing. . . . nothing very special. . . . like masturbation, kind of with bells." Do you think Joel is telling the truth or inventing the story? Why? In either case, why would he discuss the disappointment of it? If Joel's report is honest, what might explain the fact that "it was not like the books at all"?

Does the description of Joel, ". . . his looks weren't particularly masculine or clean-cut, and he wasn't a fine figure of a boy—he was merely beautiful," provide clues to the possible motive for Joel's sexual experiment? Might a similar doubt or fear in Preston—who curls the few limp hairs on his chest, who is far from handsome, and who dismisses a girl by saying "all she does is talk. She's frigid or something" explain his interest in sex and his suggestion to run away and go to a whorehouse?

Eleanor admits,

"You know, I think I'm not basically a happy person. . . . I always thought I was. . . . People expect you to be, especially if you're a girl."

Would you agree that people expect girls to be basically happy? More so than boys? For what reasons? What evidence might lead to the conclusion that the reverse is true?

The narrator's relationship with Eleanor is "first" love but not "final" love. What limitations do you find in it? On what is it based?

How relevant is the comment:

. . . To a considerable extent adolescent love is an attempt to arrive at a definition of one's identity by projecting one's diffused self-image on another and by seeing it thus reflected and gradually clarified. That is why so much of young love is conversation. [4]

Consider the following dialogue from *First Love and Other Sorrows:*

"I don't like to hear you being so dissatisfied with yourself," I mumbled. "You could undermine your self-confidence that way."
"How can I, Eleanor. How *can* I?" I cried. "I'm nobody. I've been damaged by my heredity."
"You, too!" she exclaimed happily. "Oh, that's what's wrong with me!"

How does their "young love" serve as a sort of therapy for both Eleanor and the narrator?

After leaving Eleanor's house and vaulting his own back fence, the narrator suddenly looks down at his fingertips:

> . . . they were blurred in the darkness and moist from the lilac, and I swept them to my mouth and kissed them.

Why?

In what respects are Eleanor and the narrator of *First Love and Other Sorrows* still trapped in an "I"-orientation?

RELATED QUESTIONS

The narrator says:

> I used to wonder why my mother didn't take my sister's success for granted. My sister was lovely, she had plenty of dates, the phone rang incessantly. Where was the danger?

Where *is* the danger in Dodie's attitude? With what fictional females from the "I" section might she be compared?

Joel Bush in *First Love and Other Sorrows,* Anna Jones in *Snowfall in Childhood,* Francolin and Bletts of *The Bulpington of Blup* bear out statistical findings that peers, rather than parents, are the favored sources of sex education—however faulty or partial the information.

Recent surveys suggest that considerably more girls than boys credit sex education to their homes, but even those girls are not in a majority. When asked what they found most difficult to discuss with their parents, 85 percent of college freshmen sampled in one study named sex; 80 percent cited petting as a subject impossible to talk over with their mothers and fathers [5].

From a parental perspective, most mothers seem to be glad to talk over intimate questions of life and love with their children at any time. However, surveys show that a considerable number of mothers that believe they *ought* to discuss the facts of life with their children often are tongue-tied and uneasy when confronted with their children's sex questions.

The following entries in Anne Frank's *The Diary of a Young Girl,* continuing in sequence from the selection on p. 26, also probe sexual concerns and show, from a fourteen-year-old's perspective, Anne's insight into the nature of her relationship to her parents and with Peter Van Daan.

The Diary of a Young Girl

ANNE FRANK

My longing to talk to someone became so intense that somehow or other I took it into my head to choose Peter.

Sometimes if I've been upstairs into Peter's room during the day, it always struck me as very snug, but because Peter is so retiring and would never turn anyone out who became a nuisance, I never dared stay long, because I was afraid he might think me a bore. I tried to think of an excuse to stay in his room and get him talking, without it being too noticeable, and my chance came yesterday. Peter has a mania for crossword puzzles at the moment and hardly does anything else. I helped him with them and we soon sat opposite each other at his little table, he on the chair and me on the divan.

It gave me a queer feeling each time I looked into his deep blue eyes, and he sat there with that mysterious laugh playing round his lips. I was able to read his inward thoughts. I could see on his face that look of helplessness and uncertainty as to how to behave, and, at the same time, a trace of his sense of manhood. I noticed his shy manner and it made me feel very gentle; I couldn't refrain from meeting those dark eyes again and again, and with my whole heart I almost beseeched him: oh, tell me, what is going on inside you, oh, can't you look beyond this ridiculous chatter?

But the evening passed and nothing happened, except that I told him about blushing—naturally not what I have written, but just so that he would become more sure of himself as he grew older.

When I lay in bed and thought over the whole situation, I found it far from encouraging, and the idea that I should beg for Peter's patronage was simply repellent. One can do a lot to satisfy one's longings, which certainly sticks out in my case, for I have made up my mind to go and sit with Peter more often and to get him talking somehow or other.

Whatever you do, don't think I'm in love with Peter—not a bit of it! If the Van Daans had had a daughter instead of a son, I should have tried to make friends with her too. . . .

Monday, 24 January, 1944

Something has happened to me; or rather, I can hardly describe it as an event, except that I think it is pretty crazy. Whenever anyone used to speak of sexual problems at home or at school, it was something either mysterious or revolting. Words which had any bearing on the subject were whispered, and often if someone didn't understand he was laughed at. It struck me as very odd and I thought, "Why are people so secretive and tiresome when they talk about these things?" But as I didn't think that I could change things, I kept my mouth shut as much as possible, or sometimes asked girl friends for information. When I had learned quite a lot and had also spoken about it with my parents, Mummy said one day, "Anne, let me give you some good advice; never speak about this subject to boys and don't reply if they begin about it." I remember exactly what my answer was: I said, "No, of course not! The very idea!" And there it remained.

When we first came here, Daddy often told me about things that I would really have preferred to hear from Mummy, and I found out the rest from books and things I picked up from conversations. Peter Van Daan was never as tiresome over this as the boys at school—once or twice at first perhaps—but he never tried to get me talking.

Mrs. Van Daan told us that she had never talked about these things to Peter, and for all she knew neither had her husband. Apparently she didn't even know how much he knew.

Yesterday, when Margot, Peter, and I were peeling potatoes, somehow the conversation turned to Boche. "We still don't know what sex Boche is, do we?" I asked.

"Yes, certainly," Peter answered. "He's a tom."

I began to laugh. "A tomcat that's expecting, that's marvelous!"

Peter and Margot laughed too over this silly mistake. You see, two months ago, Peter had stated that Boche would soon be having a family, her tummy was growing visibly. However, the fatness appeared to come from the many stolen bones, because the children didn't seem to grow fast, let alone make their appearance!

Peter just had to defend himself. "No," he said, "you can go with me yourself to look at him. Once when I was playing around with him, I noticed quite clearly that he's a tom."

I couldn't control my curiosity, and went with him to the warehouse. Boche, however, was not receiving visitors, and was nowhere to be seen. We waited for a while, began to get cold, and went upstairs again. Later in the afternoon I heard Peter go downstairs for the second time. I mustered up all my courage to walk through the silent house alone, and reached the warehouse. Boche stood on the packing table playing with Peter, who had just put him on the scales to weigh him.

"Hello, do you want to see him?" He didn't make any lengthy preparations, but picked up the animal, turned him over on to his back, deftly held his head and paws together, and the lesson began. "These are the male organs, these are just a few stray hairs, and that is his bottom." The cat did another half turn and was standing on his white socks once more.

If any other boy had shown me "the male organs," I would never have looked at him again. But Peter went on talking quite normally on what is otherwise such a painful subject, without meaning anything unpleasant, and finally put me sufficiently at my ease for me to be normal too. We played with Boche, amused ourselves, chattered together, and then sauntered through the large warehouse towards the door.

"Usually, when I want to know something, I find it in some book or other, don't you?" I asked.

"Why on earth? I just ask upstairs. My father knows more than me and has had more experience in such things."

We were already on the stair, so I kept my mouth shut after that.

"Things may alter," as Brer Rabbit said. Yes. Really I shouldn't have discussed these things in such a normal way with a girl.

. . . I wasn't quite my usual self for the rest of the day though, in spite of everything. When I thought over our talk, it still seemed rather odd. But at least I'm wiser about one thing, that there really are young people—and of the opposite sex too—who can discuss these things naturally without making fun of them.

I wonder if Peter really does ask his parents much. Would he honestly behave with them as he did with me yesterday? Ah, what would I know about it!

Sunday, 13 February, 1944

Since Saturday a lot has changed for me. It came about like this. I longed—and am still longing—but . . . now something has happened, which has made it a little, just a little, less.

To my great joy—I will be quite honest about it—already this morning I noticed that Peter kept looking at me all the time. Not in the ordinary way, I don't know how, I just can't explain.

I used to think that Peter was in love with Margot, but yesterday I suddenly had the feeling that it is not so. I made a special effort not to look at him too much, because whenever I did, he kept on looking too and then—yes, then—it gave me a lovely feeling inside, but which I mustn't feel too often.

I desperately want to be alone. Daddy has noticed that I'm not quite my usual self, but I really can't tell him everything. "Leave me in peace, leave me alone," that's what I'd like to keep crying out all the time. Who knows, the day may come when I'm left alone more than I would wish!

Tuesday, 28 March, 1944

I could write a lot more about politics, but I have heaps of other things to tell you today. First, Mummy has more or less forbidden me to go upstairs so often, because, according to her, Mrs. Van Daan is jealous. Secondly, Peter has invited Margot to join us upstairs; I don't know whether it's just out of politeness or whether he really means it. Thirdly, I went and asked Daddy if he thought I need pay any regard to Mrs. Van Daan's jealousy, and he didn't think so. What next? Mummy is cross, perhaps jealous too. Daddy doesn't grudge us these times together, and thinks it's nice that we get on so well. Margot is fond of Peter too, but feels that two's company and three's a crowd.

Mummy thinks that Peter is in love with me; quite frankly, I only wish he were, then we'd be quits and really be able to get to know each other. She also says that he keeps on looking at me. Now, I suppose that's true, but still I can't help it if he looks at my dimples and we wink at each other occasionally, can I?

I'm in a very difficult position. Mummy is against me and I'm against her, Daddy closes his eyes and tries not to see the silent battle between us. Mummy is sad, because she does really love me, while I'm not in the least bit sad, because I don't think she understands. And Peter—I don't want to give Peter up, he's such a darling. I admire him so; it can grow into something beautiful between us; why do the "old 'uns" have to poke their noses in all the time? Luckily I'm quite used to hiding my feelings and I manage extremely well not to let them see how mad I am about him. Will he ever say anything? Will I ever feel his cheek against mine. . . . When he lies with his head on his arm with his eyes closed, then he is still a child; when he plays with Boche, he is loving; when he carries potatoes or anything heavy, then he is strong; when he goes and watches the shooting, or looks for burglars in the darkness, then he is brave; and when he is so awkward and clumsy, then he is just a pet.

I like it much better if he explains something to me than when I have to teach him; I would really adore him to be my superior in almost everything.

What do we care about the two mothers? Oh, but if only he would speak!

Monday, 17 April, 1944

Do you think that Daddy and Mummy would approve of my sitting and kissing a boy on a divan—a boy of seventeen and a half and a girl of just under fifteen? I don't really think they would, but I must rely on myself over this. . . .

Tuesday, 2 May, 1944

On Saturday evening I asked Peter whether he thought that I ought to tell Daddy a bit about us; when we'd discussed it a little, he came to the conclusion that I should. I was glad, for it shows that he's an honest boy. As soon as I got downstairs I went off with Daddy to get some water; and while we were on the stairs I said, "Daddy, I expect you've gathered that when we're together Peter and I don't sit miles apart. Do you think it's wrong?" Daddy didn't reply immediately, then said, "No, I don't think it's wrong, but you must be careful, Anne; you're in such a confined space here." When we went upstairs, he said something else on the same lines. On Sunday morning he called me to him and said, "Anne, I have thought more about what you said." I felt scared already. "It's not really very right—here in this house, I thought that you were just pals. Is Peter in love?"

"Oh, of course not," I replied.

"You know that I understand both of you, but you must be the one to hold back. Don't go upstairs so often, don't encourage him more than you can help. It is the man who is always the active one in these things; the woman can hold him back. It is quite different under normal circumstances, when you are free, you see other boys and girls, you can get away sometimes, play games and do all kinds of other things; but here, if you're together a lot, and you want to get away, you can't; you see each other every hour of the day—in fact, all the time. Be careful, Anne, and don't take it too seriously!"

"I don't, Daddy, but Peter is a decent boy, really a nice boy!"

"Yes, but he is not a strong character; he can be easily influenced, for good, but also for bad; I hope for his sake that his good side will remain uppermost, because, by nature, that is how he is."

We talked on for a bit and agreed that Daddy should talk to him too.

On Sunday morning in the attic he asked, "And have you talked to your father, Anne?"

"Yes," I replied, "I'll tell you about it. Daddy doesn't think it's bad, but he says that here, where we're so close together all the time, clashes may easily arise."

"But we agreed, didn't we, never to quarrel; and I'm determined to stick to it!"

"So will I, Peter, but Daddy didn't think that it was like this, he just thought we were pals; do you think that we still can be?"

"I can—what about you?"

"Me too, I told Daddy that I trusted you. I do trust you, Peter, just as much as I trust Daddy, and I believe you to be worthy of it. You are, aren't you, Peter?"

"I hope so." (He was very shy and rather red in the face.)

"I believe in you, Peter," I went on, "I believe that you have good qualities, and that you'll get on in the world."

After that, we talked about other things. Later I said, "If we come out of here, I know quite well that you won't bother about me any more!"

He flared right up. "That's not true, Anne, oh no, I won't let you think that of me!"

Then I was called away.

Daddy has talked to him; he told me about it today. "Your father thought that the friendship might develop into love sooner or later," he said. But I replied that we would keep a check on ourselves.

Daddy doesn't want me to go upstairs so much in the evenings now, but I don't want that. Not only because I like being with Peter; I have told him that I trust him. I do trust him and I want to show him that I do, which can't happen if I stay downstairs through lack of trust.

No, I'm going! . . .

Friday, 5 May, 1944

Daddy is not pleased with me; he thought that after our talk on Sunday I automatically wouldn't go upstairs every evening. He doesn't want any "necking," a word I can't bear. It was bad enough talking about it, why must he make it so unpleasant now? I shall talk to him today. Margot has given me some good advice, so listen; this is roughly what I want to say:

"I believe, Daddy, that you expect a declaration from me, so I will give it you. You are disappointed in me, as you had expected more reserve from me, and I suppose you want me to be just as a fourteen-year-old should be. But that's where you're mistaken!

"Since we've been here, from July 1942 until a few weeks ago, I can assure you that I haven't had an easy time. If you only knew how I cried in the evenings, how unhappy I was, how lonely I felt, then you would understand that I want to go upstairs!

"I have now reached the stage that I can live entirely on my own, without Mummy's support or anyone else's for that matter. But it hasn't just happened in a night; it's been a bitter, hard struggle and I've shed many a tear, before I became as independent as I am now. You can laugh at me and not believe me, but that can't harm me. I know that I'm a separate individual and I don't feel in the least bit responsible to any of you. I am only telling you this because I thought that otherwise you might think that I was underhand, but I don't have to give an account of my deeds to anyone but myself.

"When I was in difficulties you all closed your eyes and stopped up your ears and didn't help me; on the contrary, I received nothing but warnings not to be so boisterous. I was only boisterous so as not to be miserable all the time. I was reckless so as not to hear that persistent voice within me continually. I played a comedy for a year and a half, day in, day out, I never grumbled, never lost my cue, nothing like that—and now, now the battle is over. I have won! I am independent both in mind and body. I don't need a mother any more, for all this conflict has made me strong.

"And now, now that I'm on top of it, now that I know that I've fought the battle, now I want to be able to go on in my own way too, the way that I think is right. You can't and mustn't regard me as fourteen, for all these troubles have made me older; I shall not be sorry for what I have done, but shall act as I think I can. You can't coax me into not going upstairs; *either* you forbid it, *or* you trust me through thick and thin, but then leave me in peace as well!"

Sunday morning, 7 May, 1944

Daddy and I had a long talk yesterday afternoon, I cried terribly and he joined in. Do you know what he said to me . . .? "I have received many letters in my life, but this is certainly the most unpleasant! You, Anne, who have received such love from your parents, you, who have parents who are always ready to help you, who have always defended you whatever it might be, can you talk of feeling no responsibility towards us? You feel wronged and deserted; no, Anne, you have done us a great injustice!

"Perhaps you didn't mean it like that, but it is what you wrote; no, Anne, we haven't deserved such a reproach as this!"

Oh, I have failed miserably; this is certainly the worst thing I've ever done in my life. I was only trying to show off with my crying and my tears, just trying to appear big, so that he would respect me.

It's right that for once I've been taken down from my inaccessible pedestal, that my pride has been shaken a bit, for I was becoming much too taken up with myself again. What Miss Anne does is by no means always right! Anyone who can cause such unhappiness to someone else, someone he professes to love, and on purpose, too, is low, very low!

And the way Daddy has forgiven me makes me feel more than ever ashamed of myself, he is going to throw the letter in the fire and is so sweet to me now, just as if he had done something wrong. No, Anne, you still have a tremendous lot to learn, begin by doing that first, instead of looking down on others and accusing them!

I have had a lot of sorrow, but who hasn't at my age? I have played the clown a lot too, but I was hardly conscious of it; I felt lonely, but hardly ever in despair! I ought to be deeply ashamed of myself, and indeed I am.

What is done cannot be undone, but one can prevent it happening again. I want to start from the beginning again and it can't be difficult, now that I have Peter. With him to support me, I can and will!

I'm not alone any more; he loves me. I love him, I have my books, my storybook and my diary. I'm not so frightfully ugly, not utterly stupid, have a cheerful temperament and want to have a good character!

Yes, Anne, you've felt deeply that your letter was too hard and that it was untrue. To think that you were even proud of it! I will take Daddy as my example, and I *will* improve.

. . . I have one outstanding trait in my character, which must strike anyone who knows me for any length of time, and that is my knowledge of myself. I can watch myself and my actions, just like an outsider. The Anne of every day I can face entirely without prejudice, without making excuses for her, and watch what's good and what's bad about her. This "self-consciousness" haunts me, and every time I open my mouth I know as soon as I've spoken whether "that ought to have been different" or "that was right as it was." There are so many things about myself that I condemn; I couldn't begin to name them all. I understand more and more how true Daddy's words were when he said: "All children must look after their own upbringing." Parents can only give good advice or put them on the right paths, but the final forming of a person's character lies in their own hands.

In addition to this, I have lots of courage, I always feel so strong and as if I can bear a great deal, I feel so free and so young! I was glad when I first realized it, because I don't think I shall easily bow down before the blows that inevitably come to everyone.

. . . "For in its innermost depths youth is lonelier than old age." I read this saying in some book and I've always remembered it, and found it to be true. Is it true then that grownups have a more difficult time here than we do? No. I know it isn't. Older people have formed their opinions about everything, and don't waver before they act. It's twice as hard for us young ones to hold our ground, and maintain our opinions, in a time when all ideals are being shattered and destroyed, when people are showing their worst side, and do not know whether to believe in truth and right and God.

Anne's confidences to her diary, written in the Secret Annexe hideout from the Nazis which she shared with her parents, her sister Margot, and the Van Daan family, seem to reinforce findings of investigations:

> Whenever anyone used to speak of sexual problems at home or at school, it was something either mysterious or revolting. Words which had any bearing on the subject were whispered, and often if someone didn't understand he was laughed at. It struck me as very odd and I thought, "Why are people so secretive and tiresome when they talk about these things?" But as I didn't think that I could change things, I kept my mouth shut as much as possible, or sometimes asked girl friends for information. . . .
>
> Mrs. Van Daan told us that she had never talked about [sexual matters with] Peter, and for all she knew neither had her husband. Apparently she didn't even know how much he knew.

Why are "words which [have] any bearing on the subject" whispered?

Why are girls more likely than boys to get sex education at home? What are they educated about? What areas of sex education are probably most frequently omitted by parents? Why?

Anne finds Peter Van Daan one of those "young people—and of the opposite sex too—who can discuss these things naturally without making fun of them."

How does Peter's attitude about Boche, the cat, and the lesson in sex suggest an approach that adults might adopt in order to put young people at ease?

What might be some of the reasons that such a large percentage of college freshmen feel unable to discuss sex with their parents?

What conditions or parental attitudes might improve lines of communication about sex between parents and young people?

Would you agree with the physician and sex educator who says:

> I don't think parents are the best people to give sex education—not reproductive information—but sex education to their kids because it imposes too great a burden on the parent-child relationship at a moment when it is most stressed. [6]

Why do you suppose parents might be "secretive," "tiresome," "tongue-tied," "uneasy," and "uncomfortable" in discussing sex with their own children? One mother who was interviewed reportedly said:

> In my growing up years we just didn't ask. We simply guessed at answers and put two and two together on our own. [7]

Might mothers feel, therefore, that their children should do the same? Might some adults' embarrassment stem from their feeling inadequately prepared to instruct? Is "the new morality," like the "new math," a totally different and frightening new approach to a familiar subject?

Do you share Anne's conviction that "older people have formed their opinions about everything, and don't waver before they act"?

Why do you think Anne would "really have preferred to hear from Mummy" the things her father told her? Why do you suppose Anne's mother didn't assume the responsibility?

Many more of today's mothers disapprove of their daughters' dates than was the case when the mother herself was a girl [8], because some of the results of the so-called sexual revolution—increased promiscuity, unwanted pregnancies, early and unsatisfactory marriages, abortion, and high incidence of venereal disease—are alien to their understanding. Thus, parents may not be certain about approaches to adopt and what to tell young people to assist them in developing a healthy basic value system. The young sense their parents' uneasiness in dealing with sexual matters. To what degree is parental disapproval, or fear of incurring it, a block to communication? How do young people also heighten the wall of silence?

Anne's father commented: "All children must look after their own upbringing." His daughter recognized that "parents can only give good advice or put them on the right paths . . . the final forming of a person's character lies in their own hands." A psychiatrist adds:

> The day for control by edict is over. Parents must recognize that their usefulness and their authority will now rest upon their own validity as parents and not upon their fast diminishing powers. Blustering, threatening and denial will fail to work now—if they ever worked at all. . . . [Parents] cannot afford to relinquish family management or family life to the uncertainties of the inexperienced youngster. Nor can they afford to insist upon the unquestioned superiority and finality of their own judgments and decisions. [9]

Why do "blustering, threatening, and denial" fail to work?

What do you think it means to say that parental usefulness and authority rest "upon their own validity as parents"? How would they demonstrate their "validity" to you?

As a parent, what would be "right paths" on which you might try to put your children? In what areas, or on what specific things would you refuse to relinquish responsibility and, therefore, authority?

Anne makes frequent reference to the establishment of self-reliance:

> Do you think that Daddy and Mummy would approve of my sitting and kissing a boy on a divan—a boy of seventeen and a half and a girl of just under fifteen? I don't really think they would, but I must rely on myself over this. . . .

> I have now reached the stage that I can live entirely on my own, without Mummy's support or anyone else's for that matter. . . . I don't have to give an account of my deeds to anyone but myself.

> I am independent both in mind and body.

How realistic is Anne's concept of independence?

Asserting her independence, Anne found she could trust her own judgment: Despite her mother's warning never to speak about sex with boys, Anne discovered through talks on the subject with Peter that she was "wiser about one thing." Has Anne reached the stage where she can live entirely on her own, without her mother's support, "or anyone else's for that matter"? Is such total independence possible? Desirable?

In her Declaration of Independence to her father, Anne adds: "You can't coax me into not going upstairs; *either* you forbid it, *or* you trust me through thick and thin." Earlier, Anne had written in her diary

> Daddy doesn't want me to go upstairs so much in the evenings now, but I don't want that. Not only because I like being with Peter; I have told him that I trust him. I do trust him and I want to show him that I do, which can't happen if I stay downstairs through lack of trust.

Anne's argument appears to center on the word "trust." What meaning does she ascribe to the word?

Does the fact that Anne's father wants her not to spend so much time alone with Peter mean that he does not trust her? Would following her father's advice lessen Anne's trust in Peter? Does Anne trust her father? Her mother? If Anne had had more experience with living what might she realize about male and female sexuality which her father recognizes?

Is Anne's self-reproach in her diary entry of May 7 genuine or is she posturing?

Does her declared knowledge of herself: "I can watch myself and my actions, just like an outsider. The Anne of every day I can face entirely without prejudice" ring true? Why might an adult be suspicious of the word "entirely"?

Would you agree with Anne's judgment: "he loves me; I love him"? What is your definition of love in this case?

Assuming that Anne and Peter had survived the war and been liberated, what might their chances have been of creating a lasting relationship? How much of the intensity of their recorded relationship results from their living in close quarters, under abnormal circumstances where neither is free to see other males or females, facing a threatening present and uncertain future, at an age where each is sexually awake and acutely sensitive to sexual desires?

Do you subscribe to the notion that a man and a woman who were forced to live with each other would eventually fall in love?

RELATED QUESTIONS

What signs of Anne's sensitivity to Peter in *The Diary of a Young Girl* are reminiscent of Tim Hazard's toward Rachel Wells in *The City of Trembling Leaves* (p. 94)? What sorts of things does Anne notice about Peter that she would not be aware of were she completely "I"-oriented?

The author of *Sex Education* (see "*Night-Lights,*" p. 548), in her growing-up years, was one of those who had to guess at answers and put two and two together for herself. What was she not told? What were the effects? What reassurance does she come to wish she had been given? How, nevertheless, through increasing insight, does she come to a genuine understanding of her own part in a frightening sexual encounter?

The author of *A High Wind in Jamaica* (p. 22) observed that "grown-ups embark on a life of deception . . . and generally fail [whereas] a child can hide the most appalling secret without the least effort" and be practically secure against detection. While the secret may not have been "appalling," Anna's strategy of silence in *Snowfall in Childhood* (p. 86) was a minor piece of calculated deception:

> I heard my mother ask where I was. Mrs. Jones answered that I was buried somewhere in the hay and Anna whispered close to me not to answer or say anything.

The narrator of *Merrymakers* (p. 100), although seemingly on reasonably good terms with his parents, says:

> I'd been cross-examined at the dinner table when the news came out that I wasn't taking JoAnne to this dance. . . . Well, who was I taking then? It seemed to me parents had no respect for a son's private life. I answered sullenly.

In similar fashion, Anne asks her diary: "Why do the old 'uns have to poke their noses in all the time? Luckily I'm quite used to hiding my feelings and I manage extremely well not to let them see how mad I am about [Peter]," and the narrator of *First Love and Other Sorrows* (p. 111) numbers among his treasures, "thirty-five pages of secret thoughts written out in longhand." How much further evidence is there for the observation that secretiveness and sensitivity to parental intrusion is part of the individual's effort to form tastes that are independent of his family's and to develop emotional freedom from parents?

How often is not telling one's parents for fear of hurting them simply a rationalization permitting us to do what we want to do, even though we know it would bring parental disapproval?

Have you ever bristled at what you knew to be well-intentioned parental help, yet almost simultaneously wished that your parents would cater to your needs and wait on you as they did when you were a small child?

In each of the following cases, parental advice in areas of sex education creates friction:

My mother would often bring up matters of propriety. Late dates were improper, flirting with boys other than one's date, breaking dates. Then, too, she would try to instruct my sister in other matters, which had to do with keeping passion in its place and so preventing embarrassment for the boy and disaster for the girl. My sister would grow irritated.

"I know what I'm saying!" my mother would cry when she argued with my sister. "You must listen to me. People talk. . . . You don't know who you'll meet on a date; it's good to accept even if you don't like the boy. . . . Girls have to be very careful. You're thoughtless. Don't you think in fifty years I've learned what makes the world go around? Now, listen to me. I know what I'm saying. . . ."

First Love and Other Sorrows (p. 114)

Mummy said one day, "Anne, let me give you some good advice; never speak about this subject to boys and don't reply if they begin about it." Daddy . . . said, ". . . you must be careful, Anne; you're in such a confined space here. . . . you must be the one to hold back. Don't go upstairs so often, don't encourage him more than you can help. It is the man who is always the active one in these things; the woman can hold him back. . . . Be careful, Anne. . . .

The Diary of a Young Girl (pp. 133, 136)

Is there any similarity in content and/or tone between the excerpts of parental instruction? How would you have reacted to each directive? Whether or not you agree with the parental advice in each, what intellectual basis can you find for it? Is some of the advice given without reason? Outdated? "Bad"? Why?

Are objections more apt to be to the actual advice given, or to the way in which that advice is presented? Even to the fact, sometimes, that the advice is given at all?

Everyone wants to feel that his ideas are valuable, his opinions worthy of attention, respect and consideration. What is it about the way parents talk to their children in *First Love and Other Sorrows* (p. 111) and *The Diary of a Young Girl* that might make the younger person feel threatened? Without altering content, can you express it differently in each case so that the listener might not feel diminished or irritated, or like a child who was going through a difficult phase?

The way in which advice is given includes, not only the tone and phrasing, but considerations of time and place. Were you to be given advice of this nature by one of your parents, when, where, by whom and in front of whom would you want it to be?

Despite an inarticulate start and the agonies of her "shy reticence," Sylvia, the daughter of an intellectual pair who appreciate the simple life, is able to discuss sexual confusions and fears with her mother, who "like a strong and beneficent magician" can rebuild a "black and shattered world" pictured in the following excerpt from Dorothy Canfield's *The Bent Twig.*

The Bent Twig

DOROTHY CANFIELD

. . . "Oh, Mother—!" she exclaimed in an unhappy tone, and said no more. She knew no words to phrase what was in her mind.

"Yes, dear," said her mother gently. She looked at her daughter anxiously, expectantly, with a passion of yearning in her eyes, but she said no more than those two words.

There was a silence. Sylvia was struggling for expression. They continued to walk swiftly through the cold, ruddy, sunset air, the hard-frozen road ringing beneath their rapid advance. Sylvia clasped her hands together hard in her muff. She felt that something in her heart was dying, was suffocating for lack of air, and yet that it would die if she brought it to light. She could find no words at all to ask for help, agonizing in a shy reticence impossible for an adult to conceive. Finally, beginning at random, very hurriedly, looking away, she brought out, faltering, "Mother, *is* it true that all men are—that when a girl marries, she must expect to—aren't there *any* men who—" she stopped, burying her burning face in her muff.

Her words, her tone, the quaver of desperate sincerity in her accent, brought her mother up short. She stopped abruptly and faced the girl. "Sylvia, look at me!" she said in a commanding voice which rang loud in the frosty silences about them. Sylvia started and looked into her mother's face. It was moved so darkly and so deeply from its usual serene composure that she would have recoiled in fear, had she not been seized upon and held motionless by the other's compelling eyes.

"Sylvia," said her mother, in a strong, clear voice, acutely contrasted to Sylvia's muffled tones, "Sylvia, it's a lie that men are nothing but sensual! There's nothing in marriage that a good girl honestly in love with a good man need fear."

"But—but—" began Sylvia, startled out of her shyness.

Her mother cut her short. "Anything that's felt by decent men in love is felt just as truly, though maybe not always so strongly, by women in love. And if a woman doesn't feel that answer in her heart to what he feels—why, he's not mate for her. Anything's better for her than going on. And, Sylvia, you mustn't get the wrong idea. Sensual feeling isn't bad in itself. It's in the world because we have bodies as well as minds—it's like the root of a plant. But it oughtn't to be a very big part of the plant. And it must be the root of the woman's feeling as well as the man's or everything's all wrong."

"But how can you *tell!*" burst out Sylvia.

"You can tell by the way you feel, if you don't lie to yourself, or let things like money or social position count. If an honest girl shrinks from a man instinctively, there's something not right—sensuality is too big a part of what the man feels for her—and look here, Sylvia, that's not always the man's fault. Women don't realize as they ought how base it is to try to attract men by their bodies," she made her position clear with relentless precision, "when they wear very low-necked dresses, for instance—" At this chance thrust, a wave of scarlet burst up suddenly over Sylvia's face, but she could not withdraw her eyes from her mother's searching, honest gaze, which, even more than her words, spoke to the girl's soul. The strong, grave voice went on unhesitatingly. For once in her life

Mrs. Marshall was speaking out. She was like one who welcomes the opportunity to make a confession of faith. "There's no healthy life possible without some sensual feeling between the husband and wife, but there's nothing in the world more awful than married life when it's the only common ground."

Sylvia gazed with wide eyes at the older woman's face, ardent, compelling, inspired, feeling too deeply, to realize it wholly, the vital and momentous character of the moment. She seemed to see nothing, to be aware of nothing but her mother's heroic eyes of truth; but the whole scene was printed on her mind for all her life—the hard, brown road they stood on, the grayed old rail-fence back of Mrs. Marshall, a field of brown stubble, a distant grove of beech-trees, and beyond and around them the immense sweeping circle of the horizon. The very breath of the pure, scentless winter air was to come back to her nostrils in after years.

"Sylvia," her mother went on, "it is one of the responsibilities of men and women to help each other to meet on a high plane and not on a low one. And on the whole—health's the rule of the world—on the whole, that's the way the larger number of husbands and wives, imperfect as they are, do live together. Family life wouldn't be possible a day if they didn't."

Like a strong and beneficent magician, she built up again and illuminated Sylvia's black and shattered world. "Your father is just as pure a man as I am a woman, and I would be ashamed to look any child of mine in the face if he were not. . . .

For the first time she moved from her commanding attitude of prophetic dignity. She came closer to Sylvia, but although she looked at her with a sudden sweetness which affected Sylvia like a caress, she but made one more impersonal statement: "Sylvia dear, don't let anything make you believe that there are not as many decent men in the world as women, and they're just as decent. Life isn't worth living unless you know that—and it's true." Apparently she had said all she had to say, for she now kissed Sylvia gently and began again to walk forward.

Because "shy reticence" is perhaps *not* "impossible for an adult to conceive," Mrs. Marshall is able to sense the nature of her daughter's distress, even from Sylvia's fragmented and hurried questions. What is the essence of Sylvia's fears?

How does Mrs. Marshall manage to help and to reassure her daughter? Why is her approach successful?

What distinction, if any, does Mrs. Marshall make between love and sex?

"Sensual," synonymous with carnal or lustful, stresses indulgence of the appetite, especially for sexual pleasure. Sensual feelings were a major source of torment for many of the young people depicted in the "I" section as they first experienced the clear, urgent overwhelming call of the flesh. From a more advanced perspective, the poet Lawrence Ferlinghetti describes the texture of sensuality in "Poem 26" from *A Coney Island of the Mind:*

> That 'sensual phosphorescence
> > my youth delighted in'
> now lies almost behind me
> > like a land of dreams

wherein an angel
                    of hot sleep
          dances like a diva
                    in strange veils
          thru which desire
                    looks and cries
    And still she dances
                    dances still
      and still she comes
                    at me
                         with breathing breasts
      and secret lips
                    and (ah)
                         bright eyes

Why isn't sensual feeling bad *in* itself, only *by* itself?

What does Mrs. Marshall mean in saying that sensuality "must be the root of the woman's feeling as well as the man's or everything's all wrong"?

There's no healthy life possible without some sensual feeling between the husband and wife, but there's nothing more awful than married life when it's the only common ground.

What other elements might be considered vital to a successful marriage? How important, for example, would mutual liking, trust, and respect be?

RELATED QUESTIONS

Which of the fictional characters already encountered demonstrate some of these and other qualities—in addition to sexual attraction—desirable for a mature, sound and durable relationship?

How does Mrs. Marshall dispose of the behavior shown by the *Girl Walking* (p. 76), the tanned blonde of *The Once-Over* (p. 74), and Frances in *Young Lonigan* (p. 48)? Why might Mrs. Marshall be more tolerant of Frances than of the others?

Francie Nolan, the "tremulously innocent" heroine of *A Tree Grows in Brooklyn,* grows up in a slum. Her father, Johnny, is a lovable drunkard; her mother, Katie, is a tender, but practical and determined woman. Like Sylvia in *The Bent Twig,* Francie finds her mother approachable and understanding about her sexual dilemma. At sixteen, Francie has found herself attracted to an experienced twenty-two-year-old man who immediately suggests that they spend the night together. Francie refuses, but when she learns of his subsequent involvement with someone else, Francie regrets her decision, feeling that she will "never love anyone as much again." In her bitter misery, Francie is partly testing an adult who represents a world in which the public ethic—despite countless private hypocrisies—frowns on premarital sex.

A Tree Grows in Brooklyn

BETTY SMITH

Katie heard the story. "It's come at last," she thought, "the time when you can no longer stand between your children and heartache. When there wasn't enough food in the house you pretended that you weren't hungry so they could have more. In the cold of a winter's night you got up and put your blanket on their bed so they wouldn't be so cold. You'd kill anyone who tried to harm them. . . . Then one sunny day, they walk out in all innocence and they walk right into the grief that you'd give your life to spare them."

Francie gave her the letter. She read it slowly and as she read, she thought she knew how it was. Here was a man of twenty-two who evidently . . . had been around. Here was a girl sixteen years old; six years younger than he. A girl—in spite of bright-red lipstick and grown-up clothes and a lot of knowledge picked up here and there—who was yet tremulously innocent; a girl who had come face to face with some of the evil of the world and most of its hardships, and yet had remained curiously untouched by the world. Yes, she could understand her appeal for him.

Well, what could she say? That he was no good or at best just a weak man who was easily susceptible to whoever he was with? No, she couldn't be so cruel as to say that. Besides the girl wouldn't believe her anyhow.

"Say something," demanded Francie. "Why don't you say something?"

"What can I say?"

"Say that I'm young—that I'll get over it. Go ahead and say it. Go ahead and lie."

"I know that's what people say—you'll get over it. I'd say it too. But I know it's not true. Oh, you'll be happy again, never fear. But you won't forget. Everytime you fall in love it will be because something in the man reminds you of *him*."

"Mother. . . ."

Mother! Katie remembered. She had called her own mother "mama" until the day she had told her that she was going to marry Johnny. She had said, "Mother, I'm going to marry . . ." She had never said "mama" after that. She had finished growing up when she stopped calling her mother "mama." Now Francie . . .

"Mother, he asked me to be with him for the night. Should I have gone?"

Katie's mind darted around looking for words.

"Don't make up a lie, Mother. Tell me the truth."

Katie couldn't find the right words.

"I promise you that I'll never go with a man without being married first—if I ever marry. And if I feel I must—without being married, I'll tell you first. That's a solemn promise. So you can tell me the truth without worrying that I'll go wrong if I know it."

"There are two truths," said Katie finally.

"As a mother, I say it would have been a terrible thing for a girl to sleep with a stranger—a man she had known less than forty-eight hours. Horrible things might have happened to you. Your whole life might have been ruined. As your mother, I tell you the truth.

"But as a woman . . ." she hesitated. "I will tell you the truth as a woman. It would have been a very beautiful thing. Because there is only once that you love that way."

Francie thought, "I should have gone with him then. I'll never love anyone as much again. I wanted to go and I didn't go and now I don't want him that way any more because *she* owns him now. But I wanted to and I didn't and now it's too late." She put her head down on the table and wept.

"There are two truths," said Katie finally. What are the distinctions between the maternal truth and the woman's truth? Are both perspectives valid? Can the two perspectives be reconciled into one absolute truth?

What position would you take were Francie to demand of you, "Say something. Why don't you say something?"

How apt is the following comment on virtue:

> You have to make your own laws and rules about that; not much you have learned in theory quite fits the praxis. Losing your virtue might be considered virtuous by the fellow you lost your virtue to. But in the eyes of the other fellow, who wasn't that lucky, or of your father and mother, you are a low and "fallen woman" by one and the same deed. If the man you lost your virtue to marries you, you are just lucky—not more virtuous than the next girl who didn't catch the guy. And later, you are a madonnalike creature to the man you leave your husband for, and again, by the same deed, you are a "rotten-to-the-core" adulteress to your husband, his kin and the neighbors. Just by these few examples, you can see how mixed up a girl can get about the meaning of virtue. So you must make, and live by, your own code of virtue. It is rewarding, as the saying goes, whereas deserting one's own code brings disastrous consequences. [10]

Had Francie followed this advice would her decision have been easier? Why?

> Francie thought, "I should have gone with him then. I'll never love anyone as much again. I wanted to go and I didn't go and now I don't want him that way any more because *she* owns him now. But I wanted to and I didn't and now it's too late."

Did Francie really love the man? What does she mean by "that way"? Why should the fact that *"she* owns him now" alter Francie's feeling? Do we tend to overrate opportunities that might have been, and things we have lost?

As a mother, Katie says, "Horrible things might have happened to you. Your whole life might have been ruined." What are some of the "horrible things" that might have happened? How could Francie's whole life have been ruined? Would such dangers be removed had Francie known the man *more* than forty-eight hours?

What does Katie mean: "It would have been a very beautiful thing. Because there is only once that you love that way"? What is "that way"? Is Katie using the phrase as Francie does when she says "I don't want him *that way* anymore"? Why does Francie's mother feel it can be so "only once"? Do you agree with her? How might the experience also have turned out to be a very ugly thing?

Why does Katie feel that it would be "cruel" and futile to share her insights and intuitions about the man with Francie?

Do you agree that, "besides, the girl wouldn't believe her anyhow"? Why? How valid do you consider the following interpretation:

Francie's mother is weak and cowardly and immoral. She withholds from her daughter, and doesn't give her a real answer in the stuff she does say. Besides hedging with Francie, Katie is actually encouraging her daughter to be promiscuous by telling her that sex with a stranger would be beautiful.

RELATED QUESTIONS

Do you think that Sylvia's mother of **The Bent Twig** (p. 144) would share Francie's mother's perspective?

How might Anne Frank's father in **The Diary of a Young Girl** (p. 133) and Dodie's mother in **First Love and Other Sorrows** (p. 111) have responded to Francie's search for "right" values?

Beneatha, a college student, is a member of the Black family in Lorraine Hansberry's **A Raisin in the Sun.** Beneatha becomes exasperated when her brother Walter foolishly invests family funds in a liquor store deal that falls through. She is disgusted with his lack of pride and manliness when he grovels before a bigoted white man, and she finds "nothing left to love" in Walter.

Her mother, however, is able to separate the doer from the deed. Mama may despise what Walter has done, but she cannot despise her son. In the following excerpt from the play, she verbalizes and exemplifies supportive love.

A Raisin in the Sun
LORRAINE HANSBERRY

BENEATHA   That is not a man. That is nothing but a toothless rat.

MAMA   Yes—death done come in this here house. *(She is nodding, slowly, reflectively)* Done come walking in my house. On the lips of my children. You what supposed to be my beginning again. You—what supposed to be my harvest. *(To* BENEATHA*)* You—you mourning your brother?

BENEATHA   He's no brother of mine.

MAMA   What you say?

BENEATHA   I said that that individual in that room is no brother of mine.

MAMA   That's what I thought you said. You feeling like you better than he is today? (BENEATHA *does not answer)* Yes? What you tell him a minute ago? That he wasn't a man? Yes? You give him up for me? You done wrote his epitaph too—like the rest of the world? Well, who give you the privilege?

BENEATHA   Be on my side for once! You saw what he just did, Mama! You saw him—down on his knees. Wasn't it you who taught me—to despise any man who would do that. Do what he's going to do.

MAMA   Yes—I taught you that. Me and your daddy. But I thought I taught you something else too . . . I thought I taught you to love him.

BENEATHA   Love him? There is nothing left to love.

MAMA   There is always something left to love. And if you ain't learned that, you ain't learned nothing. *(Looking at her)* Have you cried for that boy today? I don't mean for yourself and for the family 'cause we lost the money. I mean for him; what he been through and what it done to him. Child, when do you think is the time to love somebody the most; when they done good and made things easy for everybody? Well then, you ain't through learning—because that ain't the time at all. It's when he's at his lowest and can't believe in hisself 'cause the world done whipped him so. When you starts measuring somebody, measure him right, child, measure him right. Make sure you done taken into account what hills and valleys he come through before he got to wherever he is.

How might the principles which determine Mama's feeling for Walter apply to any male-female relationship? To any human relationship? Even to erotic love? Genuine love has been described as

> . . . an expression of productiveness [which] implies care, respect, responsibility, and knowledge. It is not an "affect" in the sense of being affected by somebody, but an active striving for the growth and happiness of the loved person, rooted in one's own capacity to love. . . . [p. 263]

and as

> . . . a principle . . . . not something we *have* or *are,* it is something we *do.* Our task is to act so that more good, (i.e., loving-kindness) will occur than any possible alternatives. We are to be "optimific," to seek an optimum of loving-kindness. It is an attitude, a disposition, a leaning, a preference, a purpose. [p. 316]

What similarities exist between the two descriptions of genuine love? How are the perspectives relevant to the situation in **A Raisin in the Sun?**

> Love and hate are closely related emotions. Loving someone does not preclude real feelings of hostility toward that person from time-to-time. Such ambivalence, a tendency to hate those we love, usually occurs when love is too ambitious or possessive to accept human limitations. Frustrated, annoyed, or displeased, love takes on a hostile quality. [11]

There are even "times when loving is so confused and bewildering that we are willing to wash our hands of it all. Then it is that we are hostile not only toward the persons whom we have been loving but, indeed, toward love itself" [12]. Yet "response is itself a kind of affirmation, even when it issues into unpleasant emotions such as anger and hatred. These need not be antithetical to love; they may even be signs of it—as every romanticist knows" [p. 220].

"**They**" forces in *The Downward Path to Wisdom* by Katherine Anne Porter consist of hate-riddled relatives who provide young Stephen with a sexual and emotional education in fear, confusion, guilt, shame, insecurity, and inconsistency.

Caught in the spider-like filaments of hostilities spun by his family and other adults, Stephen reacts by starting to spin in secret the pattern he has observed: "I hate Papa, I hate Mama, I hate Grandma, I hate Uncle David, I hate Old Janet, I hate Marjory, I hate Papa, I hate Mama. . . ."

The Downward Path to Wisdom

KATHERINE ANNE PORTER

In the square bedroom with the big window Mama and Papa were lolling back on their pillows handing each other things from the wide black tray on the small table with crossed legs. They were smiling and they smiled even more when the little boy, with the feeling of sleep still in his skin and hair, came in and walked up to the bed. Leaning against it, his bare toes wriggling in the white fur rug, he went on eating peanuts which he took from his pajama pocket. He was four years old.

"Here's my baby," said Mama. "Lift him up, will you?"

He went limp as a rag for Papa to take him under the arms and swing him up over a broad, tough chest. He sank between his parents like a bear cub in a warm litter, and lay there comfortably. He took another peanut between his teeth, cracked the shell, picked out the nut whole and ate it.

"Running around without his slippers again," said Mama. "His feet are like icicles."

"He crunches like a horse," said Papa. "Eating peanuts before breakfast will ruin his stomach. Where did he get them?"

"You brought them yesterday," said Mama, with exact memory, "in a grisly little cellophane sack. I have asked you dozens of times not to bring him things to eat. Put him out, will you? He's spilling shells all over me."

Almost at once the little boy found himself on the floor again. He moved around to Mama's side of the bed and leaned confidingly near her and began another peanut. As he chewed he gazed solemnly in her eyes.

"Bright-looking specimen, isn't he?" asked Papa, stretching his long legs and reaching for his bathrobe. "I suppose you'll say it's my fault he's dumb as an ox."

"He's my little baby, my only baby," said Mama richly, hugging him, "and he's a dear lamb." His neck and shoulders were quite boneless in her firm embrace. He stopped chewing long enough to receive a kiss on his crumby chin. "He's sweet as clover," said Mama. The baby went on chewing.

"Look at him staring like an owl," said Papa.

Mama said, "He's an angel and I'll never get used to having him."

"We'd be better off if we never *had* had him," said Papa. He was walking about the room and his back was turned when he said that. There was silence for a moment. The little boy stopped eating, and stared deeply at his Mama. She was looking at the back of Papa's head, and her eyes were almost black. "You're going to say that just once too often," she told him in a low voice. "I hate you when you say that."

Papa said, "You spoil him to death. You never correct him for anything. And you don't take care of him. You let him run around eating peanuts before breakfast."

"You gave him the peanuts, remember that," said Mama. She sat up and hugged her baby once more. He nuzzled softly in the pit of her arm. "Run along, my darling," she told him in her gentlest voice, smiling at him straight in the eyes. "Run along," she said, her arms falling away from him. "Get your breakfast."

The little boy had to pass his father on the way to the door. He shrank into himself when he saw the big hand raised above him. "Yes, get out of here and stay out," said Papa, giving him a little shove toward the door. It was not a hard shove, but it hurt the little boy. He slunk out, and trotted down the hall trying not to look back. He was afraid something was coming after him, he could not imagine what. Something hurt him all over, he did not know why.

He did not want his breakfast; he would not have it. He sat and stirred it round in the yellow bowl, letting it stream off the spoon and spill on the table, on his front, on the chair. He liked seeing it spill. It was hateful stuff, but it looked funny running in white rivulets down his pajamas.

"Now look what you're doing, dirty boy," said Marjory. "You dirty little old boy."

The little boy opened his mouth to speak for the first time. "You're dirty yourself," he told her.

"That's right," said Marjory, leaning over him and speaking so her voice would not carry. "That's right, just like your papa. Mean," she whispered, "mean."

The little boy took up his yellow bowl full of cream and oatmeal and sugar with both hands and brought it down with a crash on the table. It burst and some of the wreck lay in chunks and some of it ran all over everything. He felt better.

"You see?" said Marjory, dragging him out of the chair and scrubbing him with a napkin. She scrubbed him as roughly as she dared until he cried out. "That's just what I said. That's exactly it." Through his tears he saw her face terribly near, red and frowning under a stiff white band, looking like the face of somebody who came at night and stood over him and scolded him when he could not move or get away. "Just like your papa, *mean*."

The little boy went out into the garden and sat on a green bench dangling his legs. He was clean. His hair was wet and his blue woolly pull-over made his nose itch. His face felt stiff from the soap. He saw Marjory going past a window with the black tray. The curtains were still closed at the window he knew opened into Mama's room. Papa's room. Mommanpoppasroom, the word was pleasant, it made a mumbling snapping noise between his lips; it ran in his mind while his eyes wandered about looking for something to do, something to play with.

Mommanpoppas' voices kept attracting his attention. Mama was being cross with Papa again. He could tell by the sound. That was what Marjory always said when their voices rose and fell and shot up to a point and crashed and rolled like the two tomcats who fought at night. Papa was being cross, too, much crosser than Mama this time. He grew cold and disturbed and sat very still, wanting to go to the bathroom, but it was just next to Mommanpoppasroom; he didn't dare think of it. As the voices grew louder he could hardly hear them any more, he wanted so badly to go to the bathroom. The kitchen door opened suddenly and Marjory ran out, making the motion with her hand that meant he was to come to her. He didn't move. She came to him, her face still red and frowning, but she was not angry; she was scared just as he was. She said, "Come on, honey, we've got to go to your gran'ma's again." She took his hand and pulled him. "Come on quick, your gran'ma is waiting for you." He slid off the bench. His mother's voice rose in a terrible scream, screaming something he could not understand, but she was furious; he had seen her clenching her fists and stamping in one spot, screaming with her eyes shut; he knew how she looked. She was screaming in a tantrum, just as he remembered having heard himself. He stood still, doubled over, and all his body seemed to dissolve, sickly, from the pit of his stomach.

"Oh, my God," said Marjory. "Oh, my God. Now look at you. Oh, my God. I can't stop to clean you up."

He did not know how he got to his grandma's house, but he was there at last, wet and soiled, being handled with disgust in the big bathtub. His grandma was there in long black skirts saying, "Maybe he's sick; maybe we should send for the doctor."

"I don't think so, m'am," said Marjory. "He hasn't et anything; he's just scared."

The little boy couldn't raise his eyes, he was so heavy with shame. "Take this note to his mother," said Grandma.

She sat in a wide chair and ran her hands over his head, combing his hair with her fingers; she lifted his chin and kissed him. "Poor little fellow," she said. "Never you mind. You always have a good time at your grandma's, don't you? You're going to have a nice little visit, just like the last time."

The little boy leaned against the stiff, dry-smelling clothes and felt horribly grieved about something. He began to whimper and said, "I'm hungry. I want something to eat." This reminded him. He began to bellow at the top of his voice; he threw himself upon the carpet and rubbed his nose in a dusty woolly bouquet of roses. "I want my peanuts," he howled. "Somebody took my peanuts."

His grandma knelt beside him and gathered him up so tightly he could hardly move. She called in a calm voice above his howls to Old Janet in the doorway, "Bring me some bread and butter with strawberry jam."

"I want peanuts," yelled the little boy desperately.

"No, you don't, darling," said his grandma. "You don't want horrid old peanuts to make you sick. You're going to have some of grandma's nice fresh bread with good strawberries on it. That's what you're going to have." He sat afterward very quietly and ate and ate. His grandma sat near him and Old Janet stood by, near a tray with a loaf and a glass bowl of jam upon the table at the window. Outside there was a trellis with tube-shaped red flowers clinging all over it, and brown bees singing.

"I hardly know what to do," said Grandma, "it's very . . . "

"Yes, m'am," said Old Janet, "it certainly is . . . "

Grandma said, "I can't possibly see the end of it. It's a terrible . . . "

"It certainly is bad," said Old Janet, "all this upset all the time and him such a baby."

Their voices ran on soothingly. The little boy ate and forgot to listen. He did not know these women, except by name. He could not understand what they were talking about; their hands and their clothes and their voices were dry and far away; they examined him with crinkled eyes without any expression that he could see. He sat there waiting for whatever they would do next with him. He hoped they would let him go out and play in the yard. The room was full of flowers and dark red curtains and big soft chairs, and the windows were open, but it was still dark in there somehow; dark, and a place he did not know, or trust.

"Now drink your milk," said Old Janet, holding out a silver cup.

"I don't want any milk," he said, turning his head away.

"Very well, Janet, he doesn't have to drink it," said Grandma quickly. "Now run out in the garden and play, darling. Janet, get his hoop."

A big strange man came home in the evenings who treated the little boy very confusingly. "Say 'please,' and 'thank you,' young man," he would roar, terrifyingly, when he gave any smallest object to the little boy. "Well, fellow, are you ready for a fight?" he would say, again, doubling up huge, hairy fists and making passes at him. "Come on now, you must learn to box." After the first few times this was fun.

"Don't teach him to be rough," said Grandma. "Time enough for all that."

"Now, Mother, we don't want him to be a sissy," said the big man. "He's got to toughen up early. Come on now, fellow, put up your mitts." The little boy liked this new word for hands. He learned to throw himself upon the strange big man, whose name was Uncle David, and hit him on the chest as hard as he could; the big man would laugh and hit him back with his huge, loose fists. Sometimes, but not often, Uncle David came home in the middle of the day. The little boy missed him on the other days, and would hang on the gate looking down the street for him. One evening, he brought a large square package under his arm.

"Come over here, fellow, and see what I've got," he said, pulling off quantities of green paper and string from the box which was full of flat, folded colors. He put something in the little boy's hand. It was limp and silky and bright green with a tube on the end. "Thank you," said the little boy nicely, but not knowing what to do with it.

"Balloons," said Uncle David in triumph. "Now just put your mouth here and blow hard." The little boy blew hard and the green thing began to grow round and thin and silvery.

"Good for your chest," said Uncle David. "Blow some more." The little boy went on blowing and the balloon swelled steadily.

"Stop," said Uncle David, "that's enough." He twisted the tube to keep the air in. "That's the way," he said. "Now I'll blow one, and you blow one, and let's see who can blow up a big balloon the fastest."

They blew and blew, especially Uncle David. He puffed and panted and blew with all his might, but the little boy won. His balloon was perfectly round before Uncle David could even get started. The little boy was so proud he began to dance and shout, "I beat, I beat," and blew in his balloon again. It burst in his face and frightened him so he felt sick. "Ha ha, ho ho ho," whooped Uncle David. "That's the boy. I bet I can't do that. Now let's see." He blew until the beautiful bubble grew and wavered and burst into thin air, and there was only a small colored rag in his hand. This was a fine game. They went on with it until Grandma came in and said, "Time for supper now. No, you can't blow balloons at the table. Tomorrow maybe." And it was all over.

The next day, instead of being given balloons, he was hustled out of bed early, bathed in warm soapy water and given a big breakfast of soft-boiled eggs with toast and jam and milk. His grandma came in to kiss him good morning. "And I hope you'll be a good boy and obey your teacher," she told him.

"What's teacher?" asked the little boy.

"Teacher is at school," said Grandma. "She'll tell you all sorts of things and you must do as she says."

Mama and Papa had talked a great deal about School, and how they must send him there. They had told him it was a fine place with all kinds of toys and other children to play with. He felt he knew about School. "I didn't know it was time, Grandma," he said. "Is it today?"

"It's this very minute," said Grandma. "I told you a week ago."

Old Janet came in with her bonnet on. It was a prickly looking bundle held with a black rubber band under her back hair. "Come on," she said. "This is my busy day." She wore a dead cat slung around her neck, its sharp ears bent over under her baggy chin.

The little boy was excited and wanted to run ahead. "Hold to my hand like I told you," said Old Janet. "Don't go running off like that and get yourself killed."

"I'm going to get killed, I'm going to get killed," sang the little boy, making a tune of his own.

"Don't say that, you give me the creeps," said Old Janet. "Hold to my hand now." She bent over and looked at him, not at his face but at something on his clothes. His eyes followed hers.

"I declare," said Old Janet, "I did forget. I was going to sew it up. I might have known. I *told* your grandma it would be that way from now on."

"What?" asked the little boy.

"Just look at yourself," said Old Janet crossly. He looked at himself. There was a little end of him showing through the slit in his short blue flannel trousers. The trousers came halfway to his knees above, and his socks came halfway to his knees below, and all winter long his knees were cold. He remembered now how cold his knees were in cold weather. And how sometimes he would have to put the part of him that came through the slit back again, because he was cold there too. He saw at once what was wrong, and tried to arrange himself, but his mittens got in the way. Janet said, "Stop that, you bad boy," and with a firm thumb she set him in order, at the same time reaching under his belt to pull down and fold his knit undershirt over his front.

"There now," she said, "try not to disgrace yourself today." He felt guilty and red all over, because he had something that showed when he was dressed that was not supposed to show then. The different women who bathed him always wrapped him quickly in towels and hurried him into his clothes, because they saw something about him he could not see for himself. They hurried him so he never had a chance to see whatever it was they saw, and though he looked at himself when his clothes were off, he could not find out what was wrong with him. Outside, in his clothes, he knew he looked like everybody else, but inside his clothes there was something bad the matter with him. It worried him and confused him and he wondered about it. The only people who never seemed to notice there was something wrong with him were Mommanpoppa. They never called him a bad boy, and all summer long they had taken all his clothes off and let him run in the sand beside a big ocean.

"Look at him, isn't he a love?" Mamma would say and Papa would look, and say, "He's got a back like a prize fighter." Uncle David was a prize fighter when he doubled up his mitts and said, "Come on, fellow."

Old Janet held him firmly and took long steps under her big rustling skirts. He did not like Old Janet's smell. It made him a little quivery in the stomach; it was just like wet chicken feathers.

School was easy. Teacher was a square-shaped woman with square short hair and short skirts. She got in the way sometimes, but not often. The people around him were his size; he didn't have always to be stretching his neck up to faces bent over him, and he could sit on the chairs without having to climb. All the children had names, like Frances and Evelyn and Agatha and Edward and Martin, and his own name was Stephen. He was not Mama's "Baby," nor Papa's "Old Man"; he was not Uncle David's "Fellow" or Grandma's "Darling," or even Old Janet's "Bad Boy." He was Stephen. He was learning to read, and to sing a tune to some strange-looking letters or marks written in chalk on a blackboard. You talked one kind of lettering, and you sang another. All the children talked and sang in turn, and then all together. Stephen thought it a fine game. He felt awake and happy. They had soft clay and paper and wires and squares of colors in tin boxes to play with, colored blocks to build houses with. Afterward they all danced in a big ring, and then they danced in pairs, boys with girls. Stephen danced with Frances, and Frances kept saying, "Now you just follow me." She was a little taller than he was, and her hair stood up in short, shiny curls, the color of an ash tray on Papa's desk. She would say, "You can't dance." "I can dance too," said Stephen, jumping around holding her hands, "I can, too, dance." He was certain of it. "*You* can't dance," he told Frances, "you can't dance at all."

Then they had to change partners, and when they came round again, Frances said, "I don't *like* the way you dance." This was different. He felt uneasy about it. He didn't jump quite so high when the phonograph record started going dumdiddy dumdiddy again. "Go ahead, Stephen, you're doing fine," said Teacher, waving her hands together very fast. The dance ended, and they all played "relaxing" for five minutes. They relaxed by swinging their arms back and forth, then rolling their heads round and round.

When Old Janet came for him he didn't want to go home. At lunch his grandma told him twice to keep his face out of his plate. "Is that what they teach you at school?" she asked. Uncle David was at home. "Here you are, fellow," he said and gave Stephen two balloons. "Thank you," said Stephen. He put the balloons in his pocket and forgot about them. "I told you that boy could learn something," said Uncle David to Grandma. "Hear him say 'thank you'?"

In the afternoon at school Teacher handed out big wads of clay and told the children to make something out of it. Anything they liked. Stephen decided to make a cat, like Mama's Meeow at home. He did not like Meeow, but he thought it would be easy to make a cat. He could not get the clay to work at all. It simply fell into one lump after another. So he stopped, wiped his hands on his pull-over, remembered his balloons and began blowing one.

"Look at Stephen's horse," said Frances. "Just look at it."

"It's not a horse, it's a cat," said Stephen. The other children gathered around. "It looks like a horse, a little," said Martin.

"It is a cat," said Stephen, stamping his foot, feeling his face turning hot. The other children all laughed and exclaimed over Stephen's cat that looked like a horse. Teacher came down among them. She sat usually at the top of the room before a big table covered with papers and playthings. She picked up Stephen's lump of clay and turned it round and examined it with her kind eyes. "Now, children," she said, "everybody has the right to make anything the way he pleases. If Stephen says this is a cat, it *is* a cat. Maybe you were thinking about a horse, Stephen?"

"It's a *cat,*" said Stephen. He was aching all over. He knew then he should have said at first, "Yes, it's a horse." Then they would have let him alone. They would never have known he was trying to make a cat. "It's Meeow," he said in a trembling voice, "but I forgot how she looks."

His balloon was perfectly flat. He started blowing it up again, trying not to cry. Then it was time to go home, and Old Janet came looking for him. While Teacher was talking to other grown-up people who came to take other children home, Frances said, "Give me your balloon; I haven't got a balloon." Stephen handed it to her. He was happy to give it. He reached in his pocket and took out the other. Happily, he gave her that one too. Frances took it, then handed it back. "Now you blow up one and I'll blow up the other, and let's have a race," she said. When their balloons were only half filled Old Janet took Stephen by the arm and said, "Come on here, this is my busy day."

Frances ran after them, calling, "Stephen, you give me back my balloon," and snatched it away. Stephen did not know whether he was surprised to find himself going away with Frances' balloon, or whether he was surprised to see her snatching it as if it really belonged to her. He was badly mixed up in his mind, and Old Janet was hauling him along. One thing he knew, he liked Frances, he was going to see her again tomorrow, and he was going to bring her more balloons.

That evening Stephen boxed awhile with his uncle David, and Uncle David gave him a beautiful orange. "Eat that," he said, "it's good for your health."

"Uncle David, may I have some more balloons?" asked Stephen.

"Well, what do you say first?" asked Uncle David, reaching for the box on the top bookshelf.

"Please," said Stephen.

"That's the word," said Uncle David. He brought out two balloons, a red and a yellow one. Stephen noticed for the first time they had letters on them, very small letters that grew taller and wider as the balloon grew rounder. "Now that's all, fellow," said Uncle David. "Don't ask for any more because that's all." He put the box back on the bookshelf, but not before Stephen had seen that the box was almost full of balloons. He didn't say a word, but went on blowing, and Uncle David blew also. Stephen thought it was the nicest game he had ever known.

He had only one left, the next day, but he took it to school and gave it to Frances. "There are a lot," he said, feeling very proud and warm; "I'll bring you a lot of them."

Frances blew it up until it made a beautiful bubble, and said, "Look, I want to show you something." She took a sharp-pointed stick they used in working the clay; she poked the balloon, and it exploded. "Look at that," she said.

"That's nothing," said Stephen, "I'll bring you some more."

After school, before Uncle David came home, while Grandma was resting, when Old Janet had given him his milk and told him to run away and not bother

her, Stephen dragged a chair to the bookshelf, stood upon it and reached into the box. He did not take three or four as he believed he intended; once his hands were upon them he seized what they could hold and jumped off the chair, hugging them to him. He stuffed them into his reefer pocket where they folded down and hardly made a lump.

He gave them all to Frances. There were so many, Frances gave most of them away to the other children. Stephen, flushed with his new joy, the lavish pleasure of giving presents, found almost at once still another happiness. Suddenly he was popular among the children; they invited him specially to join whatever games were up; they fell in at once with his own notions for play, and asked him what he would like to do next. They had festivals of blowing up the beautiful globes, fuller and rounder and thinner, changing as they went from deep color to lighter, paler tones, growing glassy thin, bubbly thin, then bursting with a thrilling loud noise like a toy pistol.

For the first time in his life Stephen had almost too much of something he wanted, and his head was so turned he forgot how this fullness came about, and no longer thought of it as a secret. The next day was Saturday, and Frances came to visit him with her nurse. The nurse and Old Janet sat in Old Janet's room drinking coffee and gossiping, and the children sat on the side porch blowing balloons. Stephen chose an apple-colored one and Frances a pale green one. Between them on the bench lay a tumbled heap of delights still to come.

"I once had a silver balloon," said Frances, "a beyootiful silver one, not round like these; it was a long one. But these are even nicer, I think," she added quickly, for she did want to be polite.

"When you get through with that one," said Stephen, gazing at her with the pure bliss of giving added to loving, "you can blow up a blue one and then a pink one and a yellow one and a purple one." He pushed the heap of limp objects toward her. Her clear-looking eyes, with fine little rays of brown in them like the spokes of a wheel, were full of approval for Stephen. "I wouldn't want to be greedy, though, and blow up all your balloons."

"There'll be plenty more left," said Stephen, and his heart rose under his thin ribs. He felt his ribs with his fingers and discovered with some surprise that they stopped somewhere in front, while Frances sat blowing balloons rather halfheartedly. The truth was, she was tired of balloons. After you blow six or seven your chest gets hollow and your lips feel puckery. She had been blowing balloons steadily for three days now. She had begun to hope they were giving out. "There's boxes and boxes more of them, Frances," said Stephen happily. "Millions more. I guess they'd last and last if we didn't blow too many every day."

Frances said somewhat timidly, "I tell you what. Let's rest awhile and fix some liquish water. Do you like liquish?"

"Yes, I do," said Stephen, "but I haven't got any."

"Couldn't we buy some?" asked Frances. "It's only a cent a stick, the nice rubbery, twisty kind. We can put it in a bottle with some water, and shake it and shake it, and it makes foam on top like soda pop and we can drink it. I'm kind of thirsty," she said in a small, weak voice. "Blowing balloons all the time makes you thirsty, I think."

Stephen, in silence, realized a dreadful truth and a numb feeling crept over him. He did not have a cent to buy licorice for Frances and she was tired of his balloons. This was the first real dismay of his whole life, and he aged at least a year in the next minute, huddled, with his deep, serious blue eyes focused down his nose in intense speculation. What could he do to please Frances that would not cost money? Only yesterday Uncle David had given him a nickel, and he had thrown it away on gumdrops. He regretted that nickel so bitterly his neck and forehead were damp. He was thirsty too.

"I tell you what," he said, brightening with a splendid idea, lamely trailing off on second thought, "I know something we can do, I'll—I . . ."

"I *am* thirsty," said Frances with gentle persistence. "I think I'm so thirsty maybe I'll have to go home." She did not leave the bench, though, but sat, turning her grieved mouth toward Stephen.

Stephen quivered with the terrors of the adventure before him, but he said boldly, "I'll make some lemonade. I'll get sugar and lemon and some ice and we'll have lemonade."

"Oh, I love lemonade," cried Frances. "I'd rather have lemonade than liquish."

"You stay right here," said Stephen, "and I'll get everything."

He ran around the house, and under Old Janet's window he heard the dry, chattering voices of the two old women whom he must outwit. He sneaked on tiptoe to the pantry, took a lemon lying there by itself, a handful of lump sugar and a china teapot, smooth, round, with flowers and leaves all over it. These he left on the kitchen table while he broke a piece of ice with a sharp metal pick he had been forbidden to touch. He put the ice in the pot, cut the lemon and squeezed it as well as he could—a lemon was tougher and more slippery than he had thought—and mixed sugar and water. He decided there was not enough sugar so he sneaked back and took another handful. He was back on the porch in an astonishingly short time, his face tight, his knees trembling, carrying iced lemonade to thirsty Frances with both his devoted hands.

A pace distant from her he stopped, literally stabbed through with a thought. Here he stood in broad daylight carrying a teapot with lemonade in it, and his grandma or Old Janet might walk through the door at any moment.

"Come on, Frances," he whispered loudly. "Let's go round to the back behind the rose bushes where it's shady." Frances leaped up and ran like a deer beside him, her face wise with knowledge of why they ran; Stephen ran stiffly, cherishing his teapot with clenched hands.

It was shady behind the rose bushes, and much safer. They sat side by side on the dampish ground, legs doubled under, drinking in turn from the slender spout. Stephen took his just share in large, cool, delicious swallows. When Frances drank she set her round pink mouth daintily to the spout and her throat beat steadily as a heart. Stephen was thinking he had really done something pretty nice for Frances. He did not know where his own happiness was; it was mixed with the sweet-sour taste in his mouth and a cool feeling in his bosom because Frances was there drinking his lemonade which he had got for her with great danger.

Frances said, "My, what big swallows you take," when his turn came next.

"No bigger than yours," he told her downrightly. "You take awfully big swallows."

"Well," said Frances, turning this criticism into an argument for her rightness about things, "that's the way to drink lemonade anyway." She peered into the teapot. There was quite a lot of lemonade left and she was beginning to feel she had enough. "Let's make up a game and see who can take the biggest swallows."

This was such a wonderful notion they grew reckless, tipping the spout into their opened mouths above their heads until lemonade welled up and ran over their chins in rills down their fronts. When they tired of this there was still lemonade left in the pot. They played first at giving the rose bush a drink and ended by baptizing it. "Name father son holygoat," shouted Stephen, pouring. At this sound Old Janet's face appeared over the low hedge, with the tan, disgusted-looking face of Frances' nurse hanging over her shoulder.

"Well, just as I thought," said Old Janet. "Just as I expected." The bag under her chin waggled.

"We were thirsty," he said; "we were awfully thirsty." Frances said nothing, but she gazed steadily at the toes of her shoes.

"Give me that teapot," said Old Janet, taking it with a rude snatch. "Just because you're thirsty is no reason," said Old Janet. "You can ask for things. You don't have to steal."

"We didn't steal," cried Frances suddenly. "We didn't. We didn't!"

"That's enough from you, missy," said her nurse. "Come straight out of there. You have nothing to do with this."

"Oh, I don't know," said Old Janet with a hard stare at Frances' nurse. "*He* never did such a thing before, by himself."

"Come on," said the nurse to Frances, "this is no place for you." She held Frances by the wrist and started walking away so fast Frances had to run to keep up. "Nobody can call *us* thieves and get away with it."

"You don't have to steal, even if others do," said Old Janet to Stephen, in a high carrying voice. "If you so much as pick up a lemon in somebody else's house you're a little thief." She lowered her voice then and said, "Now I'm going to tell your grandma and you'll see what you get."

"He went in the icebox and left it open," Janet told Grandma, "and he got into the lump sugar and spilt it all over the floor. Lumps everywhere underfoot. He dribbled water all over the clean kitchen floor, and he baptized the rose bush, blaspheming. And he took your Spode teapot."

"I didn't either," said Stephen loudly, trying to free his hand from Old Janet's big hard fist.

"Don't tell fibs," said Old Janet; "that's the last straw."

"Oh, dear," said Grandma. "He's not a baby any more." She shut the book she was reading and pulled the wet front of his pull-over toward her. "What's this sticky stuff on him?" she asked and straightened her glasses.

"Lemonade," said Old Janet. "He took the last lemon."

They were in the big dark room with the red curtains. Uncle David walked in from the room with the bookcases, holding a box in his uplifted hand. "Look here," he said to Stephen. "What's become of all my balloons?"

Stephen knew well that Uncle David was not really asking a question.

Stephen, sitting on a footstool at his grandma's knee, felt sleepy. He leaned heavily and wished he could put his head on her lap, but he might go to sleep, and it would be wrong to go to sleep while Uncle David was still talking. Uncle

David walked about the room with his hands in his pockets, talking to Grandma. Now and then he would walk over to a lamp and, leaning, peer into the top of the shade, winking in the light, as if he expected to find something there.

"It's simply in the blood, I told her," said Uncle David. "I told her she would simply have to come and get him, and keep him. She asked me if I meant to call him a thief and I said if she could think of a more exact word I'd be glad to hear it."

"You shouldn't have said that," commented Grandma calmly.

"Why not? She might as well know the facts. . . . I suppose he can't help it," said Uncle David, stopping now in front of Stephen and dropping his chin into his collar, "I shouldn't expect too much of him, but you can't begin too early—"

"The trouble is," said Grandma, and while she spoke she took Stephen by the chin and held it up so that he had to meet her eye; she talked steadily in a mournful tone, but Stephen could not understand. She ended, "It's not just about the balloons, of course."

"It *is* about the balloons," said Uncle David angrily, "because balloons now mean something worse later. But what can you expect? His father—well, it's in the blood. He—"

"That's your sister's husband you're talking about," said Grandma, "and there is no use making things worse. Besides, you don't really *know*."

"I *do* know," said Uncle David. And he talked again very fast, walking up and down. Stephen tried to understand, but the sounds were strange and floating just over his head. They were talking about his father, and they did not like him. Uncle David came over and stood above Stephen and Grandma. He hunched over them with a frowning face, a long, crooked shadow from him falling across them to the wall. To Stephen he looked like his father, and he shrank against his grandma's skirts.

"The question is, what to do with him now?" asked Uncle David. "If we keep him here, he'd just be a—I won't be bothered with him. Why can't they take care of their own child? That house is crazy. Too far gone already, I'm afraid. No training. No example."

"You're right, they must take him and keep him," said Grandma. She ran her hands over Stephen's head; tenderly she pinched the nape of his neck between thumb and forefinger. "You're your Grandma's darling," she told him, "and you've had a nice long visit, and now you're going home. Mama is coming for you in a few minutes. Won't that be nice?"

"I want my mama," said Stephen, whimpering, for his grandma's face frightened him. There was something wrong with her smile.

Uncle David sat down. "Come over here, fellow," he said, wagging a forefinger at Stephen. Stephen went over slowly, and Uncle David drew him between his wide knees in their loose, rough clothes. "You ought to be ashamed of yourself," he said, "stealing Uncle David's balloons when he had already given you so many."

"It wasn't that," said Grandma quickly. "Don't say that. It will make an impression—"

"I hope it does," said Uncle David in a louder voice; "I hope he remembers it all his life. If he belonged to me I'd give him a good thrashing."

Stephen felt his mouth, his chin, his whole face jerking. He opened his mouth to take a breath, and tears and noise burst from him. "Stop that, fellow, stop that," said Uncle David, shaking him gently by the shoulders, but Stephen could not stop. He drew his breath again and it came back in a howl. Old Janet came to the door.

"Bring me some cold water," called Grandma. There was a flurry, a commotion, a breath of cool air from the hall, the door slammed, and Stephen heard his mother's voice. His howl died away, his breath sobbed and fluttered, he turned his dimmed eyes and saw her standing there. His heart turned over within him and he bleated like a lamb, "Maaaaama," running toward her. Uncle David stood back as Mama swooped in and fell on her knees beside Stephen. She gathered him to her and stood up with him in her arms.

"What are you doing to my baby?" she asked Uncle David in a thickened voice. "I should never have let him come here. I should have known better—"

"You always should know better," said Uncle David, "and you never do. And you never will. You haven't got it here," he told her, tapping his forehead.

"David," said Grandma, "that's your—"

"Yes, I know, she's my sister," said Uncle David. "I know it. But if she must run away and marry a—"

"Shut up," said Mama.

"And bring more like him into the world, let her keep them at home. I say let her keep—"

Mama set Stephen on the floor and, holding him by the hand, she said to Grandma all in a rush as if she were reading something, "Good-by, Mother. This is the last time, really the last. I can't bear it any longer. Say good-by to Stephen; you'll never see him again. You let this happen. It's your fault. You know David was a coward and a bully and a self-righteous little beast all his life and you never crossed him in anything. You let him bully me all my life and you let him slander my husband and call my baby a thief, and now this is the end. . . . He calls my baby a thief over a few horrible little balloons because he doesn't like my husband. . . ."

She was panting and staring about from one to the other. They were all standing. Now Grandma said, "Go home, daughter. Go away, David. I'm sick of your quarreling. I've never had a day's peace or comfort from either of you. I'm sick of you both. Now let me alone and stop this noise. Go away," said Grandma in a wavering voice. She took out her handkerchief and wiped first one eye and then the other and said, "All this hate, hate—what is it for? . . . So this is the way it turns out. Well, let me alone."

"You and your little advertising balloons," said Mama to Uncle David. "The big honest businessman advertises with balloons and if he loses one he'll be ruined. And your beastly little moral notions . . ."

Grandma went to the door to meet Old Janet, who handed her a glass of water. Grandma drank it all, standing there.

"Is your husband coming for you, or are you going home by yourself?" she asked Mama.

"I'm driving myself," said Mama in a far-away voice as if her mind had wandered. "You know he wouldn't set foot in this house."

"I should think not," said Uncle David.

"Come on, Stephen darling," said Mama. "It's far past his bedtime," she said, to no one in particular. "Imagine keeping a baby up to torture him about a few miserable little bits of colored rubber." She smiled at Uncle David with both rows of teeth as she passed him on the way to the door, keeping between him and Stephen. "Ah, where would we be without high moral standards," she said, and then to Grandma, "Good night, Mother," in quite her usual voice. "I'll see you in a day or so."

"Yes, indeed," said Grandma cheerfully, coming out into the hall with Stephen and Mama. "Let me hear from you. Ring me up tomorrow. I hope you'll be feeling better."

"I feel very well now," said Mama brightly, laughing. She bent down and kissed Stephen. "Sleepy, darling? Papa's waiting to see you. Don't go to sleep until you've kissed your papa good night."

Stephen woke with a sharp jerk. He raised his head and put out his chin a little. "I don't want to go home," he said, "I want to go to school. I don't want to see Papa, I don't like him."

Mama laid her palm over his mouth softly. "Darling, don't."

Uncle David put his head out with a kind of snort. "There you are," he said. "There you've got a statement from headquarters."

Mama opened the door and ran, almost carrying Stephen. She ran across the sidewalk, jerking open the car door and dragging Stephen in after her. She spun the car around and dashed forward so sharply Stephen was almost flung out of the seat. He sat braced then with all his might, hands digging into the cushions. The car speeded up and the trees and houses whizzed by all flattened out. Stephen began suddenly to sing to himself, a quiet, inside song so Mama would not hear. He sang his new secret; it was a comfortable, sleepy song: "I hate Papa, I hate Mama, I hate Grandma, I hate Uncle David, I hate Old Janet, I hate Marjory, I hate Papa, I hate Mama . . ."

His head bobbed, leaned, came to rest on Mama's knee, eyes closed. Mama drew him closer and slowed down, driving with one hand.

Why is the story titled *The Downward Path to Wisdom?* What is the "wisdom"? Why is the path to it "downward"? Must it be?

How do Stephen's parents exploit him by using him as a pawn in their marital relationship? For example, after lying comfortably between his parents, "like a bear cub in a warm litter," Stephen finds himself suddenly on the floor again, because he was spilling peanut shells all over his mother. When she tells her husband to "put him out," is it for Stephen's benefit, so that through the discipline of deprivation he will learn not to spill peanut shells in bed? Or is it for her own comfort? Or is it to punish her husband indirectly for bringing the peanuts when she had asked "dozens of times" that he not bring Stephen things to eat?

Sexual attitudes are not always communicated through direct statement: Adult conversational fragments—presumably of no interest to or over the head of the child—facial expressions, tones of voice, timing of responses, and the subtle repertoire of parental glances and gestures, can unexpectedly convey to the child through "body English," significant messages which bear directly on his sexual attitudes and emotional growth. Observe the body language by which nonverbal messages are imparted to a four-year-old:

... his back was turned when he said that.

She was looking at the back of Papa's head and her eyes were almost black.

... he saw the big hand raised above him.

... her face terribly near, red and frowning under a stiff white band. . . .

... he had seen her clenching her fists and stamping in one spot. . . .

... they examined him with crinkled eyes without any expression that he could see.

What other impressions of the world does Stephen receive through sight? How do they differ from those which a child who was a product of a tender, loving home might expect?

Even without words, what does Stephen realize from such auditory impressions as:

There was silence for a moment.

... she told him in a low voice.

... their voices rose and fell and shot up to a point and crashed and rolled like the two tomcats who fought at night.

What is ironic about Grandma's admonition to Uncle David: "Don't say that. It will make an impression—"?

Why does Stephen not only refuse breakfast, but sit and stir it? Why does he like seeing it spill? Why does he feel better after bringing his full cereal dish down with a crash on the table?

How does Old Janet and "the different women who bathed him and always wrapped him quickly in towels and hurried him into his clothes" create—out of their own superstitions, guilts, and fears—similar and unnecessary ones in Stephen?

How do Uncle David and Grandma also use Stephen for their own advantage and emotional reasons? How is he used by Old Janet to cover up her own lack of responsibility? How does Marjory take out her hostility on the innocent four-year-old?

Why does Stephen like school? How does it give him a sense of security he has never known?

What is significant about the statement:

All the children had names . . . and his own name was Stephen. He was not Mama's "Baby," nor Papa's "Old Man"; he was not Uncle David's "Fellow" or Grandma's "Darling," or even Old Janet's "Bad Boy." He was Stephen.

Much can happen to Stephen in eleven years to make speculations about him as an adolescent in large part guesswork. But recognizing the importance of the formative years of early childhood (the period in which basic attitudes are set), try to imagine Stephen at age fifteen. What conditioning factors depicted in *The Downward Path to Wisdom* forecast what he might be like?

Consider, for example, what sort of disposition or temperament he might have, or what his academic record might be: Would he be more likely to be an honor student, or the type described by teachers as "not living up to potential"? How much confidence do you think he would have in teachers? In adults in general? Why? Do you think he would go out for team sports? Many extracurriculars? Would you expect him to be popular with other males? What might his attitude toward girls be? What could be his feeling about his genitals? About masturbation? About his own sexual adequacy?

The Mob and the Mass Media

Like those of four-year-old Stephen in *The Downward Path to Wisdom,* the attitudes of five-year-old Richard in Paul Horgan's *The Dawn of Hate,* a chapter from *Things as They Are,* are learned ones.

From adults who over-react and who interpret for him, rather than from his own experience, Richard not only acquires a sexual prejudice but also bears out the author's generalization that we become "subject to what we are taught to hate."

The Dawn of Hate

PAUL HORGAN

[Anna, our cook and laundress,] began to sing gently one of her hooting tunes. She was holding one of my hands while with the other I cradled my ship. It was meant to be an ocean greyhound. I could not wait to learn whether it would float on an even keel.

We were not even half-way to the Circle when Anna stopped and halted me.

"What's the matter?" I asked.

"Never mind."

She was peering up the street at a figure which came idling into view along the sidewalk on our side of the street. It was a man. He moved slowly, with little steps that hardly advanced his progress. His body was oddly in motion, almost as if he were dancing in his shoes with tiny movements. From a distance I could see that he was dressed in old grey clothes, very shabby, which were too large for him.

"Is it a tramp?" I asked, with a leap of interest and fright—for the word tramp was one to strike terror in the women of our household, who took great precautions against tramps when my father was not at home.

"I think so. Come," said Anna, "we will cross the street and go on the other walk."

She led me abruptly across and quickened her pace. Looking proud and unafraid in case the man really was a tramp, she lifted her head and began to exhibit her idea of what a grand lady was like, striding daintily yet hugely, and making angry little tosses of her head. She picked up with thumb and one finger a fold of her dress and held it athwart her hip. She seemed to say, I'll show him, that tramp, I'll dare him to ask me for a nickel for a glass of beer, he wouldn't dare try anything, me with my boy along here with me, going to sail a boat in Yates Circle, where there's often *a policeman* around to see that the children don't fall in the water and drowned theirself!

I lagged, staring at the tramp with fascination as we approached to pass each other on opposite sides of the street. Anna refused even to see him, but kept up her lofty plan to pass him by as if he did not exist.

Now I could see him clearly and intimately. He had a wide grin on his unshaven grey face with red cheeks and nose and bleached-looking places about the eyes. He blinked at us and bowed in a friendly way. Shabby, drifting, uncertain, he seemed to be reaching for us— for me, I was sure, since all life was directed toward me. There was an ingratiating gaiety about him, and when he left his sidewalk to come toward us, in his shambling little dance, I saw something else which puzzled me.

He nodded and smiled, and I thought he nodded and smiled at me. When he was halfway across the street toward us, keeping pace now with Anna's angry, ladylike advance—her eyes forward and her head up—I tugged at her and asked,

"Anna, what's he doing?"

At the sound of my voice the tramp laughed weakly in a beery little cough, and ducked his head, and smiled and smiled, hungry for response. I then saw how his clothes were disarrayed in what was later called indecent exposure.

"Anna!" I insisted.

"Never mind, come along," she said with a toss of her head as though she wore plumes.

"But he wants to show me something," I protested.

At this, she glanced aside at the tramp, who presented himself and his antic lewdness hilariously at her.

It took her only that glance to understand.

"Holy God in heaven!" she cried, and turned and in a single sweep of her heavy arm swung me all but through the air toward home, causing me to drop my boat. At a half-run she dragged me along the walk toward our house.

"My boat! My boat!" I kept crying, but she paid no heed, only muttering and groaning the names of saints, giving forth holy ejaculations. We came breathless to the house, where she slammed and locked the front door behind us, and ran through to the kitchen door and locked that too. Hearing this, and the sound of my angry sobs at the loss of my new ship, my mother came downstairs laughing, and saying,

"Slam, slam, cry, cry—what on earth is happening? Why are you home so soon?"

"My boat!" I stormed, running against her and angrily hugging her hips and butting my head against her waist. "She made me lose it! We didn't even sail it once!"

"Anna?" called my mother through the hall.

Anna loomed in the pantry door and beckoned to my mother.

"Don't bring him," Anna said, raising her chin at me. "I must tell you."

The manly voice which Anna now used as she caught her breath conveyed to my mother an air of something ominous.

"Then, Richard," said my mother, "take your coat off and put it away, and go upstairs and wash your face. You are a fright. Wait for me in your room."

Unwillingly I took the stairs one step at a time, and as the pantry door closed after my mother, I heard in Anna's voice the words "tramp" and "crazy drunk" and then a grand, long, running line of narrative blurred away from detail by the shut door, punctuated by little screams of shock and horror from my mother.

My room was at the front of the house next to the bedroom of my father and mother. I sat in the window seat looking out, mourning for my ship, which lay broken and worthless up the street, and then I saw the tramp, of whom I still thought as my funny new friend, come idling into view along the sidewalk. Now restored to modesty, he was eating with a sad air a crust-end of a sandwich. He leaned against a tree and rubbed his back against the bark like an old dog. He nodded right and left at the afternoon in general. He was a small man, I now saw, and he seemed sleepy and lonesome. In another moment, he slid gently against the tree trunk to the ground, and fastidiously searched in his loose pockets for something, and brought it forth—it was a pint bottle, empty. He raised it to his mouth. Nothing to drink ran forth, and with a little heave, he threw the empty bottle up on the lawn of the house next door, and then he fell sideways into a deep sleep on the ground, resembling a bundle of old clothes ready for the poor.

The voices downstairs went on, now heavy and baleful, now light and firm. I heard my mother use the telephone—she was calling my father at his office. Then a long silence fell in the house, while I wondered. In a quarter of an hour I heard a thrilling sound of clanging gongs come down the street, mixed with the rattle of hooves on the pavement. I leaned to see, and sure enough, it was a police patrol wagon, all shiny black with big gold lettering on the sides of the van.

The driver slowed down before our house to let two policemen, in their long-coated blue uniforms and domed grey helmets, and carrying their gleaming clubs, jump down from the rear door. I greatly admired the police for their uniforms, their horses, and their power. Anna had threatened me with their authority many times when I misbehaved. I watched now with abstracted excitement as they went to the tree where the tramp lay asleep. They took him up and shook him awake.

With an air of courtesy, he awoke and smiled his dusty, weak-necked smile at the two policemen.

For being smiled at by a degenerate, one of the policemen struck him in the face with his immense open hand.

A look of bewilderment came into the tramp's face.

The other policeman gave an order to hold the tramp, and then ran up to our front door and jabbed at the bell. In a moment Anna was taken forth to confront the man whom she had reported as a committer of public outrage. I saw her nod when the police pointed at the tramp. She identified him, though in her agitated modesty she could only look at him over her crooked elbow.

But this was enough for the police. They told her to go, she returned to the porch, and I heard her heavy steps running for the door and then the door slam behind her.

At the street curbing, while I knelt up on the window seat to see, one policeman knocked the tramp to the ground with his club and the other kicked him in the belly to make him stand up again. He tried to become a ball like a bear asleep in the zoo against the cold of winter, but they pulled his arms away from his head and between their hands they punched his head back and forth.

They knocked his knees down from protecting his loins and kicked him there until he screamed silently. Suddenly he went to the ground of his own weight. The policemen looked at each other and in silent, expert accord took him up between them and carried him to the patrol wagon, threw him in the door, climbed in after him, and the wagon got up and away from a starting trot. I watched until they were all gone. My thoughts were slow, separate, and innocent.

Why did they beat him so?

Did they arrest him just because he was a tramp?

Or because he didn't look like everybody else?

Or because he was a "crazy-drunk?"

Or for sleeping under somebody else's tree?

Or for how he had presented himself to me and Anna?

Why didn't they want him to do what he had done up the street?

Didn't they know it hurt when they kicked and beat someone else?

In any case, it was an immense event, full of excitement and mystery, and I fell asleep on the window seat from the sheer emotion of it. When I awoke it was to find the barricade of our house lifted, and my mother, pretending that nothing whatever had happened, standing by me to say that it was time for me to get ready for supper.

"Daddy will be home soon, and he will come and see you when you have your tray."

But he did not.

I heard him come in, and then I heard the famous sounds of private, grown-up discussion in the living room, with the sliding doors closed. Anna was summoned to give all over again her account of what had happened, while my father listened in silence, and my mother made little supplementary exclamations.

The mystery grew for me as all such attention was paid to it, and it became complete when my father ran upstairs at last to put me to bed. There was something stern and righteous in his air. I understood that we had all survived a dreadful danger, though of what nature I was not sure.

"Well, Doc," he said, "it was quite a day. Sit down here on my knee and listen to me for a minute."

He pretended to knock me out with a fisted blow to my chin, and he smiled and scowled at the same moment. In his dark blue eyes there was a light like that of retained tears, as he mourned for the presence of evil in the world and the tender vulnerability of innocence. Trying his best to resolve for us all the event of the afternoon, he said,

"Doc?"

"Yes, Daddy."

"Promise me something."

"Yes, Daddy."

"Promise me to forget absolutely everything that happened this afternoon, with that tramp. Will you?"

"Yes."

"We must never keep thoughts about those things"—(what things?)—"in our heads. God does not want us to. When we see something terrible that

happens near us we must get away and forget it as fast as we can. Do you understand?"

"Yes."

"Good."

"You mean," I asked, "what the policeman did to the man?"

"No, no, I mean what the man did. He was crazy and he was drunk and
nobody else acts that way. Don't think other men are like that. They don't go
around in public that way."

"Was he a bad man?"

"Oh, yes. A very bad man. But forget him. Promise?"

"Yes."

"He can't scare you again if you forget him, you see."

"He didn't scare me. He scared Anna."

"Well, then, Doc, it is because you didn't understand." He set me down and
stood up. "All right, now? We won't have a thing to do again about it?"

"No."

"Good. Then up comes the young giant and the old giant will take him to
his castle for the night!"

And he swung me to his shoulders and walking hunchily and with great
heavy spread steps the way giants walked he took me to my bed across the room
and undressed me and put my pajamas on me and laid me down and kissed my
forehead and said. "We'll leave just a crack," and went to the door and left it
open just a crack so the upstairs hall light would stand like a golden lance of
safety all night long between me and the dark, and went downstairs to dine with
my mother. Their voices grew easier as the minutes passed and faded into sleep.

But the very first thing I thought of when I awoke was the tramp, and the
more I said to myself that I had promised to forget him and all of it, the more
I remembered. During the morning, when Anna was in the basement laundry,
I went down to see her.

"Anna, why was the tramp a bad man?"

"You are not to talk about it."

"But he didn't do anything!"

"Oh, God," she said, reviving her sense of shock with hushed pleasure.

"He was trying to make friends with me. He was doing something funny,
but—".

"Don't you know," she asked in a hoarse whisper, "what he was doing?"

"No, I don't."

She pointed to my groin.

"There, and all like that," she moaned, "and it was a terrible sin he committed, doing that, and doing it to a lady and a little boy, and Hell don't have
fires enough to punish him for what he did!"

"It doesn't?"

"Not fires enough!"

I stared at her. Her tired, sad, grey bulk was alive with some glory of rage,
some fullness of life, and suddenly I knew for the first time in my years what
it was she and all the others in the house had been talking about. From I could
not know where, the knowledge of new sins, and their power, dawned within
me, and they seemed to reside just there where Anna had pointed.

I began to jig up and down.

"Anna!" I cried, "He was a bad man, my father said he was! He was bad!"

"Well," she said with the massive placidity of vested virtue, "why do you suppose I dragged you away from seeing such a thing, and why do you suppose your Máma called your Pápa, and he called the police station, and they sent a patrol wagon for the man? Well, I know, and you know, now."

"The police beat him!" I cried exultantly.

"I saw," she said. "Nothing they could do to him would be too much."

How could I ever have liked the tramp, or have felt sorry for him?

"Bash!" I exclaimed, imitating the blows of the police, "Blong!"

"Run along now, and don't think any more about it, it is all over."

But my interest was at a high pitch since I knew how to think about the affair, and I ran next door to see my friend Tom Deterson, who was my age, and with whom I exchanged secrets.

"Did you hear about the tramp?" I asked out of breath.

"No," said Tom. "What tramp?"

I had the rich opportunity, then, to tell him everything—all that I had seen and heard and was supposed to forget. Tom and I were in the old carriage house at the foot of his yard. Nothing was kept there but the discards of the Deterson household. It made a fine playhouse, for it was removed, musty, dim, and private. As I told him what I knew, we sat on an old ruined sofa whose springs sagged into view below. Its cushions were awry and stained.

Tom's eyes were huge in his flushed, thin little face. He had curly hair and jangling nerves. He was never at rest. He was like a hot-nosed, insistent puppy climbing against all objects and persons and mysteries with an assumption of universal good will. At that time he was my best friend.

When I reached the most dreadful part of my story, I showed in pantomime what the tramp kept doing. Tom stared and jiggled as if he saw the actuality instead of a mockery of the scandal.

"What for?" he asked.

"I don't know. But he was crazy-drunk. They all do it. You know what?"

"No. What."

"He was a bad man."

"He was?"

"Yes, he was. My father said so, and Anna said so, and the police took him away."

"What did they do?"

"I'll show you what they did."

I seized an old split cushion from the sofa and threw it on the floor of the carriage house and I began to kick it.

"This is what they did!" I cried in heightening excitement. I picked up the cushion and punched it and threw it to Tom. He caught it and punched it and his eyes fired with power and purpose, and he threw the cushion down and he kicked it, and I kicked it again, and then we found some old thin brass curtain rods on the floor and we took these up and with them whipped the cushion.

"I'll tell you what I would do to that tramp!" I shouted. "I would beat him and push him until all his stuffing came out, and I would hit him"—and I did—"and I would kick him"—and I did—"and I would burn him in hell with all the fire that all the fire engines can't put out!"

"I have some matches!" cried Tom.

"Get them!"

He dug them from under the upholstery at the arm of the sofa and he lit a match and touched it to the split cushion where its dismal cotton stuffing showed through. It took on a feeble flame, making heavy white smoke. Exalted, we danced about the victim, telling each other to kick him, to whip him, to burn him. Suddenly the cushion made a spurt of fire and scared us. We had more fire than we expected.

"Say!" shouted Tom in a changed voice.

"Yes, yes, put it out!" I called.

He began to stamp with his flat sandalled feet at the burning corner of the cushion, but without much effect.

"Danged old tramp!" he said, "doing that!"

The cotton stuffing made little explosions with flying sparks.

"I know what," I said, "we can put out the fire—let's both of us—" and seeing what I did, Tom did the same, and with a sense of high glee, triumph, and even carnal fulfillment, we made our water together over the cushion and quelled the flame. The fire in the cushion guttered down into little worms of crinkling coal which finally expired yielding up a few last threads of noisome smoke.

"There!" said Tom.

"Yes, I said.

We made ourselves proper again as passion gave way to shame. We kicked the cushion against the brick wall behind the sofa and went out into the unknowing, cool, golden October morning.

This loss of innocence was not in seeing what I saw, but in hearing what I was told about it—for we are subject to what we are taught to hate.

Exhibitionism, or indecent exposure, is illustrated in **The Dawn of Hate** by a tramp in disarrayed clothes who exposes his genitals in a public place. What satisfaction might the exhibitionist derive from his behavior? Why?

Is exhibitionism restricted to males?

Is an exhibitionist dangerous? Is the indecent exposure likely to lead to more direct sexual advances?

Prejudice is acquired, not inherited. Consider the way in which the innocent narrator sees the exhibitionist:

He blinked at us and bowed in a friendly way. . . . There was an ingratiating gaiety about him. . . . my funny new friend. . . . he was eating with a sad air . . . . he seemed sleepy and lonesome. . . . with an air of courtesy he awoke and smiled his dusty, weak-necked smile at the policemen. For being smiled at by a degenerate, one of the policemen struck him in the face with his immense open hand. A look of bewilderment came into the tramp's face.

In what ways might the naïve five-year-old's perspective be said to be more sensitive, perceptive and "true" than the adults' attitude?

The direct and indirect instructional methods of sex education used by Richard's parents in explaining this particular event are two-fold:

THE SHUT-DOOR APPROACH

. . . as the pantry door closed after my mother, I heard in Anna's voice the words "tramp" and "crazy drunk," and then a grand, long, running line of narrative blurred away from detail by the shut door, punctuated by little screams of shock and horror from my mother.

. . . then I heard the famous sounds of private, grown-up discussion in the living room, with the sliding doors closed.

THE EVASIVE APPROACH

When I awoke it was to find the barricade of our house lifted, and my mother, pretending that nothing whatever had happened, standing by me to say that it was time for me to get ready for supper.

"Promise me to forget absolutely everything that happened this afternoon, with that tramp. . . . We must never keep thoughts about those things" —(what things?)—"in our heads. God does not want us to. When we see something terrible that happens near us we must get away and forget it as fast as we can."

How do both approaches, although well-intentioned, prove ironically to have exactly the reverse effect from the intended one?

His fundamental question still unanswered, Richard asks "Anna, why was the tramp a bad man?" What criticisms might be made of her explanation? What might have been told Richard in order to avoid some of Anna's negative effects?

Why did Richard and his friend Tom urinate on the fire? How is urinating on the fire connected with "carnal fulfillment"?

Are there other areas of sexuality where young people are vulnerable to adult pressures and overreactions? Instances where again it could be said:

[the] loss of innocence was not in seeing what I saw, but in hearing what I was told about it. . . .

In our society there are universally widespread and incompatible attitudes toward sexual behavior, some of them inconsistent in themselves:

If we ask . . . what is acceptable public behavior in the neighborhoods or with the neighbors, the confusion is baffling. There are islands of contradictory practice, even though these may have the identical Culture and almost the same Thought. Kids masturbating may be smiled on or ignored, or they may be barred from one's home, or they may be arrested as delinquent. Among the boys themselves, up to the age of thirteen mutual masturbation is a wicked thrill, but after thirteen it is queer and absolutely to be inhibited. Adolescent couples must pet or it is felt that something is wrong with them; but "how far?" Sometimes they may copulate, if they can get away with it; or they absolutely must not. You may admire and speak to strange girls on the street, it is flattering and shows spirit; or you may not, it is rude and threatening. But if you whistle at them while you huddle in your own group, that's bully. You may pet in public like the French; you may not pet in public, it's disgusting; you may on the beach but not on the grass. Among the boys, to boast of actual or invented prowess is acceptable, but to speak soberly of a love affair or a sexual problem in order to be understood is strictly taboo; it is more acceptable among girls. It is assumed that older teen-agers are experienced and sophisticated, but they are legal minors who must not be corrupted. More important, any relation between an older teen-aged girl and a man even in his twenties, or between an older teen-aged boy and an experienced woman, is shocking or ludicrous, though this is the staple of sexual education among the civilized.

In this tangle of incompatible and inconsistent standards, one strand is sure and predictable: that the law will judge by the most out-of-date, senseless, and unpsychological convention, even though it is against the consensus of almost every family in the neighborhood and the confessional attitude of the parish priest. They will arrest you for nude bathing a mile away on a lonely beach. (But this tendency to maintain the moral-obsolete is, of course, inevitable in our kind of democracy. A legislator may believe what he pleases, but how can he publicly propose the repeal of a statute against sin?) [13]

To what extent does the comment on incompatible and inconsistent sexual attitudes apply to *The Dawn of Hate?*

RELATED QUESTIONS

Which of the other selections you have read illustrate the "tangle of incompatible and inconsistent standards"?

Would you consider the behavior of George in *Through the First Gate* (p. 31), or the tanned blonde on the subway in *The Once-Over* (p. 74), or Richard and Tom in *The Dawn of Hate* to be exhibitionistic? Why, or why not?

The family is one of the smaller units of "**They**" forces which the growing "**I**" encounters. The mob, or the mass, often so willing to 'lend its ears', can be a carrier of public prejudice—both infectious and contagious—with tragic consequences for individuals like Wing Biddlebaum, "forever frightened and beset by a ghostly band of doubts" in Sherwood Anderson's short story *Hands.*

Hands

SHERWOOD ANDERSON

Upon the half decayed veranda of a small frame house that stood near the edge of a ravine near the town of Winesburg, Ohio, a fat little old man walked nervously up and down. Across a long field that has been seeded for clover but that had produced only a dense crop of yellow mustard weeds, he could see the public highway along which went a wagon filled with berry pickers returning from the fields. The berry pickers, youths and maidens, laughed and shouted boisterously. A boy clad in a blue shirt leaped from the wagon and attempted to drag after him one of the maidens who screamed and protested shrilly. The feet of the boy in the road kicked up a cloud of dust that floated across the face of the departing sun. Over the long field came a thin girlish voice. "Oh, you Wing Biddlebaum, comb your hair, it's falling into your eyes," commanded the voice to the man, who was bald and whose nervous little hands fiddled about the bare white forehead as though arranging a mass of tangled locks.

Wing Biddlebaum, forever frightened and beset by a ghostly band of doubts, did not think of himself as in any way a part of the life of the town where he had lived for twenty years. Among all the people of Winesburg but one had come close to him. With George Willard, son of Tom Willard, the proprietor of the new Willard House, he had formed something like a friendship. George Willard was the reporter on the *Winesburg Eagle* and sometimes in the evenings he walked out along the highway to Wing Biddlebaum's house. Now as the old man walked up and down on the veranda, his hands moving nervously about, he was hoping that George Willard would come and spend the evening with him. After the wagon containing the berry pickers had passed, he went across the field through the tall mustard weeds and climbing a rail fence peered anxiously along the road to the town. For a moment he stood thus, rubbing his hands together and looking up and down the road, and then, fear overcoming him, ran back to walk again upon the porch on his own house.

In the presence of George Willard, Wing Biddlebaum, who for twenty years had been the town mystery, lost something of his timidity, and his shadowy personality, submerged in a sea of doubts, came forth to look at the world. With the young reporter at his side, he ventured in the light of day into Main Street or strode up and down on the rickety front porch of his own house, talking excitedly. The voice that had been low and trembling became shrill and loud. The bent figure straightened. With a kind of wriggle, like a fish returned to the brook by the fisherman, Biddlebaum the silent began to talk, striving to put into words the ideas that had been accumulated by his mind during long years of silence.

Wing Biddlebaum talked much with his hands. The slender expressive fingers, forever active, forever striving to conceal themselves in his pockets or behind his back, came forth and became the piston rods of his machinery of expression.

The story of Wing Biddlebaum is a story of hands. Their restless activity, like unto the beating of the wings of an imprisoned bird, had given him his name. Some obscure poet of the town had thought of it. The hands alarmed their owner. He wanted to keep them hidden away and looked with amazement at the quiet inexpressive hands of other men who worked beside him in the fields, or passed, driving sleepy teams on country roads.

When he talked to George Willard, Wing Biddlebaum closed his fists and beat with them upon a table or on the walls of his house. The action made him more comfortable. If the desire to talk came to him when the two were walking in the fields, he sought out a stump or the top board of a fence and with his hands pounding busily talked with renewed ease.

The story of Wing Biddlebaum's hands is worth a book in itself. Sympathetically set forth it would tap many strange, beautiful qualities in obscure men. It is a job for a poet. In Winesburg the hands had attracted attention merely because of their activity. With them Wing Biddlebaum had picked as high as a hundred and forty quarts of strawberries in a day. They became his distinguishing feature, the source of his fame. Also they made more grotesque an already grotesque and elusive individuality. Winesburg was proud of the hands of Wing Biddlebaum in the same spirit in which it was proud of Banker White's new stone house and Wesley Moyer's bay stallion, Tony Tip, that had won the two-fifteen trot at the fall races in Cleveland.

As for George Willard, he had many times wanted to ask about the hands. At times an almost overwhelming curiosity had taken hold of him. He felt that there must be a reason for their strange activity and their inclination to keep hidden away and only growing respect for Wing Biddlebaum kept him from blurting out the questions that were often in his mind.

Once he had been on the point of asking. The two were walking in the fields on a summer afternoon and had stopped to sit upon a grassy bank. All afternoon Wing Biddlebaum had talked as one inspired. By a fence he had stopped and beating like a giant woodpecker upon the top board had shouted at George Willard, condemning his tendency to be too much influenced by the people about him. "You are destroying yourself," he cried. "You have the inclination to be alone and to dream and you are afraid of dreams. You want to be like others in town here. You hear them talk and you try to imitate them."

On the grassy bank Wing Biddlebaum had tried again to drive his point home. His voice became soft and reminiscent, and with a sigh of contentment he launched into a long rambling talk, speaking as one lost in a dream.

Out of the dream Wing Biddlebaum made a picture for George Willard. In the picture men lived again in a kind of pastoral golden age. Across a green open country came clean-limbed young men, some afoot, some mounted upon horses. In crowds the young men came to gather about the feet of an old man who sat beneath a tree in a tiny garden and who talked to them.

Wing Biddlebaum became wholly inspired. For once he forgot the hands. Slowly they stole forth and lay upon George Willard's shoulders. Something new and bold came into the voice that talked. "You must try to forget all you have learned," said the old man. "You must begin to dream. From this time on you must shut your ears to the roaring of the voices."

Pausing in his speech, Wing Biddlebaum looked long and earnestly at George Willard. His eyes glowed. Again he raised the hands to caress the boy and then a look of horror swept over his face.

With a convulsive movement of his body, Wing Biddlebaum sprang to his feet and thrust his hands deep into his trousers pockets. Tears came to his eyes. "I must be getting along home. I can talk no more with you," he said nervously.

Without looking back, the old man had hurried down the hillside and across a meadow, leaving George Willard perplexed and frightened upon the grassy slope. With a shiver of dread the boy arose and went along the road toward town. "I'll not ask him about his hands," he thought, touched by the memory of the terror he had seen in the man's eyes. "There's something wrong, but I don't want to know what it is. His hands have something to do with his fear of me and of everyone."

And George Willard was right. Let us look briefly into the story of the hands. Perhaps our talking of them will arouse the poet who will tell the hidden wonder story of the influence for which the hands were but fluttering pennants of promise.

In his youth Wing Biddlebaum had been a schoolteacher in a town in Pennsylvania. He was not then known as Wing Biddlebaum, but went by the less euphonic name of Adolph Myers. As Adolph Myers he was much loved by the boys of his school.

Adolph Myers was meant by nature to be a teacher of youth. He was one of those rare, little-understood men who rule by a power so gentle that it passes as a lovable weakness. In their feeling for the boys under their charge such men are not unlike the finer sort of women in their love of men.

And yet that is but crudely stated. It needs the poet there. With the boys of his school, Adolph Myers had walked in the evening or had sat talking until dusk upon the schoolhouse steps lost in a kind of dream. Here and there went his hands, caressing the shoulders of the boys, playing about the tousled heads. As he talked his voice became soft and musical. There was a caress in that also. In a way the voice and the hands, the stroking of the shoulders and the touching of the hair was a part of the schoolmaster's effort to carry a dream into the young minds. By the caress that was in his fingers he expressed himself. He was one of those men in whom the force that creates life is diffused, not centralized. Under the caress of his hands doubt and disbelief went out of the minds of the boys and they began also to dream.

And then the tragedy. A half-witted boy of the school became enamored of the young master. In his bed at night he imagined unspeakable things and in the morning went forth to tell his dreams as facts. Strange, hideous accusations fell from his loose-hung lips. Through the Pennsylvania town went a shiver. Hidden, shadowy doubts that had been in men's minds concerning Adolph Myers were galvanized into beliefs.

The tragedy did not linger. Trembling lads were jerked out of bed and questioned. "He put his arms about me," said one. "His fingers were always playing in my hair," said another.

One afternoon a man of the town, Henry Bradford, who kept a saloon, came to the schoolhouse door. Calling Adolph Myers into the school yard he began to beat him with his fists. As his hard knuckles beat down into the frightened face of the schoolmaster, his wrath became more and more terrible. Screaming with dismay, the children ran here and there like disturbed insects. "I'll teach you to put your hands on my boy, you beast," roared the saloon keeper, who, tired of beating the master, had begun to kick him about the yard.

Adolph Myers was driven from the Pennsylvania town in the night. With lanterns in their hands a dozen men came to the door of the house where he lived alone and commanded that he dress and come forth. It was raining and one of the men had a rope in his hands. They had intended to hang the schoolmaster, but something in his figure, so small, white, and pitiful, touched their hearts and they let him escape. As he ran away into the darkness they repented of their weakness and ran after him, swearing and throwing sticks and great balls of soft mud at the figure that screamed and ran faster and faster into the darkness.

For twenty years Adolph Myers had lived alone in Winesburg. He was but forty but looked sixty-five. The name of Biddlebaum he got from a box of goods seen at a freight station as he hurried through an eastern Ohio town. He had an aunt in Winesburg, a black-toothed old woman who raised chickens, and with her he lived until she died. He had been ill for a year after the experience in Pennsylvania, and after his recovery worked as a day laborer in the fields, going timidly about and striving to conceal his hands. Although he did not understand what had happened he felt that the hands must be to blame. Again and again the fathers of the boys had talked of the hands. "Keep your hands to yourself," the saloon keeper had roared, dancing with fury in the schoolhouse yard.

Upon the veranda of his house by the ravine Wing Biddlebaum continued to walk up and down until the sun had disappeared and the road beyond the field was lost in the gray shadows. Going into his house he cut slices of bread and spread honey upon them. When the rumble of the evening train that took away the express cars loaded with the day's harvest of berries had passed and restored the silence of the summer night, he went again to walk upon the veranda. In the darkness he could not see the hands and they became quiet. Although he still hungered for the presence of the boy, who was the medium through which he expressed his love of man, the hunger became again a part of his loneliness and his waiting. Lighting a lamp, Wing Biddlebaum washed the few dishes soiled by his simple meal and, setting up a folding cot by the screen door that led to the porch, prepared to undress for the night. A few stray white bread crumbs lay on the cleanly washed floor by the table; putting the lamp upon a low stool he began to pick up the crumbs, carrying them to his mouth one by one with unbelievable rapidity. In the dense blotch of light beneath the table, the kneeling figure looked like a priest in some service of his church. The nervous expressive fingers, flashing in and out of the light, might well have been mistaken for the fingers of the devotee going swiftly through decade after decade of his rosary.

The trouble is never so much the fact of what one does or says; the trouble comes with the interpretation that is put on it. What *factually* did Adolph Myers do or say? What was added to such facts as "he put his arms about me," and "his fingers were always playing in my hair," to drive out of town the schoolmaster whose caresses had made "doubt and disbelief" go out of boys freed to dream?

Adolph Myers was meant by nature to be a teacher of youth. He was one of those rare, little-understood men who rule by a power so gentle that it passes as a lovable weakness. In their feeling for the boys under their charge such men are not unlike the finer sort of women in their love of men.

Why does the author consider this characterization "crudely stated" and needing the "poet there"? How are positively intended connotations open to negative misinterpretation?

What really initiated the tragic series of causes and effects that "galvanized into beliefs" "the hidden, shadowy doubts that had been in men's minds concerning Adolph Myers"?

RELATED QUESTIONS

Homosexuality, like exhibitionism, is an unfortunate deviation from normal sexual development, yet "there is probably more nonsense written about homosexuality, more unwarranted fear of it, and less understanding of it than of any other area of human sexuality" [14].

Without condoning the tramp's behavior in **The Dawn of Hate** (p. 166), or what might have been the sexual tendencies of the schoolmaster in **Hands,** how might each situation have been more effectively handled?

The public image of prejudice is not necessarily stable; every generation and culture creates its own: The motive of Wing Biddlebaum, in whom the force that creates life was expressed by the caress that was in his fingers, might never have been challenged the way it was in **Hands** had Wing lived in France, where kissing three times on the cheeks, hugging and crying by males are accepted as signs of honest feeling rather than suspected as indications of effeminacy or homosexuality.

The promise made by Francie to her mother in **A Tree Grows in Brooklyn**—never to have intercourse with a man before marriage, at least not without telling her mother first—might warm the heart of a parent who had tried to instill respect for society's public ethic, yet, in Sweden, Francie might be scorned for her emphasis on the significance of the sexual act. "The Swedes think [Americans] are immoral, because by our silence we countenance total sexual intimacy in every orifice of the body to mutual orgasm provided the penis hasn't entered the vagina. They consider that hypocrisy" [15].

Another perspective on American sexual hypocrisy is offered in the news article *Little Brother Comes to America,* dealing with this country's alarm and protest over the imported French doll, *Petit Frère,* "a 4-pound, 21-inch, cuddly representation of a 4-month-old boy . . . anatomically correct."

Little Brother Comes to America

BARBARA W. WYDEN

"This grave danger . . . adversely affects the mental and moral growth of our very littlest children."

"If we condone that which is wrong by our silence, then in the future it will be our shame to bear."

Letters bearing these warnings are crisscrossing the country. Editorials have been written. And a certain segment of the populace is busily viewing with alarm.

For the mother and father who are not yet aware of the space-age catastrophe that threatens our children, here is the story:

The man who is perhaps the most directly responsible is Claude Refabert of Paris. Most children would consider Mr. Refabert an absolutely ideal grandfather. He owns a toy factory. Many adults, however, consider him an absolutely depraved soul.

Mr. Refabert is the manufacturer of *Petit Frère* (known in this country as Little Brother), a 4-pound, 21-inch, cuddly representation of a 4-month-old boy. He is "anatomically correct," which means that he has sex organs. The doll owes its existence to the Refaberts' young grandson, who picked up a doll one day and asked his grandmother, "Is it a boy or a girl?" He had a right to be puzzled. The doll was dressed as a boy, but had the usual neuter doll body. His grandmother, who works with her husband as a designer, asked in turn, "Why not a boy doll?"

The Refaberts were aware that such a doll, if it were to be put on the market, must be physically and artistically impeccable. Mrs. Refabert sought a prototype in the sculptures at Chartres, in the paintings of Rubens and Raphael. She visited the Alte Pinakothek in Munich and searched through the chapels and palazzos of Rome. Finally, in Florence, she found her model, the disarming cherub with a dolphin, the Verrocchio statue in the Palazzo Vecchio.

She returned to Paris triumphantly with a portfolio of photographs. A mold was made and submitted to the august Institut Pédagogique de France, a branch of the Ministry of Education. The Institut pondered and finally declared that Little Brother was a "very nice idea," but that it would prefer to see him modeled as "a real baby, not as an angel." Mrs. Refabert produced another mold and another and another. Her sixth effort won approval.

The doll went on sale in Europe late in 1966 and met with a mixed reaction. In France, a group of women shrieking, *Scandale! Scandale!"* forced shopkeepers in one town to remove the doll from sale. In Luxembourg, it created such a stir that Radio Luxembourg conducted a poll of its listeners— 25 per cent of those answering took a dim view of Little Brother. The Scandinavians, and especially the Swedes, took Little Brother to their sexually emancipated hearts immediately. More than 4,000 dolls have been sold in Sweden.

The English were not amused. There was a good deal of organized opposition, although Dr. R. Montagne, a British psychiatrist, said: "There is no risk at all of shocking children with this doll. They will find it normal. From 18 to 20 months, all babies start to identify different parts of the body, and from a very early age they realize there is a difference in sex. They are intrigued and interested by this, not shocked. There is no reason at all to hide such things from them. It is the parents who may be sensitive. It is their prejudices that will have to go."

Early this year, Frank Caplan, the general manager of Creative Playthings, a concern based in Princeton, N.J., that has pioneered in the design of intellectually stimulating toys, saw Little Brother at the Toy Fair in Nuremberg, Germany. The doll was, in fact, the talk of the fair. Toy buyers from the United States walked by the exhibit, nudged each other and snickered. "Did you see what I saw?" they would ask. "A doll with ——?" Many came to look, but none stayed to buy except Mr. Caplan who immediately saw the possibility of using Little Brother as a teaching aid. He acquired the right to sell the doll in the United States. Little Brother is now on sale in 51 stores throughout the country for a big $19.95.

"Even before anyone had seen the doll," Mr. Caplan reports, "we were in hot water. We had a call from the head of the Customs Bureau in New York. He said he had heard we were importing a doll with sex organs and they would have to refuse to let the doll in until they had a chance to inspect it.

"We got this cleared up with Washington and then a man from the Department of Commerce called and said he had heard 'from some of the fellows on the Hill' that we were importing a doll with sex organs and the department would like to know more about it.

"Then we heard from the Department of Health, Education and Welfare that they had heard we were importing a pornographic doll. A representative of the Food and Drug Administration came to our plant in Princeton to inspect it. When he saw Little Brother, he just laughed.

"A couple of New York City Councilmen came to our office and said their constituents had alerted them that we were importing pornography and what was this all about.

"I understand," Mr. Caplan sighed, "that a lot of people have even written to the President . . . about Little Brother."

All this had been set in motion by Mrs. Stephen Wetzel of Norwood, Ohio, the softspoken wife of a factory worker and mother of three children ranging from 4 to 13. Last May she bought a copy of a New York Sunday paper, something she often does "because it has the funnies a week in advance of the local papers." After she finished the funnies, Mrs. Wetzel came across a story that shocked her profoundly. It was a report that a doll from France with sex organs would be sold in this country. "I showed it to a group of women in the neighborhood," she said, "and each was more shocked than the other."

Together with a neighbor, Mrs. Paul McLane, who has 11 grandchildren, she formed the Citizens Committee to Protest Little Brother Doll. The committee's first act was to send a letter protesting Little Brother to "elected officials, churches, clubs, organizations and citizens" urging them to take a firm stand against the doll. Mrs. Wetzel and Mrs. McLane wrote: "Toys are, should be, and must remain objects of play. Sex organs are not. There must be no part on a toy that a mother reprimands her child that it is not nice to play with. A simple 'What's that?' asked by a 2-, 3- or 4-year-old must not force us into a vocabulary or subject matter beyond the realm of their understanding."

The response was immediate and encouraging. Mrs. Wetzel estimates that they have sent out more than 1,000 copies of the letter. As other Citizens Committees have been formed, they, too, have added their mite to the mailman's load.

When a doll raises such a storm, it is only natural to wonder whether or not it does indeed threaten the sensibilities of our children. Parents who have no strong feeling would probably be inclined to shrug their shoulders and sit this one out—and not buy the doll. But with the increasing emphasis on sex education in schools and the probability that this doll will be used in some school systems, the possible effects of Little Brother become of more immediate concern to parents. Is he dangerous—or is this all just a tempest in a dollhouse?

"A doll like this should be very helpful," says Dr. Milton I. Levine, clinical professor of pediatrics at Cornell University Medical College, an authority on sex education for young children.

"It is very important for little children to know the differences between boys and girls. If little girls are being brought up where there are no boys, we advise mothers to take them where there are little boy babies so they can learn the differences early. And the same for boys.

"I do not believe that little children should see their mother and father in the nude, but they should see other children. In nursery schools we advise that boys and girls use the same bathroom so they have a chance to see in a matter-of-fact way that they are different.

"Parents don't have to worry about a doll like this causing sexual excitement. If a mother comes upon her little girl playing with this doll and giggling or playing bathroom with it, these things may disturb the mother, but they are not harmful or over-stimulating to the child. This is natural play—unless adult reaction makes it unnatural play."

Helene S. Arnstein, the author of the recently published "Your Growing Child and Sex" (Bobbs-Merrill), says substantially the same thing. "If your child and her friends play with the doll and start giggling about the penis (if they already know the word) or wee-wee or using other bathroom talk, don't worry,"

Mrs. Arnstein advises. "It is better that these thoughts come out, because obviously they have been there all the time and needed expression. Now is the time for a mother to step in quietly and explain about the differences between boys and girls.

"I would suspect that after a few giggly sessions the doll will be played with just like any other doll."

Many experts feel, along with Dr. Montagne, the British psychiatrist, that the problem is with the parents. "It is likely that reaction to this doll will be stronger in parents than in children," Dr. John F. McDermott Jr., associate professor of psychiatry at the University of Michigan Medical School, says. "The impact of the family is an important factor. Most parents are aware that their preschool children have a good deal of curiosity about the difference between the sexes, which they tend to satisfy by observation or discussion with playmates and by 'playing doctor.' For parents who want to channel their child's sex curiosity into discussion rather than the outlets of exploration and experimentation, the doll may help. In other families, however, with different cultural backgrounds and attitudes, the doll might have an adverse effect on the relationship of parents and child if it serves to heighten embarrassment, self-consciousness and anxiety in the parents."

"Adults look at these things through their own eyes," Dr. Levine says. "That's wrong. They have to look at them through the eyes of children. As a matter of fact, I think we should have a similar girl doll. It would be extremely useful."

"If there is no female counterpart," says Kay Sperry Showers, a psychologist in the Bergenfield, N.J., public schools, "the major good of this product will be lost. As every parent or teacher of small boys knows, there is just as much curiosity about little girls among little boys. After all, why have small children been lurking out behind the barn and the garage for all these generations?

"Were this doll and a female counterpart standard equipment in kindergartens," Mrs. Showers says, "some of the sex education, which more and more states are legislating into their curriculums, could be started in the natural easy way that it should be."

Mrs. Wetzel and Mrs. McLane can relax though. They do not have to rev up their mimeograph machines. Claude Refabert, who obviously values his peace and his digestion, reports from Paris: "There are no plans for a *Petite Soeur.*"

In what ways could United States alarm and protest concerning the importing of *Petit Frère* be considered one of its cultural contradictions, a hypocritical sexual attitude?

One source of American parental dismay was fear that the doll would "cause sexual excitement." What sexual stimulants or examples of pornography in the American culture might be considered more grave dangers "adversely affect[ing] the mental and moral growth" of young people than a 4-pound, 21-inch, anatomically correct cuddly representation of a 4-month old boy?

If, however, adults want to protect children from exhibitionists, why should they promote a doll whose sex organs are equally apparent as the tramp's in **The Dawn of Hate** (p. 166)?

The Citizens' Committee to Protest Little Brother Doll took the stand that

Toys are, should be, and must remain objects of play. Sex organs are not. There must be no part on a toy that a mother reprimands her child that it is not nice to play with. A simple "What's that?" asked by a 2-, 3- or 4-year-old must not force us into a vocabulary or subject matter beyond the realm of their understanding.

How might each of the three arguments be countered?

What further ammunition could you give the Citizens' Committee to support their protest?

RELATED QUESTIONS

In "The *Playboy* Philosophy," editor Hugh Hefner, dealing with another perspective on censorship, asks:

Whose foot is to be the measure to which ours are all to be cut or stretched?

Those most interested in promoting censorship are usually least qualified to act as censors and those most qualified are most strongly opposed to the very idea of censorship in a free society. Even if the "ideal censor" were to be found (and the very words are, to us, incompatible)—a Solomon who truly tried to adjust his decisions, not to his own likes and dislikes, but to the Supreme Court's concept of a *community standard*—we have already seen that no single standard can ever be said to exist for the many and varied educational, social, ethnic and religious parts of a community and certainly not for the thousands of separate communities all across this broad country of ours. And we have previously quoted Justice Douglas of the Supreme Court who has stated: "Any test that turns on what is offensive to the community's standards is too loose, too capricious, too destructive of freedom of expression to be squared with the First Amendment."

If that most improbable Solomon of Censorship does exist, few communities have made any concerted attempt to find him. Instead, we are asked to shape our foot to the size of an arbitrarily selected officer of the police department or a censor board composed of housewives with spotty educational and cultural backgrounds. Attorneys for the award-winning French film *The Game of Love,* a faithful adaptation of a classic novel by Colette, clearly demonstrated the questionable qualifications of a great many censors, when they appealed to the Illinois courts the City of Chicago's refusal to grant the motion picture a permit for exhibition.

Having entered into evidence the facts that the film had been awarded the Diploma of Merit at the Edinburgh Film Festival and the *Grand Prix du Cinéma Français* (Grand Prize of the French Motion Picture Industry) and that the American premiere of the film had been sponsored by the Fresh Air Fund of the *New York Herald-Tribune,* the attorneys brought out through testimony or members of the Police Censor Unit that there were no rules of procedure under which the Censor Unit operated and that they sought no outside opinions on movies being considered — neither the distributor's, nor drama critics', nor movie reviewers'. Lt. Ignatius J. Sheehan, head of the Censor Unit, testified that he did not read many books, did not attend many plays, did not attend art exhibits, did not read the book-review sections and had never read any of Colette's novels. He knew nothing about the awards that the motion picture had received nor anything about the honors which had been given Madame Colette during her lifetime. He stated that he could not define a classic or name any classic. He stated that he took the entertainment value of a motion picture into consideration in determining whether a picture should be accepted or rejected and he did not find the film entertaining. Lt. Sheehan testified that one of the things indecent was that a group of girls in the movie presumably saw the private parts of an adolescent boy who came out of the water after swimming nude. He stated that he thought that the young girl in the picture was "sex minded" and that this was abnormal in a girl 15 years old.

A Mrs. O'Hallaren testified that she was a movie censor for the City of Chicago, for which she receives $304 a month and that she views movies eight hours a day, five days a week. She stated that she was a high school graduate and that she read movie reviews after she had passed upon a film, "but I don't read too much before. I don't go for that, because I like to see the movie my way and enjoy it and censor it, and then I am going to do it from my thinking. Then I am going to check to see how close I came." She testified that she had never read any of Colette's works and did not know too much about her. She stated that she did not think the motion picture *The Game of Love* had any entertainment value and that she thinks that movies should provide entertainment. She stated that the absence of entertainment value could be one of the reasons for rejecting a picture. She stated that it was unusual for a girl of 15 to have sexual desires. She stated that she thought the movie was offensive to the standards of decency and that it was unfit, immoral and obscene. She defined a classic as "a work accepted by the standards of excellency," stated that it was accepted by the people generally and that Shakespeare's writings were classic because she had "never heard anyone really talk against Shakespeare." She testified that "there are a lot of things true to life that we cannot put on the screen."

Mrs. Joyce, another of the movie censors, testified that she was a high school graduate, that her tastes did not lean to classics, and expressed the opinion that most classics were written in the 18th Century. She stated that she would be "surprised and amazed" to find that Colette's novels circulated freely in the Chicago Public Library and that if any books like the movie were circulating, such books ought to be looked over before they get into the Public Library. Mrs. Joyce testifed that she rejected the picture because "it was immoral, because it was against my parental rearing. Anyway, it was immoral, corrupt, indecent, against my religious principles, unclean, sinful and corrupt."

Whatever the multiple motivations that prod the prude and the censor, it should be clear that much more is involved than simply the considered protection of the public from ideas that might prove harmful. Moreover, our democracy is founded on the premise that people have a God-given right to knowledge—a *right to know*. And no human being has the right to tamper with the free flow of ideas among his fellows.

The attitude that some ideas are best kept from the citizenry advances a concept of totalitarian paternalism that is contrary to the most basic ideals of our free society. It is akin to the colonialist concept that a new nation may not yet be ready to rule itself. The only way in which the people of a country can ever *become* mature enough for self-rule is by setting them free to *practice* self-rule. Similarly, the only way in which a society can mature sexually, socially and philosophically is by allowing it naturally free and unfettered sexual, social and philosophical growth. By treating our own citizens like so many overprotected children, we have produced our present, too-often-childlike, immature, hypocritical social order.

But anti-sexualists cannot contemplate with equanimity the free acceptance of man's sexual role, nor any literature which tends to inform, educate or increase interest in that role. The best proof of this is that literature of an erotic nature is the constant and foremost target of self-appointed censors who connect this type of reading to crime and acted out violence, but who virtually ignore the vast body of books dealing with violence in the most gruesome detail. . . .

It has long seemed quite incredible—indeed, incomprehensible—to us that detailed descriptions of murder, which we consider a crime, are acceptable in our art and literature, while detailed descriptions of sex, which is not a crime, are prohibited. It is as though our society put hate above love—favored death over life. [16]

What are some of the "multiple motivations" that appear to prod the censor and preclude adherence to, much less formulation of, a "community standard"?

Is sex-mindedness abnormal in a fifteen-year-old girl? What evidence from readings thus far might counter Lieutenant Sheehan's testimony that seeing "the private parts" of an adolescent male emerging nude from swimming is "indecent" and that sex-mindedness is abnormal among fifteen-year-old females?

Why do you think the lieutenant refers to the male genitals as "private parts"?

How would you expect Lieutenant Sheehan to react to a film sequence of **Through the First Gate** (p. 31)? To a scene from **Young Lonigan** (p. 48)?

What flaws in logic appear in Mrs. O'Hallaren's definition of a classic?

How rational and objective is Mrs. Joyce's rejection of *The Game of Love?*

How would you define morality? Ideally, on what should it be based? Are issues other than sexual ones moral concerns?

What are some of the feet used as measurers of morality? Of obscenity, or pornography?

Do you feel "children under 18" should not be admitted to certain movies? Would you keep the prohibition, but lower the age limit? If so, for what kind(s) of films?

Do you agree with Hefner that only through exposure to varieties of experience and through self-rule can maturity result? Or do you feel that censorship of books, films, and plays acts as a healthy protection to society because, as FBI Director J. Edgar Hoover has stated:

We know that in an overwhelmingly large number of cases, sex crime is associated with pornography. We know that sex criminals read it, are clearly influenced by it. I believe that if we can eliminate the distribution of such items among impressionable children, we shall greatly reduce our frightening crime rate. [17]

A bather whose clothing was strewed
By breezes that left her quite nude,
Saw a man come along,
And, unless we are wrong,
You expected this line to be lewd.

Copyright 1962 *Eros Quarterly.* Reprinted with permission.

Are the authors of this limerick right or wrong? Why might they well be confident that their last-line expectations would prove correct?

. . . it is hard to grow up when the general social attitude toward sexuality is inconsistent and unpredictable. (It is hard to exist as an adult too.) In this respect our society is uniquely problematical. . . .

In the ideal theory and practice, sexuality is one of the most important natural functions and the attitude toward it ranges from permissive to enthusiastic. This is the position of all Thinking, of public spokesmen and women's magazines, and of the Supreme Court in its decisions on classics of literature; and it is somewhat put into practice by psychological parents, mental hygienists, nursery schools, and bands of adolescents and adults. Yet there are puzzling inconsistencies. What applies to brother does not apply to sister, though every girl is somebody's sister. What is affirmed and tacitly condoned, must still not be done overtly. For instance, although all Serious Thought is agreed on the simple natural function and there are colorful little abstract treatises for children, it is inconceivable for a publisher to print a sober little juvenile story about, say, playing doctor or the surprising discovery of masturbation. A character in a juvenile (or adult) adventure story may not incidentally get an erection as he may wolf a sandwich or get sleepy . . . . although most public spokesmen are for a "healthy frankness," the public schools are run quite otherwise . . . . in California (spring of '59), a high school science teacher employed the bright-idea project of tabulating the class's sexual habits as an exercise in fact finding. This got him into terrible hot water, and the School Board carefully explained, "What we teach is human reproduction, much as we discuss the functions of the human eye or ear," that is, without mentioning light or sound, color or harmony, or any other act or relation.

(I am writing this equably and satirically, but the stupidity of these people is outrageous.) [18]

How might the case of **Little Brother Comes to America,** the issue of sex education, and the instance of movie censorship described in *Playboy* all fit into this argument?

The treatment of sexuality in the popular culture and the commodities and advertising is less puzzling: it is to maximize sales. Existing lust is exploited and as far as possible there is created an artificial stimulation, with the justified confidence that the kind of partial satisfactions obtainable will involve buying something: cosmetics, sharp clothes, art magazines, dating entertainment. And since, for very many people, lust is at present accompanied by embarrassment, shame, and punishment, these too are exploited as much as possible. . . . there is an absolute incompatibility between this sexuality of popular culture and the ideal theory and practice of the "simple natural function." [19]

Sex has gone as public as AT&T. . . . our entire social scheme is based on exposure. We have to know everything. This desire for exposure . . . is reflected in our attitude about sex. Anything and everything goes, just as long as it remains public. Anyone who "views with alarm" is a blue-nosed old fogey of a Puritan. . . . Motion pictures in technicolor and twenty feet tall present for our enjoyment—indeed, our amazement—a bevy of bosoms and buttocks . . . the arts reflect the society which nurtures and supports it. . . . TV deals with sex as casually as do the other arts, perhaps not as candidly—but don't lose heart—if the competition gets tough enough they'll have to sell soap by selling sexuality. [20]

An advertisement for the Twentieth-Century Fox film *Doctor Dolittle* carried a banner headline: "It Will Charm the Pants Off You!"

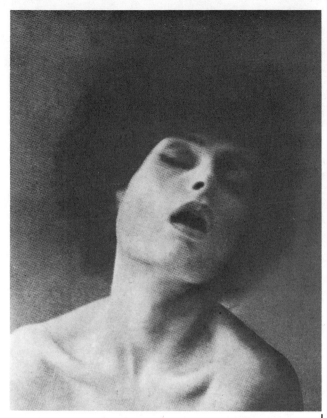

Satisfied

A manufacturer's advertisement for bedspreads shows a boudoir dominated by an orange-spreaded double bed. In the upper right corner of the ad, an inset pictures a heavy-lidded, long-haired female face looking over her shoulder toward the printed invitation: "Spend the Night with Morgan Jones."

How do advertisements illustrate the exploitation of lust to create artificial stimulation in order to market a product? Are these campaigns relevant? To what?

How have soaps, shampoos, hair preparations, toothpastes, and cars already sold sexuality to sell the product?

Do you think that the advertising business, like the arts, reflects the society that nurtures and supports it?

Suggest some answers to the caption of the cartoon on page 188.

Judging from the "Personals" on page 189, what qualities do males and fe- **187**

"I wonder what he had in mind . . ."

Reproduced by courtesy of *Medical Tribune* and J. G. Farris.

males seem to be looking for in each other? Are they typical? Are they the essential traits?

A Los Angeles button maker claims that it's the adults who buy the sexy buttons. If so, how would you explain it?

SEX: In America an obsession. In other parts of the world a fact. [21]

Can you account for the distinction between "fact" and "obsession"?

The fact that nearly every motion picture deals with love proves that sex is the most important factor in life. The interest in these films is, in the main, neurotic. It is the interest of sex-guilty, sex-frustrated people. Unable to love naturally because of sex guilt, they flock to film stories that make love romantic, even beautiful. The sex-repressed live out their interest in sex by proxy. No man, no woman with a full love life could be bothered sitting twice a week in a movie house seeing trashy pictures which are only imitations of real life.

So it is also with popular novels. They either deal with sex or with crime, usually a combination of the two. A very popular novel, *Gone with the Wind,* was a favorite, not because of the background of the tragedy of the Civil War and the slaves, but because it centered around a tiresome, egocentric girl and her love affairs.

Fashion journals, cosmetics, leg shows, highbrow sophisticated reviews, sex stories—all show clearly that sex is the most important thing in life. At the same time, they prove that only the trappings of sex are approved of—in other words, fiction, films, leg shows.

It was D. H. Lawrence who pointed out the iniquity of sex films, where

Intelligent sensitive male, age 34, desires pretty, shapely female, 18-35 who is warm, affectionate and understanding. I am 5'8", medium build, average looking, talented, compassionate & understanding, with a sense of humor. I like music, cultural activities & sports. If you desire a sincere, honest, romantic relationship and companionship & would enjoy being needed & appreciated, then please write to: I.S., P.O. Box 000, New York, N.Y. (photo optional).

Tall, handsome young male artist (32, 6'3", 185lbs.), needs lovely young nympho type girl friend for lunches and daytime or twilight togetherness. Call 000–0000, days.

Man, late 20's, seeks FEMALE partner, for indoor nudist gatherings. Only twenty minutes from NYC. Female callers only. Call 201 - 000-0000 from 6-9 p.m. only.

ORAL LOVE — Good looking magazine editor in mid-twenties desires FEMALE partner (18-30) for wild and discreet love making sessions. I can and will do anything with the right girl. Call John Buhle 000–0000, leave name and number. NO fags, please.

Tall, attractive, mature Spanish artist, 34 with apartment in West Village looking for quiet attractive female to share love, art and bed games. 8 a.m. or after 10 p.m. 000–0000.

YOU'RE SENSITIVE, a grown-up girl who loves conversation, delights in the hay? Share tall, traveled writer's warmth, bread . . . pad? Jay Robideaux, (NYC) 000–0000 (messages).

---

30 year old very handsome executive desires to learn about cunnilingus. Write Stuart Rivers c/o Craft Service, W. 74th St. NYC.

Very beautiful girl under 26 years desired for marriage to 37 year, 6' tall slender, considerate, warm professional. Write: L. Hogan, 0000 Crescent St., Queens, L.I.C., N.Y.

Male 29 desires to meet mature women, for mutual desirable sex relations. Also has friend if you have one. Reply to: Box 0000 GPO NYC, NY. 10001

Young man in 20's desires a sincere relationship and offers a home (the upper east side) to a female who enjoys taking care of a house and a man (not financially). Please write to: Mr. Lemis, P.O. Box 00, Prince St. Sta. NY, NY 10012.

Attractive professional man, 20's seeks friendly, unspoiled, uninhibited female, to lead to meaningful relationship. Write: Box 000, Bronx 10453.

Imaginative young male disciplinarian desires relationship with obedient, receptive young female in Boston Area. Write "DM" c/o P.O. Box 00, Newton Center, Mass. 02159

WANTED: Interesting, sexy, young girl for afternoon or evening dates with man, 30, tall, intelligent, generous, village apartment. PO Box 000, Cooper Station, NY. 10003

Professional man, 29 — wanted young, warm, uninhibited, intelligent WOMAN 18-35, to share bright apt. on a mutually satisfying basis. No Homo's Call Bob after 6: Phone 000-0000 or Write: Bob — apt. 4, 0000 74th St., 11373 N.Y.

Attractive, female art teacher, young, recently divorced, seeks swinging boy and girl friends for physical and emotional fun. Will call or Write. Box 00 Oakland Gardens, Flushing, NY

Generous Grad. student; 27, 6'2", 175, Cauc., Shy, Moustached. Seeks female (only) sexual partners for casual relationships. Age, Race no barrier. 609 - 000-0000. Collect 10-11:30 p.m.

Tall, handsome professional man seeks uninhibited female. G.P.O. Box 0000, Brooklyn, N.Y.

TO THE GAL WHO LEADS A DOUBLE LIFE (OR WOULD LIKE TO): Considerate, good-looking businessman (35) with luxury apartment and cultured tastes (music, theater, art, travel, sports cars), solid citizen by day, unmasks after dark. Seeks slim, lovely, intelligent gal companion or roommate. Phone Mr. Carr during office hours. 000–0000

Two young, handsome men await nympho type girls, preferably women, seeking to have sexual relationship. Please write, accompanied by photo (intriguing) if possible. No homos. 00 Carle Rd., Westbury, L.I.

Young man 32, own Manhattan apartment would like to meet girl 20-30 who desires mature companionship. Call Michael, 000–0000 late in evenings.

Cultured, successful gentleman interested in the arts - theatre, ballet, all music, etc. Would like to meet an intelligent, attractive gal to enjoy same. Be my guest, winter vacation in the islands and late spring, summer in Europe. May consider financial help for talented, creative girl. Have beautiful midtown pad which you may share. Phone anytime (212) 000–0000 and let's wine and dine.

Quietness of the mind can be found!! Even in the void of the learning room of machines . . . ZOD

Young male, (23), good-looking, medium build, 5'10", interested in music, literature, politics, etc., desires to share life in serious, hopefully long-term relationship with same. Must be good-looking, intelligent, unaffected, under 24 yrs. No brutes, no creeps, no psychos. Write, give background ad lib., enclose photos (portrait) — Box 000, Cathedral Station, N.Y., N.Y. 10025. If interested will reciprocate promptly and, if mutually satisfactory, will arrange meeting. Absolute discretion assured.

Love, love, love...if you need it — we're sexperts. Two guys with groovy ideas for fun and pleasure Call Billy 000–0000 or Allen 000–0000 evenings.

Cameraman in Boston on feature film offers sweet, young, pretty swinger(s) chance of a lifetime to meet actors, filmmakers and technicians from N.Y. and Hollywood. Call Ross (617) 000–0000 or send photo, 000 Boylston St.. No wierdos or prudes, please.

Our group, swinging in the NYC, NJ and Philadelphia areas, seeks discreet, attractive girls, guys and couples interested in the Libidinal laws of nature. A description of yourself & photo appreciated. Write: P.O. Box 00 Winslow Post Office, NJ 08095

Magic math: one times one times sixty-nine equals Zowie. Free tuition for succulent goddess. Send nude Polaroid and phone to Studio One, 000 West 58 St., New York 10019, pronto.

Good looking business executive White, 33, 6'2", well endowed seeks attractive girls or couples for intimate get-togethers. NY - NJ area. I own color polaroid if interested. Photo, phone a must. Write: W. Davis, P.O. Box 000, Ansonia Sta. NYC 10023

the sex-repressed youth, fearful of actual girls in his own circle, showers all his sex emotion on a Hollywood star—and then goes home to masturbate. Lawrence, of course, did not mean that masturbation is wrong; he meant that it is unhealthy sex that seeks masturbation with the fantasy of a film star. Healthy sex would most surely seek a partner in the neighborhood.

Think of the enormous vested interests that thrive on repressed sex: the fashion people, the lipstick merchants, the church, the theaters and movies, the best-seller novelists, and the stocking manufacturers.

It would be foolish to say that a society sexually free would abolish beautiful clothes. Of course not. Every woman would want to look her best before the man she loved. Every man would like to appear elegant when he dated his girl. What would disappear would be fetishism—the valuing of the shadow because the reality is forbidden. Sex-repressed men would no longer stare at women's lingerie in shop windows. What a horrible pity that sex interest is so repressed. The highest pleasure in the world is enjoyed with guilt. This repression enters into every aspect of human life, making life narrow, unhappy, hateful. [22]

How plausible is "the valuing of the shadow because the reality is forbidden" as an explanation of American advertising psychology?

One contemporary writer believes that our attitude toward sex and sexuality cannot be changed until it is set in the context of a philosophy of living:

. . . I think a different concept of sex is needed. We have, on the one hand, the restrictive, fearful and repressive concept . . . which essentially restricts and subdues sexual expression . . . the second concept [is] a sort of sex for sex's sake. . . . These seem to be the extremes of a continuum. . . . Yet, when you begin to examine them, they are very much alike. Both are obsessed with sex as an end in itself. In the one you must not; in the other you must. Both are rigid and demanding, and neither seem really to see or to be concerned with a fulfilled human being. [23]

Could it be argued that the old morality said "you must not," and that the new morality says "you must"? If a different concept of sex is needed, what might it be? What sort of concept might be "concerned with a fulfilled human being"?

Toward a Definition of Love and Sex

In part, perhaps, because of the deft use of sex by the "hidden persuaders," the differences between love and sex, like the nature of each, have become blurred. The fundamental connotative confusions surrounding words like "sex" and "love" are pinpointed by Irving Fineman in *Spelling Lesson:*

> SEX, (this is odd),
> isn't a four-letter word;
> it's a three-letter word,
> and so is GOD.
> While LOVE, (how absurd!),
> is a four-letter word. [24]

In the following section, poets, philosophers, and professors train their lenses on this area of sexuality. Their perspectives afford a clarification of the terms and contribute toward a definition of love and sex.

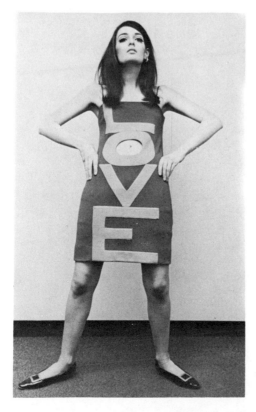

Newsweek photo by Tony Rollo.
Copyright *Newsweek* 1970.

How does the dress worn by the girl in the photograph advertise sex while claiming to advertise love? On the basis of the photograph, how is sex being defined?

Why is love so often confused with sex? In *Peyton Place* by Grace Metalious, the heroine comments:

> I used to think that the business of confusing love with sex was childish and stupid, but now I know why so many women do this. It is because it is too painful afterward, if one can remember nothing of love. [25]

What other reasons might be added?

How might the relationship—if any—between love and sex be expressed? Is sex a strictly physiological phenomenon? An expression of love of the highest kind? Is there no love without desire?

Where did sex get its bad name? From the Victorians? The Puritans? The Bible? Did Jesus say anything about courtship, perversions, masturbation, sex manners, codes of reproduction and parenthood, multiple marriage, incest, birth control, artificial insemination, or feticide?

Das Liebesleben

THOM GUNN

The theme tune occurs again!
it is now at its loudest
and thus we know that Tristan
and Isolde are at last

to be rewarded by the
ultimate in orgasms
(death). Even King Mark is sorry.
Contemplating their problems,

I weep, my neighbours weep, and
the programme sellers weep. For
this, we know, was Love: high-toned
sexual play bound for death or

disaster. Off stage, no doubt,
matters are a bit different.
If love were sex, and without
any other element,

then sex would be love, which I
know it isn't: it's my small
pink member, like a friendly
dog, nuzzling and raising hell.

Much luck to you, Member; just
try never to let me down,
and keep to your place. And lest
you be, my simple friend, in

doubt, let me clearly tell you
love involves things neither Tristan nor you could ever do:
such as washing the dishes.

In a theatrical presentation of a medieval romance, "high-toned sexual play bound for death or disaster" can, through an act of imagination, become "Love." But off stage, as **Das Liebesleben** explains, "matters are a bit different." The poet Thom Gunn recognizes that, as Singer states (p. 229):

Love is not always ecstatic; and even its poetry is often prosaic. There are quiet, comfortable, humdrum loves as well as the rhapsodic ones that seem to accompany inexperience.

What example of the "prosaic" poetry of love is given in **Das Liebesleben?** How does the poet define sex? Would the poet agree with the concept of married love presented by Dietrich (p. 352) in which:

. . . your antennas tell you . . . to look for beauty and for joy in everything you do, instead of seeing all your daily duties drab and joyless. . . . To clean your house and your machines that help you clean, and wash, and beat the eggs and mix the dough.

Would his concept of love make this attitude toward daily routines possible?

RELATED QUESTIONS

What would the author of **Das Liebesleben** probably say to Luisa's desire for "**Much More**" (p. 66)?

How fully would Gunn agree with Carl Sandburg in **Honey and Salt** (see "**Night-Lights,**" p. 583) that the key to love is

. . . in passion, knowledge, affection?
All three—along with moonlight, roses, groceries,
givings and forgivings, gettings and forgettings,
keepsakes and room rent,
pearls of memory along with ham and eggs.

Why?

Love and Orgasm

ALEXANDER LOWEN

SEX AND LOVE

. . . Sex is an expression of love. . . . If sexual activity were not an expression of love, no mature person would speak of coitus as an act of love. Sex is a biological expression of love. If the sexual act is accompanied by feelings of hostility or contempt for the sexual partner, this ambivalence denotes the dissociation of the individual's conscious feelings from his instinctive behavior. The intimate connection between sex and love can be clearly shown.

The feeling of love inspires many relationships that are not primarily sexual. We use the word "love" to describe our feelings for a brother, for a friend, for our country, and for God. All relationships in which love enters are characterized by the desire for closeness, both spiritually and physically, with the love object. "Closeness" may not be a strong enough word. In its more intense forms, the feeling of love includes the desire for fusion and union with the love object. As Erich Fromm pointed out in *The Art of Loving*, the answer to the problem of human existence "lies in the achievement of interpersonal union, of fusion with another person, in *love*." This is true not only of the love of one person for another, but also of the love that a person feels for the symbols and material objects that he cherishes. Love impels one toward closeness both in spirit (identification) and in body (physical contact and penetration). We desire to be close to those we love, and we love those toward whom we feel this desire.

In what way is sex different? Sex brings people together. It might be said that sex brings people together physically, not spiritually. This is not so. The spiritual side of life can be separated from the physical only at the risk of destroying the unity and integrity of the whole being. The physical act of sex involves the spiritual experience of identification with and knowledge of the partner. In ancient Hebrew and Greek, the word "cohabit" is expressed by the verb "to know." The Bible relates that "Adam knew Eve his wife, and she conceived and bore Cain." This choice of words is neither fortuitous nor prudish. It denotes the intimate relation between knowledge and physical closeness, between knowing and the primordial sense of touching. To know (love) an object, one must be close to it. Viewed in this light, the sexual act is the most intimate form of love.

The relation of sex to the desire for closeness is demonstrable. There are other phenomena that can be interpreted to support the thesis that sex is an expression of love. The erection of the penis depends upon the tumescence of that organ with blood. And just as tumescence is necessary for the male sexual function, congestion is necessary for the female's sexual response. The feeling of fullness in the vagina and clitoris, the flow of the lubricating secretions, and the sensation of heat result from the flow of blood into the pelvic area of the female's body. Biologically, genital excitation may be viewed as a function of the blood and the circulatory system. In the sexual act, two organs suffused with blood and so highly charged that they are often pulsatile come into the closest physical contact with each other. Erotogenic zones are characterized by the richness of their blood supply. Close contact between bloodrich organs occurs in kissing and in nursing, which are also regarded as expressions of love.

Love can also be experienced as a general or localized feeling. The feeling of love as opposed to the idea of love is often localized in or about the heart, although it also extends into the arms, when reaching out to a love object, and to other parts of the body, the lips, and the genitals.

The relation of the heart to love is expressed in common symbolism and everyday language. Cupid's arrow pierces the heart to indicate that love has been awakened. The heart is the symbol of St. Valentine's Day, the patron saint of love. We use such expressions as, "My heart is full of love," "My heart aches for love," "You have touched my heart," and so on, to express our unconscious sense of this relationship. Love songs are full of references to the heart as the symbol of love.

These ideas do not constitute scientific proof that an erection is an expression of the desire for love, but, then, the phenomenon of love is a most difficult subject for scientific investigation. In the view of science represented by physiology, the heart is only a pump that drives the blood through the body. Such scientific thinking, however, gives us no understanding of human behavior or feelings. It the heart is only a pump, if the penis is only an organ to introduce sperm cells into the female body, then the human being is only a machine that requires no feelings of love or pleasure to motivate its functions. I reject the concept that a man is only a mechanism whose behavior is explained solely in terms of physiochemical laws. I believe some credence must be given to beliefs and ideas by which the human mind has attempted to understand its own feelings and actions. . . . The suffusion of the pelvic area in the woman with blood makes the tissues of the genital apparatus full and firm. And it is the presence of the blood that accounts for the heat she experiences in sexual desire and response. In many ways, therefore, the female's sexual reactions parallel those of the male. She, too, is capable of dissociating her heart from her vaginal response in varying degrees.

An interesting example of this dissociation is the case of Suzie Wong. In the delightful picture *The World of Suzie Wong,* Suzie justified her activities as a prostitute by saying that while she gave men her body, she did not give them her heart. The sexual act became thereby emotionally meaningless to her. When she was in love, however, it was different. She gave herself fully to her lover. The difference should be obvious to any man, Suzie claimed, unless he had a small heart. Our sexual mores make no such distinctions, but there is merit in Suzie's argument.

What are the exceptions to the statement that sex is impossible without love? Are the sexual relations of a man with a prostitute to be considered an expression of love? The answer must be yes. The sexual feelings of a man for a prostitute express his love for her in his desire for closeness and in the fact of erection. Unfortunately, sexual love in our culture is not free from secondary feelings of shame, disgust, guilt, and hostility. Their presence in a person distorts the significance of the sexual act and undermines its values. They may render the expression of sexual love impossible except under conditions that permit the release of these associated feelings. The man who can function sexually only with a prostitute indicates thereby that he is capable of loving only a prostitute, not a woman of his own class or standing. However, the love for the prostitute is real. Not infrequently it has developed into a more abiding and respectable relationship. Both history and literature bear witness to the genuine affection that a man can have for a mistress or a prostitute. And not infrequently the feelings of the prostitute for her lover is more sincere and affectionate than that which the man had inspired in other women. In *The Great God Brown*, Eugene O'Neill depicts such a relationship in sympathetic terms.

How explain the rapist? Is not his sexuality an expression of sadism rather than love? To analyze pathological sexual behavior in detail would require more space than I can give to it here. I shall have to limit my comments on this problem to the observation that sadistic behavior is directed only at those who are loved. It manifests the condition of ambivalence: love and hate directed toward the same object. The element of love in a rape determines its sexual content; the element of hate denies to the act its normal pleasure and satisfaction. To the extent that the expression of sexual love is inhibited, distorted, or encumbered with secondary feelings, the sexual function is limited in its capacity to yield pleasure and satisfaction.

If love is conceived as being more than a "noble sentiment," it must be recognized that it contains a force that impels to action and that seeks fulfillment and satisfaction in all relationships in which it is present. A person is not happy unless he can do something to express his feelings for a friend. A mother is frustrated unless she feels that her efforts for her child lead to its well-being. The lover is a giver. But love is not unselfish. The need to love is as much a part of our biological makeup as the need to breathe or to move. The impulse of love aims to satisfy this need. The satisfaction of love derives from the expression of love in some concrete, material form or in some appropriate action. The universal tendency to give gifts and presents to those we care for is a manifestation of this need to give. Isn't this true of sex, too? The act of sex is a giving of the self. Satisfaction results from the full surrender of the self to the partner in the sexual embrace. Without this surrender, sexual satisfaction cannot be achieved. In other words, only when lovemaking is wholehearted, or not until the heart is joined to the genitals in the act of sex, is it possible to attain orgastic fulfillment in sexual love. If sexual happiness is relatively rare in our culture, it is because individuals have lost the ability to give themselves fully to one another. The loss of this ability to love is both cause and result of the widespread neuroses of our time.

One of my patients made an observation that, I believe, clarifies the relation of sex to love. She said, "A man can't love a woman unless he loves women." The same could be said of a woman. She can love a man only if she loves all men. Love for the opposite sex determines the ability to respond sexually to that sex. It is very closely associated with the biological drive of sex, which on the unconscious level is nondiscriminating. It can be stated that the strength of the sexual feeling in a man is proportionate to the strength of his positive feelings for the feminine sex. The misogynist and the homosexual are relatively impotent males. What is true of the male is equally true of the female.

Love in the personal sense is a conscious feeling that results from the focus of this general affection upon a specific individual. Through this personal form of love, sex becomes discriminating. The same phenomenon can be observed in infants. A newborn or very young infant will nurse any breast. Once the baby has become conscious of his mother, he will focus his feelings and desires on her. Similarly, adolescent sexuality is dominated by the unconscious element in its broad responsiveness to the opposite sex. This explains why the Don Juan type of sexual behavior is described as adolescent. Mature sexuality is selective. It has a greater conscious component. This conscious component is superimposed upon the underlying generalized instinctual reaction.

This dissociation of sex and love can be described as a split between the conscious and the unconscious feeling of love. The man who can respond only to a prostitute is reacting to her on a nonpersonal level. As "woman," she is a legitimate object for his sexual desires. Her anonymity or her role as social outcast, which removes her from the society of persons, allows him to express his sexual feelings to her. His love is directed to the female in her, divorced from her personality. The rapist has a similar attitude. He can respond sexually to the feminine in a woman only if by his violence he can destroy the integrity of her personality. The degree of dissociation of the tender, affectionate feelings and the sexual feelings varies according to the severity of the neurotic disturbance. But to whatever degree it exists, it acts to decrease orgastic potency.

. . . Sex is an expression of love. But the relationship between sex and love has other aspects. Can it be shown that love is a manifestation of sexuality?

LOVE AND SEX

. . . Love is not sex any more than sex is love. This statement, however, does not reject the idea of an intimate relationship between these two feelings. Sex is an expression of love, but there are other ways to express love besides the sexual. Love is not sex, but it can be shown that it derives from the sexual function. Support for this idea can be found both in evolutionary development of animals and in the personal development of the individual.

Love as a conscious sentiment is a relative newcomer in the field of emotions. By contrast, sex appeared early in the evolutionary scheme of life. Sexual differentiation and sexual activity appear among the lower animals long before any behavior that can be recognized as motivated by feelings of affection or love. Even the basic feelings of mother love toward offspring are completely absent from most species of fish. Yet sex as it functions among fish in mating and reproduction is not so greatly different from the sexual functions of the higher animals, including man.

As one follows the sexual evolution of animals, it is interesting to note that signs of tenderness and affection appear as physical closeness and intimacy between the sexes increase in the course of mating. In the mating of fish, the male hovers over the spot where the female has extruded her eggs and discharges his sperm cells. In this activity, there is little physical contact between male and female. Contact during sexual activity is first noted in amphibians. The male frog, for example, clasps the female with special gripper pads on his forelegs as he covers her during the discharge of the sexual gametes. Both eggs and sperm cells are discharged freely into the water, where fertilization takes place. Amphibians have an advantage over fish in that the simultaneous discharge that occurs increases the chances of fertilization.

There was neither penetration nor deposits of sperm cells into the body of the female until the evolution of animals who spend their entire lives on dry land. Perhaps there was no need for sexual penetration among the water animals. The sea was the great repository, the great mother substance. Sandor Ferenczi expressed the idea that sexual penetration among land animals has the function of providing a fluid medium of approximately the same chemical composition as the ancient seas for the process of fertilization and embryonic development.* The human embryo develops and grows in a fluid medium exactly as do the fertilized eggs of fish and amphibians. In this sense, the saying that life began in the sea is true for all living creatures. But whatever the reason, the fact is that the evolutionary development of animals is characterized by closer and more intimate sexual contact.

With the increase in physical closeness and intimacy that characterizes the sexual act among birds and mammals, there is the appearance of behavior that reflects feelings of affection, tenderness, and love. Naturalists have described actions among birds that can be understood only in terms of such feelings. Among many birds, it is customary for the female to preen the feathers of her mate as she perches beside him on a limb, an activity that he appears to relish highly. In return, he feeds her choice morsels of worms and other food as a token of his feelings.

I had occasion to watch and photograph a pair of collies who appeared to be attracted to each other at first sight and who were subsequently mated. The male ran beside the female as they romped along the sand, licking her at every moment. He was a large, handsome animal. Regularly, he placed his neck over hers, rubbing it to and fro. It was the first time I had seen true "necking." One evening when he heard her on the beach, he jumped out of a one-story window to be near her. He had been locked in his room because he had spent the whole of the previous night outside, close to the cottage where his "girl friend" was staying. It is important to add that the female was not in heat at this time. His behavior could not be explained, therefore, as sexual. In my opinion, it represented a real feeling of affection.

What I and others have observed in animals is behavior that parallels human behavior in similar circumstances. To ascribe feelings of love or affection to such behavior seems not beyond the realm of possibility. The point I wish to make is that behavior that can be described as affectionate is manifested only by the animals who are physically intimate in the reproductive process.

Among human beings, tenderness and affection between a man and a woman are commonly associated with sexual interest. One set of emotions involves the other. To argue that these feelings, love and sex, have no functional or organic relationship runs counter to common experience. Even in long-married couples in whom sexual attraction has abated, it seems unreasonable to separate the affection that remains from the sexual feelings that originally drew them together. The question is, does the feeling of affection or love derive from the

* Sandor Ferenczi, *Thalassa: A Theory of Genitality.* New York: Psychoanalytic Quarterly, Inc., 1949.

sexual attraction? If the answer is yes, it is important to know how. Some understanding can be gained from the study of the maternal behavior of animals.

The evolution of animals is also characterized by increasing physical closeness and intimacy between mother and young. Among animals who deposit eggs to be fertilized in the sea or who deposit fertilized eggs to be hatched unattended in the ground, there are no signs of maternal care or affection. Only in the higher animals, where the biological processes impose a closer physical relationship between mother and offspring, does evidence of maternal love appear. Birds not only hatch their young with the heat of their bodies, but also feed them and protect them until they are ready to leave the nest. Among mammals, the dependence of the young upon the mother is greater, and her response is broader. She cleans them, protects them, plays with them, and teaches them. Her obvious distress when separated from her young is the basis for the assumption of maternal feeling. The amount of feeling among animal mothers seems to be proportionate to the helpessness of the offspring.

The psychosexual development of the child provides good material for the study of the relationship of love to sex. Biologically, it can be said that every child is conceived in love. This follows logically from the premise that sex is an expression of love on the body level. Unfortunately, ambivalences and conflicts are present in most individuals. Sex and pregnancy are often contaminated by what Wilhelm Reich called "secondary drives." Sex may be a submissive act to avoid conflict rather than a voluntary surrender to love. Pregnancy may be motivated secondarily by a woman's desire to tie a man to her or to fill an emptiness in her life. These secondary feelings limit a mother's love, but they do not deny it. Every expression of love and attention that a woman shows her child manifests her love for him. But she may also hate him. Many mothers have told me that at times they felt like murdering a difficult child. A harsh tone, a cold glance, a humiliating remark may betray a hatred which the mother may not consciously perceive, but to which the child is sensitive. In his earliest days, the infant, like all mammalian babies, simply reacts with pleasure or pain to the satisfaction or denial of his needs. He cannot understand the emotional problems of his mother.

As he grows older, a development occurs in the child that transforms love as a biological function into love as a conscious psychological experience. This development is the emergence of self-consciousness, together with its corollary, the consciousness of the other. Early in life, the child becomes aware of his mother as an object that can provide pleasure and satisfaction. The recognition of the human face manifested by the smiling response of the infant, which usually occurs at about three months of age, indicates, according to René Spitz, that memory and anticipation are present in the infant's psyche. At about eight months of age . . . "the ego has come into its own." It cannot be said definitely that an infant of eight months is conscious of his love for his mother. This will come soon. He is conscious of his mother, he recognizes her special role in relation to his needs, and he can express his desire for closeness by appropriate actions.

However, when speech is well developed, at about the age of three years, a child expresses his feelings of affection for the "good mother" in words of love.

Anyone who has heard a child say, "I love you, Mommy," cannot fail to sense the sincerity and depth of the feeling. The words seem to come directly from the heart. What was originally a biological response of pleasure and joy at the approach of the "good mother" has become a psychological experience that the child has learned to express in language. The use of language enables the child to dissociate the feeling from its base in the action of reaching out his arms to his mother. Memory and anticipation combine to create a feeling of affection directed toward the image of the "good mother" that can be perceived consciously and expressed verbally. Marcel Proust defined beauty as the "promise of happiness." I would define love as the anticipation of pleasure and satisfaction.

Love as a psychological experience is an abstraction. By this I mean that it is a feeling divorced from its appropriate action, an anticipation that has not found its realization. It has the same quality as a hope, a wish, or a dream. These aspirations and sentiments are necessary to human existence. The appreciation of love as a psychological phenomenon must not blind one to the necessity of its fulfillment in action. Love finds its reality in the pleasure and satisfaction of the biological urge to embrace and unite. Romantic love is the handmaiden of sexuality. It serves an important function.

Love increases the tension of sexual attraction. It does this by placing a psychic distance between the lovers. This distance is the heightened consciousness of the loved person. Such heightened awareness of the other actually separates two people. It defines their differences and accents their individuality. The loved person is unique, never generic. The saying, "Absence [distance] makes the heart grow fonder," may be interpreted to mean that the greater the love, the greater the separation. This is where sex comes in. Sex has a pleasure mechanism. It aims to eliminate the distance and to discharge the tension, thereby producing pleasure. Since the amount of pleasure is in direct proportion to the amount of tension, as Freud pointed out, the more the love, the greater the distance and the fuller the pleasure of the sexual union.

The relationship between love and sex may be set forth as follows. Sex divorced from its conscious correlates, that is, sex as an instinctual drive, obeys the pleasure principle. The buildup of sexual tension leads in such conditions to an immediate attempt to discharge the tension with the nearest available object. But when love enters the scene, the reality principle becomes operative. Knowing love, one is aware that the pleasure of the sexual discharge can be heightened by certain sexual objects and lowered by others. Knowing love, one tends to hold back the action, consciously restraining the discharge of the sexual tension until the most favorable situation is available, which is, of course, a loved person. The insistence upon selectivity and discrimination in the choice of a sexual object for greater sexual pleasure is one of the main functions of love. When one looks for a special object, one becomes more conscious of the object, more sensitive to love and to the love partner.

Love can be expressed spiritually or physically. One does not rule out the other. Normally the two modes of expression are complementary. In a healthy person, the spiritual expression of love creates a tension that is discharged in some physical act of love. The pleasure that the latter yields increases consciousness and spirituality. One leads to the other and makes the other a more significant experience.

In an unneurotic individual, spirituality contributes to sexuality and vice versa. In the absence of dissociative tendencies that split the unity of the personality, more spirituality means more sexuality. For this reason, I would say that, generally speaking, the sexuality of a civilized person is superior, qualitatively and quantitatively, to that of a primitive person. Qualitatively, it contains a greater tenderness, a keener sensitivity, and deeper respect for individuality. Quantitatively, there is a greater frequency of and intensity to the sexual impulse. But this is true only in the absence of neurosis. The neurotic individual looks with longing at the sexual freedom and pleasure enjoyed by some primitive peoples.

Formerly, the primitive person envied the civilized man's seeming sexual superiority. The civilized man's sense of individuality and egoism awed the primitive man and fascinated the primitive woman. Unfortunately, the primitive mind was unprepared for civilized man's neurotic behavior, his trickery and deceit.

In *Laughing Boy,* the story of a Navajo Indian, Oliver La Farge explores the effect of the white man's sexual practices upon Indian attitudes. Laughing Boy meets and is attracted to an Indian girl who has been raised by white people and seduced by one of them. She introduces him to the excitement of love play, with its kisses and caresses, and also to alcohol. Laughing Boy falls madly in love with this girl and finds that he cannot leave her to go back to his people. On the other hand, she will not be accepted by his family. Still he must try. His dilemma is resolved by her death on the return voyage. But Laughing Boy is then left with the insurmountable difficulty of accepting one of the drab Indian girls as his wife. He decides to live alone, but he is not lonely, for the memory of his love is bright in his heart.

I have painted a one-sided picture of civilized man's love. The promise it offers is not easily fulfilled. Culture brings problems as well as promises, conflicts as well as excitement. Although love is the ally of sex, it can also betray it. The danger in any dialectical relationship is that one member of the pair will turn against the other. It is in the name of love that infantile sexuality is suppressed. The mother believes that she is acting in the best interests of her child when she stops his masturbatory activity. It is in the name of love that adult sexuality is restricted and undermined. How many women have expressed the thought, "If you loved me, you would not want such a thing from me"? True, such attitudes are less common today, but they are by no means absent. The antagonism of love and sex is also expressed in the double standard that many men follow: one does not sleep with the girl one loves, and one cannot love the girl one sleeps with. To sophisticated ears, this sounds old-fashioned, but the distinction between love and sex is emphasized by many current writers on love. The distinction is there, but to emphasize it is to dissociate love from sex, as Theodor Reik does. "I believe that love and sex are different in origin and nature." Sex, he says, is a biological instinct that aims at the release of physical tension only. Love is a cultural phenomenon that aims at happiness through the establishment of a very personal relationship. Reik believes that there is sex without love, "straight sex."‡ The

‡ Theodor Reik, *Of Love and Lust.* New York: Farrar, Straus & Co., 1957.

effect of such an attitude is to degrade sexuality. It is reduced to an animal passion, lust, which is inferior to the noble quality of love.

The dissociation of love from sex derives from the division of man's unitary nature into opposing categories—body and spirit, nature and culture, intelligent mind and animal body. These distinctions exist, but to ignore their essential unity in man's biological nature is to create a schizoid condition. Culture can oppose nature only at its peril. An intelligent mind acts to control the body in the interest of a better body function and a richer experience of its passions. Man can be human only to the degree that he is also an animal. And sex is part of man's animal nature.

All this, however, is only the philosophical explanation of the antagonism of love to sex. As was stated before, the dynamic mechanism of this antagonism goes back to infancy. The infant or the child can experience two distinct feelings in relation to his mother. One is erotic pleasure at her breast or in closeness to her body. The other is the awareness of the mother as a love object, a person who promises pleasure and fulfillment through her being. Normally, these two feelings are fused in the image of the mother. But, often, the image of the mother is split into a "good mother" and a "bad mother." The "good mother" promises happiness, and the child transfers his love to this image. The "bad mother" is the frustrating figure, the one who denies the child's need for erotic satisfaction. The child focuses his hostility upon the image of the "bad mother." Love thus becomes associated in the mind of the child with the promise of happiness, but not with its fulfillment.

In proportion as the promise is greater, the chances of its fulfillment decrease. One cannot fail to be impressed by the fact that all great love stories end in tragedy and death. *Romeo and Juliet, Tristan and Isolde* are the classic examples; *Laughing Boy* is a modern version. The list is endless. Is love an illusion that fades in the harsh reality of day? Is the world so cruel a place that a great love cannot survive in it?

I had as a patient an intelligent young woman who was very much in love. This is the way she described her feeling to me: "I said to him [her lover], 'I love you so much that nothing can satisfy me. I want to devour you, to consume you; I want to have every part of you inside me.'" Her love may be described as neurotic, infantile, irrational, and so on, but the sincerity and genuineness of her feelings could not be denied. She observed that even after the most terrific sexual experience, she never felt satisfied. And she remarked, "When I am most in love, I feel most helpless, dependent, and weak." She was intelligent enough to realize that a marriage could not be founded on such feelings. Eventually, each married some other person, but the attraction between them never fully vanished.

. . . Love is our search for paradise lost. . . . isn't there some element of this search for paradise in all feelings of love? And isn't paradise regained when we find our beloved? This is the magic of love; it transforms the ordinary into the extraordinary, earth into heaven. . . .

Divorced from its roots in man's biological function, love is tragic. If paradise is sought anywhere but on earth and in the reality of daily living, the result is death. The divine in human form is the ecstasy of orgasm. In any other form, it exists only in saints, angels, and martyrs. If we cannot be saints and do not wish to be martyrs, we can be human in the full sense of the term, which includes our animal nature. The sexual sophisticate advocates sex without love. To proclaim love without sex is to promise a kingdom that is not of this earth. The reality of our being is that life and love arose from sex, which in turn became the vehicle for the expression of love. The great mystery of life is sexual love. Love promises the fulfillment that sexuality offers.

Under what conditions can the sexual act, or coitus, be considered the most intimate form of love? What does it become when those conditions do not apply?

According to Lowen, what are the exceptions to the statement that sex is impossible without love? Why? Do you agree?

If there is merit in Suzie Wong's argument (p. 195), do you think that our sexual mores should distinguish between a sexual but emotionally meaningless act in which the body is given without the heart, and a sexual act in which one gives oneself fully?

What generalization is the author supporting by his instance of the pair of collies "necking"? Are you persuaded? If not, how would you explain apparent signs of affection, tenderness, and love among lower animals and their relationship to sexual behavior and evolutionary development?

How does Lowen respond to Reik's theory of "straight sex"?

Do you subscribe to the view that males feel "one does not sleep with the girl one loves, and one cannot love the girl one sleeps with"? Why might men make such a distinction? Of what significance is it to the relationship between sex and love? Would the fact be relevant that some men who have sexual intercourse with prostitutes do not want to kiss them?

The old saying that "Absence makes the heart grow fonder," has been dismissed as:

> A pretty and poetic thought, but quite misleading. If the person is not around to annoy you, the heart might feel fonder for a short time, but any prolonged absence weakens the bond of love.
> The French go a step further: "Absence is to love what the wind is to fire. It blows out the small one and lights the big one." [26]

What position does Lowen take? What point of view seems most valid to you? Under what circumstances?

How would you describe mature sexuality? What is it? What is it not?

While many would agree that

> . . . the minor tragedies which are caused by the misunderstandings that arise when a man and a woman, for instance, both say "I Love You," would alone justify our working toward greater clarity [27]

about the term love, fewer, perhaps, see a need for greater clarification of meanings attached to variants of the term sex. Observe Lowen's usage of "sex," "sexual," and "sexuality":

SEX:
   "the feminine *sex*"
   "the opposite *sex*"
   "*sex* becomes discriminating"
   "*sex* without love; straight *sex*"
   "*sex* brings people together"

SEXUAL:
  "*sexual* impulse"
  "*sexual* interest"
  "*sexual* attraction"
  "*sexual* desire"
  "*sexual* embrace"
  "*sexual* penetration"
  "*sexual* relations"
  "*sexual* act"
  "*sexual* feelings"
  "*sexual* behavior"
  "*sexual* function"
  "*sexual* object"
  "*sexual* tension"
  "*sexual* union"
  "*sexual* satisfaction"
  "*sexual* pleasure"
  "*sexual* happiness"
  "*sexual* love"
  "*sexual* sophisticate"
  "psycho*sexual* development of the child"
  "homo*sexual*"
  "relationships that are not primarily *sexual*"

SEXUALITY:
  "to degrade *sexuality*"
  "love is a manifestation of *sexuality*"
  "infantile *sexuality*"
  "adolescent *sexuality*"
  "adult *sexuality*"
  "mature *sexuality*"

Which of the terms are synonymous? If you were compiling dictionary definitions for "sex," "sexual," and "sexuality" what alternative meanings would you need to present for each term?

RELATED QUESTIONS

How might Lowen explain Stephen Daedalus' visit to the prostitute were he to analyze the emotional components in the scene from *A Portrait of the Artist as a Young Man* (p. 51)?

What explanation might Lowen give for the lack of sexual satisfaction described in *Entry August 29* by Walter Benton (see "**Night-Lights,**" p. 534)?

To what extent does the argument advanced by "She" in William Dickey's *Resolving Doubts* (see "**Night-Lights,**" p. 545) coincide with that of Suzie Wong as reported by Lowen in "Sex and Love" *(Love and Orgasm)*?

How might Mrs. Marshall of *The Bent Twig* (p. 144) react to Lowen's paragraph on tenderness and affection between a man and a woman on p. 198?

In *Entry November 12* by Walter Benton (see "**Night-Lights,**" p. 535), do you think the narrator had sexual relations with the girl crying by St. Mark's church? If so, what might have motivated the act in his case? How would Lowen view the situation presented in Benton's poem?

Having cited *Tristan and Isolde,* Lowen poses the question: "Is love an illusion that fades in the harsh reality of day?" How do you imagine that Gunn, author of **Das Liebesleben** (p. 192), would respond?

What connections exist between William Hazlitt's description of perfect love in **Liber Amoris** (see "**Night-Lights,**" p. 563) and Lowen's statement that "Love is our search for paradise lost"? Where and how should it be sought? Can it be found?

How does **Don Juan** by George Gordon, Lord Byron (see "**Night-Lights,**" p. 556) illustrate the Don Juan type of sexual behavior described by Lowen as adolescent since it "is dominated by the unconscious element in its broad responsiveness to the opposite sex," whereas "mature sexuality is selective," with "a greater conscious component . . . superimposed upon the underlying generalized instinctual reaction"?

The primary function of sex is to reproduce, but the sexual act may satisfy (or at least be used to meet) a variety of needs. From selections you have examined so far, and from other reading, observation, or experience, indicate some of the purposes for which sex can be used when it is other than an expression of a voluntary surrender to love.

Eros

C. S. LEWIS

By Eros I mean of course that state which we call "being in love"; or, if you prefer, that kind of love which lovers are "in." . . . Sexuality makes part of our subject only when it becomes an ingredient in the complex state of "being in love." That sexual experience can occur without Eros, without being "in love," and that Eros includes other things besides sexual activity, I take for granted. . . . The carnal or animally sexual element within Eros . . . I call Venus. And I mean by Venus . . . what is known to be sexual by those who experience it; what could be proved to be sexual by the simplest observations.

Sexuality may operate without Eros or as part of Eros. . . . I am not at all subscribing to the popular idea that it is the absence or presence of Eros which makes the sexual act "impure" or "pure," degraded or fine, unlawful or lawful. If all who lay together without being in the state of Eros were abominable, we all come of tainted stock. The times and places in which marriage depends on Eros are in a small minority. Most of our ancestors were married off in early youth to partners chosen by their parents on grounds that had nothing to do with Eros. They went to the act with no other "fuel," so to speak, than plain animal desire. And they did right; honest Christian husbands and wives, obeying their fathers and mothers, discharging to one another their "marriage debt," and bringing up families in the fear of the Lord. Conversely, this act, done under the influence of a soaring and iridescent Eros which reduces the role of the senses to a minor consideration, may yet be plain adultery, may involve breaking a wife's heart, deceiving a husband, betraying a friend, polluting hospitality and deserting your children. It has not pleased God that the distinction between a sin and a duty should turn on fine feelings. This act, like any other, is justified (or not) by far more prosaic and definable criteria; by the keeping or breaking of promises, by justice or injustice, by charity or selfishness, by obedience or disobedience. My treatment rules out mere sexuality—sexuality without Eros—on grounds that have nothing to do with morals; because it is irrelevant to our purpose.

To the evolutionist Eros (the human variation) will be something that grows out of Venus, a late complication and development of the immemorial biological impulse. We must not assume, however, that this is necessarily what happens within the consciousness of the individual. There may be those who have first felt mere sexual appetite for a woman and then gone on at a later stage to "fall in love with her." But I doubt if this is at all common. Very often what comes first is simply a delighted pre-occupation with the Beloved—a general, unspecified pre-occupation with her in her totality. A man in this state really hasn't leisure to think of sex. He is too busy thinking of a person. The fact that she is a woman is far less important than the fact that she is herself. He is full of desire, but the desire may not be sexually toned. If you asked him what he wanted, the true reply would often be, "To go on thinking of her." He is love's contemplative. And when at a later stage the explicitly sexual element awakes, he will not feel (unless scientific theories are influencing him) that this had all along been the root of the whole matter. He is more likely to feel that the incoming tide of Eros, having demolished many sand-castles and made islands of many rocks, has now at last with a triumphant seventh wave flooded this part of his nature also—the little pool of ordinary sexuality which was there on his beach before the tide came in. Eros enters him like an invader, taking over and reorganising, one by one, the institutions of a conquered country. It may have taken over many others before it reaches the sex in him; and it will reorganise that too.

No one has indicated the nature of that reorganisation more briefly and accurately than George Orwell, who disliked it and preferred sexuality in its native condition, uncontaminated by Eros. In *Nineteen Eighty-Four* his dreadful hero (how much less human than the four-footed heroes of his excellent *Animal Farm!*), before towsing the heroine, demands a reassurance, "You like doing this?" he asks, "I don't mean simply me; I mean the thing in itself." He is not satisfied till he gets the answer, "I adore it." This little dialogue defines the reorganisation. Sexual desire, without Eros, wants *it*, the *thing in itself;* Eros wants the Beloved.

The *thing* is a sensory pleasure; that is, an event occurring within one's own body. We use a most unfortunate idiom when we say, of a lustful man prowling the streets, that he "wants a woman." Strictly speaking, a woman is just what he does not want. He wants a pleasure for which a woman happens to be the necessary piece of apparatus. How much he cares about the woman as such may be gauged by his attitude to her five minutes after fruition (one does not keep the carton after one has smoked the cigarettes). Now Eros makes a man really want, not a woman, but one particular woman. In some mysterious but quite indisputable fashion the lover desires the Beloved herself, not the pleasure she can give. No lover in the world ever sought the embraces of the woman he loved as the result of a calculation, however unconscious, that they would be more pleasurable than those of any other woman. If he raised the question he would, no doubt, expect that this would be so. But to raise it would be to step outside the world of Eros altogether. . . .

. . . Eros thus wonderfully transforms what is *par excellence* a Need-pleasure into the most Appreciative of all pleasures. It is the nature of a Need-pleasure to show us the object solely in relation to our need, even our momentary need. But in Eros, a Need, at its most intense, sees the object most intensely as a thing admirable in herself, important far beyond her relation to the lover's need.

If we had not all experienced this, if we were mere logicians, we might boggle at the conception of desiring a human being, as distinct from desiring any pleasure, comfort, or service that human being can give. And it is certainly hard to explain. Lovers themselves are trying to express part of it (not much) when they say they would like to "eat" one another. Milton has expressed more when he fancies angelic creatures with bodies made of light who can achieve total interpenetration instead of our mere embraces. Charles Williams has said something of it in the words, "Love you? I *am* you."

Without Eros sexual desire, like every other desire, is a fact about ourselves. Within Eros it is rather about the Beloved. It becomes almost a mode of perception, entirely a mode of expression. It feels objective; something outside us, in the real world. That is why Eros, though the king of pleasures, always (at his height) has the air of regarding pleasure as a by-product. To think about it would plunge us back in ourselves, in our own nervous system. It would kill Eros, as you can "kill" the finest mountain prospect by locating it all in your own retina and optic nerves. Anyway, whose pleasure? For one of the first things Eros does is to obliterate the distinction between giving and receiving.

It has been widely held in the past, and is perhaps held by many unsophisticated people to-day, that the spiritual danger of Eros arises almost entirely from the carnal element within it; that Eros is "noblest" or "purest" when Venus is reduced to the minimum. . . . With all proper respect to the medieval guides, I cannot help remembering that they were all celibates, and probably did not know what Eros does to our sexuality; how, far from aggravating, he reduces the nagging and addictive character of mere appetite. And that not simply by satisfying it. Eros, without diminishing desire, makes abstinence easier. He tends, no doubt, to a pre-occupation with the Beloved which can indeed be an obstacle to the spiritual life; but not chiefly a sensual pre-occupation.

The real spiritual danger in Eros as a whole lies, I believe, elsewhere. I will return to the point. For the moment, I want to speak of the danger which at present, in my opinion, especially haunts the act of love. This is a subject on which I disagree, not with the human race (far from it), but with many of its gravest spokesmen. I believe we are all being encouraged to take Venus too seriously; at any rate, with a wrong kind of seriousness. All my life a ludicrous and portentous solemnisation of sex has been going on.

One author tells us that Venus should recur through the married life in "a solemn, sacramental rhythm." A young man to whom I had described as "pornographic" a novel that he much admired, replied with genuine bewilderment,

"Pornographic? But how can it be? It treats the whole thing so seriously"—as if a long face were a sort of moral disinfectant. Our friends who harbour Dark Gods, the "pillar of blood" school, attempt seriously to restore something like the Phallic religion. Our advertisements, at their sexiest, paint the whole business in terms of the rapt, the intense, the swoony-devout; seldom a hint of gaiety. And the psychologists have so bedevilled us with the infinite importance of complete sexual adjustment and the all but impossibility of achieving it, that I could believe some young couples now go to it with the complete works of Freud, Kraft-Ebbing, Havelock Ellis and Dr. Stopes spread out on bed-tables all round them. Cheery old Ovid, who never either ignored a mole-hill or made a mountain of it, would be more to the point. We have reached the stage at which nothing is more needed than a roar of old-fashioned laughter.

But, it will be replied, the thing *is* serious. Yes; quadruply so. First, theologically, because this is the body's share in marriage which, by God's choice, is the mystical image of the union between God and Man. Secondly, as what I will venture to call a sub-Christian, or Pagan or natural sacrament, our human participation in, and exposition of, the natural forces of life and fertility—the marriage of Sky-Father and Earth-Mother. Thirdly, on the moral level, in view of the obligations involved and the incalculable momentousness of being a parent and ancestor. Finally it has (sometimes, not always) a great emotional seriousness in the minds of the participants.

But eating is also serious; theologically, as the vehicle of the Blessed Sacrament; ethically in view of our duty to feed the hungry; socially, because the table is from time immemorial the place for talk; medically, as all dyspeptics know. Yet we do not bring bluebooks to dinner nor behave there as if we were in church. And it is *gourmets*, not saints, who come nearest to doing so. Animals are always serious about food.

We must not be totally serious about Venus. Indeed we can't be totally serious without doing violence to our humanity. It is not for nothing that every language and literature in the world is full of jokes about sex. Many of them may be dull or disgusting and nearly all of them are old. But we must insist that they embody an attitude to Venus which in the long run endangers the Christian life far less than a reverential gravity. We must not attempt to find an absolute in the flesh. Banish play and laughter from the bed of love and you may let in a false goddess. She will be even falser than the Aphrodite of the Greeks; for they, even while they worshipped her, knew that she was "laughter-loving." The mass of the people are perfectly right in their conviction that Venus is a partly comic spirit. We are under no obligation at all to sing all our love-duets in the throbbing, world-without-end, heart-breaking manner of Tristan and Isolde. . . .

Venus herself will have a terrible revenge if we take her (occasional) seriousness at its face value.

She herself is a mocking, mischievous spirit, far more elf than deity, and makes game of us. When all external circumstances are fittest for her service she will leave one or both the lovers totally indisposed for it. When every overt act is impossible and even glances cannot be exchanged—in trains, in shops, and at interminable parties—she will assail them with all her force. An hour later, when time and place agree, she will have mysteriously withdrawn; perhaps from only one of them. What a pother this must raise—what resentments, self-pities, suspicions, wounded vanities and all the current chatter about "frustration"—in those who have deified her! But sensible lovers laugh. It is all part of the game; a game of catch-as-catch-can, and the escapes and tumbles and head-on collisions are to be treated as a romp.

In Eros at times we seem to be flying; Venus gives us the sudden twitch that reminds us we are really captive balloons. It is a continual demonstration of the truth that we are composite creatures, rational animals, akin on one side to the angels, on the other to tom-cats.

Man has held three views of his body. First there is that of those ascetic Pagans who called it the prison or the "tomb" of the soul, and of Christians like Fisher to whom it was a "sack of dung," food for worms, filthy, shameful, a source of nothing but temptation to bad men and humiliation to good ones. Then there are the Neo-Pagans (they seldom know Greek), the nudists and the sufferers from Dark Gods, to whom the body is glorious. But thirdly we have the view which St. Francis expressed by calling his body "Brother Ass." All three may be—I am not sure—defensible; but give me St. Francis for my money.

Ass is exquisitely right because no one in his senses can either revere or hate a donkey. It is a useful, sturdy, lazy, obstinate, patient, lovable and infuriating beast; deserving now the stick and now a carrot; both pathetically and absurdly beautiful. So the body. There's no living with it till we recognise that one of its functions in our lives is to play the part of buffoon. Until some theory has sophisticated them, every man, woman and child in the world knows this. The fact that we have bodies is the oldest joke there is. Eros (like death, figure-drawing, and the study of medicine) may at moments cause us to take it with total seriousness. The error consists in concluding that Eros should always do so and permanently abolish the joke. But this is not what happens. The very faces of all the happy lovers we know make it clear. Lovers, unless their love is very short-lived, again and again feel an element not only of comedy, not only of play, but even of buffoonery, in the body's expression of Eros. And the body would frustrate us if this were not so. It would be too clumsy an instrument to render love's music unless its very clumsiness could be felt as adding to the total experience its own grotesque charm—a sub-plot or antimasque miming with its own hearty rough-and-tumble what the soul enacts in statelier fashion. . . . The highest does not stand without the lowest. There is indeed at certain moments a high poetry in the flesh itself; but also, by your leave, an irreducible element of obstinate and ludicrous unpoetry. If it does not make itself felt on one occasion, it will on another. Far better plant it foursquare within the drama of Eros as comic relief than pretend you haven't noticed it.

For indeed we require this relief. The poetry is there as well as the unpoetry; the gravity of Venus as well as her levity, the *gravis ardor* or burning weight of desire. Pleasure, pushed to its extreme, shatters us like pain. The longing for a union which only the flesh can mediate while the flesh, our mutually excluding bodies, renders it forever unattainable can have the grandeur of a metaphysical pursuit. Amorousness as well as grief can bring tears to the eyes. But Venus does not always come thus "entire, fastened to her prey," and the fact that she sometimes does so is the very reason for preserving always a hint of playfulness in our attitude to her. When natural things look most divine, the demoniac is just round the corner.

This refusal to be quite immersed—this recollection of the levity even when, for the moment, only the gravity is displayed—is especially relevant to a certain attitude which Venus, in her intensity, evokes from most (I believe, not all) pairs of lovers. This act can invite the man to an extreme, though short-lived, masterfulness, to the dominance of a conqueror or a captor, and the woman to a correspondingly extreme subjection and surrender. Hence the roughness, even fierceness, of some erotic play; the "lover's pinch which hurts and is desired." How should a sane couple think of this? or a Christian couple permit it?

I think it is harmless and wholesome on one condition. We must recognise that we have here to do with what I called "the Pagan sacrament" in sex. In Friendship, as we noticed, each participant stands for precisely himself—the contingent individual he is. But in the act of love we are not merely ourselves. We are also representatives. It is here no impoverishment but an enrichment to be aware that forces older and less personal than we work through us. In us all the masculinity and femininity of the world, all that is assailant and responsive, are momentarily focused. The man does play the Sky-Father and the woman the Earth-Mother; he does play Form, and she Matter. But we must give full value to the word *play*. Of course neither "plays a part" in the sense of being a hypocrite. But each plays a part or role in—well, in something which is comparable to a mystery-play or ritual (at one extreme) and to a masque or even a charade (at the other).

A woman who accepted as literally her own this extreme self-surrender would be an idolatress offering to a man what belongs only to God. And a man would have to be the coxcomb of all coxcombs, and indeed a blasphemer, if he arrogated to himself, as the mere person he is, the sort of sovereignty to which Venus for a moment exalts him. . . .

From Venus, the carnal ingredient within Eros, I now turn to Eros as a whole. Here we shall see the same pattern repeated. As Venus within Eros does not really aim at pleasure, so Eros does not aim at happiness. We may think he does, but when he is brought to the test it proves otherwise. Everyone knows that it is useless to try to separate lovers by proving to them that their marriage will be an unhappy one. This is not only because they will disbelieve you. They usually will, no doubt. But even if they believed, they would not be dissuaded. For it is the very mark of Eros that when he is in us we had rather share unhappiness with the Beloved than be happy on any other terms. Even if the two lovers are mature and experienced people who know that broken hearts heal in the end and can clearly foresee that, if they once steeled themselves to go through the present agony of parting, they would almost certainly be happier ten years hence than marriage is at all likely to make them—even then, they would not part. . . . Even when it becomes clear beyond all evasion that marriage with the Beloved cannot possibly lead to happiness—when it cannot even profess to offer any other life than that of tending an incurable invalid, of hopeless poverty, of exile, or of disgrace—Eros never hesitates to say, "Better this than parting. Better to be miserable with her than happy without her. Let our hearts break provided they break together." If the voice within us does not say this, it is not the voice of Eros.

This is the grandeur and terror of love. But notice, as before, side by side with this grandeur, the playfulness. Eros, as well as Venus, is the subject of countless jokes. And even when the circumstances of the two lovers are so tragic that no bystander could keep back his tears, they themselves—in want, in hospital wards, on visitors' days in jail—will sometimes be surprised by a merriment which strikes the onlooker (but not them) as unbearably pathetic. Nothing is falser than the idea that mockery is necessarily hostile. Until they have a baby to laugh at, lovers are always laughing at each other.

It is in the grandeur of Eros that the seeds of danger are concealed. He has spoken like a god. His total commitment, his reckless disregard of happiness, his transcendence of self-regard, sound like a message from the eternal world.

And yet it cannot, just as it stands, be the voice of God Himself. For Eros, speaking with that very grandeur and displaying that very transcendence of self, may urge to evil as well as to good. Nothing is shallower than the belief that a love which leads to sin is always qualitatively lower—more animal or more trivial—than one which leads to faithful, fruitful and Christian marriage. The love which leads to cruel and perjured unions, even to suicide-pacts and murder, is not likely to be wandering lust or idle sentiment. It may well be Eros in all his splendour; heartbreakingly sincere; ready for every sacrifc except renunciation.

There have been schools of thought which accepted the voice of Eros as something actually transcendent and tried to justify the absoluteness of his commands. Plato will have it that "falling in love" is the mutual recognition on earth of souls which have been singled out for one another in a previous and celestial existence. To meet the Beloved is to realise "We loved before we were born." As a myth to express what lovers feel this is admirable. But if one accepted it literally one would be faced by an embarrassing consequence. We should have to conclude that in that heavenly and forgotten life affairs were no better managed than here. For Eros may unite the most unsuitable yokefellows; many unhappy, and predictably unhappy, marriages were love-matches.

A theory more likely to be accepted in our own day is what we may call Shavian—Shaw himself might have said "metabiological"—Romanticism. According to Shavian Romanticism the voice of Eros is the voice of the élan vital or Life Force, the "evolutionary appetite." In overwhelming a particular couple it is seeking parents (or ancestors) for the superman. It is indifferent both to their personal happiness and to the rules of morality because it aims at something which Shaw thinks very much more important: the future perfection of our species. But if all this were true it hardly makes clear whether—and if so, why—we should obey it. All pictures yet offered us of the superman are so unattractive that one might well vow celibacy at once to avoid the risk of begetting him. And secondly, this theory surely leads to the conclusion that the Life Force does not very well understand its (or her? or his?) own business. So far as we can see the existence or intensity of Eros between two people is no warrant that their offspring will be especially satisfactory, or even that they will have offspring at all. Two good "strains" (in the stockbreeders' sense), not two good lovers, is the recipe for fine children. And what on earth was the Life

Force doing through all those countless generations when the begetting of children depended very little on mutual Eros and very much on arranged marriages, slavery, and rape? Has it only just thought of this bright idea for improving the species?

Neither the Platonic nor the Shavian type of erotic transcendentalism can help a Christian. We are not worshippers of the Life Force and we know nothing of previous existences. We must not give unconditional obedience to the voice of Eros when he speaks most like a god. Neither must we ignore or attempt to deny the god-like quality. This love is really and truly like Love Himself. In it there is a real nearness to God (by Resemblance); but not, therefore and necessarily, a nearness of Approach. Eros, honoured so far as love of God and charity to our fellows will allow, may become for us a means of Approach. His total commitment is a paradigm or example, built into our natures, of the love we ought to exercise towards God and Man. As nature, for the nature-lover, gives a content to the word *glory,* so this gives a content to the word *Charity.* It is as if Christ said to us through Eros, "Thus—just like this—with this prodigality—not counting the cost—you are to love me and the least of my brethren." Our conditional honour to Eros will of course vary with our circumstances. Of some a total renunciation (but not a contempt) is required. Others, with Eros as their fuel and also as their model, can embark on the married life. Within which Eros, of himself, will never be enough—will indeed survive only in so far as he is continually chastened and corroborated by higher principles.

But Eros, honoured without reservation and obeyed unconditionally, becomes a demon. . . . Of all loves he is, at his height, most god-like; therefore most prone to demand our worship. Of himself he always tends to turn "being in love" into a sort of religion.

Theologians have often feared, in this love, a danger of idolatry. I think they meant by this that the lovers might idolise one another. That does not seem to me to be the real danger; certainly not in marriage. The deliciously plain prose and businesslike intimacy of married life render it absurd. So does the Affection in which Eros is almost invariably clothed. Even in courtship I question whether anyone who has felt the thirst for the Uncreated, or even dreamed of feeling it, ever supposed that the Beloved could satisfy it. As a fellow-pilgrim pierced with the very same desire, that is, as a Friend, the Beloved may be gloriously and helpfully relevant; but as an object for it—well (I would not be rude), ridiculous. The real danger seems to me not that the lovers will idolise each other but that they will idolise Eros himself.

When lovers say of some act that we might blame, "Love made us do it," notice the tone. A man saying, "I did it because I was frightened," or "I did it because I was angry," speaks quite differently. He is putting forward an excuse for what he feels to require excusing. But the lovers are seldom doing quite that. Notice how tremulously, almost how devoutly, they say the word *love,* not so much pleading an "extenuating circumstance" as appealing to an authority. The confession can be almost a boast. There can be a shade of defiance in it. They "feel like martyrs." In extreme cases what their words really express is a demure yet unshakable allegiance to the god of love.

"These reasons in love's law have passed for good," says Milton's Dalila.

That is the point; *in love's law.* "In love," we have our own "law," a religion of our own, our own god. Where a true Eros is present resistance to his commands feels like apostasy, and what are really (by the Christian standard) temptations speak with the voice of duties—quasi-religious duties, acts of pious zeal to love. He builds his own religion round the lovers. . . . The "spirit" of Eros supersedes all laws, and they must not "grieve" it.

It seems to sanction all sorts of actions they would not otherwise have dared. I do not mean solely, or chiefly, acts that violate chastity. They are just as likely to be acts of injustice or uncharity against the outer world. They will seem like proofs of piety and zeal towards Eros. The pair can say to one another in an almost sacrificial spirit, "It is for love's sake that I have neglected my parents—left my children—cheated my partner—failed my friend at his greatest need." These reasons in love's law have passed for good. The votaries may even come to feel a particular merit in such sacrifices; what costlier offering can be laid on love's altar than one's conscience?

And all the time the grim joke is that this Eros whose voice seems to speak from the eternal realm is not himself necessarily even permanent. He is notoriously the most mortal of our loves. The world rings with complaints of his fickleness. What is baffling is the combination of this fickleness with his protestations of permanency. To be in love is both to intend and to promise lifelong fidelity. Love makes vows unasked; can't be deterred from making them. "I will be ever true," are almost the first words he utters. Not hypocritically but sincerely. No experience will cure him of the delusion. We have all heard of people who are in love again every few years; each time sincerely convinced that "*this* time it's the real thing," that their wanderings are over, that they have found their true love and will themselves be true till death.

And yet Eros is in a sense right to make this promise. The event of falling in love is of such a nature that we are right to reject as intolerable the idea that it should be transitory. In one high bound it has overleaped the massive wall of our selfhood; it has made appetite itself altruistic, tossed personal happiness aside as a triviality and planted the interests of another in the centre of our being. Spontaneously and without effort we have fulfilled the law (towards one person) by loving our neighbour as ourselves. It is an image, a foretaste, of what we must become to all if Love Himself rules in us without a rival. It is even (well used) a preparation for that. Simply to relapse from it, merely to "fall out of" love again, is—if I may coin the ugly word—a sort of *disredemption.* Eros is driven to promise what Eros of himself cannot perform.

Can we be in this selfless liberation for a lifetime? Hardly for a week. Between the best possible lovers this high condition is intermittent. The old self soon turns out to be not so dead as he pretended—as after a religious conversion. In either he may be momentarily knocked flat; he will soon be up again; if not on his feet, at least on his elbow, if not roaring, at least back to his surly grumbling or his mendicant whine. And Venus will often slip back into mere sexuality.

But these lapses will not destroy a marriage between two "decent and sensible" people. The couple whose marriage will certainly be endangered by them, and possibly ruined, are those who have idolised Eros. They thought he had the power and truthfulness of a god. They expected that mere feeling would do for them, and permanently, all that was necessary. When this expectation is disappointed they throw the blame on Eros or, more usually, on their partners. In reality, however, Eros, having made his gigantic promise and shown you in glimpses what its performance would be like, has "done his stuff." He, like a godparent, makes the vows; it is we who must keep them. It is we who must labour to bring our daily life into even closer accordance with what the glimpses have revealed. We must do the works of Eros when Eros is not present. This all good lovers know, though those who are not reflective or articulate will be able to express it only in a few conventional phrases about "taking the rough along with the smooth," not "expecting too much," having "a little common sense," and the like. And all good Christian lovers know that this programme, modest as it sounds, will not be carried out except by humility, charity and divine grace; that it is indeed the whole Christian life seen from one particular angle.

Thus Eros, like the other loves, but more strikingly because of his strength, sweetness, terror and high port, reveals his true status. He cannot of himself be what, nevertheless, he must be if he is to remain Eros. He needs help; therefore needs to be ruled. The god dies or becomes a demon unless he obeys God. It would be well if, in such case, he always died. But he may live on, mercilessly chaining together two mutual tormentors, each raw all over with the poison of hate-in-love, each ravenous to receive and implacably refusing to give, jealous, suspicious, resentful, struggling for the upper hand, determined to be free and to allow no freedom, living on "scenes." Read *Anna Karenina,* and do not fancy that such things happen only in Russia. The lovers' old hyperbole of "eating" each other can come horribly near to the truth.

What is C. S. Lewis' concept of "Eros"?

How would you evaluate the response "Love you? I *am* you!"? Is it "good" or "bad" to feel this way? Why? Might it represent the highest, most unselfish feeling in the fusion of one personality with another? Or might it suggest a loss of vital individuality?

Believing that one real danger haunting the act of love is our tendency to take Venus, a partly comic spirit, too seriously, the author would support the criticism that adults are unable

to admit to . . . young people that sex is marvelous, creative, varied, and a colorful experience, and *fun and funny,* incidentally. [28]

What factors can contribute to the wrong kind of "solemnisation of sex"? Is the significance attached to the wedding night one of them? How might the levity of sex be implemented? How would you go about making the admissions to young people described above?

Do public displays of mild love-making, and even fornication by daylight in parks, provide the light, casual comic touch? An antidote to the "throbbing, world-without-end, heart-breaking rendering of love-duets"?

Why is a lingering kiss between two people in public streets often frowned on? Would a time limit make the kiss more acceptable? In better taste? If the kiss were short, would it connote a shift to greetings? Are those who object simply displaying their old-fashioned unhealthy and hypocritical sexual repression? Are they jealous? Erotically aroused and frustrated? Are objections to a public display of sexual intercourse or intense love-making rooted in the same basis? Why do objectors look?

Is hand-holding in school corridors, kissing on street corners, and necking openly at parties more than a matter of meeting standards of good taste?

How much importance would you attach to reserving expressions of genuine feeling for the places, as well as for the persons, that give them most meaning?

How do you react to the assessment that "offending couples, usually the more immature and impulsive, rarely are aware of the extent to which they irritate and amuse" even their contemporaries, and that "it is only during the calf-love stage that love-making is open to the herd"? [29]

What would Lewis say to the following argument:

We're going to sleep with each other, because it's just too hard to wait when you love each other as much as we do. If we have sexual relations, we won't be so preoccupied with sexual desire all the time.

There are those who believe that sincere love comes only once in a lifetime; there are others who feel more able to appreciate it the second time around, and there are some who speak frequently of having fallen in love again. How does Lewis' view of Eros make all three attitudes plausible?

RELATED QUESTIONS

Lowen, in "Sex and Love" (p. 196) writes that

The act of sex is a giving of the self. Satisfaction results from the full surrender of the self to the partner in the sexual embrace. Without this surrender, sexual satisfaction cannot be achieved.

What kind of sexual satisfaction cannot be achieved? Does Lowen's statement eliminate what Lewis in **Eros** terms "Need-pleasure"?

How does Lewis, by dealing with "a refusal to be quite immersed," modify the view of self-surrender?

In **Eros,** Lewis writes

Sexuality [becomes] part of our subject only when it becomes an ingredient in the complex state of "being in love." That sexual experience can occur without Eros, without being "in love," and that Eros includes other things besides sexual activity, I take for granted.

If paralleled with the view presented in **Love and Orgasm** (p. 194), could this perspective be expressed by the analogy:

Venus: Eros
Sex: Love

Why, or why not?

In "Love and Sex," Lowen claims that while a distinction exists, any dissociation of love from sex degrades sex, reducing it to "an animal passion, lust, which is inferior to the noble quality of love"; in **Eros,** however, Lewis rejects "the popular idea that it is the absence or presence of Eros which makes the sexual act 'impure' or 'pure,' degraded or fine, unlawful or lawful." With what reasons does each author support his position? Can you reconcile their differences? Under what conditions would you believe the sexual act to be pure?

Lewis writes:

> To the evolutionist Eros (the human variation) will be something that grows out of Venus, a late complication and development of the immemorial biological impulse.

Would Lowen, therefore, be considered an evolutionist?

What objections does Lewis raise to the scientists' argument?

How might Lowen respond to the idea of "love's contemplative" presented in *Eros?* To the statement "he is full of desire, but the desire may not be sexually toned"?

Lowen's "Sex and Love" and Lewis' *Eros* both comment on woman as a legitimate object for male sexual desire. What transforms a woman from "the necessary piece of apparatus" to "the Beloved"? How fully do Lowen and Lewis agree on this point?

Do you believe that the degree of sexual satisfaction depends on the presence of tender, affectionate feelings as well as sexual attraction? Does your answer apply equally to males and females?

If sexual desire is an "itch," would masturbation be the ideal sexual satisfaction to remove it?

What connection, if any, can be made between the feeling "Love you? I *am* you!" and the patient's feeling reported in "Love and Sex" (p. 202): "I want to devour you, to consume you; I want to have every part of you inside me"?

Considering all samples of hidden persuasion with which you are familiar, as well as the advertisements in the "**Mass Media**" section, do you agree with Lewis that "our advertisements, at their sexiest, paint the whole business in terms of the rapt, the intense, the swoony-devout; seldom a hint of gaiety"?

Does the excerpt from *Art of Love* (See "**Night-Lights,**" p. 580) live up to Lewis' claims for "cheery old Ovid"?

Lewis comments:

> Lovers, unless their love is very short-lived, again and again feel an element not only of comedy, not only of play, but even of buffoonery, in the body's expression of Eros. . . . There is indeed at certain moments a high poetry in the flesh itself; but also, by your leave, an irreducible element of obstinate and ludicrous unpoetry.

How might this apply to Kenneth Patchen's *As We Are So Wonderfully Done with Each Other* (see "**Night-Lights,**" p. 581)? To *when i have thought of you somewhat too* by E. E. Cummings (see "**Night-Lights,**" p. 544)?

How might Lewis react to A. E. Housman's cynical observation in *Oh, When I Was in Love with You* (see "**Night-Lights,**" p. 565)?

How would Lewis answer the questions posed by Carl Sandburg in *One Parting* (see "**Night-Lights,**" p. 587)?

Appraisal and Bestowal

IRVING SINGER

I start with the idea that love is a way of valuing something. It is a positive response *toward* the "object of love"—which is to say, anyone or anything that is loved. In a manner quite special to itself, love affirms the goodness of this object. Some philosophers say that love *searches* for what is valuable in the beloved; others say that love *creates* value in the sense that it makes the beloved objectively valuable in some respect. Both assertions are often true, but sometimes false; and, therefore, neither explains the type of valuing which is love.

In studying the relationship between love and valuation, let us avoid merely semantical difficulties. The word "love" sometimes means liking very much, as when a man speaks of loving the food he is eating. It sometimes means desiring obsessively, as when a neurotic reports that he cannot control his feelings about a woman. In these and similar instances the word does not affirm goodness. Liking something very much is not the same as considering it good; and the object of an obsessive desire may attract precisely because it is felt to be bad. These uses of the word are only peripheral to the concept of love as a positive response toward a valued object. As we *generally* use the term, we imply an act of prizing, cherishing, caring about—all of which constitutes a mode of valuation.

But what is it to value or evaluate? Think of what a man does when he sets a price upon a house. He establishes various facts—the size of the building, its physical condition, the cost of repairs, the proximity to schools. He then weights these facts in accordance with their importance to a hypothetical society of likely buyers. Experts in this activity are called appraisers; the activity itself is appraisal or appraising. It seeks to find an objective value that things have in relation to one or another community of human interests. I call this value "objective" because, although it exists only insofar as there are people who want the house, the estimate is open to public verification. As long as they agree about the circumstances—what the house is like and what a relevant group of buyers prefer—all fair-minded appraisers should reach a similar appraisal, regardless of their own feelings about this particular house. In other words, appraising is a branch of empirical science, specifically directed toward the determining of value.

But now imagine that the man setting the price is not an appraiser, but a prospective buyer. The price that he sets need not agree with the appraiser's. For he does more than estimate objective value: he decides what the house is worth to *him.* To the extent that his preferences differ from other people's, the house will have a different value for him. By introducing such considerations, we relate the object to the particular and possibly idiosyncratic interests of a single person, his likings, his needs, his wants, his desires. Ultimately, all objective value depends upon interests of this sort. The community of buyers whose inclinations the appraiser must gauge is itself just a class of individuals. The appraiser merely predicts what each of them would be likely to pay for the house. At the same time, each buyer must be something of an appraiser himself; for he must have at least a rough idea of the price that other buyers will set. Furthermore, each person has to weigh, and so appraise, the relative importance of his own particular interests; and he must estimate whether the house can satisfy them. In principle these judgments are verifiable. They are also liable to mistake: for instance, when a man thinks that certain desires matter more to him than they really do, or when he expects greater benefits from an object than it can provide. Deciding what something is worth to *oneself* we may call an "individual appraisal." It differs from what the appraiser does; it determines a purely individual value, as opposed to any objective value.

Now, with this in mind, I suggest that love creates a new value, one that is not reducible to the individual or objective value that something may also have. This further type of valuing I call bestowal. Individual and objective value depend upon an object's ability to satisfy prior interests—the needs, the desires, the wants, or whatever it is that motivates us toward one object and not another. Bestowed value is different. It is created by the affirmative relationship *itself,* by the very act of responding favorably, giving an object emotional and pervasive importance regardless of its capacity to satisfy interests. Here it makes no sense to speak of verifiability; and though bestowing may often be injurious, unwise, even immoral, it cannot be erroneous in the way that an appraisal might be. For now it is the valuing alone that *makes* the value.

Think of what happens when a man comes to love the house he has bought. In addition to being something of use, something that gratifies antecedent desires, it takes on special value for him. It is now *his* house, not merely as a possession or a means of shelter but also as something he *cares about,* a part of his affective life. Of course, we also care about objects of mere utility. We need them for the benefits they provide. But in the process of loving, the man establishes another kind of relationship. He gives the house an importance beyond its individual or objective value. It becomes a focus of attention and possibly an object of personal commitment. Merely by engaging himself in this manner, the man bestows a value the house could not have had otherwise.

We might also say that the homeowner acts as if his house were valuable "for its own sake." And in a sense it is. For the value that he bestows does not depend upon the house's capacity to satisfy. Not that love need diminish that capacity. On the contrary, it often increases it by affording opportunities for enjoyment that would have been impossible without the peculiar attachment in which bestowal consists. Caring about the house, the man may find new and more satisfying ways of living in it. At the same time, the object achieves a kind of autonomy. The house assumes a presence and attains a dignity. It makes demands and may even seem to have a personality, to have needs of its own. In yielding to these "needs"—restoring the house to an earlier condition, perhaps, or completing its inherent design—the homeowner may not be guided by any other considerations.

In love between human beings something similar happens. For people, too, may be appraised; and they may be valued beyond one's appraisal. In saying that a woman is beautiful or that a man is good in some respect, we ascribe objective value. This will always be a function of *some* community of human interests, though we may have difficulty specifying which one. And in all communities people have individual value for one another. We are means to each other's satisfactions, and we constantly evaluate one another on the basis of our individual interests. However subtly, we are always setting prices on other people, and on ourselves. But we also bestow value in the manner of love. We then respond to another as something that cannot be reduced to *any* system of appraisal. The lover takes an interest in the beloved as a *person,* and not merely as a commodity (which she may also be). He bestows importance upon *her* needs and *her* desires, even when they do not further the satisfaction of his own. Whatever her personality, he gives it a value it would not have apart from his loving attitude. In relation to him, this woman has become valuable for her own sake.

In the love of persons, then, people bestow value upon one another over and above their individual or objective value. The reciprocity of love occurs when each participant receives bestowed value while also bestowing it upon the other. But since reciprocity need not occur, I shall refer to the lover as one who bestows value, and the beloved as one who receives it. The lover makes the beloved valuable merely by attaching himself to her. Though she may satisfy his needs, he refuses to use her as a mere instrument. To love a woman as a person is to desire her for the sake of values that appraisal might discover, and yet to place one's desire within a context that affirms her importance regardless of these values. Eventually, the beloved may no longer matter to us as one who is desired. Treating her as an end, we may think only of how we can be useful to *her.* But still it is we who think and act and make this affirmative response. Only in relation to *our* bestowal does another person enjoy the kind of value that love creates.

In saying that love bestows value, I am not referring to the fact that lovers shower good things upon those they love. Gifts may sometimes symbolize love, but they never prove its existence. Loving is not synonymous with giving. We do speak of one person "giving love" to another, but what is given hardly resembles what we usually mean by a gift. Even to say that the lover gives himself is somewhat misleading. Love need not be self-sacrificial. In responding affirmatively to another person, the lover creates something and need lose nothing in himself. To bestow value is to augment one's own being as well as the beloved's. Bestowal generates a new society by the sheer force of emotional attachment, a society that enables the lovers to discard many of the conventions that would ordinarily have separated them. But such intimacy is only one of the criteria by which bestowal may be identified. It shows itself in many ways, not all of which need ever be present at once or in equal strength.

A man who loves bestows value by caring about the needs and interests of the beloved, by wishing to benefit or protect her, by delighting in her achievements, by encouraging her independence and respecting her individuality, by giving her pleasure, by taking pleasures with her, by feeling glad when she is present and sad when she is not, by sharing his ideas and venting his emotions with her, by sympathizing with her weaknesses and depending upon her strength, by developing common pursuits, by allowing her to become second nature to him—"her smiles, her frowns, her ups, her downs"—by feeling a need to increase their society with other human beings upon whom they can jointly bestow value, by wanting children who may perpetuate their love. These are not necessary and sufficient conditions; but their occurrence would give us reason to think that an act of bestowal has taken place.

Through bestowal lovers have "a life" together. The lover accords the beloved the tribute of expressing *his* feelings by responding to hers. If he sends her valuable presents, they will signify that he too appreciates what she esteems; if he makes sacrifices on her behalf, he indicates how greatly her welfare matters to him. It is as if he were announcing that what is real for her is real for him also. Upon the sheer personality of the beloved he bestows a framework of value, emanating from himself but focused on her. Lovers linger over attributes that might well have been ignored. Whether sensuous or polite, libidinous or serene, brusque or tender, the lover's response is variably fervent but constantly gratuitous. It dignifies the beloved by treating her as *someone*, with all the emphasis the italics imply. Though independent of our needs, she is also the significant object of our attention. We show ourselves receptive to her peculiarities in the sense that we readily respond to them. Response is itself a kind of affirmation, even when it issues into unpleasant emotions such as anger and hatred. These need not be antithetical to love; they may even be signs of it—as every romanticist knows. Under many circumstances one cannot respond to another person without the unpleasant emotions, as a parent cannot stay in touch with a wayward child unless he occasionally punishes him. It is only when these emotions reject the other person, reducing him to a nothing or expressing our indifference, that love necessarily disappears. For then instead of bestowing value, we have withdrawn it.

In general, every emotion or desire contributes to love once it serves as a positive response to an independent being. If a woman is *simply* a means to sexual satisfaction, a man may be said to want her, but not to love her. For his sexual desire to become a part of love, it must function as a way of responding to the character and special properties of this particular woman. Desire wants what it wants for the sake of some private gratification, whereas love demands an interest in that vague complexity we call another person. No wonder lovers sound like metaphysicians; no wonder scientists are more comfortable in the study of desire, and rigorous philosophers would sooner make love in public than discuss it with their colleagues. For love is an attitude with no clear objective. Through it one human being affirms the individual significance of another, much as a painter highlights a figure by defining it in a sharpened outline. But the beloved is not a painted figure. She is not static: she is fluid, changing, indefinable—*alive*. The lover is attending to a *person*. And who can say what that is?

In the history of philosophy, bestowal and appraisal have often been confused with one another, perhaps because they are both types of valuation.* Love is related to both; they interweave in it. Unless we appraised we could not bestow a value that goes beyond appraisal; and without bestowal there would be no love. We may speak of lovers accepting one another, or even taking each other as is. But this need not mean a blind submission to some unknown being. In love we *attend* to the beloved, in the sense that we respond to what *she* is. For the effort to succeed, it must be accompanied by justifiable appraisals, objective as well as individual. The objective beauty and goodness of his beloved will delight the lover, just as her deficiencies will distress him. In her, as in every other human

---

* Though not of "*evaluation*." That word is usually reserved for appraisal.

being these are important properties. How is the lover to know what they are without a system of appraisals? Or how to help her realize her potentialities—assuming that is what she wants? Of course, in bestowing value upon this woman, the lover will "accentuate the positive" and undergo a kind of personal involvement that no disinterested spectator would. He will feel an intimate concern about the continuance of good properties in the beloved and the diminishing of bad ones. But none of this would be possible without objective appraisals.

Even more important is the role of individual appraisal. The person we love is generally one who satisfies our needs and desires. She may do so without either of us realizing the full extent of these satisfactions; and possibly all individual value is somehow based upon unconscious effects. Be this as it may, our experience of another person includes a large network of individual evaluations continually in progress and available to consciousness. At each moment our interests are being gratified or frustrated, fulfilled or thwarted, strengthened or weakened in relation to the other person. Individual value is rarely stable. It changes in accordance with our success or failure in getting what we want. And as this happens, our perception of the beloved also changes. Though the lover bestows value upon the woman as a separate and autonomous person, she will always be a person in *his* experience, a person whom he needs and who needs him, a person whose very nature may eventually conform to his inclinations, as well as vice versa. The attitude of love probably includes more, not fewer, individual appraisals than any other. How else could the lover really care about the beloved?

Love would not be love unless appraising were accompanied by the bestowing of value. But where this conjuction exists, *every* appraisal may lead on to a further bestowal. By disclosing an excellence in the beloved, appraisal (whether individual or objective) makes it easier for us to appreciate her. By revealing her faults and imperfections, it increases the importance of acting on her behalf. Love may thus encompass all possible appraisals. Once bestowal has occurred, a man may no longer care that his beloved is not the choicest of sexual objects. Given the opportunity, he may prefer her to women who are sexually more attractive. His love is a way of compensating for and even overcoming negative appraisals. If it were a means of repaying the object for value received, love would turn into gratitude; if it were an attempt to give more than the object has provided, it would become generosity or condescension. These are related attitudes, but love differs from them in bestowing value without calculation. It confers importance no matter *what* the object is worth.

When appraisal occurs alone, our attitude changes in the direction of science, ambition, or morality. To do "the right thing" we need not bestow value upon another person; we need only recognize the truth about his character and act appropriately. Admiring a woman's superiority, we may delight in her as an evidence of the good life. We feel toward her what Hume calls "the sense of approbation." We find her socially useful or morally commendable, which is not to say that she excites our love. If she has faults, they offend our moral sensibility or else elicit our benevolence. In short, we respond to this woman as an abstraction, as a something that may be better or worse, an opportunity for judgment or for action, but not a person whom we love. Appraisal without bestowal may lead us to change other people regardless of what they want. As moralists or legislators, or as dutiful parents, we may even think that this is how we *ought* to behave. The magistrate will then enforce a distance between himself and the criminal, whose welfare he is quite prepared to sacrifice for the greater good of society. The parent will discipline his child in the hope of molding him "in the most beneficial manner." On this moral attitude great institutions are often built. But it is not a loving attitude. We are not responding affirmatively toward others. We are only doing what is (we hope) in their best interests, or else society's.

When love intervenes, morality becomes more personal but also more erratic. It would be almost impossible to imagine someone bestowing value without caring about the other person's welfare. To that extent, love implies benevolence. And yet the lover does not act benevolently for the sake of doing the right thing. In loving another person, we respect *his* desire to improve himself. If we offer to help, we do so because *he* wants to be better than he is, not because *we* think he ought to be. Love and morality need not diverge, but they often do. For love is not *inherently* moral. There is no guarantee that it will bestow value properly, at the right time, in the right way. Through love we enjoy another person as he is, including his moral condition; yet this enjoyment may itself violate the demands of morality. Moral attitudes must always be governed by appraisal rather than bestowal. They must consider the individual in his relations to other people, as one among many who have equal claims. Faced with the being of a particular person, morality tells us to pick and choose those attributes that are most desirable. It is like a chef who makes an excellent stew by bringing out one flavor and muffling another. The chef does not care about the ingredients as unique or terminal entities, but only as things that are good to eat. In loving another person, however, we enact a nonmoral *loyalty*—like the mother who stands by her criminal son even though she knows he is guilty. Her loyalty need not be *im*moral; and though she loves her son, she may realize that he must be punished. But what if the value she has bestowed upon her child blinds her to the harm he has done, deters her from handing him over to the police, leads her to encourage him as a criminal? Her love may increase through such devotion, but it will be based on faulty appraisals and will not be a moral love.

Possibly the confusion between appraisal and bestowal results from the way that lovers talk. To love another person is to *treat* him with great regard, to confer a new and personal value upon him. But when lovers describe their beloved, they sometimes sound as if she were perfect just in being herself. In caring about someone, attending to her, affirming the importance of her being what she is, the lover resembles a man who has appraised an object and found it very valuable. Though he is bestowing value, the lover *seems* to be declaring the objective goodness of the beloved. It is *as if* he were predicting the outcome of all possible appraisals and insisting that they would always be favorable.

As a matter of fact, the lover is doing nothing of the sort. His superlatives are expressive and metaphoric. Far from being terms of literal praise, they betoken the magnitude of his attachment and say little about the lady's beauty or goodness. They may even be accompanied by remarks that diminish the beloved in some respect—as when a man lovingly describes a woman's funny face or inability to do mathematics. If he says she is "perfect" that way, he chooses this ambiguous word because it is used for things we refuse to relinquish. As in appraisal we may wish to accept nothing less than perfection, so too the lover calls perfect whatever he accepts despite its appraisal. The lover may borrow appraisive terminology, but he uses it with a special intent, as he might also bid the sun to warm his beloved or the winds to cool her. His language signifies that love had bestowed incalculable worth upon this particular person. Such newly given value is not a good of the sort that appraisal seeks: it is not an attribute that supplements her other virtues, like a dimple wrought by some magician to make a pretty woman prettier. For it is nothing but the importance that one person assigns to another; and in part at least, it is created by the language. The valuative terms that lovers use—"wonderful," "marvelous," "glorious," "grand," "terrific"—bestow value in themselves. They are scarcely capable of describing excellence or reporting on appraisals.

If we have any doubts about the lover's use of language, we should listen to the personal appendages he usually adds. He will not say "That woman is perfect," but rather "To *me* she is perfect" or "*I* think she is wonderful." In talking this way, he reveals that objective appraisal does not determine his attitude. For objective appraisal puts the object in relation to a community of valuers, whereas love creates its own community. The men in some society may all admire an "official beauty"— as Ortega calls her. Every male may bend the knee or doff his cap, as if the lady were a public monument; and some will want to possess her, as they would want to steal the crown jewels. But how many will be able to love her? Very few, since love involves a different kind of response, more intimate, more personal, and more creative.

For similar reasons it would be a mistake to think that the lover's language articulates an individual appraisal. When he says that to him the woman is perfect, the lover does not mean that she is perfect *for* him. Unless the beloved satisfied in some respect, no man might be able to love her. For *she* must find a place in *his* experience; she must come alive for him, stimulate new and expansive interests; and none of this is likely to happen unless she has individual value to him. But though the beloved satisfies the lover, she need not satisfy perfectly. Nor does the lover expect her to. In saying that to him she is perfect, he merely reiterates the fact that he loves this woman. Her perfection is an honorific title which he, and only he, bestows. The lover is like a child who makes a scribble and then announces "This is a tree." The child could just as easily have said "This is a barn." Until he tells us, the scribble represents nothing. Once he tells us, it represents whatever he says—as long as his attitude remains consistent.

In being primarily bestowal and only secondarily appraisal, love is never elicited by the object in the sense that desire or approbation is. We desire things or people for the sake of what will satisfy us. We approve of someone for his commendable properties. But these conditions have only a causal tie to love: as when a man loves a woman *because* she is beautiful, or *because* she satisfies his sexual, domestic, and social needs, or *because* she resembles his childhood memory of mother. Such facts indicate the circumstances under which people love one another; they explain why this particular man loves this particular woman; and if the life sciences were sufficiently developed, the facts could help us to predict who among human beings would be likely to love whom. But explaining the occurrence of love is not the same as explicating the concept. The conditions for love are not the same as love itself. In some circumstances the bestowing of value will happen more easily than in others; but *whenever* it happens, it happens spontaneously and exceeds anything in the object that might be thought to elicit it. Even if a man loves only a woman who is beautiful and looks like his mother, he does not *love* her for these attributes in the sense in which he might *admire* her for being objectively valuable or *desire* her for satisfying his needs.

For what then does a man love a woman? For being the person she is, for being herself? But that is to say that he loves her for nothing at all. Everyone is himself. Having a beloved who is what she is does not reveal the nature of love. Neither does it help us to understand the saint's desire to love all people. They are what they are. Why should they be loved for it? Why not pitied or despised, ignored or simply put to use? Though beauty and goodness are not in the eye of the beholder, love is. It supplements the human search for value with a capacity for bestowing it gratuitously. To one who has succeeded in cultivating this capacity, anything may become an object of love. The saint is a man whose earthly needs and desires are extraordinarily modest; in principle, every human being can satisfy them. That being so, the saint creates a value-system in which all persons fit equally well. This disposition, this freely given response, cannot be elicited from him: it bestows itself and (however suspect) happens to be indiscriminate.

To the man of common sense it is very upsetting that love does not limit itself to some prior value in the object. The idea goes against our purposive ways of thinking. If I wish to drink the best wine, I have every reason to prefer French champagne over American. My choice is dictated by an objective goodness in the French champagne. If instead I wish to economize, I act sensibly in choosing an inferior commodity. We reason this way whenever we use purposive means of attaining the good life, which covers a major part of our existence. But love, unlike desire, is not wholly purposive. Within the total structure of a human life it may serve as a lubricant to purposive attitudes, furthering their aims through new interests that promise new satisfactions; but in creating value, bestowing it freely, love introduces an element of risk into the economy. Purposive attitudes are safe, secure, like money in the bank; the loving attitude is speculative and always dangerous. Love is not *practical,* and sometimes borders on madness. We take our life in our hands when we allow love to tamper with our purposive habits. Without love, life might not be worth living; but without purposiveness, there would be no life.

No wonder, then, that the *fear* of love is one of the great facts of human nature. In all men and women there lurks an atavistic dread of insolvency whenever we generate more emotion than something has a right to demand of us. In everyone there is the country bumpkin who giggles nervously at an abstract painting because it looks like nothing on earth. Man finds the mere possibility of invention and spontaneous originality disquieting, even ominous. We are threatened by any new bestowal. Particularly when it means the origination of feelings, we are afraid to run the usual risks of failure and frustration, to expose ourselves in a positive response than can so easily be thwarted. As a character in D. H. Lawrence says of love: "I am almost more afraid of this touch than I was of death. For I am more nakedly exposed to it." Even Pascal, who spoke of the heart's having reasons whereof the reason does not know, seemed to think that love adheres to a secret, mysterious quality within the object that only feeling can discern. But Pascal was wrong. Love is sheer gratuity. It issues from a person like hairs on his head. It can be stimulated and developed, but it cannot be implanted: it cannot be derived from outside.

Love is like awakened genius that chooses its materials in accordance with its own creative requirements. Love does not create its object; it merely responds to it creatively. That is why one can rarely convince a man that his beloved is unworthy of him. For his love is a creative means of *making* her more worthy—in the sense that he invests her with greater value, not in making her a better human being. That may also happen. But more significantly, the lover changes *himself.* By subordinating his purposive attitudes, he transforms himself into a being who enjoys the act of bestowing. There is something magical about this, as we know from legends in which the transformations of love are effected by a philter or a wand. In making another person valuable by developing a certain disposition within oneself, the lover performs in the world of feeling something comparable to what the alchemist does in the world of matter.

The creativity of love is thus primarily a self-creation. Lovers create within themselves a remarkable capacity for affective response, an ability to use their emotions, their words, their deeds for bestowing as well as appraising value. Each enhances the other's importance through an imaginative play within valuation itself. Indeed, love may be best approached as a subspecies of the imagination. Not only does the lover speak in poetic metaphors, but also he behaves like any artist. Whatever his "realistic" aspirations, no painter can duplicate reality. The scene out there cannot be transferred to a canvas. The painter can only *paint* it: i.e., give it a new importance in human life by presenting his way of seeing it through the medium of his art and the techniques of his individual genius. These determine the values of his painting, not the external landscape that may have originally inspired him. The artist may vary the scene to his heart's content, as El Greco did when he rearranged the buildings of Toledo. What matters is his way of seeing as a function of the imagination, not the disposition in space of stones and mortar. Similarly, a lover sees a woman not as others might, but through the creative agency of bestowing value. He need not change her any more than El Greco changed the real Toledo. But he alters her personality by subsuming it within the imaginative system of his own positive responses. Through her he expresses the variety of feelings that belong to love. Artists, even the most abstract, do not create out of nothing: they recreate, create anew. So too, the lover re-creates another person. By deploying his imagination in the art of bestowing value, by caring about the independent being of another person, the lover adds a new dimension to the beloved. In relation to him, within his loving attitude, she becomes the object of an affirmative interest, even an aesthetic object. She is, as we say, "*appreciated*"—made more valuable through the special media and techniques in which love consists.

Treating love as an aspect of the imagination enables us to confront problems I have thus far ignored. For instance, I said it was *as if* the lover were predicting that no appraisal would discover any significant fault. If we now inquire into the meaning of these as ifs, I can only remind you how they operate in other situations involving the imagination. Think of yourself as a spectator in the theater, watching an engrossing drama. The hero dies, and you begin to weep. Now for whom are you crying? Surely not for the actor: you know that as soon as the curtain falls, he will scramble to his feet and prepare for a great ovation. Is it then the character in the play? But there is no such person. You are fully aware that Hamlet (at least Shakespeare's Hamlet) never existed. How can his death, which is purely fictional, sadden you? Yet it does, more so perhaps than the death of real people you may have known. What happens, I think, is that you respond *as if* the actor were really Hamlet and *as if* Hamlet really existed. The "as if" signifies that although you *know* the actor is only acting and Hamlet only fictitious, your imaginative involvement causes you to express feelings appropriate to real people. At no point are you deluded. The "illusion" of the theater is not an illusion at all. It is an act of imagination—nothing like a mistake of judgment, nothing like the derangement that causes Don Quixote to smash the cruel puppet show in order to save the unfortunate heroine. On entering the theater, you have entered the dramatic situation. You have allowed your imagination to engage itself in one specific channel. With the assistance of the realistic props, the surrounding darkness, the company of other people doing the same imagining, you have invested the actors and the characters they represent with a capacity to affect your feelings as real persons might.

In love the same kind of thing occurs. The as ifs of love are imaginative, not essentially delusional. Of course, the lover *may* be deluded about his beloved. That is the familiar joke about lovers: they live in constant illusion, Cupid is blinded by emotion, etc. That this often happens I do not care to deny. But that this should be the essence of love, that by its very nature love should be illusory, seems to me utterly absurd. Even if people frequently clambered on stage and acted like Don Quixote, we would not say that their behavior revealed what it is to be a theatrical spectator. We would say they did not know how to look at a play. Likewise, it is not in the acting out of illusions that people become lovers. Though lovers do commit errors of judgment and are sometimes carried away by their feelings, love itself is not illusory. Emotional aberrations are adventitious to it, not definitive. As love is not primarily a way of knowing, neither is it a way of making mistakes. Appraisal is a way of knowing, and emotions may always interfere with its proper employment. But love is an imaginative means of bestowing value that would not exist otherwise. To the extent that a man is a lover, rather than a person seeking knowledge or yielding to self-delusion (which he may also be), he accords his beloved the courtesy of being treated affirmatively regardless of what he knows about her. In refusing to let his appraisive knowledge deflect his amorous conduct, he bestows a tribute which can only be understood as an imaginative act. As one of Rousseau's characters says: "Love did not make me blind to your faults, but it made those faults dear to me." It is this kind of valuative gesture that the imagination uses for courtesy as a whole. The gentleman shows respect to all ladies alike, whatever their social rank. He does so as a loving gift to the female sex, the worst as well as the best, the lowest as well as the highest. He is not normally deluded about differences in society or among human beings. He does not think that women are all the same. Yet he creates a universal excellence in treating them imaginatively as better than they "really" are.

There is another respect in which the analogy from the theater elucidates the lover's imagination. I refer to the phenomenon of *presence*. The spectator responds to the fictional character as if it were a real person. He can do so, in part, because the character has been *presented to* him by a real person. Talking, laughing, shouting, the actor *makes present* to the spectator the reality of a human being. The very artificiality of his surroundings—his being in a "play," a fiction, his being placed on a stage so that everyone can see and hear, his giving a performance scheduled for a particular time, in a particular building—all this accentuates the fact that the actor himself is not artificial, but alive. The spectator makes his imaginative leap by seeing the actor as a present reality framed within the aesthetic contrivances of the theater. The greater the actor's "stage presence," the more he facilitates the spectator's feat. But ultimately the phenomenon depends upon the spectator himself, upon his dramatic sensibility, his creative capacity to infuse a fictional character with the reality of the human being right there before him. As the Prologue to Shakespeare's *Henry V* tells the audience: "And let us, ciphers to this great accompt, / On your imaginary forces work. / . . . For 't is your thoughts that now must deck our kings."

In a similar fashion the lover's attention fixes upon the sheer presence of the beloved. In that extreme condition sometimes called "falling in love," such attentiveness often approaches self-hypnosis. Freud was one of the first to recognize the kinship between hypnosis and certain types of love; but his analysis neglects the philosophical import of these occurrences, their linkage of valuation. For me the loving stare of one human being visually glued to another signifies an extraordinary bestowal of value, an imaginative (though possibly excessive) response to the presence of another person. The lover's glance illuminates the beloved. He celebrates her as a living reality to which to attends. As in celebration of any sort, his response contributes something new and expressive. He introduces the woman into the world of his own imagination—as if, through some enchantment, she were indeed his work of art and only he could contemplate her infinite detail. As long as they intensify her presence, the lover will cherish even those features in the beloved that appraisal scorns. Does the lady have a facial blemish? To her lover it may be more fascinating than her baby blue eyes: it makes her stand out more distinctly in his memory. Does she have a sharp tongue and a biting temper? Her lover may come to relish these traits, not generally but in this particular woman. They make the image of her vivid and compelling. Even the ludicrous banalities of Odette are endearing to Swann. They show him with unmistakable clarity what she is; and though he loathes the banal, as Proust himself hated the everyday world, he obviously enjoys this opportunity to compensate for his loathing by the imaginative bestowal of unmerited value.

Speaking of suitable subjects for literature, Flaubert said: "Yvetot [a provincial town in northern France] is as good as Constantinople." Likewise, one might say that everything that distinguishes the beloved, even her lack of distinction, may contribute to the lover's art. For that consists in taking a woman as she is, in opening oneself to the full impact of her presence, at the same time that one invokes aesthetic categories that give her a new significance. By his affirmative response alone, the lover places an ordinary stone within the costliest of settings. The amorous imagination bestows value upon a person as the dramatic imagination bestows theatrical import upon an actor. The beloved is put on a pedestal as the actor is put on a stage: not necessarily for purposes of adoration, but in order to concentrate, in the most imaginative way, upon the suggestive reality of her presence. The lover knows the woman is not objectively perfect, as the audience knows the actor is not Hamlet. . . .

I am sure that the similarity between love and the theater could be pushed much further. Love is the art of enjoying another person, as theater is the art of enjoying dramatic situations. Because it inevitably suggests the possibility of *enjoyment,* love is the most frequent theme in all entertainments based on human relations: it is the only subject that interests everyone. Nevertheless, the analogy between love and the theater can also be misleading. The actor portrays a character; the beloved does not portray anything, though she may symbolize a great deal. The beloved is not an image of perfection in the sense in which an actor is an image or representation of Hamlet. The lover uses his imagination to appreciate the beloved; the audience uses the actor as a vehicle for the fiction. That is why an actor rarely looks his audience in the eye. In so direct a communication his presence crowds out his aesthetic function, and we respond to him as the person he is, not as the character he represents. On the other hand, lovers may well be stereotyped (as they are often photographed or painted) in a joint posture of immediate confrontation, face to face, each searching for the other's personality, each peering into the other's eyes: "Our eyebeams twisted, and did thread / Our eyes, upon one double string."

This fundamental difference between love and the theater may help to explain some of the emotional difficulties actors often feel. Like everyone else the actor wants to be loved for himself; but his audiences know him only through the roles he portrays. He rightly senses that what they "love" is really the characters or at best his characterizations, certainly no more than that part of himself which goes into making the characters present. Succeeding as an actor, he may even identify with the type of character he best portrays. That may give him an opportunity to express much of his own personality, but the role he lives will often mask his deepest inclinations and make it difficult for anyone to respond to him as a person. For similar reasons, to which I shall return, I fail to see how Plato could be talking about the love of persons when he says that the lover sees in the beloved an "image" or "representation" of absolute beauty. Plato uses this idea to argue that all lovers are really in love with the absolute. Might we not also say that the lovers he has in mind are simply incapable of loving another person?

In love, as in the theater, imagination manifests itself in a particular set or disposition. A carpenter who happens to overhear a rehearsal may surely know that the man on stage is playing Hamlet. But he does not respond to the actor *as if* he were Hamlet. Preoccupied with his own work, the carpenter is not an audience: he has not put himself into a dramatic channel. Neither does an experimenter affirm the being of a person whom he observes with scientific detachment. He devoted himself to the experiment, not to the individual under observation. He may take the subject as is, but only in the sense of being impartial about his data. By detaching himself, the scientist refuses to enter into the relationship required for love. In that relationship one person *attaches* himself to another, and in a way that reveals his own personality as well as the other's. The reality of the beloved glows with a sense of vital importance which emanates from the lover. Or is glow too vibrant a word? Love is not always ecstatic; and even its poetry is often prosaic. There are quiet, comfortable, humdrum loves as well as the rhapsodic ones that seem to accompany inexperience. Love has infinite modulations, all possible degrees of intensity, and endless variety in its means of imaginative expression.

It is even through the amorous imagination that one person becomes sexually attractive to another. Our instincts alone would not enable us to love or even to lust in the way that human beings do. At least not the *obvious* instincts, e.g., the mechanism of genital excitement. Possibly the bestowing of value is itself instinctive. It need not be learned, and it would seen to be universal in man. Everyone feels the need for some loving relationship. All people crave a more personal society than the one to which they are born. That is why love is always a threat to the status quo, and sometimes subversive. Lovers create their own affective universe. When the amorous imagination ricochets back and forth—each person seeing himself as both lover and beloved—a new totality results, an interacting oneness. The human species could survive without the art of the theater, or of painting, or of literature, or of music; but man would not be man without the art of love. In that sense, the amorous imagination, more than any other, shows us both what we are and what, ideally, we may become.

What are the key distinctions made by Singer between appraisal and bestowal?

In *The Steep Ascent,* Anne Morrow Lindbergh writes:

People "died" all the time in their lives. Parts of them died when they made the wrong kinds of decisions—decisions against life. Sometimes they died bit by bit until finally they were just living corpses walking around. If you were perceptive you could see it in their eyes; the fire had gone out. Yet, there were a lot of people walking around who were "dead" and a lot of people killed who were "living". She couldn't explain it any more than that. But you always knew when you made a decision against life. When you denied life you were warned. The cock crowed, always, somewhere inside of you. The door clicked and you were safe inside—safe and dead.
    And usually it was fear that made you pull the door shut: emotional fear of becoming involved with people, of loving too much (because it always meant suffering to love deeply). . . . physical fear of pain and death, spiritual fear of the great and the unknown that made you stop in your mind when you came on words like God and Prayer. [30]

How does Singer explain the reasons behind an "emotional fear of becoming involved . . . of loving too much. . . ."? What are the alternatives?

How does Singer show in **Appraisal and Bestowal** that love entails both creativity and imagination?

RELATED QUESTIONS

The author of **Eros** stated: "Sexual desire, without Eros, wants *it,* the *thing in itself;* Eros wants the Beloved." How does the author of **Appraisal and Bestowal** express the same idea in his distinction between desire and love? Does Lowen's **Love and Orgasm** (pp. 196–197) make a similar distinction when he says:

Love in the personal sense is a conscious feeling that results from the focus of . . . general affection upon a specific individual. . . . This conscious component is superimposed upon the underlying generalized instinctual reaction.

How might Singer, on the basis of *Appraisal and Bestowal,* answer these questions asked by the Prince in a song from *Cinderella:* "Do I love you because you're beautiful, or are you beautiful because I love you? . . . Do I want you because you're wonderful, or are you wonderful because I want you?"

Reconsider the attitude of Richard toward Aunt Bunch in *Parma Violets* (p. 13); of William Baxter toward "Milady" in *Seventeen* (p. 40); of Stephen Daedalus toward the prostitute in *A Portrait of the Artist* (p. 51); of the subway riders toward the tanned blonde in *The Once-Over* (p. 74); of Tim Hazard toward Rachel Wells in *The City of Trembling Leaves* (p. 94); and of Anne Frank toward Peter Van Daan in *The Diary of a Young Girl* (p. 133). Which, according to Singer, make appraisals of objective value? Which make individual appraisals? Which make bestowals? Which make some of each? How?

Sonnet 116

WILLIAM SHAKESPEARE

Let me not to the marriage of true minds
Admit impediments, Love is not love
Which alters when it alteration finds,
Or bends with the remover to remove—

O, no! it is an ever-fixèd mark
That looks on tempests, and is never shaken;
It is the star to every wandering bark,
Whose worth's unknown, although his height be taken.

Love's not Time's fool, though rosy lips and cheeks
Within his bending sickle's compass come;
Love alters not with his brief hours and weeks,
But bears it out ev'n to the edge of doom—

If this be error and upon me proved,
I never writ, nor no man ever loved.

What is the most significant characteristic of love as it is emphasized in *Sonnet 116?* How is love qualified in the first four lines of the poem?

With what two constants is love compared in lines 5–8?

What is love's relationship to time?

Shakespeare suggests that love is true only if it remains unchanged despite alterations in circumstances surrounding it, and that a true lover will not stop loving even one who has ceased loving him. How would you reconcile this view with a philosophy that contends that love is possible given the one condition of mutual need?

How much *should* true love depend upon reciprocity? How much *does* true love depend on reciprocity?

Would you agree with the central character in Arthur Miller's play **After the Fall** that "you never stop loving whoever you loved. Hatred doesn't wipe it out"?

RELATED QUESTIONS

C. S. Lewis in **Eros** (p. 212) wrote:

Of all loves [Eros] is, at his height, most god-like. . . . Of himself he always tends to turn "being in love" into a sort of religion. . . . The real danger seems to me not that the lovers will idolise each other but that they will idolise Eros himself.

To what extent does the comment apply to Shakespeare's statements about love in **Sonnet 116?**

Do you feel that love is eternal, an "ever-fixed mark" like a guiding star, or that it is internal, "a self-creation" and "sheer gratuity [that] issues from a person like hairs on his head," as Singer describes it in **Appraisal and Bestowal?** Does it matter?

Does Shakespeare in **Sonnet 116** speak of an impossible love, as Lowen says (p. 202) "divorced from its roots in man's biological function"?

Does Shakespeare ignore things like "doing dishes," mentioned in **Das Liebesleben** (p. 192) and similar specifics of "the deliciously plain prose and business-like intimacy of married life" suggested by Lewis in **Eros?**

How would Shakespeare respond to Lowen's statement (p. 202) that "if paradise is sought anywhere but on earth and in the reality of daily living, the result is death"?

Does Shakespeare in **Sonnet 116** contradict the theory he dramatized in *A Midsummer Night's Dream*—that love is fickle and illusory in nature? If so, why has this sonnet on love survived more than 400 years?

How is the concept of love in **Sonnet 116** related to the Biblical versions of **I, Corinthians xiii** (see "**Night-Lights,**" p. 539)? Do the nine ingredients in Paul's "Spectrum of love—Patience; Kindness; Generosity; Humility; Courtesy; Unselfishness; Good Temper; Guilelessness; Sincerity—make up the supreme gift, the stature of the perfect man . . . and [function] in relation to men, in relation to life, in relation to the known today and the near tomorrow, and not to the unknown eternity"? [31]

What parallels are there between William Shakespeare's comments on true love in **Sonnet 116** and those of William Sylvanus Baxter in **Seventeen** (see "**Night-Lights,**" p. 588)?

Would Shakespeare support Francie Nolan of **A Tree Grows in Brooklyn** in her feeling that she will "never love anyone as much again"?

Double-Sunrise

ANNE MORROW LINDBERGH

This shell was a gift; I did not find it. It was handed to me by a friend. It is unusual on the island. One does not often come across such a perfect double-sunrise shell. Both halves of this delicate bivalve are exactly matched. Each side, like the wing of a butterfly, is marked with the same pattern; translucent white, except for three rosy rays that fan out from the golden hinge binding the two together. I hold two sunrises between my thumb and finger. Smooth, whole, unblemished shell, I wonder how its fragile perfection survived the breakers on the beach.

It is unusual; yet it was given to me freely. People are like that here. Strangers smile at you on the beach, come up and offer you a shell, for no reason, lightly, and then go by and leave you alone again. Nothing is demanded of you in payment, no social rite expected, no tie established. It was a gift, freely offered, freely taken, in mutual trust. People smile at you here, like children, sure that you will not rebuff them, that you will smile back. And you do, because you know it will involve nothing. The smile, the act, the relationship is hung in space, in the immediacy and purity of the present; suspended on the still point of here and now; balanced there, on a shaft of air, like a seagull.

The pure relationship, how beautiful it is! How easily it is damaged, or weighed down with irrelevancies—not even irrelevancies, just life itself, the accumulations of life and of time. For the first part of every relationship is pure, whether it be with friend or lover, husband or child. It is pure, simple and unencumbered. It is like the artist's vision before he has to discipline it into form, or like the flower of love before it has ripened to the firm but heavy fruit of responsibility. Every relationship seems simple at its start. The simplicity of first love, or friendliness, the mutuality of first sympathy seems, at its initial appearance—even if merely in exciting conversation across a dinner table—to be a self-enclosed world. Two people listening to each other, two shells meeting each other, making one world between them. There are no others in the perfect unity of that instant, no other people or things or interests. It is free of ties or claims, unburdened by responsibilities, by worry about the future or debts to the past.

And then how swiftly, how inevitably the perfect unity is invaded; the relationship changes; it becomes complicated, encumbered by its contact with the world. I believe this is true in most relationships, with friends, with husband or wife, and with one's children. But it is the marriage relationship in which the changing pattern is shown up most clearly because it is the deepest one and the most arduous to maintain; and because, somehow, we mistakenly feel that failure to maintain its exact original pattern is tragedy.

It is true, of course, the original relationship is very beautiful. Its self-enclosed perfection wears the freshness of a spring morning. Forgetting about the summer to come, one often feels one would like to prolong the spring of early love, when two people stand as individuals, without past or future, facing each other. One resents any change, even though one knows that transformation is natural and part of the process of life and its evolution. Like its parallel in physical passion, the early ecstatic stage of a relationship cannot continue always at the same pitch of intensity. It moves to another phase of growth which one should not dread, but welcome as one welcomes summer after spring. But there is also a dead weight accumulation, a coating of false values, habits, and burdens which blights life. It is this smothering coat that needs constantly to be stripped off, in life as well as in relationships.

Both men and women feel the change in the early relationship and hunger nostalgically for its original pattern as life goes on and becomes more complicated. For inevitably, as the relationship grows, both men and women, at least to some degree, are drawn into their more specialized and functional roles: man, into his less personal work in the world; woman, into her traditional obligations with family and household. In both fields, functional relationships tend to take the place of the early all-absorbing personal one. But woman refinds in a limited form with each new child, something resembling, at least in its absorption, the early pure relationship. In the sheltered simplicity of the first days after a baby is born, one sees again the magical closed circle, the miraculous sense of two people existing only for each other, the tranquil sky reflected on the face of the mother nursing her child. It is, however, only a brief interlude and not a substitute for the original more complete relationship.

But though both men and women are absorbed in their specialized roles and each misses something of the early relationship, there are great differences in their needs. While man, in his realm, has less chance for personal relations than woman, he may have more opportunity for giving himself creatively in work. Woman, on the other hand, has more chance for personal relations, but these do not give her a sense of her creative identity, the individual who has something of her own to say or to give. With each partner hungry for different reasons and each misunderstanding the other's needs, it is easy to fall apart or into late love affairs. The temptation is to blame the situation on the other person and to accept the easy solution that a new and more understanding partner will solve everything.

But neither woman nor man are likely to be fed by another relationship which seems easier because it is in an earlier stage. Such a love affair cannot really bring back a sense of identity. Certainly, one has the illusion that one will find oneself in being loved for what one really is, not for a collection of functions. But can one actually find oneself in someone else? In someone else's love? Or even in the mirror someone else holds up for one? I believe that true identity is found, as Eckhart once said, by "going into one's own ground and knowing oneself." It is found in creative activity springing from within. It is found, paradoxically, when one loses oneself. One must lose one's life to find it. Woman can best refind herself by losing herself in some kind of creative activity of her own. Here she will be able to refind her strength, the strength she needs to look and work at the second half of the problem — the neglected pure relationship. Only a refound person can refind a personal relationship.

But can the pure relationship of the sunrise shell be refound once it has become obscured? Obviously some relationships can never be recovered. It is not just a question of different needs to be understood and filled. In their changing roles the two partners may have grown in different directions or at different rates of speed. A brief double-sunrise episode may have been all they could achieve. It was an end in itself and not a foundation for a deeper relation. In a growing relationship, however, the original essence is not lost but merely buried under the impedimenta of life. The core of reality is still there and needs only to be uncovered and reaffirmed.

One way of rediscovering the double-sunrise is to duplicate some of its circumstances. Husband and wife can and should go off on vacations alone and also on vacations alone *together*. For if it is possible that woman can find herself by having a vacation alone, it is equally possible that the original relationship can sometimes be refound by having a vacation alone *together*. Most married couples have felt the unexpected joy of one of these vacations. How wonderful it was to leave the children, the house, the job, and all the obligations of daily life; to go out together, whether for a month or a weekend or even just a night in an inn by themselves. How surprising it was to find the miracle of the sunrise repeated. There was the sudden pleasure of having breakfast alone with the man one fell in love with. Here at the small table, are only two people facing each other. How the table at home has grown! And how distracting it is, with four or five children, a telephone ringing in the hall, two or three school buses to catch, not to speak of the commuter's train. How all this separates one from one's husband and clogs up the pure relationship. But sitting at a table alone opposite each other, what is there to separate one? Nothing but a coffee pot, corn muffins and marmalade. A simple enough pleasure, surely, to have breakfast alone with one's husband, but how seldom married people in the midst of life achieve it.

Actually, I believe this temporary return to the pure relationship holds good for one's children, too. If only, I think, playing with my sunrise shell—if only we could have each of our children alone, not just for part of each day, but for part of each month, each year. Would they not be happier, stronger and, in the end, more independent because more secure? Does each child not secretly long for the pure relationship he once had with the mother, when he was "The Baby," when the nursery doors were shut and she was feeding him at her breast —*alone*? And if we were able to put into practice this belief and spend more time with each child alone—would he not only gain in security and strength, but also learn an important first lesson in his adult relationship?

We all wish to be loved alone. "Don't sit under the apple-tree with anyone else but me," runs the old popular song. Perhaps, as Auden says in his poem, this is a fundamental error in mankind.

> For the error bred in the bone
> Of each woman and each man
> Craves what it cannot have,
> Not universal love
> But to be loved alone.

Is it such a sin? In discussing this verse with an Indian philosopher, I had an illuminating answer. "It is all right to wish to be loved alone," he said, "mutuality is the essence of love. There cannot be others in mutuality. It is only in the time-sense that it is wrong. It is when we desire *continuity* of being loved alone that we go wrong." For not only do we insist on believing romantically in the "one-and-only"—the one-and-only love, the one-and-only mate, the one-and-only mother, the one-and-only security—we wish the "one-and-only" to be permanent, ever-present and continuous. The desire for continuity of being-loved-alone seems to me "the error bred in the bone" of man. For "there is no one-and-only," as a friend of mine once said in a similar discussion, "there are just one-and-only moments."

The one-and-only moments are justified. The return to them, even if temporarily, is valid. The moment over the marmalade and muffins is valid; the moment feeding the child at the breast is valid; the moment racing with him later on the beach is valid. Finding shells together, polishing chestnuts, sharing one's treasures:—all these moments of together aloneness are valid, but not permanent.

One comes in the end to realize that there is no permanent pure-relationship and there should not be. It is not even something to be desired. The pure relationship is limited, in space and in time. In its essence it implies exclusion. It excludes the rest of life, other relationships, other sides of personality, other responsibilities, other possibilities in the future. It excludes growth. The other children are there clamoring outside the closed nursery door. One loves them, too. The telephone rings in the next room. One also wants to talk to friends. When the muffins are cleared away, one must think of the next meal or the next day. These are realities too, not to be excluded. Life must go on. That does not mean it is a waste of time to recreate for brief holiday periods together-alone experiences. On the contrary, these one-and-only moments are both refreshing and rewarding. The light shed over the small breakfast table illumines the day, many days. The race on the beach together renews one's youth like a dip in the sea. But we are no longer children; life is not a beach. There is no pattern here for permanent return, only for refreshment.

One learns to accept the fact that no permanent return is possible to an old form of relationship; and, more deeply still, that there is no holding of a relationship to a single form. This is not tragedy but part of the ever-recurrent miracle of life and growth. All living relationships are in process of change, of expansion, and must perpetually be building themselves new forms. But there is no single fixed form to express such a changing relationship. There are perhaps different forms for each successive stage; different shells I might put in a row on my desk to suggest the different stages of marriage—or indeed of any relationship.

My double-sunrise shell comes first. It is a valid image, I think, for the first stage: two flawless halves bound together with a single hinge, meeting each other at every point, the dawn of a new day spreading on each face. It is a world to itself. Is this not what the poets have always been attempting to describe?

> And now good-morrow to our waking souls
> Which watch not one another out of fear;
> For love all love of other sights controls,
> And makes one little room an everywhere.
> Let sea-discoverers to new worlds have gone,
> Let maps to other, worlds on worlds have shown,
> Let us possess one world; each hath one, and is one.

It is, however, a "little room," that Donne describes, a small world, that must be inevitably and happily outgrown. Beautiful, fragile, fleeting, the sunrise shell; but not, for all that, illusory. Because it is not lasting, let us not fall into the cynic's trap and call it an illusion. Duration is not a test of true or false. The day of the dragon-fly or the night of the Saturnid moth is not invalid simply because that phase in its life cycle is brief. Validity need have no relation to time, to duration, to continuity. It is on another plane, judged by other standards. It relates to the actual moment in time and place. "And what is actual is actual only for one time and only for one place." The sunrise shell has the eternal validity of all beautiful and fleeting things.

The author chose a double-sunrise shell as a metaphor for the pure relationship. How do the characteristics of the shell parallel elements of the first stage of love? For example, the fact that "both halves of this delicate bivalve are exactly matched. Each side . . . marked with the same pattern; translucent white, except for three rosy rays that fan out from the golden hinge binding the two together. . . . smooth, whole, unblemished . . . fragile perfection. . . ."

How is the name of the shell itself symbolic of the relationship?

In *The Pilgrim's Regress,* C. S. Lewis asks:

Do you not know how it is with love? First comes delight; then pain; then fruit. And then there is joy of the fruit, but that is different again from the first delight. And mortal lovers must not try to remain at the first step: for lasting passion is the dream of a harlot and from it we wake in despair. You must not try to keep the raptures: they have done their work. Manna kept, is worms. [32]

Lindbergh in **Double-Sunrise** agrees. What reasons does she give for the transformation of the early ecstatic stage of the relationship into more functional ones?

If "one resents any change" why do people not hold the pure relationship to this single fixed form which makes "one little room an everywhere"?

How would you expect Lindbergh to reply to the question: "Does love last?" Does her analogy—"like its parallel in physical passion, the early ecstatic stage of a relationship cannot continue always at the same pitch of intensity"—indicate that *sex* does not last?

How might Lindbergh react to the following definition of indifference:

"The tragedy of love." *Somerset Maugham.*
How do you know that love is gone? If you said you would be there at seven, you get there by nine and he or she has not called the police yet—it's gone. [33]

From your own experience, with life or literature, how would you reinforce her generalization that "there is no one-and-only . . . there are just one-and-only moments"?

Is there a difference between "togetherness" and "exclusiveness"?

What does the Indian philosopher who spoke to Lindbergh mean:

"It is all right to wish to be loved alone . . . mutuality is the essence of love. . . . It is only in the time-sense that it is wrong. It is when we desire *continuity* of being loved alone that we go wrong."

What does Lindbergh believe to be one of the differences in male and female needs? What others might be added to distinguish between male and female sexuality?

RELATED QUESTIONS

Would Lewis in **Eros** (p. 206) consider the partners in a double-sunrise relationship to be "love's contemplatives"? Why, or why not?

How might Lindbergh react to the statements made about love in **Kisses, Can You Come Back Like Ghosts?** by Carl Sandburg (see **"Night-Lights,"** p. 586), as well as to the title question?

Many writers have considered the question: "If appearances are deceptive, how can one know when love is real and when it is illusion?" Lindbergh comments:

Beautiful, fragile, fleeting, the sunrise shell; but not, for all that, illusory. Because it is not lasting, let us not fall into the cynic's trap and call it an illusion. Duration is not a test of true or false. . . . Validity need have no relation to time, to duration, to continuity. . . . The sunrise shell has the eternal validity of all beautiful and fleeting things.

"The elderly," says Auden in "Are You There?," "are always prone/To think of love as a subjective fake" [34].

In **Appraisal and Bestowal** (p. 226), Singer claims that:

The as ifs of love are imaginative, not essentially delusional. Of course, the lover *may* be deluded about his beloved. That is the familiar joke about lovers: they live in constant illusion, Cupid is blinded by emotion, etc. That this often happens I do not care to deny. But that this should be the essence of love, that by its very nature love should be illusory, seems to me utterly absurd. . . . Though lovers do commit errors of judgment and are sometimes carried away by their feelings, love itself is not illusory.

Ralph Waldo Emerson states in *Essays: Illusions:*

There are deceptions of the senses, deceptions of the passions, and the structural, beneficent illusions of sentiment and the intellect. There is the illusion of love, which attributes to the beloved person all which that person shares with his or her family, sex, age, or condition, nay, with the human mind itself. 'Tis these which the lover loves, and Anna Matilda gets the credit of them. As if one shut up always in a tower, with one window, through which the face of heaven and earth could be seen, should fancy that all the marvels he beheld belonged to that window. [35]

Evelyn Duvall, in *Love and the Facts of Life* explains:

. . . sudden, intense attraction between two persons usually is based upon one of two powerful forces. The first is sex attraction. Something about a girl, often some insignificant characteristic—the turn of an ankle, the look in the eyes, the modulation of the voice—trips off the boy's sex interest, and he may find himself head over heels in love with someone that he scarcely knows as a person. This can happen to girls, too. They report that sometimes the way a man walks, or talks, or looks at a girl may suddenly cause her to "fall for" him. Even smells may be a factor in this kind of attraction. Touch is a powerful stimulus, as many persons find to their surprise.

The second thing . . . is that he or she reminds him of a previous loved one . . . he does not consciously recognize the likeness . . . but his feelings behave as they used to with the-woman-he-sees-in-her. . . .

Infatuation and love are not the same thing. Infatuation is apt to be sudden, impulsive, and fragile. Love grows out of mutual association into a steady, long-lasting sturdy affection. [36]

Do any of these ideas overlap? Explain each other? Help provide criteria for determining when one is really in love?

On Falling in Love
ROBERT LOUIS STEVENSON

Lord, what fools these mortals be!

. . . Falling in love is the one illogical adventure, the one thing of which we are tempted to think as supernatural, in our trite and reasonable world. The effect is out of all proportion with the cause. Two persons, neither of them, it may be, very amiable or very beautiful, meet, speak a little, and look a little into each other's eyes. That has been done a dozen or so of times in the experience of either with no great result. But on this occasion all is different. They fall at once into that state in which another person becomes to us the very gist and center-point of God's creation, and demolishes our laborious theories with a smile; in which our ideas are so bound up with the one master-thought that even the trivial cares of our own person become so many acts of devotion, and the love of life itself is translated into a wish to remain in the same world with so precious and desirable a fellow creature. And all the while their acquaintances look on in stupor, and ask each other, with almost passionate emphasis, what so-and-so can see in that woman, or such-a-one in that man? I am sure, gentlemen, I cannot tell you. For my part, I cannot think what the women mean. It might be very well, if the Apollo Belvedere should suddenly glow all over into life, and step forward from the pedestal with that godlike air of his. But of the misbegotten changelings who call themselves men, and prate intolerably over dinner table, I never saw one who seemed worthy to inspire love—no, nor read of any, except Leonardo da Vinci, and perhaps Goethe in his youth. About women I entertain a somewhat different opinion; but there, I have the misfortune to be a man.

There are many matters in which you may waylay Destiny, and bid him stand and deliver. Hard work, high thinking, adventurous excitement, and a great deal more that forms a part of this or the other person's spiritual bill of fare, are within the reach of almost anyone who can dare a little and be patient. But it is by no means in the way of everyone to fall in love. You know the difficulty Shakespeare was put into when Queen Elizabeth asked him to show Falstaff in love. I do not believe that Henry Fielding was ever in love. Scott, if it were not for a passage or two in *Rob Roy*, would give me very much the same effect. These are great names and (what is more to the purpose) strong, healthy, high-strung, and generous natures, of whom the reverse might have been expected. As for the innumerable army of anemic and tailorish persons who occupy the face of this planet with so much propriety, it is palpably absurd to imagine them in any such situation as a love affair. A wet rag goes safely by the fire; and if a man is blind, he cannot expect to be much impressed by romantic scenery. Apart from all this many lovable people miss each other in the world, or meet under some unfavorable star. There is the nice and critical moment of declaration to be got over. From timidity or lack of opportunity a good half of possible love cases never get so far, and at least another quarter do there cease and determine. A very adroit person, to be sure, manages to prepare the way and out with his declaration in the nick of time. And then there is a fine solid sort of man, who goes on from snub to snub; and if he has to declare forty times, will continue imperturbably declaring, amid the astonished consideration of men and angels, until he has a favorable answer. I daresay, if one were a woman, one would like to marry a man who was capable of doing this, but not quite one who had done so. It is just a little bit abject, and somehow just a little bit gross; and marriages in which one of the parties has been thus battered into consent scarcely form agreeable subjects for meditation. Love should run out to meet love with open arms. Indeed, the ideal story is that of two people who go into love step for step, with a fluttered consciousness, like a pair of children venturing together into a dark room. From the first moment when they see each other, with a pang of curiosity, through stage after stage of growing pleasure and embarrassment, they can read the expression of their own trouble in each other's eyes. There is here no declaration properly so called; the feeling is so plainly shared, that as soon as the man knows what it is in his own heart, he is sure of what it is in the woman's.

This simple accident of falling in love is as beneficial as it is astonishing. It arrests the petrifying influence of years, disproves cold-blooded and cynical conclusions, and awakens dormant sensibilities. Hitherto the man had found it a good policy to disbelieve the existence of any enjoyment which was out of his reach; and thus he turned his back upon the strong sunny parts of nature, and accustomed himself to look exclusively on what was common and dull. He accepted a prose ideal, let himself go blind of many sympathies by disuse; and if he were young and witty, or beautiful, wilfully forwent these advantages. He joined himself to the following of what, in the old mythology of love, was prettily called *nonchaloir;* and in an odd mixture of feelings, a fling of self-respect, a preference for selfish liberty, and a great dash of that fear with which honest people regard serious interests, kept himself back from the straightforward course of life among certain selected activities. And now, all of a sudden, he is unhorsed, like St. Paul, from his infidel affectation. His heart, which has been ticking accurate seconds for the last year, gives a bound and begins to beat high and irregularly in his breast. It seems as if he had never heard or felt or seen until that moment; and by the report of his memory, he must have lived his past life between sleep and waking, or with the preoccupied attention of a brown study. He is practically incommoded by the generosity of his feelings, smiles much when he is alone, and develops a habit of looking rather blankly upon the moon and stars. But it is not at all within the province of a prose essayist to give a picture of this hyperbolical frame of mind; and the thing has been done already, and that to admiration. In *Adelaide,* in Tennyson's *Maud,* and in some of Heine's songs, you get the absolute expression of this midsummer spirit. Romeo and Juliet were very much in love; although they tell me some German critics are of a different opinion, probably the same who would have us think Mercutio a dull fellow. Poor Antony was in love, and no mistake. That lay figure Marius, in *Les Misérables,* is also a genuine case in his own way, and worth observation. A good many of George Sand's people are thoroughly in love; and so are a good many of George Meredith's. Altogether, there is plenty to read on the subject. If the root of the matter be in him, and if he has the requisite chords to set in vibration, a young man may occasionally enter, with the key of art, into that land of Beulah which is upon the borders of Heaven and within sight of the City of Love. There let him sit awhile to hatch delightful hopes and perilous illusions.

One thing that accompanies the passion in its first blush is certainly difficult to explain. It comes (I do not quite see how) that from having a very supreme sense of pleasure in all parts of life—in lying down to sleep, in waking, in motion, in breathing, in continuing to be—the lover begins to regard his happiness as beneficial for the rest of the world and highly meritorious in himself. Our race has never been able contentedly to suppose that the noise of its wars, conducted by a few young gentlemen in a corner of an inconsiderable star, does not re-echo among the courts of Heaven with quite a formidable effect. In much the same taste, when people find a great to-do in their own breasts, they imagine it must have some influence in their neighborhood. The presence of the two lovers is so enchanting to each other that it seems as if it must be the best thing possible for everybody else. They are half inclined to fancy it is because of them and their love that the sky is blue and the sun shines. And certainly the weather is usually fine while people are courting. . . . In point of fact, although the happy man feels very kindly toward others of his own sex, there is apt to be something too much of the magnifico in his demeanor. If people grow presuming and self-important over such matters as a dukedom or the Holy See, they will scarcely support the dizziest elevation in life without some suspicion of a strut; and the dizziest elevation is to love and be loved in return. Consequently, accepted lovers are a trifle condescending in their address to other men. An overweening sense of the passion and importance of life hardly conduces to simplicity of manner. To women, they feel very nobly, very purely, and very generously, as if they were so many Joan-of-Arcs; but this does not come out in their behavior; and they treat them to Grandisonian airs marked with a suspicion of fatuity. I am not quite certain that women do not like this sort of thing; but really, after having bemused myself over *Daniel Deronda,* I have given up trying to understand what they like.

If it did nothing else, this sublime and ridiculous superstition, that the pleasure of the pair is somehow blessed to others, and everybody is made happier in their happiness, would serve at least to keep love generous and great-hearted. Nor is it quite a baseless superstition after all. Other lovers are hugely interested. They strike the nicest balance between pity and approval, when they see people aping the greatness of their own sentiments. It is an understood thing in the play, that while the young gentlefolk are courting on the terrace, a rough flirtation is being carried on and a light, trivial sort of love is growing up, between the foot-man and the singing chambermaid. As people are generally cast for the leading parts in their own imaginations, the reader can apply the parallel to real life without much chance of going wrong. In short, they are quite sure this other love affair is not so deep seated as their own, but they like dearly to see it going forward. And love, considered as a spectacle, must have attractions for many who are not of the confraternity. The sentimental old maid is a commonplace of the novelists; and he must be rather a poor sort of human being, to be sure, who can look on at this pretty madness without indulgence and sympathy. For nature commends itself to people with a most insinuating art; the busiest is now and again arrested by a great sunset; and you may be as pacific or as cold-blooded as you will, but you cannot help some emotion when you read of well-disputed battles, or meet a pair of lovers in the lane.

Certainly, whatever it may be with regard to the world at large, this idea of beneficent pleasure is true as between the sweethearts. To do good and communicate is the lover's grand intention. It is the happiness of the other that makes his own most intense gratification. It is not possible to disentangle the different emotions, the pride, humility, pity and passion, which are excited by a look of happy love or an unexpected caress. To make one's self beautiful, to dress the hair, to excel in talk, to do anything and all things that puff out the character and attributes and make them imposing in the eyes of others, is not only to magnify one's self, but to offer the most delicate homage at the same time. And it is in this latter intention that they are done by lovers; for the essence of love is kindness; and indeed it may be best defined as passionate kindness: kindness, so to speak, run mad and become importunate and violent. Vanity in a merely personal sense exists no longer. The lover takes a perilous pleasure in privately displaying his weak points and having them, one after another, accepted and condoned. He wishes to be assured that he is not loved for this or that good quality, but for himself, or something as like himself as he can contrive to set forward. For, although it may have been a very difficult thing to paint the marriage of Cana, or write the fourth act of *Antony and Cleopatra*, there is a more difficult piece of art before every one in this world who cares to set about explaining his own character to others. Words and acts are easily wrenched from their true significance; and they are all the language we have to come and go upon. A pitiful job we make of it, as a rule. For better or worse, people mistake our meaning and take our emotions at a wrong valuation. And generally we rest pretty content with our failures; we are content to be misapprehended by crackling flirts; but when once a man is moonstruck with this affection of love, he makes it a point of honor to clear such dubieties away. He cannot have the Best of Her Sex misled upon a point of this importance; and his pride revolts at being loved in a mistake.

He discovers a great reluctance to return on former periods of his life. To all that has not been shared with her, rights and duties, bygone fortunes and dispositions, he can look back only by a difficult and repugnant effort of the will. That he should have wasted some years in ignorance of what alone was really important, that he may have entertained the thought of other women with any show of complacency, is a burthen almost too heavy for his self-respect. But it is the thought of another past that rankles in his spirit like a poisoned wound. That he himself made a fashion of being alive in the bald, beggarly days before a certain meeting, is deplorable enough in all good conscience. But that She should have permitted herself the same liberty seems inconsistent with a Divine providence.

A great many people run down jealousy, on the score that it is an artificial feeling, as well as practically inconvenient. This is scarcely fair; for the feeling on which it merely attends, like an ill-humored courtier, is itself artificial in exactly the same sense and to the same degree. I suppose what is meant by that objection is that jealousy has not always been a character of man; formed no part of that very modest kit of sentiments with which he is supposed to have begun the world: but waited to make its appearance in better days and among richer natures. And this is equally true of love, and friendship, and love of country, and delight in what they call the beauties of nature, and most other things worth having. Love, in particular, will not endure any historical scrutiny: to all who have fallen across it, it is one of the most incontestable facts in the world; but if you begin to ask what it was in other periods and countries, in Greece for instance, the strangest doubts begin to spring up, and everything seems so vague and changing that a dream is logical in comparison. Jealousy, at any rate, is one of the consequences of love; you may like it or not, at pleasure; but there it is.

It is not exactly jealousy, however, that we feel when we reflect on the past of those we love. A bundle of letters found after years of happy union creates no sense of insecurity in the present; and yet it will pain a man sharply. The two people entertain no vulgar doubt of each other: but this pre-existence of both occurs to the mind as something indelicate. To be altogether right, they should have had twin birth together, at the same moment with the feeling that unites them. Then indeed it would be simple and perfect and without reserve or afterthought. Then they would understand each other with a fullness impossible otherwise. There would be no barrier between them of associations that cannot be imparted. They would be led into none of those comparisons that send the blood back to the heart. And they would know that there had been no time lost, and they had been together as much as was possible. For besides terror for the separation that must follow some time or other in the future, men feel anger, and something like remorse, when they think of that other separation which endured until they met. Some one has written that love makes people believe in immortality, because there seems not to be room enough in life for so great a tenderness, and it is inconceivable that the most masterful of our emotions should have no more than the spare moments of a few years. Indeed, it seems strange; but if we call to mind analogies, we can hardly regard it as impossible.

"The blind bow-boy," who smiles upon us from the end of terraces in old Dutch gardens, laughingly hails his bird-bolts among a fleeting generation. But for as fast as ever he shoots, the game dissolves and disappears into eternity from under his falling arrows; this one is gone ere he is struck; the other has but time to make one gesture and give one passionate cry; and they are all the things of a moment. When the generation is gone, when the play is over, when the thirty years' panorama has been withdrawn in tatters from the stage of the world, we may ask what has become of these great, weighty, and undying loves, and the sweethearts who despised mortal conditions in a fine credulity; and they can only show us a few songs in a bygone taste, a few actions worth remembering, and a few children who have retained some happy stamp from the disposition of their parents.

In *On Falling in Love,* Stevenson deals primarily with the attitudes and behavior of those startled by the experience of "falling in love." What are some of the recognizable characteristics of this emotional condition? Does the author seem to exaggerate it? For example, is the effect of falling in love really "out of all proportion with the cause"? In that state does "another person [become] the very gist and center-point of God's creation"?

Stevenson claims that "it is not at all within the province of a prose essayist to give a picture of this hyperbolical frame of mind." Why does he consider it hyperbolical?

Stevenson emphasizes the startling nature and benefits of love, but are there disadvantages as well? If so, what are some of the liabilities and how can one deal with them?

What does the author mean that

> . . . the essence of love is kindness; and indeed it may be best defined as passionate kindness: kindness, so to speak, run mad and become importunate and violent.

Jealousy, according to Stevenson, "is one of the consequences of love; you may like it or not . . . but there it is." Jealousy has been called "an uncontrollable passion, the Siamese twin of love" [37], and "almost always a mark of immaturity and insecurity . . . a badge of love when a young girl says in delighted surprise 'why, you're jealous! You must care for me after all.' She may deliberately provoke jealousy to reassure herself of his feeling" [38]. What do you consider the relationship between jealousy and love? Is it an inevitable corrolary? Or does confidence in the person we love, and faith in our ability to hold that love, replace jealousy?

From his masculine perspective, Stevenson claims never to have seen one of the "misbegotten changelings who call themselves men . . . who seemed worthy to inspire love . . . nor read of any, except Leonardo da Vinci, and perhaps Goethe in his youth." As a male, would you subscribe to Stevenson's inability to fathom "what so-and-so can see . . . in that man"? What fictional or nonfictional males seem "worthy to inspire love"? As a female, could you subscribe to Stevenson's comment if rephrased to apply to women? What fictional or nonfictional females would be worthy to inspire love? How are you defining love?

Would you expect males and females to differ in their choices of names "worthy to inspire love"? Why?

As a female, would you like to marry a man Stevenson describes as capable of going on

> . . . from snub to snub; [who] if he has to declare forty times, will continue imperturbably declaring, amid the astonished consideration of men and angels, until he has a favorable answer.

As a male, would you view such a man as "a fine solid sort," as Stevenson says he does?

Stevenson suggests that:

> The lover takes a perilous pleasure in privately displaying his weak points and having them, one after another, accepted and condoned. He wishes to be assured that he is not loved for this or that good quality, but for himself. . . . He cannot have the Best of Her Sex misled upon a point of this importance; and his pride revolts at being loved in a mistake.

Is this why a man might confide to the person with whom he has fallen in love about his previous romances? Previous sexual experiences? Are there other motives?

Should the word "love" be reserved for abiding love in which two people can think as well as feel together? Or is it quite as applicable to the more spectacular "simple and astonishing accidents" which leave one moonstruck?

244 RELATED QUESTIONS

"They"
awareness of others

How does Stevenson's concept of falling in love resemble the "double-sunrise" state described by Anne Morrow Lindbergh (p. 232)?

Which of Stevenson's generalizations in *On Falling in Love* are illustrated in the following poems:

Early Love by Samuel Daniel ("**Night-Lights,**" p. 545)
Oh, When I Was in Love with You by A. E. Housman ("**Night-Lights,**" p. 565)
Apology by Amy Lowell ("**Night-Lights,**" p. 572)
Eros in the Kitchen by Phyllis McGinley ("**Night-Lights,**" p. 575)

Stevenson prefaces his argument that "falling in love is the one illogical adventure, the one thing of which we are tempted to think as supernatural, in our trite and reasonable world," with a quotation from *A Midsummer Night's Dream:* "Lord, what fools these mortals be!" Do you agree with the Shakespearian philosophy that:

> Things base and vile, holding no quantity,
> Love can transpose to form and dignity.
> Love looks not with the eyes, but with the mind,
> And therefore is wing'd Cupid painted blind.
> Nor hath Love's mind of any judgment taste;
> Wings and no eyes figure unheedy haste:
> And therefore is Love said to be a child,
> Because in choice he is so oft beguil'd.
> As waggish boys in game themselves forswear,
> So the boy Love is perjur'd everywhere. [39]

If love is not blind, why does Stevenson refer to the statue of Cupid as "the blind bow-boy who smiles upon us from the end of the terraces"? Or why do people claim "love made us do it," or "we were blinded by emotion"? Why then is it that "love makes vows unasked; can't be deterred from making them"? Why would C. S. Lewis' "two mature and experienced people who know that broken hearts heal in the end" hear a voice within them saying, "'Let our hearts break provided they break together.'"?

If love is not blind and irrational, how can Pascal argue, in *On the Passion of Love:*

> . . . when a person is in love, he seems to himself wholly changed from what he was before; and he fancies that everybody sees him in the same light. This is a great mistake, but reason being obscured by passion, he cannot be convinced, and goes on still under the delusion. [40]

Or Francis Bacon in *Essays* state:

> . . . it was well said: That it is impossible to love and to be wise. . . . For whosoever esteemeth too much of amorous affection, quitteth both riches

and wisdom. . . . They do best, who, if they cannot but admit love, yet make it keep quarter: and sever it wholly, from their serious affairs, and actions of life: for if it check once with business, it troubleth men's fortunes, and maketh men, that they can, no wise be true, to their own ends. [41]

Why would Singer, despite his distinction in **Appraisal and Bestowal** that "the as ifs of love are imaginative, not essentially delusional" also write: "Love is not *practical,* and sometimes borders on madness"?

Lindbergh's shell in **Double-Sunrise** suggests that "love all love of other sights controls"; C. S. Lewis speaks of the event of falling in love as being of such a nature that it tosses "personal happiness aside as a triviality . . . plant[ing] the interests of another in the centre of our being"; Singer in **Appraisal and Bestowal** applauds lovers who through the amorous imagination create their own affective universe; and Pascal in *On the Passion of Love* agrees with one who holds that

> . . . in love, fortune, friends, relatives, are all forgotten: this is the tendency of most elevated attachments. A man in love feels, for the time, that he wants nothing but the object of his preference: the mind is filled: there is no room for other care or solicitude. Passion always impels to extremes: thence it is that we become indifferent to the opinion of the world; we satisfy ourselves that we have right on our side, and ought not to be the object of censure. [42]

What then might be the counter-argument of poets like Edna St. Vincent Millay, in "Sonnet XXVI," who insist:

> Love is not blind. I see with single eye
> Your ugliness and other women's grace.
> I know the imperfection of your face,—
> The eyes too wide apart, the brow too high
> For beauty. Learned from earliest youth am I
> In loveliness, and cannot so erase
> Its letters from my mind, that I may trace
> You faultless, I must love until I die.
> More subtle is the sovereignty of love. [43]

Is she speaking about love's blindness, or only one facet of it?

Is Millay saying "Love [does] not make me blind to your faults, but it [makes] those faults dear to me" (p. 226)?

If Millay is realistic—even far-sighted—about the imperfections described, why does she say "I must love until I die"?

In what ways might the "sovereignty of love" be "more subtle"? More subtle than what?

What clues to the sanity and sovereignty of love does Pascal provide by saying in *Pensées* that "the heart has reasons that reason knows not of," and in *On the Passion of Love:*

> It has been usual, but without cause, to underrate, and regard, as opposed to reason, the passion of love. Reason and love are, however, consistent with each other. It is a precipitation of mind that thus carries us into partialities and extremes; but it is still reason, and we ought not to wish it to be otherwise. We should, in that case, only prove man to be a very disagreeable machine. Let us not seek to exclude reason from love; for they are inseparable. [44]

Does "sanity" suggest a distinction between the sudden strange experience of "falling in love" and a commitment to loving? Carefully separated from the commitment of loving, does falling in love seem closer to physical attraction or infatuation? Is the suddenness of falling in love a flag of suspicion rather than a mark of authenticity? Would you agree with Menninger [45] that people don't fall in love; rather, that they grow in love, and that love grows in them?

Is Love an Art?

ERICH FROMM

Is love an art? Then it requires knowledge and effort. Or is love a pleasant sensation, which to experience is a matter of chance, something one "falls into" if one is lucky? . . . Undoubtedly the majority of people today believe in the latter.

Not that people think that love is not important. They are starved for it; they watch endless numbers of films about happy and unhappy love stories, they listen to hundreds of trashy songs about love — yet hardly anyone thinks that there is anything that needs to be learned about love.

This peculiar attitude is based on several premises which either singly or combined tend to uphold it. Most people see the problem of love primarily as that of *being loved*, rather than that of *loving*, of one's capacity to love. Hence the problem to them is how to be loved, how be to lovable. In pursuit of this aim they follow several paths. One, which is especially used by men, is to be successful, to be as powerful and rich as the social margin of one's position permits. Another, used especially by women, is to make oneself attractive, by cultivating one's body, dress, etc. Other ways of making oneself attractive, used both by men and women, are to develop pleasant manners, interesting conversation, to be helpful, modest, inoffensive. Many of the ways to make oneself lovable are the same as those used to make oneself successful, "to win friends and influence people." As a matter of fact, what most people in our culture mean by being lovable is essentially a mixture between being popular and having sex appeal.

A second premise behind the attitude that there is nothing to be learned about love is the assumption that the problem of love is the problem of an *object*, not the problem of a *faculty*. People think that to *love* is simple, but that to find the right object to love — or to be loved by — is difficult. This attitude has several reasons rooted in the development of modern society. One reason is the great change which occurred in the twentieth century with respect to the choice of a "love object." In the Victorian age, as in many traditional cultures, love was mostly not a spontaneous personal experience which then might lead to marriage. On the contrary, marriage was contracted by convention — either by the respective families, or by a marriage broker, or without the help of such intermediaries; it was concluded on the basis of social considerations, and love was supposed to develop once the marriage had been concluded. In the last few generations the concept of romantic love has become almost universal in the Western world. In the United States, while considerations of a conventional nature are not entirely absent, to a vast extent people are in search of "romantic love," of the personal experience of love which then should lead to marriage. This new concept of freedom in love must have greatly enhanced the importance of the *object* as against the importance of the *function*.

Closely related to this factor is another feature characteristic of contemporary culture. Our whole culture is based on the appetite for buying, on the idea of a mutually favorable exchange. Modern man's happiness consists in the thrill of looking at the shop windows, and in buying all that he can afford to buy, either for cash or on installments. He (or she) looks at people in a similar way. For the man an attractive girl—and for the woman an attractive man—are the prizes they are after. "Attractive" usually means a nice package of qualities which are popular and sought after on the personality market. What specifically makes a person attractive depends on the fashion of the time, physically as well as mentally. During the twenties, a drinking and smoking girl, tough and sexy, was attractive; today the fashion demands more domesticity and coyness. At the end of the nineteenth and the beginning of this century, a man had to be aggressive and ambitious—today he has to be social and tolerant—in order to be an attractive "package." At any rate, the sense of falling in love develops usually only with regard to such human commodities as are within reach of one's own possibilities for exchange. I am out for a bargain; the object should be desirable from the standpoint of its social value, and at the same time should want me, considering my overt and hidden assets and potentialities. Two persons thus fall in love when they feel they have found the best object available on the market, considering the limitations of their own exchange values. Often, as in buying real estate, the hidden potentialities which can be developed play a considerable role in this bargain. In a culture in which the marketing orientation prevails, and in which material success is the outstanding value, there is little reason to be surprised that human love relations follow the same pattern of exchange which governs the commodity and the labor market.

The third error leading to the assumption that there is nothing to be learned about love lies in the confusion between the initial experience of *"falling"* in love, and the permanent state of *being* in love, or as we might better say, of "standing" in love. If two people who have been strangers, as all of us are, suddenly let the wall between them break down, and feel close, feel one, this moment of oneness is one of the most exhilarating, most exciting experiences in life. It is all the more wonderful and miraculous for persons who have been shut off, isolated, without love. This miracle of sudden intimacy is often facilitated if it is combined with, or initiated by, sexual attraction and consummation. However, this type of love is by its very nature not lasting. The two persons become well acquainted, their intimacy loses more and more its miraculous character, until their antagonism, their disappointments, their mutual boredom kill whatever is left of the initial excitement. Yet, in the beginning they do not know all this: in fact, they take the intensity of the infatuation, this being "crazy" about each other, for proof of the intensity of their love, while it may only prove the degree of their preceding loneliness.

This attitude—that nothing is easier than to love—has continued to be the prevalent idea about love in spite of the overwhelming evidence to the contrary. There is hardly any activity, any enterprise, which is started with such tremendous hopes and expectations, and yet, which fails so regularly, as love. If this were the case with any other activity, people would be eager to know the reasons for the failure, and to learn how one could do better—or they would give up the activity. Since the latter is impossible in the case of love, there seems to be only one adequate way to overcome the failure of love—to examine the reasons for this failure, and to proceed to study the meaning of love.

The first step to take is to become aware that *love is an art*, just as living is an art. . . .

The process of learning an art can be divided conveniently into two parts: one, the mastery of the theory; the other, the mastery of the practice. . . . And, maybe, here lies the answer to the question of why people in our culture try so rarely to learn this art, in spite of their obvious failures: in spite of the deep-seated craving for love, almost everything else is considered to be more important than love: success, prestige, money, power—almost all our energy is used for the learning of how to achieve these aims, and almost none to learn the art of loving.

Could it be that only those things are considered worthy of being learned with which one can earn money or prestige, and that love, which "only" profits the soul, but is profitless in the modern sense, is a luxury we have no right to spend much energy on?

Is love an art that "requires knowledge and effort"? Or is it a pleasant, chance sensation, something we "fall into" if we are lucky? Do you agree with Fromm that most people believe in the latter?

Do we tend to expect too much of love? If so, in what way? Who or what creates a false image of it?

How does Fromm in **Is Love an Art?** clarify the popular confusion between the initial experience of *falling* in love and the permanent state of *being* in love?

Fromm says that "the miracle of sudden intimacy is often facilitated if it is combined with, or initiated by, sexual attraction and consummation. However, this type of love is by its very nature not lasting." Lindbergh in **Double-Sunrise** and Lewis in *The Pilgrim's Regress* also share Fromm's notion that:

The two persons become well acquainted, their intimacy loses more and more its miraculous character, until their antagonism, their disappointments, their mutual boredom kill whatever is left of the initial excitement. Yet, in the beginning they do not know all this: in fact, they take the intensity of the infatuation, this being "crazy" about each other, for proof of the intensity of their love, while it may only prove the degree of their preceding loneliness.

In a part of *The Woman on the Stair,* and *The Happy Marriage* Archibald MacLeish describes Fromm's "falling in love" as "love not love" and as "love's true negative." MacLeish considers, in the excerpt "The Second Love" from *The Woman on the Stair* that

In love not love there never are two lovers:
There are but two together with blind eyes
Watching within what ecstasy love suffers.

One, like a shore at which the water rises,

Senses the flooding of a sea to spate
Her naked and lovely longing with its rising.

One, like the flooding of a sea, awaits
The smooth resistance of the gradual shore
To be fallen in shudder of hush from his headlong greatness.

What they remember each of the other more than
Meeting of mouths or even the profound touch
Is their own ecstasy heavy to be borne.

So it is, even with these whose touching
Makes them a moment on a bed to share
What time with all its timid gifts begrudges.

Neither her serious mouth nor pitiful hair
Nor his mouth mortal with the murderous need
Troubles their hearts to tenderness.

                              They stare
Each in the other's face like those who feed
Delight in mirrors: and as though alone
Learn from each other where their love will lead them. [46]

In an excerpt from *The Happy Marriage,* MacLeish reflects:

This was not love but love's true negative
That spends itself in passion to be spent,
And lives no longer than the wish may live
To waste itself and then is impotent,
And fails not only but confounds in fault
What love most lives upon, the very need,
The lack, the famine, the too thirsty salt,
Till wanting want love has no will to feed. [47]

What does MacLeish consider the limiting characteristics of "love's true negative," or "love not love"? What qualities are missing that are intrinsic to "being
in love," or "standing" in love?

RELATED QUESTIONS

In the excerpt from *The Woman on the Stair,* how does the poet answer
the questions raised in **Double-Sunrise:** "But can one actually find oneself in
someone else? In someone else's love? Or even in the mirror someone else holds
up for one?"

What feeling does Tim show toward Rachel in **The City of Trembling Leaves**
(p. 94) that the lovers from *The Woman on the Stair* lack?

Why does the couple in *The Woman on the Stair* not meet Saint-Exupéry's
definition of love, "Love does not consist in gazing at each other but in looking
outward together in the same direction" (p. 346)?

In *The Happy Marriage* the poet refers to "What love most lives upon, the very need,/ The lack, the famine, the too thirsty salt." What do you think it is that "love most lives upon"?

To what degree do advertisements support or contradict Fromm's first premise in **Is Love an Art?** that "most people see the problem of love primarily as that of *being loved,* rather than that of *loving,* of one's capacity to love. Hence the problem to them is how to be loved, how to be lovable."

In which category—love as an art, or love as a pleasant sensation—would you put Stevenson's concept of falling in love (p. 238)? Lindbergh's essence of the double-sunrise relationship (p. 232)? Singer's notions of appraisal and bestowal p. 217)?

How does Lindbergh's discussion of the stages of love in **Double-Sunrise** (p. 232) suggest ways to resolve the problem of "falling" in love rather than "being" in love?

What Love Must Be

LAURIE LEE

Since we in the West have chosen to live in the private grip of love—and it seems that most of us have—perhaps we might ask what such love should be.

Not the seeking of ourselves in others, certainly, but an acknowledgment of the uniqueness of the sexes, their tongue-and-groove opposites, which provides love with its natural adhesive. "We are so much alike" is the fatal phrase, suggesting a cloudy affair with a mirror, when the real balance that binds us is the polar differences of sex, the magnetic forces that grapple between.

Perhaps the most useful service we can offer love is to respect that primitive gulf. This may not be easy in the general mix-up of today with the enforced blurring of sexual identities; but man still should be man, and woman as female as she is able, so that both may know the best of their natures.

Love should be an act of will, of passionate patience—flexible, cunning, constant; proof against roasting and freezing, drought and flood, and the shifting climates of mood and age. In order to make it succeed, one must lose all preconceptions, including a reliance on milk and honey, and fashion something that can blanket the whole range of experience from ecstasy to decay.

Most of all it must be built on truth, not dream, the knowledge of what we are, rather than what we think it is the fashion to be. For no pair of lovers were ever built to an identical program. So, beware of the norm, for no one is normal.

In sexual love there is no one rule that demands what love should be. Some, of course, are possessors, and some the possessed; some placid, or deeply devious. Some need the spirit only, vessels for adoration, for comfort, peace and calm; while others must be taken with tooth and claw and can only be damaged by misplaced mercy. All such is right, if love is right, and the anarchy is shared, and neither person is used simply as the other's victim but as one whose needs should also be cherished.

The sum of love is that it should be a meeting place, an interlocking of nerves and senses, a series of constant surprises and renewals of each other's moods—best of all, a steady building, from the inside out, to extend its regions to admit a larger world where children can live and breathe.

This seems promising ground. Yet the hard fact remains that love today fails more often than it succeeds—a failure due chiefly to the intolerable pressures of the age. Love needs to seed in a certain space and quiet—and even marriage requires some single-mindedness. The present machine-jigged world allows little for this, being shrunk, overcrowded, filled with the racket of voices, never still. Worse, it provides us with all too much—inflation of experience and fragmentation of desire. Frantic mobility, mass communications, the drug fix of jazz often keep the lover at such a pitch that normal flesh-and-blood contact palls.

In the calm, empty spaces of other times, a boy made good with the girl next door; now the crowded campus and swarming life of the city see him half-paralyzed by proliferation of choice. Taking up, putting down, unable in a dementia of equal temptation to decide or hold, constantly deluded by sight and surface—such conditioning, of course, is also the fracture of marriage, with the switching of partners like automobiles, a modern compulsion, with little to show for the exchange save the junk heaps on the edge of life.

But perhaps the main cause of failure lies in our attitude toward love itself—that as soon as it drops one degree below the level of self-satisfaction it is somehow improper to attempt to preserve it. In claiming the sanction to withdraw from any relationship the moment our happiness appears less than perfect, we are acting out a delusion that results in the denial of everything but the most trivial kind of love. Worse still, it makes a paper house of marriage, flimsily built for instant collapse, haunted by rootless children whose sense of incipient desertion dooms them to an emotional wasteland.

For the wholeness of modern man love must be deeper, to adapt to the world's shifting sands; able to withstand disaffections and occasional betrayals; sufficiently constant, in the center of orgy and bedlam, to create its own area of sacred quiet; and also strong enough to take marriage, its toughest test, and sink the best of its virtues in it, so that its children may be heirs of its proper kingdom rather than trail castaways of its self-absorption.

Some readjustments of attitudes may be necessary, of course. Such as the abdication of the need for power. And the giving up of the prizefight relationship, which, particularly in marriage, consists of scoring points and knocking one another down.

Love still has intimations of immortality to offer us, if we are willing to pay it tribute. If we can learn to forget the old clichés of jealousy and pride and not be afraid to stand guard, protect, acquiesce, forgive, and even serve. Love is not merely the indulgence of one's personal taste buds; it is also the delight in indulging another's. Also, in remembering such simplicities as tenderness and care, in taking some pleasure in the act of adoring, and in being content now and then to lie by one's sleeping love and to shield his eyes from the sun.

What to Lee in **What Love Must Be** is "the sum of love"?

What are some possible "tongue-and-groove" opposites which provide love with its natural adhesive?

Would you agree with the author that love today fails more often than it succeeds chiefly because of the intolerable pressures of the age? What are some of those pressures? What makes them intolerable?

Does Lee's use of the word sex connote the sex act? Or sexuality, the essential qualities of being male or female?

What might be some of the "polar differences of sex"?

How might young people be helped to sort truth from dream?

RELATED QUESTIONS

Like Fromm in *Is Love an Art?* (p. 246), Lee emphasizes loving rather than being loved. In what ways does he present love as an active effort, involving the head as well as the heart?

Lee also shares Fromm's conviction that love is an art, requiring knowledge and effort. What sort of knowledge might be considered as important as effort?

How is Lindbergh's concept of a deep and lasting relationship, indicated in *Double-Sunrise* (p. 232), illustrative of the "sum of love" in *What Love Must Be?*

The Theory of Love
ERICH FROMM

Man—of all ages and cultures—is confronted with the solution of one and the same question: the question of how to overcome separateness, how to achieve union, how to transcend one's own individual life and find at-onement.

One way of achieving this aim lies in all kinds of *orgiastic states*. These may have the form of an auto-induced trance, sometimes with the help of drugs. Many rituals of primitive tribes offer a vivid picture of this type of solution. In a transitory state of exaltation the world outside disappears, and with it the feeling of separateness from it. Inasmuch as these rituals are practiced in common, an experience of fusion with the group is added which makes this solution all the more effective. Closely related to, and often blended with this orgiastic solution, is the sexual experience. The sexual orgasm can produce a state similar to the one produced by a trance, or to the effects of certain drugs. Rites of communal sexual orgies were a part of many primitive rituals. It seems that after the orgiastic experience, man can go on for a time without suffering too much from his separateness. Slowly the tension of anxiety mounts, and then is reduced again by the repeated performance of the ritual.

As long as these orgiastic states are a matter of common practice in a tribe, they do not produce anxiety or guilt. To act in this way is right, and even virtuous, because it is a way shared by all, approved and demanded by the medicine men or priests; hence there is no reason to feel guilty or ashamed. It is quite different when the same solution is chosen by an individual in a culture which has left behind these common practices. Alcoholism and drug addiction are the forms which the individual chooses in a non-orgiastic culture. In contrast to those participating in the socially patterned solution, such individuals suffer from guilt feelings and remorse. While they try to escape from separateness by taking refuge in alcohol or drugs, they feel all the more separate after the orgiastic experience is over, and thus are driven to take recourse to it with increasing frequency and intensity. Slightly different from this is the recourse to a sexual orgiastic solution. To some extent it is a natural and normal form of overcoming separateness, and a partial answer to the problem of isolation. But in many individuals in whom separateness is not relieved in other ways, the search for the sexual orgasm assumes a function which makes it not very different from alcoholism and drug addiction. It becomes a desperate attempt to escape the anxiety engendered by separateness, and it results in an ever-increasing sense of separateness, since the sexual act without love never bridges the gap between two human beings, except momentarily.

All forms of orgiastic union have three characteristics: they are intense, even violent; they occur in the total personality, mind *and* body; they are transitory and periodical. Exactly the opposite holds true for that form of union which is by far the most frequent solution chosen by man in the past and in the present: the union based on *conformity* with the group, its customs, practices and beliefs.

Union by conformity is not intense and violent; it is calm, dictated by routine, and for this very reason often is insufficient to pacify the anxiety of separateness. The incidence of alcoholism, drug addiction, compulsive sexualism, and suicide in contemporary Western society are symptoms of this relative failure of herd conformity. Furthermore, this solution concerns mainly the mind and not the body, and for this reason too is lacking in comparison with the orgiastic solutions. Herd conformity has only one advantage: it is permanent, and not spasmodic. The individual is introduced into the conformity pattern at the age of three or four, and subsequently never loses his contact with the herd. Even his funeral, which he anticipates as his last great social affair, is in strict conformance with the pattern.

. . . [Another] way of attaining union lies in *creative activity,* be it that of the artist, or of the artisan. In any kind of creative work the creating person unites himself with his material, which represents the world outside of himself. Whether a carpenter makes a table, or a goldsmith a piece of jewelry, whether the peasant grows his corn or the painter paints a picture, in all types of creative work the worker and his object become one, man unites himself with the world in the process of creation. This, however, holds true only for productive work, for work in which *I* plan, produce, see the result of my work. In the modern work process of a clerk, the worker on the endless belt, little is left of this uniting quality of work. The worker becomes an appendix to the machine or to the bureaucratic organization. He has ceased to be he — hence no union takes place beyond that of conformity.

The unity achieved in productive work is not interpersonal; the unity achieved in orgiastic fusion is transitory; the unity achieved by conformity is only pseudo-unity. Hence, they are only partial answers to the problem of existence. The full answer lies in the achievement of interpersonal union, of fusion with another person, in *love.*

This desire for interpersonal fusion is the most powerful striving in man.

It is the most fundamental passion, it is the force which keeps the human race together, the clan, the family, society. The failure to achieve it means insanity or destruction — self-destruction or destruction of others. Without love, humanity could not exist for a day. Yet, if we call the achievement of interpersonal union "love," we find ourselves in a serious difficulty. Fusion can be achieved in different ways — and the differences are not less significant than what is common to the various forms of love. Should they all be called love? Or should we reserve the word "love" only for a specific kind of union, one which has been the ideal virtue in all great humanistic religions and philosophical systems of the last four thousand years of Western and Eastern history?

As with all semantic difficulties, the answer can only be arbitrary. What matters is that we know what kind of union we are talking about when we speak of love. Do we refer to love as the mature answer to the problem of existence, or do we speak of those immature forms of love which may be called *symbiotic union?* In the following pages I shall call love only the former. I shall begin the discussion of "love" with the latter.

Symbiotic union has its biological pattern in the relationship between the pregnant mother and the foetus. They are two, and yet one. They live "together," *(sym-biosis),* they need each other. The foetus is a part of the mother, it receives everything it needs from her; mother is its world, as it were; she feeds it, she protects it, but also her own life is enhanced by it. In the *psychic* symbiotic union, the two bodies are independent, but the same kind of attachment exists psychologically.

The *passive* form of the symbiotic union is that of submission, or if we use a clinical term, of *masochism.* The masochistic person escapes from the unbearable feeling of isolation and separateness by making himself part and parcel of another person who directs him, guides him, protects him; who is his life and his oxygen, as it were. The power of the one to whom one submits is inflated, may he be a person or a god; he is everything, I am nothing, except inasmuch as I am part of him. As a part, I am part of greatness, of power, of certainty. The masochistic person does not have to make decisions, does not have to take any risks; he is never alone — but he is not independent; he has no integrity; he is not yet fully born. In a religious context the object of worship is called an idol; in a secular context of a masochistic love relationship the essential mechanism, that of idolatry, is the same, The masochistic relationship can be blended with physical, sexual desire; in this case it is not only a submission in which one's mind participates, but also one's whole body. There can be masochistic submission to fate, to sickness, to rhythmic music, to the orgiastic state produced by drugs or under hypnotic trance — in all these instances the person renounces his integrity, makes himself the instrument of somebody or something outside of himself; he need not solve the problem of living by productive activity.

The *active* form of symbiotic fusion is domination or, to use the psychological term corresponding to masochism, *sadism.* The sadistic person wants to escape from his aloneness and his sense of imprisonment by making another person part and parcel of himself. He inflates and enhances himself by incorporating another person, who worships him.

The sadistic person is as dependent on the submissive person as the latter is on the former; neither can live without the other. The difference is only that the sadistic person commands, exploits, hurts, humiliates, and that the masochistic person is commanded, exploited, hurt, humiliated. This is a considerable difference in a realistic sense; in a deeper emotional sense, the difference is not so great as that which they both have in common: fusion without integrity. . . .

In contrast to symbiotic union, mature *love* is *union under the condition of preserving one's integrity,* one's individuality. *Love is an active power in man;* a power which breaks through the walls which separate man from his fellow men, which unites him with others; love makes him overcome the sense of isolation and separateness, yet it permits him to be himself, to retain his integrity. In love the paradox occurs that two beings become one and yet remain two.

Love is an activity, not a passive affect; it is a "standing in," not a "falling for." In the most general way, the active character of love can be described by stating that love is primarily *giving,* not receiving.

What is giving? Simple as the answer to this question seems to be, it is actually full of ambiguities and complexities. The most widespread misunderstanding is that which assumes that giving is "giving up" something, being deprived of, sacrificing. . . . People whose main orientation is a non-productive one feel giving as an impoverishment. Most individuals of this type therefore refuse to give. Some make a virtue out of giving in the sense of a sacrifice. They feel that just because it is painful to give, one *should* give; the virtue of giving to them lies in the very act of acceptance of the sacrifice. For them, the norm that it is better to give than to receive means that it is better to suffer deprivation than to experience joy.

For the productive character, giving has an entirely different meaning. Giving is the highest expression of potency. In the very act of giving, I experience my strength, my wealth, my power. This experience of heightened vitality and potency fills me with joy. I experience myself as overflowing, spending, alive, hence as joyous. Giving is more joyous than receiving, not because it is a deprivation, but because in the act of giving lies the expression of my aliveness.

It is not difficult to recognize the validity of this principle by applying it to various specific phenomena. The most elementary example lies in the sphere of sex. The culmination of the male sexual function lies in the act of giving; the man gives himself, his sexual organ, to the woman. At the moment of orgasm he gives his semen to her. He cannot help giving it if he is potent. If he cannot give, he is impotent. For the woman the process is not different, although somewhat more complex. She gives herself too; she opens the gates to her feminine center; in the act of receiving, she gives. If she is incapable of this act of giving, if she can only receive, she is frigid. With her the act of giving occurs again, not in her function as a lover, but in that as a mother. She gives of herself to the growing child within her, she gives her milk to the infant, she gives her bodily warmth. Not to give would be painful.

. . . What does one person give to another? He gives of himself, of the most precious he has, he gives of his life. This does not necessarily mean that he sacrifices his life for the other—but that he gives him of that which is alive in him; he gives him of his joy, of his interest, of his understanding, of his knowledge, of his humor, of his sadness—of all expressions and manifestations of that which is alive in him. In thus giving of his life, he enriches the other person, he enhances the other's sense of aliveness by enhancing his own sense of aliveness. He does not give in order to receive; giving is in itself exquisite joy. But in giving, he cannot help bringing something to life in the other person, and this which is brought to life reflects back to him; in truly giving, he cannot help receiving that which is given back to him. Giving implies to make the other person a giver also and they both share in the joy of what they have brought to life. In the act of giving something is born, and both persons involved are grateful for the life that is born for both of them. Specifically with regard to love this means: love is a power which produces love; impotence is the inability to produce love. This thought has been beautifully expressed by Marx: "Assume," he says, "*man as man,* and his relation to the world as a human one, and you can exchange love only for love, confidence for confidence, etc. If you wish to enjoy art, you must be an artistically trained person; if you wish to have influence on other people, you must be a person who has a really stimulating and furthering influence on other people. Every one of your relationships to man and to nature must be a definite expression of your *real, individual* life corresponding to the object of your will. If you love without calling forth love, that is, if your love as such does not produce love, if by means of an *expression of life* as a loving person you do not make of yourself a *loved person,* then your love is impotent, a misfortune."*

Beyond the element of giving, the active character of love becomes evident in the fact that it always implies certain basic elements, common to all forms of love. These are *care, responsibility, respect* and *knowledge.*

That love implies *care* is most evident in a mother's love for her child. No assurance of her love would strike us as sincere if we saw her lacking in care for the infant, if she neglected to feed it, to bathe it, to give it physical comfort; and we are impressed by her love if we see her caring for the child. It is not different even with the love for animals or flowers. If a woman told us that she loved flowers, and we saw that she forgot to water them, we would not believe in her "love" for flowers. *Love is the active concern for the life and the growth of that which we love.* Where this active concern is lacking, there is no love.

Care and concern imply another aspect of love; that of *responsibility.* Today responsibility is often meant to denote duty, something imposed upon one from the outside. But responsibility, in its true sense, is an entirely voluntary act; it is my response to the needs, expressed or unexpressed, of another human being. To be "responsible" means to be able and ready to "respond." . . . In the love between adults it refers mainly to the psychic needs of the other person.

Responsibility could easily deteriorate into domination and possessiveness, were it not for a third component of love, *respect.* Respect is not fear and awe; it denotes, in accordance with the root of the word (*respicere* = to look at), the ability to see a person as he is, to be aware of his unique individuality. Respect means the concern that the other person should grow and unfold as he is. Respect,

---

* "Nationalökonomie und Philosophie," 1844, published in Karl Marx' *Die Frühschriften,* Alfred Kröner Verlag, Stuttgart, 1953, pp. 300, 301. (My translation, E. F.)

thus, implies the absence of exploitation. I want the loved person to grow and unfold for his own sake, and in his own ways, and not for the purpose of serving me. If I love the other person, I feel one with him or her, but with him *as he is,* not as I need him to be as an object for my use. It is clear that respect is possible only if *I* have achieved independence; if I can stand and walk without needing crutches, without having to dominate and exploit anyone else. Respect exists only on the basis of freedom: "l'amour est l'enfant de la liberté" as an old French song says; love is the child of freedom, never that of domination.

To respect a person is not possible without *knowing* him; care and responsibility would be blind if they were not guided by knowledge. Knowledge would be empty if it were not motivated by concern. There are many layers of knowledge; the knowledge which is an aspect of love is one which does not stay at the periphery, but penetrates to the core. It is possible only when I can transcend the concern for myself and see the other person in his own terms. I may know, for instance, that a person is angry, even if he does not show it overtly; but I may know him more deeply than that; then I know that he is anxious, and worried; that he feels lonely, that he feels guilty. Then I know that his anger is only the manifestation of something deeper, and I see him as anxious and embarrassed, that is, as the suffering person, rather than as the angry one.

Knowledge has one more, and a more fundamental, relation to the problem of love. The basic need to fuse with another person so as to transcend the prison of one's separateness is closely related to another specifically human desire, that to know the "secret of man." While life in its merely biological aspects is a miracle and a secret, man in his human aspects is an unfathomable secret to himself — and to his fellow man. We know ourselves, and yet even with all the efforts we may make, we do not know ourselves. We know our fellow man, and yet we do not know him, because we are not a thing, and our fellow man is not a thing. The further we reach into the depth of our being, or someone else's being, the more the goal of knowledge eludes us. Yet we cannot help desiring to penetrate into the secret of man's soul, into the innermost nucleus which is "he."

There is one way, a desperate one, to know the secret: it is that of complete power over another person; the power which makes him do what we want, feel what we want, think what we want; which transforms him into a thing, our thing, our possession.

The other path to knowing "the secret" is love. Love is active penetration of the other person, in which my desire to know is stilled by union. In the act of fusion I know you, I know myself, I know everybody — and I "know" nothing. I know in the only way knowledge of that which is alive is possible for man — by experience of union — not by any knowledge our thought can give. Sadism is motivated by the wish to know the secret, yet I remain as ignorant as I was before. I have torn the other being apart limb from limb, yet all I have done is to destroy him. Love is the only way of knowledge, which in the act of union answers my quest. In the act of loving, of giving myself, in the act of penetrating the other person, I find myself, I discover myself, I discover us both, I discover man.

Care, responsibility, respect and knowledge are mutually interdependent. They are a syndrome of attitudes which are to be found in the mature person;

that is, in the person who develops his own powers productively, who only wants to have that which he has worked for, who has given up narcissistic dreams of omniscience and omnipotence, who has acquired humility based on the inner strength which only genuine productive activity can give.

Thus far I have spoken of love as the overcoming of human separateness, as the fulfillment of the longing for union. But above the universal, existential need for union rises a more specific, biological one: the desire for union between the masculine and feminine poles. . . . Sexual polarization leads man to seek union in a specific way, that of union with the other sex. The polarity between the male and female principles exists also *within* each man and each woman. Just as physiologically man and woman each have hormones of the opposite sex, they are bisexual also in the psychological sense. They carry in themselves the principle of receiving and of penetrating, of matter and of spirit. Man—and woman—finds union within himself only in the union of his female and his male polarity. This polarity is the basis for all creativity.

The male-female polarity is also the basis for interpersonal creativity. This is obvious biologically in the fact that the union of sperm and ovum is the basis for the birth of a child. But in the purely psychic realm it is not different; in the love between man and woman, each of them is reborn. (The homosexual deviation is a failure to attain this polarized union, and thus the homosexual suffers from the pain of never-resolved separateness, a failure, however, which he shares with the average heterosexual who cannot love.)

The problem of the male-female polarity leads to some further discussion on the subject matter of love and sex. I have spoken before of Freud's error in seeing in love exclusively the expression—or a sublimation—of the sexual instinct, rather than recognizing that the sexual desire is one manifestation of the need for love and union. But Freud's error goes deeper. In line with his physiological materialism, he sees in the sexual instinct the result of a chemically produced tension in the body which is painful and seeks for relief. The aim of the sexual desire is the removal of this painful tension; sexual satisfaction lies in the accomplishment of this removal. This view has its validity to the extent that the sexual desire operates in the same fashion as hunger or thirst do when the organism is undernourished. Sexual desire, in this concept, is an itch, sexual satisfaction the removal of the itch. In fact, as far as this concept of sexuality is concerned, masturbation would be the ideal sexual satisfaction. What Freud, paradoxically enough, ignores, is the psycho-biological aspect of sexuality, the masculine-feminine polarity, and the desire to bridge this polarity by union. . . . Woman is not a castrated man, and her sexuality is specifically feminine and not of "a masculine nature."

Sexual attraction between the sexes is only partly motivated by the need for removal of tension; it is mainly the need for union with the other sexual pole. In fact, erotic attraction is by no means only expressed in sexual attraction. There is masculinity and femininity in *character* as well as in *sexual function*. The masculine character can be defined as having the qualities of penetration, guidance, activity, discipline and adventurousness; the feminine character by the qualities of productive receptiveness, protection, realism, endurance, motherliness. (It must always be kept in mind that in each individual both characteristics are

blended, but with the preponderance of those appertaining to "his" or "her" sex.)
Very often if the masculine *character* traits of a man are weakened because
emotionally he has remained a child, he will try to compensate for this lack by
the exclusive emphasis on his male role in *sex*. The result is the Don Juan, who
needs to prove his male prowess in sex because he is unsure of his masculinity
in a characterological sense. When the paralysis of masculinity is more extreme,
sadism (the use of force) becomes the main — a perverted — substitute for masculinity. If the feminine sexuality is weakened or perverted, it is transformed into
masochism, or possessiveness.

When the child grows and develops, he becomes capable of perceiving
things as they are; the satisfaction in being fed becomes differentiated from the
nipple, the breast from the mother. Eventually the child experiences his thirst,
the satisfying milk, the breast and the mother, as different entities. He learns
to perceive many other things as being different, as having an existence of their
own. . . . He learns how to handle people; that mother will smile when I eat;
that she will take me in her arms when I cry; that she will praise me when I have
a bowel movement. All these experiences become crystallized and integrated in
the experience: *I am loved.* I am loved because I am mother's child. I am loved
because I am helpless. I am loved because I am beautiful, admirable. I am loved
because mother needs me. To put it in a more general formula: *I am loved for
what I am,* or perhaps more accurately, *I am loved because I am.* This experience
of being loved by mother is a passive one. There is nothing I have to do in order
to be loved — mother's love is unconditional. All I have to do is *to be* — to be her
child. Mother's love is bliss, is peace, it need not be acquired, it need not be deserved. But there is a negative side, too, to the unconditional quality of mother's
love. Not only does it not need to be deserved — it also *cannot* be acquired, produced, controlled. If it is there, it is like a blessing; if it is not there, it is as if all
beauty had gone out of life — and there is nothing I can do to create it.

For most children before the age from eight and a half to ten, the problem
is almost exclusively that of *being loved* — of being loved for what one is. The child
up to this age does not yet love; he responds gratefully, joyfully to being loved.
At this point of the child's development a new factor enters into the picture:
that of a new feeling of producing love by one's own activity. For the first time,
the child thinks of *giving* something to mother (or to father), of producing something — a poem, a drawing, or whatever it may be. For the first time in the child's
life the idea of love is transformed from being loved into loving; into creating
love. It takes many years from this first beginning to the maturing of love. Eventually the child, who may now be an adolescent, has overcome his egocentricity;
the other person is not any more primarily a means to the satisfaction of his own
needs. The needs of the other person are as important as his own — in fact, they
have become more important. To give has become more satisfactory, more joyous, than to receive; to love, more important even than being loved. By loving, he
has left the prison cell of aloneness and isolation which was constituted by the
state of narcissism and self-centeredness. He feels a sense of new union, of sharing, of oneness. More than that, he feels the potency of producing love by loving —
rather than the dependence of receiving by being loved — and for that reason having to be small, helpless, sick — or "good." Infantile love follows the principle: "*I*

love because I am loved." Mature love follows the principle: *"I am loved because I love."* Immature love says: *"I love you because I need you."* Mature love says: *"I need you because I love you."*

. . . Eventually, the mature person has come to the point where he is his own mother and his own father. He has, as it were, a motherly and a fatherly conscience. Motherly conscience says: "There is no misdeed, no crime which could deprive you of my love, of my wish for your life and happiness." Fatherly conscience says: "You did wrong, you cannot avoid accepting certain consequences of your wrongdoing, and most of all you must change your ways if I am to like you." The mature person has become free from the outside mother and father figures, and has built them up inside. . . .

Love is not primarily a relationship to a specific person; it is an *attitude,* an *orientation of character* which determines the relatedness of a person to the world as a whole, not toward one "object" of love. If a person loves only one other person and is indifferent to the rest of his fellow men, his love is not love but a symbiotic attachment, or an enlarged egotism. Yet, most people believe that love is constituted by the object, not by the faculty. In fact, they even believe that it is a proof of the intensity of their love when they do not love anybody except the "loved" person. This is the same fallacy which we have already mentioned above. Because one does not see that love is an activity, a power of the soul, one believes that all that is necessary to find is the right object—and that everything goes by itself afterward. This attitude can be compared to that of a man who wants to paint but who, instead of learning the art, claims that he has just to wait for the right object, and that he will paint beautifully when he finds it. If I truly love one person I love all persons, I love the world, I love life. If I can say to somebody else, "I love you," I must be able to say, "I love in you everybody, I love through you the world, I love in you also myself."

Saying that love is an orientation which refers to all and not to one does not imply, however, the idea that there are no differences between various types of love, which depend on the kind of object which is loved.

The most fundamental kind of love, which underlies all types of love, is *brotherly love.* By this I mean the sense of responsibility, care, respect, knowledge of any other human being, the wish to further his life. This is the kind of love the Bible speaks of when it says: love thy neighbor as thyself. Brotherly love is love for all human beings; it is characterized by its very lack of exclusiveness. . . .

Brotherly love is love among equals; motherly love is love for the helpless. Different as they are from each other, they have in common that they are by their very nature not restricted to one person. If I love my brother, I love all my brothers; if I love my child, I love all my children; no, beyond that, I love all children, all that are in need of my help. In contrast to both types of love is *erotic love;* it is the craving for complete fusion, for union with one other person. It is by its very nature exclusive and not universal; it is also perhaps the most deceptive form of love there is.

First of all, it is often confused with the explosive experience of "falling" in love, the sudden collapse of the barriers which existed until that moment between two strangers. But, as was pointed out before, this experience of sudden intimacy is by its very nature short-lived. After the stranger has become an intimately known person there are no more barriers to be overcome, there is no more sudden closeness to be achieved. The "loved" person becomes as well known as oneself. Or, perhaps I should better say as little known. If there were more depth in the experience of the other person, if one could experience the infiniteness of his personality, the other person would never be so familiar — and the miracle of overcoming the barriers might occur every day anew. But for most people their own person, as well as others, is soon explored and soon exhausted. For them intimacy is established primarily through sexual contact. Since they experience the separateness of the other person primarily as physical separateness, physical union means overcoming separateness.

Beyond that, there are other factors which to many people denote the overcoming of separateness. To speak of one's own personal life, one's hopes and anxieties, to show oneself with one's childlike or childish aspects, to establish a common interest vis-à-vis the world — all this is taken as overcoming separateness. Even to show one's anger, one's hate, one's complete lack of inhibition is taken for intimacy, and this may explain the perverted attraction married couples often have for each other, who seem intimate only when they are in bed or when they give vent to their mutual hate and rage. But all these types of closeness tend to become reduced more and more as time goes on. The consequence is one seeks love with a new person, with a new stranger. Again the stranger is transformed into an "intimate" person, again the experience of falling in love is exhilarating and intense, and again it slowly becomes less and less intense, and ends in the wish for a new conquest, a new love — always with the illusion that the new love will be different from the earlier ones. These illusions are greatly helped by the deceptive character of sexual desire.

Sexual desire aims at fusion — and is by no means only a physical appetite, the relief of a painful tension. But sexual desire can be stimulated by the anxiety of aloneness, by the wish to conquer or be conquered, by vanity, by the wish to hurt and even to destroy, as much as it can be stimulated by love. It seems that sexual desire can easily blend with and be stimulated by any strong emotion, of which love is only one. Because sexual desire is in the minds of most people coupled with the idea of love, they are easily misled to conclude that they love each other when they want each other physically. Love can inspire the wish for sexual union; in this case the physical relationship is lacking in greediness, in a wish to conquer or to be conquered, but is blended with tenderness. If the desire for physical union is not stimulated by love, if erotic love is not also brotherly love, it never leads to union in more than an orgiastic, transitory sense. Sexual attraction creates, for the moment, the illusion of union, yet without love this "union" leaves strangers as far apart as they were before — sometimes it makes them ashamed of each other, or even makes them hate each other, because when the illusion has gone they feel their estrangement even more markedly than before. Tenderness is by no means, as Freud believed, a sublimation of the sexual instinct; it is the direct outcome of brotherly love, and exists in physical as well as in non-physical forms of love.

In erotic love there is an exclusiveness which is lacking in brotherly love and motherly love. This exclusive character of erotic love warrants some further discussion. Frequently the exclusiveness of erotic love is misinterpreted as meaning possessive attachment. One can often find two people "in love" with each other who feel no love for anybody else. Their love is, in fact, an egotism *à deux;* they are two people who identify themselves with each other, and who solve the problem of separateness by enlarging the single individual into two. They have the experience of overcoming aloneness, yet, since they are separated from the rest of mankind, they remain separated from each other and alienated from themselves; their experience of union is an illusion. Erotic love is exclusive, but it loves in the other person all of mankind, all that is alive. It is exclusive only in the sense that I can fuse myself fully and intensely with one person only. Erotic love excludes the love for others only in the sense of erotic fusion, full commitment in all aspects of life — but not in the sense of deep brotherly love.

Erotic love, if it is love, has one premise. That I love from the essence of my being — and experience the other person in the essence of his or her being. In essence, all human beings are identical. We are all part of One; we are One. This being so, it should not make any difference whom we love. Love should be essentially an act of will, of decision to commit my life completely to that of one other person. This is, indeed, the rationale behind the idea of the insolubility of marriage, as it is behind the many forms of traditional marriage in which the two partners never choose each other, but are chosen for each other — and yet are expected to love each other. In contemporary Western culture this idea appears altogether false. Love is supposed to be the outcome of a spontaneous, emotional reaction, of suddenly being gripped by an irresistible feeling. In this view, one sees only the peculiarities of the two individuals involved — and not the fact that all men are part of Adam, and all women part of Eve. One neglects to see an important factor in erotic love, that of *will.* To love somebody is not just a strong feeling — it is a decision, it is a judgment, it is a promise. If love were only a feeling, there would be no basis for the promise to love each other forever. A feeling comes and it may go. How can I judge that it will stay forever, when my act does not involve judgment and decision?

Taking these views into account one may arrive at the position that love is exclusively an act of will and commitment, and that therefore fundamentally it does not matter who the two persons are. Whether the marriage was arranged by others, or the result of individual choice, once the marriage is concluded, the act of will should guarantee the continuation of love. This view seems to neglect the paradoxical character of human nature and of erotic love. We are all One — yet every one of us is a unique, unduplicable entity. In our relationships to others the same paradox is repeated. Inasmuch as we are all one, we can love everybody in the same way in the sense of brotherly love. But inasmuch as we are all also different, erotic love requires certain specific, highly individual elements which exist between some people but not between all.

Both views then, that of erotic love as completely individual attraction, unique between two specific persons, as well as the other view that erotic love is nothing but an act of will, are true — or, as it may be put more aptly, the truth is neither this nor that. Hence the idea of a relationship which can be easily dissolved if one is not successful with it is as erroneous as the idea that under no circumstances must the relationship be dissolved. . . .

We have come now to the basic psychological premises on which the conclusions of our argument are built. Generally, these premises are as follows:

not only others, but we ourselves are the "object" of our feelings and attitudes; the attitudes toward others and toward ourselves, far from being contradictory, are basically *conjunctive*. With regard to the problem under discussion this means: love of others and love of ourselves are not alternatives. On the contrary, an attitude of love toward themselves will be found in all those who are capable of loving others. *Love*, in principle, *is indivisible as far as the connection between "objects" and one's own self is concerned.* Genuine love is an expression of productiveness and implies care, respect, responsibility and knowledge. It is not an "affect" in the sense of being affected by somebody, but an active striving for the growth and happiness of the loved person, rooted in one's own capacity to love.

To love somebody is the actualization and concentration of the power to love. The basic affirmation contained in love is directed toward the beloved person as an incarnation of essentially human qualities. Love of one person implies love of man as such. The kind of "division of labor," as William James calls it, by which one loves one's family but is without feeling for the "stranger," is a sign of a basic inability to love. Love of man is not, as is frequently supposed, an abstraction coming after the love for a specific person, but it is its premise, although genetically it is acquired in loving specific individuals.

From this it follows that my own self must be as much an object of my love as another person. *The affirmation of one's own life, happiness, growth, freedom is rooted in one's capacity to love,* i.e., in care, respect, responsibility, and knowledge. If an individual is able to love productively, he loves himself too; if he can love *only* others, he cannot love at all.

Granted that love for oneself and for others in principle is conjunctive, how do we explain selfishness, which obviously excludes any genuine concern for others? The *selfish* person is interested only in himself, wants everything for himself, feels no pleasure in giving, but only in taking. The world outside is looked at only from the standpoint of what he can get out of it; he lacks interest in the needs of others, and respect for their dignity and integrity. He can see nothing but himself; he judges everyone and everything from its usefulness to him; he is basically unable to love. Does not this prove that concern for others and concern for oneself are unavoidable alternatives? This would be so if selfishness and self-love were identical. But that assumption is the very fallacy which has led to so many mistaken conclusions concerning our problem. *Selfishness and self-love, far from being identical, are actually opposites.* The selfish person does not love himself too much but too little; in fact he hates himself. This lack of fondness and care for himself, which is only one expression of his lack of productiveness, leaves him empty and frustrated. He is necessarily unhappy and anxiously concerned to snatch from life the satisfactions which he blocks himself from attaining. He seems to care too much for himself, but actually he only makes an unsuccessful attempt to cover up and compensate for his failure to care for his real self. Freud holds that the selfish person is narcissistic, as if he had withdrawn his love from others and turned it toward his own person. *It is true that selfish persons are incapable of loving others, but they are not capable of loving themselves either. . . .*

. . . Ideas on self-love cannot be summarized better than by quoting Meister Eckhart on this topic: "If you love yourself, you love everybody else as you do yourself. As long as you love another person less than you love yourself, you will not really succeed in loving yourself, but if you love all alike, including yourself, you will love them as one person and that person is both God and man. Thus he is a great and righteous person who, loving himself, loves all others equally."‡

How does Fromm in *The Theory of Love* feel that love can provide the mature, full answer to the problem of existence?

What does Fromm mean by "interpersonal fusion"? Sexual intercourse? Intellectual, spiritual and/or emotional harmony? The loss of individuality through merger with another personality, as exemplified in the statement "Love you? I *am* you!"?

Mature love, by Fromm's definition, is union with someone outside one's own self, "under the condition of preserving one's integrity, one's individuality." An active power of giving, love further implies certain basic elements: care, responsibility, respect, and knowledge. How are each of these components of love "mutually interdependent"?

"Immature love says: *'I love you because I need you;'* Mature love says: *'I need you because I love you.'"* What is the distinction?

How might Fromm react to the following dialogue from *After the Fall* by Arthur Miller:

> LOUISE, *with intense reasonableness:* Look, Quentin, it all comes down to a very simple thing; you want a woman to provide an . . . atmosphere, in which there are never any issues, and you'll fly around in a constant bath of praise . . .
>
> QUENTIN: Well I wouldn't mind a little praise, what's wrong with praise?
>
> LOUISE: Quentin, I am not a praise machine! I am not a blur and I am not your mother! I am a separate person! . . .
>
> QUENTIN: Louise, I am asking you to explain this to me because this is when I go blind! When you've finally become a separate person, what the hell is there?
>
> LOUISE, *with a certain unsteady pride:* Maturity.
>
> QUENTIN: I don't know what that means.
>
> LOUISE: It means that you know another person exists, Quentin. [48]

How does Fromm argue that selfishness is not identical with self-love; in fact, that they are opposites?

Fromm says:

> Love is not primarily a relationship to a specific person; it is an *attitude,* an *orientation* of *character* which determines the relatedness of a person to the world as a whole, not toward one "object" of love.

Others add that "it is not sexual behavior that determines character; it is character that determines sexual behavior" [49], and that sex is not what we do, but what we are. Do these statements help to differentiate between sex (in the sense of physical relations) and sexuality?

How does the following section from *The Happy Marriage* by Archibald

‡ Meister Eckhart, trans. R. B. Blakney (New York: Harper & Brothers, 1941), p. 204.

MacLeish re-create Fromm's reasons for considering sexual orgies, herd conformity, and the use of alcohol or drugs, unsatisfactory attempts to overcome separateness (that is, a sense of isolation or loneliness)?

> They say they are one flesh:
> They are two nations.
> They cannot mix nor mesh:—
> Their conjugations
>
> Are cries from star to star.
> They would commingle,
> They couple far and far—
> Still they are single.
>
> With arms and hungry hands
> They cling together,
> They strain at bars and bands,
> They tug at tether,
>
> Still there are walls between,
> Still space divides them,
> Still are themselves unseen,
> Still distance hides them. [50]

How else might separateness be overcome?

RELATED QUESTIONS

Would Fromm view the mood of the pair pictured by Edna St. Vincent Millay in **Recuerdo** (see "**Night-Lights,**" p. 576) as interpersonal fusion?

How does Mama in **A Raisin in the Sun** (p. 149) exemplify responsibility in what Fromm terms "its true sense"—an entirely voluntary response to the needs, expressed or unexpressed, of another human being? Are her son Walter's needs expressed or unexpressed?

To what extent does Anne Frank in **The Diary of a Young Girl** (p. 133) exemplify characteristics valued by Fromm in her appreciation of Peter Van Daan?

Fromm claims that for most children under eight-and-a-half years old "the problem is almost exclusively that of *being loved.* . . . The child up to this age does not yet love; he responds gratefully, joyfully to being loved." What modifications, if any, of Fromm's view might the authors of **Parma Violets** (p. 13) and **The Downward Path to Wisdom** (p. 151) make?

Would C. S. Lewis (**Eros,** p. 205) agree with Fromm's concept of erotic love?

How fully would Laurie Lee (**What Love Must Be,** p. 250) subscribe to Fromm's view of sexual polarization as developed in **The Theory of Love?**

The biological symbiotic union is a vital and healthy relationship between a pregnant mother and her fetus. But even though the two bodies become physically independent of each other, an unhealthy psychological tie can take its place. In this psychic symbiotic union, a dependency classified by Fromm as an immature form of love, one person is passive and submits; the other person is active and dominates. In the first excerpt from **The Barretts of Wimpole Street** by Rudolf Besier (see "**Night-Lights,**" p. 536), Edward Barrett, a stern, possessive, lonely widower who focuses all his love on his eldest daughter, Elizabeth, a semi-invalid, asks her to drink a kind of beer called porter, insisting it will be good for her health.

In the second excerpt, Elizabeth, whose health has improved since her visits from Robert Browning, tries to explain to him why her father will forbid her proposed trip to Italy, recommended by doctors.

How does Edward Barrett's behavior, as seen directly or indirectly described, exhibit characteristics of the dominating or sadistic person in a symbiotic union?

How does Robert Browning show a more mature form of love for Elizabeth? Does it follow: "if you love me, you can't be afraid of me"?

What is the fallacy in Edward Barrett's argument: "And you'll prove your love by doing as I wish?"

Barrett says (see p. 536):

> Listen, dear. I told you just now that if you disobeyed me, you would incur my displeasure. I take that back. I shall never in any way reproach you. You shall never know by word, or deed, or hint of mine, how much you have grieved and wounded your father by refusing to do the little thing he asked.

Is Edward being sincere? Self-pitying? Contradictory? Using emotional blackmail?

Why does Robert Browning react so violently to Elizabeth's choice of the word "devoted" to describe her father's feeling for her?

The cast of Sidney Howard's play **The Silver Cord** (see "**Night-Lights,**" p. 565) includes Mrs. Phelps, a possessive, calculating widow; her two grown sons, David and Robert; Dave's wife, Chris; and Rob's ex-fiancée, Hester. In the first excerpt, quite late at night, Mrs. Phelps, like a "wee mousie," has entered the bedroom of her son David, an architect who has come home with his wife for a visit. The second excerpt is a conversation later that evening between Dave and his wife.

How does Mrs. Phelps resemble Mr. Barrett? What specific techniques does she employ to try to engineer her sons' worship? How does she encourage her married son's dependence? What does "a boy's mother is his best friend" mean?

To what literal "cord" does the play's title allude? Why is it "silver" in this case?

How does David's wife—like Elizabeth's fiancé Robert in **The Barretts of Wimpole Street** (p. 536)—define love differently and more maturely than the parental figure in each play?

What is your concept of a good mother and good father? Do they systematically love their children then leave them to be free when the time is right?

Psyche with the Candle

ARCHIBALD MacLEISH

Love which is the most difficult mystery
Asking from every young one answers
And most from those most eager and most beautiful—
Love is a bird in a fist:

To hold it hides it, to look at it lets it go.
It will twist loose if you lift so much as a finger.
It will stay if you cover it—stay but unknown and invisible.
Either you keep it forever with fist closed
Or let it fling
Singing in fervor of sun and in song vanish.
There is no answer other to this mystery.

The controversial nature of love accounts for the fact that it has been used to label every emotional package from the most realistically raw physical orgasm to the most idealistically pure spiritual ecstasy. Yet its magic which, as Lowen observed in **Love and Orgasm,** "transforms the ordinary into the extraordinary, earth into heaven," escapes scientific analysis and can be only partially traced in the metaphors and paradoxes of poets like Archibald MacLeish. In **Psyche with the Candle,** how does MacLeish contribute to the common spiritual ideal that "love is the mystery-of-mysteries who creates them all"? [51]

RELATED QUESTIONS

Who can read the face of love? asks Sandburg in "Solo for Saturday Night Guitar":

> Time was. Time is. Time shall be.
> Man invented time to be used.
> Love was. Love is. Love shall be.
> Yet man never invented love
> Nor is love to be used like time.
> A clock wears numbers one to twelve
> And you look and read its face
> And tell the time pre-cise-ly ex-act-ly.
> Yet who reads the face of love? [52]

Can one ever remember love? Quentin, in Arthur Miller's *After the Fall* explains:

> It's like trying to summon up the smell of roses in a cellar. You might see a rose, but never the perfume. And that's the truth of roses, isn't it—the perfume? [53]

Many of the ideas about love presented in this section converge in the statement by F. Alexander Magoun that:

> Love is the passionate and abiding desire on the part of two or more people to produce together the conditions under which each can be and spontaneously express his real self; to produce together an intellectual soil and an emotional climate in which each can flourish, far superior to what either could achieve alone. [54]

How does Magoun explain Fromm's statement in **The Theory of Love** that "in love the paradox occurs that two beings become one and yet remain two. . . . "?
How does Magoun activate Fromm's implications of giving—"to make the other person a giver also"?

How does Magoun suggest Lee's "sum of love," embodying qualities which adhere to the "act of will"?

How does Magoun amplify Singer's basic view of bestowal in **Appraisal and Bestowal** that lovers have a life together:

> When the amorous imagination ricochets back and forth—each person seeing himself as both lover and beloved—a new totality results, an interacting oneness"?

How does Magoun parallel Lowen's statement that "the loved person is unique, never generic"?

How does Magoun's perspective relate to Lindbergh's premises in **Double-Sunrise** (p. 233) concerning "true identity"?

How does Robert Johann elaborate on Magoun's definition in the following passage:

> A living thing is not merely involved in a process but is itself a process. It seeks not merely space, but growth, not merely to neutralize the other but to draw nourishment from it. The power of the person, however, is the highest of all. Its confrontation with otherness involves more than the effort to maintain physical integrity in the face of invading forces, more too than the struggle to eke out a living by converting the other into itself. The proper task of the person, and the one proportionate to his power, is to incorporate in his life the other precisely as other. It is to make of his life a comprehensive synthesis, interior to which both self and other are preserved in their distinctiveness. This is what is meant by saying that the person is called to community. It also provides the basic problem of personal life. [55]

Revolution in Sexual Ethics

ROGER L. SHINN

As long as human life has existed, people have been men and women, boys and girls. They have exulted in their sexuality, resented it, worshiped it, abused it. They have wondered about its mystery. Because of its explosive energy and its creative power, they have seen in it a symbol. It has represented the kinship of man with cosmic power and with the fertility of nature. Sexuality has been part of many religions, the occasion for exploitation and cruelty, part of the shared life of man and woman in the family.

Sexuality is part of the distinctiveness of humanity. People sometimes think of it as part of their animal nature, and in some ways, of course, it is. It can erupt in a violence that defies human rationality. But sex in man is peculiarly human. In the animals it is controlled by instinct, given full expression at limited times and mating seasons. In humanity it is freed. Man, it is said, is the only animal who makes love all year round. For man and woman sex is never solely impulse. It is the expression of selfhood. . . .

Today a major rethinking of sexuality is in process. Everywhere people are talking about the revolution in sexual ethics. Often they are wondering to what extent contemporary society is achieving a healthy appreciation of sex and to what extent it is asking for trouble. . . .

We might sum up the changed situation by saying that an old slogan, "Beware of sex," has given way to a new slogan, "Hurrah for sex!" But if there are a few people for whom one slogan or the other is an adequate expression, there are many more who are caught in the change and are perplexed.

Since the second slogan is more in vogue that the first, let us look at it. I am as ready as the next person to say, "Hurrah for sex." Sex is real, important, wonderful. But to say, "Hurrah for sex" is only the beginning of an understanding of it. If one says, "Hurrah for life!" he must still decide what he will make of his life. To approve of sex is the starting point for deciding how to appreciate sex, how to enjoy and respect it, in oneself and in others.

PRESENT PERPLEXITIES

As a brief way of describing the present situation of our culture, in its search for the meaning of sexuality, I suggest six words. Any one of them is misleading if taken by itself. All six together are misleading if taken as a glib summary. But each word stands for a real aspect of contemporary life.

1. *Confusion.* Our society is not sure where we are or where we are going. A sampling of a month's newspapers will turn up controversial and conflicting items on such subjects as what high school students do after the dance, censorship of books and movies, abortion, divorce statistics, behavior in college dormitories, birth control and contraceptives, women's styles (one season it was topless bathing suits), the antics of famous movie stars, court rulings on legislation, appeals for new legislation. Participants in the public discussion include politicians, teachers, students, artists, journalists, clergymen. Participants in private discussions include almost everybody.

2. *Liberation.* Many of the old restraints and inhibitions are gone. Others, still lingering, are on the way out. People are trying to decide what to do with their freedom. Often the first response to new freedom is to reason, "Whatever has been forbidden must be worth trying." The second response may be to realize that the first response is not intelligent in any area outside of sex and may not be in sex. Eventually persons must seek to define freedom—freedom from the tyranny of peer groups as well as from convention, freedom from the slavery of impulse as well as of inhibition. Today's society, both a little excited and a little frightened by freedom, is seeking to learn its meaning.

3. *Commercialization.* There is money in sex. There always has been (as long as there has been money), but today's world has invented new ways of commercializing sex. The old-fashioned selling of sex for money is on the decline; it is unsophisticated. Our society still cultivates some unsophisticated ways of making money from sex: pornography is reportedly a half-billion-dollar-a-year business. But far more lucrative is the deft use of sex by the "hidden persuaders" in the advertisements. The modern advertising industry has made marvelous discoveries, not about selling sex (an ancient discovery) but about using sex to sell practically everything.

4. *Mechanization.* A lot of sexual talk and activity these days is about as joyless and mechanical as driving a car through a traffic jam. A technical society has inevitably produced a huge literature on the techniques of sex. Some of the books are good, some poor. All of them mislead if they make people think that technique is a substitute for personal meaning. Psychologist Rollo May has com-

mented: "When emphasis beyond a certain point is placed upon technique in sexuality, the person finds that he has separated himself all the more from . . . his own spontaneity and joy and the surging up of his own experience of potency."*

5. *Trivialization.* Strangely the very effort to enhance and enjoy sex has often robbed it of its power. Walter Lippmann asked the cogent question some years ago: "If you start with the belief that love is the pleasure of a moment, is it really surprising that it yields only a momentary pleasure?"‡ More recently David Boroff compared today's "younger generation" with an earlier younger generation by saying, "What was tense sexual melodrama twenty years ago seems to be little more than reflex action today."‡‡

6. *Realization.* Sometimes in our society, as sometimes in man's long past, man and woman enter into a personal relation in which they realize the wonder and joy of sex. Such realization does not come through concentration on sex alone. The persons involved are concerned not simply for sex, but for each other. Yet it is not enough that they dote on each other. They seek to share life, to join together in work and joy and appreciation for the mystery of life and love. Then sexual activity is one expression of mutuality and commitment.

It is one of the wonders of sex that flashes of this realization may illumine even the more mechanized and trivialized relationships that are so common in our society. But the authentic, profound realization is rather rare in a society that often reveals a hunger for it. And, of course, it is never totally untainted. Denis de Rougemont has called marriage at its best "poise in imperfection."§ The poise is the more wonderful as men and women acknowledge their imperfection.

———

How is Shinn in **Revolution in Sexual Ethics** using the term sexuality? Is it the same as his use of "sex"? Of "the expression of selfhood"?
Shinn comments that:

A technical society has inevitably produced a huge literature on the techniques of sex. Some of the books are good, some poor. All of them mislead if they make people think that technique is a substitute for personal meaning.

Lionel Trilling writes in an essay criticizing the Kinsey report *(Sexual Behavior in the Human Male):*

The tendency to divorce sex from the other manifestations of life is already a strong one. This truly absorbing study of sex in charts and tables, in data and quantities, may have the effect of strengthening the tendency still more with people who are by no means trained to invert the process of abstraction and to put the fact back into the general life from which it has been taken.
The Report, then, is a study of sexual behavior in so far as it can be quantitatively measured. This is certainly very useful. But, as we might fear, the sexuality that is measured is taken to be the definition of sexuality itself.

* Rollo May, *Symbolism in Religion and Literature* (New York: George Braziller, 1960), p. 29.
‡ Walter Lippmann, *A Preface to Morals* (New York: Macmillan, 1929), p. 304.
‡‡ David Boroff, "Sex: The Quiet Revolution," *Esquire* (July, 1961), p. 96.
§ Denis de Rougemont, *Love in the Western World* (New York: Pantheon, 1956), p. 302.

The authors are certainly not without interest in what they call attitudes, but they believe that attitudes are best shown by "overt sexual experiences." We want to know, of course, what they mean by an experience and we want to know by what principles of evidence they draw their conclusions about attitudes.

We are led to see that their whole conception of a sexual experience is totally comprised by the physical act and that their principles of evidence are entirely quantitative and cannot carry them beyond the conclusion that the more the merrier. Quality is not integral to what they mean by experience. As I have suggested, the Report is partisan with sex, it wants people to have a good sexuality. But by good it means nothing else but frequent. "It seems safe to assume that daily orgasm would be within the capacity of the average male and that the more than daily rates which have been observed for some primate species could be matched by a large portion of the human population if sexual activity were unrestricted." The Report never suggests that a sexual experience is anything but the discharge of specifically sexual tension and therefore seems to conclude that frequency is always the sign of a robust sexuality. Yet masturbation in children may be and often is the expression not of sexuality only but of anxiety. In the same way, adult intercourse may be the expression of anxiety; its frequency may not be so much robust as compulsive.

The Report is by no means unaware of the psychic conditions of sexuality, yet it uses the concept almost always under the influence of its quantitative assumption. [56]

How does Trilling illustrate Shinn's paragraph in *Revolution in Sexual Ethics* on "mechanization"?

RELATED QUESTIONS

What selections from the "**I**" and "**They**" sections provide examples of "confusion," as Shinn explains it? Of "liberation"? Of "commercialization"? Of "trivialization"?

Why would you be unlikely to find illustrations of "realization" among the selections thus far? In what section might you expect to discover readings in which persons "seek to share life, to join together in work and joy and appreciation for the mystery of life and love," and for whom "sexual activity is one expression of mutuality and commitment"?

The poem *They Laugh* (see "**Night-Lights**," p. 532) was written by a high school senior. What phases of love or perspectives on it does the author present? In which situations in his poem is "I love you" used irresponsibly or inaccurately—a confusion between the heart and the glands? What should the speaker have said in each case to be more precise? How well do you think the poem represents real situations? What parts of *They Laugh* might prose writers whom you have read in this section particularly like? How might each quote certain lines from the poem to support one of their generalizations?

Consider the circumstances, the attitudes, the decisions and the consequences involved in each of the following readings in "**Night-Lights**." In all five, sexual relations outside marriage is an issue:

Blackburn: *The One-Night Stand* (p. 540)
Ferlinghetti: *See It Was Like This When (9)* (p. 546)
Ferlinghetti: *We Squat upon the Beach of Love (24)* (p. 547)
MacNeice: *Trilogy for X* (p. 573)
Miller: Excerpt from *After the Fall* (p. 576)

How might Miller and Ferlinghetti be said to be at opposite poles? How would you describe the "middle distance" between their extreme points of view?

How much sexual freedom outside marriage would you condone? To what extent would it depend on the circumstances? If so, what might those contingent circumstances be?

What do you now conceive to be the relationship between love and sex?

Do you hold with Reik that "sex is a biological instinct that aims at the release of physical tension only" while "love is a cultural phenomenon that aims at happiness through the establishment of a very personal relationship" (p. 201)?

Do you believe with Fromm in **The Theory of Love** (p. 261) that "because sexual desire is in the minds of most people coupled with the idea of love, they are easily misled to conclude that they love each other when they want each other physically"?

Do you agree that

Sex is dynamite. Unchanneled by high character it leads to chaos and destruction. It can be the fiercest cement of relationship, but it can also be the lever that breaks people apart. [57]

Toward a Definition of Morality

After the Fall
ARTHUR MILLER

What the hell is moral? What does that really mean? And what am I . . . to even ask that question? A man ought to know . . . a decent man knows that like he knows his own face!

"I Cain't Say No" (*from* Oklahoma)
RICHARD RODGERS and OSCAR HAMMERSTEIN II

It ain't so much a question of not knowin' what to do;
I know what's right and wrong since I've been ten.
I heard a lot of stories and I reckon they are true,
About how girls are put upon by men.
I know I mustn't fall into the pit,
But when I'm with a fellar I forgit. . . .

When a person tries to kiss a girl,
I know she oughta give his face a smack;
But as soon as someone kisses me,
I somehow sorta wanna kiss him back.

I'm just a fool when lights are low,
I cain't be prissy or quaint,
I ain't the type that can faint;
How can I be what I ain't?

For a while I act refined and cool,
A-settin' on the velveteen settee,
Then I think of that old golden rule,
And do for him what he would do for me.

I cain't resist a romeo in a sombrero and chaps,
As soon as I sit on their laps,
Something inside of me snaps,
I cain't say no.

In **After the Fall,** Quentin finds that he does not really know the meaning of morality; Ado Annie of *Oklahoma* has known "what's right and wrong" since the age of ten. If "it ain't so much a question of not knowing what to do," why doesn't she act in accord with the principles of right and wrong that she has learned? If she understands "mustn't" and "ought," why cain't she say "no" when the situation requires it?

More than 2000 years ago Confucius said: "I see what is right and I choose what is wrong." And some religious terminology recognizes that

> . . . to do is very easy and attractive, to do right is very difficult and unpleasant. Thus we speak of the "straight and narrow path" to heaven and the "primrose path" to hell. We say in regard to righteous folk that "many are called, but few are chosen," and they may be spoken of as "the elect." We sometimes speak of the "lure of sin," or of the "wiles of the devil." A common evangelistic expression for those who are seeking "salvation" is that they are "fighting through." [58]

How would you explain Millay's expression in her **Pity Me Not (Sonnet XXIX)** (see "**Night-Lights**," p. 575) "that the heart is slow to learn/What the swift mind beholds at every turn"? That often we do not practice what we preach?

Most people do not yield to all temptations, only to some: Where and why is there a dividing line?

How has Ado Annie confused ethics with being "prissy or quaint"? How has Ado Annie twisted the implications of the Golden Rule?

Quentin is shocked at his confusion, feeling that "a man ought to know . . . a decent man knows that like he knows his own face!" Might he feel that he should know because the great governor of behavior is conscience, which even the child recognizes? Because "right" and "wrong" are simple absolutes?

Are the problems with morality based on Quentin's dilemma, the inability to define the meaning of moral? Or are they based on Annie's type of inability to make practice correspond to theory? Some of each? Neither?

"What the hell *is* moral"? Is it the "virtue" associated with obedience to sexual taboos? Or does the term encompass more than success or failure in respecting sexual conventions?

Is "moral" applied to what we do or to what we are? Or to both? If to both, then what happens to Ado Annies who claim a keen inner sense of right and wrong, but who "cain't say no"?

Is moral the same as "morale"?

Is morality the same as ethics? Are morals standards? Ideals? Sanctions? Principles of right and wrong? As Hugh Hefner asked in his *Playboy* editorial (p. 183), "whose foot is to be the measure?" Who or what censors human behavior? The individual? Conscience? The law? Religion? Society? Community? Family? Under what circumstances?

Although the dictionary blurs the definitive edge of "moral" and "ethical," one distinction that has been made between them suggests that

> . . . ethical sense is the mark of the adult . . . which takes over from the ideological conviction at adolescence and the moralism of childhood. . . .
> Morality in the moralistic sense can be shown to be predicated on superstitions and irrational inner mechanisms which, in fact, ever again undermine the ethical fiber of generations; but old morality is expendable only where new and more universal ethics prevail. This is the wisdom that the words of many religions have tried to convey to man. He has tenaciously clung to the ritualized words even though he has understood them only

vaguely and in his actions has disregarded or perverted them completely. But there is much in ancient wisdom which now, perhaps, can become knowledge. [59]

In this vein:

> Our ethical interest is in the ends people seek, the goods they want, the values they live by and for. In this perspective, sex is a means to an end or ends, not an end in itself. [60]

And, therefore,

> . . . it is the *motives* of sex behavior that are the most important facts, and statistics cannot measure them or discover them.
> For example, a factual study describing premarital intercourse in three couples could record the class position, income, age, education, religion, vocation, and the like of all six persons, but the *meaning* of their behavior would be undisclosed. The first couple might be planning to marry (a committed relationship), the second merely seeking "release" from sexual tension (a mutually utilitarian view of each other), and the third couple might be "using" each other with no concern or respect at all (an exploitative relationship: what Erich Fromm calls the "nonproductive, exploitative orientation"). [61]

In his book *Tangled World,* Shinn says similarly:

> We do not know as much about the revolution in sexual ethics as some of us think we know. . . .
> Of course there are stacks of charts and statistical data about sex—in marriage, outside of marriage, before marriage. We know less about the meaning of the figures. Nobody can put on a chart the meaning of the love of two persons who have shared the joys and sorrows of life. And we know even less about behavior in the past. Former generations left no charts to be compared with ours. If we want to understand ourselves, shall we compare the behavior of people today with that of Don Juan or with the Puritans? [62]

Kirkendall, in *Searching for the Roots of Moral Judgments,* points out that moral judgments should derive from the ethical sense and stem "from the meaning of an action, rather than being based upon whether or not an act has occurred" (p. 298).

Thus with ethics, as with sex, it is not what we do, but what we are: it is the meaning behind the act; the reason behind the practice; the motive behind the behavior which gives it significance. How, by these yardsticks, does the why become more important than the what?

RELATED QUESTIONS

In *Sex Education* by Dorothy Canfield Fisher (see "**Night-Lights,**" p. 548) how do "facts" reassemble themselves with time and shift into a kaleidoscope of meanings, depending on the interpretation of them?

What does "devotion rather than dread" signify to you in the following passage:

And now what? With the loss or weakening of religious sanctions, and the disappearance of prudential sanctions under the new technology of sex, the only motivating force to turn to, to buttress our sexual ideals, is the positive one of love rather than the negative one of fear. It means that our sex standards will have to find a foundation in loyalty and devotion to some loved one—based, that is to say, in a high-commitment relationship—whether that person be human or divine. For the humanist it will be only the former; for the theist it will or can be both. *But the fundamental truth to get straight is that our sex standards in an era of medical technology and urban anonymity depend for their sanction upon devotion rather than dread.* [63]

How do **Death Wish** (p. 61) about the Jewish parochial student, and **A Portrait of the Artist as a Young Man** (p. 50) about a Catholic student, indicate the need for more "devotion" and less "dread"? How do the two readings suggest a possible reason for "the loss or weakening of religious sanctions"?

Some Observations on Sexual Morality

WARREN R. JOHNSON

At the heart of the controversy over sexual morality is the fact that there is no longer *a* sexual morality that is universally acceptable in our society—even though the law and most public utterances (including those made in most schools) would suggest otherwise. In fact, there are at least three more or less incompatible sexual moralities which are being advocated by large numbers of responsible, honest, enthusiastically "moral" individuals in our society. Perhaps . . . it is possible to consider the three prominent views as representing a model of our society's views, generally.

There are [those] men who consider the traditional Judao-Christian-puritan sex rules and regulations forever valid and unchangeable. So-called moral relative-ism is out of the question for them: a thing is right or it is wrong. If there is to be sex education at all, it must be very limited and totally within the context of traditional sexual morality which disavows the existence of sexual expression outside of marriage. (The unusual circumstances of Tarzan and Jane were no real excuse for their getting involved sexually.) Within marriage, sex is essentially for reproductory purposes.

Another group . . . —perhaps the largest group today—believes in the traditional rules but is willing to bend them to a degree in the interests of the individuals involved if there is no apparent injury to them or to society. To this group, sex within marriage is at least as much for pleasure as for procreation. Sex before marriage may *not* be intolerable if it occurs in a firmly established engagement. Homosexuality is more an illness than a sin or crime. Masturbation is not harmful if not carried to excess. In rare instances adultery might be condoned if it were to lead to good, as for example to tolerable or improved family relationships.

The third small but growing group . . . is incomprehensible to the first group and . . . extremist to the second. It maintains that the rules of the traditional sexual morality are no longer appropriate or useful and that behavior can be evaluated solely on the basis of its meaning to the people involved and to society. Sex within marriage can be as evil as any sex outside of marriage. Typically, some of this group's representatives have lectured coeds on the subject of how sex relations can be beautiful as well as responsible before marriage is contemplated at all. One's own sexual expression is none of society's business so long as others are not coerced or hurt or unwanted children conceived (in or out of marriage). As with the other two groups . . . "responsibility" is given the highest priority by this group.

What ethic constitutes the reasoning behind the position of each of the three groups as outlined by the author of **Some Observations on Sexual Morality?** In other words, what philosophical principle or principles would determine specific behavior for each group?

In which group would you place yourself: The first—moral absolutism? The second—semimoral absolutism? The third—moral relativism? Why?

RELATED QUESTIONS

Reread the selection from **A Portrait of the Artist as a Young Man** (p. 50) and the discussion questions following it. Do your responses to the "rightness" or "wrongness" of Stephen's visits to the prostitute confirm your alliance with one of the three sexual moralities specified in **Some Observations on Sexual Morality?**

There Was a Young Lady Named Wilde

There was a young lady named Wilde
Who kept herself quite undefiled
By thinking of Jesus
And social diseases
And the fear of having a child.

"There was an old woman who lived in a shoe.
She had so many children because she didn't
know what to do."'

Reproduced by permission of the editors of *Modern Medicine*

As weakening of religious structures has been accompanied by advances in technology, science has reduced the threat of venereal diseases like syphilis and gonorrhea with very short-term treatments of massive doses of penicillin or other antibiotics. The birth-control pill, taken orally, contains progesterone and estrogen hormones which suppress the follicle-stimulating hormone so that the egg in the ovary does not ripen. Thus two of Miss Wilde's fears and one of the "old woman's" can be considered minimal today.

Even so, the rates of conceptions out of wedlock, of abortions, and of disease are high. In the United States more than 250,000 babies are born to unmarried mothers each year, and about 1 out of 5 brides is pregnant at her wedding [a]. Estimates of illegal abortions in the United States range from 200,000 to one million; perhaps 1 out of 4 pregnancies ends in abortion. [64]

Assuming that the modern woman probably is familiar with several methods of birth control—douches, the diaphragm, chemical spermicides, the intrauterine device, "the Pill"—how might one account for the continuing increasing rates of illegitimate births and venereal disease? What is the meaning behind the facts?

Shall we agree with the English novelist, John Osborne, that America is a "sexual nuthouse"? Or with the anthropologist, Eric Dingwall (also an Englishman), who says that "the United States is almost, if not quite, the most sex-obsessed country in the world"? Or shall we take the judgment of Hugh Hefner that Americans are achieving a healthy enjoyment of life in rejecting the restraints of the past? Or shall we accept David Riesman's belief that American society is not notable for sexual energy or ambition, but that people without much sense of purpose look to sex as a "defense against the threat of total apathy," and for assurance that they are alive and are having the experiences they think other people are having? [65]

Are moral standards internal or external? Or a little or each?

Based on your reading and experience, would you say that sexual promiscuity is more common than it used to be? That sex standards and ideals of love are lower today than ever before? Why might both these decreases in standards have occurred? Consider the following three perspectives on the subject:

Everybody recognizes that this is a time of widespread experimentation and rejection of old inhibitions. People sometimes forget that traditional morality has always been defied. A reading of Chaucer, Rabelais, and Shakespeare makes it clear that the moral codes were not obeyed by everybody. A society that knows the stories of David and Bathsheba, of Antony and Cleopatra, of Tristan and Isolde cannot regard sexual extravagance as a modern invention. But today surely there is more open rejection of old standards and more puzzled questioning among well-intentioned people than in much of the past. [66]

There is no convincing evidence that young people today are any less conscientious than their parents, or less successful at maturing emotionally. That is to say, they are no less capable of avoiding sexual promiscuity since they are just as able as their forebears to relinquish short-term satisfactions for the sake of long-term satisfactions. (This is a criterion of maturity, of being grown-up or adult, or of "ego sovereignty over the id.") There is, in short, no reason to think that today's youth have less moral stamina or weaker fibers than their elders. *But* our patterns of moral action involve more than ideals; the *inducements or motivations or incentives* of morality include "sanctions" as well as ideals. We walk in the paths of virtue because there is an expectation of rewards and punishments in the background; this is true of some people all of the time, and of all people some of the time. (Just look at the prizes and penalties held out in the Sermon on the Mount, Matt., chs. 5 to 7!) Our *ideals* of love and of sexual expression are as high as ever but *the sanctions behind our loyalty to the ideals have changed.* [67]

"Are youth today less moral than youth of a generation ago?" I have learned by experience the kind of an answer which is expected. The questioner commonly expects me to present figures comparing the extent to which members of the two generations have indulged in forbidden sexual behavior. Here we fall back to the outmoded and unsatisfactory practice of judging morality by counting the number of omitted or committed acts.

I expect if the truth were known that this generation engages in more tabooed sex behavior than did the preceding several generations. But this is due to their confusion and uncertainty about many matters and the lack of authentic help from the older generations. Youth are confused and perplexed but not less moral.

Judging the moral standards of youth in terms of the interpersonal relationships criterion, I feel that this, at least can be said. I have no evidence which indicates to me that young people are any less concerned with creating effective and meaningful interpersonal relationships than any other generation. In fact, they sometimes seem so desirous and so much in need of such relations that I fear they become willy-nilly conformists, thus losing the very thing they are striving to attain. In any event, looking at the question asked me from the interpersonal relationships point of view, I have no reason for labeling this present generation as any less or any more moral than any other generation. Let's recognize that always, in all people, their concern for developing good interpersonal relations is a basic quality upon which we can depend, and forget about counting acts to determine the extent of goodness or badness. [68]

Which view or views seem most valid to you?

I Thought I Was Modern*

EVELYN HAVENS

I have made the daring experiment and have learned that in this year of grace, 1936, as surely as in any previous age, the end of that road, for the woman at any rate, is still confusion, unhappiness, and agony of spirit, if not absolute despair.

I was in my thirtieth year when our paths crossed. He was a man of my own age, my equal in every respect. He had married, when he was in his early twenties and extremely poor, the daughter of a well-to-do Catholic family. . . . They had parted after less than a year. . . . There was no divorce. The girl's religion forbade her to seek one. . . . I loved this man and was strongly attracted to him sexually. He felt the same about me.

With my eyes wide open, sure of my ability to take love in my stride, so to speak, and to make of the sex relationship a fine and constructive thing, I embarked on the great adventure. . . . Within three months, I, who had been so sure that legal marriage was something I could do without, found myself wanting, as I had never wanted anything in my life before, the things every normal woman has wanted since time began—a love that could declare itself in the open, a home, a husband, a child, and that sense of stability, protection, and security which, in our present social system, only marriage can give. . . .

Much is talked of the evils of frustration in the case of the woman who denies herself the physical expression of love. In my opinion that vague and generally periodic torment is as nothing compared to the frustration suffered by the woman who seeks happiness in love outside of marriage.

* This article originally appeared in *Forum*, 1938, Vol. 96, pp. 166–170.

Almost before I knew it I found myself involved in a tangle of deception, dissembling, and evasion against which my whole nature revolted and which I realized was gradually undermining the honesty and integrity of characteristics of which I had once been so proud.

My conscious judgment acquitted me of guilt, but my subconscious and infinitely more powerful judgment convicted me. And the result was a steadily growing, cumulative sense of failure, inferiority, and shame, bringing with it a troop of ugly and destructive companions—lost confidence, lost self-esteem, and a sense of lost integrity, losses for which all the tenderness and the devotion in the world cannot compensate.

Then, too, there is the fear of pregnancy. As I write this I can almost hear the derisive cries of the sophisticated younger generation which has as yet no first-hand knowledge of the situation which I am discussing. "But my dear," I can hear them saying, "no woman needs to become pregnant these days unless she wants to."

Yes, I know all about that. The first thing I did was to visit my doctor and ask for advice and information. I followed his instructions to the letter, and always. Yet, except for a brief period each month, I was never entirely free from the devastating apprehension to which I have referred. The fact that I never *had* been pregnant had only a negligible effect in allaying my fears. It is a feeling no amount of reasoning can eradicate . . . and I have never known a woman in a position similar to my own who was not perpetually haunted by this same terror.

To the unmarried woman pregnancy must always be a thing of disaster. So there must always be fear, present at the most intimate and tender moments, chilling desire and slowly but surely robbing the sex relation of the freedom and spontaneity which alone gives it significance and beauty.

Doubt, too, there must always be. The only proof a man can offer a woman of the depth and sincerity of his feeling for her, is marriage.

Only a superwoman or a woman of no sensibility whatever can hold out indefinitely against these combined forces of frustration, humiliation, guilt, fear, and doubt. Time and again I resolved to end the relationship. . . . And time and again, because I loved the man, I was hurled once more into the dizzy water of conflict, unhappiness, despair.

What added immeasurably to the agony was that my lover could find only one explanation of my behavior—that I no longer loved him.

There may be women who have carried off the irregular sex affairs happily and successfully. But if there are I have never met them, and I have known many in these past few years.

Although Miss Havens' article *I Thought I Was Modern* was written in the 1930s, elements of the moral conflict persist universally, despite "the Pill" or the Pope. In the current wave of new morality, an individual's freedom to choose his sexual codes is modified in one critically different way from Miss Haven's era: Today, with the general absence of the fear ethic and the "Thou shalt not" authoritarianism, the choice of chastity is a positive sexual decision, rather than a decision forced by negative pressures. Thus, sexual taboos today could more appropriately be termed self-restraints. Like Evelyn Havens, many females may decide to embark "on the great adventure" because their eyes are wide open, they are sure of their ability to take love in stride, and they are determined to "make of the sex relationship a fine and constructive thing." In what ways does the author try to demonstrate that there are some things you cannot possible know until it is too late?

Despite confidence in "the pill" and other contraceptive measures, what fear—however unscientific—still persists to Miss Havens' way of thinking?

How might shame and other destructive feelings defy even the conscious judgment that may acquit a man or a woman of guilt and self-reproach?

How much weight do you attach to the influence of Western tradition, of parents, of teachers who advocate chastity? Does the history of civilization show the transmission of a legacy of sin that cannot be broken, even by those who feel liberated from traditional moral values or religious considerations? Or are sexual relationships so individual, so much a matter of private moral decision, that no **"They"** force could counterbalance a personal choice?

For those contending that sexual conduct is one of the most intimate private questions, how does Miss Havens argue the opposite point of view that "sex is never entirely a private question, because a person is never solely a private individual. He lives in his culture, and his culture lives in him" [69].

Might one argue that the dangers of sexual relationships such as Miss Havens describes are not physical or even social, but that the hazards lie in emotional consequences, which vary with individuals and which cannot be fully predicted?

By the same token, if individuals differ in emotional reactions, can it be said that Miss Havens overstates the case for chastity?

The author of a report on sex and the college student chose the case of a

> . . . coed named Sally to demonstrate what they regard as an enlightened attitude suitable to the conditions of life today. Sally entered college intending to remain a virgin, but in her junior year she changed her mind when she met a young man who attracted her deeply. The authors of the Report are impressed by her ability to change her mind. They write: "Growth is shown by Sally's ability to develop flexible attitudes toward the possibility of intercourse. . . . She demonstrates a responsiveness to life experience and a capacity to learn from them and to make choices. Rigidity, the necessity to cling unyieldingly to a set of fixed attitudes without the exercise of judgment, is usually indicative of anxiety and a lack of freedom to learn."

> The authors speak favorably of the qualities revealed in Sally's change of mind. "Flexibility" and "responsiveness to life experience" are indeed desirable traits.

> The authors continue: "Issues of sexual morality are complex and confusing for the college student. The oversimplification of the moral position in which abstinence equals right and indulgence equals wrong is not at all consistent with conduct at most colleges." They deride this "oversimplification" and they prefer the "flexibility" shown by Sally. They write: "Abstinence . . . may simply reflect inability to embrace sexual pleasure during adolescence." [70]

May abstinence also be due to a belief that sex is an expression of feeling to be reserved for a relationship of highest and fullest commitment?

Havens concludes that:

There may be women who have carried off the irregular sex affairs happily and successfully. But if there are I have never met them, and I have known many in these past few years.

Might Miss Havens' reactions be modified by findings that

. . . couples, especially engaged pairs, experiencing premarital intercourse, state that it strengthens their relationships. Some research findings indicate that premarital intercourse may be related if not conducive to more effective sexual adjustments in marriage. Some counselors, therapists and philosophers see positive values in such experiences, and parents may be advised to be more lenient and accepting toward premarital intercourse. [71]

In view of advances in contraception which have upset traditional sexual morality, might Miss Havens revise her opinion today and concur with a professor of health education who writes:

An increasingly safe and potentially wholesome sex life is said to be becoming available to the married and the unmarried who desire it; and there seems to be a growing feeling that this is a decision to be made by individual women and is not the business of society at all. . . . A considerable number of people view the new era for women with alarm, [but] my personal view is that the new era for women with its opportunities for independence and choice as to way of life is one of the most important and encouraging developments of history. [72]

Miss Havens recommends chastity in theory, but she does not suggest ways to maintain it in practice. How might one cope with intense sexual desires in the long gap between their awakening and the authorized expression of them? Masturbation? Prostitution? Early marriage? A heavy program of sports, on the theory that physical exercise reduces sexual tension? Some other form of sublimation?

What do adults mean when they refer to "wholesome" activities which might be tried instead?

Chastity on the Campus
ANONYMOUS

I believe that at least seventy-five percent of college girls are not virgins. I am not one myself. I want to give you our point of view. College is a preparation primarily to teach us to live the fullest life, and, if desirable, to support ourselves. We are as interested in a home and family as our parents were, the chief difference being that we have moved forward the year at which a girl is labelled an old maid. We are as interested in moral values as the next person, perhaps a little more. We are critical of dishonesty, superficiality, and laziness. Most of us have vigorous personal moral codes which we honestly try to live up to.

We are not promiscuous. The point is important. It is for many of us the difference between immorality and morality, the difference between self-respect and shame.

And that self-respect is important. If most of us felt that intercourse before marriage were a violation of our codes of personal integrity, we would have none of it. We believe that the desire for intercourse is a natural, normal, healthy instinct. In our studies of the social sciences, we have seen disastrous consequences in the lives of many people because of incomplete and unsatisfactory social adjustment. [Freud's] contemporaries in other schools also say that inadequate sex life is the most important cause of neurosis.

Forty fraternity boys on our campus were discussing the kind of wives they wanted. Not one of them would marry a girl whom he believed to be dishonest, but only one demanded virginity in his bride!

The danger of becoming pregnant does not frighten us any more than the idea that we may someday be in a train accident.

Psychological statistics show that when the man and woman have had intercourse with other persons before marriage, there is a better chance that the marriage will be a successful one.

Though we may have intercourse with more than one boy in a period of four years, most of us do not, because we have been careful—almost as careful as if we were considering marriage—in our choice of a boy.

Most undergraduates consider the present situation ideal. College boys are no longer going to prostitutes, but are finding sexual satisfaction with girls on their own level whom they admire and respect. The double standard of morals is disappearing.

Why does the anonymous author of **Chastity on the Campus** say "we are not promiscuous. The point is important"?

The author explains: "We may have intercourse with more than one boy in a period of four years, [but] most of us do not." How many different sexual partners would you say a female college student might have in four years before you would label her "promiscuous"? How many sex partners would you permit a male college student before calling him "promiscuous"? Would you change your response in terms of high school males and females? Do you find the last three questions difficult to answer? Might your answers depend on different circumstances? On what would the answers depend?

Why are reports like the following not always reliable?

Forty fraternity boys on our campus were discussing the kind of wives they wanted. Not one of them would marry a girl whom he believed to be dishonest, but only one demanded virginity in his bride.

What factors (as indicated in readings from the "I" section) might have influenced at least some of those thirty-nine fraternity brothers to tell other than the truth?

It can also be argued that some men secretly want a virgin for a bride: some consider virginity a gift to be brought by the wife to her husband; some, who feel a need to control as much of their world as possible, resent the fact that a woman has had so important an experience with another; some fear that a woman who has had premarital sexual relations will be more likely to prove unfaithful in marriage. And there is also a theory that as males become more conservative in parenthood, they may attribute signs of adolescent rebellion in their own teenage daughters to the sexual pattern of the wife before marriage, thereby adding friction to the marital relationship.

Chastity on the Campus may be a sincere presentation, yet even when it was published in 1938, the author's conception of the facts differed somewhat from the results of more comprehensive studies; Bromley and Britten, two female journalists who studied attitudes among college students during the 1930s, found 25 percent of the females and 52 percent of the males to be nonvirgin [73] and their data suggest that probably half of the nonvirginal college girls were more or less promiscuous.

Yet, despite "stacks of charts and statistical data about sex—in marriage, outside of marriage, before marriage, we know less about the meaning of the figures" [74]. Emotional facts may well be the significant ones to consider in making decisions about sexual behavior. One sixteen-year-old, asked why she had decided against sexual relations with a seventeen-year-old she thought she loved, said: "I think I love him enough to consider it moral to sleep with him, but two years ago I was positive I loved somebody else. It's scary. When I see how much I changed from fourteen to fifteen, and then from fifteen to sixteen—so how could I be sure now I wasn't making a terrible mistake, that I could never reverse? At seventeen I might discover that I regretted it."

To arrive at your own emotional truth, at least for the present moment, how would you evaluate the following considerations:

Since the ability to love others is rooted in the ability to respect oneself, will premarital sex damage your self-respect?

Are you and your potential sexual partner sufficiently free of any early teachings or cultural conditionings that might lead to guilt and shame?

Have you a stronger reason for sexual intimacies than a mere sense that current dating practices often expect couples to seal affectionate relationships with sex?

Might you be asking of sex more than it can yield by using it as one method of rejecting traditional social values or parental perspectives? Might sexual defiance be a way of acting out your conflicts with society in general, or with your family in particular?

Are you prepared to find sexual relations disappointing under conditions that are less than ideal and fraught in part with a secrecy that may breed resentment and bitterness?

Can you accept the emotional strains a sexual liaison may entail?

As a male, the physical experience may be satisfactory, if it is true that the boy plays at love for which he is not ready, because what he wants is sex. But he will have also to contend with the consequences for the girl, should the sexual relationship prove premature, if it is equally true that the girl plays at sex for which she is not ready, because, fundamentally, what she wants is love.

As a female, can you convince yourself that the permanent fulfillment of lasting love will exist first or will grow from the sexual relationship?

RELATED QUESTIONS

Is the author of *Chastity on the Campus* one of the "sophisticated younger generation" with "derisive cries" but "as yet no first-hand knowledge" of the situation which her contemporary, Evelyn Havens, discusses in *I Thought I Was Modern* (p. 280)?

Is Evelyn Havens one whom the author of *Chastity on the Campus* might consider too culturally conditioned to recognize that "the desire for intercourse is a natural, normal, healthy instinct"?

Into which of the three categories of *Some Observations on Sexual Morality* (p. 276) would you put *Chastity on the Campus?* Why? What ethic determines sexual morality for this anonymous coed?

What attitude toward chastity is suggested or stated in each of the following selections from "**Night-Lights:**"

Since the above authors are all males, what conclusions do the selections suggest concerning what a man wants in a woman?

Sex Attitudes (from Summerhill)

A. S. NEILL

. . . I have never had a pupil who did not bring to Summerhill [School] a diseased attitude toward sexuality and bodily functions. The children of modern parents who were told the truth about where babies come from have much the same hidden attitude toward sex that the children of religious fanatics have. To find a new orientation to sex is the most difficult task of the parent and teacher.

We know so little of the causes of the sex taboo that we can only hazard guesses as to its origin. Why there is a sex taboo is of no immediate concern to me. That there *is* a sex taboo is of great concern to a man entrusted to cure repressed children.

We adults were corrupted in infancy; we can never be free about sex matters. *Consciously,* we may be free; we may even be members of a society for the sex education of children. But I fear that *unconsciously* we remain to a large extent what conditioning in infancy made of us: haters of sex and fearers of sex.

I am quite willing to believe that my unconscious attitude toward sex is the Calvinistic attitude a Scottish village imposed on me in my first years of life. Possibly there is no salvation for adults; but there is every chance of salvation for children, if we do not force on them the awful ideas of sex that were forced on us.

Early in life, the child learns that the sexual sin is the great sin. Parents invariably punish most severely for an offense against sex morality. The very people who rail against Freud because he "sees sex in everything" are the ones who have told sex stories, have listened to sex stories, have laughed at sex stories. Every man who has been in the army knows that the language of the army is a sex language. Nearly everyone likes to read the spicy accounts of divorce cases and of sex crimes in the Sunday papers, and most men tell their wives the stories they bring home from their clubs and bars.

Now our delight in a sex story is due entirely to our own unhealthy education in sex matters. The unsavory sex interest is due to repressions. The story, as Freud says, lets the cat out of the bag. The adult condemnation of sex interest in the child is hypocritical and is humbug; the condemnation is a projection, a throwing of the guilt onto others. Parents punish severely for sex offenses because they are vitally, if unhealthily, interested in sex offenses.

Why is the crucifixion of the flesh so popular? Religious people believe that the flesh drags one downward. The body is called vile: it tempts one to evil. It is this hatred of the body that makes talk of childbirth a subject for dark corners of the schoolroom, and that makes polite conversation a cover up for everyday plain facts of life.

Freud saw sex as the greatest force in human behavior. Every honest observer must agree. But moral instruction has over-emphasized sex. The first correction that a mother makes, when the child touches his sexual organ, makes sex the most fascinating and mysterious thing in the world. To make fruit forbidden is to make it delectable and enticing.

The sex taboo is the root evil in the suppression of children. I do not narrow the word *sex* down to genital sex. It is likely that the child at the breast feels unhappy if his mother disapproves of any part of her own body, or impedes his pleasure in his own body.

Sex is the basis of all negative attitudes toward life. Children who have no sex guilt never ask for religion or mysticism of any kind. Since sex is considered the great sin, children who are fairly free from sex fear and sex shame do not seek any God from whom they can ask pardon or mercy, because they do not feel guilty.

When I was six my sister and I discovered each other's genitals, and naturally played with each other. Discovered by our mother, we were severely thrashed; and I was locked in a dark room for hours, and then made to kneel down and ask forgiveness from God.

It took me decades to get over that early shock; and, indeed, I sometimes wonder if I ever fully got over it.

How many of today's adults have had a similar experience? How many of today's children are having their whole natural love of life changed into hate and aggression because of such treatment? They are being told that touching the genitals is bad or sinful and that natural bowel movements are disgusting.

Every child who is suffering from sex suppression has a stomach like a board. Watch a repressed child breathe and then look at the beautiful grace with which a kitten breathes. No animal has a stiff stomach, nor is self-conscious about sex or defecation.

In his well-known work, *Character Analysis,* Wilhelm Reich pointed out that a moralistic training not only warps the thinking process, but enters structually into the body itself, armoring it literally with stiffness in posture and contraction of pelvis. I agree with Reich. I have observed, during many years of dealing with a variety of children at Summerhill, that when fear has not stiffened the musculature, the young walk, run, jump and play with a wonderful grace.

What then can we do to prevent sex repression in children? Well, for one thing, from the earliest moment the child must be completely free to touch any and every part of his body.

A psychologist friend of mine had to say to his son of four, "Bob, you must not play with your wee-wee when you are out among strange people for they think it bad. You must do it only at home and in the garden."

My friend and I talked about it and agreed that it is impossible to guard the child against the anti-life haters of sex. The only comfort is that when the parents are sincere believers in life, the child will generally accept the parental standards and is likely to reject the outside prudery. But all the same, the mere fact that a child of five learns that he cannot bathe in the sea without pants is enough to form some kind—if only a minor kind—of sex distrust.

Today many parents put no ban on masturbation. They feel that it is natural, and they know the dangers of suppressing it. Excellent. Fine.

But some of these enlightened parents balk at the next step. Some do not mind if their little boys have sex play with other little boys, but they stiffen with alarm if a small boy and a small girl have sex play.

If my good, well-meaning mother had ignored the sex play of my year younger sister and me, our chances of growing up with some sanity toward sex would have been good.

I wonder how much impotence and frigidity in adults date from the first interference in a heterosexual relationship of early childhood. I wonder how much homosexuality dates from the tolerance of homosexual play and the forbidding of heterosexual play.

Heterosexual play in childhood is the royal road, I believe, to a healthy, balanced adult sex life. When children have no moralistic training in sex, they reach a healthy adolescence—not an adolescence of promiscuity.

I know of no argument against youth's love life that holds water. Nearly every argument is based on repressed emotion or hate of life—the religious, the moral, the expedient, the arbitrary, the pornographic. None answer the question why nature gave man a strong sex instinct, if youth is to be forbidden to use it unless sanctioned by the elders of society. Those elders, some of them, have shares in companies that run films full of sex appeal, or in companies that sell all sorts of cosmetics to make girls more delectable to boys, or companies that publish magazines which make sadistic pictures and stories a magnet to their readers.

I know that adolescent sex life is not practical today. But my opinion is that it is the right way to tomorrow's health. I can *write* this, but if in Summerhill I approved of my adolescent pupils sleeping together, my school would be suppressed by the authorities. I am thinking of the long tomorrow when society will have realized how dangerous sex repression is.

I do not expect every Summerhill pupil to be unneurotic, for who can be complex-free in society today? What I hope for is that in generations to come this beginning of freedom from artificial sex taboos will ultimately fashion a life-loving world.

The invention of contraceptives must in the long run lead to a new sex morality, seeing that fear of consequences is perhaps the strongest factor in sex morality. To be free, love must feel itself safe.

Youth today has little opportunity for loving in the true sense. Parents will not allow sons or daughters to live in sin, as they call it, so that young lovers have to seek damp woods or parks or automobiles. Thus everything is loaded heavily against our young people. Circumstances compel them to convert what should be lovely and joyful into something sinister and sinful, into smut and leers, and shameful laughter.

The taboos and fears that fashioned sex behavior are those same taboos and fears that produce the perverts who rape and strangle small girls in parks, the perverts who torture Jews and Negroes.

Sex prohibition anchors sex to the family. The masturbation prohibition forces a child to interest himself in the parents. Every time a mother smacks a child's hands for touching his genitals, the sex drive of the child gets constellated with his mother, and the hidden attitude toward the mother becomes one of desire and repulsion, love and hate. Repression flourishes in an unfree home. Repression helps to retain adult authority, but at the price of a plethora of neurosis.

If sex were allowed to go over the garden wall to the boy or girl next door, the authority of the home would be in danger; the tie to father and mother would loosen and the child would automatically leave the family emotionally. It sounds absurd but those ties are a very necessary pillar of support to the authoritative state—just as prostitution was a necessary safeguard for the morality of nice girls from nice homes. Abolish sex repression and youth will be lost to authority.

Fathers and mothers are doing what their parents did to them: bringing up respectable, chaste children, conveniently forgetting all the hidden sex play and pornographic stories of their own childhood, forgetting the bitter rebellion against their parents that they had to repress with infinite guilt. They do not realize that they are giving their own children the same guilt feelings that gave them miserable nights many long years ago.

Man's serious neurosis starts with the earliest genital prohibitions: Touch not. The impotence, frigidity, and anxiety of later life date from the tying up of the hands or the snatching away of the hands, usually with a spank. A child left to touch its genitals has every chance of growing up with a sincere, happy attitude toward sex. Sex play among small children is a natural, healthy act that ought not to be frowned on. On the contrary, it should be encouraged as a prelude to a healthy adolescence and adulthood. Parents are ostriches hiding their heads in the sand if they are ignorant that their children have sex play in dark corners. This kind of clandestine and furtive play breeds a guilt that lives on in later life, a guilt that usually betrays itself in disapproval of sex play when these same children become parents. Bringing sex play out into the light is the only sane thing to do. There would be infinitely less sex crime in the world if sex play were accepted as normal. That is what moral parents cannot see or dare not see, that sex crime and sex abnormality of any kind are a direct result of disapproval of sex in early childhood.

The famous anthropologist, Malinowski, tells us that there was no homosexuality among the Trobrianders until the shocked missionaries segregated boys and girls in separate hostels. There was no rape among the Trobrianders, no sex crimes. Why? Because small children were given no repressions about sex.

. . . there is no sitting on the fence, no neutrality. The choice is between guilty-secret sex or open-healthy-happy sex. If parents choose the common standard of morality, they must not complain of the misery of sex-perverted society, for it is the result of this moral code. Parents then must not hate war, for the hate of self that they give their children will express itself in war. Humanity is sick, emotionally sick, and it is sick because of this guilt and anxiety acquired in childhood. The emotional past is everywhere in our society.

When Zoe was six she came to me and said, "Willie has the biggest cock among the small kids, but Mrs. X (a visitor) says it is rude to say *cock."* I at once told her that it was not rude. Inwardly, I cursed that woman for her ignorant and narrow understanding of children. I might tolerate propaganda about politics or manners, but when anyone attacks a child by making that child guilty about sex, I fight back vigorously.

All our leering attitude toward sex, our guffaws in music halls, our scribbling of obscenities on urinal walls spring from the guilty feeling arising from suppression of masturbation in infancy and from driving mutual sex play into holes and corners. There is secret sex play in every family; and because of the secrecy and guilt, there are many fixations on brothers and sisters that last throughout life and make happy marriages impossible. If sex play between brother and sister at the age of five were accepted as natural, each of them would advance freely to a sex object outside the family.

The extreme forms of sex hate are seen in sadism. No man with a good sex life could possibly torture an animal, or torture a human, or support prisons. No sex-satisfied woman would condemn the mother of a bastard.

Of course, I lay myself open to the accusation: "This man has sex on the brain. Sex isn't everything in life. There is friendship, work, joy, and sorrow. Why sex?"

I answer: Sex affords the highest pleasure in life. Sex with love is the supreme from of ecstasy because it is the supreme form of both giving and receiving. Yet sex is obviously hated; otherwise no mother would forbid masturbation—no father forbid a sex life outside conventional marriage. Otherwise, there would be no obscene jokes in vaudeville halls, nor would the public waste its time seeing love films and reading love stories; it would be practicing love.

Hate sex and you hate life. Hate sex and you cannot love your neighbor. If you hate sex, your sexual life will be, at the worst, impotent or frigid; at best, incomplete. Hence the common remark by women who have had children, "Sex is an overrated pastime." If sex is unsatisfactory, it must go somewhere, for it is too strong an urge to be annihilated. It goes into anxiety and hate.

Not many adults look upon the sex act as a giving; otherwise the percentage of people afflicted with impotency and frigidity would not be about seventy per cent, as quite a few experts have claimed it is. To many men, intercourse is polite rape; to many women, a tiresome rite that has to be endured. Thousands of married women have never experienced an orgasm in their lives; and even some educated men do not know that a woman is capable of an orgasm. In such a system, giving must be minimal; and sex relations are bound to be more or less brutalized and obscene. The perverts who require to be scourged with whips or to beat women with rods are merely extreme cases of people who, owing to sex miseducation, are unable to give love except in the disguised form of hate.

Every older pupil at Summerhill knows from my conversation and my books that I approve of a full sex life for all who wish one, whatever their age. I have often been asked in my lectures if I provide contraceptives at Summerhill, and if not, why not? This is an old and vexed question that touches deep emotions in all of us. That I do not provide contraceptives is a matter of bad conscience with me, for to compromise in any way is to me difficult and alarming. On the other hand, to provide contraceptives to children either over or under the age of consent would be a sure way of closing down my school. One cannot advance in practice too much ahead of the law.

A familiar question asked by critics of child freedom is, "Why don't you let a small child see sexual intercourse?" The answer that it would give him a trauma, a severe nervous shock, is false. Among the Trobrianders, according to Malinowski, children see not only parental sexual intercourse but birth and death as matters of course, and are not affected adversely. I do not think that seeing sexual intercourse would have any bad emotional effect on a self-regulated child. The only honest answer to the question is to say that love in our culture is not a public matter.

I do not forget that many parents have religious or other negative views on the sinfulness of sex. Nothing can be done about them. They cannot be converted to our views. On the other hand, we must fight them when they infringe on our own children's right to freedom, genital or otherwise.

To other parents, I say: Your big headache will come when your daughter of sixteen wants to live her own life. She will come in at midnight. On no account ask her where she has been. If she has not been self-regulated, she will lie to you just as you lied, and I lied, to our parents.

When my daughter is sixteen, should I find her in love with some insensitive man, I shall have more than one worry. I know that I shall be powerless to do anything. I hope I will have sense not to try. Since she has been self-regulated, I do not anticipate that she will fall for an undesirable type of young man; but one can never tell.

What does Neill in **Sex Attitudes** feel to be the root evil in problem children's, and man's, "serious neurosis"?

Even those without a belief in orthodox religion cannot help carrying with them into early sexual experience a sense of sin, which they seldom lose. How does Neill explain this unconscious guilt? How does he suggest liberation from it?

Neill says that when "parents are sincere believers in life, the child will generally accept the parental standards." If positive or negative parental influence can be so strong, why do so many young people revolt against their parents and their parents' standards?

Would you agree that if sex repression is abolished, youth "will be lost to authority"?

Confronted with the situation of Neill's psychologist friend with his four-year-old son, how would you have handled it?

Is there an answer to the question: Why does man have such a strong sex instinct if in youth he is forbidden to fulfill it in ways that are not sanctioned by society?

Would you want to attend a school which approved "of a full sex life for all who wish one, whatever their age"? Why, or why not? Would you enroll your children in that school? Why, or why not?

Do you concur with Neill that "girls are not as a rule seduced; they are partners in a seduction," [75] or with the woman who believes that "anyone who was seduced wanted to be seduced" [76]?

Neill would surely subscribe to the following perspective on physical love:

> Any society that allows conditions to exist in which the adolescent begins to connect guilt with physical love raises a generation of defectives. [77]

Does Neill overstate his case, or oversimplify issues, when he concludes that "in generations to come this beginning of freedom from artificial sex taboos will ultimately fashion a life-loving world"?

RELATED QUESTIONS

How does Neill, in essence, agree with the anonymous coed who wrote *Chastity on the Campus* (p. 283)?

Would Neill concur with *Playboy* editor Hugh Hefner (p. 185) that "it is as though our society put hate above love, favored death over life"?

How does *The Dawn of Hate* (p. 166), in which Richard encounters a tramp who exposes himself, illustrate Neill's concepts?

How might Neill react to the introductory comments on masturbation prefacing *Manchild in the Promised Land* (p. 33)?

What sort of future would Neill envision for four-year-old Stephen on the basis of his early experiences in *The Downward Path to Wisdom* (p. 151)?

On which side of the controversy in *Little Brother Comes to America* (p. 179) would you expect to find Neill, and why?

Neill claims that "youth today has little opportunity for loving in the true sense." What do you think he means by "the true sense"?

Would Neill's concept of loving resemble that of Singer in *Appraisal and Bestowal* (p. 217)? C. S. Lewis in *Eros* (p. 205)? Lindbergh in *Double-Sunrise* (p. 232)? Lee in *What Love Must Be* (p. 250)? Fromm in *The Theory of Love* (p. 252) or *Is Love an Art?* (p. 246)? Yours?

How might some of the writers on the subject of love and sex react to Neill's statement:

> Not many adults look upon the sex act as a giving; otherwise the percentage of people afflicted with impotency and frigidity would not be about seventy per cent, as quite a few experts have claimed it is.

Glory of Life

LLEWELYN POWYS

Renan wrote "Nature thinks nothing of chastity." This is true enough, but in so far as we surpass Nature chastity may, for some people, have a kind of value. I would say nevertheless without hesitation that far more persons are injured by sexual restraints than by sexual indulgence. Oh what slow malign torturings of the human spirit are being done about us in the name of this most foolish human illusion!

In life everything is so involved, and every relationship so entirely unique, that to abide by any fixed rule is impossible. I myself believe that it shows the most sorry improvidence to turn aside from such felicities when opportunity offers. These moments are our golden moments and the moments that on the day of our death we are likely to value most.

When, as occasionally happens, there is an utter, impassioned, and heroical love between two people, when the thought of each other's bodies causes them day and night to stand as worshippers before the shrine of Aphrodite, quivering, shivering with idolatry, fidelity becomes as natural as to breathe. . . . When love of this kind visits the earth, as it does visit the earth rarely and by chance, then preserve it, shelter it, sacrifice everything to it! . . . To know that you will be loved, even to the grave's edge, deprives the Icarus-like falling from life to death of half its horror. . . .

It is far better to accept life simply and naturally; to recognize that soon enough our happiness will be at an end. There is no wiser word than to eat and to drink and to be merry. No word that we hear spoken, no gesture we see should be lost. In moments of profane love we should be possessed by an ultimate rapture, our spirits under their foolish bewitchment, awake with gladness, knowing the high fortune of so tender, so savage, so God-like an experience! . . .

For at the end of all—what are we? A herd of dream cattle, images of breath, passing shadows that move swiftly across the world's pastures to a graveyard where, at a single clap, eternity is as a day and a day as eternity. . . .

Powys' view of sexual morality in the excerpt from **Glory of Life** is obviously not rooted in the fear ethic—fear of religious, social, physical, or emotional consequences. How is the philosophy behind moral relativism indicated in Powys' statement:

> In life everything is so involved, and every relationship so entirely unique, that to abide by any fixed rule is impossible.

Powys acknowledges and honors those cases of "utter, impassioned, and heroical love between two people" in which "fidelity becomes as natural as to breathe," but he also considers love of this kind rare on earth. How then does he justify sexual "indulgence" in the more frequent instances?
Why does he believe that

In moments of profane love we should be possessed by an ultimate rapture, our spirits under their foolish bewitchment, awake with gladness, knowing the high fortune of so tender, so savage, so God-like an experience.

How can we feel such ecstasy if, in a large majority of cases, a guilt sense persists? If, as Havens concluded in *I Thought I Was Modern:*

. . . there must always be fear, present at the most intimate and tender moments, chilling desire and slowly but surely robbing the sex relation of the freedom and spontaneity which alone gives it significance and beauty.

What examples might support Renan's generalization in **Glory of Life** that "Nature thinks nothing of chastity"?

RELATED QUESTIONS

Who might be more likely to agree with Powys on what constitutes a "most foolish human illusion": Neill in **Sex Attitudes** (p. 286) or Havens in **I Thought I Was Modern** (p. 280)? Why?

Would Havens, Powys, and Neill agree on the cause of "slow malign torturings of the human spirit"? Why, or why not?

Havelock Ellis in *Studies in the Psychology of Sex* writes:

There are some who seem to think that they have held the balance evenly, and finally stated the matter, if they admit that sexual love may be either beautiful or disgusting, and that either view is equally normal and legitimate. "Listen in turn," Tarde remarks, "to two men who, one cold, the other ardent, one chaste, the other in love, both equally educated and large-minded, are estimating the same thing: one judges as disgusting, odious, revolting, and bestial what the other judges to be delicious, exquisite, ineffable, divine. What, for one, is in Christian phraseology, an unforgivable sin, is, for the other, the state of true grace. Acts that for one seem a sad and occasional necessity, stains that must be carefully effaced by long intervals of continence, are for the other the golden nails from which all the rest of conduct and existence is suspended, the things that alone give human life its value." Yet we may well doubt whether both these persons are equally well-educated and broad-minded. The savage feels that sex is perilous, and he is right. But the person who feels that the sexual impulse is bad, or even low and vulgar, is an absurdity in the universe, an anomaly. He is like those persons in our insane asylums, who feel that the instinct of nutrition is evil and so proceed to starve themselves. They are alike spiritual outcasts in the universe whose children they are. It is another matter when a man declares that, personally, in his own case, he cherishes an ascetic ideal which leads him to restrain, so far as possible, either or both impulses. The man who is sanely ascetic seeks a discipline which aids the ideal he has personally set before himself. He may still remain theoretically in harmony with the universe to which he belongs. But to pour contempt on the sexual life, to throw the veil of "impurity" over it, is, as Nietzsche declared, the unpardonable sin against the Holy Ghost of Life. [78]

How might Neill (**Sex Attitudes,** p. 286) and Powys each separately interpret sexual freedoms as "the golden nails from which all the rest of conduct and existence is suspended, the things that alone give human life its value"?

Would you classify supporters of the case for chastity in this section with those who feel "that the sexual impulse is bad" or with those who cherish "an ascetic ideal"? Or with neither, but with something else? Why?

Searching for the Roots of Moral Judgments

LESTER A. KIRKENDALL

Persons working in the field of human relations, including teachers, religious workers, youth workers, counselors, and social workers, are keenly aware of the concern of the average person for deciding what is "right" or "wrong." Questions beginning "Is it right to——?", "Is it wrong to——?" are common.

The essence of morality lies in the quality of interrelationships which can be established among people. Moral conduct is that kind of behavior which enables people in their relationships with each other to experience a greater sense of trust, and appreciation for others; which increases the capacity of people to work together; which reduces social distance and continually furthers one's outreach to other persons and groups; which increases one's sense of self-respect and produces a greater measure of personal harmony.

Immoral behavior is just the converse. Behavior which creates distrust; destroys appreciation for others; decreases the capacity for cooperation; lessens concern for others; causes persons or groups to shut themselves off or be shut off from others; and which decreases an individual's sense of self-respect is immoral behavior.

This is, of course, nothing new. The concept has been implicit in religions for ages. The injunction to "love thy neighbor as thyself" is a case in point. This is seemingly what is meant by the Golden Rule. It is the basic issue in the question, "Am I my brother's keeper?" Our failure has been to study its meaning, pursue its ramifications, and put it into practice.

The most important thing in the world today is the building of relationships which will enable people to communicate effectively, and in turn to live together in brotherhood. If people could communicate fully and effectively enough to understand each other, there would be little or no chance of wars. Until we can build understanding, until we can communicate, until we can feel a sense of unity and brotherhood, we will never have peace either internationally, or in our personal lives. Morally the important issue is not whether some act has, or has not, occurred but how can sound relationships be built.

Concern for the quality of interrelationships seems not only a sound, but the essential foundation for morality because it is in harmony with the nature of man. True, "the nature of man" is not unalterably established. I am making an assumption. To me, however, the evidence is conclusive enough that I am assuming man is by nature cooperative and social. One of his deep, if not his deepest, need is his unchanging desire to be associated happily, acceptably, and harmoniously with his kind. His sense of self-respect and worth comes from feeling that he has contributed to the welfare and well-being of those who have accepted him. The more we learn about man the more it appears that this is a sound concept of his nature.

The sex urge also yields to the concern for strong, satisfying personal interrelationships. When an individual finds a relationship with a member of the other sex has become important to him, he seeks to order his sexual behavior to strengthen the relationship. I have seen this a number of times in working with young people.

Occasionally the concern for satisfying relationships seems obscured by cynicism, self-centeredness, and concern for personal gratification. Experience in counseling indicates that in such cases the individual has already experienced so many immoral relationships that the sense of fellowship has been corroded and submerged by them.

Another important aspect of this concept, if accepted, is that moral judgments and practices are then based upon an unchanging factor common to all men. Racial differences, place of residence, or citizenship do not change the nature of man. His desire and need for acceptance remain, and we have no reason for believing this will change. This certainly cannot be said for social custom or authoritative statements on the nature of right and wrong.

The more we find about the universe and the principles which govern it the more we are impelled to widen our horizons, and to acknowledge that all men are kin. We find also most of the barriers we erect between groups are based upon trumped-up differences and erroneous assumptions.

Each additional bit of knowledge we gain proves that there is no inherent difference between races. Regardless of skin color men fall prey to the same diseases, and respond to the same treatments. Psychologically they have fears, ambitions, respond to love, recoil from or fight against hatred, and feel anger, jealousy, and pride. Those who try to justify barriers between racial and ethnic groups get no comfort from science.

What we need is to implement in our daily relations the philosophy expressed by Edwin Markham in his poem, "Outwitted,"

> He drew a circle that shut me out—
> Heretic, rebel, a thing to flout.
> But love and I had the wit to win:
> We drew a circle that took him in.

If this approach is accepted it immediately requires some very important reconsiderations. Immediately we have to be concerned with whatever conditions the quality of our interrelationships. Let us look at some of these reconsiderations.

First, *all of our behavior must be scrutinized to determine its moral significance.*

If we say a person is immoral we usually think he has indulged in sexual misbehavior. We have attached the term "immorality" very largely to sex. A person may steal or lie, (or impair the strength of interrelationships) but this is not immoral living. Our moral standards need to apply to all behavior, rather than having a restricted meaning which associates them with just one type of behavior.

Sarcasm is an example. Sarcasm is immoral, for it almost always has the net effect of creating a feeling of distrust and suspicion. It builds a barrier between the persons who use the sarcasm and the persons against whom it is directed. By the standard of moral judgment suggested here, sarcasm is immoral.

Corruption in government and embezzlement are immoral. Most people would agree because they realize that somebody is taking something which doesn't belong to them. But there is more to it. Corruption in government is wrong because it breaks the trust of people in their government. When we believe that our governmental leaders are corrupt and dishonest we feel we can't depend upon them. Being unable to trust our leaders, we can no longer communicate to each other, or work together so effectively through the government. Corruption destroys the fabric of cooperation. Since it destroys the capacity of the group to communicate and work together, it endangers their survival; it is immoral. The same is true of embezzlement.

Some jokes are immoral since they build barriers between people. In making their point they hurt and create a sense of distrust. They depend for their humor on stinging someone; a bit of ridicule or a jibe at someone's weakness. A very good illustration was found in our newspapers sometime ago. According to a report, the Canadian committee planning for the visit of the King and Queen had become very upset at the comments of certain American comedians. They charged that these comedians were joking at the expense of British traditions in which both the British and Canadian people took great pride. They felt that some of the jokes were very offensive and worked against friendly and cordial relations. To the extent that these jokes prevented the Americans, the British, and the Canadians from building a mutual understanding, and from working more closely together, they were immoral.

The effect of these various jokes may not be very serious; we may seem to recover from them readily. They serve to illustrate, though, how every aspect of our life may have implications for moral living. Furthermore, the residue of feeling left has a bearing upon the quality of human interrelationships.

The grading system in our schools, as it commonly operates, produces immoral consequences. Over and over again, it creates distrust and builds barriers between students and their instructors. Most conscientious teachers are aware that grades break down interrelationships. They work carefully and diligently to mark as accurately and fairly as possible. Yet they know they can never be precisely accurate in their evaluations. Finally they are forced to put this evaluation into a cold, impersonal letter grade which really doesn't tell the student anything about what he has accomplished, or what he needs to accomplish further. So the business of marking and setting in *arbitrary* judgment frequently ends by destroying the relationship which has been built up during the rest of the course.

Marks sometimes build a feeling of competition between students which impairs relationships. One student may refuse to help another, because if he did and the student he helped improved his standing, his own standing might be endangered, or depressed. The whole matter of evaluation needs re-examination.

The use of words in a deceptive, ambiguous way is immoral. It makes communication difficult, or impossible. It hampers or defeats people in their efforts to work together. We have seen much of this in international relations. A predatory nation will invade a country and shield its own aggressive designs through bandying the words "liberation" and "freedom." Some of our words have been so misused that when people use them it creates confusion rather than understanding.

Lewis Mumford, in *Faith for Living* writes, ". . . man's greatest triumph in producing order out of chaos, greater than law, greater than science, was language. To keep the channels of human communication clean is a duty as primal—and holy—as guarding the sacred fire was for primitive man. He who debases the word . . . breeds darkness and confusion and all manner of foulness."

The most immoral of all behavior seems that conduct in international affairs which confuses rather than clarifies, which creates hatred and distrust in the peoples of one nation for those of another, which tries to separate, divide and wall off. We have a full measure of such immoral conduct in international affairs today, and we are even now, and will be tomorrow, reaping the terrifying consequences.

Second, *our moral judgments would stem from the meaning of an action, rather than being based upon the determination of whether or not an act has occurred.* When immoral conduct is mentioned we commonly expect a description of an action rather than a consideration of how it affects a relationship. The relating of acts may satisfy our curiosity, but the significant question is "How did this action affect the quality of human relationships?"

Since immorality is commonly thought of in terms of sex, let us examine the matter of premarital sex standards. The moral issue relating to petting or premarital intercourse is not, did it or did it not happen? Rather the question is what does it do to the relationship. Do or can petting and premarital intercourse create trust, understanding, and appreciation? Do they build a willingness to work together? Do they create more concern for the welfare of others? Do they make them more able to reach out to others in a spirit of love? Do they instill a feeling of self-respect? Or do they result in the converse of such conditions? When we are able to answer those questions we can make a basically sound judgment about the morality of sex standards.

Another illustration of the confused thinking which results from concentrating on an act rather than the quality of the relationship is the common question asked by parents, "Is it right or wrong to spank a child?" I have led many parent discussion groups, and as a leader I was quite disturbed when that question arose. I hadn't been able to come to a conclusion myself. My uncertainty was caused by the sense of guilt I felt over having spanked my own children.

Then one day a simple experience threw an entirely different light on the issue. My two children and I were rough-housing on the living room floor. I had got about enough, so was getting up from the floor when my six-year old son ran up and shoved me over backward. I jumped up and continuing the spirit of play, chased him around the room, caught him, turned him over my knee, and spanked him. That seemed great sport. He tried to push me over again, and actually challenged me to repeat what I had just done. Afterwards I realized that in the play situation I had probably spanked him harder than I had ever spanked him as a disciplinary measure. In the play situation he had laughed about a spanking and really courted more, but when used in a disciplinary sense he acted terribly injured.

I realized then it wasn't the physical force of the spanking that made the difference. What was it?

At this point many people say in regard to the disciplinary spanking that "he knew he had done wrong." This is not a convincing answer for I know of numerous other instances in which he knew "he had done wrong" which were not so upsetting to him. For example, the time I caught him raiding the jelly jar, and I couldn't keep from smiling at the expression on his face as he looked up and saw me standing beside him. His expression was proof that he knew he had "done wrong," but on observing my smile he broke out in a broad one of his own.

A child's upset from a disciplinary spanking may come from two things. First, the child may feel outraged and demeaned that someone whom he loved and trusted should have treated him with such indignity. Second, the spanking may seem to have destroyed the relationship between himself and the parent. It seems a rejection and the child can do nothing about it. The injury is to his feelings, and his sense of belonging. He is disturbed at his inability to repair the relationship since he is unable to communicate his feelings to his parent.

The issue should be, not whether to spank or not, but what various procedures in child rearing do to the parent-child relationship. While I believe the net effect of most spankings is to damage relationships (and is therefore wrong), from my experience I realized that one could say something to a child, and without ever touching him physically, damage relationships more severely than if physical punishment had been used. Also with skillful handling a spanking and the subsequent events might result in improved relationships, in an increased feeling of unity, closeness, and a greater ability to work together.

Third, *we all become parties to the morality or immorality which characterizes a particular situation.* Cheating in schools is an example. Ordinarily our attitude is that cheating is bad and is indulged in by students who are lazy and purposeless. They are students who "just don't want to get anything out of school." *They* are the *ones* who are wrong, or immoral. That is a vast oversimplification, and one which obscures understanding so much that corrective measures are more likely to be more harmful than helpful. Cheating results essentially from a breakdown in relationships, and from the incapacity of pupils and teachers to communicate with each other.

Students do not cheat on something which they believe is important to them and their well-being. Even Al Capone would hardly have cheated in a course on how to evade the income tax. Nor do people try to outsmart leaders whom they are convinced are working sincerely for their welfare. Where relationships are good and communication is possible, cheating is most unlikely to occur.

I believe I could take almost any group of students, and regardless of how strongly they felt about honesty in their school work, teach them so that by the end of the course they would be cheating.

How would I do it? I would put on as much pressure as possible. I would schedule unexpected tests. I would include references for class recitation that the students had had little or no chance to read. I would give little chance for any exchange of feeling or opinion between myself and the students. I would show my distrust for them by saying I did not trust them. "Nobody is going to get away with anything in this course. I know your tricks and I'll be watching every one of you. Don't try to put anything over on me for it will go hard with you if you do."

I would make the course appear as purposeless as possible. I would make it seem that the students were studying things because I required it, rather than for any worthwhile objective. I would rely on my authority as a teacher to support the statements I make and the arrangements I set up. Out of this breakdown in relationships and failure in communication would come cheating in class.

Properly analyzed, this kind of a situation is a component part of most cheating in schools.

After a while, if I really taught this way, I would begin saying that all students were undependable and dishonest. Yet I myself would have created the kind of relationship which caused their dishonesty.

We tend to get from people the kind of behavior we expect, since, due to our expectations, we set up relationships which produce it. Young men say, "You can't trust any women," or young women ask, "Can't you depend on any man?" Such reactions tell more about the person speaking, than they do about men or women in general. It tells that the person has probably conducted himself towards members of the other sex so as to produce suspicion and distrust.

Fourth, *this approach to morality makes moral living a pleasant, joyous experience.* Morality is so in harmony with the nature of man, and so potentially fulfilling of the need to be accepted that moral conduct becomes more satisfying and rewarding than immoral behavior.

The feeling of satisfaction that can come with moral living has been experienced by most people, though the experience is differently named by various groups. In schools it may be called "spirit," in offices or military groups it is "morale," in religious groups it is "brotherhood."

I recall a story of a discussion group leader who had been able to build this sense of closeness and understanding in a series of discussion groups he conducted each summer. One woman attended his series for four consecutive summers, and after the first summer, she commented, "We have had a wonderful experience. These are better than average people."

At the end of the second summer, she said, "This has been a wonderful experience. These are much better than average people." At the end of the third summer she said the same thing. At the end of the fourth summer, she said, "This has been a wonderful experience. These are above average people." Then she added, "You know, I have come to think that 95% of all people are above average." She had been having a moral experience and had found it highly satisfying.

This is not to say that moral living will be all ease and without trial. It will be hard and difficult at times. Disappointments will be met, and painful decisions will have to be made. They can be made, however, in light of a meaningful and challenging criterion, the improvement of interrelationships, and the long run results have a much better chance of being satisfying.

Too much of the time moral living is made to seem glum, dour, and joyless. As a young man in my college class put it, "I should think if a person lived a moral life always, it would be a dull life." He, of course, was thinking of morality in an entirely different sense.

Some people have suggested that I entitle this article "A Viewpoint of

Ethics." Any talk about morality is suspect. I have decided against their advice for these reasons. Morality has about it a sense of deep-seated concern about behavior and the treatment which human beings accord each other. That is the concern of this paper. Furthermore so many people have construed morality as a theological concept involving professional religionists that they feel ideas of morality have little bearing on their daily living. In this they are very wrong. Morality, since it is a problem of human interrelationships, is a problem of all of us at all times.

Morality has been discussed, it is true, without reference to supernaturalism or a supernatural Deity. This has been done, as was indicated earlier, because it seems to me that morality can be soundly based upon a genuine respect for and belief in the worth of people, and the possibility of the brotherhood of man. In fact, if we accept this view of what constitutes morality that is where it must be based.

Some people say, "But you must have something bigger than yourself, something outside yourself for which to work. A religion is necessary."

With this I can only agree wholeheartedly. Yet surely the concept of working for the improvement of interrelationships, and toward the brotherhood of *all* human beings—not just males, nor just white men, or just American men, or even just Western Hemisphere men is a concept bigger than any individual. It has power and motivating force. It is the concept which religions have always advocated though in different words and by a different approach.

I have just written of the desire and capacity of men to love their fellow man. I have faith in that. It is there in all of us—so real, so tangible, so sustaining, and so universal. Those who feel that this is "too feeble a reed on which to lean" as one seeks for something on which to base one's faith, are only saying that they have never really been close to their fellow men. Of course we can never experience this if we must always go about pretending, refusing to reveal ourselves and putting up a false front.

People have sometimes said to me, in referring to the counseling work I do, which involves working with people experiencing marital and sexual difficulties, "You hear so many stories of human misconduct and mistakes, you must lose all faith in people. I can't see how you can listen to some of the things you do, and still believe in human nature and human beings."

The experience they think should cost me my faith in people is what has actually built it. I have never worked with anyone, no matter what kind of a person they seemed to be, who didn't want to be accepted and appreciated by others, and to work in harmony with people. It sometimes takes a long time before these desires are revealed, but they are there in all people. If you could get the expression of the deep, inner wishes of any person, you would find they want to live in harmony with others, to find understanding and acceptance. In other words, they want to be moral.

Our code of moral conduct, however, needs to be based upon the innate wish for and striving to be accepted and loved, and centered about the concern for the improvement of human interrelationships. First, this is where it is properly centered. Second, this concept of morality can be understood and accepted by the religious (in a theological sense) or the non-religious, by the black or yellow man as well as the white, by educated and uneducated, by old and young. The application of the concept often takes time and study but it is understandable.

Another question which is often raised is "But don't you have to have some standards?" The tone of voice and the wording implies that the concept which has been advanced wipes out all standards. Quite the contrary! It sets up a very definite standard—this time a "thou shalt" one. "Thou shalt do those things which contribute to trust, understanding, good will, and the ultimate ability of all to work together."

The trouble when this question is raised is that people have thought so commonly of standards as acts forbidden, or permitted, that they cannot think in terms of relationships.

Initially it seems so much easier to accept authority, to draw a line and say "on this side is good, on this side is bad." But in actual life these lines fail to hold. They become blurred, or wiped out entirely. When this happens the individual ordinarily follows one of two courses. He clings rigidly (but often unhappily) to the teachings which he has never understood, and which now seem to have failed him. Or he drifts about aimlessly with no criteria to help him in the decisions he must make.

This concept of morality does not eliminate conflict in choice, or even conflict in relationships. Immediate desires and long-time objectives are not always in harmony. Nor is a relationship always a good one just because it exists. It may be a close (a better term might be smothering) relationship, but a binding, inhibiting, defeating one, and consequently not moral. The reader will remember that one of the criteria for a moral relationship was that it enabled the person continually to reach out, to move toward others, to grow in his capacity to accept, until finally he can feel brotherhood with all men everywhere.

A relationship which creates solidarity and unity in one group by making them hateful, fearful, and distrustful of other groups is not a moral relationship. This is the evil genius of excessive nationalism, or of war itself. A tremendous feeling of national unity, a sense of closeness, good will and harmony may result from fearing another nation, and/or even from the effort to thoroughly defeat, or insofar as possible, to destroy another nation. But such unity, as we have learned to our sorrow, is short-lived, and the legacy even within the victorious group is hatred, distrust, and suspicion. Immoral! Nationalistic rivalries and war can be naught but immoral.

Schools, through their students and their staffs, sometimes try to create school unity and morale through creating a rivalry which ends in distrust, suspicion, and hard feeling. They, too, have created an immoral situation.

The same thing is seen in individual lives. Parents trying to bind their children to them instead of freeing them for a mature, on-going life as independent adults have created an immoral situation. Children, at the young adult level, are sometimes in an agony because their parents are making them choose between what the parents call "loyalty" to them, and freedom and a life in their own right. The parents may try to reinforce the bonds they are forging with charges of "ingratitude" and "selfish" behavior. As a moral issue the matter is clear-cut. The child must choose the path which frees him as an individual and leads him into broader and broader relationships featured by trust and understanding. This means that the break with the parents needs to be made with as much sympathy and understanding as possible, rather than with antagonistic remarks and bitterness. But if the parents cannot see their way clear to freeing their grown children, then morally speaking, the break should come.

Moral behavior, it becomes clear, is a condition in which one is satisfactorily related to others much more than it is an intellectualized acceptance of verbal injunctions. Our entire society relies far too much on exhortation for securing our so-called moral conduct, and pays scant attention to conditions which make for trust, understanding, and love. Yet it is out of the latter ingredients that genuinely moral behavior comes.

A child who has been treated as a person, and with respect and courtesy, does not want to strike at, hurt, or deceive others. The individual who has been hurt, deceived, or degraded is the person who engages in such actions in turn. Morality, then, is created and nurtured by the kind of conditions we are able to establish in our homes, schools, and communities. It is at this point that our philosophy about life, our values, our scientific knowledge in various fields, particularly psychology, psychiatry, anthropology, and sociology, join hands to provide a mature, moral individual.

The truly moral individual is not racked with conflicting desire and constantly engaged in a struggle against degrading forces within himself. Suppose a person has had the kind of experiences in growing up which enable him to respect himself as a person. That person does not have to grit his teeth and clench both fists determinedly to keep from picking up something that doesn't belong to him every time he enters a store. Young people who are sexually moral, that is do not use sex exploitively, or to demean themselves or others, or who can think of sex in the context of a relationship, are not continually fighting to curb strong, torturing sexual desires. The person who is so afflicted and for whom moral behavior becomes a problem is over and over a person who has been made to feel demeaned or degraded himself, who has been hurt or injured, who has felt himself rejected or outcast.

This concept of morality places a high premium upon communication. The term "Communication" is used in preference to "talking," for people can do much talking with little or no communication. Communication means the ability to overcome inhibitions and to rise above conventional expressions to the point where we can discuss our real feelings. Our hopes, fears, wishes, and motivations must be expressed and given honest and thoughtful consideration if we are really to communicate. It is at this point that the relationship between the emotionally mature person and the truly moral person becomes the clearest.

It also raises extremely challenging questions about the values we hold, both individually and culturally. It calls into question our definition of progress, our assumptions about cooperation and competition, and the importance of materialistic goals. If the development of interpersonal relationships is regarded as important, we are immediately plunged into the issue of values and goals.

The price of survival on this shrinking planet is a genuine morality based on the brotherhood of man as the motivating concept.

As Kirkendall points out in *Searching for the Roots of Moral Judgments,*

> Initially, it seems . . . easier to accept authority, to draw a line and say "on this side is good, on this side is bad." But in actual life these lines fail to hold. They become blurred, or wiped out entirely. When this happens the individual. . . . clings rigidly (but often unhappily) to the teachings which he has never understood, and which now seem to have failed him. Or he drifts about aimlessly with no criteria to help him in the decisions he must make.

It has also been noted that

> when people have stuck to ideals out of the fear of what will happen when they cheat, they are helpless when that crutch is gone. Fear as a motive *is* a crutch, a sign of weakness and not of strength. [79]

Fear tends to make people obedient to what cynics have called the Eleventh Commandment, "Thou Shalt Not Be Caught."

> . . . if fear is a discarded crutch, what help have we, what other motivation? Humanists will say it must be loyalty to personal integrity and the common good, social conscience. That is part of the answer, no doubt; but I do not believe it can succeed by itself. . . . As things are now, we have to act out of love, not out of fear. [80]

How does Kirkendall in *Searching for the Roots of Moral Judgments* combine the love ethic, the loyalty to personal integrity, and the common good—social conscience—in his concept of the essence of morality?

If training in discipline, a superimposing of external values, is the hand-maiden of the fear ethic, what is its counterpart in the love ethic; that is, how does Kirkendall explain cases where "the individual has already experienced . . . many immoral relationships"?

What potential internal—rather than external—value has been corroded and submerged by relationships "obscured by cynicism, self-centeredness, and concern for personal gratification"?

How does Markham's poem "Outwitted," quoted by Kirkendall in his article, express the philosophy of the love ethic?

> Our moral standards need to apply to all behavior, rather than having a restricted meaning which associates them with just one type of behavior.

When moral judgments are based, not on whether or not an act has occurred, but, rather, on its meaning, this application of standards is possible. According to Kirkendall, what is the significant question that can serve as the ethical yard-stick for the measurement of all behavior?

How does Kirkendall define "morale" and relate it to "moral"?

Some authorities claim that normal young men and women want chastity; Kirkendall claims they want to be moral. Are the two viewpoints the same? Why, or why not?

How does Kirkendall suggest that the long interval between sexual awakening and its decently authorized expression can be handled, without early marriage or a constant struggle to control torturing sexual urges?

The Puritans and the Victorians took the position of moral absolutism based on fear of consequences and guided by negative sanctions. Contemporary views, like Kirkendall's, propose a position of moral relativism based on love and guided by positive sanctions. Why, therefore, might today's sexual crisis be considered less a "sexual revolution" than a "revolution in sexual ethics"?

What distinctions might be made between the "new morality" and the "fun morality"?

What are some of the merits of the love ethic? What are some of its limitations or dangers? How might the question: "Is the love ethic or the fear ethic easier to follow?" be debated? Would the following comment be relevant to one side, both sides, or neither side in such a debate?

> . . . human selfishness is such that I do not think most people can "identify" with their neighbors completely enough for altruistic ends. By our very constitution we are too self-centered. Psychology calls it egocentricity, theology calls it sin; in either purview it makes for only limited communality of interest. [81]

It has also been stated that

> The loyalty needed to keep modern people hewing to the line of the old ideal must . . . be born out of grace, out of the spiritual power of religious conviction. Religious faith is not needed to tell us *what* is good, but it *is* needed to make us *want* it enough to do it. [82]

In what terms does Kirkendall also establish a firm connection between a morality based on the quality of human interrelations and "religion"?

What specific kind of conditions would you try to establish if "morality is created and nurtured by the kind of conditions we are able to establish in our homes, schools and communities"?

RELATED QUESTIONS

Using Kirkendall's ethical ruler—the significant question that can serve as a measure of moral behavior—how moral or immoral would you consider each of the following, and why?

- Having sexual intercourse with a very good-looking girl after a weekend party when you had both had several beers;
- Telling your four-year-old son never to play with his "wee wee";
- The parental affection of Edward Barrett in *The Barretts of Wimpole Street* (see "**Night-Lights,**" p. 536);
- The comments made by Chris to her husband, David, in *The Silver Cord* (see "**Night-Lights,**" p. 568).

What relevance has the poem "Outwitted," quoted by Kirkendall in his article, to Fromm's theory in *The Theory of Love* (p. 260) that "love is not primarily a relationship to a specific person," but rather "an attitude, an orientation of character which determines the relatedness of a person to the world as a whole, not toward one 'object' of love"?

How does Mama's speech to her daughter Beneatha in *A Raisin in the Sun* (p. 149) suggest how "love and I" can have the wit to win, as "Outwitted" explains it?

Would you consider Kirkendall more or less extreme in his views than Neill, author of *Sex Attitudes* (p. 286)?

Immoral behavior, according to Kirkendall, creates distrust and weakens the quality of an interrelationship. Re-examine Anne Frank's discussion of trust in her May 2, 1944 entry in *The Diary of a Young Girl* (p. 136). Weighing Anne's remarks, how might Kirkendall view Mr. Frank's cautionings about his daughter's visits to the attic? How might Kirkendall assess Anne's relationship with Peter? Would Kirkendall approve Anne's decision to disobey her father, since her visits to Peter would classify as moral conduct, "that kind of behavior which enables people in their relationships with each other to experience a greater sense of trust"?

How does Anne's situation in *The Diary of a Young Girl* validate Kirkendall's assertion:

> This concept of morality does not eliminate conflict in choice, or even conflict in relationships. Immediate desires and long-time objectives are not always in harmony.

How, too, does Anne Frank's situation support the view that to act out of love, not out of fear requires mature people?

The Symposium, or "Drinking Together," is a dialogue of Plato (c. 428–347 B.C.) comprising a series of speeches by Socrates and other guests made at a supper party. The professional entertainer provided by the host has been dismissed; instead, the guests speak in praise of Love and all its degrees. The first speaker extolls love as the most helpful of the gods toward the attainment of virtue; but another guest, Pausanias, who speaks in the following excerpt, is more cautious and distinguishes between the higher love of the soul and the lower love of the body, thus making Love not one, but two.

The Symposium

PLATO

We agreed that love itself, as such, was neither good nor bad, but only in so far as it led to good or bad behavior. It is base to indulge a vicious lover viciously, but noble to gratify a virtuous lover virtuously. Now the vicious lover is the follower of the earthly Love who desires the body rather than the soul; his heart is set on what is mutable and must therefore be inconstant. And as soon as the body he loves begins to pass the first flower of its beauty, he 'spreads his wings and flies away,' giving the lie to all his pretty speeches and dishonoring his vows, whereas the lover whose heart is touched by moral beauties is constant all his life, for he has become one with what will never fade.

Now it is the object of the Athenian law to make a firm distinction between the lover who should be encouraged and the lover who should be shunned. And so it enjoins pursuit in certain cases, and flight in others, and applies various touchstones and criteria to discriminate between the two classes of lover and beloved. And this is why it is immoral, according to our code, to yield too promptly to solicitation; there should first be a certain lapse of time, which is generally considered to be the most effective test. Secondly, it is immoral when the surrender is due to financial or political considerations, or to unmanly fear of ill-treatment; it is immoral, in short, if the youth fails to show the contempt he should for any advantage he may gain in pocket or position. For in motives such as these we can find nothing fixed or permanent, except, perhaps, the certainty that they have never been the cause of any noble friendship.

There remains, therefore, only one course open to the beloved if he is to yield to his lover without offending our ideas of decency. It is held that, just as the lover's willing and complete subjection to his beloved is neither abject nor culpable, so there is one other form of voluntary submission that shall be blameless—a submission which is made for the sake of virtue. And so, gentlemen, if anyone is prepared to devote himself to the service of another in the belief that through him he will find increase of wisdom or of any other virtue, we hold that such willing servitude is neither base nor abject.

Such, then, is the Love of the heavenly Aphrodite, heavenly in himself and precious alike to cities and to men, for he constrains both lover and beloved to pay the most earnest heed to their moral welfare, but all the rest are followers of the other, the earthly Aphrodite.

What distinction is made between "vicious" and "virtuous" lovers in *The Symposium*?

What are the various "touchstones and criteria used to discriminate between the two classes of lover and beloved": those to be encouraged and those to be shunned?

How does Plato's "vicious lover" exemplify qualities which might be considered exploitative today? Who, among the characters encountered thus far in this book, might serve as an example of a "vicious lover"?

Considering the time during which *The Symposium* was written, how "new" or "revolutionary" is the new morality?

RELATED QUESTIONS

How do Kirkendall in *Searching for the Roots of Moral Judgments* (p. 295) and Singer in *Appraisal and Bestowal* (p. 217) echo the Greek idea that "love itself, as such, [is] neither good nor bad, but only in so far as it [leads] to good or bad behavior"?

In which of the three classifications of sexual morality outlined by Warren Johnson in *Some Observations on Sexual Morality* (p. 276) would you place this excerpt from *The Symposium?*

Situation Ethics

JOSEPH FLETCHER

The situationist enters into every decision-making situation fully armed with the ethical maxims of his community and its heritage, and he treats them with respect as illuminators of his problems. Just the same he is prepared in any situation to compromise them or set them aside *in the situation* if love seems better served by doing so.

Situation ethics goes part of the way with natural law, by accepting reason as the instrument of moral judgment, while rejecting the notion that the good is "given" in the nature of things, objectively. It goes part of the way with Scriptural law by accepting revelation as the source of the norm while rejecting all "revealed" norms or laws but the one command—to love God in the neighbor. The situationist follows a moral law or violates it according to love's need. For example, "Almsgiving is a good thing *if* . . ." The situationist never says, "Almsgiving is a good thing. Period!" His decisions are hypothetical, not categorical. Only the commandment to love is categorically good. "Owe no one anything, except to love one another." (Rom. 13:8). If help to an indigent only pauperizes and degrades him, the situationist refuses a handout and finds some other way. . . . The legalist says that even if he tells a man escaped from an asylum where his intended victim is, if he finds and murders him, at least only one sin has been committed (murder), not two (lying as well)!

. . . We might say, from the situationist's perspective, that it is possible to derive general "principles" from whatever is the one and only universal law (*agapē* for Christians, something else for others), but not laws or rules. We cannot milk universals from a universal!

William Temple put it this way: "Universal obligation attaches not to particular judgments of conscience but to conscientiousness. What acts are right may depend on circumstances . . . but there is an absolute obligation to will whatever may on each occasion be right."* Our obligation is relative *to* the situation, but obligation *in* the situation is absolute. We are only "obliged" to tell the truth, for example, if the situation calls for it; if a murderer asks us his victim's whereabouts, our duty might be to lie. . . . We have to find out what is "fitting" to be truly ethical, to use H. R. Niebuhr's word for it in his *The Responsible Self.*‡ Situation ethics aims at a contextual appropriateness—not the "good" or the "right" but the *fitting*.

A cartoon in a fundamentalist magazine once showed Moses scowling, holding his stone tablet with its graven laws, all ten, and an eager stonecutter saying to him, "Aaron said perhaps you'd let us reduce them to 'Act responsibly in love.'" This was meant as a dig at the situationists and the new morality, but the legalist humor in it merely states exactly what situation ethics calls for! . . .

One competent situationist, speaking to students, explained the position this way. Rules are "like 'Punt on fourth down,' or 'Take a pitch when the count is three balls.' These rules are part of the wise player's know-how, and distinguish him from the novice. But they are not unbreakable. The best players are those

---

Nature, Man and God (The Macmillan Company, 1934), p. 405.
‡(Harper & Row, Publishers, Inc., 1963), pp. 60–61.

who know when to ignore them. In the game of bridge, for example, there is a useful rule which says 'Second hand low.' But have you ever played with anyone who followed the rule slavishly? You say to him (in exasperation), 'Partner, why didn't you play your ace? We could have set the hand.' And he replies, unperturbed, 'Second hand low!' What is wrong? The same thing that was wrong when Kant gave information to the murderer. He forgot the purpose of the game. . . . He no longer thought of winning the hand, but of being able to justify himself by invoking the rule."‡‡

[The core of the situation ethic] is a healthy and primary awareness that "circumstances alter cases"—i.e., that in actual problems of conscience the situational variables are to be weighed as heavily as the normative or "general" constants.

The situational factors are so primary that we may even say "circumstances alter rules and principles." . . . It is antimoralistic as well as antilegalistic, for it is sensitive to variety and complexity. It is neither simplistic nor perfectionist. . . . It is case-focused and concrete, concerned to bring Christian imperatives into practical operation. . . . It works with two guidelines from Paul: "The written code kills, but the Spirit gives life" (II Cor. 3:6), and "For the whole law is fulfilled in one word, 'You shall love your neighbor as yourself'" (Gal. 5:14).

. . . [Situation] ethics "must not be understood as an escape from the heavy burden of moral integrity. For, though its advocates truly deny the absolute value of universal norms, some are motivated by the belief that in this manner they are better safeguarding the eminent sovereignty of God."§

As we shall see, *Christian* situation ethics has only one norm or principle or law (call it what you will) that is binding and unexceptionable, always good and right regardless of the circumstances. That is "love"—the *agapē* of the summary commandment to love God and the neighbor. || Everything else without exception, all laws and rules and principles and ideals and norms, are only *contingent,* only valid *if they happen* to serve love in any situation. Christian situation ethics is not a system or program of living according to a code, but . . . the strategy of love. . . .

In non-Christian situation ethics some other highest good or *summum bonum* will, of course, take love's place as the one and only standard—such as self-realization in the ethics of Aristotle. But the *Christian* is neighbor-centered first and last. Love is for people, not for principles, i.e., it is personal—and therefore when the impersonal universal conflicts with the personal particular, the latter prevails in situation ethics.

PRINCIPLES, YES, BUT NOT RULES

It is necessary to insist that situation ethics is willing to make full and respectful use of principles, to be treated as maxims but not as laws or precepts.

‡‡ E. LaB. Cherbonnier, unpublished address, Trinity College, December 14, 1964.
§ Article, "Morality, Situation," in *Dictionary of Moral Theology,* ed. by Francesco Cardinal Roberti and Msgr. Pietro Palazzini (The Newman Press, 1962), pp. 800–802.
|| Matt. 5:43–48 and ch. 22:34–40; Luke 6:27–28; 10:25–28 and vs. 29–37; Mark 12:28–34; Gal. 5:14; Rom. 13:8–10; etc.

We might call it "principled relativism." . . . Principles or maxims or general rules are *illuminators*. But they are not *directors*. The classic rule of moral theology has been to follow laws but do it *as much as possible* according to love and according to reason. . . . Situation ethics, on the other hand, calls upon us to keep law in a subservient place, so that *only* love and reason really count when the chips are down! . . . Bishop Robinson says: "Such an ethic [situationism] cannot but rely, in deep humility, upon guiding rules, upon the cumulative experience of one's own and other people's obedience. It is this bank of experience which gives us our working rules of 'right' and 'wrong,' and without them we could not but flounder."¶ Nevertheless, in situation ethics even the most revered principles may be thrown aside if they conflict in any concrete case with love. Even Karl Barth, who writes vehemently of "absolutely wrong" actions, allows for what he calls the *ultima ratio*, the outside chance that love in a particular situation might override the absolute. The instance he gives is abortion.**

Using the terms made popular by Tillich and others, we may say that Christian situationism is a method that proceeds, so to speak, from (1) its one and only law, *agapē* (love), to (2) the *sophia* (wisdom) of the church and culture, containing many "general rules" of more or less reliability, to (3) the *kairos* (moment of decision, the fullness of time) in which *the responsible self in the situation* decides whether the *sophia* can serve love there, or not. This is the situational strategy in capsule form. To legalists it will seem to treat the *sophia* without enough reverence and obedience.

ABORTION: A SITUATION

In 1962 a patient in a state mental hospital raped a fellow patient, an unmarried girl ill with a radical schizophrenic psychosis. The victim's father, learning what had happened, charged the hospital with culpable negligence and requested that an abortion to end the unwanted pregnancy be performed at once, in an early stage of the embryo. The staff and administrators of the hospital refused to do so, on the ground that the criminal law forbids all abortion except "therapeutic" ones when the mother's life is at stake—because the *moral* law, it is supposed, holds that any interference with an embryo after fertilization is murder, i.e., the taking of an innocent human being's life.

Let's relate [two] ethical approaches to this situation. The rape has occurred and the decisional question is: May we rightly (licitly) terminate this pregnancy, begun in an act of force and violence by a mentally unbalanced rapist upon a frightened, mentally sick girl? Mother and embryo are apparently healthy on all the usual counts.

The legalists would say *NO*. Their position is that killing is absolutely wrong, inherently evil. It is permissible only as self-defense and in military service, which is held to be presumptive self-defense or justifiable homicide. If the mother's life is threatened, abortion is therefore justified, but for no other reasons. (Many doctors take an elastic view of "life" and thereby justify abortions

¶ *Honest to God,* pp. 119–120.
** Church Dogmatics (Edinburgh: T. & T. Clark, 1961), Vol. III, Bk. 4, pp. 420–421.

to save a patient's *mental* life as well as physical.) Even in cases where they justify it, it is only *excused*—it is still held to be inherently evil. Many Protestants hold this view, and some humanists.

Catholic moral theology goes far beyond even the rigid legalism of the criminal law, absolutizing their prohibition of abortion *absolutely,* by denying all exceptions and calling even therapeutic abortion wrong. (They allow killing in self-defense against malicious, i.e., deliberate, aggressors but not in self-defense against innocent, i.e., unintentional, aggressors.) Thus if it is a tragic choice of the mother's life or the baby's, as can happen in rare cases, neither can be saved.

To this ethical nightmare legalism replies: "It is here that the Church appears merciless, but she is not. It is her logic which is merciless; and she promises that if the logic is followed the woman will receive a reward far greater than a number of years of life."‡‡‡ Inexplicably, shockingly, Dietrich Bonhoeffer says the same thing: "The life of the mother is in the hand of God, but the life of the child is arbitrarily extinguished. The question whether the life of the mother or the life of the child is of greater value can hardly be a matter for a human decision."‡‡‡‡

The situationists, if their norm is the Christian commandment to love the neighbor, would almost certainly, *in this case,* favor abortion and support the girl's father's request. (Many purely humanistic decision makers are of the same mind about abortion following rape, and after incest too.) They would in all likelihood favor abortion for the sake of the patient's physical and mental health, not only if it were needed to save her life. It is even likely they would favor abortion for the sake of the victim's self-respect or reputation or happiness or simply on the ground that *no unwanted and unintended* baby should ever be born.

They would, one hopes, reason that it is *not* killing because there is no person or human life in an embryo at an early stage of pregnancy (Aristotle and St. Thomas held that opinion), or even if it *were* killing, it would not be murder because it is self-defense against, in this case, not one but *two* aggressors. First there is the rapist, who being insane was morally and legally innocent, and then there is the "innocent" embryo which is continuing the ravisher's original aggression! Even self-defense legalism would have allowed the girl to kill her attacker, no matter that he was innocent in the forum of conscience because of his madness. The embryo is no more innocent, no less an aggressor or unwelcome invader! Is not the most loving thing possible (the right thing) in this case a responsible decision to terminate the pregnancy?

What think ye?

SOME PRESUPPOSITIONS

The heart of this explanation of situation ethics lies in its six propositions. . . . But there are a few preliminary matters to be made plain first, in the reader's

‡‡‡ Alan Keenan, O.F.M., and John Ryan, M.D., *Marriage: A Medical and Sacramental Study* (Sheed & Ward, Inc., 1955), p. 53.
‡‡‡‡ *Ethics,* p. 131n.

interest, so that he can know what *presuppositions* are at work. There are four of them. If need be, then, he can correct for any bias he thinks they are imposing. Their labels look far more technical and up in the air than they really are.

FOUR WORKING PRINCIPLES

1. Pragmatism

. . . Philosophy is utterly useless as a way to bridge the gap between doubt and faith. . . . [We must appreciate] the importance of the contextual or situational, i.e., the *circumstantial* approach to the search for the right and the good. We have seen the light when we recognize that abstract and conceptual morality is a mare's nest.

The pragmatic method is a legitimate tool of ethics. American pragmatism and British empiricism have always trained their sights primarily on Pilate's question, "What is truth?" The ethical question, on the other hand, is, What is good? Yet the *verum* and the *bonum* (and for that matter, the *pulchrum* as well) are not really separable matters.

As James called truth and goodness expediency, so John Dewey saw them as what gives *satisfaction,* and F. C. S. Schiller as what *works.* §§ All are agreed: the good is what works, what is expedient, what gives satisfaction. Socrates' question, "What is goodness?" gets from pragmatism the same answer Pilate's does. The good, it replies, like the true, is whatever works.

We must realize, however, that pragmatism, as such, is no self-contained world view. It is a method, precisely. It is not a substantive faith, and properly represented it never pretends to be. Pragmatism of itself yields none of the norms we need to measure or verify the very success that pragmatism calls for! To be correct or right a thing—a thought or an action—must *work.* Yes. But work to what end, for what purpose, to satisfy what standard or ideal or norm? Like any other method, pragmatism as such is utterly without any way of answering this question. Yet this is the decisive question.

The very first question in all ethics is, *What* do I want? Only after this is settled (pleasure in hedonism, adjustment in naturalism, self-realization in eudaemonism, etc.) can we ask about the *why* and the *how* and the *who* and the *when* and the *where* and the *which!* The primary issue is the "value" problem, our choice of our *summum bonum.* This is a *pre*ethical or metaethical question, relying on some other source for a faith proposition or commitment. . . .

Christianly speaking, as we shall see, the norm or measure by which any thought or action is to be judged a success or failure, i.e., right or wrong, is *love.* . . . The situationist, whether a Christian or not, follows a strategy that is pragmatic. . . .

§§ See Dewey's *The Quest for Certainty* (Minton, Balch & Co., 1929) and *Ethics,* with J. H. Tufts (Henry Holt, 1908); F. C. S. Schiller's *Problems of Belief* (London: Hodder & Stoughton, Ltd., 1924); G. H. Mead's *Mind, Self, and Society* (1934) and *The Philosophy of the Act* (1938), both ed. by C. W. Morris (The University of Chicago Press).

2. Relativism

In our attempt to be situational, to be contemporary in our understanding of conscience, we can pin another label on our method. It is *relativistic.* As the strategy is pragmatic, the tactics are relativistic. . . . The situationist avoids words like "never" and "perfect" and "always" and "complete" as he avoids the plague, as he avoids "absolutely." . . .

To be relative, of course, means to be relative *to* something. To be "absolutely relative" (an uneasy combination of terms) is to be inchoate, random, unpredictable, unjudgeable, meaningless, amoral—rather in the antinomian mode. There must be an absolute or norm of some kind if there is to be any true relativity. This is the central fact in the normative relativism of a situation ethic. It is not anarchic (i.e., without an *archē,* an ordering principle). In *Christian* situationism the ultimate criterion is, as we shall be seeing, "agapeic love." It relativizes the absolute, it does not absolutize the relative!

. . . the divine command is always the same in its *Why* but always different in its *What,* or changeless as to the *What* but contingent as to the *How.* We are always, that is to say, commanded to act lovingly, but how to do it depends on our own *responsible* estimate of the situation. Only love is a constant; everything else is a variable. The shift to relativism carries contemporary Christians away from code ethics, away from stern iron-bound do's and don'ts, away from prescribed conduct and legalistic morality.

3. Positivism

A third presupposition is "positivism." In the case of Christian ethics this means theological positivism. When we get right down to it there are really only two ways to approach "religious knowledge" or belief. . . . One is theological *naturalism,* in which reason adduces or deduces faith propositions from human experience and natural phenomena; nature yields the evidences, natural reason grasps them. Natural theology, so-called, and "natural law" ethics are examples of this method.

The other approach is theological *positivism* (or "positive theology"), in which faith propositions are "posited" or affirmed voluntaristically rather than rationalistically. It is a-rational but not ir-rational, outside reason but not against it. Its starting point is . . . thinking supported by faith rather than faith supported by thinking. Although it does not exclude reason, reason goes to work because of the commitment and in its service. Thus Christian ethics "posits" faith in God and *reasons* out what obedience to his commandment to love requires in any situation. God's existence and belief that Christ is God in man cannot be proved, any more than a Marxist can prove that history is headed for Communism and that labor is the sole source of commodity value.

But how, then, does positive thought play a part in *non*-Christian ethics? [For example,] the simple hedonism of a Hugh Hefner (editor of *Playboy*)? . . . Any moral or value judgment in ethics, like a theologian's faith proposition, is a *decision*—not a conclusion. It is a choice, not a result reached by force of logic, Q.E.D. The hedonist cannot "prove" that pleasure is the highest good, any more than the Christian can "prove" his faith that *love* is! . . . Love like good itself is axiomatic, ostensive, categorical, like blue or sour or anything else that simply is what it is, a "primary" not definable in terms of something else. There is no way under heaven of proving that the Supreme Court was "right" in decreeing in 1954 that public schools "should" and "must" ignore racial differences in their admissions policies. This is why the end product of the judicial procedure is called a *decision,* not a conclusion. Reason can note facts and infer relations, but it cannot find values (goodness).

Value choices are made and normative standards embraced in a fashion every bit as arbitrary and absurd as the leap of faith. . . .
. . . Believers or unbelievers (theologically speaking), we are all bound to acknowledge that we simply cannot climb across the gap from descriptive to prescriptive propositions; from "is" statements to "ought" statements. We have to make jumps, faith leaps. They are not steps in logic or even in common sense.
In moral theology, or, if you prefer, theological morals or Christian ethics, the key category of love *(agapē)* as the axiomatic value is established by *deciding* to say, "Yea" to the faith assertion that "God is love" and thence by logic's inference to the value assertion that love is the highest good. . . .

. . . Ethical decisions seek justification, whereas cognitive conclusions seek verification. We cannot verify moral choices. They may be vindicated, but not validated.

The faith comes first. The Johannine proposition (I John 4: 7–12) is not that God is *love* but that *God* is love! The Christian does not understand God in terms of love; he understands love in terms of God as seen in Christ. "We love, because he first loved us." This obviously is a faith foundation for love. Paul's phrase (Gal. 5:6), "faith working through love," is the essence and pith of Christian ethics. *Nevertheless,* a perfectly sincere man, in every way as intelligent and wise as any Christian might be, can refuse to put any stock whatever in Christ, in which case he might in all seriousness also doubt the hope and love that Paul linked to faith in his triad of theological virtues (I Cor., ch. 13). But still, these are the faith commitments which identify the Christian.

4. Personalism

Ethics deals with human relations.‖ ‖ Situation ethics puts people at the center of concern, not things. Obligation is to persons, not to things; to subjects, not objects. The legalist is a *what* asker (What does the law say?); the situationist is a *who* asker (Who is to be helped?). That is, situationists are *personalistic.* In the Christian version, for example, a basic maxim is that the disciple is commanded to love people, not principles or laws or objects or any other *thing.*
There are no "values" in the sense of inherent goods—value is what *happens to* something when it happens to be useful to love working for the sake of persons. . . . Anything, material or immaterial, is "good" only because it is good for or to somebody.

‖ ‖ A fine essay on ethics as relational is H. R. Niebuhr, "The Center of Value," *Moral Principles of Action,* ed. by R. N. Anshen (Harper & Brothers, 1952), pp. 162–175.

And just as good derives from the needs of people, so people derive from society. There is nothing individualistic about personalism, nor in situation ethics. . . . Only people can exercise the freedom that is essential in the forum of conscience for decision-making. Only free persons, capable of being "the responsible self," can sustain relationship and thereby enter the field of obligation.

In *Christian* situation ethics, there is also a theological side to personalism, since God is "personal" and has created men in his own image—*imago Dei.* Personality is *therefore* the first-order concern in ethical choices. Kant's second maxim holds: Treat persons as ends, never as means. Even if in some situations a material thing is chosen rather than a person, it will be (if it is Christianly done) for the sake of the person, not for the sake of the thing itself. If a man prefers to keep his money invested instead of giving it to his son who needs it, it could only be because he believes his son will need it far more urgently later on. To repeat, values are only extrinsically, never intrinsically, "valuable." Love is of people, by people, and for people. Things are to be used; people are to be loved. It is "immoral" when people are used and things are loved. Loving actions are the *only* conduct permissible.

If we put these working principles together (pragmatism, relativism, positivism, and personalism), their shape is obviously one of action, *existence*, eventfulness. The situation ethic, unlike some other kinds, is an ethic of *decision*—of *making* decisions rather than "looking them up" in a manual of prefab rules. . . . It does not ask *what* is good but *how* to do good for *whom;* not what *is* love but how to *do* the most loving thing possible in the situation. It focuses upon *pragma* (doing), not upon *dogma* (some tenet). . . .

CONSCIENCE

[In] situation ethics . . . "conscience" is merely a word for . . . attempts to make decisions creatively, constructively, fittingly. . . .

Another feature of situation ethics is its concern with antecedent rather than consequent conscience, i.e., with prospective decision-making rather than with retrospective judgment-passing.

Only one "general" proposition is prescribed, namely, the commandment to love God through the neighbor. And this commandment is, be it noted, a normative ideal; it is *not* an operational directive. All else, all other generalities (e.g., "One should tell the truth" and "One should respect life") are at most only *maxims,* never rules. For the situationist there are no rules—none at all.

LOVE IS A PREDICATE

Apart from the helping or hurting of people, ethical judgments or evaluations are meaningless. Having as its supreme norm the neighbor love commanded of Christians, Christian situation ethics asserts firmly and definitely: *Value, worth, ethical quality, goodness or badness, right or wrong—these things are only predicates, they are not properties.* They are not "given" or objectively "real" or self-existent.¶¶ There is only one thing that is always good and right, intrinsically good regardless of the context, and that one thing is love. . . .

But love is not a substantive—nothing of the kind. It is a principle, a "formal" principle, expressing what type of real actions Christians are to call good. (Exactly the same is true of justice.) It is the *only* principle that always obliges us in conscience. Unlike all other principles you might mention, love alone when well served is always good and right in every situation. Love is the only universal. But love is not something we *have* or *are*, it is something we *do*. Our task is to act so that more good (i.e., loving-kindness) will occur than any possible alternatives; we are to be "optimific," to seek an optimum of loving-kindness. It is an attitude, a disposition, a leaning, a preference, a purpose.

When we say that love is always good, what we mean is that whatever is loving in any *particular* situation is good! Love is a way of relating to persons, and of using things.

Christian love is not desire. *Agapē* is giving love—nonreciprocal, neighbor-regarding—"neighbor" meaning "everybody," even an enemy (Luke 6:32–35). It is usually distinguished from friendship love *(philia)* and romantic love *(erōs)*, both of which are selective and exclusive. Erotic love and philic love have their proper place in our human affairs but they are not what is meant by *agapē*, agapeic love or "Christian love." Erotic and philic love are emotional, but the effective principle of Christian love is *will*, disposition; it is an *attitude*, not feeling.

. . . Love, unlike law, sets no carefully calculated limits on obligation; it seeks the most good possible in every situation. It maximizes or optimizes obligation.

When a woman is viciously attacked, fifty neighbors watch without helping, without even calling the police. A farmer destroys his barn to keep a fire from spreading to his neighbor's property, but the neighbor won't help to compensate the farmer. An indifferent passer-by watches a baby drown. A motorist sees a wheel wobbling loose on the car in front of him but merely slows down to keep out of the way of a pileup. American and English law on principle do not have a "good Samaritan" provision (Germany, Italy, the Soviet Union, France, do). The Anglo-American principle is "Mind your own business"; the law limits your obligation, you are responsible only for what you do—not for what you should or could have done. This is the prudence of self-centeredness and indifference, contrasted to the aggressive, questing prudence of *agapē*.

A noteworthy complaint is that situation ethics presumes more ability to know the facts and weigh them than most people can muster. It is true that all of us are limited in how much we know about things, and how competent we are to evaluate even what little we know or think we know. This is very plainly the case in foreign affairs. . . .

But in his more immediate situation he must make his own decisions, and should. If it is true that one's opinions are no better than his facts, then situation

¶¶ A philosophical defense of the predicative concept is in Stephen Toulmin, *An Examination of the Place of Reason in Ethics* (Cambridge: Cambridge University Press, 1950). He successfully attacks the "non-natural" property thesis of G. E. Moore.

ethics puts a high premium on our knowing what's what when we act. We are always free and often well advised to call in expert and professional advice *if we choose* to call upon it. But if law cuts down our range of free initiative and personal responsibility, by doing our thinking for us, we are so much the less for it as persons. Law easily undermines political freedom (democracy) and personal freedom (grace).

Situation ethics aims to widen freedom, which is the other face of responsibility. As much as he can, the situationist will prevent law's Procrusteanly squeezing down an iron system of prefabricated decisions upon free people in living situations. . . .

If it is supposed that the situational method of moral decision-making is too open to a conscious or unconscious rationalizing of selfish and evasive motives, we need only to remember that self-deceit and excuse-making can exploit *law* too for its own purposes, often as easily as it uses freedom. Our real motives can hide as effectively behind rules as behind free contextual choices. Law is a common camouflage, and makes a much better disguise. It is harder to hide double-dealing when you have no protective cover of law. Being legally right may mean nothing at all morally, as any acquaintance with money lenders and technical virgins will show. H. G. Wells once said that a lot of moral indignation is "only jealousy with a halo."

The old cracker-barrel phrase is: "We can't legislate morals." Experience with sex laws, as with the "noble experiment" of prohibition in the twenties, seems to support that idea. But sometimes law can encourage and inculcate higher standards of behavior, not reflecting present mores but nurturing and pioneering better ones. Situationists acknowledge that law and order are not only necessary but actually good, wherever and whenever they promote the best interests of love.

Christian ethics is concerned not only with a remedy for sin (moral evil), as in discrimination against Negroes, but also with the *restraint* of it. It needs both love-justice and law-order. Indeed, each presupposes the other. Situation ethics welcomes law for love's sake sometimes, all depending. . . .

. . . Law and freedom from law can be duties, but love is the basic principle.

In this connection we should note that the strategy of civil disobedience poses the problem neatly. We ought not to hesitate to break a law that is in all conscience unjust, that is to say, unloving. . . . But neither the state nor its laws is boss for the situationist; when there is a conflict, he decides for the higher law of love.*** He has to weigh immediate and remote consequences as well as local and broader interests, but if the scales go against law, so does he.

If his disobedience is ethical, not sheer outlawry, he will be open and above-board about it. His disobedience will be a witness to love-justice, and doing it in plain view will be his acknowledgment of order's reasonable claims.‡‡‡‡ The serious subversive is never clandestine. . . .

*** One Christian moralist condemns this view, R. C. Mortimer, *Christian Ethics* (London: Hutchinson's Universal Library, 1950), pp. 57ff.

‡‡‡‡ See J. A. Pike's thoughtful discussion, *Doing the Truth*, rev. ed. (The Macmillan Company, 1965), pp. 98–102, 106–108.

Love Is Not Liking

The Fourth Proposition: "Love wills the neigh-
bor's good whether we like him or not."

To love Christianly is a matter of attitude, not feeling. Love is discerning and critical; it is not sentimental. . . . Christian love is definitely agapeic, not erotic nor philic (not a question of romance or friendship). . . . That is, it is neighbor-concerned, outgoing, not self-concerned or selective. . . .

NEVER SENTIMENTALIZE LOVE

In Canon Quick's sensitive expression, "Whereas in *erōs* desire is the cause of love, in *agapē* love is the cause of desire.‡‡‡‡‡ *Agapē's* desire is to satisfy the neighbor's need, not one's own, but the main thing about it is that *agapē* love precedes all desire, of any kind.

A young unmarried couple might decide, if they make their decisions Christianly, to have intercourse (e.g., by getting pregnant to force a selfish parent to relent his overbearing resistance to their marriage). But as Christians they would merely say, "It's all right if we *like* each other!" Loving concern can make it all right, but mere liking cannot.

Pinned down to its precise meaning, Christian love is benevolence, literally. Goodwill. Unfortunately for us in our age, if we have any wish to stick with the New Testament's glossary of terms, the words "benevolence" and "goodwill" have by common usage taken on a tepid, almost merely polite meaning. Nevertheless, this is what Christian love is. It does not seek the deserving, nor is it judgmental when it makes its decisions—judgmental, that is, about the people it wants to serve. *Agapē* goes out to our neighbors not for our own sakes nor for theirs, really, but for God's. We can say quite plainly and colloquially that Christian love is the business of loving the unlovable, i.e., the *unlikable*.

. . . To suppose that we are required by any Christian imperative to like everybody is a cheap hypocrisy ethically and an impossibility psychologically. People often point out, quite reasonably and properly, that "it is impossible to love in obedience to a command" and that to ask it of us only encourages hypocrisy, "since all men are not lovable."§§§ Both objections are correct. But only if we *sentimentalize* love, taking it to be a matter of feeling or emotion, could they be true objections to *agapē*. Loving and liking are not the same thing.

. . . But the question remains, *how* are we to "love ourselves in the right way"? How are we to transform self-centered self-love into self-love for the sake of others? . . .

Bernard of Clairvaux, in a mystical and monkish essay, once outlined a

‡‡‡‡‡ *The Doctrines of the Creed* (Charles Scribner's Sons, 1938), p. 54.
§§§ cf. E. B. Redlich, *The Forgiveness of Sins* (Edinburgh: T. & T. Clark, 1937), pp. 294-295.

"ladder" by which we may climb: It goes from (1) love of self for self's sake, to (2) love of God, yet still for self's sake, to (3) love of God for God's sake, to (4) love of self, once more, but this time for God's sake and not one's own.|||||| In the same way, surely, we can see how it is possible, by a parallel, to ascend the ladder of neighbor-love: from (1) love of ourself for our own sake, to (2) love of our neighbor for our own sake, to (3) love of neighbor for the neighbor's sake, to (4) love of ourself again, but now *for the right reason,* i.e., for the neighbor's sake.

. . . The logic of love is that self-concern is obligated to cancel neighbor-good whenever *more* neighbor-good will be served through serving the self. The self is to be served rather than any neighbor if *many* neighbors are served through serving the self. This is strictly parallel to love's problem when facing a conflict between one neighbor's good and another's. We do not prefer one neighbor to another, but we *do* prefer the neighbor whose need is greater, and we prefer to serve *more* neighbors rather than fewer.

Therefore the ship's captain or the plane's pilot or the wagon train's or safari's master and scout—these are to keep themselves alive, even at the expense of some passengers, if need be, when disaster threatens all. This is tragedy—of the kind that is enacted constantly in peace and war. Who could seriously disagree with the situationist's opinion that the President of the United States, in the event of a bomb attack, should disregard all cries of fear, pain, and helplessness around him, and scuttle "callously" for the safety of his shelter, where his special knowledge could be brought to bear for millions of others?

The two commandments in the love Summary are really only one, and the three objects of love (God, neighbor, and self) unite its work; they do not divide it. All love is *amor sui,* self-love, i.e., all love seeks its own good. For Christians, self-love may be either right or wrong love, depending upon the good sought and the situation. If we love ourselves for our own sakes, that is wrong. If we love ourselves for God's sake and the neighbor's, then self-love is right. For to love God and the neighbor is to love one's self in the right way; to love one's neighbor is to respond to God's love in the right way; to love one's self in the right way is to love God and one's neighbors.

CALCULATION IS NOT CRUEL

All of this is thoughtful love, careful as well as care-full. It is a matter of intelligence, not sentiment. Nothing is as complex and difficult as ethics, even Christian love ethics, *once we have cut loose from law's oversimplifying pre-tailored rules, once we become situational.*

Moral choices need intelligence as much as they need concern, sound information as well as good disposition. To be "good" we have to get rid of innocence. The Victorian advice, "Be good, sweet maid, and let who will be clever," is false. The sweet maid *has* to be clever to be good.

|||||| *On the Love of God (De diligendo Deo)* newly tr. by a Religious of C.S.M.V. (Morehouse-Gorham, Inc., 1950), pp. 56–69.

Even the radical principle of enemy-love has to be qualified in the calculations of the situation; it is right to deal lovingly with the enemy *unless to do so hurts too many friends.* The enemy-neighbor has no stronger claims than a friend-neighbor, after all. In the old heart tugger, "Which should you save if you can carry only one from a burning building, the baby or Da Vinci's *Mona Lisa?*" you take the baby if you are a personalist. There are copies and photos of the painting. But if the choice is between your own father and a medical genius who has discovered a cure for a common fatal disease, you carry out the genius if you understand *agapē.* This is the agapeic calculus. . . . We choose what is most "useful" for the most people.

In Italy during World War II a priest in the underground resistance bombed a Nazi freight train. The occupying authorities began killing twenty hostages a day, "until the saboteur surrendered." When asked if he refused to give himself up because he intended to do more heroic deeds, the priest said, "No. There is no other priest available and our people's souls need my absolution for their eternal salvation." After three days a Communist, a fellow resistance fighter, betrayed the priest to stop the carnage. One may accept the priest's assumptions about salvation or not (the Communist evidently did not), but no situationist could quarrel with his *method* of ethical analysis and decision.

Only those who sentimentalize and subjectivize love look upon calculation and "figuring the angles" as cold or cruel or inimical or a betrayal of "love's warmth." . . . Love might even disguise itself, distort its face, pretend to be other than it is. In a TV play, *The Bitter Choice,* a nurse in a military hospital deliberately makes wounded soldiers hate her enough to motivate them to get them on their feet again and out of her care on the way to full recovery! Love can simulate, it can calculate. Otherwise, it is like the bride who wanted to ignore all recipes and simply let her love for her husband guide her when baking him a cake.

Make no mistake about it; love can not only make people angry, it can *be* angry too. Love makes judgments; it does not say, "Forget it" but, "Forgive it." It may not hate the sinner but it hates the sin, to use an old but fundamentally true bromide. . . .

Again, to love is not necessarily to please. *Agapē* is not gratification. It has often been remarked that the golden rule should read, "Do unto others as they would have you do unto them"—that its classic form, "as you would have them do unto you" is self-centered, cutting its cloth according to what *you* want rather than what the neighbor wants. But to accept this revision would be too close to "disinterested" love; it would be *neutral* love, which is too close to indifference. For *agapē* is concerned for the neighbor, ultimately, for God's sake; certainly not for the self's, but not even for the neighbor's own sake only. Christian love, for example, cannot give heroin to an addict just because he wants it. Or, at least, if the heroin is given, it will be given as part of a cure. And the same with all pleas—sex, alms, food, anything. All parents know this.

It is sentimental, simplistic, and romantically backward to "feel" that love cannot or ought not calculate; that it is either demeaned or diluted by having a memory, making future references, counting people, trying to figure the angles, finding its mix of alternatives and trying to win the game of optimum choice. Very much to the contrary, love grows up, is matured and actualized, when it permits a reasonable fire to warm its work but seeks more and more light, less and less heat. The heat it can leave to romance.

Love's business is not to play favorites or find friends or to "fall" for some one-and-only. It plays the field, universalizes its concern, has a social interest, is no respecter of persons.

Once we realize and truly accept that only love is good in and of itself, and that no act apart from its foreseeable consequences has any *ethical* meaning whatsoever—only then will we see that the right question to ask is, Does an evil means always nullify a good end? And the answer, on a basis of what is sometimes called "due proportion," must be, *"No."* It always depends upon the situation. When people oppose government lotteries because "gambling is wrong" they are petrified legalists; when they conclude against them as a policy carrying more evil than good, we can take them seriously—even if we do not agree.

We could, we might, decide that the whore in the Greek movie *Never on Sunday,* was right. In Piraeus near Athens she finds a young sailor who is afraid he cannot function sexually as an adult and virile man, and suffers as a prey to corrosive self-doubt and nonidentity. She manages things deliberately (i.e., responsibly) so that he succeeds with her and gains his self-respect and psychic freedom from a potential fixation on sex itself. . . .

THE FOUR FACTORS

And what is it, then, that we are to take into account as we analyze and weigh and judge the situation? What do we look for, what question do we ask? There are four questions of basic and indispensable importance to be raised about every case, four factors at stake in every situation, all of which are to be balanced on love's scales. There are no foregone decisions.

The first one, the primary one, is the *end.* What is wanted? What is the object sought; what result is aimed at? A student, for example, might want a new and highly useful thesaurus. But then, as a second factor, by what *means* could he acquire one; what method should he employ to bring about the end he seeks? It might be stealing or borrowing or buying, and to get money to buy it he might steal or save or beg or borrow or gamble. This, then, brings into view the third factor at stake, his *motive.* What is the drive or "wanting" dynamic behind the act? Is the student moved by covetousness or charity or scholarship or ostentation or bibliomania?

Finally, every serious decision maker needs to ask the fourth question, What are the foreseeable *consequences?* Given any course of action, in the context of the problem, what are the effects directly and indirectly brought about, the immediate consequences, and the remote (sequelae)? This last question means, we must note, that there are more results entailed than just the end wanted, and they *all* have to be weighed and weighted. Along with getting the thesaurus, there may come other things: impoverishment, a neurosis nurtured, professional growth, resentment by a wife or creditor, successful completion of an important thesis.

Rigoristic, intrinsicalist legalism often takes the position that to be wrong an action need be at fault on only one of these four scores, whereas in order to be right it must be right on *all four*. When Kant, the grandfather of modern ethical absolutizers, wrote his essay *On a Supposed Right to Tell Lies from Benevolent Motives,* he made it quite clear that in his ethics a lie to a would-be murderer, to save his victims' life, would be wrong. The situationist prefers the ethics of the civil law, in which the failure to tell the necessary lie might very possibly make one an accessory before the fact of the murder!

FANATIC VIRTUE

As the old adage has it, "Virtue never goes out of style," i.e., the *disposition* toward honor, chastity, loyalty, patience, humility, and all the rest. But *situations* change. There is another old saying, *Semper sed non ad semper* (Principles are always sound but not in every case). What is constructive in one era may not be in another.

For real decision-making, freedom is required, an open-ended approach to situations. Imagine the plight of an obstetrician who believed he must always respirate every baby he delivered, no matter how monstrously deformed! A century ago Thomas Huxley rather thought he would prefer being accurate and correct as a moral decision maker, even if he had to be as mechanical as a clock wound up for the day, than assume the burden of mistakes entailed by freedom. What an irony to compare his opinion to Tik-Tok's in *The Wizard of Oz!* There the mechanical man had the special grace of always doing "what he was wound up to do," but wanted instead to be *human.* And what did he lack? Freedom to choose.

As we know, for many people, sex is so much a moral problem, largely due to the repressive effects of legalism, that in newspapers and popular parlance the term "morals charge" always means a sex complaint! "Her morals are not very high" means her sex life is rather looser than the mores allow. Yet we find nothing in the teachings of Jesus about the ethics of sex, except adultery and an absolute condemnation of divorce—a correlative matter. He said nothing about birth control, large or small families, childlessness, homosexuality, masturbation, fornication or premarital intercourse, sterilization, artificial insemination, abortion, sex play, petting, and courtship. Whether any form of sex (hetero, homo, or auto) is good or evil depends on whether love is fully served.

The Christian ethic is not interested in reluctant virgins and technical chastity. What sex probably needs more than anything is a good airing, demythologizing it and getting rid of its mystique-laden and occult accretions, which come from romanticism on the one hand and puritanism on the other. People are learning that we can have sex without love, and love without sex; that baby-making can be (and often ought to be) separated from love-making. It is, indeed, for re-creation as well as for procreation. But if people do not believe it is wrong to have sex relations outside marriage, it isn't, unless they hurt themselves, their partners, or others. This is, of course, a very big "unless" and gives reasons to many to abstain altogether except within the full mutual commitment of marriage. The civil lawmakers are rapidly ridding their books of statutes making unmarried sex a crime between consenting adults. All situationists would agree with Mrs. Patrick Campbell's remark that they can do what they want "as long as they don't do it in the street and frighten the horses."

. . . Is adultery wrong? . . . One can only respond, "I don't know. Maybe. Give me a case. Describe a real situation." . . .

WHEN RIGHTS ARE RIGHT

When love reigns, not law, the decisions of conscience are relative. Love plots the course according to the circumstances. What is to be done in any situation depends on the case, and the solution of any moral issue is, therefore, quite relative. What is right is revealed in the facts. . . . But once the relative course is chosen, the obligation to pursue it is absolute. We cannot blow hot or cold, or lukewarm, sounding an uncertain note about the obligation itself. The obligation is absolute; only the decision is relative. Only the *how* is relative, not the *why*. This is why we have said that the task is "to find absolute love's relative course."

The metaphysical moralist of the classical tradition, with his intrinsic values and moral universals and code apparatus, says in effect, "Do what is right and let the chips fall where they may." The situational decision maker says right back at his metaphysical rival: "Ha! Whether what you are doing is right or not depends precisely upon where the chips fall."

The focus of this "new morality" which is, as we have seen, not so new as many suppose, is clearly focused upon *decision*. In its retrospective function, looking back upon moral choices in the past, conscience makes *judgments*; it judges after the fact whether what was done was right or wrong, good or evil. In doing so, in this retrospective role, it works with all the advantages of hindsight. But in its prospective function, facing forward toward moral choices yet to be made, conscience makes *decisions*; it decides before the fact whether one path or another will be right or wrong, good or evil. Here it has no second-guessing advantages; it is engaged in first-guessing, and much of its decision-making work entails a frightful measure of doubt and uncertainty and opacity. So much of the time we are making, at best, "educated guesses." Nevertheless, we have to decide, to choose whether we lean on law or ride out into the open for love's sake.

THE CHRISTIAN REASON WHY

Acknowledging that every moral decision involves four factors (the ends, the means, the motives, and the foreseeable results both direct and indirect), then there appears to the Christian situationist to be nothing particularly different or unique in a Christian's choices—except as to motive. *But even here* it is not true that the Christian's motive is unique because his "will" is "moved" by love. Lovingness is often the motive at work full force behind the decisions of non-Christian and nontheological, even atheist, decision makers.

The Christian love ethic is, as Paul Lehmann says, a *"koinōnia* ethic" in the sense that the Christian's reason or motive of love and his understanding of its source is peculiar to his faith community.¶¶¶

. . . Obedience to the love commandment is not a question of salvation but of *vocation*. Therefore, quoting a line of Thomas à Becket's in T. S. Eliot's play, *Murder in the Cathedral*, "The supreme treason is to do the right thing for the wrong reason."

THE QUESTION-ASKING WAY

And if we were to summarize what we have been saying in a single, simple formula, we should put it this way: "Christian ethics or moral theology is not a scheme of living according to a code but a continuous effort to relate love to a world of relativities through a casuistry obedient to love; its constant task is to work out the strategy and tactics of love, for Christ's sake."

———————

In all three of the more or less incompatible sexual moralities advocated by large numbers of responsible, honest, enthusiastically "moral" individuals in our society, all three groups give highest priority to responsibility. The situationist is a moral relativist. To be "responsible" in every decision-making situation, what factors must be taken into account?

What makes one capable of being "the responsible self"?

Where does the situationist differ from the legalist, that is, the moral absolutist? In what ways does he differ? How, for example, does the cartoon of Moses and the stone-cutter mentioned by Fletcher in **Situation Ethics** indicate areas of agreement between the legalist and the situationist?

What does Fletcher mean when describing Christian situation ethics as "the strategy of love," rather than a program of living according to a code?

In **Situation Ethics** what distinction does Fletcher make between "rules" and "principles"?

The pragmatic view of goodness boils it down to "what works." But, as Fletcher continues to explain, "Yes. But work to what end, for what purpose, to satisfy what standard or ideal or norm? This is the decisive question." How would you reply to it?

Would a situationist principal of a school announce, "All students who become pregnant while attending this school will be expelled"? Why, or why not?

What does the author mean when saying: "We cannot verify moral choices. They may be vindicated, but not validated"?

Reconsider the case Fletcher cites of abortion. Where are the situationists' working principles of pragmatism, relativism, positivism, and personalism manifested in their ethical approach and decision?

If situation ethics is concerned with "antecedent rather than consequent

¶¶¶ *In Christian Faith and Social Action*, ed. by J. A. Hutchison (Charles Scribner's Sons, 1953), pp. 102-114 .

conscience," with decision-making rather than judgment-passing, how might it counteract the following argument:

> Today people tend to deny that sex conduct is a moral issue. Thus people are supposedly free to "make up their own minds." Yet how can an intellectual process be applied to conduct like sex relations which are usually the result of runaway emotions?

Under what circumstances might a situationist break the law? All? Some? None? Why?

In his essay *Tolerance,* E. M. Forster writes:

> . . . Most people, when asked what spiritual quality is needed to rebuild civilization, will reply "Love." Men must love one another, they say; nations must do likewise, and then the series of cataclysms which is threatening to destroy us will be checked.
>
> Respectfully but firmly, I disagree. Love is a great force in private life; it is indeed the greatest of all things: but love in public affairs does not work. It has been tried again and again: by the Christian civilizations of the Middle Ages, and also by the French Revolution, a secular movement which reasserted the Brotherhood of Man. And it has always failed. The idea that nations should love one another, or that business concerns or marketing boards should love one another, or that a man in Portugal should love a man in Peru of whom he has never heard—it is absurd, unreal, dangerous. It leads us into perilous and vague sentimentalism. "Love is what is needed," we chant, and then sit back and the world goes on as before. The fact is we can only love what we know personally. And we cannot know much. [83]

How, in the face of E. M. Forster's argument, can Fletcher maintain that

> *Agapē* goes out to our neighbors not for our own sakes nor for theirs, really, but for God's. We can say quite plainly and colloquially that Christian love is the business of loving the unlovable, i.e., the *unlikable.*

What might Fletcher say in response to Forster?

How does the word "deliberately" become synonymous with "responsibly" in situation ethics?

How would you respond to the author's question "What think Ye?" concerning the abortion case (p. 310)?

Why might Fletcher feel that situation ethics applied to sexual morals represents the midpoint between "romanticism" and "puritanism"? What is your concept of "romanticism" in this context?

On what grounds might a situationist who could not absolutely declare that "chastity is important, because it is right" argue a case for chastity?

RELATED QUESTIONS

Is Fromm's interpretation of "responsibility" in **The Theory of Love** (p. 252) the same as Fletcher's in **Situation Ethics?**

Is "responsibility" a relevant term in Neill's argument for sex expression rather than sex repression in **Sex Attitudes** (p. 286)?

What factors would be considered by someone whom Kirkendall might call "responsible" on the basis of **Searching for the Roots of Moral Judgments** (p. 295)?

Using Fletcher's distinction between rules and principles, would you call Kirkendall's "very definite standard. . . . 'Thou shalt do those things which contribute to trust, understanding, good will, and the ultimate ability of all to work together'" a rule or a principle? Why?

How does Kirkendall's concept of morality in **Searching for the Roots of Moral Judgments** exemplify Fletcher's notion of personalism in **Situation Ethics?**

Fletcher says, "In non-Christian situation ethics some other highest good will be the one and only standard—such as self-realization in the ethics of Aristotle." What might Powys (**Glory of Life,** p. 293) consider this *summum bonum?*

How is the concept that "Love is not something we *have* or *are,* it is something we *do,*" demonstrated in **A Raisin in the Sun** (p. 149)? Would Fromm (**The Theory of Love,** p. 252); Singer (**Appraisal and Bestowal,** p. 217); and/or Lindbergh (**Double-Sunrise,** p. 232) agree with it? Why, or why not?

The New Morality
THOMAS A. WASSMER

It all looks so easy to say you are a situationalist and it is only love that counts. But is this decision-making method of morality so easy and so applicable?

. . . . Mature responsibility is commensurate with the deliberate knowledge and free acceptance of . . . consequences . . . initiated by our moral act in this existential moment of ethical history. Where does [its effect go], whom does it touch, with what results for good or evil; how does it develop or undermine our own selves in mature responsibility? The decision-making method of situational morality becomes an enormous calculation and extrapolation of the consequences that unavoidably follow from the particular moral act posited here and now.

WHEN THE HARD ETHICAL CHOICE MUST BE MADE

This is serious business. It it not a morality of the mere presence or absence of *agapé.* This is a morality that demands self-knowledge, mature experience, a disciplined character, an awareness of others as persons with rights and claims upon us in multiple interpersonal relations, a sensitivity to the short-term and long-term consequences of this moral act. Situational morality is most authentic when it refuses to trivialize the situation. After all, is not the principal criticism of traditional morality that it is juridicial, legalistic and indifferent to the agonizing existential moment when the hard ethical choice must be made?

This is the first reason why situational morality is so difficult: in refusing to trivialize the situation, it places the onus on the situationalist to evaluate the consequences that follow from the act. . . . No one wants to trivialize the situation, no one wants to be less mature and responsible than someone else, and situationalism seems only to compound problem upon problem for the authentic choice that has to be made.

Another difficulty with this moral theory of decision-making arises from its attitude toward moral principles, precepts or laws. For the situationalist there is no principle, precept or law that always binds; there is no universal negative principle, precept or law that always obliges. This is not to say that there is no very significant number of occasions when the principle, precept or law does have direct application. Some situationalists refer to the principle being valid and applicable in 98 out of 100 cases. Now this should cause problems for any situationalist who wants to establish himself in the very small number of cases where the law does not apply or where, because *agapé* would suffer, the law must be put aside. This ought to suggest to the responsible and mature situationalist that a possible deceptive reading might result in a too rapid conclusion that the exceptional has been found.

Before this inference can be drawn, should not the wisdom of the law and the values implicit in the law be recognized constantly? Is it not possible that while love may place some moral dimension upon the exceptional case, a certain degree of hubris has been manifest in a summary rejection of the values and the wisdom incorporated in the law? Love and law are not so incompatible that their tension cannot be resolved in most situations to the interest of both. At times it seems that some situationalists represent the extraordinary case as one in which persons can only be loved more if law is loved less. Does this represent the authentic situation? Can it really be established that in a critical case of conflict between love and law, a man necessarily loves a person more insofar as he loves law less?

A DIFFICULT MORALITY BUT FOR SOME THE ONLY KIND

. . . . All morality, properly understood, is situational, is aware of the increasing importance placed upon circumstances, motives, historical evolution, the subjectivity of the moral agent. . . . If situational morality is mature and responsible to the extent that it does not trivialize the human situation, is it a morality that is easy to adopt and apply with discernment and prudence? Situational morality is a difficult morality, but it is the only morality for the mature, responsible, conscientious person.

Dr. Joseph Fletcher, author of *Situation Ethics* (Westminster Press), has his own problems in trying to clarify for others what precisely he means by love or *agapé*. Certainly, for this proponent of situational morality, love or loving concern is central in his "new morality." The presence of love is pivotal in the moral life, and in ethical analysis everything hinges upon loving concern. Dr. John Lachs, professor of philosophy at the College of William and Mary, contends that nowhere in Dr. Fletcher's book are we told in detail what love *is*. In "Dogmatist in Disguise," an article in the *Christian Century* for Nov. 16, 1966, he has pointed to the diverse roles love plays in the ethics of situationalism, some of which are incompatible with others. Dr. Lachs identifies the pages in *Situation Ethics* where these many roles are catalogued: "Love is first said to be something we do: it is thus 1) an action or a way of behaving (p. 61). This definition is quickly revised: love becomes 2) a characteristic of certain human actions and relationships (p. 63). Again it is 3) the purpose behind the action (p. 61). Toward the end of the book it becomes 4) the motive behind the decision to act (p. 155). Elsewhere, love is 5) an attitude of persons, 6) a disposition to act in certain ways, 7) a preference for certain values, and 8) good will or a conative predisposition to take certain attitudes (pp. 79, 61, 104, 105). And it is also said to be 9) a relation, 10) a formal principle and 11) a regulative principle (pp. 105, 60, 61)." Dr. Lachs concludes that love surely cannot be all these things, and if it is identified in all these ways, then Dr. Fletcher has no clear idea of the nature of love.

Dr. Lachs argues that if love is "an action or way of behaving," it cannot also be "a characteristic of certain human actions and relationships," because actions cannot be characteristics of actions. Again, if love is "a relation," it cannot also be "the motive behind the decision to act," or "an attitude of persons," or "a disposition to act in certain ways," because relations are not motives, attitudes or dispositions. Further, if love is "the purpose behind the action," it cannot also be "a formal principle" or "a regulative principle," because purposes are not principles. Dr. Lachs insists that if Dr. Fletcher holds that love, the only ultimate value for him, is a kind of action, he is unavoidably drawn to the position that right actions are right *intrinsically;* on the other hand, if Dr. Fletcher maintains that love is a motive, a purpose or a conative attitude, he is ineluctably drawn to the position that right actions are right *extrinsically* for the intentions or personal attitudes of the agent who performs them. Finally, if love is a relation between persons, this should make Dr. Fletcher adopt the position that the moral quality of an act must be evaluated by its tendency to establish such valuable relations.

WHAT KIND OF LOVE MAKES AN ACT MORALLY GOOD?

What is the love or *agapé* that is said to make an act morally good? It is not love that is *erotic or philiac,* but a peculiar kind of love that is intrinsically good. *Erotic* love is selfish love, *philiac* love is a mutual giving that ceases when mutuality ceases. *Agapaic* love is selfless, completely other-directed, almost sacrificial, perfectly verified in Christ's love of mankind by His death on the cross. Now, is *agapaic* love even a possibility outside of the sacrificial love of a mother or the heroic act of *kenotic* love for another creature? Is it not true that we recognize many acts to be moral and ethical that are not accompanied by selfless concern? In other words, is it sensible to discriminate *agapaic* love from *erotic* and *philiac* and then speak of *agapé* as the loving, selfless concern that gives the moral quality to the human act?

It might seem to a non-specialist in moral science that there are many moral acts that are not accompanied by *agapé,* and that there are few moral acts where the love that is present is of a quality that is selfless, kenotic, sacrificial and utterly separable from the love that is *erotic* and *philiac.* The situationalist may not question this estimate, but his persistence in using the term *agapé* makes moral acts appear to be almost impossible to realize.

. . . . In these words of Brian Wicker: "Real moral dilemmas are not cases to be analyzed but agonies to be lived through. The living of these agonies, and the survival of them, *is* the moral history of mankind. And since . . . moral dilemmas have a sociological aspect, because they concern the gap between 'law' and 'love' as it is incarnated at a particular moment and at a particular place, morality has to do with the history of human social structures, that is, with our political history."

To polarize "law" and "love" is to deny the moral paradoxes that all of us frequently face in our lives. For example, in the case of a meaningful sexual relationship "outside the law," the situationalist cannot resolve the paradox by referring to it as *good and right*. Nor, equally, can the legalist resolve it by referring to it as *bad and wrong*. God has introduced us into a situation that can only validly and honestly be called *good but wrong*.

What objections or questions does Wassmer in **The New Morality** raise to the following statements of Fletcher's from **Situation Ethics** (p. 308):

(a) As much as he can, the situationist will prevent law's Procrusteanly squeezing down an iron system of prefabricated decisions upon free people in living situations. . . . Being legally right may mean nothing at all morally. . . .

(b) There are four questions of basic and indispensable importance to be raised about every case, four factors at stake in every situation, all of which are to be balanced on love's scales. . . . the end, . . . means, . . . motive, . . . [and] consequences.

(c) To love Christianly is a matter of attitude, not of feeling. Love is discerning and critical; it is not sentimental. . . . Christian love is definitely agapeic . . . not a question of romance or friendship. . . .

How might Fletcher defend his position against the charge from Wassmer in **The New Morality:** ". . . should not the wisdom of the law and the values implicit in the law be recognized constantly? . . . To polarize 'law' and 'love' is to deny the moral paradoxes that all of us frequently face in our lives"?

Modern Morals in a Muddle

RICHARD A. McCORMICK

"If there is mutual consideration, if they are committed to each other, especially if they intend to marry, if there is no danger of pregnancy, if they have talked it over and agree on the consequences, then it would be mere dogmatism to say that anything is wrong here." This is the good news of sexual freedom that enlightens and liberates. The old "thou shalt not" has given way to "thou mayest if." Promiscuous or casual premarital sex is, of course, out. But meaningful and responsible premarital sex, where there is emotional commitment and no one is hurt, is in. . . . The young couple have to make up their own minds; they must hammer out new codes to fit the facts. But in doing so they must remember one thing: gone is the day of the absolute. No longer can anyone say that something is right or wrong, black or white—except, of course, that it is never right to say something is always wrong.

Need one belong to Catullus' *senes severiores,* those censorious old men, if he entertains a sneaking suspicion that something is awry here? The source of moral conviction down the ages has been the perception of value, the grasp of significance. A shift in moral conviction, therefore, will represent the perception of new significance—or a blunting of sensitivity to the old. Our era has worried about premarital relations largely because of unwanted pregnancy and venereal disease. This suggests that our sensitivity to the true moral issues has become blunted and that we have bogged down in concern about factors not internal to the personal relationship itself.

William I. Nichols, publisher of *This Week Magazine,* noted in a January speech before the Executives' Club of Chicago: "There are signs that young people are wearied by the meaninglessness of our permissive, affluent and sex-drenched society." Yet Boston University's Robert H. Hamill stated recently that sex and cheating are "the two most obvious moral issues on the modern campus." Something is passing strange here: detached weariness plus deep moral concern. When we see these two in combination, generally we are witnessing the uneasy search for significance. And if the search still continues—even though in bizarre ways—it is a pretty good sign that the "thou mayest if" of the new moralists has been no more successful in yielding meaning than the "thou shalt not" of less troubled times.

It is here that a wisdom, very ancient but ever new, must be heard: the Bible itself. If it tells us anything about sexual intimacy, it tells us that it is a communication between persons, a sign and language so unique (ultimately because of its basic procreativity) that *of itself* it expresses a two-in-oneship, exclusive and irrevocable. Because it *sometimes* brings about procreation, it is *always* a symbol of total personal donation.

Because it expresses the person, it must correspond to the existing personal relationship. To the extent that it does not correspond to the existing relationship, it does not express the person, but something else, infrahuman and divisive. To perform or to ask another to perform an act that prescinds from the personal is to ask her or him to act in a nonhuman way, hence to do something harmful to himself. Regardless of the emotional concomitants, the high purpose, the repeated protestations of love, this cannot be an act of love toward that person, but must remain objectively, even if not consciously, an act of manipulation. And in the Christian ethic it is always immoral to manipulate another person.

This is why the cardinal rule of sexual conduct was and always will remain: physical expressions of intimacy express the person and therefore must correspond to the existing relationship of the persons. The unmarried are only preparing for the total relationship of marriage. They are learning, not chiefly but among other things, to fill their expressions of love with respect and protection, with more of the person: they are learning to drain off the elements that stifle personal communion. Since their love is protective, not possessive, they will give themselves to each other only to the extent that the person can be given at this point—in a limited way. Consequently, they will avoid those acts that of themselves signify total personal oblation, not out of blind servility to a negative "thou shalt not," but because, being in love, they will wish to speak a personal, and therefore a genuinely human, language to each other.

Since sexual intercourse and its antecedents represent total *personal* exchange, they can be separated from total personal relationship (marriage) only by undermining their truly human, their expressive character. Man has, of course, separated many things: man from life, nation from nation, permanency from marriage, even himself from God. When he does so, he indicates only that he has acted freely, not that he has acted wisely.

Why does this critic of situation ethics suspect that the "thou mayest if" of the new moralists has been no more successful in the area of sexual conduct than the previous "thou shalt not"?

Reconstruct the reasoning, the step-by-step development of McCormick's case for chastity as presented in *Modern Morals in a Muddle.* At what points could Fletcher provide counterarguments?

RELATED QUESTIONS

Can you reconcile the attitudes toward sexual intercourse outside marriage expressed by McCormick in *Modern Morals in a Muddle* and by Neill in *Sex Attitudes* (p. 286)? If so, how? If not, why must they remain at variance with each other?

Faithful Love

ROGER L. SHINN

Contemporary society, involved in its revolution in sexual ethics, is not likely to turn expectantly for understanding to the Bible. But those who do so are often surprised at what they find. This literature—which tells of polygamy, concubinage, lust and adultery, asceticism, and much else—communicates also a powerful expression of the meaning of sex. The Bible brought its own revolution in sexual ethics, a revolution often perverted and seldom understood even today.

The key passage, I think, is in the second chapter of Genesis. This chapter tells about the creation of man and woman. Long after it was written, Jesus quoted it to express his convictions about the meaning of marriage.

As we look at the record, it is important to get one problem out of the way immediately. We shall not find here a scientific description of how the human race appeared on earth. The author has no intention of writing science. He tells a story that expresses a belief that sexuality is a gift from God and the basis of a profound human relationship. He does it with a magnificent earthiness and a penetrating spirituality that are inseparable.

In Genesis 2:7 we read: "Then the Lord God formed man of dust from the ground, and breathed into his nostrils the breath of life; and man became a living being." Notice that man is akin to nature—made of dust from the ground—and akin also to God, who gave him the breath of life. There is no hint here that man's body or his physical nature is bad. It is this body that becomes the living person when God gives it the breath of life.

The story goes on to tell how God placed man in the Garden of Eden. After a while it continues: "Then the Lord God said, 'It is not good that the man should be alone; I will make him a helper fit for him.'" Man alone, this record is saying, is lonely and incomplete. He needs a companion, a helper. Other men will not be adequate. The man needs another person, akin to him, yet different.

But before we get to the creation of woman, there is a delay. God creates the animals. Once again let us notice that this is not a scientific treatise. Science tells us that animals lived on earth before man. Another author, writing in the first chapter of Genesis, puts the creation of the fish, birds, and animals ahead of the creation of man. The second chapter makes a different point. The animals are related to man. They are made of the same stuff of the earth by the same God. Man sees them and gives them names. But, the account continues, "for the man there was not found a helper fit for him." The animals are not an adequate answer to man's loneliness.

Now we come to the great event: "So the Lord God caused a deep sleep to fall upon the man, and while he slept took one of his ribs and closed up its place with flesh; and the rib which the Lord God had taken from the man he made into a woman and brought her to the man."

Let us not get literal about that rib; if we do, we simply turn a sound insight into bad zoology. But see what the writer is getting at, as he continues: "Then the man said, 'This at last is bone of my bones, and flesh of my flesh; she shall be called Woman, because she was taken out of Man.'" Here is the joyful exclamation of the man. He has lived through the loneliness, first of solitude, then of life with the animals. Now "at last" he has found what he craved.

Then come two fascinating sentences. "Therefore a man leaves his father and his mother and cleaves to his wife, and they become one flesh. And the man and his wife were both naked, and were not ashamed."

In those exuberant sentences three things are worth noticing. First, the woman whom the man cleaves to becomes his wife. She is not a plaything to be enjoyed and then forgotten, not a convenience for the man's aggressiveness or lust, but a wife. Man leaves mother and father in order to cleave to her. Second, there is a wonderful eagerness in the way man and wife become one flesh. There is no false spirituality here, no apology for the physical, no shame over nakedness, but a glad acceptance of the physical union. Third, no mention is made at this point of children. That will come later. Children in the Bible are a blessing of marriage. The married couple often long for them. But the fleshly union of husband and wife need not be justified as a means to some other end. It is good of itself. It is part of God's purpose.

In that ancient story of creation is an appreciation of sex, in its freedom and its commitment, its delight and its seriousness, that has a fresh ring even in the jaded world of today. Some, of course, will argue that it is obsolete. But we can foolishly escape responsibilities and opportunities by calling them obsolete. Interestingly some of the most contemporary psychology, using a clinical rather than a poetic language, makes the same points.

A name that would rank high on any list of American psychologists and that would head some lists is Erik Erikson. He works, generally speaking, in the Freudian tradition, which many people would try to oppose to the biblical heritage. He describes six conditions that should be included in sexual mutuality. I list them in his language:

1. mutuality of orgasm
2. with a loved partner
3. of the other sex
4. with whom one is able and willing to share a mutual trust
5. and with whom one is able and willing to regulate the cycles of
   a. work
   b. procreation
   c. recreation
6. so as to secure to the offspring, too, a satisfactory development.*

Erikson points out that any such achievement, on a widespread basis, is more than an individual accomplishment. He adds that it is more than a sexual matter also.

Our society is throwing out many an inherited set of rules and inhibitions. Some of these should have been thrown out long ago. The question is whether we will rediscover the meaning of sex or distort it to our great loss.

Sex, which often is commercial, mechanical, or trivial, can be personal. Sexual activity, which frequently is the outlet for pride or fear or hostility, can be the expression of faithful love.

That is the meaning of the traditional vows in which man and woman take each other, "for richer or for poorer, for better or for worse, in sickness and in health, to love and to cherish, until death us do part."

How does the second chapter of Genesis express a belief that sexuality is a gift from God and the basis of a profound human relationship?
Shinn says:

> Our society is throwing out many an inherited set of rules and inhibitions. Some of these should have been thrown out long ago. The question is whether we will rediscover the meaning of sex or distort it to our great loss.

What are some of the inherited sets of rules and inhibitions that Shinn believes should have been thrown out long ago?
If we were to "rediscover the meaning of sex" what do you think we might discover from Shinn's perspective?

RELATED QUESTIONS

How does McCormick in **Modern Morals in a Muddle** (p. 329) build his case on "a wisdom very ancient but ever new"?
How does John Hollander, analyzing "love's true anatomy" in **The Lady's-Maid's Song** (see **"Night-Lights,"** p. 564), also use the passage from Genesis (although in a rather different fashion from Shinn) for the basis of his argument?

* Erik Erikson, *Childhood and Society* (New York: W. W. Norton, 1950), pp. 230–231.

Among the reminders that "traditional morality has always been defied," as Shinn observed, are two inhabitants of seventeenth-century Puritan New England: Hester Prynne (to whom **The Sadder-But-Wiser Girl for Me,** "**Night-Lights,**" p. 592 alludes) and Reverend Arthur Dimmesdale. **The Scarlet Letter** by Nathaniel Hawthorne deals with the effects of sin on the human mind and spirit: Dimmesdale's inability to expiate his sin without public admission to his crime of adultery with Hester; Hester's public condemnation in front of Salem's townspeople, an "A" embroidered on her gown and the illegitimate infant in her arms as, "with natural dignity and force of character," she steps from the prison door in the first excerpt from "The Market-Place."

The second excerpt, "The Pastor and His Parishioner," takes place seven years after the first. Hester, released from jail and living in a cottage in Salem, has raised her daughter Pearl; Dimmesdale, for his unconfessed part, has been punished by conscience. His torment is aggravated by Hester's husband, an old, scholarly physician who came to America two years after his wife. Discovering her situation, he assumes the name Roger Chillingworth to seek out her unidentified lover and revenge himself. He attaches himself to the seemingly holy preacher, suspecting him to be the father of Hester's child.

The Scarlet Letter

NATHANIEL HAWTHORNE

THE MARKET-PLACE

. . . The women who were now standing about the prison-door stood within less than half a century of the period when the man-like Elizabeth had been the not altogether unsuitable representative of the sex. They were her countrywomen; and the beef and ale of their native land, with a moral diet not a whit more refined, entered largely into their composition. The bright morning sun, therefore, shone on broad shoulders and well-developed busts, and on round and ruddy cheeks, that had ripened in the far-off island, and had hardly yet grown paler or thinner in the atmosphere of New England. There was, moreover, a boldness and rotundity of speech among these matrons, as most of them seemed to be, that would startle us at the present day, whether in respect to its purport or its volume of tone.

"Goodwives," said a hard-featured dame of fifty, "I'll tell ye a piece of my mind. It would be greatly for the public behoof, if we women, being of mature age and church-members in good repute, should have the handling of such male-factresses as this Hester Prynne. What think ye, gossips? If the hussy stood up for judgment before us five, that are now here in a knot together, would she come off with such a sentence as the worshipful magistrates have awarded? Marry, I trow not!" . . .

"The magistrates are God-fearing gentlemen, but merciful overmuch,— this is a truth," added [an] autumnal matron. "At the very least, they should have put the brand of a hot iron on Hester Prynne's forehead. Madam Hester would have winced at that, I warrant me. But she,—the haughty baggage,—little will she care what they put upon the bodice of her gown! Why, look you, she may cover it with a brooch, or such like heathenish adornment, and so walk the streets as brave as ever!"

"Ah, but," interposed, more softly, a young wife, holding a child by the hand, "let her cover the mark as she will, the pang of it will be always in her heart."

"What do we talk of marks and brands, whether on the bodice of her gown, or the flesh of her forehead?" cried another female, the ugliest as well as the most pitiless of these self-constituted judges. "This woman has brought shame upon us all, and ought to die. Is there not law for it? Truly, there is, both in the Scripture and the statute-book. Then let the magistrates, who have made it of no effect, thank themselves if their own wives and daughters go astray!"

"Mercy on us, goodwife," exclaimed a man in the crowd, "is there no virtue in woman, save what springs from a wholesome fear of the gallows? That is the hardest word yet! Hush, now, gossips! for the lock is turning in the prison-door, and here comes Mistress Prynne herself."

The door of the jail being flung open from within, there appeared, in the first place, like a black shadow emerging into sunshine, the grim and grisly presence of the town-beadle, with a sword by his side, and his staff of office in his hand. This personage prefigured and represented in his aspect the whole dismal severity of the Puritanic code of law, which it was his business to administer in its final and closest application to the offender. Stretching forth the official staff in his left hand, he laid his right upon the shoulder of a young woman, whom he thus drew forward; until, on the threshold of the prison-door, she repelled him, by an action marked with natural dignity and force of character, and stepped into the open air, as if by her own free will. She bore in her arms a child, a baby of some three months old, who winked and turned aside its little face from the too vivid light of day; because its existence, heretofore, had brought it acquainted only with the gray twilight of a dungeon, or other darksome apartment of the prison.

When the young woman—the mother of this child—stood fully revealed before the crowd, it seemed to be her first impulse to clasp the infant closely to her bosom; not so much by an impulse of motherly affection, as that she might thereby conceal a certain token, which was wrought or fastened into her dress. In a moment, however, wisely judging that one token of her shame would but poorly serve to hide another, she took the baby on her arm, and, with a burning blush, and yet a haughty smile, and a glance that would not be abashed, looked around at her townspeople and neighbors. On the breast of her gown, in fine red cloth, surrounded with an elaborate embroidery and fantastic flourishes of gold-thread, appeared the letter A. . . .

THE PASTOR AND HIS PARISHIONER

Slowly as the minister walked, he had almost gone by, before Hester Prynne could gather voice enough to attract his observation. At length, she succeeded.

"Arthur Dimmesdale!" she said, faintly at first; then louder, but hoarsely. "Arthur Dimmesdale!"

"Who speaks?" answered the minister.

Gathering himself quickly up, he stood more erect, like a man taken by surprise in a mood to which he was reluctant to have witnesses. Throwing his eyes anxiously in the direction of the voice, he indistinctly beheld a form under the trees, clad in garments so sombre, and so little relieved from the gray twilight into which the clouded sky and the heavy foliage had darkened the noontide, that he knew not whether it were a woman or a shadow. It may be, that his pathway through life was haunted thus, by a spectre that had stolen out from among his thoughts.

He made a step nigher, and discovered the scarlet letter.

"Hester! Hester Prynne!" said he. "Is it thou? Art thou in life?"

"Even so!" she answered. "In such life as has been mine these seven years past! And thou, Arthur Dimmesdale, dost thou yet live?"

It was no wonder that they thus questioned one another's actual and bodily existence, and even doubted of their own. So strangely did they meet, in the dim wood, that it was like the first encounter, in the world beyond the grave, of two spirits who had been intimately connected in their former life, but now stood coldly shuddering, in mutual dread; as not yet familiar with their state, nor wonted to the companionship of disembodied beings. Each a ghost, and awe-stricken at the other ghost! They were awe-stricken likewise at themselves; because the crisis flung back to them their consciousness, and revealed to each heart its history and experience, as life never does, except at such breathless epochs. The soul beheld its features in the mirror of the passing moment. It was with fear, and tremulously, and, as it were, by a slow, reluctant necessity, that Arthur Dimmesdale put forth his hand, chill as death, and touched the chill hand of Hester Prynne. The grasp, cold as it was, took away what was dreariest in the interview. They now felt themselves, at least, inhabitants of the same sphere.

Without a word more spoken,—neither he nor she assuming the guidance, but with an unexpressed consent,—they glided back into the shadow of the woods, whence Hester had emerged, and sat down on the heap of moss where she and Pearl had before been sitting. When they found voice to speak, it was, at first, only to utter remarks and inquiries such as any two acquaintance might have made, about the gloomy sky, the threatening storm, and, next, the health of each. Thus they went onward, not boldly, but step by step, into the themes that were brooding deepest in their hearts. So long estranged by fate and circumstances, they needed something slight and casual to run before, and throw open the doors of intercourse, so that their real thoughts might be led across the threshold.

After a while, the minister fixed his eyes on Hester Prynne's.

"Hester," said he, "hast thou found peace?"

She smiled drearily, looking down upon her bosom.

"Hast thou?" she asked.

"None!—nothing but despair!" he answered. "What else could I look for, being what I am, and leading such a life as mine? Were I an atheist,—a man devoid of conscience,—a wretch with coarse and brutal instincts,—I might have found peace, long ere now. Nay, I never should have lost it! But, as matters stand with my soul, whatever of good capacity there originally was in me, all of God's gifts that were the choicest have become the ministers of spiritual torment. Hester, I am most miserable!"

"The people reverence thee," said Hester. "And surely thou workest good among them! Doth this bring thee no comfort?"

"More misery, Hester!—only the more misery!" answered the clergyman, with a bitter smile. "As concerns the good which I may appear to do, I have no faith in it. It must needs be a delusion. What can a ruined soul, like mine, effect towards the redemption of other souls?—or a polluted soul, towards their purification? And as for the people's reverence, would that it were turned to scorn and hatred! Canst thou deem it, Hester, a consolation, that I must stand up in my pulpit, and meet so many eyes turned upward to my face, as if the light of heaven were beaming from it!—must see my flock hungry for the truth, and listening to my words as if a tongue of Pentecost were speaking!—and then look inward, and discern the black reality of what they idolize? I have laughed, in bitterness and agony of heart, at the contrast between what I seem and what I am! And Satan laughs at it!"

"You wrong yourself in this," said Hester, gently. "You have deeply and sorely repented. Your sin is left behind you, in the days long past. Your present life is not less holy, in very truth, than it seems in people's eyes. Is there no reality in the penitence thus sealed and witnessed by good works? And wherefore should it not bring you peace?"

"No, Hester, no!" replied the clergyman. "There is no substance in it! It is cold and dead, and can do nothing for me! Of penance I have had enough! Of penitence there has been none! Else, I should long ago have thrown off these garments of mock holiness, and have shown myself to mankind as they will see me at the judgment-seat. Happy are you, Hester, that wear the scarlet letter openly upon your bosom! Mine burns in secret! Thou little knowest what a relief it is, after the torment of a seven years' cheat, to look into an eye that recognizes me for what I am! Had I one friend,—or were it my worst enemy!—to whom, when sickened with the praises of all other men, I could daily betake myself, and be known as the vilest of all sinners, methinks my soul might keep itself alive thereby. Even thus, much of truth would save me! But, now, it is all falsehood!—all emptiness!—all death!"

. . . the sufferer's conscience had been kept in an irritated state, the tendency of which was, not to cure by wholesome pain, but to disorganize and corrupt his spiritual being. Its result, on earth, could hardly fail to be insanity, and hereafter, that eternal alienation from the Good and True, of which madness is perhaps the earthly type.

Such was the ruin to which she had brought the man, once,—nay, why should we not speak of it?—still so passionately loved! Hester felt that the sacrifice of the clergyman's good name, and death itself, as she had already told Roger Chillingworth, would have been infinitely preferable to the alternative which she had taken upon herself to choose. And now, rather than have had this grievous wrong to confess, she would gladly have lain down on the forest-leaves, and died there, at Arthur Dimmesdale's feet.

"O Arthur," cried she, "forgive me! In all things else, I have striven to be true! Truth was the one virtue which I might have held fast, and did hold fast through all extremity; save when thy good,—thy life,—thy fame,—were put in question! Then I consented to a deception. But a lie is never good, even though death threaten on the other side! Dost thou not see what I would say? That old man!—the physician!—he whom they call Roger Chillingworth!—he was my husband!"

The minister looked at her, for an instant, with all that violence of passion, which—intermixed, in more shapes than one, with his higher, purer, softer qualities—was, in fact, the portion of him which the Devil claimed, and through which he sought to win the rest. Never was there a blacker or a fiercer frown, than Hester now encountered. For the brief space that it lasted, it was a dark transfiguration. But his character had been so much enfeebled by suffering, that even its lower energies were incapable of more than a temporary struggle. He sank down on the ground, and buried his face in his hands.

"I might have known it!" murmured he. "I did know it! Was not the secret told me in the natural recoil of my heart, at the first sight of him, and as often as I have seen him since? Why did I not understand? O Hester Prynne, thou little, little knowest all the horror of this thing! And the shame!—the indelicacy!—the horrible ugliness of this exposure of a sick and guilty heart to the very eye that would gloat over it! Woman, woman, thou are accountable for this! I cannot forgive thee!"

"Thou shalt forgive me!" cried Hester, flinging herself on the fallen leaves beside him. "Let God punish! Thou shalt forgive!"

With sudden and desperate tenderness, she threw her arms around him, and pressed his head against her bosom; little caring though his cheek rested on the scarlet letter. He would have released himself, but strove in vain to do so. Hester would not set him free, lest he should look her sternly in the face. All the world had frowned on her,—for seven long years had it frowned upon this lonely woman,—and still she bore it all, nor ever once turned away her firm, sad eyes. Heaven, likewise, had frowned upon her, and she had not died. But the frown of this pale, weak, sinful, and sorrow-stricken man was what Hester could not bear, and live!

"Wilt thou yet forgive me?" she repeated, over and over again. "Wilt thou not frown? Wilt thou forgive?"

"I do forgive you, Hester," replied the minister, at length, with a deep utterance out of an abyss of sadness, but no anger. "I freely forgive you now. May God forgive us both! We are not, Hester, the worst sinners in the world. There is one worse than even the polluted priest! That old man's revenge has been blacker than my sin. He has violated, in cold blood, the sanctity of a human heart. Thou and I, Hester, never did so!"

"Never, never!" whispered she. "What we did had a consecration of its own. We felt it so! We said so to each other! Hast thou forgotten it?"

"Hush, Hester!" said Arthur Dimmesdale, rising from the ground. "No; I have not forgotten!"

They sat down again, side by side, and hand clasped in hand, on the mossy trunk of the fallen tree. Life had never brought them a gloomier hour; it was the point whither their pathway had so long been tending, and darkening ever, as it stole along;—and yet it inclosed a charm that made them linger upon it, and claim another, and another, and after all, another moment. The forest was obscure around them, and creaked with a blast that was passing through it. The boughs were tossing heavily above their heads; while one solemn old tree groaned dolefully to another, as if telling the sad story of the pair that sat beneath, or constrained to forebode evil to come.

And yet they lingered. How dreary looked the forest-track that led backward to the settlement, where Hester Prynne must take up again the burden of her ignominy, and the minister the hollow mockery of his good name! So they lingered an instant longer. No golden light had ever been so precious as the gloom of this dark forest. Here, seen only by his eyes, the scarlet letter need not burn into the bosom of the fallen woman! Here, seen only by her eyes, Arthur Dimmesdale, false to God and man, might be, for one moment, true!

In the first excerpt from *The Scarlet Letter,* what is the prevailing attitude of the women who wait outside the jail for Hester to appear? Are they legalists or situationists?

The first opinion-giver is "a hard-featured dame of fifty"; the second is also an "autumnal" matron; the third is a "young wife, holding a child by the hand"; and the fourth is "the ugliest as well as the most pitiless of these self-constituted judges." How do their personal characteristics and situations seem to correlate with their individual reactions to Hester's situation?

Why might the male speaker be more sympathetic and flexible about Hester than those of her own sex are?

What inferences might be drawn about Hester's attitude toward her sin from the brief description of her at the end of the scene?

In the second excerpt, "The Pastor and His Parishioner," why are Hester and Arthur at first able only to "utter remarks and inquiries such as any two acquaintances might have made"? Are they eventually able to "communicate," as Kirkendall uses the term (p. 303)?

What might Dimmesdale mean in his critical distinction: "Of penance I have had enough! Of penitence there has been none."

Do you agree with Hester that "a lie is never good, even though death threaten on the other side"? If not, how would you temper her statement?

Is Dimmesdale's forgiveness of Hester's deception about Chillingworth indicative of his genuine love for her?

Is it significant that after seven years of individual and lonely torment, these two retain positive, even passionate, feelings for each other? Why, or why not?

Dimmesdale says of Roger Chillingworth:

"That old man's revenge has been blacker than my sin. He has violated, in cold blood, the sanctity of a human heart. Thou and I, Hester, never did so!"
"Never, never!" whispered she. "What we did had a consecration of its own. We felt it so!"

Is revenge "blacker" than adultery under these circumstances? Would you take into account the fact that Roger sinned out of hate, the other two out of love?

RELATED QUESTIONS

To which of Johnson's groups in *Some Observations on Sexual Morality* (p. 276) would you assign Hester Prynne and Arthur Dimmesdale? Why?

The man in the crowd outside the prison door exclaims: "Is there no virtue in woman, save what springs from a wholesome fear of the gallows?" How is this related to the fear ethic? Do you believe that morality can be strengthened by increasing the number of policemen?

Which of the emotional consequences detailed by Evelyn Havens in *I Thought I Was Modern* (p. 280) are part of Hester and Arthur's situation? Which of them are not? Why?

For what reasons might the author of **Chastity on the Campus** (p. 283) judge Hester's sexual behavior with Arthur to be moral?

How would a moral absolutist, or legalist, counter any defense made of Hester and Arthur's sexual behavior?

How might an advocate of situation ethics assess their case? Would the fact that Hester and Arthur had a child make any difference to their judgment?

To what might Neill (**Sex Attitudes,** p. 286) attribute Dimmesdale's guilt?

Do you think Kirkendall (**Searching for the Roots of Moral Judgments,** p. 295) might consider their relationship entirely moral? Would Fromm, according to his philosophy in **The Theory of Love?** (p. 252)?

Would Hester and Dimmesdale's feeling for each other qualify as that "heroical love between two people" described by Powys in **Glory of Life** (p. 293)?

Following is a list of some questions about morality asked of sex education leaders by high school students:

Do you think that it is wrong for a young, matured couple to live together?

Why does my religious belief say that it is wrong to have premarital intercourse?

Why should other people decide for us what's right or wrong when it comes to sex?

If people can't measure up to the qualifications necessary for a good marriage partner, should we let them have their sex without marriage as long as they don't produce children?

How do you decide if it's right or wrong to have sex before marriage?

What do you do about dual values? When your mother has urged you all your life to be a man and the only way you can prove it is to have sex— How can you wait until you're married?

Have they any right to take your baby away just because you aren't married?

How can I develop a sense of values?

Are morals always associated with religion?

What are morals?

What opinions have you read in the selections of this section on morality which contribute *an* answer to each one? What would your answer be to each question? Why?

How might writers you have read on the subject, and you at this point, deal with Ado Annie's question in **I Cain't Say No** (p. 273): "How can I be what I ain't?"

How would you now respond to Quentin's question from **After the Fall** (p. 273): "What the hell is moral?"

Toward a Definition of Marriage

Love and Marriage

SAMMY CAHN and JAMES VAN HEUSEN

LOVE AND MAR-RIAGE, LOVE AND MAR-RIAGE, Go to-geth-er like a horse and car-riage,

This I tell ya, broth - er, Ya can't have one with-out the oth - er.

Shinn observes

[the fact that] marriage may be a temptation, as people avoid responsibilities for the sake of the comfort and security of the family. [84]

By the same token, there are those who fear, forego, or even flee from the idea of marriage, even though, as another verse of the song declares, "it's an institute you can't disparage." What are some of the fears and resistances and doubts that might stop people from marrying? What, for example, was Sylvia's most acute fear in **The Bent Twig** (p. 144) until her mother reassured her that

There's no healthy life possible without some sensual feeling between the husband and wife, but there's nothing in the world more awful than married life when it's the only common ground.

341

In *My Fair Lady,* Henry Higgins voices some masculine objections to letting a woman in his life when he sings "I'm an Ordinary Man." He found that in his relationships with women he became "selfish and tyrannical," while they became "jealous, exacting, suspicious, and a damn nuisance." Professor Higgins claimed that a woman would redecorate your home, overhaul you, shift plans, ignore your advice, and bring "an army of her friends" to criticize you; in addition, she brings "a booming, boisterous family" and "a large, Wagnerian mother." Thus, while he styles himself as "an ordinary man," desiring "nothing more than just the ordinary chance to live exactly as he likes and do precisely what he wants," he is resigned to remaining "a confirmed old bachelor."

Given some of his premises and assuming he is serious, would Professor Higgins be capable of maintaining any sort of satisfactory relationship with a woman?

Are there others perhaps, like Alexander Portnoy, who feel plagued by insatiable sexual desire which drives them from woman to woman? As Philip Roth has Portnoy explain to his psychiatrist in **Portnoy's Complaint:**

> Look, at least I don't find myself still in my early thirties locked into a marriage with some nice person whose body has ceased to be of any genuine interest to me—at least I don't have to get into bed every night with somebody who by and large I fuck out of obligation instead of lust. I mean, the nightmarish depression some people suffer at bedtime . . . On the other hand, even I must admit that there is maybe, from a certain perspective, something a little depressing about my situation, too. Of course you can't have everything, or so I understand—but the question I am willing to face is: have I anything? How much longer do I go on conducting these experiments with women? How much longer do I go on sticking this thing into the holes that come available to it—first this hole, then when I tire of this hole, that hole over there . . . and so on. When will it end? Only *why* should it end! To please a father and mother? To conform to the norm? Why on earth should I be so defensive about being what was honorably called some years ago, a bachelor? After all, that's all this is, you know—bachelorhood. So what's the crime? Sexual freedom? In this day and age? Why should *I* bend to the bourgeoisie? Do I ask them to bend to me? Maybe I've been touched by the tarbrush of Bohemia a little—is that so awful? Whom am I harming with my lusts? I don't blackjack the ladies, I don't twist arms to get them into bed with me. I am, if I may say so, an honest and compassionate man; let me tell you, as men go I am . . . But why must I explain myself! *Excuse* myself! Why must I justify with my Honesty and Compassion my desires! So I have desires—only they're endless. Endless! [85]

What qualities of character are necessary to find total and lasting satisfaction with a husband or wife?

What is the critical distinction in the statement made by the heroine to her lover in the movie *Interlude:* "Of course I love you; I just don't want to be your wife!" If love is not enough to marry on, what other factors need to be considered?

Do you think that two congenial people who are fond of each other, but not in love, might marry and then develop feelings of deep love? On what might it depend?

One sex educator proposes the following questions to ask yourself concerning a prospective husband or wife:

1. Is this person going your way? Does he or she look forward to the same sort of life that you do? Is there a similarity of hopes and dreams and ambi-

tions for the future? Are you reasonably sure that you both are working toward the same life goals?

2. Is this your kind of person? Does he or she like the same kind of things you do? Do you come from the same general background? Are your families somewhat similar? Do you share a common religious faith? Did you grow up in the same sort of community? Are you accustomed to approximately the same standard of living? Do you agree upon most of the important issues of life?

3. Do both sets of parents approve? Does your family think that the engagement is a good idea? Are they happy for you? Does his (her) family like you? Do you like them? Do you have the blessing of your parents in this important step?

4. Do you respect and admire, as well as love, one another?

5. Are you good companions? [86]

How much weight would you attach to these criteria? Why? Name some of the "important issues of life" mentioned in the second set of questions.

Even though you may disagree with the emphasis accorded them, what reasoning might lie behind the significance attached to similarities of general background? How can extreme differences in general background cause problems in interfaith or inter-racial marriages? Quite apart from external prejudice, what specific difficulties might arise in the relationship that you can foresee? How might they be solved?

Why do you think parental approval is considered important? Are the two of you all that matters? The two of you are also becoming members of each other's families, but do you have to be concerned with in-laws?

Toward a Definition of Marriage
MONA VAN DUYN

It is to make a fill, not find a land.
Elsewhere, often, one sights americas of awareness,
suddenly there they are, natural and anarchic,
with plantings scattered but rich, powers to be harnessed—
but this is more like building a World's Fair island.
Somebody thought it could be done, contracts are signed,
and now all materials are useful, everything; sludge
is scooped up and mixed with tin cans and fruit rinds,
even tomato pulp and lettuce leaves are solid
under pressure. Presently the ground humps up and shows.
But this marvel of engineering is not all.
A hodgepodge of creatures (no bestiary would suppose
such an improbable society) are at this time
turned loose to run on it, first shyly, then more free,
and must keep, for self's sake, wiles, anger, much of their
spiney or warted nature, yet learn courtesy.

It is closest to picaresque, but essentially artless.
If there were any experts, they are dead, it takes too long.

How could its structure be more than improvising,
when it never ends, but line after line plods on,
and none of the ho hum passages can be skipped?
It has a bulky knowledge, but what symbol comes anywhere
    near
suggesting it? No, the notion of art won't fit it—
unless—when it's embodied. For digression there
is meaningful, and takes such joy in the slopes and crannies
that every bony gesture is generous, full,
all lacy with veins and nerves. There, the spirit
smiles in its skin, and impassions and sweetens to style.
So this comes to resemble a poem found in his notebooks
after the master died. A charred, balky man, yet one day
as he worked at one of those monuments, the sun guiled him,
and he turned to a fresh page and simply let play
his great gift on a small ground. Yellowed, unpublished,
he might have forgotten he wrote it. (All this is surmise.)
But it's known by heart now; it rounded the steeliest shape
to shapeliness, it was so loving an exercise.

Say, for once, that the start is a pure vision
like the blind man's (though he couldn't keep it, trees
soon bleached to familiar) when the bandage came off
and what a world could be first fell on his eyes.
Say it's when campaigns are closest to home
that farsighted lawmakers oftenest lose their way.
And repeat what everyone knows and nobody wants
to remember, that always, always expediency
must treckle the fairest wishes. Say, when documents,
stiff with history, go right into the council chambers
and are rolled up to shake under noses, are constantly read
    from,
or pounded on, or passed around, the parchment limbers;
and, still later, if these old papers are still being shuffled,
commas will be missing, ashes will disfigure a word;
finally thumbprints will grease out whole phrases, the clear
    prose
won't mean much; it can never be wholly restored.
Curators mourn the perfect idea, for it crippled
outside of its case. Announce that at least it can move
in the imperfect action, beyond the windy oratory,
of marriage, which is the politics of love.

What is the significance of the word "toward" in Van Duyn's poem *Toward
a Definition of Marriage?*

The poet's opening line, "It is to make a fill, not find a land," rejects the
popularly held notion of marriage as an end rather than a beginning. The noun
"fill" means: a full supply, especially a quantity that satisfies or satiates; and ma-

terial used to fill a receptacle. How are both these dictionary meanings relevant to Van Duyn's concept of marriage as an engineer's creation rather than an explorer's discovery? As building rather than remodeling?

What specifics in the first stanza are equivalent to the concept of love in which two people "produce together an intellectual soil and an emotional climate in which each can flourish"?

Why is it not possible for marriage to be the discovery of a land with "plantings scattered but rich, powers to be harnessed"?

What ideas do Van Duyn's final lines suggest to you:

> Curators mourn the perfect idea, for it crippled
> outside of its case. Announce that at least it can move
> in the imperfect action, beyond the windy oratory,
> of marriage, which is the politics of love.

Do we cherish illusions about married bliss which become shattered in the business of living? What is meant by "the politics of love"?

RELATED QUESTIONS

What sorts of things might Van Duyn consider some of the "ho hum passages" of marriage with which Lindbergh in *Double-Sunrise* (p. 232) might concur?

What "ho hum passage" does Gunn suggest in *Das Liebesleben* (p. 192)?

How might Stevenson (*On Falling in Love*, p. 238) and Lindbergh (*Double-Sunrise*, p. 232) describe "the start" which Van Duyn calls "a pure vision"

> like the blind man's (though he couldn't keep it, trees
> soon bleached to familiar) when the bandage came off
> and what a world could be first fell on his eyes.

How are the final lines of *Toward a Definition of Marriage* related to the following passage on "realization" in Shinn's *Revolution in Sexual Ethics* (p. 270)?

> Sometimes in our society, as sometimes in man's long past, man and woman enter into a personal relation in which they realize the wonder and joy of sex. Such realization does not come through concentration on sex alone. The persons involved are concerned not simply for sex, but for each other. Yet it is not enough that they dote on each other. They seek to share life, to join together in work and joy and appreciation for the mystery of life and love. Then sexual activity is one expression of mutuality and commitment.
>
> It is one of the wonders of sex that flashes of this realization may illumine even the more mechanized and trivialized relationships that are so common in our society. But the authentic, profound realization is rather rare in a society that often reveals a hunger for it. And, of course, it is never totally untainted. Denis de Rougemont has called marriage at its best "poise in imperfection." The poise is the more wonderful as men and women acknowledge their imperfection.

Oyster Bed

ANNE MORROW LINDBERGH

346

"They"
awareness of others

But surely we *do* demand duration and continuity of relationships, at least of marriage. That is what marriage is, isn't it—continuity of a relationship? Of course, but not necessarily continuity in one single form or stage; not necessarily continuity in the double-sunrise stage. There are other shells to help me, to put in the row on my desk. Here is one I picked up yesterday. Not rare; there are many of them on the beach and yet each one is individual. You never find two alike. Each is fitted and formed by its own life and struggle to survive. It is an oyster, with small shells clinging to its humped back. Sprawling and uneven, it has the irregularity of something growing. It looks rather like the house of a big family, pushing out one addition after another to hold its teeming life—here a sleeping porch for the children, and there a veranda for the play-pen; here a garage for the extra car and there a shed for the bicycles. It amuses me because it seems so much like my life at the moment, like most women's lives in the middle years of marriage. It is untidy, spread out in all directions, heavily encrusted with accumulations and, in its living state—this one is empty and cast up by the sea—firmly imbedded on its rock.

Yes, I believe the oyster shell is a good one to express the middle years of marriage. It suggests the struggle of life itself. The oyster has fought to have that place on the rock to which it has fitted itself perfectly and to which it clings tenaciously. So most couples in the growing years of marriage struggle to achieve a place in the world. It is a physical and material battle first of all, for a home, for children, for a place in their particular society. In the midst of such a life there is not much time to sit facing one another over a breakfast table. In these years one recognizes the truth of Saint-Exupéry's line: "Love does not consist in gazing at each other (one perfect sunrise gazing at another!) but in looking outward together in the same direction." For, in fact, man and woman are not only *looking* outward in the same direction; they are *working* outward. (Observe the steady encroachment of the oyster bed over the rock.) Here one forms ties, roots, a firm base. (Try and pry an oyster from its ledge!) Here one makes oneself part of the community of men, of human society.

Here the bonds of marriage are formed. For marriage, which is always spoken of as a bond, becomes actually, in this stage, many bonds, many strands, of different texture and strength, making up a web that is taut and firm. The web is fashioned of love. Yes, but many kinds of love: romantic love first, then a slow-growing devotion and, playing through these, a constantly rippling companionship. It is made of loyalties, and interdependencies, and shared experiences. It is woven of memories of meetings and conflicts; of triumphs and disappointments. It is a web of communication, a common language, and the acceptance of lack of language, too; a knowledge of likes and dislikes, of habits and reactions, both physical and mental. It is a web of instincts and intuitions, and known and unknown exchanges. The web of marriage is made by propinquity, in the day to day living side by side, looking outward and working outward in the same direction. It is woven in space and in time of the substance of life itself.

But the bond—the bond of romantic love is something else. It has so little to do with propinquity or habit or space or time or life itself. It leaps across all of them, like a rainbow—or a glance. It is the bond of romantic love which fastens the double-sunrise shell, only one bond, one hinge. And if that fragile link is snapped in the storm, what will hold the halves to each other? In the oyster stage of marriage, romantic love is only one of the many bonds that make up the intricate and enduring web that two people have built together.

I am very fond of the oyster shell. It is humble and awkward and ugly. It is slate-colored and unsymmetrical. Its form is not primarily beautiful but functional. I make fun of its knobbiness. Sometimes I resent its burdens and excrescences. But its tireless adaptability and tenacity draw my astonished admiration and sometimes even my tears. And it is comfortable in its familiarity, its homeliness, like old garden gloves which have moulded themselves perfectly to the shape of the hand. I do not like to put it down. I will not want to leave it.

But is it the permanent symbol of marriage? Should it—any more than the double-sunrise shell—last forever? The tide of life recedes. The house, with its bulging sleeping porches and sheds, begins little by little to empty. The children go away to school and then to marriage and lives of their own. Most people by middle age have attained, or ceased to struggle to attain, their place in the world. That terrific tenacity to life, to place, to people, to material surroundings and accumulations—is it as necessary as it was when one was struggling for one's security or the security of one's children? Many of the physical struggles have ceased, due either to success or to failure. Does the shell need to be so welded to its rock? Married couples are apt to find themselves in middle age, high and dry in an outmoded shell, in a fortress which has outlived its function. What is one to do—die of atrophy in an outstripped form? Or move on to another form, other experiences?

Perhaps, someone will suggest, this is the moment to go back to the simple self-enclosed world of the sunrise shell? Alone at last again over the muffins and the marmalade! No, one cannot go back to that tightly closed world. One has grown too big, too many-sided, for that rigidly symmetrical shell. I am not sure that one has not grown too big for any shell at all.

Perhaps middle age is, or should be, a period of shedding shells; the shell of ambition, the shell of material accumulations and possessions, the shell of the ego. Perhaps one can shed at this stage in life as one sheds in beach-living; one's pride, one's false ambitions, one's mask, one's armor. Was that armor not put on to protect one from the competitive world? If one ceases to compete, does one need it? Perhaps one can at last in middle age, if not earlier, be completely oneself. And what a liberation that would be!

It is true that the adventures of youth are less open to us. Most of us cannot, at this point, start a new career or raise a new family. Many of the physical, material, and worldly ambitions are less attainable than they were twenty years ago. But is this not often a relief? "I no longer worry about being the belle of Newport," a beautiful woman, who had become a talented artist, once said to me. And I always liked that Virginia Woolf hero who meets middle age admitting: "Things have dropped from me. I have outlived certain desires . . . I am not so gifted as at one time seemed likely. Certain things lie beyond my scope. I shall never understand the harder problems of philosophy. Rome is the limit of my travelling . . . I shall never see savages in Tahiti spearing fish by the light of a blazing cresset, or a lion spring in the jungle, or a naked man eating raw flesh. . ." (Thank God! you can hear him adding under his breath.)

The primitive, physical, functional pattern of the morning of life, the active years before forty or fifty, is outlived. But there is still the afternoon opening up, which one can spend not in the feverish pace of the morning but in having time at last for those intellectual, cultural, and spiritual activities that were pushed aside in the heat of the race. We Americans, with our terrific emphasis on youth, action, and material success, certainly tend to belittle the afternoon of life and even to pretend it never comes. We push the clock back and try to prolong the morning, over-reaching and overstraining ourselves in the unnatural effort. We do not succeed, of course. We cannot compete with our sons and daughters. And what a struggle it is to race with these over-active and under-wise adults! In our breathless attempts we often miss the flowering that waits for afternoon.

For is it not possible that middle age can be looked upon as a period of second flowering, second growth, even a kind of second adolescence? It is true that society in general does not help one accept this interpretation of the second half of life. And therefore this period of expanding is often tragically misunderstood. Many people never climb above the plateau of forty-to-fifty. The signs that presage growth, so similar, it seems to me, to those in early adolescence: discontent, restlessness, doubt, despair, longing, are interpreted falsely as signs of decay. In youth one does not as often misinterpret the signs; one accepts them, quite rightly, as growing pains. One takes them seriously, listens to them, follows where they lead. One is afraid. Naturally. Who is not afraid of pure space— that breath-taking empty space of an open door? But despite fear, one goes through to the room beyond.

But in middle age, because of the false assumption that it is a period of decline, one interprets these life-signs, paradoxically, as signs of approaching death. Instead of facing them, one runs away; one escapes—into depressions, nervous breakdowns, drink, love affairs, or frantic, thoughtless, fruitless overwork. Anything, rather than face them. Anything, rather than stand still and learn from them. One tries to cure the signs of growth, to exorcise them, as if they were devils, when really they might be angels of annunciation.

Angels of annunciation of what? Of a new stage in living when, having shed many of the physical struggles, the worldly ambitions, the material encumbrances of active life, one might be free to fulfill the neglected side of one's self. One might be free for growth of mind, heart, and talent; free at last for spiritual growth; free of the clamping sunrise shell. Beautiful as it was, it was still a closed world one had to outgrow. And the time may come when—comfortable and adaptable as it is—one may outgrow even the oyster shell.

How does the oyster shell symbolize the middle years of marriage?
What might Lindbergh use to enlarge on Van Duyn's image in *Toward a Definition of Marriage:*

. . . Presently the ground humps up and shows,
But this marvel of engineering is not all.

How does Lindbergh elaborate on Van Duyn's question: "How could [the structure of marriage] be more than improvising,/ when it never ends, but line after line plods on,/ and none of the ho hum passages can be skipped"?

RELATED QUESTIONS

Lindbergh feels that marriage is many bonds, many strands "fashioned of . . . . many kinds of love: romantic love first, then a slow-growing devotion and, playing through these, a constantly rippling companionship. It is made of loyalties, and interdependencies, and shared experiences." On the basis of her concept described in **Oyster Bed,** what criticism might Lindbergh make of the relationship portrayed in **Trilogy for X** by Louis MacNeice (see "**Night-Lights,**" p. 573)? How might one say that the couple in MacNeice's poem have more than those in the "double-sunrise" stage (p. 232), but less than those in the marital relationship of **Oyster Bed?**

Married Love: Strategy of

MARLENE DIETRICH

Love him. Unconditionally and with devotion.

You chose him. He must be wonderful.

If you chose him for any other reason, your problem, whatever it may be, lies in a realm of which I know nothing.

If your brain, instead of your heart, pilots your emotions, there must be regrets. You *cannot* trust your brain. You *can* trust your heart.

If you follow your heart there are no regrets, because there was no choice. Regretting is a fruitless, destructive occupation. Regretting, that is, what you did to yourself. Regretting the harm you did to others is a different matter. The feelings of others, particularly those of the man you live with, are very important. Much more important than your own.

You are a woman with a thousand little pockets in your being where you can tuck away little pains until tomorrow. A man hasn't got those pockets. His emotional system isn't quite as vast a labyrinth as yours. He is simpler, straighter than you are. This is not man's personal achievement, he is just made that way.

In order to love him well, you must try to be simpler, and straighter. This is much easier than it sounds. Just feel your way backward to the time when you first started to feel love. Before you started to play the game. Before you heard about and started to adopt the muddled values, tricks, the pride, the fencing, which make so many women lose their men.

You were young and felt love. This alone made you happy. The object of your love did not even have to belong to you. You were grateful if you could see him, and when he noticed you, your heart leaped. The fact that you loved him made your life wonderful. You didn't demand anything in those days—you wouldn't have dared. You just lived in a dream, and your hopes were humble. Just to be near him, you felt, was heaven. You did not think any further. The world was a beautiful place.

You had the optimism and the trust of youth. You were basically gay, with frequent melancholy hours, having the blues.

Youth is wise in matters of emotions. It takes the bad with the good in easy strides.

And then you grow up. You fall in love. Your heart leaps when he notices you. But now you want him for your own. At all times you and your heart wear your Sunday dress—and he falls in love with you. The world and life are wonderful.

But every day is not Sunday and you soon take off your Sunday dress. You and your heart. And somewhere back in your fairy-tale-hungry mind you are disappointed. And you think it must be somebody's fault. You "analyze," and find fault with the world. When you don't succeed in arriving at a fruitful conclusion you try to find the fault in a tangible object.

He does not necessarily have to be the reason. He just happens to be around when the constant Sundays become weekdays, with a few Sundays here and there and far apart, when you find out about life as you see it now in your weekday clothes. He knows too little about women and is too bewildered by your accusations to fence with half the skill you show. He thinks twice before he says words that might hurt you. You do not think at all. You find your target and you shoot. You have a vast supply of ammunition to draw on.

Your complaints range wide: from daily chores around the house and tired bones, to market prices, hot stoves, relatives, the neighbors—and the mink coat of your dreams.

He braves all your assaults because he loves you and wants peace. And for this peace and quiet that he wants, he soon trades in his age-old possession: his right to be the master of the house.

This is regrettable because you both are losers. The role of master of the house is not a lucky one for you if you obtain it by such unfair means. You lose your femininity. Let me . . . cite Goethe: "The eternal feminine draws us on." But you must be completely feminine, not just in bits and pieces and here and there where it fits the scheme of things.

To be completely woman you need a master, and in him a compass for your life. You need a man you can look up to and respect. If you dethrone him it's no wonder that you are discontented, and discontented women are not loved for long.

Your erstwhile king is loser too. His new role is unmanly and he knows it, but he resigns in hopes for armistice. Too bad for you if he discovers that indifference serves well as a shield against your whizzing arrows.

If you could stop and look at your battered target as a mother would or as a friend might do, you would not like the tactics you used—tactics you would not dare to use with anyone except the man you chose, the man whose love you want, to whom you said: "I want you for my own, forever after."

You were right in saying "forever after"—Cinderella-minded as you are. The fairy tale leaves you with the beautiful sentence about happiness forever after. But you forget that *before* it came to that poetic ending, there were dangers and sorrows and hardships. In real life, dangers and sorrows and hardships continue.

You face the bad ones together, the real sorrow and hardships. But only those. The other little sorrows, disappointments, annoyances, inconveniences you must face alone. Your sadness that has no apparent reason—face it alone and with yourself. It only proves that you are a sensitive, imaginative woman. Yield to it, it will pass more quickly that way. But don't try to find the reason in your present life, your man, your home, your routine chores of every day. Or even your duties to your children, if you are so blessed as to have them.

As our times "progress," women searching for a solution to emotional problems are steered further and further away from their own responsibility, and more and more into believing that others are responsible for their predicament. It is even becoming convenient to blame Mother for putting them the wrong way around into the cradle, or Father for doing something equally harmful to their future security.

This, to my way of thinking, has never solved anything. On the contrary, it tends to make those women more self-centered than they already are. It leads them further into complete preoccupation with themselves. Therefore, they cannot make someone else happy. Therefore, they are, themselves, unhappy.

To make a man happy is a full-time job. It leaves us very little time to take ourselves too seriously. And if you have children, you have no time at all. Or you *should* have no time at all. And when the work is directed toward the making and the keeping of a happy home, it makes you rich in contentment and puts occupational afflictions, like aching bones, into the only place where they belong, a hot bath.

This rich contentment will make you do a lot of things you had forgotten. You will remember your instinct's aerial, the tender, fine antennas you used to stretch his way in the beginning. Although neglected, they are still with you, dusty and bent, but you can straighten them. They'll help you know what he would like before he says it, as long ago when you were thrilled, and kissed, because you found another mystic link between your mind and his.

With your antennas at work, life should be easy. They'll tell you many things. His desires of each day and night and his dislikes. When to be quiet, when to talk, when to give an opinion on his problems and when just to listen, when to ask questions on how his work is going and when to wait until he wants to think of work and talk about it. When to welcome him with kisses, and when your hand in his for a moment is enough. If it was kisses you wanted, do not fret—you will be kissed, but later and surely better.

Do let him read the papers. But not while you accusingly tiptoe around the room, or perch much like a silent bird of prey on the edge of your most uncomfortable chair. (He will read them anyway, and he *should* read them, so let him choose his own good time.) Don't make a big exit. Just go. But kiss him quickly, before you go, otherwise he might think you are angry; *he is used to suspecting he is doing something wrong.*

Your antennas will make you wear the dress he likes and not the one he thinks too loud, too clinging, or too low in front. They'll tell you never to interrupt him while he is telling a story to friends, never to say, "Oh, that's not what happened, let *me* tell it." Tell your own stories if you have to talk, but leave his alone. And listen well, although you know his stories. He knows yours, too, and has to listen. Cherish the intimacy that your life together brings rather than dwell on the boring aspects. And continue to listen to your antennas. You will then not remark about his shortcomings or "the stupid thing he said this morning."

You will then, on the other hand, not (except in the company of your very closest and intimate friends) gloat over him, boast about his looks, his suits, his taste, his genius in all sorts of departments, and kiss him, hug or cuddle up to him in front of people. He is a man and it embarrasses him. People will know that you love him by the way you look at him, or by the way you take from his hand the glass he offers you.

Don't ever fight with him in public. There is nothing uglier than that. Wait till you are home, if fight you must. If he has hurt you, remember: Only the one you love can hurt you. But wait. Don't make your man impatient by crying, or accusing him of cruelty. Wait till you can think clearly, or you might say words too harsh or not quite to the point. It is more than possible that later you might not even want to mention it, or if you do you will be able to make your point much clearer. You'll find your man receptive only if there is no distortion of the facts, and if there's logic, most of all. Now, woman's logic is a muddled thing, as we all know. So all you have to do is think you are defending him against a woman and you will see your logic rise like Venus out of water, with your own love right there to give it a good leg up.

Your peace-loving antennas will make you stay at home when he is tired, when he prefers to look at baseball or at you (in moments when the game is dull) instead of twenty faces at a party. When the game is on, you can serve his dinner on a table so placed he doesn't have to strain his neck.

Don't make him do things. When he does them because he wants to do them, they'll be much better done. Let his timetable be *the* timetable.

Don't look upon him as a habit, or an object. The fact that objects like his bed, his comb, his toothbrush are with you can blind you into believing he cannot leave his bed, his toothbrush, comb, and you. He can, you know. And if he doesn't, but often has the thought that he would like to, you've lost him, even though you sleep beside him.

Your antennas tell you other things. To look for beauty and for joy in everything you do, instead of seeing all your daily duties drab and joyless (for which you need no effort). To clean your house and your machines that help you clean, and wash, and beat the eggs and mix the dough. To clean your children with your hands *(thank God there is no machine for that),* dress them, go to the market which abounds in food so you can choose, push carriages or hold the hands of children on streets, in sunny parks, or sit on benches watching them play, walk home to feed them, make them rest. Then, in that quiet hour in your home, to feel the beauty of the day gone by, the joy in all the things you did, to start again the shorter afternoon, dress children, play, feed, wash them and listen for the sound of his key and the homecoming slam of the door.

Like the moon, the woman needs the man so she can shine and glow and put the tender silver into the strong reality of gold. The need to shine and glow makes her alive. Her tender presence will make the man want her as he wants sun and air. For what he dreams of is a tender woman who is at once a mother and a child.

Why is **Married Love** subtitled **"Strategy of"**? In what way do Dietrich's remarks parallel the definition of strategy: "the science and art of employing the political, economic, psychological and military forces of a nation or group of nations to afford the maximum support to adopted policies in peace or war"?

What might be specific examples of "the muddled values, tricks, the pride, the fencing, which make so many women lose their men"?

Would you agree with the author's distinction between the emotional systems of the male and female:

> . . . a woman [has] a thousand little pockets in [her] being where [she] can tuck away little pains until tomorrow. A man hasn't got those pockets. His emotional system isn't quite as vast a labyrinth. . . . He is simpler, straighter. . . . This is not a man's personal achievement, he is just made that way.

Why then is it the female who cries more often than the male?

To what extent might Dietrich support the concept of marriage implied by the manufacturers of His and Hers sweatshirts labelled "master" and "slave" respectively and advertised: "Let Them Know Who's Boss!"

Is the husband the "boss" in a marital relationship? Or do women really "wear the pants" in the partnership?

In Chaucer's *Canterbury Tales,* the Wife of Bath concluded her tale with the following philosophy of marriage:

> . . . Jesu Crist us sende
> Housbondes meke, yonge, and fresshe a-bedde,
> And grace t'overbyde hem that we wedde.
> And eek I preye Jesu shorte hir lyves
> That wol nat be governed by hir wyves;
> And olde and angry nigardes of dispence,
> God sende hem sone verray pestilence. [87]

Is this perspective on power in marriage—expressed by a woman granted grace "t'overbyde hem that we wedde" (she had outlived five husbands)—still relevant? Do women today want husbands who are meek, young and lively in bed? Do they resent those who will not be governed by their wives as well as those old and angry niggards of money?

What does it mean to say that what the man dreams of in a wife "is a tender woman who is at once a mother and a child"? Would you agree? How should the working wife carry out Dietrich's advice?

What does the author mean: "Every day is not Sunday and you soon take off your Sunday dress. You and your heart"? Why must one ever change into weekday clothes?

RELATED QUESTIONS

Fromm, in **The Theory of Love** (p. 262), wrote:

> Love should be essentially an act of will, of decision to commit [one's] life completely to that of one other person. This is, indeed, the rationale behind the idea of the insolubility of marriage. . . . To love somebody is not just a strong feeling—it is a decision, it is a judgment, it is a promise.

Lewis, in **Eros** (p. 214), wrote:

In reality . . . Eros, having made his gigantic promise and shown you in glimpses what its performance would be like, has "done his stuff." He . . . makes the vows; it is we who must keep them.

Lee, in **What Love Must Be** (p. 250), wrote:

Love should be an act of will, of passionate patience—flexible, cunning, constant; proof against roasting and freezing; drought and flood, and the shifting climates of mood and age. In order to make it succeed, one must lose all preconceptions . . . and fashion something that can blanket the whole range of experience from ecstasy to decay.

What do these three writers, along with Van Duyn (**Toward a Definition of Marriage,** p. 343), who spoke of "the politics of love," and Dietrich, who presents its strategy, suggest that marriage requires over, above, and through strong emotions? What sorts of problems require that it be a commitment, or an act of will, if there is to be any guarantee of love's continuation?

In the comments of these writers, can you find a basis for the arguments against teenage marriages? What elements, which these authors deem requisite for successful marriage, are generally associated with greater maturity than most teenagers have acquired?

Beneath the legal labels of "incompatibility," "adultery," and "mental cruelty" what reasons do you think lead to "grounds for divorce"? What do you imagine to be the most common cause of broken marriages? Could the main cause "lie in our attitude toward love itself—that as soon as it drops one degree below the level of self-satisfaction it is somehow improper to preserve it," (p. 251) and that, therefore, as Lindbergh suggests in **Double-Sunrise** (p. 233), "the temptation is to blame the situation on the other person and to accept the easy solution that a new and more understanding partner will solve everything"? How does Dietrich express a similar idea in **Married Love: Strategy of**?

What alternative explanations for marital failures exist? Could you subscribe to the following view:

Few marriages are happy. Considering the infant training that the majority of people have had, it is a matter of great astonishment that there should be any happy marriages at all. If sex is dirty in the nursery, it cannot be very clean in the wedding bed.

Where the sex relationship is a failure, everything else in the marriage is a failure. [88]

If so, would you emphasize, as strongly as this author does, that marital problems lie more with sex than with love?

How might some marital difficulties be avoided, or remedied once they have occurred? What solution does Robert Creeley suggest in **A Marriage** (see "**Night-Lights**" p. 544)? What does Creeley mean in the final lines of the poem: "he gave up loving and lived with her"? Does the phrase connote apathy? Resignation? Indifference? Life without love? The absence of sex? Recognition that giving a symbolic golden wedding ring and making gestures of physical intimacy are only two aspects of marriage which is "to make a fill"? Something else?

Review the complaints of the supposedly ordinary Henry Higgins who will never let a woman in his life (p. 342) and Portnoy, whose problems are described in the questions following **Love and Marriage** (p. 342). How would some of the writers on sex, love, morality and marriage assess their situations? Why might both men make very poor husbands?

Just as there is a case for chastity, is there a case for bachelorhood? For spinsterhood?

Alice Duer Miller's narrative poem *Forsaking All Others,* which concludes with the following excerpt, portrays an extramarital affair between the narrator of the poem and Lee. During the course of their relationship, the narrator's wife, Ruth, dies.

Forsaking All Others
ALICE DUER MILLER

"Dear Lee:—
        I've tried so many times to write,
And now I must write, for I sail next week
For Italy—Sardinia—I might
Go on to Egypt later, and the Greek
Islands. I may be several years away.

"I loved you, Lee. I wonder if I can
Explain at all what's happened? From your wealth
You gave me freely—more than any man
Has ever had—beauty, wit, youth and health—
I loved you passionately; and now my wife
Is dead. One might expect a mild distress,
A briefly pensive mood . . . Instead, my life
Is shattered . . . is dissolved . . . is meaningless . .
She whom of late I thought so little of
And saw so little, was, I find, the spring
Of all I did and felt—even of my love
Of you . . . What an insane, incredible thing!
But there it is.

        "Dear Lee, this is the truth:
That any marriage founded on devotion
Though that devotion die, as mine for Ruth,
Is not a state, but a unique emotion,
Potent, unalterable—not romantic
Love, though romantic love is where it starts—
Marriage begins only when those hot, frantic
Fires have finished welding human hearts.
It is not love, friendship, or partnership,
But this emotion—marriage, of a force
That when it once has held you in its grip
Nothing will free you wholly—not divorce,
Or death, for these destroy not it, but you,
As I am now destroyed.

"Beware, dear Lee,
Of a true marriage, if you are not true
Yourself—or you will be destroyed—like me."

The narrator explains that any marriage founded on devotion, even though that devotion dies, is "not a state, but a unique emotion." How would you distinguish between a "state" of marriage and an "emotion" of marriage?

How does the narrator react to his wife's death? What realization does it bring? Would you have expected that he might feel liberated to marry Lee? Would you have thought he might feel guilty and turn it on Lee, writing that he now realized he had never really cared for her? Would you imagine he might have felt so guilty that he would turn it on himself and suicide? Would you have expected him to decide he had never truly cared for his wife and to justify his affair with Lee by rationalizing that she fulfilled needs which Ruth could not satisfy?

What are his feelings for Lee? Did they change because of Ruth's death?

What were his feelings for Ruth? Did her death change them?

Instead of experiencing a "mild distress, a briefly pensive mood" following his wife's death, the narrator finds that his life "is shattered . . . is dissolved . . . is meaningless." Why?

What does he mean by "what an insane, incredible thing!" Why does it strike him as "insane" and "incredible"? Does it seem equally ironic to you?

RELATED QUESTIONS

The narrator separates the unique emotion of marriage from "those hot, frantic fires" characteristic of romantic love. In what other terms have those hot, frantic fires been described in previous selections?

How are romantic love and marriage connected by Alice Duer Miller? Does Creeley in *A Marriage* (see "**Night-Lights**," p. 544) feel similarly or differently?

What does the narrator mean: "Marriage is not love, friendship, or partnership"? Would Lindbergh (p. 346), Van Duyn (p. 343) and/or Dietrich (p. 349) agree?

Do Lindbergh, Van Duyn, and/or Dietrich view marriage as a "state" or as a "unique emotion"? Why?

To what extent does Elizabeth Barrett Browning in *Sonnet VI* (see "**Night-Lights**," p. 542) subscribe to Miller's perspective in *Forsaking All Others?*

In *Sonnet 116* (p. 230), Shakespeare speaks of the "marriage of true minds" in defining characteristics of true love. Would Alice Duer Miller agree with him? Why, or why not?

"You–I"

INTERRELATIONSHIPS

Environmental "**They**" forces—contemporaries, family, mob, and media, not to mention writers of psychology, philosophy, poetry, and prose—provide young people with food for thought. Yet, since "knowledge springs not from thinking, but from thinking about what happens when we act" [1], theoretical advice, cultural "oughts," family standards, media's "might-be's," and peer-group practices must be tested out in concrete, individualized relationships that an "**I**" experiences with a "**You.**"

But a mutually satisfying love relationship between two individuals—a selective "**I**" and a selective "**You**"—is sometimes difficult to establish and often difficult to maintain. Since physiological maturation seems to outstrip psychological growth, adolescents are apt to be bigger "outside" than "inside." When the value of investments in others has yet to be learned, alliances are apt to be either experimental efforts to discover what the opposite sex is like and how one rates in relation to it, or desperate attempts to delineate one's ego identity. Early love relationships are likely to be founded on one's search for emotional feedback on love, much like those answers sold for a penny to those who play the "Love Machine" (see p. 362).

All readings in this "**You-I**" section view fairly intense heterosexual interactions between two people establishing a sexual and/or loving and/or marital relationship. One couple is as young as the eleven-year-old in *Manchild in the Promised Land;* several couples approach the chronological maturity of the narrator in *My Last Duchess.*

While a "**We**" potential glimmers through some of the relationships; while the bittersweet romantic moments depicted in *Marjorie Morningstar* may contribute to psychosexual maturity and may be underestimated by adults, the "**You-I**" relationships in these selections are nevertheless failures. They are failures of the flesh, or the ego, or the intellect, or the spirit, and such flaws preclude, either **359** in or out of wedlock, that "welding [of two] human hearts" intrinsic to the emotion of marriage.

Characters in the first section—"I and you"—subordinate the human worth of another to the satisfaction of their own needs. The respiratory system of the eighteen-year-old in *I Can't Breathe* is clogged with self-importance, magnified crises, and spectres of her superficial, indiscriminate "loves," as they relate to her well-being. Role-players like Philip in *Of Human Bondage* conduct clinical studies in feeling, or like the train passengers in *Romance* test the effectiveness of an ego image. A sense of power derives also from the quasi-harmless exaggerations and rationalizations about Tonka in *The Well of Days* when sex is idealized as love, or from the more honestly faced thrills of "straight sex" in *I like my body when it is with your* and *Homage to Sextus Propertius.* More destructive reductions of a person to "thing" status can be viewed from the Duke's perspective in *My Last Duchess,* or from Betty Anderson's attitude toward Rodney in *Peyton Place* where sexual weapons are used to avenge ego hurt and to gain a sense of power.

By a variety of exploitative means, characters like Harry in *Rabbit, Run* use others to reassure themselves. In imposing their terms on those they exploit, they deny the joint freedom and responsibility essential to a "**We**" relationship.

By the same token, the second section's "YOU and i" relationships lack the community which implies mutuality because, as Elizabeth Barrett Browning's *I Think of Thee (Sonnet XXIX)* illustrates, characters who accept another's terms without demur abandon their own integrity, like the woman in *I Hereby Swear; (Sonnet XVI)* or, in maintaining it, fall victim to romantic idealization, like the female in *A Lodging for the Night.*

Whether by exaggeration through fantasy (the projection of supposed virtues onto another) or self-denegration, "YOU and i" characters establish equally unsatisfactory imbalances in love. Love, for them, is built on a dream rather than on a foundation in truth. Thus adolescents like Charley in *The Return of the Native* hold only a few minutes of hero-worship in their hands.

"YOU and i" lovers suffer from deceptions of the senses, hence deceptions of the passions. In some cases the illusion is so dazzling or so necessary that the self-deception must believe the lie. In *Marjorie Morningstar,* Wally gains insight into "puppy love" only in retrospect; in *Great Expectations,* Pip recognizes his idealization of Estella at the time, but is painfully powerless to correct its distortive influence. In some cases "falling in love" means to fall into one's mirror image, hurting oneself and damaging the mirror, as Housman suggests in *Look Not in My Eyes, for Fear.*

The relationships in the third section—"YOU and I"—involve two more or less emotional equals as partners, but while there may be a "love begetting and a love begotten," there is no "love proceeding." The faltering, failing, or fizzling out of these relationships can be traced to at least two sources: (1) communication failures because the love is not strong enough to cast out fear, to replace doubt and mistrust with understanding, as evident in *Difficulty with a Bouquet* where traditional shibboleths block a generous impulse, in *Too Late the Phalarope,* and in *Home Burial,* where off-key communication between husband and wife creates discord in marital harmony; (2) mistaken notions concerning the magical properties of sex. Partners like Lili and Arne in *A Night of Watching,* who use sex as a protection against fear and loneliness in a game of touch-and-go, ask of sex more than it can do. Lovers like Paula and Henri in *The Mandarins* illustrate a sexual relationship in which one avoids responsibility and the other uses sex as a hold. Sexual acrobats like the performers in *may i feel said he* enjoy the pure fun in the carnal element, and are spared the fate of those in *Carnal Knowledge* for whom sex has become "a comical act within a tragic game." **Philander Musing** pictures a man who collects people and sexual triumphs. The limitations on satisfaction in these relationships support the notion that sex is not what we do, but what we are. Sex here is a disillusionment to those who lack self-respect or operate from false pride, self-deception, and deception of others.

Sex is also a trap for the emotionally naïve, unaware of its deceptive nature, like Mick and Harry whose impulses bring them misery in **The Heart is a Lonely Hunter.** For older couples like Hal and Ellie in **Winter Term** the sexual element becomes a razor-sharp irritant of guilt, shame, and restlessness. If prematurely explored it may contribute to misjudgments as in **Manchild in the Promised Land;** if the key differences between male and female sexuality are ignored it may bring the drastic consequences implicit in **In the Orchard.**

Divorced from the totality of love as the **"We's"** experience it, sexual attraction and sexual relations provide emotional and spiritual strangers with a common language. The "conversation" may be momentarily exciting, even unequalled; but because of the restricted vocabulary only limited communication is possible.

I and you

Play the Love Machine

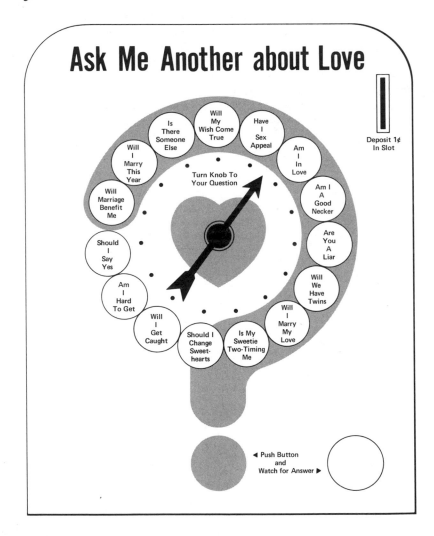

The "attitude—that nothing is easier than to love—has continued," as Fromm points out in *Is Love an Art?* (p. 247), "to be the prevalent idea about love in spite of the overwhelming evidence to the contrary." He continues:

There is hardly any activity, any enterprise, which is started with such tremendous hopes and expectations, and yet, which fails so regularly, as love. If this were the case with any other activity, people would be eager to know the reasons for the failure, and to learn how one could do better—or they would give up the activity. Since the latter is impossible in the case of love, there seems to be only one adequate way to overcome the failure of love—to examine the reasons for this failure, and to proceed to study the meaning of love.

It would indeed be a bargain if for a penny, a turn of a knob, and a push of a button, the Love Machine would answer the question "Am I in love?" Why do individuals seem to have difficulty answering the question themselves? How do you answer it for yourself? What criteria do you use? Are the six tests of love on p. 42 useful?

The love machine invites you to "ask [it] another about love": What answer would you like the machine to give you to "Am I hard to get?" Why?

If you had only one penny, which question would you ask it? Why?

I Can't Breathe

RING LARDNER

I am staying here at the Inn for two weeks with my Uncle Nat and Aunt Jule and I think I will keep a kind of a diary while I am here to help pass the time and so I can have a record of things that happen though goodness knows there isn't likely to anything happen, that is, anything exciting with Uncle Nat and Aunt Jule making the plans as they are both at least 35 years old and maybe older.

Dad and mother are abroad to be gone a month, and me coming here is supposed to be a recompense from them not taking me with them. A fine recompense to be left with old people that come to a place like this to rest. Still it would be a heavenly place under different conditions, for instance, if Walter were here, too. It would be heavenly if he were here, the very thought of it makes my heart stop.

I can't stand it. I won't think about it.

This is our first separation since we have been engaged, nearly 17 days. It will be 17 days tomorrow. And the hotel orchestra at dinner this evening played that old thing "Oh how I miss you tonight" and it seemed as if they must be playing it for my benefit though, of course, the person in that song is talking about how they miss their mother though, of course, I miss mother, too, but a person gets used to missing their mother and it isn't like Walter or the person you are engaged to.

But there won't be any more separations much longer, we are going to be married in December even if mother does laugh when I talk to her about it because she says I am crazy to even think of getting married at 18.

She got married herself when she was 18, but of course that was "different," she wasn't crazy like I am, she knew whom she was marrying. As if Walter were a policeman or a foreigner or something. And she says she was only engaged once while I have been engaged at least five times a year since I was 14, of course, it really isn't as bad as that and I have really only been really what I call engaged six times altogether, but is getting engaged my fault when they keep insisting and hammering at you and if you didn't say yes they would never go home.

But it is different with Walter. I honestly believe if he had not asked me I would have asked him. Of course I wouldn't have, but I would have died. And this is the first time I have ever been engaged to be really married. The other times when they talked about when should we get married I just laughed at them, but I hadn't been engaged to Walter ten minutes when he brought up the subject of marriage and I didn't laugh. I wouldn't be engaged to him unless it was to be married. I couldn't stand it.

Anyway mother may as well get used to the idea because it is "No Foolin'" this time and we have got our plans all made and I am going to be married at home and go out to California and Hollywood on our honeymoon. December, five months away. I can't stand it. I can't wait.

There were a couple of awfully nice looking boys sitting together alone in the dining room tonight. One of them wasn't so much, but the other was cute. And he—

There's the dance orchestra playing "Always," what they played at the Biltmore the day I met Walter. "Not for just an hour not for just a day." I can't live. I can't breathe.

July 13

This has been a much more exciting day than I expected under the circumstances. In the first place I got two long night letters, one from Walter and one from Gordon Flint. I don't see how Walter ever had the nerve to send his, there was everything in it and it must have been horribly embarrassing for him while the telegraph operator was reading it over and counting the words to say nothing of embarrassing for the operator.

But the one from Gordon was a kind of a shock. He just got back from a trip around the world, left last December to go on it and got back yesterday and called up our house and Helga gave him my address and his telegram, well it was nearly as bad as Walter's. The trouble is that Gordon and I were engaged when he went away, or at least he thought so and he wrote to me right along all the time he was away and sent cables and things and for a while I answered his letters, but then I lost track of his itinerary and couldn't write to him any more and when I got really engaged to Walter I couldn't let Gordon know because I had no idea where he was besides not wanting to spoil his trip.

And now he still thinks we are engaged and he is going to call me up tomorrow from Chicago and how in the world can I explain things and get him to understand because he is really serious and I like him ever and ever so much and in lots of ways he is nicer than Walter, not really nicer but better looking and there is no comparison between their dancing. Walter simply can't learn to dance, that is really dance. He says it is because he is flat footed, he says that as a joke, but it is true and I wish to heavens it wasn't.

All afternoon I thought and thought and thought about what to say to Gordon when he calls up and finally I couldn't stand thinking about it any more and just made up my mind I wouldn't think about it any more. But I will tell the truth though it will kill me to hurt him.

I went down to lunch with Uncle Nat and Aunt Jule and they were going out to play golf this afternoon and were insisting that I go with them, but I told them I had a headache and then I had a terrible time getting them to go without me. I didn't have a headache at all and just wanted to be alone to think about Walter and besides when you play with Uncle Nat he is always correcting your stance or your swing or something and always puts his hands on my arms and shoulders to show me the right way and I can't stand it to have old men touch me, even if they are your uncle.

I finally got rid of them and I was sitting watching the tennis when that boy that I saw last night, the cute one, came and sat right next to me and of course I didn't look at him. So we got to talking and he is even cuter than he looks, the most original and wittiest person I believe I ever met and I haven't laughed so much in I don't know how long.

For one thing he asked me if I had heard Rockefeller's song and I said no and he began singing "Oil alone." Then he asked me if I knew the orange juice song and I told him no again and he said it was "Orange juice sorry you made me cry." I was in hysterics before we had been together ten minutes.

His name is Frank Caswell and he has been out of Dartmouth a year and is 24 years old. That isn't so terribly old, only two years older than Walter and three years older than Gordon. I hate the name Frank, but Caswell is all right and he is so cute.

He was out in California last winter and visited Hollywood and met everybody in the world and it is fascinating to listen to him. He met Norma Shearer and he said he thought she was the prettiest thing he had ever seen. What he said was "I did think she was the prettiest girl in the world, till today." I was going to pretend I didn't get it, but I finally told him to be sensible or I would never be able to believe anything he said.

Well, he wanted me to dance with him tonight after dinner and the next question was how to explain how we had met each other to Uncle Nat and Aunt Jule. Frank said he would fix that all right and sure enough he got himself introduced to Uncle Nat when Uncle Nat came in from golf and after dinner Uncle Nat introduced him to me and Aunt Jule and we danced together all evening, that is not Aunt Jule. They went to bed, thank heavens.

He is a heavenly dancer, as good as Gordon. One dance we were dancing and for one of the encores the orchestra played "In a cottage small by a waterfall" and I simply couldn't dance to it. I just stopped still and said "Listen, I can't bear it, I can't breathe" and poor Frank thought I was sick or something and I had to explain that that was the tune the orchestra played the night I sat at the next table to Jack Barrymore at Barney Gallant's.

I made him sit out that encore and wouldn't let him talk till they got through playing it. Then they played something else and I was all right again and Frank told me about meeting Jack Barrymore. Imagine meeting him. I couldn't live.

I promised Aunt Jule I would go to bed at eleven and it is way past that now, but I am all ready for bed and have just been writing this. Tomorrow Gordon is going to call up and what will I say to him? I just won't think about it.

July 14

Gordon called up this morning from Chicago and it was wonderful to hear his voice again though the connection was terrible. He asked me if I still loved him and I tried to tell him no, but I knew that would mean an explanation and the connection was so bad that I never could make him understand so I said yes, but I almost whispered it purposely, thinking he wouldn't hear me, but he heard me all right and he said that made everything all right with the world. He said he thought I had stopped loving him because I had stopped writing.

I wish the connection had been decent and I could have told him how things were, but now it is terrible because he is planning to get to New York the day I get there and heaven knows what I will do because Walter will be there, too. I just won't think about it.

Aunt Jule came in my room just after I was through talking to Gordon, thank heavens. The room was full of flowers. Walter had sent me some and so had Frank. I got another long night letter from Walter, just as silly as the first one. I wish he would say those things in letters instead of night letters so everybody in the world wouldn't see them. Aunt Jule wanted me to read it aloud to her. I would have died.

While she was still in the room, Frank called up and asked me to play golf with him and I said all right and Aunt Jule said she was glad my headache was gone. She was trying to be funny.

I played golf with Frank this afternoon. He is a beautiful golfer and it is thrilling to watch him drive, his swing is so much more graceful than Walter's. I asked him to watch me swing and tell me what was the matter with me, but he said he couldn't look at anything but my face and there wasn't anything the matter with that.

He told me the boy who was here with him had been called home and he was glad of it because I might have liked him, the other boy, better than himself. I told him that couldn't be possible and he asked me if I really meant that and I said of course, but I smiled when I said it so he wouldn't take it too seriously.

We danced again tonight and Uncle Nat and Aunt Jule sat with us a while and danced a couple of dances themselves, but they were really there to get better acquainted with Frank and see if he was all right for me to be with. I know they certainly couldn't have enjoyed their own dancing, no old people really can enjoy it because they can't really do anything.

They were favorably impressed with Frank I think, at least Aunt Jule didn't say I must be in bed at eleven, but just not to stay up too late. I guess it is a big surprise to a girl's parents and aunts and uncles to find out that the boys you go around with are all right, they always seem to think that if I seem to like somebody and the person pays a little attention to me, why he must be a convict or a policeman or a drunkard or something queer.

Frank had some more songs for me tonight. He asked me if I knew the asthma song and I said I didn't and he said "Oh, you must know that. It goes, Yes, sir, asthma baby." Then he told about the underwear song, "I underwear my baby is tonight." He keeps you in hysterics and yet he has his serious side, in fact he was awfully serious when he said good night to me and his eyes simply shone. I wish Walter were more like him in some ways, but I mustn't think about that.

July 15

I simply can't live and I know I'll never sleep tonight. I am in a terrible predicament or rather I won't know whether I really am or not till tomorrow and that is what makes it so terrible.

After we had danced two or three dances, Frank asked me to go for a ride with him and we went for a ride in his car and finally he told me he loved me and I said not to be silly, but he said he was perfectly serious and he certainly acted that way. He asked me if I loved anybody else and I said yes and he asked if I didn't love him more than anybody else and I said yes, but only because I thought he wouldn't remember it anyway and the best thing to do was humor him under the circumstances.

Then all of a sudden he asked me when I could marry him and I said, just as a joke, that I couldn't possibly marry him before December. He said that was a long time to wait, but I was certainly worth waiting for and he said a lot of other things and maybe I humored him a little too much, but that is just the trouble, I don't know.

I was absolutely sure he would forget the whole thing. If he doesn't remember anything about it, of course, I am all right. But if he does remember and if he took me seriously, I will simply have to tell him about Walter and maybe about Gordon, too. And it isn't going to be easy. The suspense is what is maddening and I know I'll never live through this night.

July 16

I can't stand it, I can't breathe, life is impossible. Frank remembered everything about last night and firmly believes we are engaged and going to be married in December. His people live in New York and he says he is going back when I do and have them meet me.

Of course it can't go on and tomorrow I will tell him about Walter or Gordon or both of them. I know it is going to hurt him terribly, perhaps spoil his life and I would give anything in the world not to have had it happen. I hate so to hurt him because he is so nice besides being so cute and attractive.

He sent me the loveliest flowers this morning and called up at ten and wanted to know how soon he could see me and I hope the girl wasn't listening in because the things he said were, well, like Walter's night letters.

And that is another terrible thing, today I didn't get a night letter from Walter, but there was a regular letter instead and I carried it around in my purse all this afternoon and evening and never remembered to read it till ten minutes ago when I came up in the room. Walter is worried because I have only sent him two telegrams and written him one letter since I have been here. He would be a lot more worried if he knew what has happened now, though of course it can't make any difference because he is the one I am really engaged to be married to and the one I told mother I was going to marry in December and wouldn't dare tell her it was somebody else.

I met Frank for lunch and we went for a ride this afternoon and he was so much in love and so lovely to me that I simply did not have the heart to tell him the truth, I am surely going to tell him tomorrow and telling him today would have just meant one more day of unhappiness for both of us.

He said his people had plenty of money and his father had offered to take him into partnership and he might accept, but he thinks his true vocation is journalism with a view to eventually writing novels and if I was willing to undergo a few hardships just at first we would probably both be happier later on if he was doing something he really liked. I didn't know what to say, but finally I said I wanted him to suit himself and money wasn't everything.

He asked me where I would like to go on my honeymoon and I suppose I ought to have told him my honeymoon was all planned, that I was going to California, with Walter, but all I said was that I had always wanted to go to California and he was enthusiastic and said that is where we would surely go and he would take me to Hollywood and introduce me to all those wonderful people he met there last winter. It nearly takes my breath away to think of it, going there with someone who really knows people and has the entrée.

We danced again tonight, just two or three dances, and then went out and sat in the tennis court, but I came upstairs early because Aunt Jule had acted kind of funny at dinner. And I wanted to be alone, too, and think, but the more I think the worse it gets.

Sometimes I wish I were dead, maybe that is the only solution and it would be best for everyone concerned. I *will* die if things keep on the way they have been. But of course tomorrow it will be all over, with Frank I mean, for I must tell him the truth no matter how much it hurts us both. Though I don't care how much it hurts me. The thought of hurting him is what is driving me mad. I can't bear it.

July 18

I have skipped a day. I was busy every minute of yesterday and so exhausted when I came upstairs that I was tempted to fall into bed with all my clothes on. First Gordon called me up from Chicago to remind me that he would be in New York the day I got there and that when he comes he wants me all to himself all the time and we can make plans for our wedding. The connection was bad again and I just couldn't explain to him about Walter.

I had an engagement with Frank for lunch and just as we were going in another long distance call came, from Walter this time. He wanted to know why I haven't written more letters and sent him more telegrams and asked me if I still loved him and of course I told him yes because I really do. Then he asked me if I had met any men here and I told him I had met one, a friend of Uncle Nat's. After all it was Uncle Nat who introduced me to Frank. He reminded me that he would be in New York on the 25th which is the day I expect to get home, and said he would have theater tickets for that night and we would go somewhere afterwards and dance.

Frank insisted on knowing who had kept me talking so long and I told him it was a boy I had known a long while, a very dear friend of mine and a friend of my family's. Frank was jealous and kept asking questions till I thought I would go mad. He was so serious and kind of cross and gruff that I gave up the plan of telling him the truth till some time when he is in better spirits.

I played golf with Frank in the afternoon and we took a ride last night and I wanted to get in early because I had promised both Walter and Gordon that I would write them long letters, but Frank wouldn't bring me back to the Inn till I had named a definite date in December. I finally told him the 10th, and he said all right if I was sure that wasn't a Sunday. I said I would have to look it up, but as a matter of fact I know the 10th falls on a Friday because the date Walter and I have agreed on for our wedding is Saturday the 11th.

Today has just been the same thing over again, two more night letters, a long distance call from Chicago, golf and a ride with Frank, and the room full of flowers. But tomorrow I am going to tell Frank, and I am going to write Gordon a long letter and tell him, too, because this simply can't go on any longer. I can't breathe. I can't live.

July 21

I wrote to Gordon yesterday, but I didn't say anything about Walter because I don't think it is a thing a person ought to do by letter. I can tell him when he gets to New York and then I will be sure that he doesn't take it too hard and I can promise him I will be friends with him always and make him promise not to do anything silly, while if I told it to him in a letter there is no telling what he would do, there all alone.

And I haven't told Frank because he hasn't been feeling well, he is terribly sunburned and it hurts him terribly so he can hardly play golf or dance, and I want him to be feeling his best when I do tell him, but whether he is all right or not I simply must tell him tomorrow because he is actually planning to leave here on the same train with us Saturday night and I can't let him do that.

Life is so hopeless and it could be so wonderful.

It is only half past ten, the earliest I have gone to bed in weeks, but I am worn out and Frank went to bed early so he could put cold cream on his sunburn.

Listen, diary, the orchestra is playing "Limehouse Blues," the first tune I danced to with Merle Oliver, two years ago. I can't stand it. And how funny that they should play that old tune tonight of all nights, when I have been thinking of Merle off and on all day, and I hadn't thought of him before in weeks and weeks. I wonder where he is, I wonder if it is just an accident or if it means I am going to see him again. I simply mustn't think about it or I'll die.

July 22

I knew it wasn't an accident. I knew it must mean something, and it did.

Merle is coming here today, here to this Inn, and just to see me. And there can only be one reason. And only one answer, I knew that when I heard his voice calling from Boston. How could I ever have thought I loved anyone else? How could he ever have thought I meant it when I told him I was engaged to George Morse?

A whole year and he still cares and I still care. That shows me we were always intended for each other and for no else. I won't make *him* wait till December. I doubt if we even wait till dad and mother get home. And as for a honeymoon I will go with him to Long Beach or the Bronx Zoo, wherever he wants to take me.

After all, this is the best way out of it, the only way. I won't have to say anything to Frank, he will guess when he sees me with Merle. And when I get home Sunday and Walter and Gordon call me up, I will invite them both to dinner and Merle can tell them himself. With two of them there it will only hurt each one half of much as if they were alone.

The train is due at 2:40, almost three hours from now. I can't wait. And what if it should be late? I can't stand it.

What satisfaction do the girl's relationships with Walter, Gordon, Frank, and Merle provide? Does she seriously believe that she is truly in love with each one in turn?

Although she says "life is so hopeless and it could be so wonderful," is it possible that she sometimes enjoys her own feeling that she "can't breathe . . . can't live . . . can't stand it"?

Are there girls like this, or is the author intending primarily to be humorous?

If the girl's relationships are not stamped with honesty, or some of the other desirable characteristics outlined by writers who have attempted to define love, what satisfactions do her relationships provide? Excitement? Antidotes to boredom? Prestige? Power? Fun? Playful activity? Something else?

Among the virtues of those to whom she gets engaged and plans marriage, she lists "cuteness," "wit," gracefulness of golf swing, ability to keep her "in hysterics," entrée to Hollywood people, good looks, ability to dance, and originality. How would you characterize her sense of values?

However, the girl claims also to appreciate the "serious side" of men. How does she interpret this term? What more descriptively accurate adjective might be substituted for "serious"? Why?

In which instances does the girl rationalize her actions—that is, invent "good" reasons (though not real ones) as acceptable explanations to justify her behavior?

Is the central character of *I Can't Breathe* more in love with persons, or more in love with love?

To what degree do the generalizations made by Archibald MacLeish in the following poem, "The Rape of the Swan," apply to the girl in *I Can't Breathe:*

To love love and not its meaning
Hardens the heart in monstrous ways.
No one is ours who has this leaning.
Those whose loyalty is love's betray us.

They are not girls with a girl's softness.
They love not us at all but love.
They have hard and fanatical minds most often.
It is not we but a dream that must cover them.

A woman who loves love cannot give it.
Her part is not to give but take.
Even the great swan by the river—
Her fingers strangle and the feathers break. [2]

How do reasons for loving a person differ from reasons for liking, admiring, respecting, and/or enjoying them?

Must one have a *reason* for loving a person? Millay, in "Sonnet XL," suggests that the feeling of love transcends reason:

Loving you less than life, a little less
Than bitter-sweet upon a broken wall
Or brush-wood smoke in autumn, I confess
I cannot swear I love you not at all.
For there is that about you in this light—
A yellow darkness, sinister of rain—
Which sturdily recalls my stubborn sight

To dwell on you, and dwell on you again.
And I am made aware of many a week
I shall consume, remembering in what way
Your brown hair grows about your brow and cheek
And what divine absurdities you say:
Till all the world, and I, and surely you,
Will know I love you, whether or not I do. [3]

William Whitehead, in *The Je Ne Sais Quoi,* acknowledges only a "provoking charm of Celia altogether" [4], perhaps the equivalent of the references to the way "your brown hair grows about your brow and cheek/ And what divine absurdities you say" in Millay's sonnet.

Both Elizabeth Barrett Browning in "Sonnet XIV" and the anonymous author of "Love Not Me for Comely Grace" protest "any outward part" as a basis for loving. The former explains:

If thou must love me, let it be for nought
Except for love's sake only. Do not say
"I love her for her smile—her look—her way
Of speaking gently,—for a trick of thought
That falls in well with mine, and certes brought
A sense of pleasant ease on such a day"—
For these things in themselves, Belovèd, may
Be changed, or change for thee,—and love, so wrought,
May be unwrought so. Neither love me for
Thine own dear pity's wiping my cheeks dry,—
A creature might forget to weep, who bore
Thy comfort long, and lose thy love thereby!
But love me for love's sake, that evermore
Thou may'st love on, through love's eternity. [5]

The latter insists:

Love not me for comely grace,
For my pleasing eye or face,
Nor for any outward part:
No, nor for my constant heart!
   For these may fail or turn to ill:
   So thou and I shall sever:
Keep therefore a true woman's eye,
And love me still, but know not why!
   So hast thou the same reason still
   To doat upon me ever. [6]

In what ways do Browning and the author of "Love Not Me for Comely Grace" support Stevenson's assertion in *On Falling in Love* (p. 241) that

the lover . . . wishes to be assured that he is not loved for this or that good quality, but for himself, or something as like himself as he can contrive to set forward.

What is the danger in being loved for "comely grace," or for a "smile"?

What does Browning mean by "love's sake only"?

Singer, who also ponders the question "For what then does a man love a woman?" in **Appraisal and Bestowal** (p. 224), raises the possibility: "for being the person she is, for being herself." He continues:

> But that is to say that he loves her for nothing at all. Everyone is himself. Having a beloved who is what she is does not reveal the nature of love. Neither does it help us to understand the saint's desire to love all people. They are what they are. Why should they be loved for it?

Is there an answer to Singer's objection? Can these contradictory views be reconciled?

RELATED QUESTIONS

In what ways does the character in **I Can't Breathe** show characteristics of the "double-sunrise" state described by Lindbergh (p. 232)? In what ways is her emotional state *not* characteristic of the double-sunrise relationship?

In what respect does Ring Lardner's story **I Can't Breathe** show the nature of that "love which creates only a self," first illustrated in Horgan's **Parma Violets** (p. 13)?

Romance

WILLIAM SAROYAN

The red-cap figured the young man was a clerk who was going to have a little Sunday holiday, riding in a train from a big city to a little one, going and coming the same day, but what he didn't understand was why the young man seemed so lost, or, as the saying is, dead to the world. The boy was young, not perhaps a college graduate, more likely a boy who'd gone through high school and gotten a job in an office somewhere, maybe twenty-three years old, and perhaps in love. Anyhow, the red-cap thought, the young man looked to be somebody who might at any moment fall in love, without much urging. He had that sad or dreamy look of the potential adorer of something in soft and colorful cloth with long hair and smooth skin.

. . . The red-cap left the car. The young man looked out the window and then turned just in time to notice that the girl across the aisle was looking at him and was swiftly turning her head away, and he himself, so as not to embarrass her, swiftly continued turning his head so that something almost happened to his neck. Almost instantly he brought his head all the way back to where it had been, near the window, looking out, and felt an awful eagerness to look at the girl again and at the same time a wonderful sense of at last beginning to go places, in more ways than one, such as meeting people like her and marrying one of them and settling down in a house somewhere.

He didn't look at the girl again, though, for some time but kept wanting to very eagerly, so that finally when he did look at her he was embarrassed and blushed and gulped and tried very hard to smile but just couldn't quite make it. The girl just couldn't make it either.

That happened after they'd been moving along for more than ten minutes, the train rolling out among the hills and rattling pleasantly and making everything everywhere seem pleasant and full of wonderful potentialities, such as romance and a good deal of good humor and easy-going naturalness, especially insofar as meeting her and being friendly and pleasant and little by little getting to know her and falling in love.

They saw one another again after about seven minutes more and then again after four minutes, and then they saw one another more steadily by pretending to be looking at the landscape on the other side, and finally they just kept seeing one another steadily for a long time, watching the landscape.

At last the young man said, are you from New York?

He didn't know what he was saying. He felt foolish and unlike young men in movies who do such things on trains.

Yes, I am, the girl said.

What? the young man said.

Didn't you ask if I was from New York? the girl said.

Oh, the young man said. Yes, I did.

Well, the girl said, I am.

I didn't know you were from New York, the young man said.

I know you didn't, the girl said.

The young man tried very hard to smile the way they smiled in pictures.

How did you know? he said.

Oh, I don't know, the girl said. Are you going to Sacramento?

Yes, I am, the young man said. Are you?

Yes, I am, the girl said.

What are you doing so far from home? the young man said.

New York isn't my home, the girl said. I was born there, but I've been living in San Francisco most of my life.

So have I most of mine, the young man said. In fact all of it.

I've lived in San Francisco practically all of my life too, the girl said, with the possible exception of them few months in New York.

Is that all the time you lived in New York? the young man said.

Yes, the girl said, only them first five months right after I was born in New York.

I was born in San Francisco, the young man said. There's lots of room on these two seats, he said with great effort. Wouldn't you like to sit over here and get the sun?

All right, the girl said.

She stepped across the aisle and sat across from the young man.

I just thought I'd go down to Sacramento on the special Sunday rate, the young man said.

I've been to Sacramento three times, the girl said.

The young man began to feel very happy. The sun was strong and warm and the girl was wonderful. Unless he was badly mistaken, or unless he got fired Monday morning, or unless America got into a war and he had to become a soldier and go away and get himself killed for no good reason, he had a hunch some day he would go to work and get acquainted with the girl and marry her and settle down.

He sat back in the sunlight while the train rattled along and smiled romantically at the girl, getting ready for the romance.

What evidence in the story suggests the young man's romanticism? Is the young man a philanderer?—that is, one who makes love or carries on a flirtation without serious intentions. Does he resemble the subject of the following epigram by Donald Hall:

> Poetical Philander only thought to love:
> He went to bed with what the girls were symbols of. [7]

What are the girls symbols of? What, if anything, does the girl across the aisle symbolize for the young man in **Romance?** Does she contribute to his self-image? What qualities does he seem to appreciate in or about her? On what does the young man base his judgment that "the sun was strong and warm and the girl was wonderful"?

Is there anything illogical about the sequence in his statement, "he had a hunch someday he would go to work and get acquainted with the girl and marry her and settle down"? Is there anything significant about the fact that in the last paragraph of the story he is "getting ready for the romance"? What sort of preparations is he making?

Comment on the following contrasting analyses of the young man:

1. I believe this man is really in love. Lee and Fromm say that love should be "an act of will," and that's just what the young man is showing when he decides to fall in love and gets ready for the romance.

   He also shows the patience that Lee was talking about in **What Love Must Be.** For example, Saroyan says "they saw one another again after about seven minutes more, and then again after four minutes"— quite a long time when they're just looking at each other on a train! The young man also recognizes the pleasure of "little by little getting to know her and falling in love" and of the "someday" when he will marry her. He's not just rushing blindly into things or acting infatuated.

2. I believe this man is putting himself on. He enjoys the picture of himself about to fall in love (as if it were something you could calculate!) He's a little like William Baxter in **Seventeen,** another big romantic.

   I'm not sure the young man in **Romance** ever will really grow up. He may stay a "potential adorer of something in soft and colorful cloth with long hair and smooth skin." Then he'll miss the real thing, or be frightened by it and run right back to a romantic impossibility like the man in "Escapist's Song" by Theodore Spencer:

   > The first woman I loved, he said—
   > Her skin was satin and gold.
   > The next woman I loved, he said—
   > Her skin was satin and gold.
   > The third woman I loved, he said—
   > Was made in a different mold.
   > She was deeper than me, and said so;

She was stronger than me, and said so;
She was wiser than me, and proved it;
I shivered, and grew cold.
The fourth woman I loved, he said—
Her skin was satin and gold. [8]

RELATED QUESTIONS

How does the behavior of the young man in **Romance** differ from the behavior of the young girl in *I Can't Breathe* (p. 363)? Are their motives in love similar or different?

The Well of Days

IVAN BUNIN

Our neighbor, Alferov, who used to lead a lonely life, died. My brother Nicholas, who had long dreamt of living on his own, leased his vacated manor and lived there that winter instead of with us. Among his servants there was a maid called Tonka. She had just married, but immediately after the wedding had been forced by poverty and homelessness to part with her husband: he was a saddler and after marrying went off again on his ambulant work, whilst she took up work with my brother.

She was about twenty. In the village people called her "the jackdaw," "the savage," and thought her, for her quietness, quite stupid. I myself had known her, of course, since childhood, as I knew everybody in our village, and I always liked her. She had a very dark complexion, a gracefully and firmly built girl's body, small and strong limbs, black nut-brown, narrow-slitted eyes. She resembled a Red Indian: the straight but rather rough features of a dark face, the coarse jet of lank hair. But in that, too, I found some charm, though truly a somewhat savage one. As for stupidity, I never heard her say anything silly—perhaps because she said only what was quite necessary and commonplace, keeping silence as easily and naturally as if she were speechless.

I used to go nearly every day to my brother's; I admired her; I even liked the firm, swift tread of her feet when she brought the samovar or soup-tureen to table, the way in which she would meaninglessly look up: that stamping and that look, the coarse blackness of her hair parted in the middle and showing beneath an orange-coloured kerchief, the somewhat flat, bluish lips of her slightly elongated mouth, the slope of the dark youthful neck passing into shoulders—all this invariably roused in me a sweet and uneasy yearning. Sometimes, meeting her in the hall, or the anteroom, I would jestingly catch at her as she went, and press her to the wall. Laughing silently, she would adroitly slip away—and with that the matter ended. There was no amorous feeling between us.

But once, walking in soft winter dusk through the village, I turned absent-mindedly to Alferov's manor, passed between the snow-heaps to the house, mounted to the porch. In the dark anteroom, especially dark at the top, a pile of red-hot embers in the freshly lighted stove showed red, gloomy and fantastic as in a black cave, and Tonka, bareheaded, straddling her bare legs, their tibias shining against the light with their smooth skin, was sitting on the floor against its mouth, illumined by its dark flames, holding a poker in her hand, its white-hot end touching the embers; slightly averting from the glowing heat her dark flaming face, she was dreamily gazing at the embers, at their crimson mounts, frail and translucent, here already dying away under the fine lilac efflorescence, and there still burning with blue-green gas. I banged the door when entering— she did not even turn round.

"Why is it dark here? Is no one at home?" I asked, approaching her.

She threw her face further back, and, without looking at me, smiled somewhat uneasily and languidly.

"As if you don't know!" she said mockingly, and pushed the poker a little further into the stove.

"Know what?"

"Come on, stop it. . . ."

"Stop what?"

"You must know where they are, as they've gone to you. . . ."

"I've been taking a walk, I haven't seen them."

"Tell me about walks . . ."

I squatted on the floor, looking at her bare legs and at her bare black head, already full of inward tremors, but laughing and pretending also to admire the embers and their hot dark-crimson glow. . . . Then suddenly I sat down beside her, embraced her, and threw her on the floor, catching her reluctant lips, hot because of the fire. The poker rattled, some sparks flew up from the stove. . . .

When afterwards I jumped out to the porch, I looked like a man who had suddenly committed murder, I held my breath and quickly turned round to see whether someone was not coming. But there was no one; everything to my surprise was ordinary and quiet; in the village, in the accustomed winter darkness, the lights burned in the cottages with an incredible calmness—as if nothing had happened. . . . I looked up, listened—and quickly walked away. I could not feel the ground beneath me, for two clashing emotions: the sense of a sudden, terrible, irremediable catastrophe in my life, and that of an exultant, victorious triumph. . . .

At night, through my anxious sleep, I was now and then seized by deadly anguish, by the sense of something terrible, criminal, and shameful that had suddenly caused my undoing. "Yes, everything is over," I would think, waking up, recovering my senses with difficulty. "Everything, everything is finished, destroyed, spoilt; obviously this must be so; it can no longer be remedied or put straight. And the terrible thing is that one cannot tell it to anyone: everybody is asleep; they know nothing; they suspect nothing; and to crown it all, I am now a stranger to everybody, alone in the wide world. . . ."

Waking up in the morning, I looked with quite new eyes around me, at that room so familiar to me, lit evenly by the fresh snow which had fallen in the night: there was no sun, but in the room it was quite light from the bright whiteness. My first thought on opening my eyes was, of course, about what had happened. But that thought no longer frightened me; of the anguish, despair, shame, feeling of guilt, there was none in my soul. On the contrary. But how can I go down to tea now?—I thought. And what should I do in general? Well, nothing, I thought; nobody knows anything, and nobody will ever know, and in the world everything is just as nice as before and even more so than before; outside is my favourite, still, white weather; the garden, its bare branches covered with shaggy snow, is all piled over with white snowheaps; in the room it is warm because of the stove lit by somebody while I slept and now roaring and cracking evenly, flutteringly drawing in the brass lid. . . . It smells bitter and fresh, through the warmth, from the frosted and thawing aspen brushwood lying next to it on the floor. . . . And what happened is only that natural, necessary thing which had to happen—after all I am already seventeen and why should I be worse than the others? I am not only no worse, but even better than they, and at least I have matched them in that too. I was once more overwhelmed with triumph, pride, happiness—here I am a man, I've got a mistress! How silly were all my night-time thoughts! How wonderful and terrible was the happening of yesterday! And it will be repeated again, perhaps even to-day! With what a lovely, unexpectedly childish fear, with what obvious hopelessness did she manage to whisper something rapid and imploring! O, how I do and will love her!

Although the narrator in *The Well of Days* appears to have more knowledge of Tonka, more feeling for a "you" than the central characters of *I Can't Breathe* and *Romance* can claim, the "**I**," rather than "YOU and I," seems to receive the emphasis in the relationship. What are some of the signs that "**I**" is the dominant factor in the scene between Tonka and the narrator?

Although he concludes: "O, how I do and will love her!" do you think the thought arises to justify his sexual act? Thus, that he is rationalizing his confused feelings of guilt and joy? His

. . . two clashing emotions: the sense of a sudden, terrible, irremediable catastrophe in my life, and that of an exultant, victorious triumph?

Is his love "real"? Or is it an illusion of love, greatly helped by the deceptive character of sexual desire, as Fromm explains in *The Theory of Love* (p. 261)?

In what various ways do males react to premarital experiences such as the narrator's with Tonka? Would the emotional aftermath be the same for Tonka? How do you imagine she might have felt the next morning?

Did the narrator seduce Tonka? Or did Tonka seduce him? Who, generally, seems to you the more aggressive in a relationship of this sort: the male or the female?

Is the narrator of *The Well of Days* using sex as a proof? If so, of what?

Looking back on the experience, the narrator reflects:

. . . after all I am already seventeen and why should I be worse than the others? I am not only no worse, but even better than they, and at least I have matched them in that too.

What does he mean by "worse"? By "better"? In what has he "matched them"?

What is the significance of his statement: "here I am a man, I've got a mistress!"

It has been said that

In many instances the guilt over the sexual relationship necessitates idealizing it as love, which may in turn result in marriage. This effects a closure of the adolescent process; a pseudo-resolution that once and for all terminates the search for identity around a premature commitment to a permanent sexual relationship. For an adolescent, it is putting on the cloak of adulthood while carrying into the relationship the unresolved conflicts of the past, and an identity that remains dependent on the childhood image of the parents. Obviously, it is wrong to assume that adolescent sexual behavior and attitudes can be explained only on the basis of a desire for physical pleasure. [9]

On what other basis is adolescent sexual behavior explained in the above comment? How is it relevant to the situation in *The Well of Days?*

RELATED QUESTIONS

What parallels are there between the seventeen-year-old's "deadly anguish . . . sense of something terrible, criminal and shameful" in *The Well of Days* and Stephen Daedalus' torment in *A Portrait of the Artist as a Young Man* (p. 50)?

What are the differences in the process by which Stephen Daedalus in *A Portrait of the Artist* and the narrator of *The Well of Days* try to rid their souls of guilt? Is one way more satisfactory than the other? More permanent? Why?

Of Human Bondage

W. SOMERSET MAUGHAM

Miss Wilkinson was very different. She wore a white muslin gown stamped with gray little bunches of flowers, and pointed, high-heeled shoes, with open-work stockings. To Philip's inexperience it seemed that she was wonderfully dressed; he did not see that her frock was cheap and showy. Her hair was elaborately dressed, with a neat curl in the middle of the forehead: it was very black, shiny and hard, and it looked as though it could never be in the least disarranged. She had large black eyes and her nose was slightly aquiline; in profile she had somewhat the look of a bird of prey, but full face she was prepossessing. She smiled a great deal, but her mouth was large and when she smiled she tried to hide her teeth, which were big and rather yellow. But what embarrassed Philip most was that she was heavily powdered: he had very strict views on feminine behaviour and did not think a lady ever powdered; but of course Miss Wilkinson was a lady because she was a clergyman's daughter, and a clergyman was a gentleman.

Philip made up his mind to dislike her thoroughly. She spoke with a slight French accent; and he did not know why she should, since she had been born and bred in the heart of England. He thought her smile affected, and the coy sprightliness of her manner irritated him. For two or three days he remained silent and hostile, but Miss Wilkinson apparently did not notice it. She was very affable. She addressed her conversation almost exclusively to him, and there was something flattering in the way she appealed constantly to his sane judgment. She made him laugh too, and Philip could never resist people who amused him:

he had a gift now and then of saying neat things; and it was pleasant to have an appreciative listener.

. . . He was flattered at Miss Wilkinson's laughter.

"I'm quite frightened of you," she said. "You're so sarcastic."

Then she asked him playfully whether he had not had any love affairs at Heidelberg. Without thinking, he frankly answered that he had not; but she refused to believe him.

"How secretive you are!" she said. "At your age is it likely?" He blushed and laughed.

"You want to know too much," he said.

"Ah, I thought so," she laughed triumphantly. "Look at him blushing."

He was pleased that she should think he had been a sad dog, and he changed the conversation so as to make her believe he had all sorts of romantic things to conceal. He was angry with himself that he had not. There had been no opportunity.

Miss Wilkinson was dissatisfied with her lot. . . .

She began to talk of Paris. She loved the boulevards and the Bois. There was grace in every street, and the trees in the Champs Elysées had a distinction which trees had not elsewhere. They were sitting on a stile now by the high-road, and Miss Wilkinson looked with disdain upon the stately elms in front of them. And the theatres; the plays were brilliant, and the acting was incomparable. She often went with Madame Foyot, the mother of the girls she was educating, when she was trying on clothes.

"Oh, what a misery to be poor!" she cried. "These beautiful things, it's only in Paris they know how to dress, and not to be able to afford them! Poor Madame Foyot, she had no figure. Sometimes the dressmaker used to whisper to me: 'Ah, Mademoiselle, if she only had your figure.'"

Philip noticed then that Miss Wilkinson had a robust form, and was proud of it.

"Men are so stupid in England. They only think of the face. The French, who are a nation of lovers, know how much more important the figure is."

Philip had never thought of such things before, but he observed now that Miss Wilkinson's ankles were thick and ungainly. He withdrew his eyes quickly.

"You should go to France. Why don't you go to Paris for a year? You would learn French, and it would—*déniaiser* you."

"What is that?" asked Philip.

She laughed slyly.

"You must look it out in the dictionary. Englishmen do not know how to treat women. They are so shy. Shyness is ridiculous in a man. They don't know how to make love. They can't even tell a woman she is charming without looking foolish."

Philip felt himself absurd. Miss Wilkinson evidently expected him to behave very differently; and he would have been delighted to say gallant and witty things, but they never occurred to him; and when they did he was too much afraid of making a fool of himself to say them.

"Oh, I love Paris," sighed Miss Wilkinson. "But I had to go to Berlin. I was with the Foyots till the girls married, and then I could get nothing to do, and I had the chance of this post in Berlin. They're relations of Madame Foyot, and I accepted. I had a tiny apartment in the Rue Bréda, on the *cinquième:* it wasn't at all respectable. You know about the Rue Bréda—*ces dames,* you know."

Philip nodded, not knowing at all what she meant, but vaguely suspecting, and anxious she should not think him too ignorant.

"But I didn't care. *Je suis libre, n'est-ce-pas?*" She was very fond of speaking French, which indeed she spoke well. "Once I had such a curious adventure there."

She paused a little and Philip pressed her to tell it.

"You wouldn't tell me yours in Heidelberg," she said.

"They were so unadventurous," he retorted.

"I don't know what Mrs. Carey would say if she knew the sort of things we talk about together."

"You don't imagine I shall tell her."

"Will you promise?"

When he had done this, she told him how an art-student who had a room on the floor above her—but she interrupted herself.

"Why don't you go in for art? You paint so prettily."

"Not well enough for that."

"That is for others to judge. *Je m'y connais,* and I believe you have the making of a great artist."

"Can't you see Uncle William's face if I suddenly told him I wanted to go to Paris and study art?"

"You're your own master, aren't you?"

"You're trying to put me off. Please go on with the story."

Miss Wilkinson, with a little laugh, went on. The art-student had passed her several times on the stairs, and she had paid no particular attention. She saw that he had fine eyes, and he took off his hat very politely. And one day she found a letter slipped under her door. It was from him. He told her that he had adored her for months, and that he waited about the stairs for her to pass. Oh, it was a charming letter! Of course she did not reply, but what woman could help being flattered? And the next day there was another letter! It was wonderful, passionate, and touching. When next she met him on the stairs she did not know which way to look. And every day the letters came, and now he begged her to see him. He said he would come in the evening, *vers neuf heures,* and she did not know what to do. Of course it was impossible, and he might ring and ring, but she would never open the door; and then while she was waiting for the tinkling of the bell, all nerves, suddenly he stood before her. She had forgotten to shut the door when she came in.

"*C'était une fatalité.*"

"And what happened then?" asked Philip.

"That is the end of the story," she replied, with a ripple of laughter.

Philip was silent for a moment. His heart beat quickly, and strange emotions seemed to be hustling one another in his heart. He saw the dark staircase and the chance meetings, and he admired the boldness of the letters—oh, he would never have dared to do that—and then the silent, almost mysterious entrance. It seemed to him the very soul of romance.

"What was he like?"

"Oh, he was handsome. *Charmant garçon.*"

"Do you know him still?"

Philip felt a slight feeling of irritation as he asked this.

"He treated me abominably. Men are always the same. You're heartless, all of you."

"I don't know about that," said Philip, not without embarrassment.

"Let us go home," said Miss Wilkinson.

Philip could not get Miss Wilkinson's story out of his head. It was clear enough what she meant even though she cut it short, and he was a little shocked. That sort of thing was all very well for married women, he had read enough French novels to know that in France it was indeed the rule, but Miss Wilkinson was English and unmarried; her father was a clergyman. Then it struck him that the art-student probably was neither the first nor the last of her lovers, and he gasped: he had never looked upon Miss Wilkinson like that; it seemed incredible that anyone should make love to her. In his ingenuousness he doubted her story as little as he doubted what he read in books, and he was angry that such wonderful things never happened to him. It was humiliating that if Miss Wilkinson insisted upon his telling her of his adventures in Heidelberg he would have nothing to tell. It was true that he had some power of invention, but he was not sure whether he could persuade her that he was steeped in vice; women were full of intuition, he had read that, and she might easily discover that he was fibbing. . . .

. . . He looked at her more narrowly. He liked her much better in the evening than in the morning. In the morning she was rather lined and the skin of her neck was just a little rough. He wished she would hide it, but the weather was very warm just then and she wore blouses which were cut low. She was very fond of white; in the morning it did not suit her. At night she often looked very attractive, she put on a gown which was almost a dinner dress, and she wore a chain of garnets round her neck; the lace about her bosom and at her elbows gave her a pleasant softness, and the scent she wore (at Blackstable no one used anything but *Eau de Cologne,* and that only on Sundays or when suffering from a sick headache) was troubling and exotic. She really looked very young then.

Philip was much exercised over her age. He added twenty and seventeen together, and could not bring them to a satisfactory total. He asked Aunt Louisa more than once why she thought Miss Wilkinson was thirty-seven; she didn't look more than thirty, and everyone knew that foreigners aged more rapidly than English women; Miss Wilkinson had lived so long abroad that she might almost be called a foreigner. He personally wouldn't have thought her more than twenty-six.

"She's more than that," said Aunt Louisa.

Philip did not believe in the accuracy of the Careys' statements. All they distinctly remembered was that Miss Wilkinson had not got her hair up the last time they saw her in Lincolnshire. Well, she might have been twelve then: it was so long ago and the Vicar was always so unreliable. They said it was twenty years ago, but people used round figures, and it was just as likely to be eighteen years, or seventeen. Seventeen and twelve were only twenty-nine, and hang it all, that wasn't old, was it? Cleopatra was forty-eight when Antony threw away the world for her sake.

. . . He ought to make love to her. They had talked a good deal of love. There was the art-student in the Rue Bréda, and then there was the painter in whose family she had lived so long in Paris: he had asked her to sit for him, and he had started to make love to her so violently that she was forced to invent excuses not to sit for him again. It was clear enough that Miss Wilkinson was used to attentions of that sort. She looked very nice now in a large straw hat: it was hot that afternoon, the hottest day they had had, and beads of sweat stood in a line on her upper lip. . . . Miss Wilkinson was practically French, and that added zest to a possible adventure. When he thought of it at night in bed, or when he sat by himself in the garden reading a book, he was thrilled by it; but when he saw Miss Wilkinson it seemed less picturesque.

At all events, after what she had told him, she would not be surprised if he made love to her. He had a feeling that she must think it odd of him to make no sign: perhaps it was only his fancy, but once or twice in the last day or two he had imagined that there was a suspicion of contempt in her eyes.

"A penny for your thoughts," said Miss Wilkinson, looking at him with a smile.

"I'm not going to tell you," he answered.

He was thinking that he ought to kiss her there and then. He wondered if she expected him to do it; but after all he didn't see how he could without any preliminary business at all. . . .

"Twopence for your thoughts," smiled Miss Wilkinson.

"I was thinking about you," he answered boldly.

That at all events committed him to nothing.

"What were you thinking?"

"Ah, now you want to know too much."

"Naughty boy!" said Miss Wilkinson.

There it was again! Whenever he had succeeded in working himself up she said something which reminded him of the governess. She called him playfully a naughty boy when he did not sing his exercises to her satisfaction. This time he grew quite sulky.

"I wish you wouldn't treat me as if I were a child."

"Are you cross?"

"Very."

"I didn't mean to."

She put out her hand and he took it. Once or twice lately when they shook hands at night he had fancied she slightly pressed his hand, but this time there was no doubt about it.

He did not quite know what he ought to say next. Here at last was his chance of an adventure, and he would be a fool not to take it; but it was a little ordinary, and he had expected more glamour. He had read many descriptions of love, and he felt in himself none of that uprush of emotion which novelists described; he was not carried off his feet in wave upon wave of passion; nor was Miss Wilkinson the ideal: he had often pictured to himself the great violet eyes and the alabaster skin of some lovely girl, and he had thought of himself burying his face in the rippling masses of her auburn hair. He could not imagine himself burying his face in Miss Wilkinson's hair, it always struck him as a little sticky. All the same it would be very satisfactory to have an intrigue, and he thrilled with the legitimate pride he would enjoy in his conquest. He owed it to himself to seduce her. He made up his mind to kiss Miss Wilkinson; not then, but in the evening; it would be easier in the dark, and after he had kissed her the rest would follow. He would kiss her that very evening. He swore an oath to that effect.

He laid his plans. After supper he suggested that they should take a stroll in the garden. Miss Wilkinson accepted, and they sauntered side by side. Philip was very nervous. He did not know why, but the conversation would not lead in the right direction; he had decided that the first thing to do was to put his arm round her waist; but he could not suddenly put his arm round her waist when she was talking of the regatta which was to be held next week. He led her artfully into the darkest parts of the garden, but having arrived there his courage failed him. They sat on a bench, and he had really made up his mind that here was his opportunity when Miss Wilkinson said she was sure there were earwigs and insisted on moving. They walked round the garden once more, and Philip promised himself he would take the plunge before they arrived at that bench again; but as they passed the house, they saw Mrs. Carey standing at the door.

"Hadn't you young people better come in? I'm sure the night air isn't good for you."

"Perhaps we had better go in," said Philip. "I don't want you to catch cold."

He said it with a sigh of relief. He could attempt nothing more that night. But afterwards, when he was alone in his room, he was furious with himself. He had been a perfect fool. He was certain that Miss Wilkinson expected him to kiss her, otherwise she wouldn't have come into the garden. She was always saying that only Frenchmen knew how to treat women. Philip had read French novels. If he had been a Frenchman he would have seized her in his arms and told her passionately that he adored her; he would have pressed his lips on her *nuque*. He did not know why Frenchmen always kissed ladies on the *nuque*. He did not himself see anything so very attractive in the nape of the neck. Of course it was much easier for Frenchmen to do these things; the language was such an aid; Philip could never help feeling that to say passionate things in English sounded a little absurd. He wished now that he had never undertaken the siege of Miss Wilkinson's virtue; the first fortnight had been so jolly, and now he was wretched; but he was determined not to give in, he would never respect himself again if he did, and he made up his mind irrevocably that the next night he would kiss her without fail.

Next day when he got up he saw it was raining, and his first thought was that they would not be able to go into the garden that evening. He was in high spirits at breakfast. Miss Wilkinson sent Mary Ann in to say that she had a headache and would remain in bed. She did not come down till tea-time, when she appeared in a becoming wrapper and a pale face; but she was quite recovered by supper, and the meal was very cheerful. After prayers she said she would go straight to bed, and she kissed Mrs. Carey. Then she turned to Philip.

"Good gracious!" she cried. "I was just going to kiss you too."

"Why don't you?" he said.

She laughed and held out her hand. She distinctly pressed his.

The following day there was not a cloud in the sky, and the garden was sweet and fresh after the rain. Philip went down to the beach to bathe and when he came home ate a magnificent dinner. They were having a tennis party at the vicarage in the afternoon and Miss Wilkinson put on her best dress. She certainly knew how to wear her clothes, and Philip could not help noticing how elegant she looked beside the curate's wife and the doctor's married daughter. There were two roses in her waistband. She sat in a garden chair by the side of the lawn, holding a red parasol over herself, and the light on her face was very becoming. . . .

"It'll be lovely in the garden tonight. The stars are all out."

He was in high spirits.

"D'you know, Mrs. Carey has been scolding me on your account?" said Miss Wilkinson, when they were sauntering through the kitchen garden. "She says I musn't flirt with you."

"Have you been flirting with me? I hadn't noticed it."

"She was only joking."

"It was very unkind of you to refuse to kiss me last night."

"If you saw the look your uncle gave me when I said what I did!"

"Was that all that prevented you?"

"I prefer to kiss people without witnesses."

"There are no witnesses now."

Philip put his arm round her waist and kissed her lips. She only laughed a little and made no attempt to withdraw. It had come quite naturally. Philip was very proud of himself. He said he would, and he had. It was the easiest thing in the world. He wished he had done it before. He did it again.

"Oh, you mustn't," she said.

"Why not?"

"Because I like it," she laughed. . . .

Next day after dinner they took their rugs and cushions to the fountain, and their books; but they did not read. Miss Wilkinson made herself comfortable and she opened the red sun-shade. Philip was not at all shy now, but at first she would not let him kiss her.

"It was very wrong of me last night," she said. "I couldn't sleep, I felt I'd done so wrong."

"What nonsense!" he cried. "I'm sure you slept like a top."

"What do you think your uncle would say if he knew?"

"There's no reason why he should know."

He leaned over her, and his heart went pit-a-pat.

"Why d'you want to kiss me?"

He knew he ought to reply: "Because I love you." But he could not bring himself to say it.

"Why do you think?" he asked instead.

She looked at him with smiling eyes and touched his face with the tips of her fingers.

"How smooth your face is," she murmured.

"I want shaving awfully," he said.

It was astonishing how difficult he found it to make romantic speeches. He found that silence helped him much more than words. He could look inexpressible things. Miss Wilkinson sighed.

"Do you like me at all?"

"Yes, awfully."

When he tried to kiss her again she did not resist. He pretended to be much more passionate than he really was, and he succeeded in playing a part which looked very well in his own eyes.

"I'm beginning to be rather frightened of you," said Miss Wilkinson.

"You'll come out after supper, won't you?" he begged.

"Not unless you promise to behave yourself."

"I'll promise anything."

He was catching fire from the flame he was partly simulating, and at teatime he was obstreperously merry. Miss Wilkinson looked at him nervously.

Philip threw away the cigarette he had just lighted, and flung his arms round her. She tried to push him away.

"You promised you'd be good, Philip."

"You didn't think I was going to keep a promise like that?"

"Not so near the house, Philip," she said. "Supposing someone should come out suddenly?"

He led her to the kitchen garden where no one was likely to come. . . . He kissed her passionately. It was one of the things that puzzled him that he did not like her at all in the morning, and only moderately in the afternoon, but at night the touch of her hand thrilled him. He said things that he would never have thought himself capable of saying; he could certainly never have said them in the broad light of day; and he listened to himself with wonder and satisfaction.

"How beautifully you make love," she said.

That was what he thought himself.

"Oh, if I could only say all the things that burn my heart!" he murmured passionately.

It was splendid. It was the most thrilling game he had ever played; and the wonderful thing was that he felt almost all he said. It was only that he exaggerated a little. He was tremendously interested and excited in the effect he could see it had on her. It was obviously with an effort that at last she suggested going in.

"Oh, don't go yet," he cried.

"I must," she muttered. "I'm frightened."

He had a sudden intuition what was the right thing to do then.

"I can't go in yet. I shall stay here and think. My cheeks are burning. I want the night-air. Good-night."

He held out his hand seriously, and she took it in silence. He thought she stifled a sob. Oh, it was magnificent! When, after a decent interval during which he had been rather bored in the dark garden by himself, he went in he found that Miss Wilkinson had already gone to bed.

After that things were different between them. The next day and the day after Philip showed himself an eager lover. He was deliciously flattered to discover that Miss Wilkinson was in love with him: she told him so in English, and she told him so in French. She paid him compliments. No one had ever informed him before that his eyes were charming and that he had a sensual mouth. He had never bothered much about his personal appearance, but now, when occasion presented, he looked at himself in the glass with satisfaction. When he kissed her it was wonderful to feel the passion that seemed to thrill her soul. He kissed her a good deal, for he found it easier to do that than to say the things he instinctively felt she expected of him. It still made him feel a fool to say he worshipped her. He wished there were someone to whom he could boast a little, and he would willingly have discussed minute points of his conduct. Sometimes she said things that were enigmatic, and he was puzzled. . . . He could not make up his mind whether he ought to rush things or let them take their time. There were only three weeks more.

"I can't bear to think of that," she said. "It breaks my heart. And then perhaps we shall never see one another again."

"If you cared for me at all, you wouldn't be so unkind to me," he whispered.

"Oh, why can't you be content to let it go on as it is? Men are always the same. They're never satisfied."

And when he pressed her, she said:

"But don't you see it's impossible. How can we here?"

He proposed all sorts of schemes, but she would not have anything to do with them.

"I daren't take the risk. It would be too dreadful if your aunt found out."

A day or two later he had an idea which seemed brilliant.

"Look here, if you had a headache on Sunday evening and offered to stay at home and look after the house, Aunt Louisa would go to church."

When he made the suggestion, Miss Wilkinson did not speak for a moment, then shook her head.

"No, I won't," she said.

But on Sunday at tea-time she surprised Philip.

"I don't think I'll come to church this evening," she said suddenly. "I've really got a dreadful headache."

So after six o'clock Philip was left alone in the house with Miss Wilkinson. He felt sick with apprehension. He wished with all his heart that he had not suggested the plan; but it was too late now; he must take the opportunity which he had made. What would Miss Wilkinson think of him if he did not! He went into the hall and listened. There was not a sound. He wondered if Miss Wilkinson really had a headache. Perhaps she had forgotten his suggestion. His heart beat painfully. He crept up the stairs as softly as he could, and he stopped with a start when they creaked. He stood outside Miss Wilkinson's room and listened; he put his hand on the knob of the door-handle. He waited. It seemed to him that he waited for at least five minutes, trying to make up his mind; and his hand trembled. He would willingly have bolted, but he was afraid of the remorse which he knew would seize him. It was like getting on the highest diving-board in a swimming-bath; it looked nothing from below, but when you got up there and stared down at the water your heart sank; and the only thing that forced you to dive was the shame of coming down meekly by the steps you had climbed up. Philip screwed up his courage. He turned the handle softly and walked in. He seemed to himself to be trembling like a leaf.

Miss Wilkinson was standing at the dressing-table with her back to the door, and she turned round quickly when she heard it open.

"Oh, it's you. What d'you want?"

She had taken off her skirt and blouse, and was standing in her petticoat. It was short and only came down to the top of her boots; the upper part of it was black, of some shiny material, and there was a red flounce. She wore a camisole of white calico with short arms. She looked grotesque. Philip's heart sank as he stared at her; she had never seemed so unattractive; but it was too late now. He closed the door behind him and locked it.

Philip woke early next morning. His sleep had been restless; but when he stretched his legs and looked at the sunshine that slid through the Venetian blinds, making patterns on the floor, he sighed with satisfaction. He was delighted with himself. He began to think of Miss Wilkinson. She had asked him to call her Emily, but, he knew not why, he could not; he always thought of her as Miss Wilkinson. . . . She had begun as Miss Wilkinson, and it seemed inseparable from his impression of her. He frowned a little: somehow or other he saw her now at her worst; he could not forget his dismay when she turned round and he saw her in her camisole and the short petticoat; he remembered the slight roughness of her skin and the sharp, long lines on the side of the neck. His triumph was short-lived. He reckoned out her age again, and he did not see how she could be less than forty. It made the affair ridiculous. She was plain and old. His quick fancy showed her to him, wrinkled, haggard, made-up, in those frocks which were too showy for her position and too young for her years. He shuddered; he felt suddenly that he never wanted to see her again; he could not bear the thought of kissing her. He was horrified with himself. Was that love?

He was taken aback by the change in her. She told him in a voice thrilling with emotion immediately after breakfast that she loved him; and when a little later they went into the drawing-room for his singing lesson and she sat down on the music-stool she put up her face in the middle of a scale and said:

"*Embrasse-moi.*"

When he bent down she flung her arms round his neck. It was slightly uncomfortable, for she held him in such a position that he felt rather choked.

"*Ah, je t'aime. Je t'aime. Je t'aime,*" she cried, with her extravagantly French accent.

Philip wished she would speak English.

"I say, I don't know if it's struck you that the gardener's quite likely to pass the window any minute."

"*Ah, je m'en fiche du jardinier. Je m'en refiche, et je m'en contrefiche.*"

Philip though it was very like a French novel, and he did not know why it

388

"You—I"
interrelationships

At last he said:

"Well, I think I'll tootle along to the beach and have a dip."

"Oh, you're not going to leave me this morning—of all mornings?"

Philip did not quite know why he should not, but it did not matter.

"Would you like me to stay?" he smiled.

"Oh, you darling! But no, go. Go. I want to think of you mastering the salt sea waves, bathing your limbs in the broad ocean."

He got his hat and sauntered off.

"What rot women talk!" he thought to himself.

But he was pleased and happy and flattered. She was evidently frightfully gone on him. As he limped along the high street of Blackstable he looked with a tinge of superciliousness at the people he passed. He knew a good many to nod to, and as he gave them a smile of recognition he thought to himself, if they only knew! He did want someone to know very badly. He thought he would write to Hayward, and in his mind composed the letter. He would talk of the garden and the roses, and the little French governess, like an exotic flower amongst them, scented and perverse: he would say she was French, because—well, she had lived in France so long that she almost was, and besides it would be shabby to give the whole thing away too exactly, don't you know; and he would tell Hayward how he had seen her first in her pretty muslin dress and of the flower she had given him. He made a delicate idyl of it: the sunshine and the sea gave it passion and magic, and the stars added poetry. . . .

He wrote his letter to Hayward. . . . There were eight pages of it.

The fortnight that remained passed quickly, and though each evening, when they went into the garden after supper, Miss Wilkinson remarked that one day more had gone, Philip was in too cheerful spirits to let the thought depress him. . . . He spoke a little too freely of all he meant to do, and allowed Miss Wilkinson to see that already he was longing to be off.

"You wouldn't talk like that if you loved me," she cried.

He was taken aback and remained silent.

"What a fool I've been," she muttered.

To his surprise he saw that she was crying. He had a tender heart, and hated to see anyone miserable.

"Oh, I'm awfully sorry. What have I done? Don't cry."

"Oh, Philip, don't leave me. You don't know what you mean to me. I have such a wretched life, and you've made me so happy."

He kissed her silently. There really was anguish in her tone, and he was frightened. It had never occurred to him that she meant what she said quite, quite seriously.

"I'm awfully sorry. You know I'm frightfully fond of you. I wish you would come to London."

"You know I can't. Places are almost impossible to get, and I hate English life."

Almost unconscious that he was acting a part, moved by her distress, he pressed her more and more. Her tears vaguely flattered him, and he kissed her with real passion.

But a day or two later she made a real scene. There was a tennis-party at the vicarage, and two girls came, daughters of a retired major in an Indian regiment who had lately settled in Blackstable. They were very pretty, one was Philip's age and the other was a year or two younger. . . . Some devil within him prompted him to start a violent flirtation with them both, and as he was the only young man there, they were quite willing to meet him half-way. . . .

"I've given you the greatest thing a woman can give a man—oh, what a fool I was—and you have no gratitude. You must be quite heartless. How could you be so cruel as to torment me by flirting with those vulgar girls. We've only got just over a week. Can't you even give me that?"

Philip stood over her rather sulkily. He thought her behaviour childish. He was vexed with her for having shown her ill-temper before strangers.

"But you know I don't care twopence about either of the O'Connors. Why on earth should you think I do?"

Miss Wilkinson put away her handkerchief. Her tears had made marks on her powdered face, and her hair was somewhat disarranged. Her white dress did not suit her very well just then. She looked at Philip with hungry, passionate eyes.

"Because you're twenty and so's she," she said hoarsely. "And I'm old."

Philip reddened and looked away. The anguish of her tone made him feel strangely uneasy. He wished with all his heart that he had never had anything to do with Miss Wilkinson.

"I don't want to make you unhappy," he said awkwardly.

"You'd better go down and look after your friends. They'll wonder what has become of you."

"All right."

He was glad to leave her.

The quarrel was quickly followed by a reconciliation, but the few days that remained were sometimes irksome to Philip. He wanted to talk of nothing but the future, and the future invariably reduced Miss Wilkinson to tears. At first her weeping affected him, and feeling himself a beast he redoubled his protestations of undying passion; but now it irritated him: it would have been all very well if she had been a girl, but it was silly of a grown-up woman to cry so much. She never ceased reminding him that he was under a debt of gratitude to her which he could never repay. He was willing to acknowledge this since she made a point of it, but he did not really know why he should be any more grateful to her than she to him. He was expected to show his sense of obligation in ways which were rather a nuisance: he had been a good deal used to solitude, and it was a necessity to him sometimes; but Miss Wilkinson looked upon it as an unkindness if he was not always at her beck and call. . . .

She flung her arms passionately round his neck. He was embarrassed sometimes by the demonstrations of her affection. He would have preferred her to be more passive. It shocked him a little that she should give him so marked a lead: it did not tally altogether with his prepossessions about the modesty of the feminine temperament.

At length the day came on which Miss Wilkinson was to go, and she came down to breakfast, pale and subdued, in a serviceable travelling dress of black and white check. She looked a very competent governess. Philip was silent too, for he did not quite know what to say that would fit the circumstance; and he was terribly afraid that, if he said something flippant, Miss Wilkinson would break down before his uncle and make a scene. They had said their last good-bye to one another in the garden the night before, and Philip was relieved that there was now no opportunity for them to be alone. He remained in the dining-room after breakfast in case Miss Wilkinson should insist on kissing him on the stairs. . . . Just as the train was leaving she leaned out and kissed Mr. Carey.

"I must kiss you too, Philip," she said.

"All right," he said, blushing.

He stood up on the step and she kissed him quickly. The train started, and Miss Wilkinson sank into the corner of her carriage and wept disconsolately. Philip as he walked back to the vicarage felt a distinct sensation of relief.

"Well, did you see her safely off?" asked Aunt Louisa, when they got in.

"Yes, she seemed rather weepy. She insisted on kissing me and Philip."

"Oh, well, at her age it's not dangerous." Mrs. Carey pointed to the side-board. "There's a letter for you, Philip. It came by the second post."

It was from Hayward and ran as follows:

My dear boy,

I answer your letter at once. I ventured to read it to a great friend of mine, a charming woman whose help and sympathy have been very precious to me, a woman withal with a real feeling for art and literature; and we agreed that it was charming. You wrote from your heart and you do not know the delightful naïveté which is in every line. And because you love you write like a poet. Ah, dear boy, that is the real thing: I felt the glow of your young passion, and your prose was musical from the sincerity of your emotion. You must be happy! I wish I could have been present unseen in that enchanted garden while you wandered hand in hand, like Daphnis and Chloe, amid the flowers. I can see you, my Daphnis, with the light of young love in your eyes, tender, enraptured, and ardent; while Chloe in your arms, so young and soft and fresh, vowing she would ne'er consent — consented. Roses and violets and honeysuckle! Oh, my friend, I envy you. It is so good to think that your first love should have been pure poetry. Treasure the moments, for the immortal gods have given you the Greatest Gift of All, and it will be a sweet, sad memory till your dying day. You will never again enjoy that careless rapture. First love is best love; and she is beautiful and you are young, and all the world is yours. I felt my pulse go faster when with your adorable simplicity you told me that you buried your face in her long hair. I am sure that it is that exquisite chestnut which seems just touched with gold. I would have you sit under a leafy tree side by side, and read together *Romeo and Juliet*; and then I would have you fall on your knees and on my behalf kiss the ground on which her foot has left its imprint; then tell her it is the homage of a poet to her radiant youth and to your love for her.

Yours always,
G. Etheridge Hayward.

"What damned rot!" said Philip, when he finished the letter.

Miss Wilkinson oddly enough had suggested that they should read *Romeo and Juliet* together; but Philip had firmly declined. Then, as he put the letter in his pocket, he felt a queer little pang of bitterness because reality seemed so different from the ideal.

———————

Less able to rationalize than the narrators of *I Can't Breathe* and *The Well of Days,* Philip Carey feels "a queer little pang of bitterness" after his affair with thirty-seven-year-old Emily Wilkinson "because reality seemed so different from the ideal." Where do we get the romantic notions, such as Hayward summarizes in his letter, that first love is best, consisting of pure poetry, careless rapture, and the denial of reason in a glowing atmosphere of roses and violets and honeysuckle?

Have we also been led to believe that sexual acts are always glamorous expressions of young passion? That wedding nights and honeymoons are rapturous? Must only the disillusionment of private experience teach us, as it did Philip, that many views on love and sex are "damned rot"? Or is Philip's case unique, and the logical consequence of deliberate attempts to delude himself? Why?

In what ways does Philip's romanticism make a "**You-I**" balance impossible in his relationship with Miss Wilkinson?

What other factors condition the relationship so that only an "**I**" can dominate?

Consider Philip's reactions in the following passages from Fromm's perspective (p. 261) that "sexual desire can easily blend with and be stimulated by any strong emotion, of which love is only one":

He saw the dark staircase and the chance meetings, and he admired the boldness of the letters—oh, he would never have dared to do that—and then the silent, almost mysterious entrance. It seemed to him the very soul of romance.

In his ingenuousness he doubted her story as little as he doubted what he read in books, and he was angry that such wonderful things never happened to him. It was humiliating that if Miss Wilkinson insisted upon his telling her of his adventures in Heidelberg he would have nothing to tell.

He ought to make love to her. They had talked a good deal of love.

Miss Wilkinson was practically French, and that added zest to possible adventure.

Here at last was his chance of an adventure, and he would be a fool not to take it. . . .

. . . it would be very satisfactory to have an intrigue, and he thrilled with the legitimate pride he would enjoy in his conquest. He owed it to himself to seduce her.

Philip put his arm around her waist and kissed her lips. . . . Philip was very proud of himself. He said he would, and he had.

When he tried to kiss her again she did not resist. He pretended to be much more passionate than he really was, and he succeeded in playing a part which looked very well in his own eyes.

He said things that he would never have thought himself capable of saying; he could certainly never have said them in the broad light of day; and he listened to himself with wonder and satisfaction.

It was splendid. It was the most thrilling game he had ever played; and the wonderful thing was that he felt almost all he said. It was only that he exaggerated a little. He was tremendously interested and excited in the effect he could see it had on her.

He held out his hand seriously, and she took it in silence. He thought she stifled a sob. Oh, it was magnificent!

He was deliciously flattered to discover that Miss Wilkinson was in love with him: she told him so in English, and she told him so in French.

When he kissed her it was wonderful to feel the passion that seemed to thrill her soul. He kissed her a good deal, for he found it easier to do that than to say the things he instinctively felt she expected of him.

He wished that there were someone to whom he could boast a little, and he would willingly have discussed minute points of his conduct.

He wished with all his heart that he had not suggested the plan; but it was too late now; he must take the opportunity which he had made. What would Miss Wilkinson think of him if he did not! . . . Philip's heart sank as he stared at her; she had never seemed so unattractive; but it was too late now.

Philip woke early next morning. . . . he sighed with satisfaction. He was delighted with himself.

. . . he was pleased and happy and flattered. She was evidently frightfully gone on him.

He did want someone to know very badly.

In which of the cited passages is any concern for Miss Wilkinson indicated? Who or what is the prime object of Philip's concern, pride, and satisfaction?

If mutualism, the essence of love, is absent, what motives appear to stimulate Philip's desire for Miss Wilkinson? Before having sexual relations with Miss Wilkinson, Philip

. . . felt sick with apprehension. . . . His heart beat painfully. . . . his hand trembled. He would willingly have bolted. . . . It was like getting on the highest diving-board . . . it looked nothing from below, but when you got up there and stared down at the water your heart sank. . . . He seemed to himself to be trembling like a leaf.

Do you think this description of Philip's fears over a situation he himself engineered is atypical?

What are some of the realities about Emily Wilkinson that Philip refuses to face? Why does he refuse to face them? Had he not deluded himself into playing a romantic role, might Philip have been spared the realistic aftermath of a short-lived triumph:

She was plain and old. His quick fancy showed her to him, wrinkled, haggard, made-up, in those frocks which were too showy for her position and too young for her years. He shuddered; he felt suddenly that he never wanted to see her again; he could not bear the thought of kissing her. He was horrified with himself. Was that love?

Why is Philip's reaction so acute and extreme? In what ways did Philip's conduct get him into more than he had expected?

What does Philip mean by his constant references to "ought": he "ought to make love to her," "he was thinking that he ought to kiss her there and then," "he knew he ought to reply: 'Because I love you.' But he could not bring himself to say it."

How much of Philip's sex is in his head? How much of it is a circulatory phenomenon called "thrill," of quick breathing, pounding heart, and generalized tension that is easily confused with being in love?

Do you feel sorry for Miss Wilkinson? And/or did she get exactly what she deserved? Why?

Do you think that her voice "thrilling with emotion" as she told Philip that she loved him, her scene after the tennis party, her excessive demonstrativeness and her tears were facets of a thirty-seven-year-old woman's put-on? Or the consequences of her genuine emotional involvement with Philip after their affair? Something of each, or neither?

Might her jealousy of the O'Connor girls be real? How do they threaten her, and thus aggravate her possessiveness about Philip?

Do you believe Miss Wilkinson's declaration:

> "Oh, Philip, don't leave me. You don't know what you mean to me. I have such a wretched life, and you've made me so happy."

What *does* Philip mean to her?

Is Miss Wilkinson acting, or responding genuinely when she says:

> "I've given you the greatest thing a woman can give a man—oh, what a fool I was—and you have no gratitude. You must be quite heartless. How could you be so cruel as to torment me by flirting with those vulgar girls. We've only got just over a week. Can't you even give me that?"

Did her sexual surrender to Philip produce this intensity of feeling in her? If not, what did? If her emotions are feigned, why is she pretending?

How accurate is her analysis of Philip? Does he lack "gratitude"? Is he "heartless and cruel"? Philip reacts with a sulky stance, the thought that her behavior is childish, and vexation with her having displayed ill-temper before strangers. Why is Philip not more understanding? What was the "devil" which prompted him to start a violent flirtation with both O'Connors?

What conclusions are implied about the psychological differences between male and female reactions to premarital sex? Will a girl keep hanging around a fellow after she has had sex with him, even if she has been told that he doesn't want her anymore? Why, or why not?

Miss Wilkinson supplies considerable evidence that refutes the saying: "Flattery will get you nowhere." How does she use the technique on Philip? In what ways is flattery also part of his strategy with her? What sort of person is apt to be susceptible to flattery? Why?

What motivates Miss Wilkinson's behavior? Do you think she had ever been seduced by anyone before Philip? If not, why does she tell him that she has been? Is she as "romantic" as he is? Is she in any way genuinely interested in Philip as a person? Concerned with his welfare? Why does she never cease "reminding him that he was under a debt of gratitude to her which he could never repay"?

Why might she have suggested that they read *Romeo and Juliet* together? What is she looking for in their relationship? What needs of hers does she hope it will fulfill? Does it?

Both Emily and Philip generalize about male and female sexuality. In considering whether to rush into things or let them take their time since they have only three weeks more together, she asks Philip:

> "Oh, why can't you be content to let it go on as it is? Men are always the same. They're never satisfied."

Embarrassed sometimes by Miss Wilkinson's demonstrations of affection, Philip is shocked by her aggressiveness:

> That she should give him so marked a lead . . . did not tally altogether with his prepossessions about the modesty of the feminine temperament.

Do you believe that "men are never satisfied"? With what? In what way? Would you expect males and females to disagree in responding to this question?

Do you believe that the feminine temperament is basically modest? "Modest" about what? In what way?

Although the male is usually the one held responsible for the sexual act itself, to what extent is it the "Eve" who has offered him the apple in tempting situations? What tactics does Emily use to tempt Philip into undertaking the "siege of [her] virtue"?

RELATED QUESTIONS

What parallels exist between Philip Carey in *Of Human Bondage* and the young man in *Romance* (p. 372)?

In what respect does Philip resemble K.B. in *Manchild in the Promised Land* (p. 577) and *Fred Apollus at Fava's* (see "Night-Lights," p. 577)?

i like my body
when it is with your
E. E. CUMMINGS

i like my body when it is with your
body. It is so quite new a thing.
Muscles better and nerves more.
i like your body. i like what it does,
i like its hows. i like to feel the spine
of your body and its bones, and the trembling
-firm-smoothness and which i will
again and again and again
kiss, i like kissing this and that of you,
i like, slowly stroking the, shocking fuzz
of your electric fur, and what-is-it comes
over parting flesh . . . . And eyes big lov-crumbs,

and possibly i like the thrill

of under me you so quite new

Homage to Sextus Propertius

Orfeo: "Quia pauper amavi."

EZRA POUND

VII

Me happy, night, night full of brightness;
Oh couch made happy by my long delectations;
How many words talked out with abundant candles;
Struggles when the lights were taken away;
Now with bared breasts she wrestled against me,
               Tunic spread in delay;
And she then opening my eyelids fallen in sleep,
Her lips upon them; and it was her mouth saying: Sluggard!

In how many varied embraces, our changing arms,
Her kisses, how many, lingering on my lips.
"Turn not Venus into a blinded motion,
          Eyes are the guides of love,
Paris took Helen naked coming from the bed of Menelaus,
Endymion's naked body, bright bait for Diana,"—such at
   least is the story.

While our fates twine together, sate we our eyes with love;
For long night comes upon you
                    and a day when no day returns.
Let the gods lay chains upon us
              so that no day shall unbind them.

Fool who would set a term to love's madness,
For the sun shall drive with black horses,
                    earth shall bring wheat from barley,
The flood shall move toward the fountain
          Ere love know moderations,
          The fish shall swim in dry streams.
No, now while it may be, let not the fruit of life cease.
Dry wreaths drop their petals,
                    their stalks are woven in baskets,
To-day we take the great breath of lovers,
                    to-morrow fate shuts us in.

Though you give all your kisses
                    you give but few.
Nor can I shift my pains to other,
          Hers will I be dead,
If she confer such nights upon me,
                    long is my life, long in years,
If she give me many,
          God am I for the time.

What human needs does sex appear to satisfy in the final lines of Cummings' poem *i like my body when it is with your* and the excerpt from Pound's *Homage to Sextus Propertius?*

Are the male figures in each of these poems "I"-oriented? Is an "I"-orientation synonymous with self-centeredness? With selfishness?

What does Pound suggest in saying, "Eyes are the guides of love"? What kind of love? Is he talking about the same thing when he says, "while our fates twine together, sate we our eyes with *love.* . . . Fool who would set a term to love's madness"?

Why should love know moderation? Is there anything more healthy than the truthful celebration and total enjoyment of "raw sex"?

Would Pound and Cummings agree with the high-school girl who commented, "If you have sex, you both will have a lot of fun. Sex is an active sport, more enjoyable than tennis or bowling."

In *Situation Ethics* (p. 322), Fletcher maintains:

People are learning that we can have sex without love, and love without sex. . . . [Sex] is, indeed, for re-creation as well as for procreation. . . . if people do not believe it is wrong to have sex relations outside marriage, it isn't, unless they hurt themselves, their partners, or others.

Is there any evidence in either Cummings' or Pound's poem that anyone is being hurt?

Do the subjects in the poems give any indication of anxiety or guilt or confusion about their sexual experiences?

For sexual desire to become part of love (that is, for it to be more than a sport), Singer in *Appraisal and Bestowal* (p. 220) insists that:

. . . it must function as a way of responding to the character and special properties of [a] particular woman. Desire wants what it wants for the sake of some private gratification, whereas love demands an interest in that vague complexity we call another person. . . . If a woman is *simply* a means to sexual satisfaction, a man may be said to want her, but not to love her.

Is there any evidence that either Pound or Cummings "loves" as well as "wants"? Is there anything wrong with simply wanting a person and enjoying the "getting"?

Fromm in *The Theory of Love* (p. 253) states that

All forms of orgiastic union have three characteristics: they are intense, even violent; they occur in the total personality, mind *and* body; they are transitory and periodical. . . . To some extent it is a natural and normal form of overcoming separateness, and a partial answer to the problem of isolation. But in many individuals in whom separateness is not relieved in other ways, the search for the sexual orgasm. . . . becomes a desperate attempt to escape the anxiety engendered by separateness, and it results in an ever-increasing sense of separateness, since the sexual act without love never bridges the gap between two human beings, except momentarily.

Does Fromm's theory imply limitations for the sexual relationships described in *i like my body when it is with your* and *Homage to Sextus Propertius?* Why does the addition of love—as Fromm and Lee (*What Love Must Be*, p. 250) in particular conceive it—provide a better chance for harmony and durability in a relationship?

How might marriage strengthen the bond evident in these two poems?

Is there reason to believe that any of the sexual partners depicted in these poems wants more than a temporary bridging of the gap between two human beings?

Do either, neither, or both poems exemplify the following passage from *Eros* by C. S. Lewis (p. 210):

[The] refusal to be quite immersed—this recollection of the levity even when for the moment, only the gravity is displayed—is especially relevant to a certain attitude which Venus, in her intensity, evokes from most . . . pairs of lovers. This act can invite the man to an extreme, though short-lived, masterfulness, to the dominance of a conqueror or a captor, and the woman to a correspondingly extreme subjection and surrender.

RELATED QUESTIONS

Would Plato in *The Symposium* (p. 306) consider Cummings and Pound to be "vicious" or "virtuous" lovers? Why?

In Singer's terms, would the poets' feelings be viewed as "appraisals" or "bestowals," or as some of each?

How do the feelings described in *i like my body when it is with your* and *Homage to Sextus Propertius* compare or contrast with "that sensual phosphorescence" described by Ferlinghetti in his poem on p. 145?

How do the feelings described in *i like my body when it is with your* and *Homage to Sextus Propertius* compare or contrast with those in the sexual relationship described by Walt Whitman in *A Woman Waits for Me* (see "**Night-Lights,**" p. 590)?

Both of the following excerpts from Grace Metalious' novel *Peyton Place* deal with the relationship between sixteen-year-old Rodney Harrington and fifteen-year-old Betty Anderson, whose father works as a mill hand for Rodney's wealthy father.

Despite Betty's behavior with Rodney in the parking lot of the high school gymnasium during the first scene—a dance to which Rodney came with another date—he continues his relationship with Betty, for reasons suggested in the second scene which takes place some time later.

Peyton Place (1)

GRACE METALIOUS

Outside, Betty Anderson was leading Rodney by the hand across the dark field that served as a parking lot for the high school. John Pillsbury's car was parked a short distance away from the others, under a tree, and when Betty and Rodney reached it, she opened the back door and got in.

"Hurry up," she whispered, and Rodney climbed in behind her.

Swiftly, she pressed down the buttons on the four doors that locked them, and then she collapsed into the back seat, laughing.

"Here we are," she said. "Snug as peas in a pod."

"Come on, Betty," whispered Rodney. "Come on."

"No," she said petulantly, "I won't. I'm mad at you."

"Aw, come on, Betty. Don't be like that. Kiss me."

"No," said Betty, tossing her head. "Go get skinny Allison MacKenzie to kiss you. She's the one you brought to the dance."

"Don't be mad, Betty," pleaded Rodney. "I couldn't help it. I didn't want to. My father made me do it."

"Would you rather be with me?" asked Betty in a slightly mollified tone.

"*Would* I?" breathed Rodney, and it was not a question.

Betty leaned her head against his shoulder and ran one finger up and down on his coat lapel.

"Just the same," she said, "I think it was mean of you to ask Allison to the dance."

"Aw, come on, Betty. Don't be like that. Kiss me a little."

Betty lifted her head and Rodney quickly covered her mouth with his. She could kiss, thought Rodney, like no one else in the world. She didn't kiss with just her lips, but with her teeth and her tongue, and all the while she made noises deep in her throat, and her fingernails dug into his shoulders.

"Oh, honey, honey," whispered Rodney, and that was all he could say before Betty's tongue went between his teeth again.

Her whole body twisted and moved when he kissed her, and when his hands found their way to her breasts, she moaned as if she were hurt. She writhed on the seat until she was lying down, with only her legs and feet not touching him, and Rodney fitted his body to her without taking his mouth from hers.

"Is it up, Rod?" she panted, undulating her body under his. "Is it up good and hard?"

"Oh, yes," he whispered, almost unable to speak. "Oh, yes."

Without another word, Betty jacknifed her knees, pushed Rodney away from her, clicked the lock on the door and was outside of the car.

"Now go shove it into Allison MacKenzie," she screamed at him. "Go get the girl you brought to the dance and get rid of it with her!"

Before Rodney could catch his breath to utter one word, she had whirled and was on her way back to the gymnasium. He tried to get out of the car to run after her, but his legs were like sawdust under him, and he could only cling to the open door and curse under his breath.

"Bitch," he said hoarsely, using one of his father's favorite words. "Goddamned bitch!"

He hung onto the open car door and retched helplessly, and the sweat poured down his face.

"Bitch!" he said, but it did not help.

At last, he straightened up and wiped his face with his handkerchief, and fumbled in his pockets for a comb. He still had to go back into the gymnasium to get that goddamned Allison MacKenzie. His father would drive up at eleven-thirty and expect to find him waiting with her.

"Oh, you rotten bitch," he said under his breath to the absent Betty. "Oh, you stinking, rotten, goddamned bitchy sonofabitch!"

He racked his brain to think of new swear words to direct at her, but he could think of nothing. He began to comb his hair, almost in tears.

Betty Anderson in **Peyton Place** uses sex as an expression of hostility toward Rodney. What has made her so angry that she exploits Rodney to revenge herself?

Why was the method of revenge she chose so highly effective—a physical and emotional humiliation?

Why is Betty able to control the situation?

Isn't she physically aroused by Rodney's kisses, his manipulation of her breasts and the pressure of his body? If not, why does the author describe Betty making "noises deep in her throat," her whole body twisting and moving when he kissed her? Is the female capable of faking sexual response this way? Is the male equally able to deceive his partner?

Is Rodney's inability to recover his senses quickly explained solely by the fact that he was startled by Betty's unexpected behavior?

How do the following comments clarify the scientific basis for the differences in sexual response exhibited by Betty and Rodney:

> The man's sex response tends to be rapid and definite. His excitation is readily recognized in the change in his sex organs. The woman's sex response is slower and less definite. She experiences an all-over excitement in which there may or may not be local sensations in her genitals. Usually it is only the more sexually experienced, mature woman who is aware of sexual excitation as soon as the average man is.
>
> In the . . . man sex excitement builds up rapidly to ejaculation and then rapidly declines. Woman's response develops more slowly to climax and the more gradually tapers off. [10]

> The "sex act", so far as women are concerned, consists of the extrusion of an ovum into a tube. Thereafter, all she has to do is wait for a sperm to find it. There is no sensation of pleasure, let alone of ecstasy, associated with this female sex act. . . .
>
> The "male sex act," ejaculation of sperm, is quite different in all respects. Orgasmic paroxysm, totally irrelevant in the female's extrusion of the ovum, is an important ingredient in ejaculation of the sperm. [11]

> The whole personality, with its overall needs, is reflected in sex behavior, but there are some important psychological as well as physical differences between the sexes. Girls generally prefer a close personal tie with affectionate petting even more than coition, and many admit that they "gave in" to sexual intercourse hoping that they would, in this way, gain a permanent marriage partner. Generally, men can be more easily aroused physically, do not linger so long over preparatory acts and endearments, and turn more quickly to other interests. [12]

> Lovers' Lane: The desire engendered in the male glands is a hundred times more difficult to control than the desire bred in the female glands. All girls agreeing to a lovers' lane *tête-à-tête* in a car, knowing that they will limit their actions to arousing desire and then defend their "virtue," should be horsewhipped. [13]

If the judgment, based on the physiological differences in male and female sexual response, is valid, how hard would you "horsewhip" Betty?

Would you describe Betty as a "tease"? In a sexual context, what does teasing mean?

Would you, like Rodney, term Betty a "bitch"? What does the word connote? What does it denote?

Does Betty meet the following qualifications of the term:

. . . the bitch . . . has been especially powerful in our society. D. H. Lawrence first articulated the so-called bitch theory of American society. His thesis was that women in America were the dominant sex: they had assumed, he said, so much power that men could hardly stand up to them, and as a result they had, in effect, castrated the men. James Thurber's name has come to stand for the same view of the battle of the sexes. The bitch is "a woman without heart, who . . . [loves] merely power over men and the momentary satisfaction to vanity or flesh which they . . . [can] give her." They are the women who dominate men, who have power over them, who outmaneuver them, who successfully compete against them (especially if they make something of it). [14]

How does Betty get that "momentary satisfaction to vanity"?
In **The Theory of Love** (p. 256), Fromm stipulates:

Beyond the element of giving, the active character of love becomes evident in the fact that it always implies certain basic elements, common to all forms of love. These are *care, responsibility, respect* and *knowledge.*

Which of these four elements does Betty totally ignore? How? Which of these four elements does she distort the meaning of, twisting it for her own ends?
How is the following comment on the uses of sex applicable to Betty Anderson:

The feeling of power that comes from realizing that one can attract the opposite sex acts as a further stimulus to sex play and to sexual intercourse. . . . we sometimes try through sex experiences to make up for other lacks or needs in our life. Sex is not bad, but such an irresponsible use of sex can be. . . . it is highly important that you feel that you have meaning as a person, and that you have not been used, as a sexual object. [15]

Peyton Place (2)
GRACE METALIOUS

At sixteen, Rodney Harrington had not changed substantially from the boy he had been at fourteen. He was an inch or so taller, which made him five feet eight now, and he had filled out a bit with the result that he looked more than ever like his father. Other than that, Rodney was unchanged. His hair, which he wore just a trifle too long, was still black and curly, and his heavy mouth still showed a lack of discipline and self-control. There were a few people in Peyton Place who said that it was too late for Rodney Harrington. He would always be just what he had always been—the indulged child of a rich widowered father. They cited his expulsion from the New Hampton School for Boys as proof of what they said. New Hampton, which had attempted to teach Rodney, had ended by expelling him for laziness and insubordination after two years of trying. New Hampton had a good reputation, and had succeeded in the past, where other schools had failed with other problem youngsters, but it had been unable to leave its mark on Rodney Harrington. Apparently, the only thing that Rodney had learned while away at school was that all boys of good family had sexual intercourse with girls before reaching prep school age, and those who had not were either fairies or material for the priesthood. Rodney had learned quickly, and by the time he had been at New Hampton for less than a year he could outtalk the best of them. According to Rodney, he had deflowered no less than nine maidens in his own home town before reaching the age of fifteen, and he had almost been shot twice by the irate husband with whose wife he had carried on a passionate affair for six months.

Rodney had the sensual good looks, the money and the glib tongue to make himself believed. He had been considered quite a man among men by the time he was kicked out of New Hampton. Even his own father believed him, although he made his stories much weaker for Leslie, and named fictitious girls from White River as the heroines of his tales. Rodney had told his stories of successful seduction so often, to so many different people, that most of the time he could believe them himself. Actually he had never had a sexual experience in his life, and at times when the truth smote him, he felt as if someone had flung a glass of cold water in his face for no reason. The frightening thought that he would not know how to go about completing the act, if he ever once had the chance to get started, affected him like the sun going behind a cloud on a hot day. It left him chilled, and lent a dreary aspect to his otherwise cheerful world. What horrified him the most about the truth was not the possible personal humiliation to himself, but that the girl with whom he failed might talk. Whenever Rodney thought of what his many friends would say if they ever discovered that he had been spinning fantasies, and that he was in reality, as inexperienced as a seven-year-old, he turned cold with horror.

He was thinking along this depressing line now, as he swung his car into Ash Street which was a narrow, tumble-down street in the neighborhood where the mill hands lived. He pulled up smartly in front of the Anderson house and sounded his horn with a bravado he was far from feeling. Determinedly, he made the effort to shrug off his fears, and for Rodney Harrington the shaking off of depression or fear had never been a difficulty.

What the hell? he thought, and the sun came back out from behind its dark cloud. What the hell? He had money to spend, a car to get around in, and a pint of rye whisky in the glove compartment. What the hell? He'd know what to do if he ever got old Betty to take her pants off. He'd heard it described enough times, hadn't he? He'd described it enough times himself, hadn't he? What the hell? He had not only talked and heard about it, he had read books about it and seen pictures of it. What the hell was he worried about?

Betty strolled down the short walk in front of her house, undulating her hips fully, as she had seen a musical comedy queen do in a movie the week before. She moved slowly toward Rodney's car.

"Hi, kid," she said.

She was exactly one year and fourteen days younger than he, but she unfailingly called him kid. Tonight she wore a pair of tight green shorts and a small yellow halter. As always, whenever he looked at her, Rodney felt his speech thicken in his throat. The only way he could explain his reaction to Betty was to say that it was just like the way it had been when he was small and old Pratte had let him watch her make pudding. One minute, there was the liquid in the pan, so thin and runny that you thought it would never be any other way, and in the very next minute the stuff turned thick and syrupy, so that old Pratte really had to work to get a spoon through the mess. That was the way he was about Betty. Like pudding. Until he saw her, his mind was clear and cool and liquid, but the minute she leaned over the car door and said, "Hi, kid," his speech thickened, his eyes grew heavy lidded, and he struggled to pull breath through the syrupy mass in his chest.

"Hi," he said.

"It's too hot to get all dressed up to go somewhere," said Betty. "I just want to go for a ride and stop at a drive-in to eat."

Rodney was wearing a shirt and sports jacket because he had planned to take her to a restaurant and then somewhere to dance, but he capitulated without a murmur.

"Sure," he said.

Without another word, Betty opened the car door and flopped into the seat next to him.

"Why don't you take off that coat?" she demanded crossly. "It makes me hot and itchy all over just to look at you."

Rodney immediately took off his coat and put it on the back seat. From the Anderson house, two sullen, tired faces watched him as he put the convertible into gear and roared off down Ash Street. As soon as Rodney had turned the corner, Betty wiggled her fingers at him and he passed her his cigarettes.

"How come you couldn't go out with me last night?" he asked.

"I had other things to do," replied Betty coolly. "Why?"

"I just wondered. Seems funny to me that you have time for me only a couple of times a week, that's all."

"Listen, kid," she said. "I don't have to account to you or anybody like you for my time. Get it?"

"Don't get sore. I was just wondering."

"If it'll make you feel any better, I went dancing last night. Marty Janowski took me over to White River and we went to the China Dragon to eat and dance. Any more questions?"

Rodney knew that he should keep quiet, but he could not let it go at that. "What did you do later?" he asked.

"Went parking over at Silver Lake," replied Betty without hesitation. "Why?"

"I just wondered. Have fun?"

"As a matter of fact, I did. Marty's a swell dancer."

"That's not what I meant."

"What did you mean?"

"I mean after. Parking."

"Yes I did, if it's any of your business."

"What did you do?" asked Rodney, not wanting to hear but unable to keep himself from asking.

"Oh, for Christ's sake," said Betty disgustedly. "Find a drive-in, will you? I'm starved. We mill hands are used to getting our supper at five-thirty. We're not like high mucky muck mill owners who have servants to give them dinner at eight."

"I'll stop at the next one," said Rodney. "Listen, Betty. I don't think it's right for you to go parking with Marty Janowski."

"What!" The word was not so much a question as an exclamation of rage.

"I don't think it's right for you to go parking with Marty Janowski. Not after I've asked you a thousand times to be my girl."

"Turn this car around and take me home," demanded Betty. "At once."

Rodney stepped on the gas and kept going. "I won't let you out until you promise not to fool around with Marty any more," he said doggedly.

"I didn't tell you to let me out," said Betty furiously. "I told you to turn around and take me home."

"If you don't want to go for a ride with me," said Rodney, hating himself for not keeping his mouth shut, "I'll stop the car right here and you can walk back."

"All *right*," said Betty. "You just stop and let me out. I won't have to walk far, I'll guarantee you that. The first car that comes along with a good-looking fellow in it is the car I'll stick out my thumb for. I don't come from a mill-owning family. I don't mind hitch-hiking one damned bit. Now let me out."

"Aw, come on, Betty," pleaded Rodney. "Don't be mad. I wouldn't let you out on the highway like that. Come on, don't be mad."

"I am mad. Damned good and mad. Who do you think you are, telling me who I can go out with, and who I can't?"

"I didn't mean anything. I just got jealous for a minute, that's all. I have asked you, thousands of times, to be my girl. It makes me jealous to think of you with another fellow, that's all."

"Well keep it to yourself from now on," ordered Betty. "I don't take orders from anybody. Besides, why should I be your girl and go steady with you? When you go away to school next fall, I'd be left high and dry. It's hard for a girl to get back in circulation after she's gone steady for a while."

"I thought that maybe you liked me better than anyone else," said Rodney. "I like you better than any other girl. That's why I want to go steady with you."

Betty's expression softened a trifle. "I like you all right, kid," she said. "You're O.K."

"Well, then?"

"I'll think it over."

Rodney turned into a drive-in and a spurt of gravel flew up from behind one of his rear wheels.

"Would you go parking at Silver Lake with me?" he asked.

"I might," she said, "if you'd hurry up and feed me. I want a couple of cheeseburgers and a chocolate shake and a side of French fries."

Rodney got out of the car. "Will you?" he asked.

"I said I might, didn't I?" said Betty impatiently. "What more do you want, a written agreement?"

Much later, after they had eaten and the night had turned thoroughly dark, Rodney drove around Silver Lake. It was Betty who showed him one of the good parking places. When he had cut the motor and turned off the lights, the humid night closed in on them like a soggy black blanket.

"God, it's hot," complained Betty.

"There's a bottle in the glove compartment," said Rodney, "and I bought some ginger ale at the drive-in. A good drink will cool you off."

He mixed two drinks quickly and expertly, by the dashboard light. They were warm and tasted vaguely of the paper cups which contained them.

"Whew!" said Betty, and spit a mouthful of the warm, strong drink over the low car door. "Jeez! What swill!"

"It takes getting used to," commented Rodney, suddenly feeling very man-of-the-world. If there was one thing he knew, it was good liquor and the drinking of it. "Take another sip," he suggested. "It grows on you."

"To hell with that," said Betty. "I'm going in for a swim."

"Did you bring a suit?"

"What's the matter with you, anyway? Haven't you ever been swimming in the raw with a girl?"

"Sure, I have," lied Rodney. "Dozens of times. I was just asking if you'd brought a suit is all."

"No, I didn't bring a suit," mimicked Betty. "Are you coming?"

"Of course," said Rodney, hurriedly finishing his drink.

Before he could get his shirt unbuttoned, Betty had shed her shorts and halter and was running, naked, down the beach toward the water. When Rodney reached the water's edge, feeling very naked and more than a little foolish, Betty was nowhere to be seen. He inched himself slowly into the water, and when he had waded in as far as his waist, she was suddenly beside him. Her head emerged silently from the water, and she spit a stream straight into the middle of his back. He fell forward and when he came up, Betty was standing up and laughing at him. He tried to catch her, but she swam away from him, laughing, taunting, calling him names.

"Wait 'til I get you," he called to her. "You've got to come out sooner or later, and I'll be right here waiting."

"Don't let your teeth chatter," she yelled, "or I'll be able to find you in the dark."

As it turned out, he did not catch her. A few minutes later the blatant sound of his horn rang out in the dark, and he started violently.

"I've had enough," shouted Betty from the car.

Goddamn it. Rodney cursed savagely. He had planned to catch her and throw her down in the sand and roll her around good, feeling her, touching her. He had never been close to her when she was completely undressed before, and now, goddamn it, she had gone and beat him to the car. She must have eyes like a cat to find her way around in this moonless dark. He stumbled several times before he finally discerned the bulk of his automobile up ahead of him.

Betty waited while he stumbled again and nearly fell. She waited until he was directly in front of the car, and then she turned on the head lights. Her hoot of laughter filled the night, and Rodney was only too painfully aware of the ridiculous picture he must make as he stood and stared like a startled animal and tired to cover himself with his hands.

"You bitch!" he shouted, but she was laughing so hard that she did not hear him.

He made his way to the car and grabbed for his trousers, cursing her silently while she laughed.

"Oh, Rod!" she cried, and went off into another spasm of laughter. "Oh, Rod! What a picture to put on a postcard and send home to Mother!"

Rodney got into the car, clad only in his trousers, and immediately pressed the starter. The car's powerful motor roared to life, and Betty reached over and turned off the ignition.

"What's the matter, honey," she asked softly, running her finger tips over his bare chest. "You mad, honey?"

Rodney exhaled his breath sharply. "No," he said, "I guess not."

"Kiss me, then," she said, prettily petulant. "Kiss me to show me you aren't mad."

With something that was almost a sob, Rodney turned to her. This was the thing he could never understand about Betty. For hours, she could act as if the last thing she wanted was for him to touch her. She could make him feel as if she did not even like him particularly, but the minute he kissed her she began to make small sounds in her throat and her body twisted and turned against him as if she could not get enough of his kisses. This was the moment he waited for every time he saw her. It made everything else bearable, from the way she taunted him with her other boy friends to the way she teased him by pretending not to like him.

"Quick!" she said. "Down on the beach. Not here."

She ran ahead of him, and he followed, carrying the car robe. Before he could get the blanket smooth on the soft sand, she was lying down, holding her arms out to him.

"Oh, baby, baby," he said. "I love you. I love you so."

She nibbled hungrily at his lower lip. "Come on, honey," she said, and her body moved ceaselessly. "Come on, honey. Love me a little."

His fingers found the tie of her halter, and in less than half a minute the garment lay on the sand next to the blanket. Betty's back arched against his arms as she thrust her breasts up to him. This was not new to Rodney. She let him do this often, but it never failed to arouse him to near frenzy. Her nipples were always rigid and exciting and the full, firm flesh around them always hot and throbbing.

"Come on, honey," she whimpered. "Come on, honey," and his mouth and hands covered her. "Hard," she whispered. "Do it hard, honey. Bite me a little. Hurt me a little."

"Please," murmured Rodney against her skin. "Please. Please."

His hand found the V of her crotch and pressed against it.

"Please," he said. "Please."

It was at this point that Betty usually stopped him. She would put both her hands in his hair and yank him away from her, but she did not stop him now. Her tight shorts slipped off as easily as if they had been several sizes too large, and her body did not stop its wild twisting while Rodney took off his trousers.

"Hurry," she moaned. "Hurry. Hurry."

For only a moment, Rodney was panicky, and after that he did not care, not even when she had to help him. For less than a moment he wondered if all the stories he had read and heard and told about virgins could be wrong. Betty did not scream in pain or beg him to stop hurting her. She led him without a fumble, and her hips moved quickly, expertly. She did not cry out at all. She moaned deep in her throat the way she did when he kissed her, and the only word she uttered was, "Hurry. Hurry. Hurry."

After that, Rodney did not notice what she did or said. He was lost in her, drowning in her, and he did not think at all. In a very few minutes he lay shivering on the blanket next to her, and her voice seemed to be coming from very far away.

"Smart guy," she was hissing at him. "Smart guy who knew all about it. So smart he doesn't even know enough to wear a safe. Get me home, you dumb jackass. Quick!"

But, unfortunately, Rodney did not get her home quickly enough, or her douche was not strong enough, or, as Rodney was inclined to believe, the Fates were out to foul him up good. It was five weeks later, during the third week of August, when Betty faced him with the worst.

"I'm a month overdue."

"What does that mean?"

"It means I'm pregnant, smart guy."

"But how can you tell so soon?" stammered Rodney.

"I was supposed to come around the week after we were at the lake. That was five weeks ago," said Betty tonelessly.

"What are we going to do?"

"We're going to get married, that's what. Nobody's sticking me with a kid and then running out on me, like that bastard from White River did to my sister."

"Married! But what will my father say?"

"That's for you to find out, smart guy. Ask him."

How many different kinds and examples of deception can you identify in this excerpt from **Peyton Place?**

Would you agree with and/or accept as inevitable the following comment:

Deceit is commonly strategic in nature. In fact, the feint and the bluff have been strategic techniques from time immemorial. . . .

A considerable amount of deception is built into civilized life for both sexes. No matter how they feel, people have to put up a civilized front. A deceptive calm pervades the hostile breakfast table; a deceptive smile masks the wife's resentment; a deceptively calm voice masks the husband's anger. The amenities prescribed by convention demand a high-level performance of deception: boredom masked by flattery, annoyance masked by attention, the whole repertoire of propriety and good breeding.

Then there is the deception imposed by role specifications. The norms of masculinity and femininity demand that impulses and tastes which go counter to them be hidden, kept from view, even denied. The man who would enjoy knitting or needlepoint—why not?—hides this damaging fact; and the woman who would like to roister with the boys smiles demurely instead at the cocktail lounge. [16]

Why?

If the "bitch" is a woman who dominates a man, has power over him, outmaneuvers him, and successfully competes against him, how does Betty fulfill all the requirements? For what are she and Rodney competing?

How are the following passages indicative of her tactics or strategy for outmaneuvering or overpowering him:

Betty strolled down the short walk in front of her house, undulating her hips fully. . . .

"Hi, kid," she said.

"Find a drive-in, will you? I'm starved. We mill hands are used to getting our supper at five-thirty. We're not like high mucky muck mill owners who have servants to give them dinner at eight. . . . I don't come from a mill-owning family. I don't mind hitch-hiking one damned bit."

"All *right,*" said Betty. "You just stop and let me out. I won't have to walk far. . . . The first car that comes along with a good-looking fellow in it is the car I'll stick out my thumb for."

She waited until he was directly in front of the car, and then she turned on the head lights.

"What's the matter, honey," she asked softly, running her finger tips over his bare chest. "You mad, honey?"

"Kiss me to show me you aren't mad."

. . . the minute he kissed her she began to make small sounds in her throat and her body twisted and turned against him as if she could not get enough of his kisses.

"Hurry," she moaned. "Hurry. Hurry."

Why, since Betty usually stopped Rodney's sexual advances before inter course, did she permit him to "go all the way" this time?

Does Betty's behavior and character confirm, partially support, or refute the following observations:

On love regarded as an amusement the last word is surely this of Robert Burns:

> *I waive the quantum of the sin,*
> *The hazard of concealing;*
> *But oh! it hardens all within*
> *And petrifies the feeling.*

Nothing is more dreadful than a cold, unimpassioned indulgence. And cold and unimpassioned love infallibly becomes when it is too lightly made. It is not good, as Pascal remarked, to have too much liberty. [17]

Some people advance the argument: "If you loved me, you would sleep with me." Under what conditions would this seem logically reasoned to you?

How might you also argue, on the basis of Betty's behavior, that the converse could also be valid: "If you hated me, you would sleep with me."

Rodney's troubles are not only of the haunted imaginings variety that plagued Jean-Christophe (p. 63), they are manifest ones—as shown by the real dilemma he faces when he discovers that Betty is pregnant. How do you feel he should act? Although we know that Rodney did have intercourse with Betty, given her sexual motivation and behavior, have we reason to believe that Rodney must be the father of her child? What chances do you think a marriage between these two individuals might have of turning out well eventually? Under what circumstances might Betty have an abortion? Have the child and surrender it at birth for adoption? Marry Rodney and establish a home for their child?

Why do many adults tend to equate lack of discipline and self-control at age seventeen with irresponsibility and the confusion of freedom with license in adulthood?

Kirkendall in **Searching for the Roots of Moral Judgments** (p. 298) wrote:

Since immorality is commonly thought of in terms of sex, let us examine the matter of premarital sex standards. The moral issue relating to petting or premarital intercourse is not, did it or did it not happen? Rather the question is what does it do to the relationship. Do or can petting and premarital intercourse create trust, understanding, and appreciation? Do they build a willingness to work together? Do they create more concern for the welfare of others? Do they make them more able to reach out to others in a spirit of love? Do they instill a feeling of self-respect? Or do they result in the converse of such conditions?

Examine each of Kirkendall's questions singly in terms of Betty and Rodney's relationship. What evidence can you produce for their immorality when measured by this yardstick? In formulating your own premarital sex standards, what questions or topics would you retain? Discard? What additions would you suggest?

Distinguishing between sexual sophistication and sexual maturity, Alexander Lowen writes:

It is my contention that the sexual behavior of a person reflects his personality, just as the personality of an individual is an expression of his sexual feelings. The point of view that underlies this study is that the sexual behavior of an individual can be understood only by reference to his personality. To define and establish this point of view it is necessary to distinguish sexual sophistication from sexual maturity, the pretended from the real. Sexual sophistication manifests itself most clearly in the attitude towards: (1) the sexual act, (2) masturbation, and (3) the body.

The sexual sophisticate regards the sexual act as a performance instead of an expression of feeling for the sexual partner. In the sophisticated view sexual intercourse is considered a victory for the ego while masturbation is seen as a defeat. . . .

The idea that sexual activity involves a performance, the skills of which can be learned from books or developed through practice, is expounded by numerous books on sexual love. We should take heed at the very mention of "performance" in relation to sex. A performance suggests the execution of an act in such a way as to call attention to the special skill or artistry of the performer. There is a public quality to a performance in the sense that the execution of the act is subject to the observation and criticism of another person or of an audience. A performance is gauged by standards that are external to the performer. . . . The concept of performance distinguishes public actions from private ones. We can see, however, that any action can become a performance if it is executed with an eye to impressing others or, what is the same thing, if it is subject to evaluation by objective criteria rather than subjective ones.

Normally the sexual act is a private action, but it becomes a public one when it is exposed to observation. It becomes so exposed when the style or manner of its execution is questioned and discussed apart from the feelings that the action is intended to express. It becomes a performance if we lose sight of the feelings that give it validity. It loses its personal meaning when the criteria by which it is judged are other than subjective ones. The sexual act is a performance if it is used more to impress one's partner than to express an inner feeling. It is a performance if the partner's satisfaction takes precedence over one's own need. It is a performance if ego values are more important than feeling or sensation. The sexual sophisticate is a sexual performer.

The body is the common ground upon which sex and personality meet. Not only is the body the physical reflection of the personality, it is the instrument of the sexual impulse. Every bodily disturbance is reflected equally in the personality and in the sexual function. . . . the biological basis of man's emotions lies in the natural functions and needs of the body. The sexually sophisticated person is unaware of this relationship. To the degree of his sophistication it can be said that his "sex is in his head." This means that he functions with illusions instead of reality.

The sexually mature person, as I see him, is neither sophisticated nor burdened with sexual guilt. He is not a performer; his sexual behavior is a direct expression of his feelings. He is not an ideal, but neither is he a pretender. He is not sexually fulfilled in every experience, because the vicissitudes of life do not allow for perfection. Success or failure is not a criterion by which he judges his sexual behavior. He knows that sexual satisfaction cannot be divorced from overall satisfaction in living. Yet these satisfactions are his because his maturity represents a realistic and wholehearted commitment to life and love. [18]

In the light of Lowen's distinction, would you call Betty "sexually sophisticated" or "sexually mature"? How would you classify Rodney? What adolescent characteristics resemble those of the sexual sophisticate?

RELATED QUESTIONS

Are the central characters in *I Can't Breathe* (p. 363) and *Romance* (p. 372) "sexually sophisticated" or "sexually mature"? How would you classify Tonka's lover from *The Well of Days* (p. 375)? Philip Carey in *Of Human Bondage* (p. 378)?

In *Of Human Bondage,* Miss Wilkinson asked Philip

. . . playfully whether he had not had any love affairs at Heidelberg. Without thinking, he frankly answered that he had not; but she refused to believe him.
"How secretive you are!" she said. "At your age is it likely?"
He blushed and laughed.
"You want to know too much," he said.
"Ah, I thought so," she laughed triumphantly. "Look at him blushing."
He was pleased that she should think he had been a sad dog, and he changed the conversation so as to make her believe he had all sorts of romantic things to conceal. He was angry with himself that he had not. There had been no opportunity.

How does the characterization of Rodney at the beginning of this excerpt from *Peyton Place* shed light on Miss Wilkinson's question and conclusion? And on Philip's reaction?

If "to boast of actual or invented prowess [among boys] is acceptable, but to speak soberly of a love affair or a sexual problem in order to be understood is strictly taboo" (p. 35) how might the situation be changed to provide opportunity for honesty and clarity?

My Last Duchess

ROBERT BROWNING

That's my last Duchess painted on the wall,
Looking as if she were alive; I call
That piece a wonder, now; Fra Pandolf's hands
Worked busily a day, and there she stands.
Will 't please you sit and look at her? I said
"Fra Pandolf" by design, for never read
Strangers like you that pictured countenance,
The depth and passion of its earnest glance,
But to myself they turned (since none puts by
The curtain I have drawn for you, but I)
And seemed as they would ask me, if they durst,
How such a glance came there; so, not the first

Are you to turn and ask thus. Sir, 'twas not
Her husband's presence only, called that spot
Of joy into the Duchess' cheek: perhaps
Fra Pandolf chanced to say, "Her mantle laps
Over my lady's wrist too much," or, "Paint
Must never hope to reproduce the faint
Half flush that dies along her throat"; such stuff
Was courtesy, she thought, and cause enough
For calling up that spot of joy. She had
A heart . . . how shall I say? . . . too soon made glad,
Too easily impressed; she liked whate'er
She looked on, and her looks went everywhere.
Sir, 'twas all one! My favor at her breast,
The dropping of the daylight in the West,
The bough of cherries some officious fool
Broke in the orchard for her, the white mule
She rode with round the terrace—all and each
Would draw from her alike the approving speech,
Or blush, at least. She thanked men—good; but thanked
Somehow . . . I know not how . . . as if she ranked
My gift of a nine-hundred-year-old name
With anybody's gift. Who'd stoop to blame
This sort of trifling? Even had you skill
In speech—which I have not—to make your will
Quite clear to such an one, and say, "Just this
Or that in you disgusts me; here you miss
Or there exceed the mark"—and if she let
Herself be lessoned so, nor plainly set
Her wits to yours, forsooth, and made excuse
—E'en then would be some stooping, and I choose
Never to stoop. Oh, sir, she smiled, no doubt,
Whene'er I passed her; but who passed without
Much the same smile? This grew; I gave commands;
Then all smiles stopped together. There she stands
As if alive. Will 't please you rise? We'll meet
The company below, then. I repeat,
The Count your Master's known munificence
Is ample warrant that no just pretense
Of mine for dowry will be disallowed;
Though his fair daughter's self, as I avowed
At starting, is my object. Nay, we'll go
Together down, sir! Notice Neptune, though,
Taming a sea horse, thought a rarity,
Which Claus of Innsbruck cast in bronze for me.

This Italian nobleman of the Renaissance is showing a painting of his former wife (and last Duchess) to an envoy from the Count whose daughter the Duke is soon to marry. As the Duke discusses the details of his arranged second marriage, what does he reveal about his concept of a wife's role?

Do you believe that we can love only whatever we possess?

How would you contrast the characters of the husband and his wife as Browning portrays them in the poem?

What characteristics of the Duke may be inferred from the following statements he makes:

> . . . none puts by
> The curtain I have drawn for you, but I. . . .

> . . . she ranked
> My gift of a nine-hundred-year-old name
> With anybody's gift.

> . . . Who'd stoop to blame. . . .
> . . . I choose
> Never to stoop.

> . . . thought a rarity,
> Which Claus of Innsbruck cast in bronze for me.

In weighing opinions, it is important to consider the sources of them. Is the Duke's description of his wife colored by his own character traits?

Why was the Duke dissatisfied with his last Duchess? Was it sexual jealousy? When the Duke complains that "her looks went everywhere," does he mean that she was a flirt? A tease? A slut? A "bitch"? Something else?

From the facts apparent in this poem, is another perspective on the Duchess implicit? Could her behavior be interpreted equally well as innocent, artless, even admirable?

> Years of social research are yielding some good generalizations about marriage. One that has stood the test of time is summed up in the expression "likes marry likes," for it seems that mates are selected from a "field of eligibles" determined by similarities of race, social class, age, religion, and proximity and availability. . . . With . . . cultural similarities assumed, personality needs then become the dominant forces in the choice of partners. Here it seems "opposites attract." That mate is selected who offers the greatest probability of satisfying maximum needs, as the partners act according to a complementary pattern of motives. [19]

If opposites attract, and the Duke and Duchess shared cultural similarities, why wasn't the alliance a perfect match? What strikes you as the single most important element lacking in the marriage between the Duke and his last Duchess? What do you think the chances are that his next marriage will be more successful?

Dietrich in *Married Love: Strategy of* (p. 350) wrote: "to be completely woman you need a master." How does the situation in *My Last Duchess* distort this concept?

To what degree would you attribute the Duke's marital difficulties to Renaissance conditions where marriages were arranged? To what extent to some other factors?

The Duke comments to the envoy that the Count, his prospective father-in-law, is known for his wealth and generosity; thus whatever the Duke might request as dowry will surely be granted. What is the significance of the fact that the Duke quickly adds:

> Though his fair daughter's self as I avowed
> At starting, is my object. . . .

Is the Duke sincere? If insincere, does the Duke know this about himself? If insincere, what are his real values?

RELATED QUESTIONS

What elements make the relationship between the Duke and his last Duchess a chronologically "grown up" variation on the relationship between Aunt Bunch and Richard in *Parma Violets* (p. 13)?

In *The Ballad of Reading Gaol* (see **Night-Lights,** p. 591), Oscar Wilde claims that "each man kills the thing he loves." Does Wilde's judgment apply to the situation in *My Last Duchess?* Does it also apply to the case of *Porphyria's Lover* (see **Night-Lights,** p. 543) by Robert Browning? How are you defining "love" in responding to the last two questions?

In what ways are the natures of the Duke and Porphyria's lover similar? In what ways different?

The sexual behavior of "Rabbit," formally Harry Angstrom, a married man and father of a small son Nelson, is viewed from two perspectives in the following four excerpts from *Rabbit, Run* by John Updike: one is his relationship with Ruth, a prostitute; the other is his relationship with Janice, his pregnant wife.

In the third excerpt, Rabbit is summoned while at Ruth's by a telephone call from Jack Eccles, his close friend and the minister with whom he plays golf regularly, announcing that Janice has just started to give birth to their second child, Rebecca June.

Rabbit, Run (1)

JOHN UPDIKE

She lives one flight up. Her door is the one at the far end of a linoleum hall, nearest the street. He stands behind her as she scratches her key at the lock. Abruptly, in the cold light of the streetlamp which comes through the four flawed panes of the window by his side, blue panes so thin-seeming the touch of one finger might crack them, he begins to tremble, first his legs, and then the skin of his sides. The key fits and her door opens.

Once inside, as she reaches for the light switch, he knocks her arm down, pulls her around, and kisses her. It's insanity, he wants to crush her, a little gauge inside his ribs doubles and redoubles his need for pressure, just pure pressure, there is no love in it, love that glances and glides along the skin, he is unconscious of their skins, it is her heart he wants to grind into his own, to comfort her completely. By nature in such an embrace she grows rigid. The small moist cushion of slack willingness with which her lips had greeted his dries up and turns hard, and when she can get her head back and her hand free she fits her palm against his jaw and pushes as if she wanted to throw his skull back into the hall. Her fingers curl and a long nail scrapes the tender skin below one eye. He lets her go. The nearly scratched eye squints and a tendon in his neck aches.

"Get out," she says, her chunky mussed face ugly in the light from the hall.

He kicks the door shut with a backwards flip of his leg. "Don't," he says.

"I had to hug you." He sees in the dark she is frightened; her big black shape has that pocket in it, that his instinct feels like a tongue probing a pulled tooth. The air tells him he must be motionless; for no reason he wants to laugh. Her fear and his inner knowledge are so incongruous; he knows there is no harm in him.

"Hug," she says. "Kill felt more like it."

"I've been loving you so much all night," he says. "I had to get it out of my system."

"I know all about your systems. One squirt and done."

"It won't be," he promises.

"It better be. I want you out of here."

"No you don't."

"You all think you're such lovers."

"I am," he assures her. "I am a lover." And on a tide of alcohol and stirred semen he steps forward, in a kind of swoon. Though she backs away, it is not so quickly that he cannot feel her socket of fear healing. The room they are in, he sees by streetlight, is small, and two armchairs and a sofa-bed and a table furnish it. She walks into the next room, a little larger, holding a double bed. The shade is half drawn, and low light gives each nubbin of the bedspread a shadow.

"All right," she says. "You can get into that."

"Where are you going?" Her hand is on a doorknob.

"In here."

"You're going to undress in there?"

"Yeah."

"Don't. Let me undress you. Please." In his concern he has come to stand beside her, and touches her arm now.

She moves her arm from under his touch. "You're pretty bossy."

"Please. Please."

Her voice grates with exasperation: "I have to go to the *john*."

"But come out dressed."

"I have to do something else, too."

"Don't do it. I know what it is. I hate them."

"You don't even feel it."

"But I know it's there. Like a rubber kidney or something."

Ruth laughs. "Well aren't you choice? Do you have the answer then?"

"No. I hate them even worse."

"Look. I don't know what you think your fifteen dollars entitles you to, but I got to protect myself."

"If you're going to put a lot of gadgets in this, give me the fifteen back."

She tries to twist away, but now he holds the arm he touched. She says, "Say do you think we're married or something the way you boss me around?"

The transparent wave moves over him again and he calls to her in a voice that is almost inaudible, "Yes; let's be." So quickly her arms don't move from hanging at her sides, he kneels at her feet and kisses the place on her fingers where a ring would have been. Now that he is down there, he begins to undo the straps of her shoes. "Why do you women wear heels?" he asks, and yanks her one foot up, so she has to grab the hair on his head for support. "Don't they hurt you?" He heaves the shoe, sticky web, through the doorway into the next room, and does the same to the other. Her feet being flat on the floor gives her legs firmness all the way up. He puts his hands around her ankles and pumps them up and down briskly, between the boxy ankle bones and the circular solid fat of her calves. He has a nervous habit of massage.

"Come on," Ruth says, in a voice slightly tense with the fear of falling, his weight pinning her legs. "Get into bed."

He senses the trap. "No," he says, and stands up. "You'll put on a flying saucer."

"No, I won't. Listen, you won't know if I do or don't."

"Sure I will. I'm very sensitive."

"Oh Lord. Well anyway I got to take a leak."

"Go ahead, I don't care," he says, and won't let her close the bathroom door. She sits, like women do, primly. At home he and Janice had been trying to toilet-train Nelson, so leaning there in the doorway he feels a ridiculous paternal impulse to praise her. She is so tidy.

"Good girl," he says when she rises, and leads her into the bedroom. The edges of the doorway they pass through seem very vivid and sharp. They will always be here. Behind them, the plumbing vibrates and murmurs. She moves with shy stiffness, puzzled by his will. Trembling again, shy himself, he brings her to a stop by the foot of the bed and searches for the catch of her dress. He finds buttons on the back and can't undo them easily; his hands come at them reversed.

"Let me do it."

"Don't be in such a hurry; I'll do it. You're supposed to enjoy this. This is our wedding night."

"Ha ha."

He hates this mocking reflex in her. He turns her roughly, and, in a reflex of his own, falls into a deep wish to give comfort. He touches her caked cheeks; she seems small as he looks down into the frowning planes of her set, shadowed face. He moves his lips into one eye socket, gently, trying to say this night has no urgency in it, trying to listen through his lips to the timid pulse beating in the bulge of her lid. With a careful impartiality he fears she will find comic, he kisses also her other eye; then, excited by the thought of his own tenderness, his urgency spills; his mouth races across her face, nibbling, licking, so that she does laugh, tickled, and pushes away. He locks her against him, crouches, and presses his parted teeth into the fat hot hollow at the side of her throat. Ruth tenses at his threat to bite, and her hands shove at his shoulders, but he clings there, his teeth bared in a silent exclamation, crying out against her smothering throat that it is not her crotch he wants, not the machine; but her, her.

Though there are no words she hears this, and says, "Don't try to prove you're a lover on me. Just come and go."

"You're *so* smart," he says, and starts to hit her, checks his arm, and offers instead, "Hit me. Come on. You want to, don't you? Really pound me."

"My Lord," she says, "this'll take all night." He plucks her limp arm from her side and swings it up toward him, but she manages her hand so that five bent fingers bump against his cheek painlessly. "That's what poor Maggie has to do for your old bastard friend."

He begs, "Don't talk about them."

"Damn men," she continues, "either want to hurt somebody or be hurt."

"I don't, honest. Either one."

"Well then undress me and stop screwing around."

He sighs through his nose. "You have a sweet tongue," he says.

"I'm sorry if I shock you." Yet in her voice is a small metallic withdrawal, as if she really is.

"You don't," he says and, business-like, stoops and takes the hem of her dress in his hands. His eyes are enough accustomed to the dark now to see the cloth as green. He peels it up her body, and she lifts her arms, and her head gets caught for a moment in the neck-hole. She shakes her head crossly, like a dog with a scrap, and the dress comes free, skims off her arms into his hands floppy and faintly warm. He sails it into a chair hulking in a corner. "God," he says, "you're pretty." She is a ghost in her silver slip. Dragging the dress over her head has loosened her hair. Her solemn face tilts as she quickly lifts out the pins. Her hair falls out of heavy loops.

"Yeah," she says. "Pretty plump."

"No," he says, "you are," and in the space of a breath goes to her and picks her up, great glistening sugar in her sifty-grained slip, and carries her to the bed, and lays her on it. "So pretty."

"You lifted me," she says. "That'll put you out of action."

Harsh direct light falls on her face; the creases on her neck show black. He asks, "Shall I pull the shade?"

"Please. It's a dismal view."

He goes to the window and bends to see what she means. There is only the church across the way, gray, somber, confident. Lights behind its rose window are left burning, and this circle of red and purple and gold seems in the city night a hole punched in reality to show the abstract brilliance burning underneath. He feels gratitude to the builders of this ornament, and lowers the shade on it guiltily. He turns quickly, and Ruth's eyes watch him out of shadows that also seem gaps in a surface. The curve of her hip supports a crescent of silver; his sense of her weight seems to make an aroma.

"What's next?" He takes off his coat and throws it; he loves this throwing things, the way the flying cloth puts him in the center of a gathering nakedness. "Stockings?"

"They're tricky," she says. "I don't want a run."

"You do it then." In a sitting position, with the soft-pawed irritable deftness of a cat, she extricates herself from a web of elastic and silk and cotton; he helps clumsily. His uncertain touches gather in his own body, bending him into a forest smelling of spice. He is out of all dimension, and in a dark land, and a tender entire woman seems an inch away around a kind of corner. When he straightens up on his knees, kneeling as he is by the bed, Ruth under his eyes is an incredible continent, the pushed-up slip a north of snow.

"So much," he says.

"Too much."

"No, listen. You're good." He kisses her lips; her lips expect more than they get. Into their wet flower he drops a brief bee's probe. Cupping a hand behind her hot sheltered neck, he pulls her up, and slides her slip over her head. In just the liquid ease it comes off with he feels delight; how clothes just fall from a woman who wants to be stripped. The cool hollow his hand finds in the small of her back mixes in his mind with the shallow shadows of the stretch of skin that slopes from the bones of her shoulders. He kisses this expanse. Where her skin is whiter it is cooler. She shrugs off her bra. He moves away and sits on the corner of the bed and drinks in the pure sight of her. She keeps her arm tight against the one breast and brings up her hand to cover the other; a ring glints. Her modesty praises him; it shows she is feeling. The straight arm props her weight. Light lies along her right side where it can catch her body as it turns in stillness; this pose, embarrassed and graceful, she holds; rigidity is her one defense against his eyes and her figure does come to seem to him inviolable; absolute; her nakedness swings in tides of stone. So that when her voice springs from her form he is amazed to hear a perfect statue, unadorned woman, beauty's home image, speak: "What about you?"

He is still dressed, even to his necktie. While he is draping his trousers over a chair, arranging them to keep the crease, she scurries under the covers. He stands over her in his underclothes and asks, "Now you really don't have anything on?"

"You wouldn't let me."

He remembers the glint. "Give me your ring."

She brings her right hand out from under the covers and he carefully works a thick brass ring, like a class ring, past her bunching knuckle. In letting her hand drop she grazes the distorted front of his Jockey shorts.

He looks down at her, thinking. The covers come up to her throat and the pale arm lying on top of the bedspread has a slight serpent's twist. "There's nothing else?"

"I'm all skin," she says. "Come on. Get in."

"You want me?"

"Don't flatter yourself. I want it over with."

"You have all that crust on your face."

"God, you're insulting!"

"I just love you too much. Where's a washrag?"

"I don't want my God-damned face washed!"

He goes into the bathroom and turns on the light and finds a facecloth and holds it under the hot faucet. He wrings it out and turns off the light. As he comes back across the room Ruth laughs from the bed. He asks, "What's the joke?"

"In those damned underclothes you *do* look kind of like a rabbit. I thought only kids wore those elastic kind of pants."

He looks down at his T-shirt and snug underpants, pleased and further stirred. His name in her mouth feels like a physical touch. She sees him as special. When he puts the rough cloth to her face, it goes tense and writhes with a resistance like Nelson's, and he counters it with a father's practiced method. He sweeps her forehead, pinches her nostrils, abrades her cheeks and, finally, while her whole body is squirming in protest, scrubs her lips, her words shattered and smothered. When at last he lets her hands win, and lifts the washrag, she stares at him, says nothing, and closes her eyes.

Her wet face, relaxed into slabs, is not pretty; the thick lips, torn from most of their paint, are the pale rims of a loose hole. He stands and presses the cloth against his own face, like a man sobbing. He goes to the foot of the bed, throws the rag toward the bathroom, peels out of his underclothes, bobs, and hurries to hide in the bed. The long dark space between the sheets buries him.

He makes love to her as he would to his wife. After their marriage, and her nerves lost that fineness, Janice needed coaxing; he would begin by rubbing her back. Ruth submits warily when he tells her to lie on her stomach. To lend his hands strength he sits up on her buttocks and leans his weight down through stiff arms into his thumbs and palms as they work the broad muscles and insistent bones of the spine's terrain. She sighs and shifts her head on the pillow. "You should be in the Turkish-bath business," she says. He goes for her neck, and advances his fingers around to her throat, where the columns of blood give like reeds, and massages her shoulders with the balls of his thumbs, and his fingertips just find the glazed upper edges of her pillowing breasts. He returns to her back, until his wrists ache, and flops from astride his mermaid truly weary, as if under a sea-spell to sleep. He pulls the covers up over them, to the middle of their faces.

Janice was shy of his eyes so Ruth heats in his darkness. His lids flutter shut though she arches anxiously against him. Her hand seeks him, and angles him earnestly for a touch his sealed lids feel as red. He sees blue when with one deliberate hand she pries open his jaw and bows his head to her burdened chest. Lovely wobbly bubbles, heavy: perfume between. Taste, salt and sour, swirls back with his own saliva. She rolls away, onto her back, the precious red touch breaking, twists. Cool new skin. Rough with herself, she forces the dry other into his face, coated with cool pollen that dissolves. He opens his eyes, seeking her, and sees her face a soft mask gazing downward calmly, caring for him, and closes his eyes on the food of her again: his hand abandoned on the breadth of her body finds at arm's length a split pod, an open fold, shapeless and simple. They enter a lazy space. He wants the time to stretch long, to great length and thinness. As they deepen together he feels impatience that through all their twists they remain separate flesh; he cannot dare enough, now that she is so much his friend in this search; everywhere they meet a wall. The body lacks voice to sing its own song. Impatience tapers; she floats through his blood as under his eyelids a salt smell, damp pressure, the sense of her smallness as her body hurries everywhere to his hands, her breathing, bedsprings' creak, accidental slaps, and the ache at the parched root of his tongue each register their colors.

Nudge enters his softness, "Now?" Her voice croaky. He kneels in a kind of sickness between her spread legs, her body blurred white, distended willingly under him. With her help their blond loins fit. Something sad in the capture. He braces himself on his arms above her, afraid, for it is here he most often failed Janice, by being too quick. Yet, what with the alcohol drifting in his system, or his good fortune stunning him, his love is slow to burst in her warmth. He hides his face beside her throat, in her mint hair. With thin, thin arms she hugs him and presses him down and rises above him. From her high smooth shoulders down she is one long underbelly erect in light above him; he says in praise softly, "Hey."

She answers, "Hey."

"You're pretty."

"Come on. Work."

Galled, he shoves up through her and in addition sets his hand under her jaw and shoves her face so his fingers slip into her mouth and her slippery throat strains. As if unstrung by this anger, she tumbles and carries him over and he lies on top of her again, the skin of their chests sticking together; her breathing snags. Her thighs throw open wide and clamp his sides and throw open again so wide it frightens him, she wants, impossible, to turn inside out; the muscles and lips and bones of her expanded underside press against him as a new anatomy, of another animal. She feels transparent; he sees her heart. She suspends him, subsides, and in the folds of her withering, his love and pride revive. So she is first, and waits for him while at a trembling extremity of tenderness he traces again and again the arc of her eyebrow with his thumb. His sea of seed buckles, and sobs into a still channel. At each shudder her mouth smiles in his and her legs, locked at his back, bear down.

She asks in time, "O.K.?"

"You're pretty."

Ruth takes her legs from around him and spills him off her body like a pile of sand. He looks in her face and seems to read in its shadows a sad expression of forgiveness, as if she knows that at the moment of release, the root of love, he betrayed her by feeling despair. Nature leads you up like a mother and as soon as she gets her little price leaves you with nothing. The sweat on his skin is cold in the air; he brings the blankets up from her feet.

"You were a beautiful piece," he says from the pillow listlessly, and touches her soft side. Her flesh still soaks in the act; it ebbs slower in her.

"I had forgotten," she says.

"Forgot what?"

"That I could have it too."

"What's it like?"

"Oh. It's like falling through."

"Where do you fall to?"

"Nowhere. I can't talk about it."

He kisses her lips; she's not to blame. She lazily accepts, then in an after-flurry of affection flutters her tongue against his chin.

He loops his arm around her waist and composes himself against her body for sleep.

"Hey. I got to get up."

"Stay."

"I got to go into the bathroom."

"No." He tightens his hold.

"Boy, you better let me up."

He murmurs, "Don't scare me," and snuggles more securely against her side. His thigh slides over hers, weight on warmth. Wonderful, women, from such hungry wombs to such amiable fat; he wants the heat his groin gave given back in gentle ebb. Best bedfriend, done woman. Bit of bowl about their bellies always. Oh, how! when she got up on him like the bell of a big blue lily slipped down on his slow head. He could have hurt her shoving her jaw. He reawakens enough to feel his dry breath drag through sagged lips as she rolls from under his leg and arm. "Hey get me a glass of water," he says suddenly.

She stands by the edge of the bed, baggy in nakedness, and goes off into the bathroom to do her duty. There's that in women repels him; handle themselves like an old envelope. Tubes into tubes, wash away men's dirt, insulting, really. Faucets cry. The more awake he gets the more depressed he is. From deep in the pillow he stares at the horizontal strip of stained-glass church window that shows under the window shade. Its childish brightness seems the one kind of comfort left to him.

Light from behind the closed bathroom door tints the air in the bedroom. The splashing sounds are like the sounds his parents would make when as a child Rabbit would waken to realize they had come upstairs, that the whole house would soon be dark, and the sight of morning would be his next sensation. He is asleep when like a faun in moonlight Ruth, washed, creeps back to his side, holding a glass of water.

Do you believe that since whores are willing to sell their bodies they are essentially unlovable?

Since Ruth is a prostitute, has she any "right" to object to Rabbit's sexual demands or techniques?

At first, Ruth's approach to the sexual act seems mechanical, almost as if she were resigned to the ritual and simply wanted "it over with." She "submits warily" when told to lie on her stomach, yet she reaches orgasm, a psychophysiological peak of sexual response. Does this suggest that she loves Rabbit? Was there any aspect of his lovemaking that might account for Ruth's sexual pleasure?

How might Ruth's attitude toward men, sex, and marriage be described? Consider, for example, the implications of her following comments:

"I know all about your systems. One squirt and done."

"You all think you're such lovers."

"Say do you think we're married or something the way you boss me around?"

"Damn men . . . either want to hurt somebody or be hurt."

Which of Ruth's judgments are verified by Rabbit's behavior? What else might be a source of Ruth's negative feelings? How realistic a picture has she of herself? How well does she like herself? How much self-respect has she?

In the novel *From Here to Eternity* by James Jones, one of the characters involved in an extramarital relationship reflects on the sexual experience:

But that's not love, he thought, that's not what she wants, nor what any of them want, they do not want you to find yourself in them, they want instead that you should lose yourself in them. And yet, he thought, they are always trying to find themselves in you. . . .

And it seemed to him then that every human was always looking for himself, in bars, in railway trains, in offices, in mirrors, in love, especially in love, for the self of him that is there, someplace, in every other human. Love was not to give oneself, but to find oneself, describe oneself. And that the whole conception had been written wrong. Because the only part of any man that he can ever touch or understand is that part of himself he recognizes in him. And that he is always looking for the way in which he can escape his sealed bee cell and reach the other airtight cells with which he is connected in the waxy comb. [20]

To what degree does the comment relate to Rabbit's and Ruth's experience? To other relationships you could cite?

Updike describes Rabbit as stepping forward "in a kind of swoon, on a tide of alcohol and stirred semen." Is the sex urge greater after drinking? Why? Is the sex act itself more satisfying? Why?

Why does Rabbit want to undress Ruth himself rather than have her take off her clothes in the bathroom?

Why does Rabbit object to Ruth's wearing a contraceptive "like a rubber kidney or something"? Had "the Pill" been available, do you think Rabbit would have approved Ruth's use of it? Why does Rabbit refuse to use a contraceptive himself? Does he *want* Ruth to risk pregnancy?

What does "it is her heart he wants to grind into his own, to comfort her completely" mean?

Why does Rabbit move with shy stiffness? Why is Rabbit shy himself? His hug feels more like "kill" to Ruth. Why does Rabbit "want to crush her"? Are biting and hitting sexually pleasurable? Why, and under what conditions might they be?

When Ruth "keeps her arm tight against one breast and brings up her hand to cover the other," Rabbit concludes that "her modesty praises him; it shows she is feeling." What does he think she is feeling?

How does Rabbit transfer his love-making with his wife to his relationship with Ruth? Does it help or hinder their sexual pleasure?

What does it mean: "Nature leads you up like a mother and as soon as she gets her little price leaves you with nothing"? How is it connected with the statement preceding it:

> He looks in her face and seems to read in its shadows a sad expression of forgiveness, as if she knows that at the moment of release, the root of love, he betrayed her by feeling despair.

Why might he feel despair? Why does it constitute a betrayal of her?

RELATED QUESTIONS

What distinction does Updike suggest in describing Rabbit "crying out against her smothering throat that it is not her crotch he wants, not the machine; but her, her"? How is it similar to C. S. Lewis' discussion of "the necessary piece of apparatus" in *Eros* (p. 206)?

How is Updike's description of Ruth and Rabbit

> As they deepen together he feels impatience that through all their twists they remain separate flesh; he cannot dare enough, now that she is so much his friend in this search; everywhere they meet a wall. The body lacks voice to sing its own song.

partially explained in MacLeish's *The Happy Marriage* (p. 265)?

How much of Jean Ruiz' advice in the excerpt from *The Book of True Love* (see "**Night-Lights,**" p. 582) does Rabbit take? Are Ruiz' characterizations of female behavior and attitudes substantiated by Ruth?

Since this is Rabbit's first sexual experience with Ruth, would you think that Cummings' description in *i like my body when it is with your* (p. 394) and his conclusion, "possibly i like the thrill/of under me you so quite new" was adequate explanation of Rabbit's sexual satisfaction? If not, what other factors might be relevant?

Does Rabbit share with Pound in *Homage to Sextus Propertius* (p. 395) a need for power that will make him feel "God am I for the time"? Would Updike agree with Pound that "eyes are the guides of love"?

Is Rabbit's motive in having sexual relations with a prostitute the same as that of Stephen Daedalus in *A Portrait of the Artist as a Young Man?* What was Stephen trying to find? What is Rabbit seeking? Is one more "moral" than the other? Is Rabbit less moral because he has a wife? Would you need to know more about his wife before making a judgment?

Rabbit, Run (2)

JOHN UPDIKE

These eyes sting her and she turns her head away to hide the tears, thinking, That's one of the signs, crying easily. God, at work she has to get up from the typewriter and rush into the john like she had the runs and sob, sob, sob. Standing there in a booth looking down at a toilet laughing at herself and sobbing till her chest hurts. And sleepy. God, after coming back from lunch it's all she can do to keep from stretching out in the aisle right there on the filthy floor between Lilly Orff and Rita Fiorvante where that old horse's neck Honig would have to step over her. And hungry. For lunch an ice-cream soda with the sandwich and then a doughnut with the coffee and still she has to buy a candy bar at the cash register. After she's been trying to slim down for him and *had* lost six pounds, at least one scale said. For him, that was what was rich, changing herself for him when he was worth nothing, less than nothing, he was a menace, for all his mildness. He had that mildness. The others didn't. The thing was, when they knew you were one, they didn't think you were human, and thought they were entitled. Which they were, but still, some of the things. It was like they hated women and used *her.* But now she forgives them because it all melts, the next day is the next day and you're still the same and there, and they're away. The older they were, the more like presidents they looked, the wiser they should have been, the worse they were. Then they wanted some business their wives wouldn't give, in from the back which she didn't mind it was like being a hundred miles away once you get adjusted, or with the mouth. That. What do they see in it? It can't be as deep, she doesn't know. After all it's no worse than them at your bees and why not be generous, the first time it was Harrison and she was drunk as a monkey anyway but when she woke up the next morning wondered what the taste in her mouth *was.* But that was just being a superstitious kid there isn't much taste to it a little like seawater, just harder work than they probably think, women are always working harder than they think. The thing was, they wanted to be admired there. They really did want that. They weren't that ugly but they thought they were. That was the thing that surprised her in high school how ashamed they were really, how grateful they were if you just touched them there and how quick word got around that you would. What did they think, they were monsters? If they'd just thought they might have known you were curious too, that you could like that strangeness there like they liked yours, no worse than women in their way, all red wrinkles, my God, what was it in the end? No mystery. That was the great thing she discovered, that it was no mystery, just a stuck-on-looking bit that made them king and if you went along with it could be good and anyway put you with them against those others, those little snips running around her at hockey in gym like a cow in that blue uniform like a baby suit she wouldn't wear it in the twelfth grade and took the demerits. God she hated some of those girls. But she got it back at night, taking that urgency they didn't know existed like a queen. Boy, there wasn't any fancy business then, you didn't even need to take off your clothes, just a little rubbing through the cloth, your mouths tasting of the onion on the hamburgers you'd just had at the diner and the car heater ticking as it cooled, through all the cloth, everything, off they'd go. They couldn't have felt much it must have been just the *idea* of you. All their ideas. Sometimes just French kissing not that she ever really got with that, sloppy tongues and nobody can breathe, but all of a sudden you knew from the way their lips went hard and opened and then eased shut and away that it was over. That there was no more push for you and you better back off if you wanted to keep your dress dry. That made you dirty. You, their stickum. They couldn't forgive her that. Her forgiving them. She didn't blame them though that was their mothers making them write her name on the lavatory walls. Allie told her about that, kindly. But she had some sweet things with Allie; once after school with the sun still up they drove along a country road and up an old lane and stopped in a leafy place where they could see Mt. Judge, the town against the mountain both, dim in the distance, and he put his head in her lap, her sweater rolled up and her bra undone, and it was like a baby gently, her bees (who called them her bees? not Allie) firmer and rounder then, more sensitive; his waiting wet mouth so happy and blind and the birds making their warm noises overhead in the sunshine. Allie blabbed. He had to blab. She forgave him but it made her wiser. She began the older ones; the mistake if there was one but why not? Why not? was the question and still held; wondering if there was a mistake makes her tired just thinking, lying there wet from swimming and seeing red through her eyelids, trying to move back through all that red wondering if she was wrong. She was wise. With them being young did for being pretty, and them being older it wasn't such a rush. Boy some bastards you think *never,* like their little contribution's the greatest thing the world's ever going to see if it ever gets here.

But *this* one. What a nut. He had though that mildness. At least he saw you as being there. Boy that first night when he said that so sort of proudly "Hey" she didn't mind so much going under in fact it felt like she should. She forgave them all then, his face all their faces gathered into a scared blur and it felt like she was falling under to something better than she was. But then after all it turns out he's not that different, hanging on you all depressed and lovey and then sick of you or less just bored really when it's done. It's getting quicker, and quicker, more like a habit, he really hurries now when senses or she tells him she's lost it. Then she can just lie there and in a way listen and it's soothing; but then she can't go to sleep afterward. Some nights he tries to bring her up but she's just so sleepy and so heavy down there it's nothing; sometimes she just wants to push him off and shake him and shout, I *can't,* you dope, don't you know you're a *father!* But no. She mustn't tell him. Saying a word would make it final; it's just been one period and the next is coming up in a day maybe she'll have it and then she won't have anything. As much of a mess as it is she doesn't know how happy that would make her really. At least this way she's doing something, sending those candy bars down. God she isn't even sure she doesn't want it because *he* wants it from the way he acts, with his damn no stripper just a nice clean piece. She isn't even sure she didn't just deliberately bring it on by falling asleep under his arm just to show the smug bastard. For the thing about him he didn't mind her getting up when he was asleep and crawling into the lousy bathroom just so long as he didn't have to watch anything or do anything. That was the thing about him, he just lived in his skin and didn't give a thought to the consequences of anything. Tell him about the candy bars and feeling sleepy he'll probably get scared and off he'll go, him and his good clean piece and his cute little God and his cute little minister playing golf every Tuesday. For the damnedest thing about that minister was that, before, Rabbit at least had the idea he was acting wrong but with him he's got the idea he's Jesus Christ out to save the world just by doing whatever comes into his head. I'd like to get hold of the bishop or whoever and tell him that minister of his is a menace. Filling poor Rabbit full of something nobody can get at and even now, filling her ear, his soft cocksure voice answers her question with an idle remote smugness that infuriates her so the tears *do* come.

"I'll tell you," he says. "When I ran from Janice I made an interesting discovery." The tears bubble over her lids and the awful taste of the pool-water is sealed into her mouth. "If you have the guts to be yourself," he says, "other people'll pay your price."

What distinction does Ruth make between most men's attitude toward women whom they know to be whores, and Rabbit's? What does she mean by Rabbit's "mildness"? What examples of it are shown in his behavior with her?

No individual is suddenly normal or suddenly a deviate or a compulsive. Whatever one is has been in the making since he was born. Thus, one's psychosexual history is cumulative. Although Updike does not reveal Ruth's life story, what clues from her reflections in this excerpt from **Rabbit, Run** help to explain why she may have become a prostitute?

How have repeated sexual relations between Ruth and Rabbit been different from their affair of the first night?

Would you agree that Rabbit "just lives in his skin and doesn't give a thought to the consequences of anything"?

One sex educator lists the characteristics of physical love as follows:

Sex doesn't necessarily have other dimensions of love.
Sex can exist without the partners having any meaningful relationship.
Sex desire ends with the release of tensions.
A purely sexual experience could occur with a succession of partners.
A sexual experience can occur without concern for a partner's needs.
A purely physical experience can occur with no other form of communication.
Sex, by its very nature, is directed toward physical release.
A purely physical experience runs a course. It is finished at a point, although it could build up anew.
Sex is often limited to a very personal experience that does not lend a pervading quality of love that can sustain good family life.
Physical sex does not endure frustration. Its rhythm can be disturbed by even a minor interruption. [21]

Does the relationship between Ruth and Rabbit suggest more than "physical love"? As much as? Why?

How might it be said that Ruth's attitude toward having Rabbit's baby illustrates the use of sex as a weapon, a punishment? For what? Against whom?

RELATED QUESTIONS

In what respect do the excerpts from **Peyton Place** (pp. 397) support Ruth's comments on her high school sexual experiences? Do Ruth's reflections on times when "there wasn't any fancy business . . . you didn't even need to take off your clothes, just a little rubbing through the cloth, your mouths tasting of the onion on the hamburgers" indicate possible motives for Betty Anderson's behavior with Rodney?

Ruth believes that males consider their genitals ugly. Does the apparent pride of Adam in the limerick (p. 30) contradict her notion?

To what extent do Fromm's comments about masculine character traits and Don Juan in *The Theory of Love* (p. 259) explain Rabbit's needs and desire to be considered a "good lover"?

Rabbit, Run (3)

JOHN UPDIKE

. . . Rabbit feels he's been worked into a corner where he can't give her hell without giving her up entirely, without obliterating the sweet things. But she did that by taking him to that stinking place. "You've laid for Harrison, haven't you?"

"I guess. Sure."

"You guess. You don't know?"

"I said sure."

"And how many others?"

"I don't know."

"A hundred?"

"It's a pointless question."

"Why is it pointless?"

"It's like asking how many times you've been to the movies."

"They're about the same to you, is that it?"

"No they're not the same but I don't see what the count matters. You knew what I was."

"I'm not sure I did. You were a real hooer?"

"I took some money. I've told you. There were boy friends when I was working as a stenographer and they had friends and I lost my job because of the talk maybe I don't know and some older men got my number I guess through Margaret, I don't know. Look. It's by. If it's a question of being dirty or something a lot of married women have had to take it more often than I have."

"Did you pose for pictures?"

"You mean like for high-school kids? No."

"Did you blow guys?"

"Look, maybe we should say bye-bye." At the thought of that her chin softens and eyes burn and she hates him too much to think of sharing her secret with him. Her secret inside her seems to have no relation to him, this big body loping along with her under the street lamps, hungry as a ghost, wanting to hear the words to whip himself up. That was the thing about men, the importance they put on the mouth. Rabbit seems like another man to her, with this difference: in ignorance he has welded her to him and she can't let go.

With degrading gratitude she hears him say, "No I don't *want* to say bye-bye. I just want an answer to my question."

"The answer to your question is yes."

"Harrison?"

"Why does Harrison mean so much to you?"

"Because he stinks. And if Harrison is the same to you as me then I stink."

They are, for a moment, the same to her—in fact she would prefer Harrison, just for the change, just because he doesn't insist on being the greatest thing that ever was—but she lies. "You're not at all the same. You're not in the same league."

"Well I got a pretty funny feeling sitting across from you two in that restaurant. What all did you do with him?"

"Oh, I don't know, what *do* you do? You make love, you try to get close to somebody."

"Well, would you do everything to me that you did to him?"

This stuns her skin in a curious way, makes it contract so that her body feels squeezed and sickened inside it. "If you want me to." After being a wife her old skin feels tight.

His relief is boyish; his front teeth flash happily. "Just once," he promises, "honest. I'll never ask you again." He tries to put his arm around her but she pulls away. Her one hope is that they aren't talking about the same thing.

Up in the apartment he asks plaintively, "Are you going to?" She is struck by the helplessness in his posture; in the interior darkness, to which her eyes have not adjusted, he seems a suit of clothes hung from the broad white knob of his face.

She asks, "Are you sure we're talking about the same thing?"

"What do you think we're talking about?" He's too fastidious to mouth the words.

She says.

"Right," he says.

"In cold blood. You just want it."

"Uh-huh. Is it so awful for you?"

This glimmer of her gentle rabbit emboldens her. "May I ask what I've done?"

"I didn't like the way you acted tonight."

"How did I act?"

"Like what you were."

"I didn't mean to."

"Even so. I saw you that way tonight and I felt a wall between us and this is the one way through it."

"That's pretty cute. You just want it, really." She yearns to hit out at him, to tell him to go. But that time is past.

He repeats, "Is it so awful for you?"

"Well it is because you think it is."

"Maybe I don't."

"Look, I've loved you."

"Well, I've loved *you.*"

"And now?"

"I don't know. I want to still."

Now those damn tears again. She tries to hurry the words out before her voice crumbles. "That's good of you. That's heroic."

"Don't be smart. Listen. Tonight you turned against me. I need to see you on your knees."

"Well just that—"

"No. Not just that."

The two tall drinks have been a poor experiment; she wants to go to sleep and her tongue tastes sour. She feels in her stomach her need to keep him and wonders, Will this frighten him? Will this kill her in him?

"If I did it what would it prove?"

"It'd prove you're mine."

"Shall I take my clothes off?"

"Sure." He takes his off quickly and neatly and stands by the dull wall in his brilliant body. He leans awkwardly and brings one hand up and hangs it on his shoulder not knowing what to do with it. His whole shy pose has these wings of tension, like he's an angel waiting for a word. Sliding her last clothes off, her arms feel cold touching her sides. This last month she's felt cold all the time; her temperature being divided or something. In the growing light he shifts slightly. She closes her eyes and tells herself, They're not ugly. Not.

"Is that you, Harry? It didn't sound like you. Were you asleep?"

"In a way."

"Harry, your wife has started to have the baby. Her mother called here around eight and I just got in." Eccles closes his eyes; in the dark tipping silence he feels his ministry, sum and substance, being judged.

"Yeah," the other breathes in the far corner of the darkness. "I guess I ought to go to her."

"I wish you would."

"I guess I should. It's mine I mean too."

"Exactly. I'll meet you there. It's St. Joseph's in Brewer. You know where that is?"

"Yeah, sure. I can walk it in ten minutes."

"You want me to pick you up in the car?"

"No, I'll walk it."

"All right. If you prefer. Harry?"

"Huh?"

"I'm very proud of you."

"Yeah. O.K. I'll see you."

Eccles had reached for him, it felt like, out of the ground. Voice had sounded tinny. Ruth's bedroom is dim; the street lamp like a low moon burns shadows into the inner planes of the armchair, the burdened bed, the twisted sheet he tossed back finally when it seemed the phone would never stop. The bright rose window of the church opposite is still lit: purple red blue gold like the notes of different bells struck. His body, his whole frame of nerves and bone, tingles, as if with the shaking of small bells hung up and down his silver skin. He wonders if he had been asleep, and how long, ten minutes or five hours. He finds his underclothes and trousers draped on a chair and fumbles with them; not only his fingers but his vision itself trembles in the luminous gloom. His white shirt seems to crawl, like a cluster of glow-worms in grass. He hesitates a second before poking his fingers into the nest, that turns under his touch to safe cloth, dead. He carries it in his hand to the sullen laden bed.

"Hey. Baby."

The long lump under the covers doesn't answer. Just the top of Ruth's hair peeks up out of the pillow. He doesn't feel she is asleep.

"Hey. I got to go out."

No answer, no motion. If she wasn't asleep she heard everything he said on the phone, but what did he say? He remembers nothing except this sense of being reached. Ruth lies heavy and silent and her body hidden. The night is hot enough for just a sheet but she put a blanket on the bed saying she felt cold. It was just about the only thing she did say. He shouldn't have made her do it. He doesn't know why he did except it felt right at the time. He thought she might like it or at least like the humbling. If she didn't want to, if it made her sick, why didn't she say no like he half-hoped she would anyway? He kept touching her cheeks with his fingertips. He kept wanting to lift her up and hug her in simple thanks and say Enough you're mine again but somehow couldn't bring himself to have it stop and kept thinking the *next* moment, until it was too late, done. With it went instantly that strange floating feeling of high pride. Shame plunged in.

"My wife's having her baby. I got to go see her through it I guess. I'll be back in a couple of hours. I love you."

Still the body under the covers and the frizzy crescent of hair peeking over the top edge of the blanket don't move. He is so sure she is not asleep he thinks, *I've killed her.* It's ridiculous, such a thing wouldn't kill her, it has nothing to do with death; but the thought paralyzes him from going forward to touch her and make her listen.

"Ruth. I got to go this once, it's my baby she's having and she's such a mutt I don't think she can do it by herself. Our first one came awfully hard. It's the least I owe her."

Perhaps this wasn't the best way to say it but he's trying to explain and her stillness frightens him and is beginning to make him sore.

"Ruth. Hey. If you don't say anything I'm not coming back. Ruth."

She lies there like some dead animal or somebody after a car accident when they put a tarpaulin over. He feels if he went over and lifted her she would come to life but he doesn't like being manipulated and is angry. He puts on his shirt and doesn't bother with a coat and necktie but it seems to take forever putting on his socks; the soles of his feet are tacky.

When the door closes the taste of seawater in her mouth is swallowed by the thick grief that mounts in her throat so fully she has to sit up to breathe. Tears slide from her blind eyes and salt the corners of her mouth as the empty walls of the room become real and then dense. It's like when she was fourteen and the whole world trees sun and stars would have swung into place if she could lose twenty pounds just twenty pounds what difference would it make to God Who guided every flower in the fields into shape? Only now it's not that she's asking she knows now that's superstitious all she wants is what she had a minute ago *him* in the room him who when he was good could make her into a flower who could undress her of her flesh and turn her into sweet air Sweet Ruth he called her and if he had just said "sweet" talking to her she might have answered and he'd still be between these walls. No. She had known from the first night the wife would win they have the hooks and anyway she feels really lousy: a wave of wanting to throw up comes over her and washes away caring much about anything. She goes into the john and kneels on the tiles and watches the still oval of water in the toilet as if *it's* going to do something. She doesn't think after all she has it in her to throw up but stays there anyway because it pleases her, her bare arm resting on the icy porcelain lip, and grows used to the threat in her stomach, which doesn't dissolve, which stays with her, so in her faint state it comes to seem that this thing that's making her sick is some kind of friend.

Ruth claims Rabbit's interest in her sexual past is motivated by his "wanting to hear the words to whip himself up." Is talking about sex sexually stimulating? Does Rabbit have another reason for his seemingly prurient curiosity?

Why is it so difficult for Rabbit to say that he wants oral-genital contact with Ruth? What makes language toxic and embarrassing? Updike writes: "Rabbit wondered why she didn't say 'no,' like he half-hoped she would anyway." Do males really want the female to make the negative decisions? And the positive ones? Under what circumstances?

How would you respond to a high-school male's question, such as:

If the boy wants sex intercourse and the girl says 'no,' does she really mean 'no' or is she just trying to control it, but actually feels the same way about it as the boy?

RELATED QUESTIONS

What explanation might Neill (*Sex Attitudes,* p. 286) offer for Ruth's resistance to one type of sex practice and for Rabbit's verbal inhibitions?

Among questions asked by high-school males is:

Why is it that when adults tell younger people about sex, that they 'beat around the bush'? Why don't adults explain just how, step by step, intercourse is accomplished?

Does *Rabbit, Run* suggest that—apart from inhibitions that interfere with parent-child communication, as discussed in **"They"** ("Peers and Parents") selections— adults might also find the question impossible to answer since no single step-by-step formula exists? If so, what might account for varieties in love-making, especially if sex is a reflection of one's entire personality?

Is intercourse a technique? An acquired skill? An individualized expression of natural feeling? A combination of elements? How does Vernon Scannell in *Act of Love* (see **"Night-Lights,"** p. 587) answer this question?

Rabbit, Run (4)

JOHN UPDIKE

On Friday Janice comes home. For the first days the presence of the baby fills the apartment as a little casket of incense fills a chapel. Rebecca June lies in a bassinet of plaited rushes painted white and mounted on a trundle. When Rabbit goes over to look at her, to reassure himself that she is there, he sees her somehow dimly, as if the baby has not gathered to herself the force that makes a silhouette. Her averted cheek, drained of the bright red he glimpsed at the hospital, is mottled, yellow, and blue, marbled like the palms of his hands when he is queasy; when Janice suckles Rebecca, yellow spots well up on her breast as if in answer to the fainter shadows of this color in the baby's skin. The union of breast and baby's face makes a globular symmetry to which both he and Nelson want to attach themselves. When Rebecca nurses, Nelson becomes agitated, climbs against them, pokes his fingers into the seam between the baby's lips and his mother's udder and, scolded and pushed away, wanders around the bed intoning, a promise he has heard on television, "Mighty Mouse is on the way." Rabbit himself loves to lie beside them watching Janice manipulate her swollen breasts, the white skin shiny from fullness. She thrusts the thick nipples like a weapon into the blind blistered mouth, that opens and grips with birdy quickness. "Ow!" Janice winces, and then the glands within the baby's lips begin to bubble in tune with her milk-making glands; the symmetry is established; her face relaxes into a downward smile. She holds a diaper against the other breast, mopping the waste milk it exudes in sympathy. Those first days, full of rest and hospital health, she has more milk than the baby takes. Between feedings she leaks; the bodices of all her nighties bear two stiff stains. When he sees her naked, naked all but for the elastic belt that holds her Modess pad in place, her belly shaved and puffed and soft, his whole stomach stirs at the fierce sight of her breasts, braced high by the tension of their milk, jutting from her slim body like glossy green-veined fruit with coarse purple tips. Top-heavy, bandaged, Janice moves gingerly, as if she might spill, jarred. Though with the baby her breasts are used without shame, tools like her hands, before his eyes she is still shy, and quick to cover herself if he watches too openly. But he feels a difference between now and when they first loved, lying side by side on the borrowed bed, his eyes closed, together making the filmy sideways descent into one another. Now, she is intermittently careless, walks out of the bathroom naked, lets her straps hang down while she burps the baby, seems to accept herself with casual gratitude as a machine, a white, pliant machine for loving, hatching, feeding. He, too, leaks, thick sweet love burdens his chest, and he wants her—just a touch, he knows she's a bleeding wound, but just a touch, just enough to get rid of his milk, give it to her. Though in her ether trance she spoke of making love, she turns away from him in bed, and sleeps with a heaviness that feels sullen. He is too grateful, too proud of her, to disobey. He in a way, this week, worships her.

He persuades Janice to have a drink. He makes it—he doesn't know much about alcoholic things—of half whisky and half water. She says it tastes hateful. But after a while consumes it.

In bed he imagines that he can feel its difference in her flesh. There is that feeling of her body coming into his hand, of fitting his palm, that makes a welcome texture. All under her nightie up to the pit of her throat her body is still for him. They lie sideways, facing each other. He rubs her back, first lightly, then toughly, pushing her chest against his, and gathers such a feel of strength from her pliancy that he gets up on an elbow to be above her. He kisses her dark hard face scented with alcohol. She does not turn her head, but he reads no rejection in this small refusal of motion, that lets him peck away awkwardly at a profile. He stifles his tide of resentment, reschooling himself in her slowness. Proud of his patience, he resumes rubbing her back. Her skin keeps its secret, as does her tongue; is she feeling it? She is mysterious against him, a sullen weight whose chemistry is impervious to ideas, impregnable to their penetration. Is he kindling the spark? His wrist aches. He dares undo the two buttons of her nightie front and lifts the leaf of cloth so a long arc is exposed in the rich gloom of the bed, and her warm breast flattens against the bare skin of his chest. She submits to this maneuver and he is filled with the joyful thought that he has brought her to this fullness. He is a good lover. He relaxes into the warmth of the bed and pulls the bow on his pajama waist. She has been shaved and scratches; he settles lower, on the cotton patch. This unnaturalness, this reminder of her wound makes his confidence delicate, so he is totally destroyed when her voice—her thin, rasping, dumb-girl's voice—says by his ear, "Harry. Don't you know I want to go to sleep?"

"Well why didn't you tell me before?"

"I didn't know. I didn't know."

"Didn't know what?"

"I didn't know what you were doing. I thought you were just being nice."

"So this isn't nice."

"Well, it's not nice when I can't *do* anything."

"You can do *some*thing.

"No I can't. Even if I wasn't all tired and confused from Rebecca's crying all day I can't. Not for six weeks. You know that.

"Yeah, I know, but I thought—" He's terribly embarrassed.

"*What* did you think?"

"I thought you might love me anyway."

After a pause she says, "I *do* love you."

"Just a touch, Jan. Just let me touch you."

"Can't you go to sleep?"

"No I can't. I can't. I love you too much. Just hold still."

It would have been easy a minute ago to get it over with but all this talk has taken the fine point off. It's a bad contact and her stubborn limpness makes it worse; she's killing it by making him feel sorry for her and ashamed and foolish. The whole sweet thing is just sweat and work and his ridiculous inability to finish it against the dead hot wall of her belly. She pushes him back. "You're just using me," she says. "It feels horrible."

"Please, baby. I'm almost there."

"It feels so cheap."

Her daring to say this infuriates him; he realizes she hasn't had it for three months and in all that time has gotten an unreal idea of what love is. She exaggerates its importance, has imagined it into something rare and precious she's entitled to half of when all he wants is to get rid of it so he can move on, on into sleep, down the straight path, for her sake. It's for her sake.

"Roll over," he says.

"I love you," she says with relief, misunderstanding, thinking he's dismissing her. She touches his face in farewell and turns her back.

He scruches down and fits himself between her buttocks, cool. It's beginning to work, steady, warm, when she twists her head and says over her shoulder, "Is this a trick your whore taught you?"

He thumps her shoulder with his fist and gets out of bed and his pajama bottoms fall down. The night breeze filters in through the window screen. She turns on her back into the center of the bed and explains out of her dark face, "I'm not your whore, Harry."

"Damn it," he says, "that was the first thing I've asked from you since you came home."

"You've been wonderful," she says.

"Thanks."

"Where are you going?"

He is putting on his clothes. "I'm going out. I've been cooped up in this damn hole all day."

"You went out this morning."

He finds his suntans and puts them on. She asks, "Why can't you try to imagine how I *feel*? I've just had a baby."

"I can. I can but I don't want to, it's not the thing, the thing is how *I* feel. And I feel like getting out."

"Don't. Harry. Don't."

"You can just lie there with your precious ass. Kiss it for me."

"Oh for God's sake," she cries, and flounces under the covers, and smashes her face down into her pillow.

Even this late he might have stayed if she hadn't accepted defeat by doing this. His need to love her is by, so there's no reason to go. He's stopped loving her at last so he might as well lie down beside her and go to sleep. But she asks for it, lying there in a muddle sobbing, and outside, down in the town, a motor guns and he thinks of the air and the trees and streets stretching bare under the streetlamps and goes out the door.

The strange thing is she falls asleep soon after he goes; she's been used to sleeping alone lately and it's a physical relief not having him in bed kicking his hot legs and twisting the sheets into ropes. That business of his with her bottom made her stitches ache and she sinks down over the small pain all feathers. Around four in the morning Becky cries her awake and she gets up; her nightie taps her body lightly. Her skin feels unnaturally sensitive as she walks about. She changes the baby and lies down on the bed to nurse her. As Becky takes the milk it's as if she's sucking a hollow place into her mother's body; Harry hasn't come back. By this time if he just went out to cool off he would be back.

The baby keeps slipping off the nipple because she can't keep her mind on her; a taste like dry toast keeps touching her lips; she keeps listening for Harry's key to scratch at the door.

Mother's neighbors will laugh their heads off if she loses him again, she doesn't know why she should think of Mother's neighbors except that all the time she was home Mother kept reminding her of how they sneered and there was always that with Mother the feeling she was dull and plain and a disappointment, and she thought when she got a husband it would be all over, all that. She would be a woman with a house on her own. And she thought when she gave this baby her name it would settle her mother but instead it brings her mother against her breast with her blind mouth poor thing and she feels she's lying on top of a pillar where everyone in the town can see she is alone. She feels cold. The baby won't stay on the nipple nothing will hold to her.

She gets up and walks around the room with the baby on her shoulder patting to get the air up and the baby poor thing so floppy and limp keeps sliding and trying to dig its little boneless legs into her to hold tight and the nightie blown by the breeze keeps touching her calves the backs of her legs her ass as he called it. Makes you feel filthy they don't even have decent names for parts of you.

If there would be a scratch at the lock and he would come in the door he could do whatever he wanted with her have any part of her if he wanted what did she care that was marriage. But when he tried tonight it just seemed so unfair, she still aching and him sleeping with that prostitute all those weeks and him just saying Roll over in that impatient voice like it was just something he wanted to have done with and who was she not to let him after she had let him run off what right had she to any pride? Any self-respect. That was just why she had to have some because he didn't think she dared have any after she let him run off that was the funny thing it was his bad deed yet she was supposed not to have any pride afterwards to just be a pot for his dirt. When he did that to her back it was so practiced and reminded her of all those weeks he was off doing what he pleased and she was just helpless Mother and Peggy feeling sorry for her and everybody else laughing she couldn't bear it.

And then his going off to church and coming back full of juice. What right did he have to go to church? What did he and God talk about behind the backs of all these women exchanging winks that was the thing she minded if they'd just think about love when they make it instead of thinking about whatever they do think about whatever they're going to do whenever they've got rid of this little hot clot that's bothering them. You can feel in their fingers if they're thinking about you and tonight Harry was at first and that's why she let him go on it was like lying there in an envelope of yourself his hands going around you but then he began to be rough and it made her mad to feel him thinking about himself what a good job he was doing sucking her along and not at all any more about how she felt exhausted and aching, poking his thing at her belly like some elbow. It was so *rude*.

Just plain rude. Here he called her dumb when he was too dumb to have any idea of how she felt any idea of how his going off had changed her and how he must nurse her back not just wade in through her skin without having any idea of what was there. That was what made her panicky ever since she was little this thing of nobody knowing how you felt and whether nobody could know or nobody cared she had no idea. She didn't like her skin, never had it was too dark made her look like an Italian even if she never did get pimples like some of the other girls and then in those days both working at Kroll's she on the salted nuts when Harry would lie down beside her on Mary Hannacher's bed the silver wallpaper he liked so much and close his eyes it seemed to melt her skin and she thought it was all over she was with somebody. But then they were married (she felt awful about being pregnant before but Harry had been talking about marriage for a year and anyway laughed when she told him and said Great she was terribly frightened and he said Great and lifted her put his arms around under her bottom and lifted her like you would a child he could be so wonderful when you didn't expect it in a way it seemed important that you didn't expect it there was so much nice in him she couldn't explain to anybody she had been so frightened about being pregnant and he made her be proud) they were married and she was still little clumsy dark-complected Janice Springer and her husband was a conceited lunk who wasn't good for anything in the world Daddy said and the feeling of being alone would melt a little with a drink. It wasn't so much that it dissolved the lump as made the edges nice and rainbowy.

She's been walking around patting the baby until her wrists and ankles hurt and poor tiny Rebecca is asleep with her legs around the breast that still has its milk in it. She wonders if she should try to make her take some and thinks no if she can sleep let her sleep. She lifts the poor tiny thing weighing nothing off the sweaty place on her shoulder and lays her down in the cool shadows of the crib.

Already the night is dimming, dawn comes early to the town facing east on its mountainside. Janice lies down on the bed but the sense of light growing beside her on the white sheets keeps her awake. Pleasantly awake at first; the coming of morning is so clean and makes her feel like she did through the second month Harry was hiding. Mother's great Japanese cherry tree blooming below her window and the grass coming up and the ground smelling wet and ashy and warm. She had thought things out and was resigned to her marriage being finished. She would have her baby and get a divorce and never get married again. She would be like a kind of nun she had just seen that beautiful picture with Audrey Hepburn. And if he came back it would be equally simple: she would forgive him everything and stop her drinking which annoyed him so though she didn't see why and they would be very nice and simple and clean together because he would have gotten everything out of his system and love her so because she had forgiven him and she would know now how to be a good wife. She had gone to church every week and talked with Peggy and prayed and had come to understand that marriage wasn't a refuge it was a sharing and she and Harry would start to share everything. And then it was a miracle, these last two weeks had been that way.

And then Harry had suddenly put his whore's filthiness into it and asked her to love it and the unfairness makes her cry aloud softly, as if startled by something in the empty bed with her.

The last hours are like some narrow turn in a pipe that she can't force her thought through. Again and again she comes up to the sound of him saying "Roll over" and can't squeeze through it, can't not feel panicked and choked. She gets out of bed and wanders around with her one tight breast the nipple stinging and goes into the kitchen in her bare feet and sniffs the empty glass Harry made her drink whisky out of. The smell is dark and raw and soft and deep, and she thinks maybe a sip will cure her insomnia. Make her sleep until the scratch at the door awakens her and she sees his big white body ramble in sheepishly and she can say Come to bed, Harry it's all right, do me, I want to share it, I really want it, really.

What is the effect on Rabbit of seeing his wife nursing their baby? Does it make him jealous of the attention given another? Does the sight of Janice's breasts excite him sexually? Does it reveal Rabbit's dependency? Pride? Something else?

Rabbit says: "I thought you might love me anyway." After a pause she says: "I *do* love you." Are Rabbit and Janice using the word love in the same ways?

From Rabbit's behavior in bed with Janice, why might it be said that the pleasures of sexual intercourse depend on more than intuition and animal passion —that, in fact, they require help and direction from each partner, even in long-term marriages?

Janice pushes Rabbit back: "You're just using me," she says. "It feels horrible." *Is* she being used? If so, for what? Are your sympathies more with Janice, who, having just delivered a baby must refrain from intercourse for six weeks; or with Rabbit, whose physiological tension has built up and who is rebuffed by his wife when he tries to compromise?

Since Rabbit's sexual desire passes—by his own admission, "his need to love her is by, so there's no reason to go"—why doesn't he simply "lie down beside her and go to sleep"?

In **Parma Violets** (p. 13), the author said: "when children love they do not give; they only receive. The aching desire to create life beyond the self calls boy into man." Is Rabbit a "boy" or a "man"?

Is Rabbit a sexual performer? Has his sexual behavior a "compulsive element that is based upon his need to impress himself and others with his sexual prowess" [22]?

To what degree might it be said of Rabbit that his sex is "in his head"? Is Janice sexually more mature? Where would you classify Ruth?

What evidence does Updike furnish to show ways in which pride, including false pride, hinder honesty and understanding? Is Janice less guilty of it than Rabbit? Is Rabbit less guilty of it than Ruth? Why, or why not? Why can't all three characters openly admit their feelings?

How does Janice's childhood apparently condition her sexual attitude (her feeling that Rabbit is rude, for example)?

Both Ruth and Janice recall their earliest sexual experiences with Rabbit as being more satisfactory than the later ones. Wife or prostitute, what seems to be part of the female lover's requirements for maximum sexual pleasure?

Why do some people feel that the sexual act, once the honeymoon ends and the real test of marriage begins, becomes a mechanical habit? How might some of the "**They**" writers in "Toward a Definition of Marriage" and "Toward a Definition of Love and Sex" suggest this attitude could be remedied, if not prevented?

RELATED QUESTIONS

The sexual behavior of a person reflects his personality, and his sexual acts can convey a wide range of messages. Reconsidering the selections in this "I and you" section, which of the following uses of sex are illustrated:

> Sex as a purely playful activity,
> Sex as a way to have babies,
> Sex as fun,
> Sex as an expression of hostility,
> Sex as a punishment,
> Sex as a mechanical duty,
> Sex as an outlet from physiological or psychological tension,
> Sex as a protection against alienation,
> Sex as a way of overcoming separateness or loneliness,
> Sex as a way to communicate deep involvement in the welfare of
>   another,
> Sex as a form of "togetherness,"
> Sex as a reward,
> Sex as a revenge,
> Sex as an act of rebellion,
> Sex as an experiment,
> Sex as an adventure,
> Sex as a deceit,
> Sex as a form of self-enhancement,
> Sex as an exploitation for personal gain,
> Sex as proof.

Which of these uses overlap because of similar components? Which uses appear most frequently in this section? Which appear least often? What correlation might be made between the high and low scorers on the uses of sex and the type of person who dominates the "**I and you**" relationship?

YOU and i

As Shinn pointed out in **Revolution in Sexual Ethics** (p. 269): "There is money in sex. There always has been . . . but today's world has invented new ways of commercializing sex."

In yesterday's world, as depicted in **The Return of the Native** by Victorian writer Thomas Hardy, sex has a bartering power, as shown by nineteen-year-old Eustacia Vye in her exploitation of sixteen-year-old Charley.

Charley, living an unsophisticated adolescence in rural nineteenth-century England, exchanged his role in a Christmas play to be performed at the neighboring Yeobrights' house for fifteen minutes of holding hands with the sophisticated Eustacia who wants his part so that she can be closer to Clym Yeobright, with whom she is infatuated.

The Return of the Native
THOMAS HARDY

The lads and men prepared to leave the premises, and Eustacia returned to her fireside. She was immersed in thought, but not for long. In a few minutes the lad Charley, who had come to ask permission to use the place, returned with the key to the kitchen. Eustacia heard him, and opening the door into the passage said, 'Charley, come here.'

The lad was surprised. He entered the front room not without blushing; for he, like many, had felt the power of this girl's face and form.

She pointed to a seat by the fire, and entered the other side of the chimney-corner herself. It could be seen in her face that whatever motive she might have had in asking the youth indoors would soon appear.

'Which part do you play, Charley—the Turkish Knight, do you not?' inquired the beauty, looking across the smoke of the fire to him on the other side.

'Yes, miss, the Turkish Knight,' he replied diffidently.

'Is yours a long part?'

'Nine speeches, about.'

'Can you repeat them to me? If so I should like to hear them.'

The lad smiled into the glowing turf and began—

> 'Here come I, a Turkish Knight,
> Who learnt in Turkish land to fight,'

continuing the discourse throughout the scenes to the concluding catastrophe of his fall by the hand of Saint George.

Eustacia had occasionally heard the part recited before. When the lad ended she began, precisely in the same words, and ranted on without hitch or divergence till she too reached the end. It was the same thing, yet how different. **435**

Like in form, it had the added softness and finish of a Raffaelle after Perugino, which, while faithfully reproducing the original subject, entirely distances the original art.

Charley's eyes rounded with surprise. 'Well, you be a clever lady!' he said, in admiration. 'I've been three weeks learning mine.'

'I have heard it before,' she quietly observed. 'Now, would you do anything to please me, Charley?'

'I'd do a good deal, miss.'

'Would you let me play your part for one night?'

'O, miss! But your woman's gown—you couldn't.'

'I can get boy's clothes—at least all that would be wanted besides the mumming dress. What should I have to give you to lend me your things, to let me take your place for an hour or two on Monday night, and on no account to say a word about who or what I am? You would, of course, have to excuse yourself from playing that night, and to say that somebody—a cousin of Miss Vye's— would act for you. The other mummers have never spoken to me in their lives, so that it would be safe enough; and if it were not, I should not mind. Now, what must I give you to agree to this? Half a crown?'

The youth shook his head.

'Five shillings?'

He shook his head again. 'Money won't do it,' he said, brushing the iron head of the fire-dog with the hollow of his hand.

'What will, then, Charley?' said Eustacia in a disappointed tone.

'You know what you forbade me at the maypoling, miss,' murmured the lad, without looking at her, and still stroking the fire-dog's head.

'Yes,' said Eustacia, with a little more hauteur. 'You wanted to join hands with me in the ring, if I recollect?'

'Half an hour of that, and I'll agree, miss.'

Eustacia regarded the youth steadfastly. He was three years younger than herself, but apparently not backward for his age. 'Half an hour of what?' she said, though she guessed what.

'Holding your hand in mine.'

She was silent. 'Make it a quarter of an hour,' she said.

'Yes, Miss Eustacia—I will, if I may kiss it too. A quarter of an hour. And I'll swear to do the best I can to let you take my place without anybody knowing. Don't you think somebody might know your tongue, miss?'

'It is possible. But I will put a pebble in my mouth to make it less likely. Very well; you shall be allowed to have my hand as soon as you bring the dress and your sword and staff. I don't want you any longer now.'

Charley departed, and Eustacia felt more and more interest in life. Here was something to do: here was some one to see, and a charmingly adventurous way to see him. 'Ah,' she said to herself, 'want of an object to live for—that's all is the matter with me!'

Eustacia's manner was as a rule of a slumberous sort, her passions being of the massive rather than the vivacious kind. But when aroused she would make a dash which, just for the time, was not unlike the move of a naturally lively person.

On the question of recognition she was somewhat indifferent. By the acting lads themselves she was not likely to be known. With the guests who might be assembled she was hardly so secure. Yet detection, after all, would be no such dreadful thing. The fact only could be detected, her true motive never. It would be instantly set down as the passing freak of a girl whose ways were already considered singular. That she was doing for an earnest reason what would most naturally be done in jest was at any rate a safe secret.

The next evening Eustacia stood punctually at the fuel-house door, waiting for the dusk which was to bring Charley with the trappings. Her grandfather was at home to-night, and she would be unable to ask her confederate indoors.

He appeared on the dark ridge of heathland, like a fly on a negro, bearing the articles with him, and came up breathless with his walk.

'Here are the things,' he whispered, placing them upon the threshold. 'And now, Miss Eustacia —'

'The payment. It is quite ready. I am as good as my word.'

She leant against the door-post, and gave him her hand. Charley took it in both his own with a tenderness beyond description, unless it was like that of a child holding a captured sparrow.

'Why, there's a glove on it!' he said in a deprecating way.

'I have been walking,' she observed.

'But, miss!'

'Well — it is hardly fair.' She pulled off the glove, and gave him her bare hand.

They stood together minute after minute, without further speech, each looking at the blackening scene, and each thinking his and her own thoughts.

'I think I won't use it all up to-night,' said Charley devotedly, when six or eight minutes had been passed by him caressing her hand. 'May I have the other few minutes another time?'

'As you like,' said she without the least emotion. 'But it must be over in a week. Now, there is only one thing I want you to do: to wait while I put on the dress, and then to see if I do my part properly. But let me look first indoors.'

She vanished for a minute or two, and went in. Her grandfather was safely asleep in his chair. 'Now, then,' she said, on returning, 'walk down the garden a little way, and when I am ready I'll call you.'

Charley walked and waited, and presently heard a soft whistle. He returned to the fuel-house door.

'Did you whistle, Miss Vye?'

'Yes; come in,' reached him in Eustacia's voice from a back quarter. 'I must not strike a light till the door is shut, or it may be seen shining. Push your hat into the hole through to the wash-house, if you can feel your way across.'

Charley did as commanded, and she struck the light, revealing herself to be changed in sex, brilliant in colours, and armed from top to toe. Perhaps she quailed a little under Charley's vigorous gaze, but whether any shyness at her male attire appeared upon her countenance could not be seen by reason of the strips of ribbon which used to cover the face in mumming costumes, representing the barred visor of the mediaeval helmet.

'It fits pretty well,' she said, looking down at the white overalls, 'except that the tunic, or whatever you call it, is long in the sleeve. The bottom of the overalls I can turn up inside. Now pay attention.'

Eustacia then proceeded in her delivery, striking the sword against the staff or lance at the minatory phrases, in the orthodox mumming manner, and strutting up and down. Charley seasoned his admiration with criticism of the gentlest kind, for the touch of Eustacia's hand yet remained with him.

'And now for your excuse to the others,' she said. 'Where do you meet before you go to Mrs. Yeobright's?'

'We thought of meeting here, miss, if you have nothing to say against it. At eight o'clock, so as to get there by nine.'

'Yes. Well, you of course must not appear. I will march in about five minutes late, ready-dressed, and tell them that you can't come. I have decided that the best plan will be for you to be sent somewhere by me, to make a real thing of the excuse. Our two heath-croppers are in the habit of straying into the meads, and to-morrow evening you can go and see if they are gone there. I'll manage the rest. Now you may leave me.'

'Yes, miss. But I think I'll have one minute more of what I am owed, if you don't mind.'

Eustacia gave him her hand as before.

'One minute,' she said, and counted on till she reached seven or eight minutes. Hand and person she then withdrew to a distance of several feet, and recovered some of her old dignity. The contract completed, she raised between them a barrier impenetrable as a wall.

'There, 'tis all gone; and I didn't mean quite all,' he said, with a sigh.

'You had good measure,' said she, turning away.

'Yes, miss. Well, 'tis over, and now I'll get home-along.'

Do you find Charley's behavior comical? Tragic? Sick? Touching? Retarded? Incredible? Why?

What signs might classify Charley's attitude toward Eustacia as hero-worship? Are there some positive aspects of "crushes"?

Charley took Eustacia's hand "in both his own with a tenderness beyond description, unless it was like that of a child holding a captured sparrow." What are the implications of the simile? Why does the author focus on Charley's tender, rather than sexual, feelings? Is tenderness "greater proof than the most passionate of vows"?

Is it possible that Charley's sexual feelings have been romantically transformed because he has idealized Eustacia? Is Charley's feeling akin to that "towering feeling" familiar to those who walk down the street where she lives, and find themselves suddenly several stories high, almost out of touch with the pavement and the other pedestrians? To what degree is the enchantment rooted in fantasy? In reality?

What needs might make a person talk himself into this kind of attraction? What ideas might be flowing through Charley's mind as "they stood together minute after minute, without further speech . . . each thinking his and her own thoughts"? What might Eustacia be thinking as she pays her debt?

Sex as a negotiable asset is not usually viewed favorably. Why? Is there anything about the transaction between Charley and Eustacia that makes it more acceptable?

Is Charley more concerned with himself, or with Eustacia? Is his love an unselfish one?

In what ways does Charley remind you of William Baxter in **Seventeen** (p. 40)? Might Charley, too, adopt the sacrificial pose of Sydney Carton?

Does Charley in any way resemble Philip Carey in **Of Human Bondage** (p. 378)?

Like Eustacia in **The Return of the Native,** Marjorie Morgenstern, who aspires to a theatrical career as "Marjorie Morningstar," is nineteen, and the "beautiful young love" maddeningly beyond the reach of Wally Wronken, whom she likes, but regards as a younger brother.

More rewarded than Charley by Eustacia, Wally gets a solitary kiss from Marjorie under the rainy lilacs at the New York City Cloisters in the first excerpt from **Marjorie Morningstar** by Herman Wouk.

In the second scene from the novel, some fifteen years later, Wally, having just seen Marjorie, the "beautiful elusive girl [he] was so mad about"—now Mrs. Milton Schwartz, a run-of-the-mill wife and mother—realizes that she was never more than "an ordinary girl," except in the image which existed in his own mind.

Marjorie Morningstar

HERMAN WOUK

Wally telephoned one May morning after a long silence. "Ever been to the Cloisters?"

"No. What's the Cloisters?"

"The Cloisters is heaven on earth. Let's drive up there tomorrow morning. The lilacs are in bloom. I want you to see the lilacs."

Tomorrow was Saturday. She felt that Wally should be discouraged, but this was hardly a date, a Saturday-morning drive to look at lilacs. "Well, sure, Wally. It's nice of you to think of me."

Next morning it was pouring rain. She perched on the window seat of her bedroom in a lounging robe, reading a new novel greedily. It was a very agreeable way to pass the time, with rain clattering on the panes and the blue-gray light of a storm falling across the page. The hero of the novel looked like Noel Airman, even to the red-blond hair, and he was the same kind of dashing reprobate. When the doorbell rang she paid no attention to it. In a moment her mother poked her head into the room. "That boy Wally is here. Says you have a date to go driving. Is he crazy, coming out in this rain?"

"Oh, Lord. Tell him to wait a minute, Mom." She glanced at herself in the full-length mirror on the closet door. Her hair was combed, but her face was wanly empty of makeup, and the robe was simply a maroon wool thing, not quite covering the frilly bottom of her nightgown. To show herself in this condition to a date was impossible; but she hated to get all dressed and painted just to tell Wally to go home and stop being an idiot. She decided that Wally wasn't a date, exactly, more like a younger brother; and she went out into the living room tying the belt of her robe more closely. He was sitting at the piano in his yellow raincoat, gaily playing one of Noel's songs. "Wally, sometimes I think you have no sense. D'you expect me to go driving in this weather?"

"Why, sure, Marge. This rain is a break. We'll have the Cloisters all to ourselves."

"You'll have it all to yourself, boy. I know enough to stay in out of the wet if you don't."

The narrow shoulders sagged; the big head drooped; the long nose seemed to grow longer. She had seen dogs make this instant change from frisky joy to deep gloom, but never a human being. "Oh, look, Wally, I'm glad you came, just give me a minute to put on some clothes. We'll sit around and drink coffee and talk about the summer."

"Okay," he said mournfully.

When she came out again, hastily dressed as for a school day, he was slouched in an armchair, still wearing the raincoat. "What's the matter with you?" she said.

"Marge, I guess you haven't ever lived in the country. The best time to look at flowers is in the rain."

"I don't think you'll ever smile again," she said, laughing, "if we don't go to see those lilacs."

"Well, I do believe you'll like them."

"What the devil. I've done stupider things. Let's go."

As often happens, Marjorie was glad Wally had dragged her out, once they were driving along the river. She had forgotten how snug and exciting it was to roll through a rainstorm in a car, especially a new powerful one like Wally's father's Buick; to be dry, and cushioned at one's ease, while the storm whistled at the windows and beat on the roof, and the windshield wipers danced to and fro, wiping patches of clarity in a blurred gray world. She accepted a mentholated cigarette and curled on the seat. She did not have the habit of smoking yet, but mentholated cigarettes always seemed less sinful to her, almost medicine or candy. "This is fun," she said. "Sorry I was a slug about it."

"This is nothing," Wally said happily. "Wait."

They passed under the colossal piers of the bridge, turned away from the bubbling black river, and drove through an arch and up a steep rocky road. "See?" he said, as they pulled into a deserted parking space. "Saturday morning, but we have it to ourselves."

The medieval museum on the bluff overlooking the Hudson was new to Marjorie. Strolling through the Gothic corridors, she said, "How on earth did you discover this?"

"Fine arts course."

Their steps echoed in the dank stone galleries. The gorgeous tapestries, the great wooden saints and madonnas, the jeweled swords and suits of armor, the vaulted halls, all woke in her mind the atmosphere of the novel she had been reading; she could picture turning a corner in one of these empty corridors and coming on the tall blond hero. Wally, shambling along in his flat-footed way, with his hands in the pockets of his yellow raincoat, and the straight black hair falling over his eyes, was a comic misfit in this setting. But she was feeling very kindly toward him, all the same. He was giving her the kind of explorer's pleasure

Marsha had first opened to her when they had gone to concerts and art galleries together.

They had coffee in a bleak empty dining room. "Game for a walk in the gardens?" Wally said. "I think the rain's letting up."

"Sure, I'm game."

The trees were dripping copiously, so that it still seemed to be raining; but when they walked into an open space among the flower beds they saw that the storm was over. White clouds tumbling and rolling overhead were uncovering patches of blue. Rich perfume rose on the damp air from purple banks of iris, and across the river a shaft of sunlight was whitening the great cables of the bridge. A quiet breeze stirred the flowers, shaking raindrops from them. "Ah, Lord, it's beautiful, Wally," Marjorie said. He took her hand and she allowed him to hold it; if a palm could feel remote and respectful, Wally's did. He led her around a corner of thick bushes into a curving shadowy path filled with a curious watery lavender light.

It was an avenue solidly arched and walled with blooming lilacs. The smell, sweet and poignant beyond imagining, saturated the air; it struck her senses with the thrill of music. Water dripped from the massed blooms on Marjorie's upturned face as she walked along the lane hand in hand with Wally. She was not sure what was rain and what was tears on her face. She wanted to look up at lilacs and rolling white clouds and patchy blue sky forever, breathing this sweet air. It seemed to her that, whatever ugly illusions existed outside this lane of lilacs, there must be a God, after all, and that He must be good.

She heard Wally say, "I kind of thought you would like it." The voice brought her out of a near-trance. She stopped, turned, and looked at him. He was ugly, and young, and pathetic. He was looking at her with shining eyes.

"Wally, thank you." She put her arms around his neck—he was taller than she, but not much—and kissed him on the mouth. The pleasure of the kiss lay all in expressing her gratitude, and that it did fully and satisfyingly. It meant nothing else. He held her close while she kissed him, and loosed her the moment she stepped away. He peered at her, his mouth slightly open. He seemed about to say something, but no words came. They were holding each other's hands, and raindrops were dripping on them from the lilacs.

After a moment she uttered a low laugh. "Well, why do you look at me like that? Do I seem so wicked? You've been kissed by a girl before."

Wally said, putting the back of his hand to his forehead, "It doesn't seem so now." He shook his head and laughed. "I'm going to plant lilac lanes all over town." His voice was very hoarse.

"It won't help," she said firmly, putting her arm through his, and starting to walk again, "that was the first one and the last, my lad."

He said nothing. When they reached the end of the lane they turned back, and paced the length of it slowly. Rain dripped on the path with a whispering sound. "It's no use," she said after a while.

"What?"

"It's fading. I guess your nerves can't go on vibrating that way. It's becoming just a lane full of lilacs."

"Then let's leave." Wally quickened his steps, and they were out of the lane and in the bright open air again.

They drove downtown in sunlight along a drying roadway, with the windows open and warm fragrant air eddying into the Buick. "Come up and have lunch," she said when he stopped at her house.

"I have to go straight to the library, Marge. Term paper due Monday. Thanks anyway."

"Thanks for the lilacs, Wally. It was pure heaven."

She opened the door. Suddenly his hand was on her arm. "Maybe not," he said.

She looked at him. "Maybe not what?"

"Maybe it wasn't the last. The kiss."

With a light laugh, she said, "Wally, darling, don't lose sleep over it. I don't know. Maybe when we find such lilacs again."

He nodded, and drove off.

• • • • •

And there you are. The circle is closed.

Or is it? The mystery is solved. Or will it ever be, really? Writing this entry has stirred me up in an unaccountable way. I've gone on and on, and I meant to dispose of the whole thing in a page or so. I feel dissatisfied. I haven't managed to say what I wanted, or to indicate the quality of the meeting at all.

The thing is, this was a triumph I promised myself fifteen years ago. I can remember so clearly how I daydreamed of presenting myself to Marjorie, a successful playwright, when she'd be just another suburban housewife gone to seed. Well, I did it at last, and it wasn't a triumph at all. *There's* the point I'm trying to get at. The person I wanted to triumph over is gone, that's the catch. I can't carry my achievements backward fifteen years and flaunt them in the face of Marjorie Morgenstern, the beautiful elusive girl I was so mad about. And what satisfaction is there in crowing over the sweet-natured placid gray mama she has turned into? For that matter, what satisfaction is it to the poor ambitious skinny would-be writer of twenty years ago, little Wally, the South Wind stage manager, that I met Mrs. Schwartz and got such awe and deference? It's too late. He doesn't exist either.

But why should I care about all this? That's the strange part. It's all so dead, so forgotten. Marjorie doesn't haunt me; I haven't thought about her, except casually and without a trace of emotion, in a dozen years. Seeing her now, I can only be glad she didn't yield to my frantic puppy worship. The only remarkable thing about Mrs. Schwartz is that she ever hoped to be remarkable, that she ever dreamed of being Marjorie Morningstar. She couldn't be a more run-of-the-mill wife and mother.

What troubles me, I guess, is the thought of the bright vision that has faded. To me, she really was Marjorie Morningstar. I didn't know whether she had any talent. I didn't care. She was everything sweet, radiant, pure, and beautiful in the world. I know now that she was an ordinary girl, that the image existed only in my own mind, that her radiance was the radiance of my own hungry young desires projected around her. Still, I once saw that vision and loved it. Marjorie Morgenstern . . . What music that name used to have for me! I still hear a faint echo, sweet as a far-off flute playing Mozart, when I write the name. No doubt the land is full of nineteen-year-old boys to whom names like Betty Jones, Hazel Klein, Sue Wilson have the same celestial sound. It's a sound I shall hear no more.

And if she wasn't the bright angel I thought, she was a lovely girl; and where is that girl now? She doesn't even remember herself as she was. I am the only one on the face of God's earth, I'm sure, who still holds that picture in a dim corner of memory. When I go, that will be the end of Marjorie Morningstar, to all eternity.

Yet how beautiful she was! She rises up before me as I write—in a blue dress, a black raincoat, her face wet with rain, nineteen years old, in my arms and yet maddeningly beyond my reach, my beautiful young love, kissing me once under the lilacs in the rain. I have known most of the pleasant things I can expect in this life. I'm not famous or distinguished, but I never really hoped I would be; and my limits have been clear to me for a long time. I've had the success I aimed for. I'll go on working, and I'll have more success, I'm reasonably sure. I've had the love of good-looking women. If I'm fortunate, I may some day have what Milton Schwartz has, and what's been denied me: a wife I love, and children, and a warm happy home. But one thing I know now I will never have—the triumph I once wanted above everything on earth, the triumph I promised myself when I was a heartsick boy, the triumph that slipped through my fingers yesterday, once for all. I will never have that second kiss from Marjorie under the lilacs.

In the first excerpt, how might Wally be considered an adolescent in what Mencken has termed "a state of perceptual anesthesia"? [23].

The time spot when Marjorie kissed Wally, holding hands while raindrops dripped on them from the lilacs, could be called a heavenly moment that never comes twice. What elements combine to make such a moment special and unique?

Trace the sequential components from Marjorie's initial resistance to go out in pouring rain but her reluctance to disappoint Wally, to his realization, fifteen years later, that he would "never have that second kiss from Marjorie under the lilacs."

To what extent does Lindbergh's description in **Double-Sunrise** (p. 232) apply to Wally's and Marjorie's relationship on the lilac morning:

> . . . the first part of every relationship is . . . . pure, simple, and unencumbered. . . . The smile, the act, the relationship is hung in space, in the immediacy and purity of the present; suspended on the still point of here and now; balanced there, on a shaft of air, like a seagull. . . .
>
> But can the pure relationship of the sunrise shell be refound once it has become obscured? Obviously some relationships can never be recovered. It is not just a question of different needs to be understood and filled. In their changing roles the two partners may have grown in different directions or at different rates of speed. A brief double-sunrise episode may have been all they could achieve.

If a brief double-sunrise episode was all Marjorie and Wally could achieve, what limited their relationship? If not, on what basis might a deeper relationship have been founded? In either case, how would Lindbergh, who says, "what is actual is actual only for one time and one place," view their experience as valid rather than illusory?

How did the setting contribute to or intensify the experience? Do you believe that Nature can heighten feelings? How would you respond to the high school male who asked: "Why is it that a couple would much rather park on a hill-side and merely talk than sit at home together and do the same thing?"

Would you agree, from Wally's retrospective view of the lilac scene with Marjorie, that we tend to overrate things we have lost? That, as Whittier said, "For of all sad words of tongue or pen, the saddest are these: It might have been!"

From the vantage point of age thirty-four, Wally recognizes his adolescent feeling for Marjorie as "frantic puppy worship" and "the radiance of [his] own hungry desires projected around her." What motivated his "puppy worship"? What qualities in her appealed to him, and to his needs at that moment?

Wally's special blend of fantasy-reality serves a useful and necessary purpose: what is it that makes his observation universally true—that "the land is full of nineteen-year-old boys to whom names like Betty Jones, Hazel Klein, Sue Wilson have the same celestial sound"? What useful and necessary purpose does Wally's special blend of fantasy-reality serve?

RELATED QUESTIONS

Is Wally's and Marjorie's experience in any way parallel to that of the young boy and Anna in *Snowfall in Childhood* (p. 86)?

In *The Return of the Native* (p. 435), Charley allowed Eustacia to take his part in the play; she allowed him to hold her hand for a quarter of an hour. In *Marjorie Morningstar,* Wally introduced Marjorie to the gorgeous tapestries of the Cloisters and the beauties of a lane of lilacs after a rain; she put her arms around his neck and kissed him on the mouth. In each case a gift was given and gratitude for it was shown. In what ways do Marjorie's feelings and behavior differ from Eustacia's? How might you contrast Wally and Charley?

Pip, of Charles Dickens' novel *Great Expectations,* is one of those boys "the land is full of . . . to whom names like Betty Jones, Hazel Klein, Sue Wilson"—and in Pip's case, Estella—"have the same celestial sound."

In the following scene, Pip confides to his "old acquaintance," Biddy, how he feels about the scornful Estella, "the beautiful young lady" and ward of Miss Havisham, an eccentric old lady once disappointed in love.

Great Expectations

CHARLES DICKENS

. . . . When we came to the river-side and sat down on the bank, with the water rippling at our feet, making it all more quiet than it would have been without that sound, I resolved that it was a good time and place for the admission of Biddy into my inner confidence.

"Biddy," said I, after binding her to secrecy, "I want to be a gentleman."

"Oh, I wouldn't, if I was you!" she returned. "I don't think it would answer."

"Biddy," said I, with some severity, "I have particular reasons for wanting to be a gentleman."

"You know best, Pip; but don't you think you are happier as you are?"

"Biddy," I exclaimed, impatiently, "I am not at all happy as I am. I am disgusted with my calling and with my life. I have never taken to either since I was bound. Don't be absurd."

"Was I absurd?" said Biddy, quietly raising her eyebrows; "I am sorry for that; I didn't mean to be. I only want you to do well, and be comfortable."

"Well, then, understand once for all that I never shall or can be comfortable —or anything but miserable—there, Biddy!—unless I can lead a very different sort of life from the life I lead now."

"That's a pity!" said Biddy, shaking her head with a sorrowful air.

Now, I too had so often thought it a pity, that, in the singular kind of quarrel with myself which I was always carrying on, I was half inclined to shed tears of vexation and distress when Biddy gave utterance to her sentiment and my own. I told her she was right, and I knew it was much to be regretted, but still it was not to be helped.

"If I could have settled down," I said to Biddy, plucking up the short grass within reach, much as I had once upon a time pulled my feelings out of my hair and kicked them into the brewery wall: "if I could have settled down and been but half as fond of the forge as I was when I was little, I know it would have been much better for me. You and I and Joe would have wanted nothing then, and Joe and I would perhaps have gone partners when I was out of my time, and I might even have grown up to keep company with you, and we might have sat on this very bank on a fine Sunday, quite different people. I should have been good enough for *you;* shouldn't I, Biddy?"

Biddy sighed as she looked at the ships sailing on, and returned for answer, "Yes; I am not over-particular." It scarcely sounded flattering, but I knew she meant well.

"Instead of that," said I, plucking up more grass and chewing a blade or two, "see how I am going on. Dissatisfied, and uncomfortable, and—what would it signify to me, being coarse and common, if nobody had told me so!"

Biddy turned her face suddenly towards mine, and looked far more attentively at me than she had looked at the sailing ships.

"It was neither a very true nor a very polite thing to say," she remarked, directing her eyes to the ships again. "Who said it?"

I was disconcerted, for I had broken away without quite seeing where I was going to. It was not to be shuffled off, now, however, and I answered, "The beautiful young lady at Miss Havisham's, and she's more beautiful than anybody ever was, and I admire her dreadfully, and I want to be a gentleman on her account." Having made this lunatic confession, I began to throw my torn-up grass into the river, as if I had some thoughts of following it.

"Do you want to be a gentleman, to spite her or to gain her over?" Biddy quietly asked me, after a pause.

"I don't know," I moodily answered.

"Because, if it is to spite her," Biddy pursued, "I should think—but you know best—that might be better and more independently done by caring nothing for words. And if it is to gain her over, I should think—but you know best— she was not worth gaining over."

Exactly what I myself had thought, many times. Exactly what was perfectly manifest to me at the moment. But how could I, a poor dazed village lad, avoid that wonderful inconsistency into which the best and wisest of men fall every day?

"It may be all quite true," said I to Biddy, "but I admire her dreadfully."

In short, I turned over on my face when I came to that, and got a good grasp on the hair, on each side of my head, and wrenched it well. All the while knowing the madness of my heart to be so very mad and misplaced, that I was quite conscious it would have served my face right, if I had lifted it up by my hair, and knocked it against the pebbles as a punishment for belonging to such an idiot.

Biddy was the wisest of girls, and she tried to reason no more with me. She put her hand, which was a comfortable hand though roughened by work, upon my hands, one after another, and gently took them out of my hair. Then she softly patted my shoulder in a soothing way, while with my face upon my sleeve I cried a little—exactly as I had done in the brewery yard—and felt vaguely convinced that I was very much ill-used by somebody, or by everybody; I can't say which.

"I am glad of one thing," said Biddy, "and that is, that you have felt you could give me your confidence, Pip. And I am glad of another thing, and that is, that of course you know you may depend upon my keeping it and always so far deserving it. If your first teacher (dear! such a poor one, and so much in need of being taught herself!) had been your teacher at the present time, she thinks she knows what lesson she would set. But it would be a hard one to learn, and you have got beyond her, and it's of no use now." So, with a quiet sigh for me, Biddy rose from the bank, and said, with a fresh and pleasant change of voice, "Shall we walk a little further, or go home?"

"Biddy," I cried, getting up, putting my arm around her neck, and giving her a kiss, "I shall always tell you everything."

"Till you're a gentleman," said Biddy.

"You know I never shall be, so that's always. Not that I have any occasion to tell you anything, for you know everything I know—as I told you at home the other night."

"Ah!" said Biddy, quite in a whisper, as she looked away at the ships. And then repeated, with her former pleasant change; "shall we walk a little further, or go home?"

I said to Biddy we would walk a little further, and we did so, and the summer afternoon toned down into the summer evening, and it was very beautiful. I began to consider whether I was not more naturally and wholesomely situated, after all, in these circumstances, than playing beggar my neighbour by candlelight in the room with the stopped clocks, and being despised by Estella. I thought it would be very good for me if I could get her out of my head with all the rest of those remembrances and fancies, and could go to work determined to relish what I had to do, and stick to it, and make the best of it. I asked myself the question whether I did not surely know that if Estella were beside me at that moment instead of Biddy, she would make me miserable? I was obliged to admit that I did know it for a certainty, and I said to myself, "Pip, what a fool you are!"

We talked a good deal as we walked, and all that Biddy said seemed right. Biddy was never insulting, or capricious, or Biddy today and somebody else tomorrow; she would have derived only pain, and no pleasure, from giving me pain; she would far rather have wounded her own breast than mine. How could it be, then, that I did not like her much the better of the two?

"Biddy," said I, when we were walking homeward, "I wish you could put me right."

"I wish I could!" said Biddy.

"If I could only get myself to fall in love with you—you don't mind my speaking so openly to such an old acquaintance?"

"O dear, not at all!" said Biddy. "Don't mind me."

"If I could only get myself to do it, *that* would be the thing for me."

"But you never will, you see," said Biddy.

It did not appear quite so unlikely to me that evening, as it would have done if we had discussed it a few hours before. I therefore observed I was not quite sure of that. But Biddy said she *was*, and she said it decisively. In my heart I believed her to be right; and yet I took it rather ill, too, that she should be so positive on the point.

———————

How does Pip's motivation for "becoming a gentleman" justify placing this excerpt in the "YOU and i" section?

How does Biddy show her understanding of the importance of autonomy— that is, a clear self-concept, a stable set of internal values, self-direction, self-control, and self-respect? The autonomous person is sure of himself, can give himself, and thus can love. Is Biddy herself autonomous?

Would you classify Pip's feeling as "frantic puppy worship"? As "the radiance of [his] own hungry desires projected around" Estella? A Charley-like worship as in **The Return of the Native** (p. 435)? Something else?

What binds Pip to Estella when he knows "the madness of [his] heart to be so very mad and misplaced"?

From the excerpt from **Great Expectations** would you conclude with Shakespeare in *A Midsummer Night's Dream* that love is blind? Or with Millay in "Sonnet XXVI" that love is not blind?

How much of Pip's so-called blindness in love is self-deception? How much is a case of Millay's "pity me that the heart is slow to learn/what the swift mind beholds at every turn" (see "**Night-Lights,**" p. 575)?

If Pip is already aware of the truth in Biddy's comments, if he has admitted to himself that Biddy—unlike Estella—is never insulting or capricious or inconsistent, why is he not able to fall in love with Biddy?

Given the nature of Pip's problem, why was Biddy "the wisest of girls" in trying "to reason no more" with him? In what other ways does Biddy demonstrate her understanding, her responsible, protective, and sensitive concern for Pip's well-being? How does she demonstrate honesty in her relationship with him? Does Pip exploit Biddy?

RELATED QUESTIONS

Would you call Pip and/or Wally of **Marjorie Morningstar** (p. 439) "romantics"? Why, or why not?

What similarities might be found between Biddy and Katie Nolan, Francie's mother in **A Tree Grows in Brooklyn** (p. 147)?

A Lodging for the Night

ELINOR WYLIE

If I had lightly given at the first
The lightest favours that you first demanded;
Had I been prodigal and open-handed
Of this dead body in its dream immersed;
My flesh and not my spirit had been pierced:
Your appetite was casual and candid;
Thus, for an hour, had endured and ended
My love, in violation and reversed.

Alas, because I would not draw the bolt
And take you to my bed, you now assume
The likeness of an angel in revolt
Turned from a low inhospitable room,
Until your fiery image has enchanted
And ravished the poor soul you never wanted.

The narrator, feeling that the man in *A Lodging for the Night* was interested only in a "one-night stand," refused to sleep with him. She remarks on his "casual, candid appetite"; she recognizes that though he wanted her body, he did not want her soul.

How then, "because [she] would not draw the bolt . . ." has he managed to assume "the likeness of an angel in revolt" to her? How has his "fiery image" since her refusal of him succeeded in enchanting and ravishing her?

How has he achieved the status of "YOU" in their relationship?

RELATED QUESTIONS

How might Wylie's reaction following her rejection of an opportunity be compared with that of Francie Nolan in *A Tree Grows in Brooklyn* (p. 147) who, after refusing an affair with a twenty-two-year-old man, had to contend with the fact that she "didn't and now it's too late"?

In what ways might "SHE" in William Dickey's poem *Resolving Doubts* (see "**Night-Lights,**" p. 545) be sympathetic with the narrator in *A Lodging for the Night?*

Sonnet XXIX

ELIZABETH BARRETT BROWNING

I think of thee!—my thoughts do twine and bud
About thee, as wild vines, about a tree,
Put out broad leaves, and soon there's nought to see
Except the straggling green which hides the wood.
Yet, O my palm-tree, be it understood
I will not have my thoughts instead of thee
Who art dearer, better! rather, instantly
Renew thy presence. As a strong tree should,
Rustle thy boughs and set thy trunk all bare,
And let these bands of greenery which insphere thee
Drop heavily down,—burst, shattered, everywhere!
Because, in this deep joy to see and hear thee
And breathe within thy shadow a new air,
I do not think of thee—I am too near thee.

In *Sonnet XXIX* of the forty-three which record emotional landmarks in her relationship with Robert Browning, Elizabeth Barrett points to the danger noted by C. S. Lewis in *Eros* (p. 207): "Love you? I *am* you." Fromm defines mature love as "union under the condition of preserving one's integrity, one's individuality." It might be added that such a mature relationship permits the loved one to be viewed as a person, beyond the "amorous imagination which bestows value" in ways noted by Singer.

How does Browning indicate the danger of losing her autonomy when she says: "my thoughts do twine and bud/About thee, as wild vines, about a tree . . . soon there's nought to see/Except the straggling green which hides the wood"? What "wood" will her "vines" strangle? What will her "straggling green" thereby mask?

Why does she want him to "rustle [his] boughs" and "let these bands of greenery which insphere thee/Drop heavily down"? What then will she be able to see?

How does "this deep joy to see and hear thee/And breathe within thy shadow a new air," destroy her emotional perspective?

What does "I am too near thee" signify? Too near for what?

How does the poet confirm the notion that getting away from a person for a while, or dating other people, permits a more accurate assessment of one's feelings for that person?

Look Not in My Eyes, for Fear

A. E. HOUSMAN

Look not in my eyes, for fear
  They mirror true the sight I see,
And there you find your face too clear
  And love it and be lost like me.
One the long nights through must lie
  Spent in star-defeated sighs,
But why should you as well as I
  Perish? gaze not in my eyes.

Eyes may express feelings, or they may function as mirrors reflecting those of the viewer. Could the situation in which Housman's subjects find themselves be described as MacLeish's love which is not love in "The Woman on the Stair" (p. 248)?

> In love not love there never are two lovers:
> There are but two together with blind eyes
> Watching within what ecstasy love suffers.
>
> • • • •
>   They stare
> Each in the other's face like those who feed
> Delight in mirrors: and as though alone
> Learn from each other where their love will lead them.

Singer in **Appraisal and Bestowal** (p. 227) notes that in the theater

> The spectator makes his imaginative leap by seeing the actor as a present reality framed within the aesthetic contrivances of the theater. . . . the phenomenon depends upon the spectator himself, upon his dramatic sensibility, his creative capacity to infuse a fictional character with the reality of the human being right there before him. . . . In a similar fashion the lover's attention fixes upon the sheer presence of the beloved. In that extreme condition sometimes called "falling in love," such attentiveness often approaches self-hypnosis.

Lindbergh in **Double-Sunrise** (p. 233) asks:

> . . . can one actually find oneself in someone else? In someone else's love? Or even in the mirror someone else holds up for one?

The character in From Here to Eternity described earlier (p. 419) was speaking from a sexual context when he generalized that females want males to lose themselves in them, although the female is always trying to discover herself in the male. But his philosophizing extended to the observation that:

> . . . every human was always looking for himself, in bars, in railway trains, in offices, in mirrors, in love, especially in love, for the self of him that is there, someplace, in every other human. Love was not to give oneself, but to find oneself, describe oneself.

How does Housman's poem substantiate any or all of these reflections? What is the result? Why must one "lie through long nights spent in star-defeated sighs"?

How does the poet acknowledge that losing oneself to love—of self or other person—results in a more serious state of loss?

RELATED QUESTIONS

How does Lindbergh in **Double-Sunrise** (p. 232) elaborate on the opposite approach to this problem, that of finding true identity by "going into one's own ground and knowing oneself"?

How does the narrator's relationship with Eleanor in **First Love and Other Sorrows** (p. 111) have elements of this "reflected" love?

Laurie Lee in **What Love Must Be** (p. 250) suggests that "we are so much alike" is a fatal phrase, suggesting a cloudy affair with a mirror. What does he claim is "the real balance that binds us"?

How does Louis MacNeice in **Circe** (see **"Night-Lights,"** p. 573) elaborate on the ideas of Housman, and others who deal with this aspect of "YOU and i" attractions?

Sonnet XVI

ELINOR WYLIE

I hereby swear that to uphold your house
I would lay my bones in quick destroying lime
Or turn my flesh to timber for all time;
Cut down my womanhood; lop off the boughs
Of that perpetual ecstasy that grows
From the heart's core; condemn it as a crime
If it be broader than a beam, or climb
Above the stature that your roof allows.

I am not the hearthstone nor the cornerstone
Within this noble fabric you have builded;
Not by my beauty was its cornice gilded;
Not on my courage were its arches thrown:
My lord, adjudge my strength, and set me where
I bear a little more than I can bear.

In what ways does Elinor Wylie in her sonnet to her "lord," deny or under-value her own human worth? To what extremes is she willing to go to please him?

How is she guilty of what Fromm in **The Theory of Love** (p. 255) called

. . . the most widespread misunderstanding . . . which assumes that giving is "giving up" something, sacrificing . . . the virtue of giving to (some people) lies in the very act of acceptance of the sacrifice.

What are the likely outcomes of a relationship based on submission to an imagined ideal, on "fusion without integrity" (p. 255)?

What are the connotations of "perpetual ecstasy that grows/From the heart's core"?

Why do we idealize people? Inflate and enhance reality?

If the poet were addressing her husband would you find her feeling more acceptable than if the sonnet were addressed to a lover? Why, or why not?

Does Wylie's sonnet illustrate what Dietrich might have had in mind when she wrote in *Married Love: Strategy of* (p. 350) that "to be completely woman you need a master"?

RELATED QUESTIONS

Anne Frank in *The Diary of a Young Girl* (p. 136) wrote about Peter Van Daan:

> I like it much better if he explains something to me than when I have to teach him; I would really adore him to be my superior in almost everything.

Would Elinor Wylie share Anne's perspective on males? If so, why might the point of view be more understandable in Anne's case than in the poet's?

Charley in *The Return of the Native* (p. 435), Wally of *Marjorie Morningstar* (p. 439), Pip in *Great Expectations* (p. 444), and the narrator of Wylie's *I Hereby Swear (Sonnet XVI)* all subordinate themselves to another in varying ways and degrees. How would you interpret Elizabeth Barrett Browning's degree of autonomy from her feelings in *Go from Me (Sonnet VI)* (see "Night-Lights," p. 542)? When she tells Robert that even were he to leave her she would "stand/Henceforward in [his] shadow. . . Nevermore alone upon the threshold . . . of individual life"; that no matter how wide their geographic separation, it would "leave [his] heart in [hers] with pulses that beat double"; that what she does and dreams have the same relationship to him as does the wine to its source, the grapes, is she being submissive? Indicating dependency? Devaluating herself? Why?

In Elizabeth Barrett Browning's *And Yet, Because Thou Overcomest So (Sonnet XVI)* (see "Night-Lights," p. 542), is her statement: "If thou invite me forth, I rise above abasement at the word/Make thy love larger to enlarge my worth" the same as the idea in Wylie's plea: "adjudge my strength, and set me where/I bear a little more than I can bear"? Why, or why not? Is Browning's concept of "lordly" behavior the same as that implied by Wylie's address, "my lord"? Is there a difference in the degree to which each will surrender herself to another's sovereignty?

In what way does Denise Levertov in *The Wife* (see "Night-Lights," p. 571) react to her master? Does she diminish herself in describing herself as a "frog," "dog," or "swallow"? Would Wylie in *I Hereby Swear (Sonnet XVI)* be capable of reacting as Levertov does in the final stanza of *The Wife?*

YOU and I

Difficulty with a Bouquet

WILLIAM SANSOM

Seal, walking through his garden, said suddenly to himself: "I would like to pick some flowers and take them to Miss D."

The afternoon was light and warm. Tall chestnuts fanned themselves in a pleasant breeze. Among the hollyhocks there was a good humming as the bees tumbled from flower to flower. Seal wore an open shirt. He felt fresh and fine, with the air swimming coolly under his shirt and around his ribs. The summer's afternoon was free. Nothing pressed him. It was a time when some simple, disinterested impulse might well be hoped to flourish.

Seal felt a great joy in the flowers around him and from this a brilliant longing to give. He wished to give quite inside himself, uncritically, without thinking for a moment: "Here am I, Seal, wishing something." Seal merely wanted to give of his flowers to a fellow being. It had happened that Miss D. was the first person to come to mind. He was in no way attached to Miss D. He knew her slightly, as a plain, elderly girl of about twenty who had come to live in the flats opposite his garden. If Seal had ever thought about Miss D. at all, it was because he disliked the way she walked. She walked stiffly, sailing with her long body while her little legs raced to catch up with it. But he was not thinking of this now. Just by chance he had glimpsed the block of flats as he had stooped to pick a flower. The flats had presented the image of Miss D. to his mind.

Seal chose some common, ordinary flowers. As the stems broke he whistled between his teeth. He had chosen these ordinary flowers because they were the nearest to hand; in the second place, because they were fresh and full of life. They were neither rare nor costly. They were pleasant, fresh, unassuming flowers.

With the flowers in his hand, Seal walked contentedly from his garden and set foot on the asphalt pavement that led to the block of flats across the way. But as his foot touched the asphalt, as the sly glare of an old man fixed his eye for the moment of its passing, as the traffic asserted itself, certain misgivings began to freeze his impromptu joy.

"Good heavens," he suddenly thought, "what am I doing?" He stepped outside himself and saw Seal carrying a bunch of cheap flowers to Miss D. in the flats across the way.

"These are cheap flowers," he thought. "This is a sudden gift. I shall smile as I hand them to her. We shall both know that there is no ulterior reason for the gift and thus the whole action will smack of goodness—of goodness and simple brotherhood. And somehow . . . for that reason this gesture of mine will appear to be the most calculated pose of all. Such a simple gesture is impossible. The improbable is to be suspected. My gift will certainly be regarded as an affectation. **453**

"Oh, if only I had some reason—aggrandizement, financial gain, seduction—any of the accepted motives that would return my flowers to social favor. But no—I have none of these in me. I only wish to give and to receive nothing in return."

As he walked on, Seal could see himself bowing and smiling. He saw himself smile too broadly as he apologized by exaggeration for his good action. His neck flinched with disgust as he saw himself assume the old bravadoes. He could see the mocking smile of recognition on the face of Miss D.

Seal dropped the flowers into the gutter and walked slowly back to his garden.

From her window high up in the concrete flats, Miss D. watched Seal drop the flowers. How fresh they looked! How they would have livened her barren room! "Wouldn't it have been nice," thought Miss D., "if that Mr. Seal had been bringing *me* that pretty bouquet of flowers! Wouldn't it have been nice if he had picked them in his own garden and—well, just brought them along, quite casually, and made me a present of the delightful afternoon." Miss D. dreamed on for a few minutes.

Then she frowned, rose, straightened her dress, hurried into the kitchen. "Thank God he didn't," she sighed to herself. "I should have been most embarrassed. It's not as if he wanted me. It would have been just too maudlin for words."

In **The Theory of Love** (p. 260), Fromm maintains that "the most fundamental kind of love, which underlies all types of love, is brotherly love. . . . the kind of love the *Bible* speaks of when it says: love thy neighbor as thyself. Brotherly love is love for all human beings; it is characterized by its very lack of exclusiveness." How does Seal's "brilliant longing to give" illustrate such feeling?

How does Seal's simple, disinterested impulse to make Miss D. a present of the delightful afternoon resemble the spirit in which Mrs. Lindbergh was given the double-sunrise shell? Could Seal have been one of those strangers who, according to Lindbergh (p. 232), "smile at you on the beach, come up and offer you a shell, for no reason, lightly, and then go by and leave you alone again. Nothing is demanded of you in payment, no social rite expected, no tie established. . . . a gift, freely offered, freely taken, in mutual trust"?

What shattered Seal's trust in himself? What caused "certain misgivings. . . . to freeze [his] impromptu joy"? What does Seal think the old man thinks? What does he suspect Miss D. will assume?

Ironically, Miss D.'s feelings parallel Seal's, although neither will ever know the pleasure missed by mutual lack of trust. Do you think such moments of self-doubt, indecision and fear of being misunderstood are common? Do the simplest gestures appear to be most calculated? Are they suspect because society expects one to have an "ulterior reason"?

When is it better to stop and think through a situation as Seal did? When is it better to act immediately on impulse? What might be lost or saved in each case?

Why have we a particular fear of approaching other people with love? Is it worse to approach too slowly than too rapidly?

The adults in **Difficulty with a Bouquet** are equals in a potential "**We**" relationship. Why did it abort? Had Seal believed his heart rather than his head—the heart that "has reasons that reason knows not of"—what "might have been"?

Does the light, warm, free afternoon contribute to Seal's mood? If so, how? Is the setting as instrumental in *Difficulty with a Bouquet* as it is in *Snowfall in Childhood* (p. 86)? In *Marjorie Morningstar* (p. 439)?

Like the excerpts from *Marjorie Morningstar,* the following two extracts from Claude Brown's *Manchild in the Promised Land,* dealing with the narrator's relationship with Sugar, present "before" and "after" views, separated by a few years.

Manchild in the Promised Land (1)

CLAUDE BROWN

My eleventh birthday — the first birthday party I had ever had — was really something. On the night before the party, I took Knoxie and Bucky down to Delancey Street, where we waited until three o'clock in the morning for a nightclub to close. It was a Roumanian nightclub, but to us it was a Jewish nightclub. It had to be Jewish, because being white and talking funny so nobody could understand you was what made people Jewish. When the Jewish nightclub closed we went in with three shopping bags. Only a little bit of change was in the cash register, but we ate a lot of turkey and other kinds of funny-tasting meat. When we left the place, the three shopping bags were full of champagne for my birthday party.

It was the best party Eighth Avenue had ever seen. The people came all afternoon and all night. Ages ranged from twelve to thirty-five. Most of the people there didn't know me, and I didn't know them, and nobody cared about not knowing somebody. The word got out about the champagne, and everybody who passed by the house came in to get some champagne and pigs' feet.

After all that foolishness with the cake, I forgot about everybody at the party. Everybody but Sugar. Sugar was one of my best friends now, and I told her so. She had on a pretty white dress; her hair was curled; she looked as if somebody had worked some magic on her. Sugar must have known she looked brand new, because she didn't act the way she acted most of the time. She didn't laugh — she only smiled; and she didn't talk loud. She seemed to know that it was my party and that she was just a guest. This was the first time I had ever seen Sugar act that way, and I didn't expect her to do it for long. I kept looking at her and waiting for her to do something crazy like come over to me and stick her tongue out at me and start playing. But every time I looked at Sugar, she was still sitting there and still looking brand new.

I don't know how I got to her in that crowded living room. Sugar never said a word; she just held my hand and followed me quietly from one room to another until we found one with nobody in it. Sugar seemed to know I wanted to say something to her, but she didn't know what. She acted like she was waiting for something to happen and like that something was about to happen. Sugar seemed to know that what I said to her was going to be something real good, something I had never told her before. I had that same feeling about it. I didn't know what I was going to say to her, but I knew I wasn't going to tell her that she was ugly like I did most of the time. And I knew that Sugar wasn't going to argue and jump all over me when I got her where I was taking her to. I couldn't understand what had happened to Sugar, but she sure was different. She was still ugly, but there seemed to be so many pretty things about her that pretty girls didn't have.

Me and Sugar stayed in that room for a long time, and when we came out it seemed like the world had changed colors. I still don't know all of what happened to me in that room with Sugar. I knew it wasn't the champagne that did it. For the next two years whenever I was in the city, Sugar and I never had to say anything to each other. We came out of that room with a whole lot of understanding. Sugar could look at me and make me smile or even laugh, and it wasn't because she looked funny either; it was just that sometimes when she looked at me, I felt so good I just had to laugh or at least smile. And I could look at her and make her whole face light up. When we would hit each other, the hit always meant something that both of us understood. Our hitting wasn't like before, when we would hit each other kind of hard. Now we only tapped each other just hard enough to say what we wanted to say.

Chronologically, both Sugar and Claude are children. But what elements in their relationship seem emotionally "adult"? How do they communicate with each other?

If Claude and Sugar were ten years older, might they be able to sustain a "**We**" relationship of mature love? Why, or why not?

What does the author mean when he says "We came out of that room with a whole lot of understanding"? What do you think happened to him in that room with Sugar? Would he have experimented sexually with her?

Although "she was still ugly . . . there seemed to be so many pretty things about her that pretty girls didn't have." In what sense is Sugar "ugly"? What might some of the "so many pretty things" be? What connection do they have with being "feminine"?

Manchild in the Promised Land (2)
CLAUDE BROWN

I tried to get tight with her again. I didn't beg her or anything like that. I asked her to be my girl, but Sugar said she didn't feel the way she used to feel about me. She didn't think she could be going through what she went through before. She was a big girl now, she was older, and she felt it would be silly to go back into her childhood thing with me. . . . I felt sort of bad when she reminded me how I had mistreated her. I didn't feel bad about having mistreated her. I felt bad about her remembering this and not wanting to go with me, as fine as she was. I just said, "Hell wit it," but I sure wanted her to be my girl. When she told me no, it was a big letdown. I felt that she wasn't supposed to say this. She was supposed to be mine. I guess this was one of the hardest things I ever had to accept. Sugar had declared her independence and become a person.

How have Sugar's feelings changed? Can you account for it? Do you think that Claude, from whose perspective we viewed the first scene, misinterpreted Sugar's reactions?

People tend to have selective memories: What parts of their childhood relationship does each recall? What parts does each overlook?

Why might Claude have said, "When she told me no, it was a big letdown. I felt she wasn't supposed to say this. She was supposed to be mine." How is it a blow to Claude's masculine pride? Is it something else as well?

How would you define *person* in the context Claude places it when saying, "Sugar had declared her independence and become a person"?

The Heart Is a Lonely Hunter

CARSON McCULLERS

Mick split open the biscuits and put slices of fried white meat inside them. She sat down on the back steps to eat her breakfast. The morning was warm and bright. Spareribs and Sucker were playing with George in the back yard. Sucker wore his sun suit and the other two kids had taken off all their clothes except their shorts. They were scooting each other with the hose. The stream of water sparkled bright in the sun.

Sprays of the water blew into her face, and once the kids turned the hose on her legs. She was afraid her box would get wet, so she carried it with her through the alley to the front porch. Harry was sitting on his steps reading the newspaper. She opened her box and got out the notebook. But it was hard to settle her mind on the song she wanted to write down. Harry was looking over in her direction and she could not think.

She and Harry had talked about so many things lately. Nearly every day they walked home from school together. They talked about God. Sometimes she would wake up in the night and shiver over what they had said. Harry was a Pantheist. That was a religion, the same as Baptist or Catholic or Jew. Harry believed that after you were dead and buried you changed to plants and fire and dirt and clouds and water. It took thousands of years and then finally you were a part of all the world. He said he thought that was better than being one single angel. Anyhow it was better than nothing.

Harry threw the newspaper into his hall and then came over. 'It's hot like summer,' he said. 'And only March.'

'Yeah. I wish we could go swimming.'

'We would if there was any place.'

'There's not any place. Except that country club pool.'

'I sure would like to do something—to get out and go somewhere.'

'Me too,' she said. 'Wait! I know one place. It's out in the country about fifteen miles. It's a deep, wide creek in the woods. The Girl Scouts have a camp there in the summer-time. Mrs. Wells took me and George and Pete and Sucker swimming there one time last year.'

'If you want I can get bicycles and we can go tomorrow. I have a holiday one Sunday a month.'

'We'll ride out and take a picnic dinner,' Mick said.

'O.K. I'll borrow the bikes.'

It was time for him to go to work. She watched him walk down the street. He swung his arms. Halfway down the block there was a bay tree with low branches. Harry took a running jump, caught a limb, and chinned himself. A happy feeling came in her because it was true they were real good friends. Also he was handsome. Tomorrow she would borrow Hazel's blue necklace and wear the silk dress. And for dinner they would take jelly sandwiches and Nehi. Maybe Harry would bring something queer, because they ate orthodox Jew. She watched him until he turned the corner. It was true that he had grown to be a very good-looking fellow.

Harry in the country was different from Harry sitting on the back steps reading the newspapers and thinking about Hitler. They left early in the morning. The wheels he borrowed were the kind for boys—with a bar between the legs. They strapped the lunches and bathing-suits to the fenders and were gone before nine o'clock. The morning was hot and sunny. Within an hour they were far out of town on a red clay road. The fields were bright green and the sharp smell of pine trees was in the air. Harry talked in a very excited way. The warm wind blew into their faces. Her mouth was very dry and she was hungry.

'See that house up on the hill there? Less us stop and get some water.'

'No, we better wait. Well water gives you typhoid.'

'I already had typhoid. I had pneumonia and a broken leg and a infected foot.'

'I remember.'

'Yeah,' Mick said. 'Me and Bill stayed in the front room when we had typhoid fever and Pete Wells would run past on the sidewalk holding his nose and looking up at the window. Bill was very embarrassed. All my hair came out so I was bald-headed.'

'I bet we're at least ten miles from town. We've been riding an hour and a half—fast riding, too.'

'I sure am thirsty,' Mick said. 'And hungry. What you got in that sack for lunch?'

'Cold liver pudding and chicken salad sandwiches and pie.'

'That's a good picnic dinner.' She was ashamed of what she had brought. 'I got two hard-boiled eggs—already stuffed—with separate little packages of salt and pepper. And sandwiches—blackberry jelly with butter. Everything wrapped in oil paper. And paper napkins.'

'I didn't intend for you to bring anything,' Harry said. 'My Mother fixed lunch for both of us. I asked you out here and all. We'll come to a store soon and get cold drinks.'

They rode half an hour longer before they finally came to the filling-station store. Harry propped up the bicycles and she went in ahead of him. After the bright glare the store seemed dark. The shelves were stacked with slabs of white meat, cans of oil, and sacks of meal. Flies buzzed over a big, sticky jar of loose candy on the counter.

'What kind of drinks you got?' Harry asked.

The storeman started to name them over. Mick opened the ice box and looked inside. Her hands felt good in the cold water. 'I want a chocolate Nehi. You got any of them?'

'Ditto,' Harry said. 'Make it two.'

'No, wait a minute. Here's some ice-cold beer. I want a bottle of beer if you can treat as high as that.'

Harry ordered one for himself, also. He thought it was a sin for anybody under twenty to drink beer—but maybe he just suddenly wanted to be a sport. After the first swallow he made a bitter face. They sat on the steps in front of the store. Mick's legs were so tired that the muscles in them jumped. She wiped the neck of the bottle with her hand and took a long, cold pull. Across the road there was a big empty field of grass, and beyond that a fringe of pine woods. The trees were every color of green—from a bright yellow-green to a dark color that was almost black. The sky was hot blue.

'I like beer,' she said. 'I used to sop bread down in the drops our Dad left. I like to lick salt out my hand while I drink. This is the second bottle to myself I've ever had.'

'The first swallow was sour. But the rest tastes good.'

The storeman said it was twelve miles from town. They had four more miles to go. Harry paid him and they were out in the hot sun again. Harry was talking loud and he kept laughing without any reason.

'Gosh, the beer along with this hot sun makes me dizzy. But I sure do feel good,' he said.

'I can't wait to get in swimming.'

There was sand in the road and they had to throw all their weight on the pedals to keep from bogging. Harry's shirt was stuck to his back with sweat. He still kept talking.

Then finally they reached the place she had been looking for. 'This is it! See that sign that says PRIVATE? We got to climb the bob-wire fence and then take that path there—see!'

The woods were very quiet. Slick pine needles covered the ground. Within a few minutes they had reached the creek. The water was brown and swift. Cool. There was no sound except from the water and a breeze singing high up in the pine trees. It was like the deep, quiet woods made them timid, and they walked softly along the bank beside the creek.

'Don't it look pretty.'

Harry laughed. 'What makes you whisper? Listen here!' He clapped his hand over his mouth and gave a long Indian whoop that echoed back at them. 'Come on. Let's jump in the water and cool off.'

'Aren't you hungry?'

'O.K. Then we'll eat first. We'll eat half the lunch now and half later on when we come out.'

She unwrapped the jelly sandwiches. When they were finished Harry balled the papers neatly and stuffed them into a hollow tree stump. Then he took his shorts and went down the path. She shucked off her clothes behind a bush and struggled into Hazel's bathing-suit. The suit was too small and cut her between the legs.

'You ready?' Harry hollered.

She heard a splash in the water and when she reached the bank Harry was already swimming. 'Don't dive yet until I find out if there are any stumps or shallow places,' he said. She just looked at his head bobbing in the water. She had never intended to dive, anyway. She couldn't even swim. She had been in swimming only a few times in her life—and then she always wore water wings or stayed out of parts that were over her head. But it would be sissy to tell Harry. She was embarrassed. All of a sudden she told a tale:

'I don't dive any more. I used to dive, high dive, all the time. But once I busted my head open, so I can't dive any more.' She thought for a minute. 'It was a double jack-knife dive I was doing. And when I came up there was blood all in the water. But I didn't think anything about it and just began to do swimming tricks. These people were hollering at me. Then I found out where all this blood in the water was coming from. And I never have swam good since.'

Harry scrambled up the bank. 'Gosh! I never heard about that.'

She meant to add on to the tale to make it sound more reasonable, but instead she just looked at Harry. His skin was light brown and the water made it shining. There were hairs on his chest and legs. In the tight trunks he seemed very naked. Without his glasses his face was wider and more handsome. His eyes were wet and blue. He was looking at her and it was like suddenly they got embarrassed.

'The water's about ten feet deep except over on the other side and there it's shallow.'

'Less us get going. I bet that cold water feels good.'

She wasn't scared. She felt the same as if she had got caught at the top of a very high tree and there was nothing to do but just climb down the best way she could—a dead-calm feeling. She edged off the bank and was in the ice-cold water. She held to a root until it broke in her hands and then she began to swim. Once she choked and went under, but she kept going and didn't lose any face. She swam and reached the other side of the bank where she could touch bottom. Then she felt good. She smacked the water with her fists and called out crazy words to make echoes.

'Watch here!'

Harry shimmied up a tall, thin little tree. The trunk was limber and when he reached the top it swayed down with him. He dropped into the water.

'Me too! Watch me do it!'

'That's a sapling.'

She was as good a climber as anybody on the block. She copied exactly what he had done and hit the water with a hard smack. She could swim, too. Now she could swim O.K.

They played follow the leader and ran up and down the bank and jumped in the cold brown water. They hollered and jumped and climbed. They played around for maybe two hours. Then they were standing on the bank and they both looked at each other and there didn't seem to be anything new to do. Suddenly she said:

'Have you ever swam naked?'

The woods was very quiet and for a minute he did not answer. He was cold. His titties had turned hard and purple. His lips were purple and his teeth chattered. 'I—I don't think so.'

This excitement was in her, and she said something she didn't mean to say. 'I would if you would. I dare you to.'

Harry slicked back the dark, wet bangs of his hair. 'O.K.'

They both took off their bathing-suits. Harry had his back to her. He stumbled and his ears were red. Then they turned toward each other. Maybe it was half an hour they stood there—maybe not more than a minute.

Harry pulled a leaf from a tree and tore it to pieces. 'We better get dressed.'

All through the picnic dinner neither of them spoke. They spread the dinner on the ground. Harry divided everything in half. There was the hot, sleepy feeling of a summer afternoon. In the deep woods they could hear no sound except the slow flowing of the water and the songbirds. Harry held his stuffed egg and mashed the yellow with his thumb. What did that make her remember? She heard herself breathe.

Then he looked up over her shoulder. 'Listen here. I think you're so pretty, Mick. I never did think so before. I don't mean I thought you were very ugly— I just mean that—'

She threw a pine cone in the water. 'Maybe we better start back if we want to be home before dark.'

'No,' he said. 'Let's lie down. Just for a minute.'

He brought handfuls of pine needles and leaves and gray moss. She sucked her knee and watched him. Her fists were tight and it was like she was tense all over.

'Now we can sleep and be fresh for the trip home.'

They lay on the soft bed and looked up at the dark-green pine clumps against the sky. A bird sang a sad, clear song she had never heard before. One high note like an oboe—and then it sank down five tones and called again. The song was sad as a question without words.

'I love that bird,' Harry said. 'I think it's a vireo.'

'I wish we was at the ocean. On the beach and watching the ships far out on the water. You went to the beach one summer—exactly what is it like?'

His voice was rough and low. 'Well—there are the waves. Sometimes blue and sometimes green, and in the bright sun they look glassy. And on the sand you can pick up these little shells. Like the kind we brought back in a cigar box. And over the water are these white gulls. We were at the Gulf of Mexico—these cool bay breezes blew all the time and there it's never baking hot like it is here. Always—'

'Snow,' Mick said. 'That's what I want to see. Cold, white drifts of snow like in pictures. Blizzards. White, cold snow that keeps falling soft and falls on and on and on through all the winter. Snow like in Alaska.'

They both turned at the same time. They were close against each other. She felt him trembling and her fists were tight enough to crack. 'Oh, God,' he kept saying over and over. It was like her head was broke off from her body and thrown away. And her eyes looked up straight into the blinding sun while she counted something in her mind. And then this was the way.

This was how it was.

They pushed the wheels slowly along the road. Harry's head hung down and his shoulders were bent. Their shadows were long and black on the dusty road, for it was late afternoon.

'Listen here,' he said.

'Yeah.'

'We got to understand this. We got to. Do you—any?'

'I don't know. I reckon not.'

'Listen here. We got to do something. Let's sit down.'

They dropped the bicycles and sat by a ditch beside the road. They sat far apart from each other. The late sun burned down on their heads and there were brown, crumbly ant beds all around them.

'We got to understand this,' Harry said.

He cried. He sat very still and the tears rolled down his white face. She could not think about the thing that made him cry. An ant stung her on the ankle and she picked it up in her fingers and looked at it very close.

'It's this way,' he said. 'I never had even kissed a girl before.'

'Me neither. I never kissed any boy. Out of the family.'

'That's all I used to think about—was to kiss this certain girl. I used to plan about it during school and dream about it at night. And then once she gave me a date. And I could tell she meant for me to kiss her. And I just looked at her in the dark and I couldn't. That was all I had thought about—to kiss her—and when the time came I couldn't.'

She dug a hole in the ground with her finger and buried the dead ant.

'Listen here. If you think we ought to we can get married—secretly or any other way.'

Mick shook her head. 'I didn't like that. I never will marry with any boy.'

'I never will marry either. I know that. And I'm not just saying so—it's true.'

His face scared her. His nose quivered and his bottom lip was mottled and bloody where he had bitten it. His eyes were bright and wet and scowling. His face was whiter than any face she could remember. She turned her head from him. Things would be better if only he would just quit talking. Her eyes looked slowly around her—at the streaked red-and-white clay of the ditch, at a broken whiskey bottle, at a pine tree across from them with a sign advertising for a man for county sheriff. She wanted to sit quietly for a long time and not think and not say a word.

'I'm leaving town. I'm a good mechanic and I can get a job some other place. If I stayed home Mother could read this in my eyes.'

'Tell me. Can you look at me and see the difference?'

Harry watched her face a long time and nodded that he could. Then he said:

'There's just one more thing. In a month or two I'll send you my address and you write and tell me for sure whether you're all right.'

'How you mean?' she asked slowly.

He explained to her. 'All you need to write is "O.K." and then I'll know.'

They were walking home again, pushing the wheels. Their shadows stretched out giant-sized on the road. Harry was bent over like an old beggar and kept wiping his nose on his sleeve. For a minute there was a bright, golden glow over everything before the sun sank down behind the trees and their shadows were gone on the road before them. She felt very old, and it was like something was heavy inside her. She was a grown person now, whether she wanted to be or not.

They had walked the sixteen miles and were in the dark alley at home. She could see the yellow light from their kitchen. Harry's house was dark—his mother had not come home. She worked for a tailor in a shop on a side street. Sometimes even on Sunday. When you looked through the window you could see her bending over the machine in the back or pushing a long needle through the heavy pieces of goods. She never looked up while you watched her. And at night she cooked these orthodox dishes for Harry and her.

'Listen here——' he said.

She waited in the dark, but he did not finish. They shook hands with each other and Harry walked up the dark alley between the houses. When he reached the sidewalk he turned and looked back over his shoulder. A light shone on his face and it was white and hard. Then he was gone.

She stood outside the room and watched them. The doorway framed the kitchen like a picture. Inside it was homey and clean.

She went into the room. It was like she had expected them to move back when they saw her and stand around in a circle and look. But they just glanced at her. She sat down at the table and waited.

'Here you come traipsing in after everybody done finished supper. Seem to me like I never will get off from work.'

Nobody noticed her. She ate a big plateful of cabbage and salmon and finished off with junket. It was her Mama she was thinking about. The door opened and her Mama came in and told Portia that Miss Brown had said she found a bedbug in her room. To get out the gasoline.

'Quit frowning like that, Mick. You're coming to the age where you ought to fix up and try to look the best you can. And hold on—don't barge out like that when I speak with you—I mean you to give Ralph a good sponge bath before he goes to bed. Clean his nose and ears good.'

Ralph's soft hair was sticky with oatmeal. She wiped it with a dishrag and rinched his face and hands at the sink. Bill and Hazel finished their game. Bill's long fingernails scraped on the table as he took up the matches. George carried Ralph off to bed. She and Portia were alone in the kitchen.

'Listen! Look at me. Do you notice anything different?'

'Sure I notice, Hon.'

Portia put on her red hat and changed her shoes.

'Well—?'

'Just you take a little grease and rub it on your face. Your nose already done peeled very bad. They say grease is the best thing for bad sunburn.'

She stood by herself in the dark back yard, breaking off pieces of bark from the oak tree with her fingernails. It was almost worse this way. Maybe she would feel better if they could look at her and tell. If they knew.

Her Dad called her from the back steps. 'Mick! Oh, Mick!'

'Yes, sir.'

'The telephone.'

George crowded up close and tried to listen in, but she pushed him away. Mrs. Minowitz talked very loud and excited.

'My Harry should be home by now. You know where he is?'

'No, ma'am.'

'He said you two would ride out on bicycles. Where should he be now? You know where he is?'

'No, ma'am,' Mick said again.

Like Sugar and Claude, Mick and Harry were good friends. Taken by surprise, they found themselves involved in a sexual act. How did the event occur? Of what was it an expression? Does it seem plausible to you that Harry, who "never had even kissed a girl before" would have intercourse with a girl who had "never kissed any boy"?

Although Mick may not have been fully conscious of them, what signs are present—before Mick asks "have you ever swam naked?"—that she is aware of Harry physically and sexually?

"'We got to understand this. We got to. Do you—any?'

"'I don't know. I reckon not,'" Mick replies. What explanation might be given them?

Who was the aggressor? Mick when she dared Harry to take off his bathing suit? Harry when he said "Let's lie down. Just for a minute"?

What in Mick's and Harry's behavior—especially in their effort to curb each other's most impulsive suggestion—makes it probable that the act was neither premeditated nor engineered?

What does the author mean when she says of Mick, "This *excitement* was in her"? What kind of excitement? Is it sexual?

What might the author intend to indicate by the statement: "Maybe it was half an hour they stood there—maybe not more than a minute"? What is the effect of seeing each other naked?

What does the author mean in saying: "It was like her head was broke off from her body and thrown away"?

What are the after-effects of the sexual experience for each? Who seems the more distressed, Harry or Mick? Why? What is Mick most concerned about? With what is Harry concerned?

Which of the characters seems to you the more responsible? More mature? Less self-centered?

Could an experience like this one suddenly happen to anyone? By examining the sequence of observations, feelings, attitudes, behaviors, actions, and reactions in the case of Mick and Harry, what advice could you deduce to pass on to a young daughter or son innocently planning to picnic in the country with a good friend?

RELATED QUESTIONS

To what extent do Harry in **The Heart is a Lonely Hunter** and Rodney in **Peyton Place** (pp. 397, 400) confirm the theory that male sexuality seems to have its own laws, regardless of the norms.

How much of Harry's acute reaction might be traced to his orthodox Jewish upbringing? What light does **Death Wish** (p. 61) shed?

In the Orchard

MURIEL STUART

"I thought you loved me. " "No, it was only fun. "
"When we stood there, closer than all?" "Well, the harvest moon
"Was shining and queer in your hair, and it turned my head."
"That made you?" "Yes." "Just the moon and the light it made
"Under the tree?" "Well, your mouth, too." "Yes, my mouth?"
"And the quiet there that sang like the drum in the booth.
"You shouldn't have danced like that." "Like what?" "So close,
"With your head turned up, and the flower in your hair, a rose
"That smelt all warm." "I loved you. I thought you knew
"I wouldn't have danced like that with any but you."
"I didn't know. I thought you knew it was fun."
"I thought it was love you meant." "Well, it's done." "Yes, it's done.
"I've seen boys stone a blackbird, and watched them drown
"A kitten . . . it clawed at the reeds, and they pushed it down
"Into the pool while it screamed. Is that fun, too?"
"Well, boys are like that . . . Your brothers . . ." "Yes, I know.
"But you, so lovely and strong! Not you! Not you!"
"They don't understand it's cruel. It's only a game."
"And are girls fun, too?" "No, still in a way it's the same.
"It's queer and lovely to have a girl . . ." "Go on."
"It makes you mad for a bit to feel she's your own,
"And you laugh and kiss her, and maybe you give her a ring,
"But it's only in fun." "But I gave you everything."
"Well, you shouldn't have done it. You know what a fellow thinks
"When a girl does that." "Yes, he talks of her over his drinks
"And calls her a—" "Stop that now. I thought you knew."
"But it wasn't with anyone else. It was only you."
"How did I know? I thought you wanted it too.
"I thought you were like the rest. Well, what's to be done?"
"To be done?" "Is it all right?" "Yes." "Sure?" "Yes, but why?"
"I don't know. I thought you were going to cry.
"You said you had something to tell me." "Yes, I know.
"It wasn't anything really . . . I think I'll go."
"Yes, it's late. There's thunder about, a drop of rain
"Fell on my hand in the dark. I'll see you again
"At the dance next week. You're sure that everything's right?"
"Yes." "Well, I'll be going." "Kiss me . . ." "Good night" . . . "Good
    night."

The girl plays at sex, for which she is not ready, because fundamentally she wants love; the boy plays at love for which he is not ready, because he wants sex. How is this theory apparent in Muriel Stuart's poem *In the Orchard?*

How does the boy explain what activated his behavior? What sorts of things does his connotation of "fun" include?

How different was the girl's motivation? What was she going to tell him? Why doesn't she? Should she have? Why, or why not? How might more open and direct communication between members of opposite sexes be encouraged in order to avoid the painful consequences of well-intentioned but meaningless gestures and dissembling?

Was the physical experience sufficient for this boy? Was it enough for the girl? Or must fulfillment for her entail the promise of love and permanence?

Winter Term

SALLIE BINGHAM

It was inconvenient. And worse: Hal watched the woman behind the desk ruffle through filing cards and wondered if she had noticed that he came to the library every evening. She must have noticed, for during the past month he had looked at her so often that he had begun to recognize her dresses and the two ways she fixed her hair. He often felt that she was watching him and Ellie and feeling surprised that they came every night. During the day Hal sometimes planned a new kind of evening, in the library still, for the dancing-and-movie Saturday nights he spent with Ellie were even more stereotyped. Sometimes he imagined that Eleanor would be there when he came, or that she would not be wearing lipstick, as when he had first seen her. He knew that the small change in details could not alter the whole evening. And so in the past week he had begun to imagine the only possible change: that Eleanor would not come at all. Hal planned to wait at the library until a quarter past seven, and then if she had not come he would leave, not pausing to button his coat and turning at once onto the street.

"Why don't you take off your coat?" the librarian asked him. He had never heard her voice before. It was pleasantly colorless, and he was surprised that with such a voice she had spoken to him at all.

"Oh, that's all right," he said vaguely. "I may have to leave in a few minutes." She pulled out another drawer of filing cards and began to go through them from the back. As he watched her Hal became more and more surprised that she had spoken to him. It reminded him that he was still an intruder, even after a month; there were usually only one or two other boys in the library, so few that the girls stared openly. He walked over to the reading room door and looked in; the red-haired boy whom he had begun to speak to on the street was studying with his girl. Eleanor said they were engaged, although Hal pointed out that the girl was not wearing a ring. Eleanor said that it did not really matter: they never went out except with each other, and on Saturdays and Sundays she had seen them having breakfast together in the Waldorf. Hal remembered asking her what they had been eating; it was a new way he had of testing Ellie, to see how long it would be before she laughed; he knew that if he teased her for a certain amount of time she would more probably cry. "French toast," she had answered promptly, "three orders, with maple syrup," and then she had asked him why he had laughed, and when he shook his head and went on laughing her mouth had begun to quiver in the way that made him tighten, and she had asked: "Why do you always laugh at me?" They had had a bad evening. The tightening had started it, Hal knew; he granted that to her in the careless objectivity of his remembering. He wondered if he would ever be able to prevent himself from feeling like that when she didn't laugh with him, or when she was inexplicably depressed, or when she asked him: "What are you thinking?"

He looked at the clock. She was already seven minutes late. It happened every night; he imagined her dawdling over combing her hair, watching the clock and planning not to leave in time. She often warned him against taking each other for granted. Surprised by his own bitterness, he thought, Oh, God, why do I always have to be so hard on her; lately she can't do anything right. He remembered the way he used to feel when she came toward him, running because she was late, or to get in out of the rain; she would shake the rain out of her hair (too vain to wear a scarf), and her face would be flecked with drops. Then her coming had canceled his irritation.

Eleanor came in the door before he could decide when the change had begun. She started toward him, red-faced from the wind she had fought for four blocks. "Hello!" she said, and he knew that if he looked permissive she would have kissed him, in spite of the librarian. It was one of the things that he first liked about her: she was willing to kiss him on the Saturday night subway, when the whole row of people on the other side of the car was watching them. Hal remembered how surprised he had been when they first danced together and she had pulled close; the action did not suit the mild, high-necked dress she was wearing, or even the coolness of her cheek.

She was peeling off her coat and sweater, and he noticed how limberly she bent to unfasten her boots because he was watching. Her figure had improved since she gave up sweets. He remembered proudly that she had started to diet because he had told her once that a dress was too tight; he never had to tell her again. Now her hips were straight under her skirt, and he knew from looking at them how they would feel, very firm as she clenched the big muscles and smooth through her slippery underpants.

They went into the reading room. Hal had grown accustomed to the people who looked up as they walked down the corridor between the tables, but he knew from the way Ellie was smiling they still made her uncomfortable. When they sat down she whispered to him fiercely, "You'd think they'd learn not to stare every night!" and he whispered back, leaning so close her hair touched his mouth, "It's just because you're beautiful."

"You've said that before," she told him, mocking and pleased, but he had already realized it; it did not matter how often he repeated the compliment, for each time the situation was the same, until the lie had become as familiar as the library room. He did not think he would tell Ellie that she was beautiful if they were in a new place, a city or a green park. He looked at the clock.

"Bored?" she asked quickly.

"No." He tried not to frown. She made a little face at him and bent over her notebook.

Hal wished that he had not learned to translate her expressions; when he first met her he had been charmed by her good-humored pout or her wide-eyed expression after they kissed. But now he knew that the pout was made to conceal the quiver in her mouth, and if he watched her he would see that she was not reading; she was staring at the page and trying not to look at him. And as for her expression after they kissed—it always seemed to Hal that he was watching her rise through deep water—he did not know what it meant but it irritated him. It reminded him of the way she acted after they made love. She went into it as exuberantly as she jumped up to dance, she left it to him to make sure that his roommates were out and that the shades were down. By the time he had checked she would have pulled her dress over her head, rumpling her hair in bangs like a little boy's. He began to undress, folding his clothes on the chair—"Ellie, won't you hang up your dress?"—but when he turned around and saw her waiting, naked under her slip, he went to her and forgot what he had been about to say.

But afterward, if she did not cry, she would not let him go. She clenched him in her arms when he tried to get up, and he had to hurt her in order to break away. When she clung to him with her fingernails pricking his back he tried to force himself out of his sleepiness, to smooth her hair and kiss her. But her mouth tasted stale when he was so tired, and he was afraid she might think he wanted to do it again.

"I'm sorry I was late," she said, not looking up from her book, and he realized that for the last five minutes she had been trying to decide why he seemed irritated.

"I thought we said we wouldn't apologize any more." He wanted to sound gay, but he noticed at once that she was still raw to the subject; she said softly: "I wish you could forget that." She was bending down the corner of a page and he wanted to tell her to stop; the little mechanical action irritated him out of all proportion, and he wondered if he was so tense because they hadn't made love for four days. How did she feel about tonight? He knew that his roommates were out. He looked at her, but he could tell from the way she was hunched over her book that she was not thinking about making love but about the evening a week before when they had quarreled and then made a list of resolutions over coffee in The Grill. One of them had been not to apologize to each other any more for they had agreed it was hypocritical: apologies were only dog-in-the-manger ways of saying, I was right all along but I'll give in for the sake of peace. It had been a terrible evening and he wished that they had not gone to The Grill, for before they had both associated it with one of their first evenings together, when he had held her hand between the salt and pepper.

"Oh, I forgot to ask you about the exam." She had not whispered, and the girl at the next table glanced up, frowning. "How was it?"

"Terrible!" The word did not relieve him; he had come back in the winter darkness, coffee-nerved and fingering the three pencils in his pocket whose points were worn flat. He remembered cursing himself for not reviewing more, and he wondered if he could have written at the end of the thin, scratched-out bluebook, "Circumstances beyond my control . . ."

"But I thought you were so well prepared; you've been reviewing for practically a week."

He tried not to say it, but the words promised too much relief: "Yes, but I can't really study here." He knew before he looked at her that she was hurt. As soon as he saw her mouth he felt the tightening; he wanted to laugh out loud and throw his head back and yell with laughter, and at the same time he wanted to pull her into his arms and fold her so tightly that her breath came in gasps and she groaned, Hal, Hal, you're hurting me . . .

"You never told me you couldn't study here," she said, and he knew how carefully she had weeded the hurt out of her voice.

"Well, I mean, what do you expect? How can I concentrate with you around?" He had meant it to be a compliment—he wanted to see her smile, flushing a little and looking up at him—but it sounded like an accusation. As she turned her face sharply away he thought, Oh, God, not another scene! And then he noticed abruptly how thin she had grown; he could see the point of her collarbone through her sweater, and her little breasts stood out almost too sharply.

Ellie had bent down the corner of the page so often that it broke off in her hand. She turned to Hal, smiling brightly. "You should have seen the dormitory tonight." In spite of the new-paint smile, Hal wanted to kiss her for changing the subject. He thought that afterward he would buy her an ice cream cone at the drugstore on the way back to her dormitory. She loved sweets, and she hadn't had any for at least two weeks; he remembered her inexpensive salad dinners, even on Saturdays. And she was really almost too thin.

"You know Wednesday night's usually bad anyway," she was saying. The girl at the next table looked up again, annoyed, and Ellie put her hand to her mouth. She would not have gone on if Hal had not asked, "Well, what happened?" and then she turned to him and whispered so softly, hesitantly that he could hardly hear. "You know Wednesday night is boy night, and they have candles and ice cream for dessert. Just because we eat at a quarter past six instead of six! Tonight I sat at a table with three other girls and their dates and I literally didn't say a word!" Hal had heard it often before; he looked around the room, trying to distract his attention from his own irritation. Why was she proud of not talking for a whole meal? He noticed the pretty girl who was in his humanities class; she was winding a shank of hair around her finger as she studied. Pretty hair. But she looked even more tense than the rest of them. During exam period you could cut the atmosphere in the reading room with a knife. Most of the girls looked overtired and ugly, and they had not bothered to comb their hair. Hal remembered that the library was the one place they had not expected to see any boys. But Eleanor hated the men's library. She said she felt too stared-at when there were so few girls. Hal had seen some of the looks boys gave her when they walked down the corridor, and he agreed. She had such a damn good figure.

"You're not listening," she said. "I know—don't apologize; I shouldn't be bothering you." As though her rigidly calm tone really expressed her feelings, Eleanor neatly wrote the date at the top of a notebook page and began to read.

"I am interested!" he lied, feeling her hurt. "It's just that I'm interested in this place too." She did not answer, and he slammed his book open and turned the pages roughly, looking for his place. They sat for ten minutes in silence. Hal tried to read but he was too conscious of the tip of her elbow, almost touching his; it looked a little chapped, and he remembered how hard the winter weather was on her blond skin. Then he wondered how he had known that—he had been through no other winter with her, or even a spring or summer—and inconsequentially he wondered what she looked like in a bathing suit. He hunched his shoulders and bent closer to the book, trying to force the words into his attention.

There were long, ruler-straight lines under some of the sentences, and minute notes were printed in the margins. He had written them in October, when for a week he had devoted himself to Schopenhauer, reading each page passionately and proud of the learned comments he wrote in the margins. He had even found time to go into town to visit the museum, where there was a portrait of the philosopher, and he remembered how his head had pounded as he climbed the long steps and hurried down the corridor to the door of the room where the portrait hung. It had been a disappointment: an old, placid gentleman in conventional black. Did pessimism embodied look like that, he remembered wondering, like your own grandfather? But he had come back with a feeling of accomplishment.

Now he could not read his own notes. When Ellie was hurt the consciousness of it ticked like a clock at the back of his mind and he could not concentrate on anything. He gave up trying to ignore the point of her elbow. He wondered if she would move first, as she often did, slipping her hand into his or turning into his arms as soon as they were alone or touching the back of his neck. He noticed how rigidly she was sitting; why did they both keep on pretending to study? He looked at the clock. Already half an hour wasted. God, I wish we'd had a chance to so I wouldn't feel like I'm going crazy! Exams—we couldn't afford the time. He remembered how self-righteously they had avoided his room, knowing that once they were there, where they had first told each other that they were in love, their resolution would dissolve in a panic of desire. Their coming together was always too violent, he thought, like the too big lunch you ate after missing breakfast, snatching and tearing at the food if no one was watching. But I bet she needs it now, he thought, that's why she's so quivery, close to tears, and maybe that's why I loused up that exam. He knew it was not an excuse; he felt his resentment heating as he wondered why he had not really reviewed. But she's right: I spent all last week on it, he thought, and then he added, enjoying his own bitterness, Yes, but you know what studying here means, jockeying for position for three hours with our knees always about to touch or our hands, and she's always looking up or else I'm looking at her until finally we give up and hold hands though that means I can't write or else she can't. Why didn't I have sense enough to tell her I had to study; two evenings would have done it . . . but I know she'd cry. Not over the phone but in the booth after I hung up, so she couldn't go back to her room without the other girls seeing she'd been crying. He wanted to turn to her and break the thin, unreal wall of her concentration by asking, Why does everything hurt you too much? And why do I always have to know? Although he knew the last, at least, was not her fault.

He heard eight strike in silver, feminine notes from the clock over the girls' gym. That clock would never let him forget the amount of time he was wasting; all evening he would have to listen to its reproachful chiming. The thought drove him to the peak of his irritation and he slammed his books closed and began to stack them together. Eleanor looked up and he saw the terror in her eyes that he had seen once before when he told her that he would have to go home for the weekend. She had said: "You know that means three days without talking to anyone." And he had answered, trying to laugh: "But there must be someone— all those girls."

"You know I'm not a girl's girl; I don't really know how to talk to them.

And anyway I haven't been spending my extra time in the smoker, so they hardly even know my name." He had understood what she had been unwilling to say, that he had taken up the evenings she might have spent padding herself with girl acquaintances against the time when she would be alone. In the end he had left without telling her goodbye and the weekend had been spoiled because he had known how she was feeling.

He stood up, although he had not decided what he was going to do; only, no more waste. "You want to leave?" she asked hurriedly gathering up her books, and Hal knew that she thought he was going to walk out without her. If she began to cry he would be more than ashamed; he would feel that his hands were as clumsy as trays as he tried to soothe her, and when he struggled to think of something gentle to say he would begin to go mad with irritation. He started toward the reading room door before she was ready, and he heard the almost hysterical ruffling of pages as she closed her books. He waited for her on the other side of the door, and when she came, almost running, he saw her face become young again as she smiled with relief that he was waiting.

"I agree with you; let's get out of this dreary place," she said, and Hal wished that she had been angry.

"Look, I'm going to walk you back now," he said as they went out into the sudden coldness. She began to fumble awkwardly with her scarf, adjusting it inside her coat collar.

"Right now?" Her voice was carefully casual.

"Look, Eleanor, I've got to get something done tonight. Friday's the Phil 101 exam."

"Oh, I understand." They began to walk, conscious of not holding hands. The quadrangle was dark except for the library windows and the illumined clock over the gym. It was always five minutes fast, on purpose, Hal knew, so that the girls who were late starting would still get to class on time. In spite of the clock Ellie was always coming in late; she would drop into the seat beside him, panting, and snatch off her gloves.

"You taking our history class next term?" Ellie asked. He wished that she would not keep her voice cheerful, trying to pretend to him but not to herself that they had not silently quarreled.

"I guess so. You can't divide it." He was ashamed of his grudging tone, although it was easy to justify it; even if he broke with her now and finally (it was incredible, the idea of pushing off her hands and running without hearing her calling), he would still have to see her every Monday, Wednesday and Friday at ten in the history class where they tried not to look at each other.

Her dormitory was full of lights. "At last they've taken down the wreath!" he said.

"And high time!"

Her voice had revived with his cheerfulness—real, this time, although he knew it was ridiculous that the tarnished wreath should have depressed him. It had been a soiled reminder of the Christmas vacation they had spent straining to be together, through long-distance calls, which they spent saying goodbye, and too many letters.

They stood under the porch light and she held out her hands. He took them and slipped his fingers inside her gloves. Her palms were soft and lined.

"Look at the bikes," he said, "you'd think they'd give up in this bad weather," and they both looked out at the heaped, stone snow. He remembered that he had a long walk back, but as he bent hurriedly to kiss her she slipped her arms around him and he had to pull back hard in order to get away. She let go at last and, no longer smiling, she whispered: "Hal, don't go." He hesitated. "Please. Don't go. Please." She was rigidly controlling her voice, but he knew the limit of her endurance and he wanted to be away before she began to cry, for then he would never to able to leave. He would have to stay until she was calm, rocking her in his arms and kissing her hair. Afterward when he walked back to his dormitory he would avoid looking at clocks. But when he was in his room he would see the tin alarm clock that was already set for the morning and then he would throw his books violently into a chair. He would go out and buy coffee so that with luck he could study until three. By that time nearly all of the lights across the courtyard would have gone out, and often it would have begun to snow.

Eleanor was watching him. "About tomorrow," she said lightly, wiping a fleck off one of her books, "I know we both have a lot of work. I'll call you up in the morning and we can decide then. Maybe we ought to study by ourselves tomorrow night." Her voice was so matter-of-fact that if he had not known the pattern Hal would not have believed that next day, when they came to the deciding, she would plead with him to study with her—"Really, I promise, we'll get something done"—and offer to sign a pledge that she would not speak to him for three hours. Now she was looking down and running her fingers along the edges of her books. "Hal," she said, "I'm sorry about tonight. You know how I get sometimes." He put his arms around her, trying not to tell her how sorry he was, trying to choke back his softness. "Oh, God, Ellie," he said, and he heard the almost-tears in his own voice, the rawness that was both tenderness and irritation. She strained up to kiss him and when she opened her mouth he felt tricked, for if he put his tongue between her lips he would not be able to leave. He kissed her, beginning half consciously to forget that he should go. She dropped her books and they tumbled over their feet. He was only vaguely conscious of the porch and the staring light as he pulled her against him, hearing her moan with pain and excitement. Then he drew back and said, his voice already labored: "Isn't there anywhere we can go?" Her face was flushed, reminding him in a twisted way of a child waking up, damp and fresh. She was trying to think of somewhere to go and holding his hands tightly as though she could brace his desire.

"It's too late to have you in the dormitory," she said, and they silently checked their short list of private places. It was too cold for the park—they had been nervous there, on the bench behind the thin screen of shrubbery—and it was too late to go to his room. Parietal rules! He wondered how many people they had forced into marriage. They had talked now and then of renting a room but Hal knew they would never do it; they were still too aware of the connotations. And although they prided themselves on their indifference to surroundings, Ellie's face seemed to reflect the gray walls when they lay together on his bed.

"At least let's get out of this porch light," he said, and they went down the steps and stood hesitating on the sidewalk. She was looking around eagerly and hopefully, and he wondered again how much of her desire was passion and how much grasping; girls used sex to get a hold on you, he knew—it was so easy for them to pretend to be excited.

They wandered down the sidewalk. As they passed the parking lot Eleanor hesitated. "Look, we could—" She did not go on but Hal knew that she meant the cars, the college-girl cars with boxes of tissues and clean seat covers that were parked in the lot behind the dormitories. "All right," he said, knowing that the whole time they would be afraid of someone coming, listening for steps. They walked around the lot, comparing cars, and Ellie was laughing so that he would not think it was sordid. Hal wondered why it had become so easy to accept the back seats of cars and student beds with broken springs. Finally she chose a station wagon, and he felt himself growing more excited as she climbed into the back. He followed her and she turned to him and they sank together down onto the seat. For a moment her willing softness seemed to cancel the whole tense evening. He began to unbutton her blouse, feeling her stiffen and gasp as he traced her breast. Across the quadrangle the gymnasium clock chimed. Nine o'clock. Suddenly violent, he tore her blouse open, and as she whimpered, terrified and trying to push him off, he pulled at her slip. "Stop it, Eleanor, God, stop it," he said when she tried to hold his hands, and as he dragged the straps off her shoulders she began to cry.

Fletcher wrote: "Sex is dynamite. . . . It can be the fiercest cement of a relationship, but it can also be the lever that breaks people apart" [24]. In **Winter Term** does sex act as the "cement," as the "lever," as neither or as both? In what way is it "dynamite"?

How would you assess the comment: Sex as cement or lever has nothing to do with Hal and Ellie's problems. They are simply victims of what Lee (**What Love Must Be,** p. 251) called "the intolerable pressures of the age"?

What appears to be the major change in Hal and Ellie's relationship, dating from the Saturday night when Eleanor kissed Hal on the subway, "when the whole row of people on the other side of the car was watching them"? Is the change due to Ellie, to Hal, to both, to neither? To the dreary rut of college life?

Why is Hal so sensitive to clocks?

Why is Hal unable to enjoy study dates with Ellie?

How might Hal and Ellie react to C. S. Lewis' observation in **Eros** (p. 207) that

> . . . far from aggravating, [Eros] reduces the nagging and addictive character of mere appetite. And that not simply by satisfying it. Eros, without diminishing desire, makes abstinence easier. He tends, no doubt, to a pre-occupation with the Beloved which can indeed be an obstacle to the spiritual life; but not chiefly a sensual preoccupation.

If, as Lee (p. 250) says, "love should be an act of will," why do Hal's testing Ellie, to see how long it would be before she laughed; their resolution not to apologize any more; her offer to sign a pledge that she would not speak to him for three hours prove to be failures? Why is it that rules and bargains of this nature do not work?

How does the theory that the girl plays at sex because what she wants is love, while the boy plays at love because what he wants is sex clarify Hal's indifference to surroundings while "Ellie's face seemed to reflect the gray walls when they lay together on his bed"? Does it explain Ellie's reactions to Hal's at first welcomed advances in the car:

> Suddenly violent, he tore her blouse open, and as she whimpered, terrified and trying to push him off, he pulled at her slip. "Stop it, Eleanor, God, stop it," he said when she tried to hold his hands, and as he dragged the straps off her shoulders she began to cry.

In what ways and areas does Hal understand Ellie? In what ways and areas does Ellie understand Hal? In what ways is each insensitive to the other's human rights, needs and feelings? For example, how would you assess the "terror in her eyes that he had seen once before when he told her that he would have to go home for the weekend"? Is Ellie's reaction a significant comment on the maturity of their relationship?

Hal wondered how much of her desire was passion and how much grasping; "girls used sex to get a hold on you, he knew—it was so easy for them to pretend to be excited." Do you believe that "girls use sex to get a hold" on males? Do you think Ellie is like such females?

How does the fragment of the final scene in the car illumine all their problems and reveal the sources of conflict? Since acts define us, and our sexual acts reveal our personalities, what is it that we already know about Hal and about Ellie that emerges again in the final sentences?

Since they have some good things in their relationship, do you feel that Hal and Ellie's future is salvageable? Possibly permanent? How? What would each have to learn, and/or be willing to change?

RELATED QUESTIONS

Which males in selections you have read would most firmly insist that "girls use sex to get a hold on you—it [is] so easy for them to pretend to be excited"? What convincing evidence could they give?

Which females in selections you have read share Ellie's objections indicated in the final car scene of **Winter Term?**

It has been noted (p. 270) that

> When emphasis beyond a certain point is placed upon technique in sexuality, the person finds that he has separated himself all the more from . . . his own spontaneity and joy and the surging up of his own experience of potency.

How does this judgment—evident in Rabbit's diminution of sexual urge when Janice focused on the "how's" of intercourse in **Rabbit, Run** (p. 430)—apply to the rules, regulations, and strictures which Hal and Ellie introduce into their relationship? How is the truth of the judgment phrased as a poetic warning in Kennedy's **Ars Poetica** (see "**Night-Lights,**" p. 571)?

In what ways is Hal an older edition of Jean-Christophe (p. 63), or of Theodore, the Bulpington of Blup (p. 45) who suffered "from the powerful, perplexing influence of heightened sexual awareness"?

Theodore in **The Bulpington of Blup,** knew about the "sublimating genius," fantasy. Does Hal? What forms of sublimation does he use? What forms might he have tried?

To which of Kirkendall's questions for judging premarital sex standards (**Searching for the Roots of Moral Judgments,** p. 298) could Ellie and Hal answer "yes"?

may i feel said he

E. E. CUMMINGS

may i feel said he
(i'll squeal said she
just once said he)
it's fun said she

(may i touch said he
how much said she
a lot said he)
why not said she

(let's go said he
not too far said she
what's too far said he
where you are said she)

may i stay said he
(which way said she
like this said he
if you kiss said she

may i move said he
is it love said she)
if you're willing said he
(but you're killing said she

but it's life said he
but your wife said she
now said he)
ow said she

(tiptop said he
don't stop said she
oh no said he)
go slow said she

(cccome?said he
ummm said she)
you're divine!said he
(you are Mine said she)

How would the partners in *may i feel said he* answer the high school boy who asked: "Do you think a person should enjoy sexual intercourse during the act"? Do they?

Is his conclusion, "you're divine!" any more logical than her "you are Mine"? Why, or why not? How did each come to such a conclusion?

One writer suggests:

> The name of the game is touch-and-go. For sex just for fun cannot be serious; it cannot require a lifelong commitment; it implies no responsibility.
> The sex-as-play concept constitutes the central core of much erotic or pornographic writing. [25]

Is Cummings' poem "erotic or pornographic"?

Are there signs that the couple have more than a sort of genital harmony? Are there evidences of genuine respect? Liking? Affection? Understanding of each other?

Since, as Montaigne observed in his *Essays:*

> Nature in mockery left us the most troublesome of our actions, the most common: thereby to equal us, and without distinction to set the foolish and the wise, us and the beasts all in one rank: no barrell better herring, [26]

what difference does the choice of sexual object make?

Would you agree with a statement attributed to George Bernard Shaw that love is based on a gross exaggeration of the differences between one girl and another, and that, therefore, sexuality should glorify the instinct rather than emphasizing the object since "all women are the same in the dark" [27]?

Can sexual pleasure be justified as an end in itself? Under what circumstances?

How would you answer her question: "is it love?"

Does Cummings heed the admonition of C. S. Lewis in **Eros** that "we must not be totally serious about Venus"?

Might C. S. Lewis support the behavior of the couple in **may i feel said he** because they exemplify the "Brother Ass" view of the body expressed by St. Francis (in **Eros,** p. 209):

> . . . give me St. Francis for my money. *Ass* is exquisitely right because no one in his senses can either revere or hate a donkey. It is a useful, sturdy, lazy, obstinate, patient, lovable and infuriating beast. . . . So the body. There's no living with it till we recognise that one of its functions in our lives is to play the part of the buffoon.

RELATED QUESTIONS

Would Lowen (**Love and Orgasm,** p. 194) feel that the two in **may i feel said he** had reduced love to lust? Would Lewis (**Eros,** p. 205) think it mattered? Do you? Why?

How does Howard Moss in **Rain** (see "**Night-Lights,**" p. 579) take exception to the philosophy of the couple in **may i feel said he?**

A Night of Watching

ELLIOTT ARNOLD

. . . Arne Johansen and Lili Lund were lying naked in bed in a small flat overlooking one of the harbors in the city. For quite a little while now they had contemplated each other's bodies in the morning light, remembering pleasantly how those bodies had pleasured each other, Lili remembering as though her body was separate from her, as separate and removed as was his, an instrument she put to use.

Lili Lund was a creamy-skinned Norwegian twenty-five years old, perhaps a year or two older, but no more. She was from a very good family; her father, now in a prison camp in Stavanger, had been an important Norwegian industrialist. Her mother was related to Swedish nobility. She was tall and slender, with an oval face, a cleft chin and the eyes of a Siamese cat. The eyes were always watchful, lustrous, lazy, waiting, all somehow at the same time. She had a low voice and the accents of her upbringing and education; she was an attractive woman but she possessed something more than beauty, a quality that drew men, made them turn away from more beautiful women to look at her, react to her, remember her.

There was that in her face, in those aware eyes, in the broad, rich mouth, that said she considered sex fun, not a commitment, not necessarily a romance, perhaps better not a romance, emotions could interfere, nothing but astounding, marvelous, unequalled fun, certain fun, something to be totally enjoyed; more, something she was ready to enjoy at any time, at any place, in any way, and afterward, if that was the way it was, to wiggle a hand, to smile and walk away. And the greatest charm of all about Lili Lund was that when all this invitation and promise was put to the test she demonstrated that, if anything, she had understated herself.

She felt Arne move. It was not even a movement, it was something inside.

"You're restless," she said, knowing now that the change had come over him, that what had happened had passed on; he was able to hold onto it for just so long and then his mind lashed out and the tension was there again, as though he were alone in a jungle.

He pushed himself up with one arm, reaching over her to the bedside table for a cigarette. Her body was nothing to him now, something between him and a smoke.

"It's always that way," she said, reaching for a match, striking it, holding it out for him, seeing the tight, contained face, the muscles that corrugated his belly, the twisting torso, the chest, the body that had taken her the long distance and now had left her. "When it's over, a woman wants to get closer and a man wants to get away."

"You know. You know all about that," he said.

"Only you're not like anybody else. I can feel it creeping up. I could give it a name."

The cigarette curled smoke past his gray eyes. "What would you call it?" he asked indifferently.

"Lots of things. Fear. Loneliness. The enemy. Life."

"All of those?"

"Give me time. I could turn up some more but they'd all mean the same thing."

He lay back in the bed, disinterested, and somehow it was as though he was across the room. She thought how much of a stranger he was, how close he came and how far he went. That was part of it, not being able to hold.

Arne Johansen was not quite twenty-three. He was not small, five feet seven or eight, but he was built compactly, assembled with the economy of a watch, a ship, a fine gun. He moved thriftily and he seemed smaller than he was. The surprise about his face was his hair, a bright, true red. He didn't have the rest of the face to go with that. His light eyes appeared lighter under the hair; they could become so pale they seemed transparent.

"I don't know you," she said, trying to hold to something, knowing she couldn't, finding pleasure in the futile effort.

"Nothing to know."

"I don't know you at all."

"Nobody knows anybody."

"I know that, but with you it's more. Even now it's as though you're not here. I feel more alone than if you weren't."

He twisted his head and there was something about his mouth, something unexpected. "I'm sorry, Lili."

"No." She touched his lips. "I suppose when it goes so far one way, it has to go that far the other way, every way. How long do we know each other?"

"Four weeks, five."

"And I don't know you at all."

"You're the mystery."

"I? I'm as wide open as a barn door."

"A woman like you, taking up with me."

"What is a woman like me?"

"I used to read about women like you—society, the money, everything that goes with it. Sometimes when I see you somewhere, waiting for me, dressed up, I still can't believe the way it is."

She grinned. "Only when I'm dressed. The rest of the time you know."

He looked at her for a moment. "What do you want of me?"

"You'd know that better than anyone."

"Only that?"

"Until I can think of something better. And I've tried and I can't."

She watched him smoke the cigarette; his movements had frugality. They were controlled and nothing was wasted and they finished what they set out to do and nothing more. Maybe that's what made it so complete, to see all that management explode and break apart.

"You're worse than I am," she said.

"Worse how?"

"It goes away from me for a little while, a little while anyway. It comes back but it does go away. It goes away from you too, but not far, and then it's back, only it's something else, not us. Maybe it never really goes away at all."

"Wasn't it any good? Was it that bad?"

"You're beautiful," she said, feeling it inside her again, talking about it to him, he could bring it back faster than it had ever been brought back before and it never had taken long. "You're beautiful and it's always beautiful and when you come in me it makes me want to cry, but it doesn't stay with you, not even long enough for you to get off me sometimes; sometimes before you get off me you're back like a knot."

She looked at the red hair. It was wrong. The red hair was an after thing and he was always before.

"Why is that?" she asked, still trying to hold. "What I just said. Why doesn't it last a little longer?"

He leaned over her again, putting out the cigarette. She kissed his belly.

"I don't care," she said, pressing her cheek against his skin. "I ask questions but I don't really care. I'm always so damned frightened and those are the only times when it all doesn't seem such hell, and I'm trying to spread it a little, like now, with you next to me and we just did it and maybe we'll have time to do it again, maybe we'll have time and you'll feel like it before the world moves in again. That's all I have, Arne, that and you and here. It's what you do for me. You keep the world away."

After a moment he asked, "Have you heard anything about your father?"

"They tell me he's alive."

"That's something."

"I get so frightened when I go to Dagmar House. After the way it was at home I just have to look at them, the ones in the black uniforms especially, and it's all there again."

She shivered slightly. He drew her closer to him and pulled up the cover. "Fuck them," he said. "As the British say."

"I'm so afraid of them," she said in a low voice. "Every time I go there and try to find out something, and it doesn't go away until we're together and it doesn't go all the way away until we make love and then it's as though for a moment we defeated everything else."

He stroked her body. She stretched slightly and closed her eyes.

"That's the answer," she said, her body responding as the strings of a cello, giving off a rich music, the eyes half opening now and the mouth called back from wherever it had gone, everything returning, readying. "That's the whole answer. Wouldn't it be wonderful if this were really all there was, that the damned fighting would get itself over with and this would be all there was?"

"You women," he said. "All you think about. You think that's all there is."

"Isn't it? Is there anything you'd rather do now?"

"Now isn't all the time."

"No it isn't and it never could be, but it's lovely to think about it." She felt his hand go away and the protection was gone. "Do you think it will ever end, Arne, the war?"

"Has to. They always do."

"And my father. Will I see him again?"

"Probably."

She shook her head suddenly. "Oh, this damned war, this damned, damned war."

"Ah, things aren't so bad. Business is good. Germans buy anything we offer."

She looked at him and chuckled unexpectedly. "I always find it funny. You, a silk salesman."

"Why is that funny?"

"I don't know. There's nothing of a silk salesman about you."

"What do you think would suit me better?"

"I don't know. Every once in a while I seem to feel something. I don't know. Sometimes it frightens me."

"You just said I took that away."

"You do, the other kind, the world kind. But yours is something else. I'm not saying I mind it. It's exciting. When I think of you doing dangerous things, almost getting killed, I can feel it, I can feel it right here." She took his hand and placed it flat on her thighs. "Here. I can feel it start here and then move up."

"I must seem pretty sorry when you come down to earth again."

She ran her hand through his hair, pushing it back from his eyes. "There's a fire there. They ought to give the Blaze a rest and give you a try. I think you could make him look like a schoolboy."

"We're on that now."

She kissed him and pressed her body against his. "I've got a flame of my own, Arne. Please do something."

"You never get enough, do you?"

"Don't blame me for that. Whoever put the parts together, blame him. Please, Arne."

"Lili, we had all night."

"I know, but it's started again. You know how I'll be all day. I'll go crazy. Here, let me do something for you. Here. How does that feel? Oh, I can tell."

"Yes," he said.

"Then do something to me. Anywhere. Anything. Start anywhere and make a slow trip."

The telephone rang.

She seized his wrist as he reached out. "Don't answer it."

"Yes," he said into the mouthpiece. "Good. I'll be over."

There was a click on the other end and Arne cradled the receiver. He tossed aside the cover and swung over her. She made no move to stop him, knowing he was already gone.

"Who was that?" she asked, knowing it was going to be a bad day.

"Pal of mine down the store," he said, getting dressed. "Some new stuff just came in from Sweden and he was tipping me off. I'll get down there and get some of it before the other salesmen gobble it up. Can't get enough of that material. The supermen keep sending it home to their superwomen. Maybe I can scrounge a piece for you."

"Did you ever study dancing?" she asked. "You can't make a wrong move. It's all in such order."

"Keep that to yourself." He smiled, slipping into his jacket. "Silk salesman is bad enough. But a silk salesman who moves like a dancer." He rolled his eyes.

"When will I see you?"

"Can't tell exactly."

"You don't have to go out of town today?"

"I won't know until I look at my book."

He was dressed now, moving toward the door. Taking himself, she thought, to catch up with himself, wherever that was.

"Aren't you going to kiss me good-bye?"

He returned to the bed, moving lightly, like a dancer, like a boxer coming out of his corner, silk salesman my foot, but was he, could he be, that Buhle, suspicions crawling around in his head like worms, what a world, what a miserable world, just to remain alive, just to remain alive and without pain.

She took his face between her hands and kissed him gently on the lips. "You've made up for so much."

He nodded. That expression, she thought, she rarely saw it and it was something to see, his face unlocked the way it was at the big moment and seldom any time else and look at it now. Oh God, this awful, awful world.

"Hurry back," she said. She watched him go.

She lay back on the bed touching herself. Because it's close, that close, she told him. They all of them had that, the boys in Norway, nothing about them alike except that, the closeness to the truth. And with them it was lying with it, as close as they were, almost going and not going and having it when they finally went, dying with them, each time, the supreme coming, the supreme, final, ultimate coming, and touching with their new world, briefly, fleetingly, just the fingertips reaching out and meeting and then the vision and the peace.

Arne was different, her hand moving. But they were all different. But he was the closest. It was in everything he did and with him the fingertips had touched from the beginning.

. . . she possessed something more than beauty, a quality that drew men. . . . There was that in her face, in those aware eyes, in the broad, rich mouth, that said she considered sex fun, not a commitment, not necessarily a romance, perhaps better not a romance, emotions could interfere, nothing but astounding, marvelous, unequalled fun, certain fun, something to be totally enjoyed.

Why would love spoil the game for Lili?

Given Lili's concept of sex-as-fun, how would you account for her view of her own body as "an instrument she put to use"? What else could it be?

Why can sex-as-fun thrive only under rather special circumstances? Why must it be, in any case, temporary and short-lived?

It has been noted that even under these conditions

. . . such social, if not truly emotional relationships, may be quite different from sheer fun: they may be a refuge from loneliness, an antidote to alienation, a reassurance for some ego hurt. [28]

Which of these uses of sex seem relevant to Lili's needs?

What common denominator makes "Fear. Loneliness. The enemy. Life . . . and some more" that Lili "could turn up . . . all mean the same thing"? What illusion might it create? Where does Lili explain the comfort sex provides?

Are Lili and Arne "sexual performers," as the quotation from Lowen (p. 408) defines them? Why, or why not?

Do you concur with their separation of love and sex?

What does Lili mean in saying that with Arne "the fingertips had touched from the beginning"?

In what ways do Lili and Arne resemble the couple in Cummings' *may i feel said he* (p. 475)?

Lili says, "When it's over, a woman wants to get closer and a man wants to get away." Is this a sound generalization about the difference in male and female sexuality? Is it borne out by Rabbit's behavior with Ruth in *Rabbit, Run* (p. 412)? By other sexual partners who have appeared in these readings?

The Mandarins

SIMONE DE BEAUVOIR

. . . In his imagination he was lying on a beach of soft, white sand, looking out upon the blue sea and calmly thinking of times gone by, of faraway friends. He was delighted at being alone and free. He was completely happy.

At four in the morning, he once again found himself in the red living room. Many of the guests had already gone and the rest were preparing to leave. In a few moments he would be alone with Paula, would have to speak to her, caress her.

"Darling, your party was a masterpiece," Claudie said, giving Paula a kiss. "And you have a magnificent voice. If you wanted to, you could easily be one of the sensations of the postwar era."

"Oh," Paula said gaily, "I'm not asking for that much."

No, she didn't have any ambition for that sort of thing. He knew exactly what she wanted: to be once more the most beautiful of women in the arms of the most glorious man in the world. It wasn't going to be easy to make her change her dream. The last guests left; the studio was suddenly empty. A final shuffling on the stairway, and then steps clicking in the silent street. Paula began gathering up the glasses that had been left on the floor.

"Claudie's right," Henri said. "Your voice is still as beautiful as ever. It's been so long since I last heard you sing! Why don't you ever sing any more?"

Paula's face lit up. "Do you still like my voice? Would you like me to sing for you sometimes?"

"Certainly," he answered with a smile. "Do you know what Anne told me? She said you ought to begin singing in public again."

Paula looked shocked. "Oh, no!" she said. "Don't speak to me about that. That was all settled a long time ago."

"Well, why not?" Henri asked. "You heard how they applauded; they were all deeply moved. A lot of clubs are beginning to open up now, and people want to see new personalities."

Paula, interrupted him. "No! Please! Don't insist. It horrifies me to think of displaying myself in public. Please don't insist," she repeated pleadingly.

"It horrifies you?" he said, and his voice sounded perplexed. "I'm afraid I don't understand. It never used to horrify you. And you don't look any older, you know; in fact, you've grown even more beautiful."

"That was a different period of my life," Paula said, "a period that's buried forever. I'll sing for you and for no one else," she added with such fervor that Henri felt compelled to remain silent. But he promised himself to take up the subject again at the first opportunity.

There was a moment of silence, and then Paula spoke.

"Shall we go upstairs?" she asked.

Henri nodded. "Yes," he said.

Paula sat down on the bed, removed her earrings, and slipped her rings off her fingers. "You know," she said, and her voice was calm now, "I'm sorry if I seemed to disapprove of your trip."

"Don't be silly! You certainly have the right not to like traveling, and to say so." Henri replied. The fact that she had scrupulously stifled her remorse all through the evening made him feel ill at ease.

"I understand perfectly your wanting to leave," she said. "I even understand your wanting to go without me."

"It's not that I want to."

She cut him off with a gesture. "You don't have to be polite." She put her hands flat on her knees and, with her eyes staring straight ahead and her back very straight, she looked like one of the infinitely calm priestesses of Apollo. "I never had any intention of imprisoning you in our love. You wouldn't be you if you weren't always looking for new horizons, new nourishment." She leaned forward and looked Henri squarely in the face. "It's quite enough for me simply to be necessary to you."

Henri did not answer. He wanted neither to dishearten nor encourage her. "If only I had something against her," he thought. But no, not a single grievance, not a complaint.

Paula stood up and smiled; her face became human again. She put her hands on Henri's shoulders, her cheek against his. "Could you get along without me?"

"You know very well I couldn't."

"Yes, I know," she said happily. "Even if you said you could, I wouldn't believe you."

She walked toward the bathroom. It was impossible not to weaken from time to time and speak a few kind words to her, smile gently at her. She stored those treasured relics in her heart and extracted miracles from them whenever she felt her faith wavering. "But in spite of everything, she knows I don't love her any more," he said to himself for reassurance. He undressed and put on his pajamas. She knew it, yes, but as long as she didn't admit it to herself it meant nothing. He heard a rustle of silk, then the sound of running water and the clinking of glass, those sounds which once used to make his heart pound. "No, not tonight, not tonight," he said to himself uneasily. Paula appeared in the doorway, grave and nude, her hair tumbling over her shoulders. She was nearly as perfect as ever, but for Henri all her splendid beauty no longer meant anything. She slipped in between the sheets and, without uttering a word, pressed her body to his. He could find no pretext to repulse her. In an instant she began breathing ecstatically, pressing herself ever more tightly against him. He began caressing her shoulders, her familiar flanks, and he felt the blood flow into his sex. "Well, so much the better," he thought. Paula was in no mood to be satisfied with a peck on the brow, and it would take a lot less time satisfying her than offering explanations. He kissed her burning mouth which, as always, opened greedily at the touch of his lips. But after a moment Paula withdrew her lips slightly, and, embarrassed, he heard her murmuring old endearments he never spoke to her now.

"Am I still your beautiful wisteria vine?"

"Now and always."

"And do you love me?" she said, placing her hand around his swollen sex. "Do you really still love me?"

He did not have the courage at that moment to provoke a scene, he was resigned to avow anything—and Paula knew it. "Yes, I do."

"Do you belong to me?"

"To you alone."

"Tell me you love me, say it."

"I love you."

She uttered a long moan of satisfaction. He embraced her violently, smothered her mouth with his lips, and to get it over with as quickly as possible immediately penetrated her. Inside her it was red, a deep dark red as in the too-red living room. She began to groan and to utter words and phrases the way she used to. But in those days, Henri's love shielded her; her cries, groans, laughs, bites were sacred offerings. Tonight he was lying atop a frenzied woman who spoke obscene words and whose scratches hurt. He was horrified by her and by himself. Her head bent back, her eyes half-closed, her teeth bared, she had given herself so totally to love, was so frightfully lost, that he felt like slapping her to bring her back to earth, felt like saying. "It's just you and I and we're making love, that's all." It seemed to him as if he were raping a dead woman, or a lunatic, and yet he could not keep himself from enjoying it. When finally he fell limp on Paula, he heard a triumphant moan.

"Are you happy?" she murmured.

"Of course."

"I'm so terribly happy!" Paula exclaimed, looking at him through shining tear-brimmed eyes. He hid her unbearably bright face against his shoulder. "The almond trees will be in bloom . . . " he said to himself, closing his eyes. "And there'll be oranges hanging from the orange trees."

Is Paula one of those females who "use sex to get a hold on you"? Or, in this case, use it to keep a hold on you?

As sex moves out of love, should people face up honestly? What might have happened had Henri told Paula how his feelings have changed?

Is Henri being hypocritical? Cowardly? Considerate of her dream and need to be "the most beautiful of women in the arms of the most glorious man in the world"? Convinced that being explicit is unnecessary since Paula, "in spite of everything, knows [Henri] doesn't love her any more"?

In this case, would you agree with Hawthorne that "a lie is never good, even though death threatens on the other side"?

If Paula's "splendid beauty no longer meant anything," and if "it seemed to him as if he were raping a dead woman, or a lunatic," why could he not keep himself from enjoying it? Has it become merely the sex-as-fun game played by Lili and Arne in *A Night of Watching* (p. 477)?

What makes people fall *out* of love, seemingly without reason, when, as Henri confesses, "if only I had something against her... But no, not a single grievance, not a complaint"?

Does Henri's sexual performance truly convince Paula that he loves her? Do you feel his answers to her questions reassure her? Is she genuinely happy? Or simply trying to deceive herself, to protect herself against the realization that she is no longer "necessary" to him?

RELATED QUESTIONS

What comment might Lindbergh offer about the relationship between Henri and Paula as inferred from *Double-Sunrise* (p. 232)?

Carnal Knowledge

THOM GUNN

Even in bed I pose: desire may grow
More circumstantial and less circumspect
Each night, but an acute girl would suspect
That my self is not like my body, bare.
I wonder if you know, or knowing, care?
You know I know you know I know you know.

I am not what I seem, believe me, so
For the magnanimous pagan I pretend
Substitute a forked creature as your friend.
When darkness lies without a roll or stir
Flaccid, you want a competent poseur.
I know you know I know you know I know.

Cackle you hen, and answer when I crow.
No need to grope: I'm still playing the same
Comical act inside the tragic game.
Yet things perhaps are simpler: could it be
A mere tear-jerker void of honesty?
You know I know you know I know you know.

Leave me. Within a minute I will stow
Your greedy mouth, but will not yet to grips.
'There is a space between the breast and lips.'
Also a space between the thighs and head,
So great, we might as well not be in bed.
I know you know I know you know I know.

I hardly hoped for happy thoughts, although
In a most happy sleeping time I dreamt

We did not hold each other in contempt.
Then lifting from my lids night's penny weights
I saw that lack of love contaminates.
You know I know you know I know you know.

Abandon me to stammering, and go;
If you have tears, prepare to cry elsewhere—
I know of no emotion we can share,
Your intellectual protests are a bore
And even now I pose, so now go, for
I know you know.

What does "carnal knowledge" connote? What does the poet mean that "lack of love contaminates"? What does "a forked creature" is her friend suggest? Why is the carnal pose a "comical act inside the tragic game"?

From the last lines in each of the six stanzas, how much can be concluded concerning what is known and by whom? Does the poet's admission, "And even now I pose," thereby negate the sentiments expressed in the first five stanzas? Is it impossible to break the circular reasoning and discover the core of truth?

Does the poet by his very ambiguity confirm Fletcher's view that "sex is dynamite"? That sexual desire is deceptive?

RELATED QUESTIONS

Which of the final lines might have been spoken by Henri in reference to his situation with Paula in **The Mandarins** (p. 482)? Would Henri agree that "lack of love contaminates" a relationship? Would the couple in **may i feel said he** (p. 475)? Would Lili or Arne in **A Night of Watching** (p. 477)?

Philander Musing
JUDSON JEROME

NO WORDS: I swallow this, as you,
no doubt, are swallowing last words, too.
But, dear, had you not known, I might
have juggled a dozen loves. Delight
for you in being grasped and flung;
for me, a game of staying young
by keeping all those shapes in air—
and if none knew, why, none would care.

Knowledge is evil: now what I know
of how you twinge behind your show
of ease, and how you bite to cling,
contemptuous of the bitten thing,
unwilling, though, to let it go . . .

How can we love, with what we know?
How painful to shred all and then
laboriously build deceits again!

Is the girl in *Philander Musing* more miserable with the knowledge or without it, as her conflict is presented in the second stanza? If she is contemptuous of the "bitten thing" why is she unwilling to let it go?

Philander asks, "how can we love, with what we know?" Do you think he really loved before the truth came out? What assumption does Philander make about love when he reasons:

How painful to shred all and then
laboriously build deceits again!

What is a philanderer? Does the definition help to explain his philosophy of love?

As detailed in the sixth line of the first stanza, how does Philander characterize love?

How deep and satisfying do you consider the "delight" he thinks girls find in love?

In his contemplation of the possibility of juggling "a dozen loves," what attitude does Philander reveal toward the human worth of an individual?

RELATED QUESTIONS

In Donald Hall's poem "Philander" (p. 374) is the motivation of the central character the same as in *Philander Musing?*

If you feel that Henri should have been truthful with Paula in *The Mandarins* (p. 482), how would you argue against the rationale for deceit in *Philander Musing?*

Too Late the Phalarope

ALAN PATON

When I reached my home I was calm and quiet, and I must have kissed Nella with especial tenderness, for I could see at once that she was touched.

—A fire, I said.

—I thought you'd be cold, Pieter.

She felt my hands.

—You are cold, she said.

I saw that she was solicitous for me, but nervous, and for that I was ashamed.

—Coffee, she said.

I smiled at her, and suddenly she was weeping. I took her in my arms, and she clung to me hungrily, like a child taken back into affection.

—Why are you weeping, I asked.

—Because . . .

—Yes.

—Because you smiled at me.

—I'm sorry, I whispered, I'm sorry.

—I try to love you, she said. I try every way to love you. I pray to love you more. Then . . .

—Yes, I whispered.

—You shut me out.

I held her close to me, confessing it without words. Then she drew away from me, and wiped her eyes.

—Let's have the coffee, she said.

I sat down by the fire, and she came and put the tray on the floor, and drew the small footstool against my knees, and sat on it, attending to the coffee. Then suddenly she looked up at me.

—Remember, she said.

Yes, I remembered, for so had we sat the first time I had ever touched her, in the courtship that had been so shy and simple, advancing day by day, week by week, by a word or a look, or by the accidental brushing of a hand, long enough and yet not long enough, so that it might be meant and might not be meant, so that I could lie awake afterwards and wonder, was it meant, or was it not? Our courtship was like that, long and shy and protracted; some people said it was the times, but it was not only the times, it was also our natures. I had put my hand on her shoulders, shy and my heart beating, almost as though I had made some mistake and had meant to put them somewhere else, and might take them away at any moment. Then suddenly she had put up her own, and drawn mine down to her breasts, and so astonishing was this action from one so timid and gentle, that I had buried my face in her hair, but she would have none of it, and turned up her face to my own, so that after the fashion of those times we had agreed at once to be married.

As I thought of it now I caught my breath suddenly, to think that I should have turned from that guileless boy into the grave and sombre man, not proud and self-possessed as the world took him to be, but full of unnameable desires and penitences, of resolves and defeats, not understanding himself, withdrawing and cold and silent, a creature of sorrow and evil. Why had it come about? Some people said that boys should grow up wild, and they would settle down into model husbands and fathers. Would that have been better for me?

But my upbringing could hardly have been otherwise, with a father and mother such as I had had, one strict and stern, and the other tender and loving; for one I could never openly have disobeyed, and the other I could never knowingly have hurt. My father had a code about women, as strict and stern as himself, and once I had heard him say, in a company where I was by many years the youngest, that he had never touched a woman, as a man touches a woman, other than his wife, nor had he ever desired to do so.

I remembered it well, for the company had been telling rough stories; then suddenly there was a lull, and my father suddenly said this thing, naturally and simply, as though it were a fitting part of the conversation. I felt a sudden pride, I remember, and a sudden feeling of love for him, and for his strength and certitude: and a feeling of envy too, and wonder that I was otherwise. And as he was, so was my brother Frans; but Frans was gentle and simpler, more like my mother, and every thought he ever had could be seen in his very face, even if he did not speak it.

Then I thought I had perhaps been too obedient as a boy, too anxious to please and win approval, so that I learned to show outwardly what I was not within. Yet I was no mother's son, but could shoot and ride with them all. I can still remember, when we were all at the farm Vredendal, that my mother's cousin Hester took me suddenly into her arms and said, Pieter, you come like a wind into the house.

But perhaps when you were too obedient, and did not do openly what others did, and were quiet in the church and hardworking at school, then some unknown rebellion brewed in you, doing harm to you, though how I do not understand.

—You're quiet, Pieter. What are you thinking?

And I thought, what I am thinking would frighten the wits from your mind and the peace from your eyes, and I would tell it if I could.

—I was thinking, I said with part of the truth, of what you told me to remember.

And I would have liked to remind her of it, by slipping my hands down to her breasts, but could not do it, because something had gone wrong with it, and it would embarrass her now, here in a lighted room. She put her head back on my knees, and I put my hand on her cheek and throat.

—How did the new dominee preach, she asked.

—Well, I said.

—I am thinking, Pieter, she said with her eyes shut and her voice earnest, that I need to be better, not to worry, worry, worry, but to trust in God's providence.

And my voice caught in my throat, and I said to her, you need to be better?

—Yes, I, Pieter. When you're down, and I get down, there's no help in either of us. It grieves me to see you down.

—Does it, liefste?

—Yes. I want to help you, to get you out of the mood. But if I'm down, you think only that I'm angry, and being sorry for myself, and you hate me for it, don't you, Pieter?

I bent down and pressed my face against hers with sudden fierceness and penitence.

—I couldn't hate you, I said. Only sometimes I'm grieved for you.

—Shall we go to bed, she whispered.

I smiled at her invitation in grave agreement, for such a thing had never been a jest between us.

—Do you want to, I said.

—Yes, she whispered.

Up in the room she prayed for a long time, much longer than usual. After a while I stood up and watched her, knowing for what she prayed, for the black moods and the angers and the cold withdrawals that robbed her of the simple joys of her quiet and humble life. I said to myself, God listen to her, God listen to her, ask and it shall be given, knock and it shall be opened, search and it shall be found, before the gift and the opening and the finding are too late.

In the bed she turned on her side and pressed against me and pulled my head down to her own, and kissed me on eyes and mouth and cheeks, with a kind of fierce protection, and touched me as she knew I hungered to be touched by her, and put my hand on her breasts, and pressed the tresses of her hair against my eyes and lips, and yielded herself to me with all the childlike arts of love; and finished, curled up away from me but pressed close and sighed with happiness and content. And I lay against her, pressing my face against her hair.

After a time I said to her, are you asleep?

—Nearly, she said.

—Why did you say, the other day, you couldn't go over it all again?

She made no answer, and I spoke quickly to reassure her, as though if I did not she might fly away.

—It was this that I meant, I said.

I raised myself up on my elbow, and looked down at her.

—You think I'm talking of physical things, I said, but I'm not. It's all together, the body and mind and soul, between a man and a woman. When you love me as you've done, I'm comforted in them all. And when I love you as I've done, it's you I love, your body and mind and soul. I'm healed, strengthened, I'll live my life as it's appointed, without the black moods and the angers.

I stopped and could not go on; but I wanted to go on, and she knew enough to know that.

—Yes, Pieter.

I knew that I was taking her again into the world that she feared, foolishly, not knowing it was the same world where she was safe and sure, not knowing that it could be yet safer and surer, but fearing it because she feared some foolish unknown that was not there at all. But it was urgent, and it must be done, and if not now and in this kind of place and at this kind of time, then never at all.

So I said to her, if you could love me more often, I'd be safe, I said.

She turned over towards me.

—Safe? Against what, Pieter?

—Against anything, my love. Against fear and danger. And the black moods.

I wanted to say, against temptation, I wanted to say, against the thing that tempts me, the thing I hate; I wanted to tell her every word, to strip myself naked before her, so that she could see the nature of the man she loved, with all his fears and torments, and be filled by it with such compassion as would heal and hold him forever.

—I pray to be made more patient and understanding, she said.

And I wanted to cry out at her that I could not put the body apart from the soul, and that the comfort of her body was more than a thing of the flesh, but was also a comfort of the soul, and why it was, I could not say, and why it should be, I could not say, but there was in it nothing that was ugly or evil, but only good. But how can one find such words?

So I said to her, I love you for that, but I ask no more than you have given me tonight.

And she was at once silent, and she was unsure, because of some idea she had, some idea that was good and true but twisted in some small place, that the love of the body, though good and true, was apart from the love of the soul, and had a place where it stayed and had to be called from, and when it was called and done then it went back to its place, and stayed till it was called again, according to some rule and custom.

—A woman has her nature, Pieter. I've told you that.

But I was silent.

—And if she goes against her nature . . . well . . .

—Well, what?

—It wouldn't be the love you want.

—I'm not talking of physical love, I said.

And she was helpless, because I was talking of that, and because I was not. I bent down and kissed her.

—I'm sorry, I said.

She put her arms round me.

—I'm stupid, she said. But I'm going to get better.

—Thank you for loving me, I said.

—I'm going to try to do better, she said. Honestly.

Then she was suddenly bright and gay, and smoothed the pillow for me, and made me lie down first, and tucked in the clothes behind my back, as you would to a child. Then she lay down too with her back to me, and nestled against me, with pleasure and content, and took my arm that was over her, and put my hand against her breast, and said, I'm happy, and in a moment was asleep.

Pieter finds safety in being loved, safety "against fear and danger. And the black moods," not unlike Lili in **A Night of Watching.** But his concept of love and sex is hardly hers. How does Pieter see sex as other than a game, as more than sex-as-fun?

Nella's view differs from Pieter's because "of some idea she had, some idea that was good and true but twisted in some place." What is her idea that is essentially good and true? Where is its twist? If she were able to smooth out the twist would the love she could then offer Pieter satisfy him more fully? Protect him "against the thing that tempts [him], the thing [he] hates"?

Would it be possible for Pieter to "find words" to explain his view to Nella?

What elements in the relationship between Pieter and Nella might characterize it as a truly loving one? What prevents it from being a "**We**" relationship? What limitation restricts it to "YOU and I"?

Pieter recalls with pride and love his father's saying, naturally and simply, "that he had never touched a woman, as a man touches a woman, other than his wife, nor had he ever desired to do so." He recalls also his envy, and wonder that he was otherwise. Is it unnatural for a man to be attracted to several women at the same time? Even if he is married? Is Pieter's father perhaps more likely to be the exception than the rule?

How might "it's not what you feel, it's what you *do* with those feelings" become relevant reassurance for Pieter?

How is the function of an engagement period clarified by the comment, "our courtship was . . . long and shy and protracted; some people said it was the times, but it was not only the times, it was also our natures"?

RELATED QUESTIONS

What qualities listed in *I Corinthians xiii* (see "**Night-Lights**," p. 539) are implicit in Nella and Pieter's relationship?

Home Burial

ROBERT FROST

He saw her from the bottom of the stairs
Before she saw him. She was starting down,
Looking back over her shoulder at some fear.
She took a doubtful step and then undid it
To raise herself and look again. He spoke
Advancing toward her: 'What is it you see
From up there always—for I want to know.'
She turned and sank upon her skirts at that,
And her face changed from terrified to dull.
He said to gain time: 'What is it you see,'
Mounting until she cowered under him.
'I will find out now—you must tell me, dear.'
She, in her place, refused him any help
With the least stiffening of her neck and silence.
She let him look, sure that he wouldn't see,
Blind creature; and a while he didn't see.
But at last he murmured, 'Oh,' and again, 'Oh.'

'What is it—what?' she said.

'Just that I see.'

'You don't,' she challenged. 'Tell me what it is.'

'The wonder is I didn't see at once.
I never noticed it from here before.
I must be wonted to it—that's the reason.
The little graveyard where my people are!
So small the window frames the whole of it.
Not so much larger than a bedroom, is it?
There are three stones of slate and one of marble,
Broad-shouldered little slabs there in the sunlight
On the sidehill. We haven't to mind *those*.
But I understand: it is not the stones,
But the child's mound—'

'Don't, don't, don't, don't,' she cried.

She withdrew shrinking from beneath his arm
That rested on the banister, and slid downstairs;
And turned on him with such a daunting look,
He said twice over before he knew himself:
'Can't a man speak of his own child he's lost?'

'Not you! Oh, where's my hat? Oh, I don't need it!
I must get out of here. I must get air.
I don't know rightly whether any man can.'

'Amy! Don't go to someone else this time.
Listen to me. I won't come down the stairs.'
He sat and fixed his chin between his fists.
'There's something I should like to ask you, dear.'

'You don't know how to ask it.'

                        'Help me, then.'
Her fingers moved the latch for all reply.

'My words are nearly always an offence.
I don't know how to speak of anything
So as to please you. But I might be taught
I should suppose. I can't say I see how.
A man must partly give up being a man
With women-folk. We could have some arrangement
By which I'd bind myself to keep hands off
Anything special you're a-mind to name.
Though I don't like such things 'twixt those that love.
Two that don't love can't live together without them.
But two that do can't live together with them.'
She moved the latch a little. 'Don't—don't go.
Don't carry it to someone else this time.
Tell me about it if it's something human.
Let me into your grief. I'm not so much
Unlike other folks as your standing there
Apart would make me out. Give me my chance.
I do think, though, you overdo it a little.
What was it brought you up to think it the thing
To take your mother-loss of a first child
So inconsolably—in the face of love.
You'd think his memory might be satisfied—'

'There you go sneering now!'

                        'I'm not, I'm not!
You make me angry. I'll come down to you.
God, what a woman! And it's come to this,
A man can't speak of his own child that's dead.'

'You can't because you don't know how to speak.
If you had any feelings, you that dug
With your own hand—how could you?—his little grave;

I saw you from that very window there,
Making the gravel leap and leap in air,
Leap up, like that, like that, and land so lightly
And roll back down the mound beside the hole.
I thought, Who is that man? I didn't know you.
And I crept down the stairs and up the stairs
To look again, and still your spade kept lifting.
Then you came in. I heard your rumbling voice
Out in the kitchen, and I don't know why,
But I went near to see with my own eyes.
You could sit there with the stains on your shoes
Of the fresh earth from your own baby's grave
And talk about your everyday concerns.
You had stood the spade up against the wall
Outside there in the entry, for I saw it.'

'I shall laugh the worst laugh I ever laughed.
I'm cursed. God, if I don't believe I'm cursed.'

'I can repeat the very words you were saying.
'Three foggy mornings and one rainy day
Will rot the best birch fence a man can build.'
Think of it, talk like that at such a time!
What had how long it takes a birch to rot
To do with what was in the darkened parlour.
You *couldn't* care! The nearest friends can go
With anyone to death, comes so far short
They might as well not try to go at all.
No, from the time when one is sick to death,
One is alone, and he dies more alone.
Friends make pretence of following to the grave,
But before one is in it, their minds are turned
And making the best of their way back to life
And living people, and things they understand.
But the world's evil. I won't have grief so
If I can change it. Oh, I won't, I won't!'

'There, you have said it all and you feel better.
You won't go now. You're crying. Close the door.
The heart's gone out of it: why keep it up.
Amy! There's someone coming down the road!'

'*You*—oh, you think that talk is all. I must go—
Somewhere out of this house. How can I make you—'

'If—you—do!' She was opening the door wider.
'Where do you mean to go? First tell me that.
I'll follow and bring you back by force. I *will!*—'

In *Oyster Bed* (p. 346), Lindbergh declares that marriage, which is always spoken of as a bond, becomes actually, in this stage, many bonds, many strands, of different texture and strength, making up a web that is taut and firm. She says:

> It is made of loyalties, and interdependencies, and shared experiences. It is woven of memories of meetings and conflicts; of triumphs and disappointments. It is a web of communication, a common language, and the acceptance of lack of language, too; a knowledge of likes and dislikes, of habits and reactions, both physical and mental. It is a web of instincts and intuitions, and known and unknown exchanges. The web of marriage is made by propinquity, in the day to day living side by side, looking outward in the same direction. It is woven in space and in time of the substance of life itself.

In *Home Burial,* Amy and her husband face a real-life sorrow: the death of their first child. In this marital scene, the sight of the baby's grave as Amy looks out the window while coming downstairs, triggers the memory, renewing her grief. In this crisis, what puts strain on their "web of marriage"?

Why does Amy consider her husband insensitive? Why does he consider his wife hypersensitive?

Is he a less feeling person because he was able to dig his child's grave, even to come in and stand the spade against the wall, and talk about everyday concerns? Does this make him practical-minded? Or a brute? Is Amy a more feeling person because she can cry and continually relive her grief? Does this make her overemotional? Or compassionate?

What cultural factors might condition the husband to take a stoical approach to the death of his child? What cultural factors might explain Amy's taking the "mother-loss of a first child so inconsolably"? Has Amy more reason to suffer since she, as the mother, had carried the child for nine months? Is it less the father's tragedy because his role in creating it was briefer?

Which of the pair seems to be making the greater effort to understand the other? To strengthen the web of communication? For example, what is Amy's response to his inquiry, "What is it you see/. . . . I will find out now—You must tell me, dear"? Should he have known intuitively, without blundering into this vulnerable area? Should he have phrased the question differently? If so, how?

Even if Amy had cause to resent his manner of inquiry, does her refusing "him any help/ With the least stiffening of her neck and silence" help the situation?

Does Amy prejudge her husband?

What is the effect of her challenge, "You don't," immediately after he has said, "I see"? Why did she demand proof that "he saw"? Do you admire and/or respect him for giving it to her?

Even in the face of her "You don't know how to ask it," he begs her

> Help me, then. . . .
> My words are nearly always an offence.
> I don't know how to speak of anything
> So as to please you. But I might be taught. . . .

How does he undo his loving understanding, losing all the ground he has gained? Again, having asked her to let him into her grief, to give him a chance, what does he say that reverses the direction in which he has been going? How does she interpret his truthful criticism? How does his reaction to her misappraisal of his comment add fuel to the fire? What should she have done instead? When? What should he have done? When?

What does he mean: "A man must partly give up being a man/ With women-folk"? What does he feel he must give up? How is it connnected with her comment: "Not you! . . . I don't know rightly whether any man can."

Amy apparently talks to others in an effort to work through her grief. Does it help? Or does the problem remain internally unreconciled while she tries to get sympathy?

At the end he threatens her: "If—you—do! . . . I'll follow and bring you back by force I *will!*—" What does force imply when present in a relationship between two people?

What implications does Lee's comment in **What Love Must Be** (p. 251) have for Amy and her husband. Lee says:

> For the wholeness of modern man love must be deeper, to adapt to the world's shifting sands; able to withstand disaffections and occasional betrayals. . . . Some readjustments of attitudes may be necessary. . . . Such as the abdication of the need for power. And the giving up of the prizefight relationship, which particularly in marriage, consists of scoring points and knocking one another down.

At which points do Amy and her husband each "score" in their figurative marital prizefight?

Is Amy being realistic in her criticism that

> Friends make pretence of following to the grave,
> But before one is in it, their minds are turned
> And making the best of their way back to life
> And living people, and things they understand.
> But the world's evil.

Is she realistic in her desire not to "have grief so,/ If [she] can change it"? What would her proposed change accomplish?

Are you more sympathetic with Amy or with her husband? Why?

In an effort to restore harmony, the husband offers to stay off certain subjects which might upset Amy. How productive or practical is such an arrangement? How well did it work for Hal and Ellie in **Winter Term** (p. 466)?

What are the husband's reservations about such an arrangement "'twixt those that love" when he says:

> Two that don't love can't live together without them.
> But two that do can't live together with them.

Why does the concept of mature love make secrets or withholdings unnecessary?

What relevance has the following passage from Paul Tournier's *The Meaning of Persons* for situations like the one in **Home Burial:**

> The true dialogue is not that first easy communion, wonderful though it be —the impression one has of sharing the same feelings, saying the same things and thinking the same thoughts. The true dialogue is inevitably the confrontation of two personalities, differing in their past, their upbringing, their view of life, their prejudices, their idiosyncrasies and failings. . . . Sooner or later they will find out that they are less alike than they thought.

Either, one will dominate the other, and there will no longer be a dialogue because one of the persons is eclipsed, his power of self-determination paralyzed. Or else the course of the dialogue will take it through some very dangerous waters. One of the partners will find himself saying to the other: "I can't understand why you are acting like this." And then there arises the risk of being judged or betrayed, of which we have spoken, and the temptation to run away from it by keeping back certain confidences.

In many homes it is actually, by a strange paradox, concern for harmony and the desire to safeguard love, which gradually turns the partners away from transparency. "I don't talk about that with my husband; it irritates him. . . . All it does is to put us further apart." . . . they become more and more strangers to one another. Real dialogue becomes more and more difficult between them.

It is always a denial of love, and to some extent a disavowal of marriage, to begin to calculate what one says and does not say, even when it is done with the excellent motive of safeguarding one's love. . . . even in the happiest marriage personal contact cannot be a permanent state, acquired once and for all. The windows of our houses have to be cleaned from time to time if the light is to penetrate. . . . Between man and wife, too, the true dialogue has periodically to be reestablished by the confession of some secret, and the higher and more sincere our ideal of marriage, the more irksome it is to admit that we have hidden something.

The Figures on the Frieze

ALASTAIR REID

Darkness wears off, and, dawning into light,
they find themselves unmagically together.
He sees the stains of morning in her face.
She shivers, distant in his bitter weather.

Diminishing of legend sets him brooding.
Great goddess-figures conjured from his book
blur what he sees with bafflement of wishing.
Sulky, she feels his fierce, accusing look.

Familiar as her own, his body's landscape
seems harsh and dull to her habitual eyes.
Mystery leaves, and, mercilessly flying,
the blind fiends come, emboldened by her cries.

Avoiding simple reach of hand for hand
(which would surrender pride) by noon they stand
withdrawn from touch, reproachfully alone,
small in each other's eyes, tall in their own.

Wild with their misery, they entangle now
in baffling agonies of why and how.
Afternoon glimmers, and they wound anew,
flesh, nerve, bone, gristle in each other's view.

"What have you done to me?" From each proud heart,
new phantoms walk in the deceiving air.
As the light fails, each is consumed apart,
he by his ogre vision, she by her fire.

When night falls, out of a despair of daylight,
they strike the lying attitudes of love,
and through the perturbations of their bodies,
each feels the amazing, murderous legends move.

What character trait, exhibited by both people in *The Figures on the Frieze* most threatens their "YOU and I" relationship?

"Dawning into light," why do they find themselves *unmagically* together"? How would you account for his seeing "the stains of morning in her face" and her shivering, "distant in his bitter weather"?

Is it delusional to think that sex is a way to satisfy the need for a warm, human relationship? If used as a substitute is even sexual gratification less intense?

What does the poet mean, "When night falls, out of a despair of daylight,/ they strike the lying attitudes of love"? What relevance would the connotations of "striking a pose" have in the context of the last stanza?

Why are the legends called "murderous"? What do they kill? Is this good or bad?

Explain the title: *The Figures on the Frieze.*

What line of the poem indicates that each is behaving in an "I and you" fashion?

How do the following lines reflect one facet of "YOU and i" behavior?

Diminishing of legend sets him brooding.
Great goddess-figures conjured from his book
blur what he sees with bafflement of wishing.

Surely in marriage, couples will find each "body's landscape" "familiar as his or her own," yet, when the "mystery leaves" the love relationship sustains them and the sexual relationship is not something which "seems harsh and dull to . . . habitual eyes," even though repetition of the act has changed the honeymoon aspect of it. What provides or insures the sustenance missing in *The Figures on the Frieze?*

Why would a "simple reach of hand for hand" surrender pride? How does pride, as evidenced here, increase separateness rather than insure identity? What new problems does an insistence on maintaining pride create here?

RELATED QUESTIONS

Would a "simple reach of hand for hand" have helped the communication problems in *Home Burial* (p. 493)? Why, or why not?

Are the reactions of the couple in the first stanza of *The Figures on the Frieze,* particularly the female's, similar to Ruth's experience in *Rabbit, Run* (p. 418) once the height of sexual excitement is over?

How does Fromm in *The Theory of Love* (p. 261) explain the "morning-after" disenchantment of the figures on the frieze in his discussion of sexual attraction and the illusion of union?

Hughes observed in *A High Wind in Jamaica* (p. 24) that:

> . . . grown-ups embark on a life of deception and usually fail [whereas] a child can hide the most appalling secret without the least effort, and is practically secure against detection.

From readings in the "**You-I**" section, would you concur with Hughes? Contrasting the relationships between children with those between adults, which seem to you the more honest ones? Why?

"A considerable amount of deception is built into civilized life for both sexes" [29]. Why? When is it useful? Necessary?

Examine the deceits in relationships like those in *The Scarlet Letter* (p. 334), *I Can't Breathe* (p. 363), *Peyton Place* (p. 397), *Rabbit, Run* (p. 412), *Winter Term* (p. 466), *The Mandarins* (p. 482), *Carnal Knowledge* (p. 485), *Philander Musing* (p. 486), and *The Figures on the Frieze.* Which seem to you the most serious? Why? The most necessary? To what? Are the deceptions of self? Of others? Of both? Are the deceptions recognized or unrecognized? Does this change your evaluation of them?

Why is deceit "commonly strategic in nature" [30]? Why is it employed?

"We"

"WONDERFUL ONE TIMES ONE"

what's wholly
marvellous my

Darling

is that you &
i are more than you

& i(be

ca
us

e It's we)

[1]

As Kirkendall points out in **Searching for the Roots of Moral Judgments** (p. 303) "communication, [a term] used in preference to 'talking' . . . means the ability to overcome inhibitions and to rise above conventional expressions to the point where we can discuss our real feelings. Our hopes, fears, wishes and motivations must be expressed and given honest and thoughtful consideration if we are really to communicate. It is at this point that the relationship between the emotionally mature person and the truly moral person becomes the clearest."

"**We**"-oriented characters know that to be human is to be in danger, to be terribly vulnerable to the damage that people are capable of inflicting upon one another; thus each partner in a "**We**" relationship is particularly careful for the other.

In such an atmosphere, characters in the "**We**" section like the couple in **The Measure of Friendship** feel "a live thread begin to spin itself" between them, and the narrator of **somewhere i have never travelled** grows in the creative, loving, intensely fragile silence.

"**We**"-oriented characters understand the applied meaning of abstractions discussed in the "**They**" section: "mutualism," "commitment," "act of will," giving, and receiving. Their orientation is to past and to future, as well as being strongly anchored in the real present. They can distinguish love from lust, the heart from the glands, bestowals from appraisals, Eros from Venus, appreciative from need pleasures. They know the cherished nourishment (as well as the heady intoxication) that love provides in **A Decade;** the tender understanding of **Sophistication;** the virtues of laughter in **The Crisis;** the foolishly wise sacrifices of **The Gift of the Magi;** the antidotes to guilt and fear offered by trusting love in **That Night When Joy Began;** the infinite scope of feeling suggested in **How Do I Love Thee? (Sonnet XLIII)** and the enduring quality of love stated in **John Anderson.**

Relationships rooted in care, responsibility, respect, and knowledge incorporate sexual feeling in a wider context. That a genuine fusion of elements, as inseparable as welded human hearts, can take place is apparent from testaments made in **Gather; Plaque for a Brass Bed; Part of Plenty; Twenty-third Street Runs into Heaven; Night Song;** and **Slowly, Slowly.**

Joy and wonder increase the spiritual as well as the bodily circulation, and human beings discover that the "**We**" of "me" can be created by infinite multiplications of the "wonderful one times one."

503

The Member of the Wedding

CARSON McCULLERS

. . . A thought and explanation suddenly came to her, so that she knew and almost said aloud: *They are the we of me.* Yesterday, and all the twelve years of her life, she had only been Frankie. She was an *I* person who had to walk around and do things by herself. All other people had a *we* to claim, all other except her. When Berenice said *we,* she meant Honey and Big Mama, her lodge, or her church. The *we* of her father was the store. All members of clubs have a *we* to belong to and talk about. The soldiers in the army can say *we,* and even the criminals on chain-gangs. But the old Frankie had had no *we* to claim, unless it would be the terrible summer *we* of her and John Henry and Berenice—and that was the last *we* in the world she wanted. Now all this was suddenly over with and changed. There was her brother and the bride, and it was as though when first she saw them something she had known inside of her: *They are the we of me.*

Although Frankie's absorption in and of her brother and sister-in-law in **The Member of the Wedding** is not a productive "**We**" answer to a universal need, Frankie illumines a critical question: where is the "**We**" of "me?"—when she searches for the element that will transform an "**I**" person who has to walk around and do things by herself into one who by incorporation and by sharing has a "**We**" to claim—a "**We**" that, in Fromm's terms, allows two beings to become one, yet remain two.

As a psychoanalyst puts it:

. . . the human environment is social: the outer-world of the ego is made up of the egos of others significant to it. They are significant because on many levels of crude or subtle communication my whole being perceives in them a hospitality for the way in which my inner world is ordered and includes them, which makes me, in turn, hospitable to the way they order their world and include me—a mutual affirmation, then, which can be depended upon to activate my being as I can be depended upon to activate theirs. To this . . . I would restrict the term *mutuality,* which is the secret of love. [2]

The Measure of Friendship

SEAN O'FAOLAIN

She came in, and her wide smile and her blush did not make it easy to tell her why I came: it was a greeting for myself alone. And when we sat before the fire I felt immediately a live thread begin to spin itself between us . . . like a cobweb spinning across the road of a spring day. This was something I had not foreseen, and what with, in her, a shyness that she could not conceal and, in me, that sense of the night outside, suddenly becoming vast and multitudinous, pitying to no one, according as the warmth of the room and her companionship came stealing over me; what, too, with the memory of the summer that had been so solitary and calm, I felt about us and our talk an atmosphere quite new to me.

It was akin to benevolence and far more deep and mysterious than friendship, because it was friendship in its first stage when one is giving all, spreading out all one's little riches, not yet having discovered either how much it is vain to offer or expect. That I knew now, who have for years tried to live alone, is how people do meet and join: a first slight bridge, a wavering feeler out of the shell of self; then a gush of willingness, giving with both hands; then, when all is given, the secret measuring by each of what—not of what the other has given but of what each has taken. The end and measure of utter friendship, the only release from the cave of loneliness, is with him who knows how to accept most. That discovery has meant everything to me. For as it is with men, so it is with life which we understand and love in proportion as we accept without question what it gives, without question as to whether we need it, not even questioning whether its gift seems cruel or kind. It is the supreme generosity because we do not even know who the Giver is; why He has given; or what.

In **The Measure of Friendship,** an excerpt from *Bird Alone,* how is the process of "mutual affirmation" depicted by the statement: "when we sat before the fire I felt immediately a live thread begin to spin itself between us"?

How is "when all is given, the secret measuring by each of what—not of what the other has given but of what each has taken" related to the finding of the "**We**" of "me"?

"The end and measure of utter friendship, the only release from the cave of loneliness, is with him who knows how to accept most." Why does the author say "accept" rather than "give" most?

Is accepting love a passive act? If so, how? If not, what does it entail?

What is the relationship of friendship to love? Of friendship to sex?

RELATED QUESTIONS

How is O'Faolain's concept that "when all is given, the secret measuring by each of what—not of what the other has given but of what each has taken" related to Singer's concept in *Appraisal and Bestowal* (p. 217)?

O'Faolain in **The Measure of Friendship,** like Lindbergh in *Double-Sunrise* (p. 232), uses a shell image to suggest how two people "meet and join: a first slight bridge, a wavering feeler out of the shell of self." Is he describing the same stage of a relationship as Lindbergh? The same as Stevenson is in **On Falling in Love** (p. 238) where the couple have "scales on their eyes"? The same as Dietrich is in *Married Love: Strategy of* (p. 349) where each still wears "Sunday clothes"?

Sonnet XLIII

ELIZABETH BARRETT BROWNING

506

"We"
"wonderful one
times one"

How do I love thee? Let me count the ways.
I love thee to the depth and breadth and height
My soul can reach, when feeling out of sight
For the ends of Being and ideal Grace.
I love thee to the level of every day's
Most quiet need, by sun and candlelight.
I love thee freely, as men strive for Right;
I love thee purely, as they turn from Praise.
I love thee with the passion put to use
In my old griefs, and with my childhood's faith.
I love thee with a love I seemed to lose
With my lost saints,—I love thee with the breath,
Smiles, tears, of all my life!—and, if God choose,
I shall but love thee better after death.

Why does Elizabeth Barrett Browning say she loves him to the depth, breadth, and height her *soul* can reach? What restrictions would be placed on her feelings if she said "mind" instead of "soul"? If she said "body"?

What part(s) of the human being—body, mind, soul—would the poet probably believe to be vital to an awareness of that "live thread begin[ning] to spin itself" in O'Faolain's *The Measure of Friendship?*

The poet declares that she loves him "freely." What do you think she means?

What are some of the reasons or needs or motives that lead one into a love which is *not* a free choice?

What might be some of everyday's "quiet needs" by sun and candlelight?

RELATED QUESTIONS

Does Elizabeth's feeling for Robert—at the stage described in *Go from Me (Sonnet VI)* (see "**Night-Lights**," p. 542)—seem to you part of a "**We**" relationship or a "YOU and i" one?

Among the "**You-I**" selections, which characters would have to admit "I do *not* love thee freely"? Why?

Which of the ways of love enumerated by Browning in *Sonnet XLIII* are true of *I Can't Breathe* (p. 363), *Of Human Bondage* (p. 378), *i like my body when it is with your* (p. 394), *Homage to Sextus Propertius* (p. 395), *Peyton Place* (p. 397), *My Last Duchess* (p. 409), and *may i feel said he* (p. 475)? What conclusions can you draw about the nature of love on the basis of your responses to the preceding questions?

Sophistication

SHERWOOD ANDERSON

507

"We"

"wonderful one
times one"

At the upper end of the Fair Ground, in Winesburg, there is a half-decayed old grandstand. It has never been painted and the boards are all warped out of shape. The fairground stands on top of a low hill rising out of the valley of Wine Creek and from the grandstand one can see at night, over a cornfield, the lights of the town reflected against the sky.

George and Helen climbed the hill to the Fair Ground, coming by the path past Waterworks Pond. The feeling of loneliness and isolation that had come to the young man in the crowded streets of his town was both broken and intensified by the presence of Helen. What he felt was reflected in her.

In youth there are always two forces fighting in people. The warm unthinking little animal struggles against the thing that reflects and remembers, and the older, the more sophisticated thing had possession of George Willard. Sensing his mood, Helen walked beside him filled with respect. When they got to the grand stand they climbed up under the roof and sat down on one of the long bench-like seats.

There is something memorable in the experience to be had by going into a fair ground that stands at the edge of a Middle Western town on a night after the annual fair has been held. The sensation is one never to be forgotten. On all sides are ghosts, not of the dead, but of living people. Here, during the day just passed, have come the people pouring in from the town and the country around. Farmers with their wives and children and all the people from the hundreds of little frame houses have gathered within these board walls. Young girls have laughed and men with beards have talked of the affairs of their lives. The place has been filled to overflowing with life. It has itched and squirmed with life and now it is night and the life has all gone away. The silence is almost terrifying. One conceals oneself standing silently beside the trunk of a tree and what there is of a reflective tendency in his nature is intensified. One shudders at the thought of the meaninglessness of life while at the same instant, and if the people of the town are his people, one loves life so intensely that tears come into the eyes.

In the darkness under the roof of the grand stand, George Willard sat beside Helen White and felt very keenly his own insignificance in the scheme of existence. Now that he had come out of town where the presence of the people stirring about, busy with a multitude of affairs, had been so irritating, the irritation was all gone. The presence of Helen renewed and refreshed him. It was as though her woman's hand was assisting him to make some minute readjustment of the machinery of his life. He began to think of the people in the town where he had always lived with something like reverence. He had reverence for Helen. He wanted to love and to be loved by her, but he did not want at the moment to be confused by her womanhood. In the darkness he took hold of her hand and when she crept close put a hand on her shoulder. A wind began to blow and he shivered. With all his strength he tried to hold and to understand the mood that had come upon him. In that high place in the darkness the two oddly sensitive human atoms held each other tightly and waited. In the mind of each was the same thought. "I have come to this lonely place and here is this other," was the substance of the thing felt.

In Winesburg the crowded day had run itself out into the long night of the late fall. Farm horses jogged away along lonely country roads pulling their portion of weary people. Clerks began to bring samples of goods in off the sidewalks and lock the doors of stores. In the Opera House a crowd had gathered to see a show and further down Main Street the fiddlers, their instruments tuned, sweated and worked to keep the feet of youth flying over a dance floor.

In the darkness in the grand stand Helen White and George Willard remained silent. Now and then the spell that held them was broken and they turned and tried in the dim light to see into each other's eyes. They kissed but that impulse did not last. At the upper end of the Fair Ground a half dozen men worked over horses that had raced during the afternoon. The men had built a fire and were heating kettles of water. Only their legs could be seen as they passed back and forth in the light. When the wind blew the little flames of the fire danced crazily about.

George and Helen arose and walked away into the darkness. They went along a path past a field of corn that had not yet been cut. The wind whispered among the dry corn blades. For a moment during the walk back into town the spell that held them was broken. When they had come to the crest of Waterworks Hill they stopped by a tree and George again put his hands on the girl's shoulders. She embraced him eagerly and then again they drew quickly back from that impulse. They stopped kissing and stood a little apart. Mutual respect grew big in them. They were both embarrassed and to relieve their embarrassment dropped into the animalism of youth. They laughed and began to pull and haul at each other. In some way chastened and purified by the mood they had been in, they became, not man and woman, not boy and girl, but excited little animals.

It was so they went down the hill. In the darkness they played like two splendid young things in a young world. Once, running swiftly forward, Helen tripped George and he fell. He squirmed and shouted. Shaking with laughter, he rolled down the hill. Helen ran after him. For just a moment she stopped in the darkness. There is no way of knowing what woman's thoughts went through her mind but, when the bottom of the hill was reached and she came up to the boy, she took his arm and walked beside him in dignified silence. For some reason they could not have explained they had both got from their silent evening together the thing needed. Man or boy, woman or girl, they had for a moment taken hold of the thing that makes the mature life of men and women in the modern world possible.

Twice in this excerpt the author uses the word respect:

Sensing his mood, Helen walked beside him filled with *respect.*

They stopped kissing and stood a little apart. Mutual *respect* grew big in them.

Respect is defined as: a relation to or concern with something usually specified; an act of giving particular attention—consideration; high or special regard—

esteem—or the quality or state of being esteemed—honor; particular, detail. Which of the meanings seem most suitable to the context in which the author uses the term? Why? What is being respected in each instance?

How do Helen and George illustrate Lee's view in **What Love Must Be** (p. 250) that "the sum of love is that it should be a meeting place, an interlocking of nerves and senses, a series of constant surprises and renewals of each other's moods"?

What does the author of **Sophistication** suggest by saying, "What he felt was reflected in her"? Is this a negative or positive or neutral comment about Helen?

What does George mean, "he wanted to love and to be loved by her, but he did not want at the moment to be confused by her womanhood"?

"They kissed, but that impulse did not last." Why was sex not the answer to George or Helen's needs?

Why did they laugh, pull, haul at each other? Why did Helen trip George? Does their behavior seem childish and silly for two seemingly mature people? How can they then walk together in dignified silence? How might George and Helen's behavior be termed regressive? What did it accomplish?

"Man or boy, woman or girl," the author concludes, "they had for a moment taken hold of the *thing* that makes the mature life of men and women in the modern world possible." What is the "thing"? Is it the same as "the *thing* needed that both got from their silent evening together"?

Do you agree that "in youth there are always two forces fighting in people: the warm unthinking little animal struggles against the thing that reflects and remembers"? Why is it not so true with maturity? What to you constitute the essential components of a mature relationship? If Helen and George had been less mature, how might the story **Sophistication** have ended?

Communication of one's deep involvement in the welfare of the other, the communication of one's profound interest in the realization of the other's potentialities for being the kind of human being you are being to him, the communication of the feeling that you will always be standing by, that you will never commit the supreme treason that human beings so frequently commit against their fellow man, of letting him down when he most stands in need of you, but that you will be standing by giving him all the supports and sustenances and stimulations he requires for becoming what it is in him to be, and knowing that to be human is to be in danger, to be terribly vulnerable to the damage that people are capable of inflicting upon one another, that you will be particularly careful for the other not to commit such errors against him.

If one can communicate these messages to the other, then I believe one can be said to love him. [3]

How successfully did Helen "communicate these messages" to George?

RELATED QUESTIONS

In what ways does Helen's understanding of George in **Sophistication** resemble Biddy's understanding of Pip in **Great Expectations** (p. 444)?

How does George's "reverence" for Helen differ from Charley's reverence for Eustacia in **The Return of the Native** (p. 435)?

How might you argue that "the older, the more sophisticated thing that had possession of George Willard" did *not* have possession of Mick in **The Heart Is a Lonely Hunter** (p. 457)? What other youthful characters appear dominated by the

"wonderful one times one"

"warm unthinking little animal" force? What could or might they have done about it?

In which selections have characters been confused by another's "womanhood"—or confused by another's "manhood"—so that they mistake one feeling for another?

The Gift of the Magi

O. HENRY

One dollar and eighty-seven cents. That was all. And sixty cents of it was in pennies. Pennies saved one and two at a time by bulldozing the grocer and the vegetable man and the butcher until one's cheeks burned with the silent imputation of parsimony that such close dealing implied. Three times Della counted it. One dollar and eighty-seven cents. And the next day would be Christmas.

There was clearly nothing to do but flop down on the shabby little couch and howl. So Della did it. Which instigates the moral reflection that life is made up of sobs, sniffles, and smiles, with sniffles predominating.

While the mistress of the home is gradually subsiding from the first stage to the second, take a look at the home. A furnished flat at $8 per week. It did not exactly beggar description, but it certainly had that word on the lookout for the mendicancy squad.

In the vestibule below was a letter-box into which no letter would go, and an electric button from which no mortal finger could coax a ring. Also appertaining thereunto was a card bearing the name "Mr. James Dillingham Young."

The "Dillingham" had been flung to the breeze during a former period of prosperity when its possessor was being paid $30 per week. Now, when the income was shrunk to $20, the letters of "Dillingham" looked blurred, as though they were thinking seriously of contracting to a modest and unassuming D. But whenever Mr. James Dillingham Young came home and reached his flat above he was called "Jim" and greatly hugged by Mrs. James Dillingham Young, already introduced to you as Della. Which is all very good.

Della finished her cry and attended to her cheeks with the powder rag. She stood by the window and looked out dully at a gray cat walking a gray fence in a gray backyard. Tomorrow would be Christmas Day, and she had only $1.87 with which to buy Jim a present. She had been saving every penny she could for months, with this result. Twenty dollars a week doesn't go far. Expenses had been greater than she had calculated. They always are. Only $1.87 to buy a present for Jim. Her Jim. Many a happy hour she had spent planning for something nice for him. Something fine and rare and sterling—something just a little bit near to being worthy of the honor of being owned by Jim.

There was a pier-glass between the windows of the room. Perhaps you have seen a pier-glass in an $8 flat. A very thin and very agile person may, by observing his reflection in a rapid sequence of longitudinal strips, obtain a fairly accurate conception of his looks. Della, being slender, had mastered the art.

Suddenly she whirled from the window and stood before the glass. Her eyes were shining brilliantly, but her face had lost its color within twenty seconds. Rapidly she pulled down her hair and let it fall to its full length.

Now, there were two possessions of the James Dillingham Youngs in which they both took a mighty pride. One was Jim's gold watch that had been his father's and his grandfather's. The other was Della's hair. Had the Queen of Sheba lived in the flat across the airshaft, Della would have let her hair hang out the window some day to dry just to depreciate Her Majesty's jewels and gifts. Had King Solomon been the janitor, with all his treasures piled up in the basement, Jim would have pulled out his watch every time he passed, just to see him pluck at his beard from envy.

So now Della's beautiful hair fell about her rippling and shining like a cascade of brown waters. It reached below her knee and made itself almost a garment for her. And then she did it up again nervously and quickly. Once she faltered for a minute and stood still while a tear or two splashed on the worn red carpet.

On went her old brown jacket; on went her old brown hat. With a whirl of skirts and with the brilliant sparkle still in her eyes, she fluttered out the door and down the stairs to the street.

Where she stopped the sign read: "Mme. Sofronie. Hair Goods of All Kinds." One flight up Della ran, and collected herself, panting. Madame, large, too white, chilly, hardly looked the "Sofronie."

"Will you buy my hair?" asked Della.

"I buy hair," said Madame. "Take yer hat off and let's have a sight at the looks of it."

Down rippled the brown cascade.

"Twenty dollars," said Madame, lifting the mass with a practised hand.

"Give it to me quick," said Della.

Oh, and the next two hours tripped by on rosy wings. Forget the hashed metaphor. She was ransacking the stores for Jim's present.

She found it at last. It surely had been made for Jim and no one else. There was no other like it in any of the stores, and she had turned all of them inside out. It was a platinum fob chain simple and chaste in design, properly proclaiming its value by substance alone and not by meretricious ornamentation—as all good things should do. It was even worthy of The Watch. As soon as she saw it she knew that it must be Jim's. It was like him. Quietness and value—the description applied to both. Twenty-one dollars they took from her for it, and she hurried home with the 87 cents. With that chain on his watch Jim might be properly anxious about the time in any company. Grand as the watch was, he sometimes looked at it on the sly on account of the old leather strap that he used in place of a chain.

When Della reached home her intoxication gave way a little to prudence and reason. She got out her curling irons and lighted the gas and went to work repairing the ravages made by generosity added to love. Which is always a tremendous task, dear friends—a mammoth task.

Within forty minutes her head was covered with tiny, close-lying curls that made her look wonderfully like a truant schoolboy. She looked at her reflection in the mirror long, carefully, and critically.

"If Jim doesn't kill me," she said to herself, "before he takes a second look at me, he'll say I look like a Coney Island chorus girl. But what could I do—oh! what could I do with a dollar and eighty-seven cents?"

At 7 o'clock the coffee was made and the frying-pan was on the back of the stove hot and ready to cook the chops.

Jim was never late. Della doubled the fob chain in her hand and sat on the corner of the table near the door that he always entered. Then she heard his step on the stair away down on the first flight, and she turned white for just a moment. She had a habit of saying little silent prayers about the simplest every-day things, and now she whispered: "Please God, make him think I am still pretty."

The door opened and Jim stepped in and closed it. He looked thin and very serious. Poor fellow, he was only twenty-two—and to be burdened with a family! He needed a new overcoat and he was without gloves.

Jim stopped inside the door, as immovable as a setter at the scent of quail. His eyes were fixed upon Della, and there was an expression in them that she could not read, and it terrified her. It was not anger, nor surprise, nor disapproval, nor horror, nor any of the sentiments that she had been prepared for. He simply stared at her fixedly with that peculiar expression on his face.

Della wriggled off the table and went for him.

"Jim, darling," she cried, "don't look at me that way. I had my hair cut off and sold it because I couldn't have lived through Christmas without giving you a present. It'll grow out again—you won't mind, will you? I just had to do it. My hair grows awfully fast. Say 'Merry Christmas!' Jim, and let's be happy. You don't know what a nice—what a beautiful, nice gift I've got for you."

"You've cut off your hair?" asked Jim, laboriously, as if he had not arrived at that patent fact yet even after the hardest mental labor.

"Cut it off and sold it," said Della. "Don't you like me just as well, anyhow? I'm me without my hair, ain't I?"

Jim looked about the room curiously.

"You say your hair is gone?" he said, with an air almost of idiocy.

"You needn't look for it," said Della. "It's sold, I tell you—sold and gone, too. It's Christmas Eve, boy. Be good to me, for it went for you. Maybe the hairs of my head were numbered," she went on with a sudden serious sweetness, "but nobody could ever count my love for you. Shall I put the chops on, Jim?"

Out of his trance Jim seemed quickly to wake. He enfolded his Della. For ten seconds let us regard with discreet scrutiny some inconsequential object in the other direction. Eight dollars a week or a million a year—what is the difference? A mathematician or a wit would give you the wrong answer. The magi brought valuable gifts, but that was not among them. This dark assertion will be illuminated later on.

Jim drew a package from his overcoat pocket and threw it upon the table.

"Don't make any mistake, Dell," he said, "about me. I don't think there's anything in the way of a haircut or a shave or a shampoo that could make me like my girl any less. But if you'll unwrap that package you may see why you had me going a while at first."

White fingers and nimble tore at the string and paper. And then an ecstatic scream of joy; and then, alas! a quick feminine change to hysterical tears and wails, necessitating the immediate employment of all the comforting powers of the lord of the flat.

For there lay The Combs—the set of combs, side and back, that Della had worshipped for long in a Broadway window. Beautiful combs, pure tortoise shell, with jewelled rims—just the shade to wear in the beautiful vanished hair. They were expensive combs, she knew, and her heart had simply craved and yearned over them without the least hope of possession. And now, they were hers, but the tresses that should have adorned the coveted adornments were gone.

But she hugged them to her bosom, and at length she was able to look up with dim eyes and a smile and say: "My hair grows so fast, Jim!"

And then Della leaped up like a little singed cat and cried, "Oh, oh!"

Jim had not yet seen his beautiful present. She held it out to him eagerly upon her open palm. The dull precious metal seemed to flash with a reflection of her bright and ardent spirit.

"Isn't it a dandy, Jim? I hunted all over town to find it. You'll have to look at the time a hundred times a day now. Give me your watch. I want to see how it looks on it."

Instead of obeying, Jim tumbled down on the couch and put his hands under the back of his head and smiled.

"Dell," said he, "let's put our Christmas presents away and keep 'em a while. They're too nice to use just at present. I sold the watch to get the money to buy your combs. And now suppose you put the chops on."

The magi, as you know, were wise men—wonderfully wise men—who brought gifts to the Babe in the manger. They invented the art of giving Christmas presents. Being wise, their gifts were no doubt wise ones, possibly bearing the privilege of exchange in case of duplication. And here I have lamely related to you the uneventful chronicle of two foolish children in a flat who most unwisely sacrificed for each other the greatest treasures of their house. But in a last word to the wise of these days let it be said that of all who give gifts these two were the wisest. Of all who give and receive gifts, such as they are wisest. Everywhere they are wisest. They are the magi.

How does O. Henry's story confirm one perspective on sacrifice as "the best measuring cup of your love" [4]?

Why is Della's act of selling her hair "generosity added to love"?

O. Henry terms Jim and Della "two foolish children." How is the adjective "foolish" entirely justified? Why does it make no difference that they were so unwise?

What qualities do Jim and Della show that justify their being called "children"? In what sense is it a compliment, even though Jim is twenty-two-years old?

Might Jim also be termed "man" by Horgan's yardstick in **Parma Violets** (p. 13):

The aching desire to give, to create life beyond the self, calls boy into man. Gratified, this love creates an analogue of heaven on earth.

O. Henry concludes:

But in a last word to the wise of these days let it be said that of all who give gifts these two were the wisest.

What distinction is implied between "the wise of these days" and the magi's "wisdom"? What gift did the magi bring?

What invaluable present did Jim and Della receive?

Is the measure of love in *The Gift of the Magi,* like O'Faolain's measure of friendship, "With him who knows how to *accept* most"?

Does Fromm contradict O'Faolain's *The Measure of Friendship* when he says, in *The Theory of Love* (p. 255):

> Giving is the highest expression of potency. In the very act of giving, I experience my strength, my wealth, my power. This experience of heightened vitality and potency fills me with joy. I experience myself as overflowing, spending, alive, hence as joyous. Giving is more joyous than receiving, not because it is a deprivation, but because in the act of giving lies the expression of my aliveness.

Is Fromm's comment relevant to Jim and Della?

How big a role does sex play in O. Henry's love story?

RELATED QUESTION

How is Thomas Traherne's *Centuries of Meditations* (see "**Night-Lights,**" p. 589) manifested in *The Gift of the Magi?*

A Decade

AMY LOWELL

When you came, you were like red wine and honey,
And the taste of you burnt my mouth with its sweetness.
Now you are like morning bread,
Smooth and pleasant.
I hardly taste you at all for I know your savour,
But I am completely nourished.

From the poet's perspective, which part of the ten-year period seems more important: the "red wine and honey," or the "morning bread" phase? Why? What are the connotations of "red wine"? Of "honey"? Do they apply to the sensuous and sensual elements of infatuation? What are the connotations of "morning bread"? In what sense does the poet use "nourished"?

Does "I hardly taste you at all for I know your savour" mean that sexual relations have become mechanical and habitual over ten years, and that, therefore, the relationship has lost its "flavor" and meaning? Or that over the decade the "welding of human hearts" described by Miller in *Forsaking All Others* (p. 355) has taken place, so that the "red wine" plays a smaller part in the total "meal"?

RELATED QUESTIONS

Were Lili and Arne in *A Night of Watching* (p. 477) "nourished"? Were the figures in *The Figures on the Frieze* (p. 497)? Della and Jim in *The Gift of the Magi* (p. 510)? Henri and Paula in *The Mandarins* (p. 482)?

Night Song

PHILIP BOOTH

Beside you,
lying down at dark,
my waking fits your sleep.

Your turning
flares the slow-banked fire
between our mingled feet,

and there,
curved close and warm
against the nape of love,

held there,
who holds your dreaming
shape, I match my breathing

to your breath;
and sightless, keep my hands
on your heart's breast, keep

nightwatch
on your sleep to prove
there is no dark, nor death.

How is the "nightwatch" a part of the "tongue-and-groove relationship" described by Lee in **What Love Must Be** (p. 250)?

What are some of the signs of mutuality in **Night Song?**

RELATED QUESTIONS

How is the lyrical feeling in **Night Song** different from what might be termed Rabbit's "night howl" with Janice in **Rabbit, Run** (p. 428)? Would Updike, like Booth, say "curved close and warm/against the nape of love"? Or might he say "nape of sex"?

How does the kind of "nightwatch on your sleep to prove there is no dark, nor death" in Booth's poem differ from the "night of watching" of Lili and Arne (p. 477), although similar needs are implied?

How does Booth's poem **Night Song** depict a "**We**" relationship fusion whereas Arnold's **A Night of Watching** describes a "**You-I**" split?

somewhere i have never travelled, gladly beyond (lvii)

E. E. CUMMINGS

somewhere i have never travelled,gladly beyond
any experience,your eyes have their silence:
in your most frail gesture are things which enclose me,
or which i cannot touch because they are too near

your slightest look easily will unclose me
though i have closed myself as fingers,
you open always petal by petal myself as Spring opens
(touching skilfully,mysteriously)her first rose

or if your wish be to close me,i and
my life will shut very beautifully,suddenly,
as when the heart of this flower imagines
the snow carefully everywhere descending;

nothing which we are to perceive in this world equals
the power of your intense fragility:whose texture
compels me with the colour of its countries,
rendering death and forever with each breathing

(i do not know what it is about you that closes
and opens;only something in me understands
the voice of your eyes is deeper than all roses)
nobody,not even the rain,has such small hands

A romantic song advocates, "Try a little tenderness"; a proverb declares that "a soft answer turneth away wrath"; Cummings asserts that "nothing which we are to perceive in this world equals/the power of your intense fragility." What does the poet mean: "your eyes have their silence:/in your most frail gesture are things which enclose me"? How is the incorporative process related to finding the "**We**" of "me"? Might you say that the process also involves a reversible reaction—that is, finding the "me" of "**We**"?

Why are silences sometimes uncomfortable and embarrassing? Why do you suppose that one of the most frequent questions asked by young people concerns what to talk about on a date? For what reasons do some older people develop a protective shield of "small talk"?

What does pseudocommunication, or protection against the dangling conversation, hide? Is it necessary between two who truly love each other?

Negative silences of the sullen, hostile sort block out another person. But there can be positive, constructive silences which result from so much understanding, sensitivity, and mutuality that words become unnecessary. What elements must be present in a relationship to feel comfortable with silence?

How is silence in Cummings' poem creative? What elements does it share with the taming process described by the following writer:

> "Please—tame me!" he said.
> "I want to, very much," the little prince replied. "But I have not much time. I have friends to discover, and a great many things to understand."
> "One only understands the things that one tames," said the fox. "Men have no more time to understand anything. They buy things all ready made at the shops. But there is no shop anywhere where one can buy friendship, and so men have no friends any more. If you want a friend, tame me . . ."
> "What must I do, to tame you?" asked the little prince.
> "You must be very patient," replied the fox. "First you will sit down at a little distance from me—like that—in the grass. I shall look at you out of the corner of my eye, and you will say nothing. Words are the source of mis-understandings. But you will sit a little closer to me, every day . . ." [5]

Do we "tame" the people we love? Are we forever responsible for the things we have tamed?

RELATED QUESTIONS

How did the husband and wife in **Home Burial** (p. 493), by using physical and verbal violence to "communicate," bring out the beast in each other instead of "taming" each other? What role did patience, or its absence, play?

How does the taming process as suggested in Cummings' **somewhere i have never travelled (lvii)** compare with that in Elizabeth Barrett Browning's **And Yet, Because Thou Overcomest So (Sonnet XVI)** (see "**Night-Lights**," p. 542)?

Which of the characters in selections you have read had difficulty handling silence, or exhibited a negative, alienating kind? Which found silence construc-tive and comfortable?

The Crisis

ROBERT CREELEY

Let me say (in anger) that since the day we were married
we have never had a towel
where anyone could find it,
the fact.

Notwithstanding that I am not
simple to live with, not
my own judgement, but no
matter.

There are other things:

to kiss you is not
to love you.

Or not so simply.

Laughter releases rancor, the quality of mercy is not
strained.

It has been written:

Without the continuous struggle to come to terms acceptable to both parties and compromise the reality of neither, a truly personal union cannot be achieved. But struggle implies power. One does not enter the lists armed only with good will and kind thoughts. Besides a readiness to search out what is objectively fair, one needs the force to also resist what falls short of it. Love without power is not enough, because love without power soon ceases to be love. Without the strength to resist encroachments, openness to the other comes down simply to "giving in." The person, then, is called to do battle; there is no advance without it. If he is also called to know peace, it is because peace is not a state but a process, not just a matter of avoiding conflicts, but of keeping our conflicts constructive. [6]

In what sense does Creeley in *The Crisis* show that marital harmony entails a process of keeping conflicts constructive?

Would you say that the marriage depicted in *The Crisis* is a poor one because the linen closet is disorganized, the husband speaks in anger, and has a difficult personality? Why?

Is marriage the assurance of years of unending excitement, bliss, and harmony? Or is happiness in marriage to be built by loving persons who care about each other enough to work at it, thus, as Magoun says (p. 267), "producing together an intellectual soil and emotional climate in which each can spontaneously express his real self"?

By what process are human hearts welded together? Does it happen automatically after a wedding? Accidentally? Do people fall in love, or do people grow into love just as love grows in them?

Is dealing with inevitable problems—even rancor—a critical part of marriage? Is anger settled once and for all, or does community imply "a mutuality of distinct initiatives that . . . exist . . . as an ongoing project," so that "the order of persons is an order of continuous and inevitable tension"? [7]

What does the poet mean, "Laughter releases rancor, the quality of mercy is not strained"?

In relationships built on "truth, not dream," what are some of the ways in which problems can be eased or hammered out? Under what circumstances is laughter a good solution? When might tears be beneficial? When is silence the constructively better part of wisdom?

RELATED QUESTIONS

How did the husband in Frost's *Home Burial* (p. 493) express the idea that "peace is not a state but a process, not just a matter of avoiding conflicts"?

Part of Plenty

BERNARD SPENCER

When she carries food to the table and stoops down
—Doing this out of love—and lays soup with its good
Tickling smell, or fry winking from the fire
And I look up, perhaps from a book I am reading

Or other work: there is an importance of beauty
Which can't be accounted for by there and then,
And attacks me, but not separately from the welcome
Of the food, or the grace of her arms.

When she puts a sheaf of tulips in a jug
And pours in water and presses to one side
The upright stems and leaves that you hear creak,
Or loosens them, or holds them up to show me,
So that I see the tangle of their necks and cups
With the curls of her hair, and the body they are held
Against, and the stalk of the small waist rising
And flowering in the shape of breasts;
Whether in the bringing of the flowers or the food
She offers plenty, and is part of plenty,
And whether I see her stooping, or leaning with the flowers,
What she does is ages old, and she is not simply,
No, but lovely in that way.

How is the fact that "she offers plenty, and is part of plenty" related to the "**We**" of "me" concept?

Does the poet intend the word plenty to suggest "fullness" or "ample" or both?

Why might the poet have used sexually tinged words like "lays soup with its good *tickling* smell," "fry *winking* from the fire," "an importance of beauty . . . *attacks* me"?

In **The Crisis** (p. 517), Creeley said:

> to kiss you is not
> to love you.
>   Or not so simply.

How does Spencer in **Part of Plenty** elaborate on Creeley's statement?

When Spencer says, "she is not simply,/No, but lovely in that way," is he using the word "simply" in the same sense that Creeley intends it in **The Crisis?**

RELATED QUESTIONS

In what ways do both Creeley and Spencer recognize what Gunn pointed out in **Das Liebesleben** (p. 192); that "love involves things neither Tristan nor you could ever do:/such as washing the dishes"?

To what degree and in what ways do Spencer in **Part of Plenty;** Creeley in **The Crisis** (p. 517) and Creeley in **A Marriage** (see "**Night-Lights**," p. 544); Gunn in **Das Liebesleben** and Gunn in **Carnal Knowledge** (p. 485) and Moss in **Rain** (see "**Night-Lights**," p. 579) separate love and sex?

Gather

MICHAEL DENNIS BROWNE

520

"We"
"wonderful one
times one"

Sometimes still wet from the shower
she will come to me to lie by me,
saying she could not wait to be with me,

and then do I take her head in my hands,
gather all to her grace, the fields
of my childhood, all songs I have sung,

all hill-paths taken, all evenings
among friends, the summer waters, the flame
of the white farm, the filling of all flowers,

her head in my hands, her eyes wide, gather
all that I was and am, all I shall be,
and love.

Where is the "**We**" of "me"? How is the process of its discovery suggested by the title of Browne's poem?

What does "gather all to her grace" mean?

How does *Gather* illustrate the very complex psychological phenomena that comprise the healthy sex act? To what extent does it depend on the spiritual merger of personalities? Does it involve both giving in Fromm's concept in *The Theory of Love* (p. 252) and accepting in O'Faolain's terms (p. 504)?

"Sometimes in our society," said Shinn in *Revolution in Sexual Ethics* (p. 270),

> man and woman enter into a personal relation in which they realize the wonder and joy of sex. Such realization does not come through concentration on sex alone. The persons involved are concerned not simply for sex, but for each other.

How does *Gather* reveal sexual activity as an expression of mutuality and commitment?

How do "**We**" relationships include a past and future orientation, not merely a living in the present?

Do you think it is necessary for a couple to be legally married to achieve the "**We**" type of relationship? Why, or why not?

RELATED QUESTIONS

What similarities exist between *Gather* and *How Do I Love Thee? (Sonnet XLIII)* by Elizabeth Barrett Browning (p. 506)? For example, what connection is there between Browne's "fields of my childhood, all songs I have sung," and Browning's "I love thee with a passion put to use/in my old griefs, and with my childhood's faith . . . I love thee with the breath,/smiles, tears of all my life!"

What is the importance of "grace" in *Gather,* and "beauty" in *Part of Plenty* (p. 518)?

Both Spencer in *Part of Plenty* and Browne in *Gather* deal with love as a part of plenty. What are the other parts?

Did the couple in *may i feel said he* (p. 475) realize the wonder and joy of sex? If so, how? If not, why not? What would you term the pleasure which made him say "you're divine" and her say "You are Mine"?

What does "joy" connote that "pleasure" lacks? How is it connected with Lewis' Need-pleasure versus the "most Appreciative of all Pleasures" in *Eros* (p. 207)?

Although the situation was not a specifically sexual one, how were the same elements of Joy evident in *The Gift of the Magi* (p. 510)? How are they connected with being loved and cherished?

Slowly, Slowly

MARK VAN DOREN

The lover loves the eyes that close,
And closing, shut the world to shame;
Then parted lips; then helpless blood;
Then breast and breast, the two, the same,
The all in one, awaiting there
Himself, the other—hears his name—
And answers; but he loves the most
What now he neither hears nor sees,
Yet has at last—oh, wonder then—
Down there—his very own—the knees
That slowly, slowly melt his bones
As summer sun drowns honey bees.

How does Van Doren in *Slowly, Slowly* portray Fromm's paradox: "in love two beings become one and yet remain two"?

In the sexual act as pictured by Van Doren are they "sexual performers", as Lowen describes them (p. 408)? Why, or why not?

From a physiological point of view an orgasm is an orgasm is an orgasm. No matter how achieved, the physiological response is the same—congestion of blood vessels, increase in muscle tension and their release at orgasm. Generally the male partner is physiologically capable of reaching orgasm more quickly than the female partner, and he may have to delay his orgasm to help the female partner to reach hers. Intercourse is successful only when both partners receive some satisfaction. An orgasm is achieved gradually, particularly for the woman. The way the partners feel about each other and the act they are performing has more influence on their capacity to respond to each other with orgasm than does the skill of either as a lover. A married man who typically achieves orgasm with his wife may fail in extramarital attempts. A woman who finds sexual contacts distasteful, may not respond with orgasm in any situation. The emotional climate of a sexual relationship seems to determine the satisfaction it yields. Female orgasm and the satisfaction derived therefrom is sometimes revealed more by emotional than by physical manifestations—tenderness toward her male partner and a certain emotional release in her body and manner. Although a woman can simulate orgasm (to reinforce the male ego?) her gentle warmth may be somewhat lacking afterward. In the male, ejaculation and orgasm are practically simultaneous and synonymous—a spurt of semen and a spasm of muscles in the genital area, followed by loss of erection and sexual excitement. If a woman achieves orgasm her feeling of satisfaction and sexual excitement diminishes more slowly than that of the male. Women who have experienced an orgasm are able to describe it in physical terms only about as well as men could were there no ejaculation to describe. Descriptions of feelings and symptoms at orgasm range from "my whole body bursting with pleasure and stars" to "it is a very good feeling."

From a psychological point of view, Ruth in *Rabbit, Run* (p. 418) explained the sensation of female orgasm by "it's like falling through—to Nowhere." From the male standpoint, Joel, in *First Love and Other Sorrows* (p. 118) claimed it was disappointing, "like masturbation, kind of with bells." In Cummings' *may i feel said he* (p. 475), "he" reacts with "tiptop"; she wit"ummm. . . ." Is there a distinction between the physical emphasis which stamps the remarks of Ruth, Joel, and "he," as opposed to some additional element which marks sexual fusion in Van Doren's *Slowly, Slowly* and Browne's *Gather* (p. 520)?

Why are the elements of joy and wonder not mentioned by those in "**You-I**" relationships? How might the reason be indicated in Fromm's earlier comment (p. 261) that "sexual desire aims at fusion—and is by no means only a physical appetite, the relief of a painful tension"? Does the distinction clarify a belief of many who advance the case for chastity—namely, that the human sex impulse is tied to the deepest emotions and should be integrated with love in the truest, finest sense of the word; and that while an adolescent may physically be mature enough for sexual intercourse, he may lack the emotional preparedness to appreciate the full joy and wonder and realization of the act? Do you agree with the argument?

RELATED QUESTIONS

How do Van Doren in *Slowly, Slowly;* Browne in *Gather* (p. 520); and Spencer in *Part of Plenty* (p. 518) help to explain the paradox stated by Lindbergh (p. 233) that to find oneself, one must lose oneself?

Twenty-third Street Runs into Heaven

KENNETH PATCHEN

You stand near the window as lights wink
On along the street. Somewhere a trolley, taking
Shop-girls and clerks home, clatters through
This before-supper Sabbath. An alley cat cries
To find the garbage cans sealed; newsboys
Begin their murder-into-pennies round.

We are shut in, secure for a little, safe until
Tomorrow. You slip your dress off, roll down
Your stockings, careful against runs. Naked now,
With soft light on soft flesh, you pause

For a moment; turn and face me—
Smile in a way that only women know
Who have lain long with their lover
And are made more virginal.

Our supper is plain but we are very wonderful.

Can you resolve the seeming contradiction between "lain long with their lover" and "made more virginal"?

A virgin, by definition, is: free of impurity or stain; chaste; fresh, unspoiled. Chaste, by definition, means: innocent of unlawful sexual intercourse; celibate, the state of not being married (and, hence, presumably abstaining from sexual intercourse); pure in thought and act. In **Twenty-third Street Runs into Heaven** which of the meanings of "chaste" is the poet emphasizing? How does Patchen suggest all three dictionary meanings of chaste, even though "virginal" and "lain long with [a] lover" appear to be mutually exclusive?

Why are "we . . . very wonderful"?

Assuming these two people are not married, how might their relationship be defended as a moral one? By what standards?

RELATED QUESTIONS

In what sense does "our supper is plain but we are very wonderful" resemble the mood and tone in Spencer's **Part of Plenty** (p. 518)?

Both Ruth in **Rabbit, Run** (p. 412) and the woman in Patchen's poem roll down stockings, "careful against runs," as they undress. Contrast the behavior and attitudes of the partners in each selection depicted in the moments before the sexual act. How do the preliminary minutes differ? How might it condition the act itself and the pleasure to be derived from it?

As in **Slowly, Slowly** (p. 521) and **Rabbit, Run** the lovers in **Twenty-third Street Runs into Heaven** try to shut out the world. In doing so, in establishing a "self-enclosed perfection" described in **Double-Sunrise** (p. 232) are they shutting out reality? Why, or why not?

Given the circumstances of **Twenty-third Street Runs into Heaven,** how might Lindbergh (**Double-Sunrise,** p. 232) react?

That Night When Joy Began

W. H. AUDEN

524

"We"
"wonderful one
times one"

That night when joy began
Our narrowest veins to flush,
We waited for the flash
Of morning's levelled gun.

But morning let us pass,
And day by day relief
Outgrew his nervous laugh,
Grows credulous of peace.

As mile by mile is seen
No trespasser's reproach,
And love's best glasses reach
No fields but are his own.

As many authorities have observed, couples may be firmly convinced that they are free of conventional moral scruples, and that they view sex as another outlet for expression of affection. Yet early family training and conditioning by Western society may prove as difficult to erase as Neill in *Sex Attitudes* (p. 286) claims it is. Thus guilt and shame and disappointment may flaw sexual pleasures. What might be assumed to have been the past experiences with love in the case of the two people in *That Night When Joy Began?* What is their current experience with love?

What do key words like the "wait," the "gun," the "trespasser," the "glasses," and the "fields" signify? For example, does "We waited for the flash of morning's levelled gun" suggest that they expected to be killed? Literally? Figuratively? Shot at? If so, by whom? For what? In what sense might they be "trespassers"?

The couple in Auden's poem are allows to "pass." Pass what? By what? What is the effect? To what do anxiety and nervousness yield? What, in the poem, makes their peace credible?

Does "No trespasser's reproach" mean that no trespasser reproaches the lovers, or that no one reprimands the lovers for being trespassers? Why?

Are the "glasses" drinking glasses? Eyeglasses? Field glasses? Why is the word modified by "best" and by "love's"?

What does "no fields but are his own" mean? How are the glasses instrumental in determining this?

Displacing guilt and fear, what other qualities are now in the circulatory systems of the two lovers since that night when joy began to flush their narrowest veins?

What does joy connote that happiness or peace need not?

RELATED QUESTIONS

Is there anything about the quality of joy—as seen in *Slowly, Slowly* (p. 521), in *The Wife* (see "**Night-Lights,**" p. 571) and in *The Gift of the Magi* (p 510) that would explain the diminution of guilt and fear?

How does the experience of the couple in **That Night When Joy Began** contradict the view of Evelyn Havens in **I Thought I Was Modern** (p. 280)?

Were the figures in **The Figures on the Frieze** (p. 497) aware of "the flash of morning's levelled gun"? What did the daylight reveal to them?

Plaque for a Brass Bed

CHARLES PHILBRICK

Everything else is just furniture. This bed
Is frame on which, in light or dark, forgiveness
Weaves itself, and failure fails to matter.
Here love has worked, and pain has visited;
Here life has struck; here death may still the sheets:
This bed our garden, altar, engine-room,
The tablet of whatever testament our blood
Has written in our more than twenty years.

How might the bed in the Philbrick poem have functioned as "garden"? As "altar"? As "engine-room"?

How might the "testament" be "an act of will," the commitment outlined by Lee in **What Love Must Be** (p. 250)?

In **Winter Term** (p. 472) the author says:

. . . They had talked now and then of renting a room but Hal knew they would never do it; they were still too aware of the connotations. And although they prided themselves on their indifference to surroundings, Ellie's face seemed to reflect the gray walls when they lay together on his bed.

What "connotations" were Hal and Ellie "still too aware of"? How are the connotations markedly changed in **Plaque for a Brass Bed?**

RELATED QUESTIONS

What would the **Plaque for a Brass Bed** in a room rented by Hal and Ellie in **Winter Term** (p. 466) have to say? Anything more than "Hal and Ellie Slept Here"?

What elements of **Gather** (p. 520) and **Part of Plenty** (p. 518) appear in Philbrick's poem?

How does **Plaque for a Brass Bed** clarify the statements about marriage in **Forsaking All Others** (p. 355)?

How might Philbrick's concept of the bed as the frame in a twenty-year relationship fit into Lindbergh's concept of marriage in **Oyster Bed** (p. 346)?

John Anderson

ROBERT BURNS

Tune—*John Anderson my Jo.*

John Anderson my jo, John,
    When we were first acquent,
Your locks were like the raven,
    Your bonny brow was brent;
But now your brow is beld, John,
    Your locks are like the snaw;
But blessings on your frosty pow,
    John Anderson my jo.

John Anderson my jo, John,
    We clamb the hill thegither,
And monie a canty day, John,
    We've had wi' ane anither:
Now we maun totter down, John,
    But hand in hand we'll go,
And sleep thegither at the foot,
    John Anderson my jo.

Can love last? Which of the tests of love on p. 42 does the "**We**" relationship in *John Anderson* meet?

What is at the core of all "**We**" relationships?

RELATED QUESTIONS

How does Burns' poem reflect the view of love expressed by Shakespeare in *Sonnet 116* (p. 230)?

How are the views of marriage set forth by Lindbergh in *Oyster Bed* (p. 346) and by Dietrich in *Married Love: Strategy of* (p. 349) implicit in Burns' phrase "we clamb the hill thegither"?

if everything happens
that can't be done

E. E. CUMMINGS

if everything happens that can't be done
(and anything's righter
than books
could plan)
the stupidest teacher will almost guess

(with a run
skip
around we go yes)
there's nothing as something as one

one hasn't a why or because or although
(and buds know better
than books
don't grow)
one's anything old being everything new
(with a what
which
around we come who)
one's everyanything so

so world is a leaf so tree is a bough
(and birds sing sweeter
than books
tell how)
so here is away and so your is a my
(with a down
up
around again fly)
forever was never till now

now i love you and you love me
(and books are shuter
than books
can be)
and deep in the high that does nothing but fall
(with a shout
each
around we go all)
there's somebody calling who's we

we're anything brighter than even the sun
(we're everything greater
than books
might mean)
we're everyanything more than believe
(with a spin
leap
alive we're alive)
we're wonderful one times one

In love, where no formulas exist, can the whole be greater than the sum of its parts?

RELATED QUESTIONS

Like love, Cummings' poem is filled with mysteries, contradictions, and paradoxes. Yet he, with child-like joy in adulthood, examines the same problem that Frankie Addams in *The Member of the Wedding* (p. 504) articulated with adult-like perception in her childhood: Where is the "**We**" of "me?"

In terms of all selections you have read which are relevant to it, how might one explain each of the following phrases in Cummings' poem:

    (a) there's nothing as something as one
    (b) one hasn't a why or because or although
    (c) one's everyanything
    (d) so your is a my
    (e) forever was never till now
    (f) now i love you and you love me . . .
        there's somebody calling who's we
    (g) we're anything brighter than ever the sun
    (h) (we're everything greater
        than books
        might mean)
    (i) we're everyanything more than believe
        (with a spin
        leap
    (j) alive we're alive)
    (k) we're wonderful one times one

"Night-Lights"

REFLECTIONS ON SEXUAL THEMES

To write grossly of sex, to labor in a
story the physical side of love, is to err
aesthetically — to overpaint, for the imagination of readers requires little stimulus
in this direction, and the sex impulse is so
strong that any emphatic physical description
pulls the picture out of perspective. . . .
if it were not for the physical side of love
we should none of us be here, and the least
sophisticated of us knows intuitively . . . much
about it. . . . But the atmosphere and psychology of passion are other matters, and
the trackless maze in which the average
reader wanders where his feelings are concerned is none the worse for a night-light
or two. [1]

All the selections grouped as "**Night-Lights**" have been previously cited in the text as high-intensity sources of illumination, affording a closer look at an "**I**," a "**They**," a "**You-I**" or a "**We**" scene.

These cross-references play like searchlights across a night sky, and suggest the continuing reciprocal relationships that weave all arbitrarily categorized selections into the vast panorama of human sexuality. But by a direct focus on the light source itself—not simply the objects and views illumined by them—the integrity of each "**Night-Light**," whether flare or firefly, may be seen.

Because the selections in the first four categories more sharply clarify facets of "**I**," "**They**," "**You-I**," and "**We**" dimensions of psychosexual development, these "**Night-Lights**" were not included among them. Yet, there is nothing secondary or subordinate about these readings. Each has a valuable content and theme of its own and should be viewed and reviewed for its message about human sexuality in its many protean forms, as well as for the meaning it shares or enlarges with other selections in this book.

The following "**Night-Lights**" are alphabetically arranged by author and are not followed by specific questions for discussion. The authors' philosophy, commiting individuals to make up their own minds, extends here to encouraging readers to formulate their own questions—thus those that may be questions for others—to uncover as many perspectives as possible on a situation, and to root out the moral issues implicit or explicit in the "**Night-Lights**."

And—in courage and honesty—to answer them as responsible individuals. **531**

To His Forsaken Mistress

ROBERT AYTOUN

I do confess thou'rt smooth and fair,
    And I might have gone near to love thee,
Had I not found the slightest prayer
    That lips could speak, had power to move thee;
But I can let thee now alone,
As worthy to be loved by none.

I do confess thou'rt sweet, but find
    Thee such an unthrift of thy sweets,
Thy favours are but like the wind,
    That kisses everything it meets;
And since thou can with more than one,
Thou'rt worthy to be kiss'd by none.

The morning rose that untouch'd stands,
    Arm'd with her briars, how sweetly smells;
But, pluck'd and strain'd through ruder hands,
    Her sweet no longer with her dwells.
But scent and beauty both are gone,
And leaves fall from her, one by one.

Such fate ere long will thee betide,
    When thou hast handled been a while;
Like sere flowers to be thrown aside;—
    And I will sigh, while some will smile,
To see thy love for more than one
Hath brought thee to be loved by none.

They Laugh

RODERICK BATES

I

"Don't worry ma'am, we'll find the man,
and when we do, he'll pay for what he done."
In the back corner sat youth.
He held her hand, greasy with popcorn.
She leaned on his shoulder
and glanced carefully at his face.
Caught, she looked away;
distracted by the burst of gunfire
she watched several men die,

then turned again,
He looked down at her smile,
leaned toward her.
She shrank away
then met him . . .
The man had been found, and he
had paid,
It was bright with the lights on.
On the street, holding hands again,
they talked
    "I love you."
    "I love you, too."
    "I've never said that before, have you?"
    "Nope, me neither."
    "Gosh, love is cool!"
    "Yeah"

II

    "and now to keep you informed of what's
    happening, here's the news."
In the back seat Lust sprawled uncomfortably,
she shifted and stretched out
He looked at her legs and smiled.
She glanced down,
reached to straighten her skirt,
then stopped.
She smiled up at him,
and he bent down . . .
    "and here we have the headlines on the half hour."
Moving to the front seat,
They sat and smoked.
    "I love you a hell of a lot."
    "I love you too."
    "Wanna come here again tomorrow night?"
    "Sure"
    "Gee, Love's a hell of a lot of fun"
    "Yeah"

III

The breeze played across the sand,
the moon was sinking into the ocean.
On the beach lay Infatuation.
she held her new ring to the moon,
They watched as it caught
the white fire and burned.
He kissed her hair . . .
The sea slapped against the shore. From the

hills a breeze whistled through the pines.
The moon was gone.
   She sighed . . .
      "I just met you last week, but
      it seems as though I've known you forever"
      "It's strange isn't it?"
      "But I love you."
      "And I love you."
      "I guess that love just doesn't
      happen the way you expect it to."
      "Yes, I guess so."

IV

Pale moonlight fell on the path,
It hit the stones, and the
names stood out.
Love walked slowly
through the night.
He came to the end of the path,
and moved to the left.
He knelt beside a small stone,
brushed away a dry leaf
and laid a flower in the grass . . .
From the road they saw him kneeling.
They laughed at the old man.
He stood, and gazed at the stone.
With a gasp, he clutched his heart and fell.
They ran to him but they could do
nothing. Slowly they separated,
and walked away.
Youth said "But it's so far in the
            future and we have love,
            let's not think about it."
Lust said "Let's love now and to hell with later"
Infatuation said, "Our love is too strong, it cannot end."
But Love was gone.

Entry August 29
WALTER BENTON

It was like something done in fever, when nothing fits,
mind into mind nor body into body . . . when nothing
meets or equals—when dimensions lie and perceptions go haywire.

With what an alien sense my fingers curved about her breasts
and searched the tangled dark where love lay hiding!

I closed my eyes better to imagine you—
but the rehearsed body would not ratify the mind's deception.

The kisses of her mouth, the rhythm natural to love—and the exciting
musk with which love haloes itself . . . these thwarted my imagination.
Her love, too, was centered and intent,

it did not reach her eyes and forehead, or light her throat
as your love did—
it did not fill the room . . . or spread all over the ceiling of the sky.
It did not span the years and miles and hold hands with beast and God.

Nor did her thighs rise with that splendid grade I stroked from memory.
Her body met me unlike your body
and I entered the heaven of her uneasily . . . and could not stay—
for my heart being yours released no blood to make ready for love.

Entry November 12

WALTER BENTON

I waited years today . . . one year for every hour,
all day—though I knew you could not come till night
I waited . . . and nothing else in this God's hell meant anything.

I had everything you love—shellfish and saltsticks . . . watercress,
black olives. Wine (for the watch I pawned), real cream
for our coffee. Smoked cheese, currants in port, preserved wild cherries.

I bought purple asters from a pushcart florist and placed them where
they would be between us—
imagining your lovely face among them . . .

But you did not come . . . you did not come,
You did not come. And I left the table lit and your glass filled—
and my glass empty . . . and I went into the night, looking for you.

The glittering pile, Manhattan, swarmed like an uncovered dung heap.
Along the waterfront
manlike shapes all shoulders and collar walked stiffly like shadow figures.

Later, the half-moon rose.
                    Everywhere the windows falling dark.
By St. Mark's church, under the iron fence, a girl was crying. And the old
steeple was mouldy with moonlight, and I was tired . . . and very lonely.

The Barretts of Wimpole Street

RUDOLF BESIER

BARRETT   Elizabeth.

ELIZABETH   *(in a whisper)* Yes?

BARRETT   Why do you look at me like that, child? *(Placing hand on her head and bending it slightly back)* Are you frightened?

ELIZABETH   *(as before)* No.

BARRETT   *(moving to center of sofa, behind it)* You're trembling, why?

ELIZABETH   I—I don't know.

BARRETT   You're not frightened of me? (ELIZABETH *is about to speak; he continues quickly.*) No—no—you mustn't say it. I couldn't bear to think that. You're everything in the world to me—you know that. Without you I should be quite alone—you know that, too. And you—if you love me, you can't be afraid of me. For love casts out fear. You love me, my darling? You love your father?

ELIZABETH   *(in a whisper)* Yes.

BARRETT   *(eagerly)* And you'll prove your love by doing as I wish?

ELIZABETH   I don't understand. I was going to drink—

BARRETT   *(quickly)* Yes, out of fear, not love. Listen, dear. I told you just now that if you disobeyed me, you would incur my displeasure. I take that back. I shall never in any way reproach you. You shall never know by word, or deed, or hint of mine, how much you have grieved and wounded your father by refusing to do the little thing he asked.

ELIZABETH   Oh please, please, don't say any more. It's all so petty and sordid. Please give me the tankard.

BARRETT   You are acting of your own free will—?

ELIZABETH   Oh, Papa, let us get this over and forget it. I can't forgive myself for having made the whole house miserable over a tankard of porter.

• • • •

ELIZABETH   *(quickly and nervously)* Oh, it's hard to explain to someone who doesn't know all the circumstances. You see, Papa is very devoted to me, and—

BROWNING   Devoted?

ELIZABETH   He's very devoted to me and depends a great deal on my companionship. He hasn't many points of contact with my brothers and sisters. If I were away for six months, he—

BROWNING   *(visibly restraining himself, rising and going toward her)* Miss Barrett, may I speak plainly?

ELIZABETH   Oh, do you think you'd better? I know—more or less—how you feel about this. But you see, you don't quite understand all the situation. How should you?

BROWNING   *(walking up to center window)* Oh, very well—then I'll say nothing. *(His control suddenly gives way, and his words pour out. Returns down to upper right corner of sofa.)* You tell me I don't understand. You are quite right. I don't. You tell me he is devoted to you. I don't understand a devotion that demands favors as if they were rights, demands duty and respect, and obedience and love, demands all and takes all, and gives nothing in return. I don't understand a devotion that spends itself in petty tyrannies and gross bullying. I don't understand a devotion that grudges you any ray of light and glimpse of happiness, and doesn't even stop at risking your life to gratify its colossal selfishness. Devotion! Give me good sound, honest hatred, rather than devotion like that! At our first meeting you forbade me to speak of love—there was nothing more than friendship between us. I obeyed you, but I knew very well—we both knew—that I was to be much more than just your friend. Even before I passed that door, and our eyes first met across the room, I loved you, and I've gone on loving you—and I love you more now than words can tell— and I shall love you to the end and beyond. You know that? You've always known?

ELIZABETH *(brokenly)*   Yes—I've always known. And now, for pity's sake—for pity's sake—leave me. *(Rising.)*

BROWNING *(with a firm grasp of both her hands, rises, comes around right end of sofa)*   No!

ELIZABETH   Oh, please—please—let me go! Leave me. We must never see each other again.

BROWNING *(maintaining his grasp)*   I shall never let you go—I shall never leave you! *(Draws her into his arms.)* Elizabeth—Elizabeth!

ELIZABETH *(struggling feebly in his embrace)*   No—no—Oh, Robert, have mercy on me—

BROWNING   Elizabeth, my darling—*(He kisses her, and at the touch of his lips her arms go round his neck.)*

ELIZABETH   Oh, Robert—I love you—I love you—I love you.

[*They kiss again, then she sinks onto sofa and he sits right of her, holding her hands.*]

BROWNING   And yet you ask me to take my marching orders, and go out of your life?

ELIZABETH   Yes, Robert, for what have I to give you? I have so little of all that love asks for. I have no beauty and no health—and I'm no longer young—

BROWNING   I love you.

ELIZABETH *(speaking with restrained spiritual ecstasy)*   I should have refused to see you after our first meeting. For I loved you then, though I denied it even to myself. Oh, Robert, I think Eve must have felt as I did when her first dawn broke over Paradise—the terror—the wonder—the glory of it. I had no strength to put up any kind of resistance, except the pitiful pretense of mere friendship. I was paralyzed with happiness that I had never dreamt it was possible to feel. That's my only excuse—and God knows I need one—for not having sent you away from me at once.

BROWNING   I love you.

ELIZABETH *(continuing as before)*   My life had reached its lowest ebb. I was worn out, and hope was dead. Then you came. Robert, do you know what you have done for me? I could have laughed when Dr. Chambers said that I had cured myself by wanting to live. He was right—oh, he was right. I wanted to live— eagerly, desperately, passionately—and all because life meant you—you—*(He leans down to kiss her hands.)*—and the sight of your face, and the sound of your voice, and the touch of your hand. Oh, and so much more than that! Because of you the air once more was sweet to breathe, and all the world was good and green again.

BROWNING *(rising from kissing her hands)*   And with those words singing in my ears, I'm to turn my back on you and go?

ELIZABETH   But, Robert, can't you see how impossible—?

BROWNING   I've never yet turned my back on a friend or an enemy. Am I likely to turn it on you?

ELIZABETH   But how is it all to end? What have we to look forward to? And how—?

BROWNING   I love you, and I want you for my wife.

ELIZABETH   Robert, I can't marry you. How can I, when—?

BROWNING   Not today or tomorrow. Not this year, perhaps, or next. Perhaps not for years to come—

ELIZABETH   I may never be able to marry you.

BROWNING   What then? If you remain to the last beyond my reach I shall die proud and happy in having spent a lifetime fighting to gain the richest prize a man was ever offered.

ELIZABETH   Oh, Robert, put aside your dream of me and look on me as I am. I love you too well to let you waste your manhood pursuing the pale ghost of a woman.

BROWNING   Do you think I'm a boy to be swept off my feet by an impulse, or a sentimental dreamer blind to reality? There's no man alive who sees things clearer than I do, or has his feet more firmly planted on the earth. And I tell you in all soberness that my need of you is as urgent as your need of me. If your weakness asks my strength for support, my abundant strength cries out for your weakness to complete my life and myself.

ELIZABETH *(after a pause, turning to lie down)*   Robert, have you thought what your position here would be like if you went on seeing me after today?

BROWNING   Yes.

ELIZABETH *(continuing)*   We should have to keep our love secret from everyone lest a whisper of it get to my father's ears.

BROWNING   I know.

ELIZABETH   If he had the least suspicion that you were more than a friend, the door would be slammed in your face, my letters supervised, and my life made unbearable.

BROWNING   I know.

ELIZABETH   And you, my dear, you're as frank and open as the day. How would you enjoy coming here under false pretenses, and all the subterfuges and intrigues we'd be forced to use?

BROWNING *(smiling)*   I shall detest it—I shall hate it with all my heart and soul— and I thank God for that.

ELIZABETH   But, Robert—

BROWNING   For it's splendid and right that I should suffer some discomfort at least for such a reward as you. The immortal garland was never won without dust and heat.

I Corinthians xiii (The Holy Bible)

KING JAMES VERSION

Though I speak with the tongues of men and of angels, and have not charity, I am become as sounding brass, or a tinkling cymbal. And though I have the gift of prophecy, and understand all mysteries, and all knowledge; and though I have all faith, so that I could remove mountains, and have not charity, I am nothing. And though I bestow all my goods to feed the poor, and though I give my body to be burned, and have not charity, it profiteth me nothing.

Charity suffereth long, and is kind; charity envieth not; charity vaunteth not itself, is not puffed up, doth not behave itself unseemly, seeketh not her own, is not easily provoked, thinketh no evil; rejoiceth not in iniquity, but rejoiceth in the truth; beareth all things, believeth all things, hopeth all things; endureth all things. Charity never faileth: but whether there be prophecies, they shall fail, whether there be tongues, they shall cease; whether there be knowledge, it shall vanish away. For we know in part, and we prophesy in part. But when that which is perfect is come, then that which is in part shall be done away.

When I was a child, I spake as a child, I understood as a child, I thought as a child: but when I became a man, I put away childish things. For now we see through a glass, darkly; but then face to face: now I know in part; but then shall I know even as also I am known. And now abideth faith, hope, charity, these three; but the greatest of these is charity.

REVISED STANDARD VERSION

If I speak in the tongues of men and angels, but have not love, I am a noisy gong or a clanging cymbal. And if I have prophetic powers, and understand all mysteries and all knowledge, and if I have all faith, so as to remove mountains, but have not love, I am nothing. If I give away all I have, and if I deliver my body to be burned, but have not love, I gain nothing.

Love is patient and kind; love is not jealous or boastful; it is not arrogant or rude. Love does not insist on its own way; it is not irritable or resentful; it does not rejoice at wrong, but rejoices in the right. Love bears all things, believes all things, hopes all things, endures all things.

Love never ends; as for prophecies, they will pass away; as for tongues, they will cease; as for knowledge, it will pass away. For our knowledge is imperfect and our prophecy is imperfect; but when the perfect comes, the imperfect will pass away. When I was a child, I spoke like a child, I thought like a child, I reasoned like a child; when I became a man, I gave up childish ways. For now we see in a mirror dimly, but then face to face. Now I know in part; then I shall understand fully, even as I have been fully understood. So faith, hope, love abide, these three; but the greatest of these is love.

The One-Night Stand:
An Approach to the Bridge

PAUL BLACKBURN

Migod, a picture window
both of us sitting there
on the too-narrow couch
variously unclothed
watching sky lighten over the city

You compile your list of noes
it is incomplete
I add another
there is no anger
we keep it open
trying,
shying
away, your all
too-solid body melts, revives, stif-
fens, clears and dis-
solves, an i-
dentity emerges, disappears, it is
like watching a film, the takes dis-
solving into other takes,
spliced suddenly to a closeup
the window tints pink

                                              I wait

We sleep a bit. Your
identity goes and comes
it is never for me, it
is never sure of itself

                                            I wait, you

ask too much of yourself, why
of the moment, why
is your fear of feeding off other people? Must
you always feed off yourself
and find it unreal food you eat, unreal
water you drink from the source of yourself, unreal liquor you take from the hand of a friend, and
never grow gloriously drunk, but stay
eating yourself
finding the fare thin,
stay in a dark room holding
uneasily, in an unreal hand

a thin man's unreal cock who stays
and grows more unreal to himself?

                                                  We both sleep

New day's sun
doubles itself in the river
A double string of blue lights
glares to mark the bridge, the
city huddles under a yellow light
the sodium flares
gleam under oblique
sun's double in the stream,

                                                  I wake

ready, make my move.
"You'll make me pregnant" you murmur
and barely audible, "I'll die"
neither will stop me
your legs are open
I am there at the wet edge
of life, the moist living lips

It will not do
I have been at this life's edge
and hurt too many hours
It will be all me for a moment
then all you
Identities will dissolve
under this new act, or
six quick strokes
you move once
toward me, say
one word, even
moan, I will be finished
done
dissolved

become real, alone, no
it will not do
You are no victim and
I no rapist hero, I can
still, I
stop at life's edge

Later
we are too real
separate, try
to recover

dully, our-
selves gone out
The coffee does not warm
there is an orange sun in the river
there are blue lights on the bridge
Animal tenderness and
sadness is all we salvage, is
all the picture window
mirrors and maintains

Sonnet VI

ELIZABETH BARRETT BROWNING

Go from me. Yet I feel that I shall stand
Henceforward in thy shadow. Nevermore
Alone upon the threshold of my door
Of individual life, I shall command
The uses of my soul, nor lift my hand
Serenely in the sunshine as before,
Without the sense of that which I forbore—
Thy touch upon the palm. The widest land
Doom takes to part us, leaves thy heart in mine
With pulses that beat double. What I do
And what I dream include thee, as the wine
Must taste of its own grapes. And when I sue
God for myself, He hears that name of thine,
And sees within my eyes the tears of two.

Sonnet XVI

ELIZABETH BARRETT BROWNING

And yet, because thou overcomest so,
Because thou art more noble like a king,
Thou canst prevail against my fears and fling
Thy purple round me, till my heart shall grow
Too close against thine heart, henceforth to know
How it shook when alone. Why, conquering
May prove as lordly and complete a thing
In lifting upward, as in crushing low!
And as a vanquished soldier yields his sword
To one who lifts him from the bloody earth,—
Even so, Belovèd, I at last record,
Here ends my strife. If *thou* invite me forth,
I rise above abasement at the word.
Make thy love larger to enlarge my worth.

Porphyria's Lover

ROBERT BROWNING

The rain set early in tonight,
  The sullen wind was soon awake,
It tore the elm-tops down for spite,
  And did its worst to vex the lake:
  I listened with heart fit to break.
When glided in Porphyria; straight
  She shut the cold out and the storm,
And kneeled and made the cheerless grate
  Blaze up, and all the cottage warm;
  Which done, she rose, and from her form
Withdrew the dripping cloak and shawl,
  And laid her soiled gloves by, untied
Her hat and let the damp hair fall,
  And, last, she sat down by my side
  And called me. When no voice replied,
She put my arm about her waist,
  And made her smooth white shoulder bare,
And all her yellow hair displaced,
  And, stooping, made my cheek lie there,
  And spread, o'er all, her yellow hair,
Murmuring how she loved me—she
  Too weak, for all her heart's endeavor,
To set its struggling passion free
  From pride, and vainer ties dissever,
  And give herself to me for ever.
But passion sometimes would prevail,
  Nor could tonight's gay feast restrain
A sudden thought of one so pale
  For love of her, and all in vain:
  So, she was come through wind and rain.
Be sure I looked up at her eyes
  Happy and proud; at last I knew
Porphyria worshiped me; surprise
  Made my heart swell, and still it grew
  While I debated what to do.
That moment she was mine, mine, fair,
  Perfectly pure and good: I found
A thing to do, and all her hair
  In one long yellow string I wound
  Three times her little throat around,
And strangled her. No pain felt she;
  I am quite sure she felt no pain.
As a shut bud that holds a bee,
  I warily oped her lids: again

Laughed the blue eyes without a stain.
And I untightened next the tress
  About her neck; her cheek once more
Blushed bright beneath my burning kiss:
  I propped her head up as before,
  Only, this time my shoulder bore
Her head, which droops upon it still:
  The smiling rosy little head,
So glad it has its utmost will,
  That all it scorned at once is fled,
  And I, its love, am gained instead!
Porphyria's love: she guessed not how
  Her darling one wish would be heard.
And thus we sit together now,
  And all night long we have not stirred,
  And yet God has not said a word!

A Marriage

ROBERT CREELEY

The first retainer
he gave to her
was a golden
wedding ring.

The second—late at night
he woke up,
leaned over on an elbow,
and kissed her.

The third and the last—
he died with
and gave up loving
and lived with her.

when i have thought of
you somewhat too (vi)

E. E. CUMMINGS

when i have thought of you somewhat too
much and am become perfectly and
simply Lustful. . . .sense a gradual stir
of beginning muscle, and what it will do

to me before shutting. . . .understand
i love you. . . .feel your suddenly body reach
for me with a speed of white speech

(the simple instant of perfect hunger
Yes)
        how beautifully swims
the fooling world in my huge blood,
cracking brains A swiftlyenormous light
—and furiously puzzling through, prismatic, whims,
the chattering self perceives with hysterical fright

a comic tadpole wriggling in delicious mud

Early Love

SAMUEL DANIEL

Ah! I remember well (and how can I
But evermore remember well) when first
Our flame began, when scarce we knew what was
The flame we felt; when as we sat and sigh'd
And look'd upon each other, and conceived
Not what we ail'd—yet something we did ail;
And yet were well, and yet we were not well,
And what was our disease we could not tell.
Then would we kiss, then sigh, then look; and thus
In that first garden of our simpleness
We spent our childhood. But when years began
To reap the fruit of knowledge, ah, how then
Would she with graver looks, with sweet, stern brow,
Check my presumption and my forwardness;
    Yet still would give me flowers, still would me show
    What she would have me, yet not have me know.

Resolving Doubts

WILLIAM DICKEY

SHE   If to demands of others I agree,
      Then I will be another, but not me.

HE   If their requiring voices shake your ear,
      How will your very spirit help but hear?

SHE   It will, a bird, desert its builded nest,
      And in the virgin cloudbank only rest.

HE   If they have wings like other birds of prey,
How will it from those raptors keep away?

SHE   It will seek out the ocean's whitest curl,
And sink within it and become a pearl.

HE   But when they dive as glittering fishers dive,
Will they not take your luster all alive?

SHE   Venue shall make no difference to disguise,
Nor shall my center open to their eyes.

HE   But if by chance, by force, by God knows how,
You all unguarded should some night allow
Another there beside you in your bed,
Body is body, and will not lie dead.

SHE   Body is body, but the heart stays true,
And should that happen, I will think him you.

See It Was Like This When (9)

LAWRENCE FERLINGHETTI

See
     it was like this when
           we waltz into this place
a couple of Papish cats
        is doing an Aztec two-step
And I says
      Dad let's cut
but then this dame
      comes up behind me see
        and says
      You and me could really exist
Wow I says
     Only the next day
      she has bad teeth
       and really hates
         poetry

We Squat Upon the Beach of Love (24)

LAWRENCE FERLINGHETTI

We squat upon the beach of love
 among Picasso mandolins struck full of sand
  and buried catspaws that know no sphinx
  and picnic papers
   dead crabs' claws
   and starfish prints

We squat upon the beach of love
 among the beached mermaids
  with their bawling babies and bald husbands
  and homemade wooden animals
  with icecream spoons for feet
  which cannot walk or love
   except to eat

We squat upon the brink of love
 and are secure as only squatters are
 among the puddled leavings
   of salt sex's tides
 and the sweet semen rivulets
  and limp buried peckers
in the sand's soft flesh

And still we laugh
 and still we run
  and still we throw ourselves
   upon love's boats
 but it is deeper
  and much later
   than we think
 and all goes down
  and all our lovebuoys fail us

And we drink and drown

Sex Education

DOROTHY CANFIELD FISHER

It was three times—but at intervals of many years—that I heard my Aunt Minnie tell about an experience of her girlhood that had made a never-to-be-forgotten impression on her. The first time she was in her thirties, still young. But she had been married for ten years, so that to my group of friends, all in the early teens, she seemed quite of another generation.

The day she told us the story we had been idling on one end of her porch as we made casual plans for a picnic supper in the woods. Darning stockings at the other end, she paid no attention to us until one of the girls said, "Let's take blankets and sleep out there. It'd be fun."

"No," Aunt Minnie broke in sharply, "you mustn't do that."

"Oh, for goodness sake, why not!" said one of the younger girls, rebelliously. "The boys are always doing it. Why can't we, just once?"

Aunt Minnie laid down her sewing. "Come here, girls," she said, "I want you should hear something that happened to me when I was your age."

Her voice had a special quality which, perhaps, young people of today would not recognize. But we did. We knew from experience that it was the dark voice grown-ups used when they were going to say something about sex.

Yet at first what she had to say was like any dull family anecdote. She had been ill when she was fifteen; and afterwards she was run down, thin, with no appetite. Her folks thought a change of air would do her good, and sent her from Vermont out to Ohio—or was it Illinois? I don't remember. Anyway, one of those places where the corn grows high. Her mother's Cousin Ella lived there, keeping house for her son-in-law.

The son-in-law was the minister of the village church. His wife had died some years before, leaving him a young widower with two little girls and a baby boy. He had been a normally personable man then, but the next summer, on the Fourth of July, when he was trying to set off some fireworks to amuse his children, an imperfectly manufactured rocket had burst in his face. The explosion had left one side of his face badly scarred. Aunt Minnie made us see it, as she still saw it, in horrid detail—the stiffened, scarlet scar-tissue distorting one cheek, the lower lip turned so far out at one corner that the moist red mucous membrane lining always showed, one lower eyelid hanging loose, and watering.

After the accident, his face had been a long time healing. It was then that his wife's elderly mother had gone to keep house and take care of the children. When he was well enough to be about again, he found his position as pastor of the little church waiting for him. The farmers and village people in his congregation, moved by his misfortune, by his faithful service and by his unblemished character, said they would rather have Mr. Fairchild, even with his scarred face, than any other minister. He was a good preacher, Aunt Minnie told us, "and the way he prayed was kind of exciting. I'd never known a preacher, not to live in the same house with him, before. And when he was in the pulpit, with everybody looking up at him, I felt the way his children did, kind of proud to think we had just eaten breakfast at the same table. I liked to call him 'Cousin Malcolm' before folks. One side of his face was all right, anyhow. You could see from that that he *had* been a good-looking man. In fact, probably one of those ministers that all the women—" Aunt Minnie paused, drew her lips together, and looked at us uncertainly.

Then she went back to the story as it happened—as it happened that first time I heard her tell it. "I thought he was a saint. Everybody out there did. That was all *they* knew. Of course, it made a person sick to look at that awful scar— the drooling corner of his mouth was the worst. He tried to keep that side of his face turned away from folks. But you always knew it was there. That was what kept him from marrying again, so Cousin Ella said. I heard her say lots of times that he knew no woman would touch any man who looked the way he did, not with a ten-foot pole.

"Well, the change of air did do me good. I got my appetite back, and ate a lot and played outdoors a lot with my cousins. They were younger than I (I had my sixteenth birthday there) but I still liked to play games. I got taller and laid on some weight. Cousin Ella used to say I grew as fast as the corn did. Their house stood at the edge of the village. Beyond it was one of those big cornfields they have out West. At the time when I first got there, the stalks were only up to a person's knee. You could see over their tops. But it grew like lightning, and before long, it was the way thick woods are here, way over your head, the stalks growing so close together it was dark under them.

"Cousin Ella told us youngsters that it was lots worse for getting lost in than woods, because there weren't any landmarks in it. One spot in a cornfield looked just like any other. 'You children keep out of it,' she used to tell us almost every day, *'especially you girls.* It's no place for a decent girl. You could easy get so far from the house nobody could hear you if you hollered. There are plenty of men in this town that wouldn't like anything better than—' she never said what.

"In spite of what she said, my little cousins and I had figured out that if we went across one corner of the field, it would be a short-cut to the village, and sometimes, without letting on to Cousin Ella, we'd go that way. After the corn got really tall, the farmer stopped cultivating, and we soon beat a path in the loose dirt. The minute you were inside the field it was dark. You felt as if you were miles from anywhere. It sort of scared you. But in no time the path turned and brought you out on the far end of Main Street. Your breath was coming fast, maybe, but that was what made you like to do it.

"One day I missed the turn. Maybe I didn't keep my mind on it. Maybe it had rained and blurred the tramped-down look of the path. I don't know what. All of a sudden, I knew I was lost. And the minute I knew that, I began to run, just as hard as I could run. I couldn't help it, any more than you can help snatching your hand off a hot stove. I didn't even know I *was* running, till my heart was pounding so hard I had to stop.

"The minute I stood still, I could hear Cousin Ella saying, 'There are plenty of men in this town that wouldn't like anything better than—' I didn't know, not really, what she meant. But I knew she meant something horrible. I opened my mouth to scream. But I put both hands over my mouth to keep the scream in. If I made any noise, one of those men would hear me. I thought I heard one just behind me, and whirled around. And then I thought another one had tiptoed up behind me, the other way, and I spun around so fast I almost fell over. I stuffed my hands hard up against my mouth. And then—I couldn't help it—I ran again—

but my legs were shaking so I soon had to stop. There I stood, scared to move for fear of rustling the corn and letting the men know where I was. My hair had come down, all over my face. I kept pushing it back and looking around, quick, to make sure one of the men hadn't found out where I was. Then I thought I saw a man coming toward me, and I ran away from him—and fell down, and burst some of the buttons off my dress, and was sick to my stomach—and thought I heard a man close to me and got up and staggered around, knocking into the corn because I couldn't even see where I was going.

"And then, off to one side, I saw Cousin Malcolm. Not a man - The minister. He was standing still, one hand up to his face, thinking. He hadn't heard me.

"I was so *terrible* glad to see him, instead of one of those men, I ran as fast as I could and just flung myself on him, to make myself feel how safe I was."

Aunt Minnie had become strangely agitated. Her hands were shaking, her face was crimson. She frightened us. We could not look away from her. As we waited for her to go on, I felt little spasms twitch at the muscles inside my body. "And what do you think that *saint,* that holy minister of the Gospel, did to an innocent child who clung to him for safety? The most terrible look came into his eyes—you girls are too young to know what he looked like. But once you're married, you'll find out. He grabbed hold of me—that dreadful face of his was *right on mine*— and began clawing the clothes off my back."

She stopped for a moment, panting. We were too frightened to speak. She went on: "He had torn my dress right down to the waist before I—then I *did* scream—all I could—and pulled away from him so hard I almost fell down, and ran and all of a sudden I came out of the corn, right in the backyard of the Fairchild house. The children were staring at the corn, and Cousin Ella ran out of the kitchen door. They had heard the screaming. Cousin Ella shrieked out, 'What is it? What happened? Did a man scare you?' And I said, 'Yes, yes, yes, a man—I ran—!' And then I fainted away. I must have. The next thing I knew I was on the sofa in the living-room and Cousin Ella was slapping my face with a wet towel."

She had to wet her lips with her tongue before she could go on. Her face was gray now. "There! That's the kind of thing girls' folks ought to tell them about—so they'll know what men are like."

She finished her story as if she were dismissing us. We wanted to go away, but we were too horrified to stir. Finally, one of the youngest girls asked in a low trembling voice, "Aunt Minnie, did you tell on him?"

"No, I was ashamed to," she said briefly. "They sent me home the next day, anyhow. Nobody ever said a word to me about it. And I never did either. Till now."

By what gets printed in some of the modern child psychology books, you would think that girls to whom such a story had been told would never develop normally. Yet, as far as I can remember what happened to the girls in that group, we all grew up about like anybody. Most of us married, some happily, some not so well. We kept house. We learned—more or less—how to live with our husbands; we had children and struggled to bring them up right—we went forward into life just as if we had never been warned not to.

Perhaps, young as we were that day, we had already had enough experience of life so that we were not quite blank paper for Aunt Minnie's frightening story. Whether we thought of it then or not, we couldn't have failed to see that at this very time Aunt Minnie had been married for ten years or more, comfortably and well married, too. Against what she tried by that story to brand into our minds, stood the cheerful homelife in that house, the good-natured, kind, hard-working husband, and the children—the three rough-and-tumble, nice little boys, so adored by their parents, and the sweet girl baby who died, of whom they could never speak without tears. It was such actual contact with adult life that probably kept generation after generation of girls from being scared by tales like Aunt Minnie's into a neurotic horror of living. . . .

Of course, since Aunt Minnie was so much older than we were, her boys grew up to be adolescents and young men while our children were still little enough so that our worries over them were nothing more serious than whooping cough and trying to get them to make their own beds. Two of our aunt's three boys followed, without losing their footing, the narrow path which leads across adolescence into normal adult life. But the middle one, Jake, repeatedly fell off into the morass. "Girl trouble," as the succinct family phrase put it. He was one of those boys who have "charm," whatever we mean by that, and he was always being snatched at by girls who would be "all wrong" for him to marry. And once, at nineteen, he ran away from home, whether with one of these girls or not we never heard, for through all her ups and downs with this son, Aunt Minnie tried fiercely to protect him from scandal that might cloud his later life.

Her husband had to stay on his job to earn the family living. She was the one who went to find Jake. When it was gossiped around that Jake was "in bad company" his mother drew some money from the family savings-bank account, and silent, white-cheeked, took the train to the city where rumor said he had gone.

Some weeks later he came back with her. With no girl. She had cleared him of that entanglement. As of others, which followed later. Her troubles seemed over when, at a "suitable" age, he fell in love with a "suitable" girl, married her and took her to live in our shire town, sixteen miles away, where he had a good position. Jake was always bright enough.

Sometimes, idly, people speculated as to what Aunt Minnie had seen that time she went after her runaway son, wondering where her search for him had taken her—very queer places for Aunt Minnie to be in, we imagined. And how could such an ignorant home-keeping woman ever have known what to say to an errant wilful boy to set him straight?

Well, of course, we reflected, watching her later struggles with Jake's erratic ways, she certainly could not have remained ignorant, after seeing over and over what she probably had; after talking with Jake about the things which, a good many times, must have come up with desperate openness between them.

She kept her own counsel. We never knew anything definite about the facts of those experiences of hers. But one day she told a group of us—all then married women—something which gave us a notion about what she had learned from them. . . .

We were hastily making a layette for a not especially welcome baby in a poor family. In those days, our town had no such thing as a district-nursing service. Aunt Minnie, a vigorous woman of fifty-five, had come in to help. As we sewed, we talked, of course; and because our daughters were near or in their teens, we were comparing notes about the bewildering responsibility of bringing up girls.

After a while, Aunt Minnie remarked: "Well, I hope you teach your girls some *sense*. From what I read, I know you're great on telling them 'the facts,' facts we never heard of when we were girls. Like as not, some facts I don't know, now. But knowing the facts isn't going to do them any more good than *not* knowing the facts ever did, unless they have some sense taught them too."

"What do you mean, Aunt Minnie?" one of us asked her uncertainly.

She reflected, threading a needle: "Well, I don't know but what the best way to tell you what I mean, is to tell you about something that happened to me, forty years ago. I've never said anything about it before. But I've thought about it a good deal. Maybe—"

She had hardly begun when I recognized the story—her visit to her Cousin Ella's midwestern home, the widower with his scarred face and saintly reputation and, very vividly, her getting lost in the great cornfield. I knew every word she was going to say—to the very end, I thought.

But no, I did not. Not at all.

She broke off, suddenly, to exclaim with impatience: "Wasn't I the big ninny? But not so big a ninny as that old cousin of mine. I could wring her neck for getting me in such a state. Only she didn't know any better, herself. That was the way they brought young people up in those days, scaring them out of their wits about the awfulness of getting lost, but not telling them a thing about how *not* to get lost. Or how to act, if they did.

"If I had had the sense I was born with, I'd have known that running my legs off in a zigzag was the worst thing I could do. I couldn't have been more than a few feet from the path when I noticed I wasn't on it. My tracks in the loose ploughed dirt must have been perfectly plain. If I'd h' stood still, and collected my wits, I could have looked down to see which way my footsteps went and just walked back over them to the path and gone on about my business.

"Now I ask you, if I'd been told how to do that, wouldn't it have been a lot better protection for me—if protection was what my cousin thought she wanted to give me—than to scare me so at the idea of being lost that I turned deef-dumb-and-blind when I thought I was?

"And anyhow that patch of corn wasn't as big as she let on. And she knew it wasn't. It was no more than a big field in a farming country. I was a well-grown girl of sixteen, as tall as I am now. If I couldn't have found the path, I could have just walked along one line of cornstalks—*straight*—and I'd have come out somewhere in ten minutes. Fifteen at the most. Maybe not just where I wanted to go. But all right, safe, where decent folks were living."

She paused, as if she had finished. But at the inquiring blankness in our faces, she went on: "Well now, why isn't teaching girls—and boys, too, for the Lord's sake don't forget they need it as much as the girls—about this man-and-woman business, something like that? If you give them the idea—no matter whether it's *as* you tell them the facts, or as you *don't* tell them the facts, that it is such a terribly scary thing that if they take a step into it, something's likely to happen to them so awful that you're ashamed to tell them what—well, they'll lose their heads and run around like crazy things, first time they take one step away from the path.

"For they'll be trying out the paths, all right. You can't keep them from it. And a good thing, too. How else are they going to find out what it's like. Boys' and girls' going together is a path across one corner of growing up. And when they go together they're likely to get off the path some. Seems to me it's up to their folks to bring them up so, when they do, they don't start screaming and running in circles, but stand still, right where they are, and get their breath and figure out how to get back.

"And, anyhow, you don't tell 'em the truth about sex" (I was astonished to hear her use the actual word, tabu to women of her generation) "if they get the idea from you that it's all there is to living. It's not. If you don't get to where you want to go in it, well, there's a lot of landscape all around it a person can have a good time in.

"D'you know, I believe one thing that gives girls and boys the wrong idea is the way folks *look*! My old cousin's face, I can see her now, it was as red as a rooster's comb when she was telling me about men in that cornfield. I believe now she kind of *liked* to talk about it."

(Oh, Aunt Minnie—and yours! I thought.)

Someone asked, "But how *did* you get out, Aunt Minnie?"

She shook her head, laid down her sewing. "More foolishness. That minister my mother's cousin was keeping house for—her son-in-law—I caught sight of him, down along one of the aisles of cornstalks, looking down at the ground, thinking, the way he often did. And I was so glad to see him I rushed right up to him, and flung my arms around his neck and hugged him. He hadn't heard me coming. He gave a great start, put one arm around me and turned his face full toward me—I suppose for just a second he had forgotten how awful one side of it was. His expression, his eyes—well, you're all married women, you know how he looked, the way any able-bodied man thirty-six or seven, who'd been married and begotten children, would look—for a minute, anyhow, if a full-blooded girl of sixteen, who ought to have known better, flung herself at him without any warning, her hair tumbling down, her dress half-unbuttoned, and hugged him with all her might.

"I was what they called innocent in those days. That is, I knew just as little about what men are like as my folks could manage I should. But I was old enough to know all right what that look meant. And it gave me a start. But, of course, the real thing of it was that dreadful scar of his, so close to my face—that wet corner of his mouth, his eye drawn down with the red inside of the lower eyelid showing—

"It turned me so sick, I pulled away with all my might, so fast that I ripped one sleeve nearly loose, and let out a screech like a wildcat. And ran. Did I run! And in a minute, I was through the corn and had come out in the backyard of the house. I hadn't been more than a few feet from it, probably, any of the time. And then I fainted away. Girls were always fainting away; it was the way our corset-strings were pulled tight, I suppose, and then—oh, a lot of fuss."

"But, anyhow," she finished, picking up her work and going on, setting neat, firm stitches with steady hands, "there's one thing; I never told anybody it was Cousin Malcolm I had met in the cornfield. I told my old cousin that 'a man had scared me.' And nobody said anything more about it to me, not ever. That was the way they did in those days. They thought if they didn't let on about something, maybe it wouldn't have happened. I was sent back to Vermont right away and Cousin Malcolm went on being minister of the church."

"I've always been," said Aunt Minnie moderately, "kind of proud that I didn't go and ruin a man's life for just one second's slip-up. If you could have called it that. For it *would* have ruined him. You know how hard as stone people are about other folks' let-downs. If I'd have told, not one person in that town would have had any charity. Not one would have tried to understand. One slip, *once,* and they'd have pushed him down in the mud. If I had told, I'd have felt pretty bad about it, later—when I came to have more sense. But I declare, I can't see how I came to have the decency, dumb as I was then, to know that it wouldn't be fair. . . ."

It was not long after this talk that Aunt Minnie's elderly husband died, mourned by her, by all of us. She lived alone then. It was peaceful October weather for her, in which she kept a firm roundness of face and figure, as quiet-living countrywomen often do, on into her late sixties.

But then Jake, the boy who had girl trouble, had wife trouble. We heard he had taken to running after a young girl, or was it that she was running after him? It was something serious. For his nice wife had left him and come back with the children to live with her mother in our town. Poor Aunt Minnie used to go to see her for long talks which made them both cry. And she went to keep house for Jake, for months at a time.

She grew old, during those years. When finally she (or something) managed to get the marriage mended so that Jake's wife relented and went back to live with him, there was no trace left of her pleasant brisk freshness. She was stooped and slow-footed and shrunken. We, her kinspeople, although we would have given our lives for any one of our own children, wondered whether Jake was worth what it had cost his mother to—well, steady him, or reform him. Or perhaps just understand him. Whatever it took.

She came of a long-lived family and was able to go on keeping house for herself well into her eighties. Of course, we and the other nieghbors stepped in often to make sure she was all right. Mostly, during those brief calls, the talk turned on nothing more vital than her geraniums. But one midwinter afternoon, sitting with her in front of her cozy stove, I chanced to speak in rather hasty blame of someone who had, I thought, acted badly. To my surprise this brought from her the story about the cornfield which she had evidently quite forgotten telling me, twice before.

This time she told it almost dreamily, swaying to and fro in her rocking-chair, her eyes fixed on the long slope of snow outside her window. When she came to the encounter with the minister she said, looking away from the distance and back into my eyes: "I know that I had been, all along, kind of *interested* in him, the way any girl as old as I was would be in any youngish man living in the same house with her. And a minister, too. They have to have the gift of gab so much more than most men, women get to thinking they are more alive than men who can't talk so well. I *thought* the reason I threw my arms around him was because I had been so scared. And I certainly had been scared by my old cousin's horrible talk about the cornfield being full of men waiting to grab girls. But that wasn't all the reason I flung myself at Malcolm Fairchild and hugged him. I know that now. Why in the world shouldn't I have been taught *some* notion of it then?

'Twould do girls good to know that they are just like everybody else—human nature *and* sex, all mixed up together. I didn't have to hug him. I wouldn't have, if he'd been dirty or fat and old, or chewed tobacco."

I stirred in my chair, ready to say, "But it's not so simple as all that to tell girls—" and she hastily answered my unspoken protest. "I know, I know, most of it can't be put into words. There just aren't any words to say something that's so both-ways-at-once all the time as this man-and-woman business. But look here, you know as well as I do that there are lots more ways than in words to teach young folks what you want 'em to know."

The old woman stopped her swaying rocker to peer far back into the past with honest eyes. "What was in my mind back there in the cornfield—partly, anyhow—was what had been there all the time I was living in the same house with Cousin Malcolm—that he had long straight legs, and broad shoulders, and lots of curly brown hair, and was nice and flat in front, and that one side of his face was good-looking. But most of all, that he and I were really alone, for the first time, without anybody to see us.

"I suppose, if it hadn't been for that dreadul scar, he'd have drawn me up, tight, and—most any man would—kissed me. I know how I must have looked, all red and hot and my hair down and my dress torn open. And, used as he was to big cornfields, he probably never dreamed that the reason I looked that way was because I was scared to be by myself in one. He may have thought—you know what he may have thought.

"Well—if his face had been like anybody's, when he looked at me the way he did, the way a man does look at a woman he wants to have, it would have scared me—some. I'd have cried, maybe. And probably he'd have kissed me again. You know how such things go. I might have come out of the cornfield halfway engaged to marry him. Why not? I was old enough, as people thought then. That would have been Nature. That was probably what he thought of, in that first instant.

"But what did I do? I had one look at his poor horrible face, and started back as though I'd stepped on a snake. And screamed and ran.

"What do you suppose *he* felt, left there in the corn? He must have been sure that I would tell everybody he had attacked me. He probably thought that when he came out and went back to the village he'd already be in disgrace and put out of the pulpit.

"But the worst must have been to find out, so rough, so plain from the way I acted—as if somebody had hit him with an ax—the way he would look to any woman he might try to get close to."

"That must have been," she drew a long breath, "well, pretty hard on him."

After a silence, she murmured pityingly, "Poor man!"

Don Juan

GEORGE GORDON, LORD BYRON

In her first passion woman loves her lover,
    In all the others all she loves is love,
Which grows a habit she can ne'er get over,
    And fits her loosely – like an easy glove,
As you may find, whene'er you like to prove her:
    One man alone at first her heart can move;
She then prefers him in the plural number,
    Not finding that the additions much encumber.

Real Women

ROBERT GRAVES

The most important historical study of all, utterly dwarfing all economic and political ones, is for me the changing relationship between men and women down the centuries—from prehistoric times to the present moral chaos in which both sexes have become equally confused about their roles. But I am a poet by calling, and have lived outside ordinary civilization for so many years that anything I write about real women must read oddly. Except perhaps to real women themselves, and the occasional man whom some accident of birth or experience tempts to agree with me.

A real woman, by my definition, neither despises nor worships men, but is proud not to have been born a man, does everything she can to avoid thinking of acting like one, knows the full extent of her powers, and feels free to reject all arbitrary man-made obligations. She is her own oracle of right and wrong, firmly believing in her five sound senses and the intuitive sixth. Once a real woman has been warned by her nose that those apples are tasteless, or assured by her finger-tips that this material is shoddy, no salesman in the world can persuade her to the contrary. Nor, once she has met some personage in private, and summed him up with a single keen glance as weak, vain or crooked, will his mounting public reputation convince her otherwise. She takes pleasure in the company of simple, happy, undemanding women; but seldom or never finds a friend worthy of her full confidence. Since she never settles for the second best in love, what most troubles her is the rareness of real men. Wherever she goes, her singularity will arouse strong feelings: adulation, jealousy, resentment, but never pity for her loneliness. Real women are royal women; the words once had the same meaning. Democracy has no welcome for queens.

It would be wrong to identify the real woman with the typical wild one who, after a difficult childhood, has left home early to live by her wits at the expense of men. The wild woman is incapable either of friendship for other women, whom she cannot fail to regard as rivals, or of love for a man, her declared enemy. But at least she keeps her eyes open and ridicules the view that women must enthusiastically accept this glorious modern world of plenty bestowed on them by their hardworking menfolk, and that they enjoy being passionately swept off their feet and afterward treated with amused indulgence. There was never, of course, any truth in the comic-strip legend of a primitive he-man who would grab his woman by the hair, threaten her with a knobbed club if she refused his advances, and haul her off panting ecstatically to his cave. In ancient Majorca, the island which I have made my home for more than thirty years, the woman, not the man, owned their cave; and, according to the Roman historian Strabo, if he took things too much for granted, she would merely say, "Begone, and take your possessions with you," and out he had to go—the children were hers in any case.

To reach some understanding of real women, one must think back to a primitive age, when men invariably treated women as the holier sex, since they alone perpetuated the race. Women were the sole agriculturists, guardians of springs, fruit trees, and the sacred hearth fire, and lived unaffected by any notions of progress. Tribal queens never thought in terms of historical time, but only of seasons; judged each case on its own merits, not by a legal code, as real women still do; and showed little regard for trade or mechanical invention. Chance discoveries or new techniques in arts and crafts were welcome, so long as these neither upset tribal economy nor enhanced the importance of individuals. It was the queen's task to restrain men from letting their ambition or intellectual curiosity override practical common sense, as it is still the woman's task to ask her husband: "Must you kill yourself making money? Haven't we enough for the next five years at least, even if you stopped working altogether? Surely you don't enjoy your martyrdom?" But even if he cared to listen, social pressures compel him to provide for his family until he drops dead.

History begins with the emergence of men from female rule. They had at last discovered that a woman cannot conceive without male assistance—and brooded over the implications of this surprising fact. After long whispered conferences it was agreed that men ought to claim their freedom. They asked, "Why should descent be reckoned in the female line, not the male? Why should a man when he marries go to the woman's home, not contrariwise? Why should a woman, not a man, sow the seed corn? Why should women control the tribe? Surely men are the true creators, sowers of seed, and therefore the holier sex, as well as being physically stronger?" Thus the male habit of reasoning from irrelevant facts, rather than relying on woman's practical wisdom, began the war between the sexes that has been raging ever since.

Men gradually usurped women's prerogatives in farming, magic, handicrafts, war—the Amazons are no mere figment—and government. The story is epitomized in a classical Greek myth: how the goddess Hera pitied a poor, bedraggled cuckoo and warmed him at her breast. This cuckoo was her brother Zeus in disguise, who ravished and humiliated her by seizing throne and scepter. Later, when Hera and her kinsfolk rebelled against Zeus, he hung her from the vault of heaven, with an anvil tied to each foot. . . .

Men consolidated their victory. They reckoned descent in the male line, brought wives to their own homes, invented historical annals, legal codes, weights and measures, standing armies, engineering, logic and philosophy. On the excuse of protecting the weaker sex, they placed woman under male tutelage: henceforward she must serve her father's or husband's domestic needs as though not only spiritually but mentally inferior to him.

Greek myths record an occasional dramatic protest against this state of affairs: how the fifty Danaides stabbed their husbands, the sons of Aegyptus, on their common wedding night, and were punished in hell for this crime: how the Lemnian women murdered theirs for importing concubines from Thrace; how Amazons attacked Athens. . . . Yet, as a rule, the sex war has been fought sporadically in the home between father and daughter, husband and wife, mother-in-law and son-in-law. Only isolated regions, such as Galicia, Majorca and Pictish Scotland, kept their matriarchal traditions.

It seems puzzling that the real women of those days let all this happen to them. The sole reason I can suggest is that they thought far ahead. Since man had a certain undeveloped intellectual capacity, of which it would have been wrong to deny him full use, the real women sat back patiently, prepared to give him a free hand for some hundreds or thousands of years. Only a long series of disastrous experiments could make him realize the error of his headstrong ways. Eventually he must return to them in willing and chastened dependence.

Priests of the new male gods even modified the ancient myth of a sole goddess who had created the world, giving her a male assistant; and in Genesis — a comparatively late book — Jehovah creates the world entirely by Himself; and models Eve, the first woman, from man's rib! It is added that this woman's disobedience to God caused man to stumble and sin. In fact, the story is based on a Hebrew pun: the same word means both "rib" and "make to stumble." According to Hesiod's contemporary Greek myth, an inquisitive woman named Pandora opened a divine jar entrusted to her and let loose on mankind all the evils that now plague us. Yet "Eve" was orginally a title of the sole creatrix; as was also "Pandora."

Financial pressures of men's own making brought about the recent so-called emancipation of women. Grown daughters could no longer stay idling at home, a burden to their parents and to themselves until married off. Industry was booming and, with appropriate moral safeguards, they might fill the widening gaps in manpower. Women, who can now earn and keep their own money, even when wives, and have been granted the franchise — "franchise" originally meant "freedom from being a serf" — need show men no gratitude for this liberality. Their freedom is still limited. They remain citizens of the second degree, auxiliary male personnel barred from all the highest offices; and would never have got where they are so quickly had it not been for two world wars and such loveless male inventions as machine guns, submarines, bombing planes and universal conscription.

Strangely enough, it is easier to be a real woman in backwaters of Christianity or Islam or Hinduism, where codes of behavior have not changed for centuries, than in urbanized Europe or America. There she knows what part she must play, and can guard her inborn dignity. Although the husband, as head of the family, makes all decisions, he will never dare overrule even her unspoken protests. Among Majorcan peasants who live beyond the tourist range, no man would ever think of buying or selling so much as a hen without his wife's approval. She is always referred to as *la madonna,* the titular guardian of the home.

What is home? In ancient days it meant a clan settlement, a camp or kraal, ruled by elders, where men had comrades and women their gossips, and children ran about in packs; and where a happy man-woman relationship could exist in some small corner away from the communal bustle.

Among us Westerners, because of man's jealous insistence on marital privacy, *home* has shrunk from settlement to farmhouse, thence to the cottage, thence to the ten-roomed apartment, thence to three rooms and a kitchenette with the usual labor-saving devices, in a huge residential block full of utter strangers. The housewife has her washing machine, telephone, television, refrigerator, electric cookstove, car and door keys, to pay for which a husband must be out working all week. She cannot regret (because she never knew) the easy companionship of her great-grandmother's day: quilting bees and husking bees, taking the cousins to do a week's washing down at the creek, lending a hand with the shearing and harvest, making jams and pickles, getting up round dances, singing and playing practical jokes. But no real woman can ever accept the present situation.

Man's logic has defeated itself. Boredom often drives the married woman back to a job as soon as she can leave her children at a nursery school; or to infidelity; or to an analyst. Home is home for only two days of the week. Which is why some paternally minded industrialists take advice from professors of sociology and plant their employees all together in a wholesome suburban neighborhood, where the company's standards of taste and respectability must rule their lives. Husband obeys boss; wife obeys husband, and preserves amicable relations with her fellow company wives or else. . . . Spouses are thus shackled by a well-paid job to which the husband need no longer commute, by house, garden and swimming pool, by children, by hope of advancement and the prospect of a pension. Any sign of noncompliance is scored against both. No real woman can ever accept this situation either.

Attempts to liven things up socially are all too often masked under the dubious name of charity. It is characteristic of a real woman never to support public charities—on the ground that she neither knows the person to whom her money goes nor has any assurance that it will be properly distributed. She gives only to those whose needs are familiar to her, and then from friendship, not pity. She will not be found at bridge clubs or at cocktail parties. Bridge, which is, after all, a money contest between individual players, cannot be a substitute for the good humor of a communal washday; nor can a cocktail party for the intimate gossip of a quilting bee.

Wild women take advantage of this artificial state of affairs by exploiting the dormant dissatisfactions of husbands. One of them told me the other day, "Yes, you may call me a mean, greedy, undependable, lazy, treacherous, spendthrift bitch. That's true enough a good part of the time; but it isn't the whole story. In fact, I've given myself to myself, and to no one else. My beauty is my own, and I take good care of it. If I choose a lover, I grant the lucky fellow no right over me; and if he has sense, he won't claim any. As for breaking up a home, nobody can do that unless it's already cracked!"

A real woman likes beautiful things of her own choosing. She prefers a handleless cup, a backless chair, a mattress on the floor and a packing case for the table to good taste conferred on her wholesale by interior decorators. There is an eighteenth-century English song, "Sally in Our Alley":

Her father, he sells cabbage nets
And through the streets doth cry 'em.
Her mother, she sells laces long
To such as care to buy 'em —
Who'd think such rascals could beget
So sweet a girl as Sally?
She is the darling of my heart
And lives in our alley . . .

The lover was a square: an honest, idealistic London apprentice, intent on becoming a journeyman, a master craftsman and eventually a rich merchant—perhaps even Lord Major:

When Eastertide comes round again
Oh, then I'll have some money —
I'll save it up, and box and all
I'll give it to my honey . . .
And then my seven years' time is o'er
Oh, then I'll marry Sally,
Ay, then we'll wed, and then we'll bed—
But not in our alley!

The broken-down, foul-smelling alley was a settlement, a home, the denizens of which were bound together by common poverty, shiftlessness, pugnacity, humor and a hatred of landlords and police. Yet no well-planned housing estate can ever compete with its spirit, which a Sally was always found to keep alive. From 1940 to '43 the German blitz leveled what remained of these alleys, and their sites are now occupied by large all-glass office blocks. The last of the Sallies found herself in a surburban life-box—one of hundreds built to the same design and set down in parallel rows—longing for a return to poverty, vice, dirt and even flying bombs.

Marriage, like money, is still with us; and, like money, progressively devalued. The ties between these two male inventions get closer and closer. Originally marriage meant the sale of a woman by one man to another; now most women sell themselves though they have no intention of delivering the goods listed in the bill of sale. Not only is the wife, on an average, five years younger than her husband, but she lives statistically longer. So money power passes progressively into the hands of women. Also, divorce legislation (forced on guilt-ridden legislators by nagging spouses) grossly favors the wife. A youthful rival figures in most divorce suits, and though she and the wife seldom act collusively, they share an old-fashioned insistence on the honorable state of marriage, which enriches both. Wild women will commit matrimony when things go hard for them, without the least thought of keeping their obligations. The entranced husbands never know what has hit them, nor do they profit by the experience.

The United States, though often described as a matriarchy in all but name, remains patriarchal. Matriarchy, to be effective, needs real women. When women organize themselves intellectually on masculine lines, they merely stimulate the feminization of men, who, for terror of husband-hunting viragoes, are apt to seek refuge in the cul-de-sac of homosexuality.

Though men are more conventional than women and fear to infringe the Mosaic law (Deuteronomy XXII.5) which forbids their wearing of women's clothes, women have no scruples about flouting the companion law: "The woman shall not wear that which pertaineth unto a man . . . for all that do so are abomination unto the Lord. . . ." Even matrons now unblushingly wear blue jeans zipped in front.

The pseudopatriarchal trend encourages women to respect legality, which they had hitherto found distasteful. A real woman, giving evidence in a court of law, scorns factual truth. Should her sense of equity run counter to the formal demands of justice, she will perjure herself in replies of cool and convincing honesty. When obliged to exercise a vote, she scorns the male axiom that the majority is always right.

A few real women survive in the old royal sense among West African queens, who rule with a silver knot-of-wisdom scepter and claim the moon goddess Ngame as their remote ancestress. A "knot of wisdom"—known in English as the "true lover's knot"—is the sort that tightens more securely the harder you tug at either end. Symbolically it means, "My command can never be disobeyed!"

In civilized society royal women have neither thrones nor territorial queendoms, but the moon inspires them still, and they can wield formidable powers in times of emergency. Yet, since they avoid becoming public figures—the personality cult is another male invention—their names pass into history far more seldom than those of notorious wild women. A remarkable exception was Elizabeth I of England, whom her poets addressed as Cynthia—"The Moon"—and whose cynical disparagement of herself as "but a weak woman" concealed an unshaken faith in her royal wisdom. Elizabeth ruled through awe and love, was on playful terms with her ladies-in-waiting, inspired her male subjects to feats of heroism and flights of poetry never known before or since among the English, always said "No" to a doubtful petition and then slept on it.

A real woman's main concern is her beauty, which she cultivates for her own pleasure—not to ensnare men. Though she despises fashion as a male financial business, she will not make herself conspicuous by a defiance of conventions. The materials, colors and cut of her clothes, her hair style and her jewels are all chosen to match a sense of personal uniqueness. She can dress in advance of fashion, yet seem to lead it; and to any irregular features she may have, she lends a lovely ugliness denied to common beauty queens. Perfect detachment from the artificial or secondhand keeps her face unclouded. She has no small talk on current topics, and will suddenly vanish from a party, however grand, as soon as it grows boring.

If she plays games, it will be for fun, not competition; and if up against a win-at-all-costs opponent in tennis or golf, she will take care to lose handsomely —as one who competes only against herself. If she drinks, it will because she likes the taste; and if she smokes, it will be for the same reason, not to steady her nerve.

She misses real men—men who would recognize her potentiality and agree that our world, despite its appearance of rational organization, is a wholly haphazard one, clanking on noisily to its fate along a random course once defined as "progress." And that a calamitous collapse must come before a new start can be made—from the point where the sex war was first declared and woman's conservative instinct as the guiding force of humankind repudiated. Because woman-hood remains incomplete without a child, most real women marry—preferring simple, affectionate husbands who cannot understand them. This is not a renunciation of real love, since they agree with the thirteenth-century Countess of Narbonne: "Conjugal affection has absolutely nothing in common with love. We say 'absolutely,' and with all consideration, that love cannot exist between husband and wife."

Man's biological function is to do; woman's is to be. This difference is not a contrast of mere activity with mere passivity. "To be" is indeed a full-time occupation. A real woman has no leisure in the modern economic sense—leisure as a consumer's relaxed insistence on commercial entertainment—but is always thinking, taking stock of herself, setting a stage on which actors can perform. If she paints or writes, this will be for her own private amusement, not to satisfy ambition; and if forced to earn her livelihood in this way, she repudiates the public personage forced on her by dealers and critics.

A real woman is content to dress with a difference, to make her home unmistakably her own, to illuminate any company she enters, to cook by instinct, not by the cookbook. This is her evidence of being, the proof of which lies in her sense of certitude. She is no feminist; feminism, like all "isms," implies an intellectual approach to a subject; and reality can be understood only by transcending the intellect.

Mental institutions on both sides of the Atlantic house hundreds of young, beautiful, silently brooding girls, victims of the sex war—defeated before they could come to terms with life. Their tragedy has been brilliantly described in *The Ha-Ha*, a novel by Jennifer Dawson, whose heroine is almost a real woman, because: "she never just plays a game with herself or other people, and refuses to learn the rules of society—meaning the worthy, useful, ordinary women who are so busy finding husbands and houses and good income brackets that they just haven't time to be conscious of themselves, and who see the world as an inventory, a container of so many things, and other people as so many tin-openers to undo it for them."

The friendly and intelligent staff of the mental institution cannot persuade her that she should realign herself with the orderly outside male world. Being not quite real enough to escape defeat by pretending conformity, she loses all pride in her appearance, ceases to concentrate on any self-imposed task; and when at last she desperately breaks out, the police, we know, cannot fail to fetch her back for sedation and still closer surveillance.

A real woman somehow avoids suicide, or virtual suicide, or the mental institution; but is always painfully aware of having been born out of her true epoch; considered as either the past, or as the long-distant future. A sense of humor saves her from defeat. "This is not worthy of me," she will remind herself ten times a day, "but to preserve my inner self I must once more act an alien part."

None of her women neighbors, idly content with money and what it will buy, feel any need for drastic change in the man-woman relationship; she treats them politely, and has patience. If she ever comes across a real man, the thin thread of human hope—that eventually the world will make practical sense again—cannot yet have snapped.

Woman and Tree

ROBERT GRAVES

To love one woman, or to sit
    Always beneath the same tall tree,
Argues a certain lack of wit
    Two steps from imbecility.

A poet, therefore, sworn to feed
    On every food the senses know,
Will claim the inexorable need
    To be Don Juan Tenorio.

Yet if, miraculously enough,
    (And why set miracles apart?)
Woman and tree prove of a stuff
    Wholly to glamour his wild heart?

And if such visions from the void
    As shone in fever there, or there,
Assemble, hold and are enjoyed
    On climbing one familiar stair . . . ?

To change and chance he took a vow,
    As he thought fitting. None the less,
What of a phoenix on the bough,
    Or a sole woman's fatefulness?

Liber Amoris

WILLIAM HAZLITT

Perfect love has this advantage in it, that it leaves the possessor of it nothing farther to desire. There is one object (at least) in which the soul finds absolute content, for which it seeks to live, or dares to die. The heart has, as it were, filled up the moulds of the imagination. The truth of passion keeps pace with and outvies the extravagance of mere language. There are no words so fine, no flattery so soft, that there is not a sentiment beyond them, that it is impossible to express, at the bottom of the heart where true love is. What idle sounds the common phrases *adorable creature, angel, divinity,* are! What a proud reflection it is to have a feeling answering to all these rooted in the breast, unalterable, unutterable, to which all other feelings are light and vain! Perfect love reposes on the object of its choice, like the halcyon on the wave; and the air of heaven is around it.

The Poet Loves a Mistress but Not to Marry

ROBERT HERRICK

I do not love to wed,
Though I do like to woo;
And for a maidenhead
I'll beg and buy it too.

I'll praise and I'll approve
Those maids that never vary;
And fervently I'll love,
But yet I would not marry.

I'll hug, I'll kiss, I'll play,
And, cock-like, hens I'll tread,
And sport in any way
But in the bridal bed.

For why? that man is poor
Who hath but one of many,
But crown'd he is with store
That, single, may have many.

Why, then, say what is he,
To freedom so unknown,
Who, having two or three,
Will be content with one?

The Lady's-Maid's Song

JOHN HOLLANDER

When Adam found his rib was gone
　　He cursed and sighed and cried and swore
And looked with cold resentment on
　　The creature God had used it for.
All love's delights were quickly spent
　　And soon his sorrows multiplied:
He learned to blame his discontent
　　On something stolen from his side.

And so in every age we find
　　Each Jack, destroying every Joan,

Divides and conquers womankind
  In vengeance for the missing bone.
By day he spins out quaint conceits
  With gossip, flattery, and song,
And then at night, between the sheets,
  He wrongs the girl to right the wrong.

Though shoulder, bosom, lip, and knee
  Are praised in every kind of art,
Here is Love's true anatomy:
  His rib is gone; he'll have her heart.
So women bear the debt alone
  And live eternally distressed,
For though we throw the dog his bone
  He wants it back with interest.

Oh, When I Was in Love with You

A. E. HOUSMAN

Oh, when I was in love with you,
Then I was clean and brave,
And miles around the wonder grew
How well did I behave.

And now the fancy passes by,
And nothing will remain,
And miles around they'll say that I
Am quite myself again.

The Silver Cord

SIDNEY HOWARD

MRS. PHELPS   Why do you look so startled? It's only Mother!

DAVID *(Laconic)*   Hello, Mother!

MRS. PHELPS   I came in to ask if you needed anything and . . .

DAVID   Not a thing, thanks.

MRS. PHELPS   And to warn you against opening the window in this weather. Oh, and I brought you that extra cover. I've been picking up after you, too!

DAVID *(Looking gloomily about)*   You needn't have troubled.

MRS. PHELPS   It took me back to the old days when I used to tuck you up in that same little bed . . .

DAVID *(A strong hint)*   Yeah. . . . I'm just turning in, Mother.

MRS. PHELPS *(Regardless)*   . . . And then sit in this very chair and talk over all my problems with you. I feel that I must talk to my big boy tonight. . . . I must get acquainted with my Dave again.

DAVID (*An even stronger hint*) We're not exactly strangers, are we? And besides, it's getting late.

MRS. PHELPS (*Even more persistent*) It was always in these late hours that we had our talks in the old days when we were still comrades. Oh, are those days gone forever? Don't you remember how we used to play that we had an imaginary kingdom where we were king and queen?

DAVID (*Moribund*) Did we? I wish Chris 'ud come up.

MRS. PHELPS (*A frown, and she speaks quickly*) Have you noticed, Dave, boy, that your room is just as you left it? I've made a little shrine of it. The same curtains. . . . And every day I dusted in here myself and every night I prayed in here for . . .

DAVID (*A little too dryly for good manners*) Thanks.

MRS. PHELPS   . . . I need my big boy so! Because I'm facing the gravest problem of my life, Dave. And you've got to help me.

DAVID   What is it?

MRS. PHELPS   Is it true that I'm of no more use to my two sons?

DAVID   Whatever put such an idea in your head?

MRS. PHELPS   You did.

DAVID (*Shocked*) I?

MRS. PHELPS (*Nodding*) You weren't really glad to see me this afternoon.

DAVID (*In all sincerity*) I was. . . . I was delighted!

MRS. PHELPS (*Bravely stopping him*) Not glad as I was to see you. I noticed, Dave! . . . And that made me wonder whether this scientific age—because it is a scientific age, Dave—isn't making more than one boy forget that the bond between mother and son is the strongest bond on earth. . . .

DAVID (*Not quite sure of the superlative*) Well, it's certainly strong.

MRS. PHELPS   Do you realize how sinful any boy would be to want to loosen it?

DAVID   Sure I realize that!

MRS. PHELPS   I see so many poor mothers, no less deserving of love and loyalty than I, neglected and discarded by their children, set aside for other interests.

DAVID   What interests?

MRS. PHELPS   All kinds of things. . . . Wives. . . .

DAVID (*Shying*) Nonsense, Mother!

MRS. PHELPS   The Chinese never set any relationship above their filial piety. They'd be the greatest people on earth if only they'd stop smoking opium.

DAVID   You haven't any kick, have you? I mean: Rob and I haven't let you down?

MRS. PHELPS   Not yet, Dave. But, you know the old saying?

DAVID   What old saying?

MRS. PHELPS   That a boy's mother is his best friend.

DAVID   Oh! Bet I do!

MRS. PHELPS   Do you think of *your* mother as *your* best friend?

DAVID   None better, certainly.

MRS. PHELPS   None better! H'm! You *can* say, though, that you haven't entirely outgrown me?

DAVID   Of course I haven't! Why, I'd hate to have you think that just because I'm a grown man, I . . .

MRS. PHELPS   No son is ever a grown man to his mother! *(A knock at the door)* Who can that be at this hour?

DAVID   I hope it's Chris.

(He starts for the door.)

MRS. PHELPS *(Freezing suddenly as she rises)*   Dave!

DAVID *(Turning)*   What?

MRS. PHELPS   Wait. . . . I mustn't intrude. . . . Good-night. . . .

DAVID *(Calling out)*   Just a minute! *(To his mother, politely)* You wouldn't be intruding!

MRS. PHELPS   Not on you, I know. But . . .

DAVID   Not on Chris either!

MRS. PHELPS   I know best. Kiss me goodnight.

DAVID   Good-night, Mother.

(He kisses her cheek.)

MRS. PHELPS *(A quick hug)*   God bless my big boy!

(She goes as she came. DAVID'S *look, as he watches her door close behind her, is baffled. He goes quickly to the other door.* ROBERT *is standing outside.)*

DAVID   For Pete's sake, Rob! I thought it was Chris! . . . Why didn't you walk in?

ROBERT   I thought Mother was in here.

DAVID   She was. She just went to bed.

ROBERT *(Entering)*   She must have thought it was Chris, too!

DAVID   How do you mean?

ROBERT   I shouldn't rush things if I were you.

DAVID   Maybe you're right. Women are too deep for me.

ROBERT   I came in for a smoke. I had to talk to you. I've been sitting in my room wondering what you think of all this.

DAVID *(Cigarette business)*   I don't think much and that's the truth!

ROBERT   Good God, Dave, can't you be a little easier on me? Didn't you ever feel any doubts when you were engaged? Were you always so sure of Christina that you . . .

DAVID   The first time I asked Chris to marry me, she made if perfectly clear that, as far as she was concerned, I was to consider myself dripping wet. After that I was too damned scared I wouldn't get her to think whether she loved me or not.

ROBERT *(Darkly)*   And I never had one comfortable moment from the time Hester accepted me.

DAVID   Oh, being in love's like everything else. You've got to put some guts in it.

ROBERT *(Bitter anger)*   You think I haven't got any guts. You want to make me look like a callous cad! All right, I'll *be* a cad. I don't care what people think about me! But I'll tell you one thing! I'm damned if I'm going to let you turn Mother against me!

DAVID   Do *what?*

ROBERT   You heard me!

DAVID   My God, haven't you outgrown that old stuff yet?

ROBERT   I know from experience what to expect when you and Mother get together. I used to listen at that door, night after night, night after night, while you and Mother sat in here and talked me over. Then I'd watch for the change in her next morning at breakfast when I hadn't slept a wink all night. The way you used to own the earth at those breakfasts! Well, if you try any of that old stuff tonight, I'll lose the only prop I've got left.

DAVID   Isn't it about time you let go of Mother's apronstrings?

ROBERT   You would say that! You don't realize that I'm desperate.

DAVID   Desperate, hell! You're crazy! Mother's gone to bed and . . . *(The wee mousie scratches at the door again.)* What's that?

MRS. PHELPS *(Entering)*   It's only Mother. Are my two beaux quarreling? Jealous, jealous Robin! What's the matter?

DAVID   Nothing.

MRS. PHELPS   A fine man is a frank man, David! Do you think I didn't hear every word you said? Surely you must know that Hester wasn't worthy of your brother?

DAVID   Wasn't she? Well, let's not talk any more about it.

MRS. PHELPS   Oh, but we must. For all our sakes, we must clear the air. *I* have always taken the stand that my boys could do absolutely no wrong and that is the proper stand for a mother to take. Didn't I always side with you in your school scrapes? Even against the masters? Even when you were clearly in the wrong? Of course, I did! And I shall not permit one word of criticism against your brother now. Loyalty, Dave! Loyalty! Come, now! Tell Mother all about it!

DAVID   But if you overheard every word we said!

MRS. PHELPS   "Overheard," David? Am I given to eavesdropping?

DAVID   I didn't say so.

MRS. PHELPS   I simply want to make sure I didn't miss anything while I was in my bath.

•　　•　　•　　•　　•

CHRISTINA   Dave. . . .

DAVID   Yes?

CHRISTINA   Whom do you love?

DAVID   You. Why?

CHRISTINA   I wondered, that's all. I want to be kissed.

DAVID   That's easy.

(He takes her in his arms.)

CHRISTINA   Such a tired girl, Dave. . . . I want to be held on to and made much of. . . . I want to feel all safe and warm. . . . I want you to tell me that you're in love with me and that you enjoy being in love with me. Because just loving isn't enough and it's being in love that really matters. . . . Will you tell me all that, please, Dave?

DAVID *(Hugging her)*   Darling!

CHRISTINA   You haven't kissed me yet.

DAVID *(Complying, a trifle absent-mindedly)*   There!

CHRISTINA *(As she draws back from him)*   That isn't what I call making love in a big way.

DAVID *(Repeating the kiss with more energy)*   Is that better?

CHRISTINA   There's still something lacking. . . . What's the matter? There's nobody watching us.

DAVID   That's a funny thing to say.

CHRISTINA   You take me right back to my first beau in Germany. He never got very far, either. All the English he knew was "water closet."

DAVID   Chris! Shame on you!

CHRISTINA   Shame on *you*, making me take to low jokes to amuse you. . . . I love you.

DAVID   Darling, darling, Chris!

CHRISTINA   I love you! I love you! *(For a moment she clings to him wildly).* I hate being so far from you tonight, Dave. 'Way off there at the other end of the hall!

DAVID   I'm none too pleased myself. It's just one of Mother's fool ideas.

(*He lowers his voice whenever he mentions his mother.*)

CHRISTINA   She naturally wanted you near *her*!

DAVID   That's it. *(His eyes fall beneath her steady gaze.)* We mustn't talk so loud. We'll keep Mother awake. She can hear every sound we make.

CHRISTINA   Let her hear! It'll do her good!

DAVID   That's no way to talk, Chris!

CHRISTINA   Excuse me. I didn't mean to snap. I've been fearfully shaken up tonight.

DAVID   I know you have.

CHRISTINA   And I'm awfully tired.

DAVID   Poor girl!

CHRISTINA   Poor Hester! . . . I don't feel like going to bed yet. I want to talk. Do you mind?

DAVID   Go to it.

CHRISTINA   I've never come up against anything like this before; I've heard of it, but I've never met it. I don't know what to do about it. And it scares me.

DAVID   What does?

CHRISTINA   I don't know how to tell you. *(Then, with sudden force.)* But I've got to tell you, Dave. I've got to tell you. There are no two ways about that.

DAVID   What are you driving at?

CHRISTINA   Well . . . *(But she changes her mind.)* May I ask you a question? Rather an intimate one?

DAVID   If you must!

CHRISTINA   Being your wife, I thought I might.

DAVID   Shoot!

CHRISTINA   Do you look on me as apart from all other women? I mean, do you think of all the women in the world and then think of me quite, quite differently? Do you, Dave.

DAVID   I'll bite. Do I?

CHRISTINA   Please answer me. It's awfully important to me just now.

DAVID   Of course I do. . . . Why is it so important just now?

CHRISTINA   Because that's how I feel about you and all the other men in the world. Because that's what being in love must mean and being properly and happily married. Two people, a man and a woman, together by themselves, miles and miles from everybody, from *everybody* else, glancing around, now and then, at all the rest of mankind, at *all* the rest, Dave, and saying: "Are you still there? And getting along all right? Sure there's nothing we can do to help?"

DAVID   Only we do help, don't we?

CHRISTINA   Only really if we feel that way about one another. Only *by* feeling that way.

DAVID   That's pretty deep! You do go off on the damnedest tacks!

CHRISTINA   Don't you see how that feeling between a man and a woman is what keeps life going?

DAVID   Is it?

CHRISTINA   What else could be strong enough?

DAVID   Perhaps you're right. *(Then, unaccountably, he shies.)* But what's the idea in getting so worked up about it?

CHRISTINA   This! . . . Who comes first with you? Your mother or me?

DAVID   Now what's the good of putting things that way?

CHRISTINA   That's what things come to! If your mother and I ever quarreled about anything, if it ever came up to you to choose between sticking by me and sticking by her, which would you stick by?

DAVID   I'd . . . I'd try to do the right thing. . . .

CHRISTINA   That isn't an answer. That's another evasion.

DAVID   But why ask such a question?

CHRISTINA   Because I love you. Because I've got to find out if you love me. And I'm afraid . . . I'm afraid. . . .

DAVID   Why?

CHRISTINA   Because you won't see the facts behind all this. I'm trying to tell you what they are and you won't listen. You can't even hear me.

DAVID   I *can* hear you. And a worse line of hooey I've never listened to in my life.

CHRISTINA   *(Gravely, but with steadily increasing fervor)*   Have you ever thought what it would be like to be trapped in a submarine in an accident? I've learned tonight what that kind of panic would be like. I'm in that kind of panic now, this minute. I've been through the most awful experience of my life tonight. And I've been through it alone. I'm still going through it alone. It's pretty awful to have to face such things alone. . . . No, don't interrupt me. I've got to get this off my chest. Ever since we've been married I've been coming across queer rifts in your feeling for me, like arid places in your heart. Such vast ones, too! I mean, you'll be my perfect lover one day, and the next I'll find myself floundering in sand, and alone, and you nowhere to be seen. We've never been really married, Dave. Only now and then, for a little while at a time, between your retirements into your arid places. . . . I used to wonder what you did there. At first, I thought you did your work there. But you don't. Your work's in my part of your heart, what there is of my part. Then I decided the other was just No-Man's Land. And I thought: little by little, I'll encroach upon it and pour my love upon it, like water on the western desert, and make it flower here and bear fruit there. I thought: then he'll be all alive, all free and all himself; not partly dead and tied and blind; not partly some one else—or nothing. You see, our marriage and your architecture were suffering from the same thing. They only worked a little of the time. I meant them both to work all the time. I meant you to work all the time and to win your way, *all* your way, Dave, to complete manhood. And that's a good deal farther than you've got so far. . . . Then we came here and this happened with Hester and your brother and you just stepped aside and did nothing about it! You went to bed. You did worse than that. You retired into your private wastes and sat tight. . . . I've shown you what you should do and you won't see it. I've called to you to come out to me, and you won't come. So now I've discovered what keeps you. Your mother keeps you. It isn't No-Man's Land at all. It's your mother's land. Arid, sterile, and your mother's! You won't let me get in there. Worse than that, you won't let life get in there! Or she won't! . . . That's what I'm afraid of, Dave—your mother's hold on you. And that's what's kept me from getting anywhere with you, all these months. I've seen what she can do with Robert. And what she's done to Hester. I can't help wondering what she may not do with you and to me and to the baby. That's why I'm asking you to take a stand on this business of Hester's, Dave. You'll never find the right any clearer than it is here. It's a kind of test case for me. Don't you see? What you decide about this is what you may, eventually, be expected to decide about . . . about our marriage.

Ars Poetica

X. J. KENNEDY

The goose that laid the golden egg
Died looking up its crotch
To find out how its sphincter worked.

Would you lay well? Don't watch.

The Wife

DENISE LEVERTOV

A frog under you,
knees drawn up
ready to leap out of time,

a dog beside you,
snuffing at you, seeking
scent of you, an idea unformulated,

I give up on
trying to answer my question,
Do I love you enough?

It's enough to be so much here. And
certainly when I catch

your mind in the
act of plucking
truth from the dark surroundingnowhere

as a swallow skims a
gnat from the
deep sky,

I don't stop to ask myself
Do I love him? but
laugh for joy.

Apology

AMY LOWELL

Be not angry with me that I bear
  Your colours everywhere,
All through each crowded street,
  And meet
The wonder-light in every eye,
  As I go by.

Each plodding wayfarer looks up to gaze,
  Blinded by rainbow haze,
The stuff of happiness,
  No less,
Which wraps me in its glad-hued folds
  Of peacock golds.

Before my feet the dusty, rough-paved way
  Flushes beneath its gray.
My steps fall ringed with light,
  So bright,
It seems a myriad suns are strown
  About the town.

Around me is the sound of steepled bells,
  And rich perfuméd smells
Hang like a wind-forgotten cloud,
  and shroud
Me from close contact with the world.
  I dwell impearled.

You blazon me with jewelled insignia.
  A flaming nebula

Rims in my life. And yet
  You set
The word upon me, unconfessed
  To go unguessed.

Circe

LOUIS MacNEICE

". . . . vitreamque Circen."

Something of glass about her, of dead water,
Chills and holds us,
Far more fatal than painted flesh or the lodestone of live hair
This despair of crystal brilliance.
Narcissus' error
Enfolds and kills us—
Dazed with gazing on that unfertile beauty
Which is our own heart's thought.
Fled away to the beasts
One cannot stop thinking; Timon
Kept on finding gold.
In parrot-ridden forest or barren coast
A more importunate voice than bird or wave
Escutcheoned on the air with ice letters
Seeks and, of course, finds us
(Of course, being our echo).
Be brave, my ego, look into your glass
And realize that that never-to-be-touched
Vision is your mistress.

Trilogy for X

LOUIS MacNEICE

I

When clerks and navvies fondle
  Beside canals their wenches,
In rapture or in coma
  The haunches that they handle,
And the orange moon sits idle
  Above the orchard slanted—
Upon such easy evenings
  We take our loves for granted.

But when, as now, the creaking
   Trees on the hills of London
Like bison charge their neighbours
   In wind that keeps us waking
And in the draught the scalloped
   Lampshade swings a shadow,
We think of love bound over—
   The mortgage on the meadow.

And one lies lonely, haunted
   By limbs he half remembers,
And one, in wedlock, wonders
   Where is the girl he wanted;
And some sit smoking, flicking
   The ash away and feeling
For love gone up like vapour
   Between the floor and ceiling.

But now when winds are curling
   The trees do you come closer,
Close as an eyelid fasten
   My body in darkness, darling;
Switch the light off and let me
   Gather you up and gather
The power of trains advancing
   Further, advancing further.

II

And love hung still as crystal over the bed
   And filled the corners of the enormous room;
The boom of dawn that left her sleeping, showing
   The flowers mirrored in the mahogany table.

O my love, if only I were able
   To protract this hour of quiet after passion,
Not ration happiness but keep this door for ever
   Closed on the world, its own world closed within it.

But dawn's waves trouble with the bubbling minute,
   The names of books come clear upon their shelves,
The reason delves for duty and you will wake
   With a start and go on living on your own.

The first train passes and the windows groan,
   Voices will hector and your voice become
A drum in tune with theirs, which all last night
   Like sap that fingered through a hungry tree
Asserted our one night's identity.

Eros in the Kitchen

PHYLLIS McGINLEY

575

"Night-Lights"
reflections on
sexual themes

Our cook is in love. Love hangs on the house like a mist.
It embraces us all.
The spoons go uncounted. Confused is the grocery list,
But light each footfall.
Astonished, we notice how lyric the dishwasher sings.
(Did it always sing thus?)
And the mop has a lilt. And the telephone ceaselessly rings,
Although seldom for us.
Here nothing seems quite the same as it did before.
Something ineffably hovers
Over the household. All of us plunge or soar
With the mood of the lovers.
We dine to distraction on delicate viands today
Who, likely, tomorrow
Must scrabble with timorous forks at a fallen soufflé
More sodden than sorrow.
And salad's served up with dessert and the napkin's forgot,
The butter's unformed by the mold,
And the bouillon's barbarically cold,
Or the aspic comes hot.
And the message for Mister or Madam's a fortnight untold.

But who's such a churl as to care
With amour like a mist on the air,
On the house like a bloom—
When so blithe is the broom,
And the voice of the kettle, the beat of the brush on the tile
Sound gayer than springtime peeper?
We smile at each other at breakfast. At dinner we smile.
There's a smile on the face of the sleeper.
Our years have grown younger. We sally to parties at night
In tall hat and long glove.
We remember what we had forgotten. The hallways are bright.
Our cook is in love.

Sonnet XXIX

EDNA ST. VINCENT MILLAY

Pity me not because the light of day
At close of day no longer walks the sky;
Pity me not for beauties passed away
From field and thicket as the year goes by;

Pity me not the waning of the moon,
Nor that the ebbing tide goes out to sea,
Nor that a man's desire is hushed so soon,
And you no longer look with love on me.
This have I known always: Love is no more
Than the wide blossom which the wind assails,
Than the great tide that treads the shifting shore,
Strewing fresh wreckage gathered in the gales:
Pity me that the heart is slow to learn
What the swift mind beholds at every turn.

Recuerdo

EDNA ST. VINCENT MILLAY

We were very tired, we were very merry—
We had gone back and forth all night on the ferry.
It was bare and bright, and smelled like a stable—
But we looked into a fire, we leaned across a table,
We lay on the hill-top underneath the moon;
And the whistles kept blowing, and the dawn came soon.

We were very tired, we were very merry—
We had gone back and forth all night on the ferry;
And you ate an apple, and I ate a pear,
From a dozen of each we had bought somewhere;
And the sky went wan, and the wind came cold,
And the sun rose dripping, a bucketful of gold.

We were very tired, we were very merry,
We had gone back and forth all night on the ferry.
We hailed, "Good morrow, mother!" to a shawl-covered head,

And bought a morning paper, which neither of us read;
And she wept, "God bless you!" for the apples and the pears,
And we gave her all our money but our subway fares.

After the Fall

ARTHUR MILLER

QUENTIN   I keep forgetting . . . how beautiful you are. Your eyes make me
    shiver.
        (She is silent, adoring. He breaks it, sitting.)
MAGGIE   Like to see my new apartment? There's no elevator even, or a door-

man. Nobody would know. If you want to rest before you go to Washington.
  (He doesn't reply.)
'Cause I just found out, I go to Paris after London. I'm on for two weeks, which is supposed to be unusual. But I won't be back for a while.

QUENTIN How long will you be gone?

MAGGIE About . . . six weeks, I think.
  (They both arrive at the same awareness: the separation is pain. Tears are in her eyes.)
Quentin?

QUENTIN Honey . . . *(Takes her hand)* Don't look for anything more from me.

MAGGIE I'm not! See, all I thought, if I went to Washington—. . .

QUENTIN What a lovely thought.

MAGGIE And it would make you happy.

QUENTIN *(smiling warmly at her)* And nervous. But it is a lovely thought.

MAGGIE Because it should all be one thing, you know? Helping people, and sex. You might even argue better the next day!

QUENTIN *(with a new awareness, astonishment)* You know?—There's one word written on your forehead.

MAGGIE What?

QUENTIN "Now."

MAGGIE But what else is there?

QUENTIN A future. And I've been carrying it around all my life, like a vase that must never be dropped. So you cannot ever touch anybody, you see?

MAGGIE But why can't you just hold it in one hand?
  (He laughs.)
And touch with the other! I would never bother you, Quentin.
  (He looks at his watch, as though beginning to calculate if there might not be time.)
Can't somebody just give you something? Like when you're thirsty. And you drink, and walk away, that's all.

QUENTIN But what about you?

MAGGIE Well . . . I would have what I gave. *(Slight pause.)*

QUENTIN You're all love, aren't you?

Fred Apollus at Fava's

NICHOLAS MOORE

My sexual feats—
It is accounts of these
Each friend entreats.
They do not care what women wear or what artistic fashion
 meets
My best approval.

Love is all.

There are no swans
But Leda's, and its hiss,
Majestic once,
Grows tame with telling over tea and the inevitable buns.
They hate Picasso—
Art's no go.

They only like the rude
Reclining nude
The shiny-covered magazines all show,
This svelte form,
This velvet norm
Of their romantic discipline,
Whose wild imaginations flow
Towards flesh more bright than I have ever seen.

And am I like a god
Who sit and nod
At their remarks? Experienced in all
The ways of love,
Each subtle move?
I hate them as their hard words rise
Over their plates of pork and fall
Against my ear. They take me by surprise;

For, suddenly, I know myself a jealous man,
An also-ran
Unfit to face the company of such,
Who obviously touch
Such transports of delight as I
Have never known. How can I qualify?

It only seems I have my dreams and hopes,
Those bitter shapes
Of unloved breasts and thighs that pass,
(Each one my golden ass!)—
My sexual feats are all my friends',
Not mine. Not me to whom the red tongue sends

Such thrills.
(It is the thought that kills!)

These men
(How vainly!) turn towards me again.

A Problem in Morals

HOWARD MOSS

Promiscuous lovers
Pine to have,
Under the covers,
One faithful love,
And treat their lust,
Being overwrought,
With rare disgust
On second thought.

Faithful lovers
Soon develop
The eye of rovers:
Satyr, trollope,
Long out of mind,
Becoming enticing
And come around—
The cake needs icing.

Though most have tried
A bit of both,
Lied and denied,
And nothing loth
To lie again,
They've never found,
With women and men,
A middle ground.

Rain

HOWARD MOSS

Dear, on a day of dumb rain,
When cats sleep and trees grow,
And, outside the windowpane,
Imaginary fish flow,
We, as lovers, lace our arms
Securely round each other's back,
Hoping to stave off lightning's harm,
To counter thunder's crack.

Then pleasure is as easy as
The body's closeness, and the mind's;

There is a kind of love that has
Them separate, but body finds
Body too tasteless without thought,
And lovers feel, when face to face,
That mere intellect falls short,
Short of an embrace.

Dwindling, the slim rain makes us seem
As green as any world that grows;
Intransitive in sleep, we dream
Ourselves curled tightly as the rose,
Whose bud we cannot praise too much:
This is the start of every song
That no philosophy can touch—
And only the dead are wrong.

Art of Love

OVID

Translated from the Latin by John Dryden

Kiss, if you can: Resistance if she make,
And will not give you Kisses, let her take.
Fie, fie, you naughty Man, are Words of Course;
She struggles, but to be subdu'd by Force.
Kiss only soft, I charge you, and beware,
With your hard Bristles not to brush the Fair.
He who has gain'd a Kiss, and gains no more,
Deserves to lose the Bliss he got before.
If once she kiss, her Meaning is exprest;
There wants but little Pushing for the rest.
Which if thou dost not gain, by Strength or Art,
The Name of Clown then suits with thy Desert;
'Tis downright Dulness, and a shameful Part.
Perhaps, she calls it Force; but, if she scape,
She will not thank you for th' omitted Rape.
The Sex is cunning to conceal their Fires;
They would be forc'd, ev'n to their own Desires.
They seem t' accuse you, with a down-cast Sight,
But in their Souls confess you did them right.
Who might be forc'd, and yet untouched depart,
Thank with their Tongues, but curse you with their Heart.

As We Are So Wonderfully Done with Each Other

KENNETH PATCHEN

As we are so wonderfully done with each other
We can walk into our separate sleep
On floors of music where the milkwhite cloak of childhood lies

Oh my love, my golden lark, my soft long doll
Your lips have splashed my dull house with print of flowers
My hands are crooked where they spilled over your dear curving

It is good to be weary from that brilliant work
It is being God to feel your breathing under me

A waterglass on the bureau fills with morning . . .
Don't let anyone in to wake us

When in My Arms

ALEXANDER PUSHKIN

Translated from the Russian by Babette Deutsch

When in my arms your slender beauty
Is locked, O you whom I adore,
And from my lips in gusts of rapture
Love's tender murmurs stintless pour,
In silence from my tight embraces
Your supple form you gently free,
And with a skeptic's smile, my dear one,
You mockingly reply to me:
The sad tradition of betrayal
You have remembered all too well;
You listen with a sad indifference,
Not heeding what I have to tell . . .
I curse the naughty zeal, the cunning,
The hot pursuit after delight
That filled my youth, the assignations,
The garden trysts in the hushed night;
I curse the whispered lovers' discourse,
The magic spells that lay in verse,
The gullible young girls' caresses,
Their tears, their late regrets I curse.

The Book of True Love

JEAN RUIZ

Translated from the Spanish by Hubert Creekmore

"When you're together with her, and you have a good excuse,
As if you're scared but lustful, squeeze and paw her all you can,
And often sigh and yearn for what she's going to refuse.
She'll give more than you hope for, if you're not an idle goose.

"All women love those men of force who make their will be
    done.
They long for such a man more than for money by the ton.
Their hands dissolve in languor, their heels collapse when they
    would run.
They'll go part way or all the way, but grudge it like a nun.

"A woman much prefers to be just slightly raped, they claim,
Than have to say: 'Go right ahead,' as if she had no shame,
With but a little force she feels almost excused of blame.
Among all animals this trait has proved to be the same.

"All females of whatever species share this coaxing trait:
When you begin your suit, they seemed affronted, would depart,
Pretend they're angry, act evasive—but this is merely bait.
They threaten, but withhold the blow—they're crafty in this art.

"Though ladies who are wooed may well react with roaring rage,
The honest suitors never let themselves be balked by that.
For women who get angry, on whom you men your wars must
    wage,
Are conquered by your homage, though they're fierce as a wild
    cat.

"Its fear and modesty that make the women, as a clan,
Not do what they would wish to do as heartily as you.
They don't run out through lack of lust for being with a man.
Take from the lady what you yearn for every time you can. . . ."

a stream of consciousness

JOHN C. SAMUELSON

it must be today
they say i was born right on schedule
so 9 months back from the twelfth of march is the
twelfth of june today is the anniversary of my conception
16 years ago i first was

let's celebrate   the three of us
Mom Dad and me their son
how come we have birthdays when this is so much more
    important?
there was no question at birth   that necessarily followed
predictable as it was
but on this day the decision was made
the beginnings of life arose   me the product of their love
the result of a beautiful merger   the new life
to carry on the gift of men

it will be a spiritual reunion once again
i'll ask "how was it mom? fantastic?"   "was it real good Dad?"
I'll thank them   Dad'll say "it was a pleasure"
such a corny sense of humor
they'll tell me what a great kid i am and love
will pervade over all

but how do i remind them?   what if they laugh?
if they've forgotten how it was?   if it wasn't a decision
if they never really knew which day it happened?
and maybe the love was   oh hell

Honey and Salt

CARL SANDBURG

A bag of tricks—is it?
    And a game smoothies play?
If you're good with a deck of cards
or rolling the bones—that helps?
If you can tell jokes and be a chum
and make an impression—that helps?
When boy meets girl or girl meets boy—
                    what helps?
They all help: be cozy but not too cozy:

be shy, bashful, mysterious, yet only so-so:
then forget everything you ever heard about love
for it's a summer tan and a winter windburn
and it comes as weather comes and you can't change it:
it comes like your face came to you, like your legs came
and the way you walk, talk, hold your head and hands—
and nothing can be done about it—you wait and pray.
  Is there any way of measuring love?
  Yes but not till long afterward
  when the beat of your heart has gone
  many miles, far into the big numbers.
Is the key to love in passion, knowledge, affection?
All three—along with moonlight, roses, groceries,
givings and forgivings, gettings and forgettings,
  keepsakes and room rent,
  pearls of memory along with ham and eggs.
Can love be locked away and kept hid?
  Yes and it gathers dust and mildew
  and shrivels itself in shadows
  unless it learns the sun can help,
  snow, rain, storms can help—
  birds in their one-room family nests
  shaken by winds cruel and crazy—
  they can all help:
  lock not away your love nor keep it hid.

  How comes the first sign of love?
  In a chill, in a personal sweat,
  in a you-and-me, us, us two,
  in a couple of answers,
  an amethyst haze on the horizon,
  two dance programs criss-crossed,
  jackknifed initials interwoven,
  five fresh violets lost in sea salt,
  birds flying at single big moments
  in and out a thousand windows,
  a horse, two horses, many horses,
  a silver ring, a brass cry,
  a golden gong going ong ong ong-ng-ng,
  pink doors closing one by one
  to sunset nightsongs along the west,
  shafts and handles of stars,
  folds of moonmist curtains,
  winding and unwinding wisps of fogmist.

  How long does love last?
As long as glass bubbles handled with care
or two hot-house orchids in a blizzard

or one solid immovable steel anvil
tempered in sure inexorable welding—
or again love might last as
six snowflakes, six hexagonal snowflakes,
six floating hexagonal flakes of snow
or the oaths between hydrogen and oxygen
                in one cup of spring water
                or the eyes of bucks and does
or two wishes riding on the back of a
                morning wind in winter
or one corner of an ancient tabernacle
held sacred for personal devotions
or dust   yes   dust in a little solemn heap
                played on by changing winds.

                There are sanctuaries
                        holding honey and salt.
                There are those who
                        spill and spend.
                There are those who
                        search and save.
                And love may be a quest
                        with silence and content.
                Can you buy love?
Sure   every day with money, clothes, candy,
with promises, flowers, big-talk,
with laughter, sweet-talk, lies,
every day men and women buy love
and take it away and things happen
                and they study about it
                and the longer they look at it
the more it isn't love they bought at all:
                bought love is a guaranteed imitation.

                Can you sell love?
Yes   you can sell it and take the price
                and think it over
                and look again at the price
                and cry and cry to yourself
and wonder who was selling what and why.
Evensong lights floating black night waters,
a lagoon of stars washed in velvet shadows,
a great storm cry from white sea-horses—
                these moments cost beyond all prices.

                Bidden or unbidden? how comes love?
Both bidden and unbidden, a sneak and a shadow
                a dawn in a doorway throwing a dazzle

or a sash of light in a blue fog,
a slow blinking of two red lanterns in river mist
or a deep smoke winding one hump of a mountain
and the smoke becomes a smoke known to your own
twisted individual garments:
the winding of it gets into your walk, your hands,
your face and eyes.

"Night-Lights"
reflections on
sexual themes

Kisses, Can You Come Back Like Ghosts?

CARL SANDBURG

If we ask you to gleam through the tears,
Kisses, can you come back like ghosts?

Today, tomorrow, the gateways take them.
"Always some door eats my shadow."

Love is a clock and the works wear out.
Love is a violin and the wood rots.
Love is a day with night at the end.
Love is a summer with falltime after.
Love dies always and when it dies it is dead
And when it is dead there is nothing more to it
And when there is nothing more to it then we say
This is the end, it comes always, it came to us.
And now we will bury it and put it away
Beautifully and decently, like a clock or a violin,
Like a summer day near falltime,
Like any lovely thing brought to the expected end.

Yes, let it go at that.
The clock rang and we answered.
The moon swept an old valley.
And we counted all its rings.
The water-birds flipped in the river
And flicked their wing-points in sunset gold.
To the moon and the river water-birds,
To these we answered as the high calls rang.
And now? Now we take the clock and put it away.
Now we count again the rings of the valley moon
and put them away as keepsakes.

Now we count the river-birds once more and let
    them slip loose and slip up the valley curve.
This is the end, there is always an end.

    Kisses, can you
    come back
        like ghosts?

One Parting

CARL SANDBURG

Why did he write to her,
"I can't live with you"?
And why did she write to him,
"I can't live without you"?
For he went west, she went east,
And they both lived.

Act of Love

VERNON SCANNELL

This is not the man that women choose,
This honest fellow, stuffed to the lips with groans,
Whose passion cannot even speak plain prose
But grunts and mumbles in the muddiest tones.
His antics are disgusting or absurd,
His lust obtrusive, craning from its nest
At awkward times its blind reptilian head;
His jealousy and candour are a pest.

Now, here is the boy that women will lie down for:
The snappy actor, skilled in the lover's part,
A lyric fibber and subvocal tenor
Whose pleasure in the play conceals his art;
Who, even as he enters her warm yes,
Hears fluttering hands and programmes in the vast
Auditorium beyond her voice
Applauding just one member of the cast.

Wax

WINFIELD TOWNLEY SCOTT

A covey of cotton-dressed, apple-breasted girls
Squealed from the hut as the two boys crossed the field
And were gone when the boys reached the hut,
Entered and saw the wax thing on the floor.

Not a candle. By projecting themselves
Immensely (so it seemed to them) older,
The boys knew—there in the damp shadows
Of musty ruins—what the replica was.

Glans end hung broken on the central string.
Half as thick as their wrists the thing made
A frightening excitement when their thin fingers
Explored the hard rod of dirty yellow.

They hid it under a rotted floorboard,
Not knowing why they hid it, any more
Than they imagined why, unlike themselves,
The girls had not merely touched for future luck.

Seventeen

BOOTH TARKINGTON

"Don't you think love is sacred?" he repeated in the deepest tone
of which his vocal cords were capable.

"Ess," said Miss Pratt.

"*I* do!" William was emphatic. "I think love is the most sacred thing there
is. I don't mean *some* kinds of love. I mean *real* love. You take some people, I
don't believe they even know what real love means. They *talk* about it, maybe,
but they don't understand it. Love is something nobody can understand unless
they feel it and—and if they don't understand it they don't feel it. Don't *you*
think so?"

"Ess."

"Love," William continued, his voice lifting and thrilling to the great theme
—"love is something nobody can ever have but one time in their lives, and if they
don't have it then, why prob'ly they never will. Now, if a man *really* loves a girl,
why he'd do anything in the world she wanted him to. Don't *you* think so?"

"Ess, 'deedums!" said the silvery voice.

"But if he didn't, then he wouldn't," said William vehemently. "But when
a man really loves a girl he will. Now, you take a man like that and he can generally do just about anything the girl he loves wants him to. Say, f'rinstance, she

wants him to love her even more than he does already—or almost anything like that—and supposin' she asks him to. Well, he would go ahead and do it. If they really loved each other he would!"

He paused a moment, then in a lowered tone he said, "I think *real* love is sacred, don't you?"

"Ess."

"Don't you think love is the most sacred thing there is—that is, if it's *real* love?"

"Ess."

"*I* do," said William, warmly. "I—I'm glad you feel like that, because I think real love is the kind nobody could have but just once in their lives, but if it isn't *real* love, why—why most people never have it at all, because—" He paused, seeming to seek for the exact phrase which would express his meaning. "—Because the *real* love a man feels for a girl and a girl for a man, if they *really* love each other, and, you look at a case like that, of course they would *both* love each other, or it wouldn't be real love—well, what *I* say is, if it's *real* love, well, it's—it's sacred, because I think that kind of love is always sacred. Don't you think love is sacred if it's the real thing?"

Centuries of Meditations
THOMAS TRAHERNE

In all love there is a love begetting, and a love begotten, and a love proceeding. Which though they are one in essence subsist nevertheless in three several manners. For love is benevolent affection to another. Which is of itself, and by itself relateth to its object. It floweth from itself and resteth in its object. Love proceedeth of necessity from itself, for unless it be of itself it is not Love. Constraint is destructive and opposite to its nature. The Love from which it floweth is the fountain of Love. The Love which streameth from it, is the communication of Love, or Love communicated. The Love which resteth in the object is the Love which streameth to it. So that in all Love, the Trinity is clear. By secret passages without stirring it proceedeth to its object, and is as powerfully present as if it did not proceed at all. The Love that lieth in the bosom of the Lover, being the love that is perceived in the spirit of the Beloved: that is, the same in substance, though in the manner of substance, or subsistence, different. Love in the bosom is the parent of Love, Love in the stream is the effect of Love, Love seen, or dwelling in the object proceedeth from both. Yet are all these, one and the self-same Love: though three Loves.

A Woman Waits for Me

WALT WHITMAN

A woman waits for me, she contains all, nothing is lacking,
Yet all were lacking if sex were lacking, or if the moisture of the
  right man were lacking.

Sex contains all, bodies, souls,
Meanings, proofs, purities, delicacies, results, promulgations,
Songs, commands, health, pride, the maternal mystery, the
  seminal milk,
All hopes, benefactions, bestowals, all the passions, loves,
  beauties, delights of the earth,
All the governments, judges, gods, follow'd persons of the earth,
These are contain'd in sex as parts of itself and justifications of
  itself.

Without shame the man I like knows and avows the deliciousness
  of his sex,
Without shame the woman I like knows and avows hers.

Now I will dismiss myself from impassive women,
I will go stay with her who waits for me, and with those women
  that are warm-blooded and sufficient for me,
I see that they understand me and do not deny me,
I see that they are worthy of me, I will be the robust husband
  of those women.

They are not one jot less than I am,
They are tann'd in the face by shining suns and blowing winds,
Their flesh has the old divine suppleness and strength,
They know how to swim, row, ride, wrestle, shoot, run, strike,
  retreat, advance, resist, defend themselves,
They are ultimate in their own right—they are calm, clear, well-
  possess'd of themselves.

I draw you close to me, you women,
I cannot let you go, I would do you good,
I am for you, and you are for me, not only for our own
  sake, but for others' sakes,
Envelop'd in you sleep greater heroes and bards,
They refuse to awake at the touch of any man but me.

It is I, you women, I make my way,
I am stern, acrid, large, undissuadable, but I love you,
I do not hurt you any more than is necessary for you,
I pour the stuff to start sons and daughters fit for these States,
  I press with slow rude muscle,

I brace myself effectually, I listen to no entreaties,
I dare not withdraw till I deposit what has so long accumulated
within me.

Through you I drain the pent-up rivers of myself,
In you I wrap a thousand onward years,
On you I graft the grafts of the best-beloved of me and America,
The drops I distil upon you shall grow fierce and athletic girls,
new artists, musicians, and singers,
The babes I beget upon you are to beget babes in their turn,
I shall demand perfect men and women out of my love-
spendings,
I shall expect them to interpenetrate with others, as I and you
interpenetrate now,
I shall count on the fruits of the gushing showers of them, as I
count on the fruits of the gushing showers I give now,
I shall look for loving crops from the birth, life, death, im-
mortality, I plant so lovingly now.

The Ballad of Reading Gaol

OSCAR WILDE

. . . Yet each man kills the thing he loves,
  By each let this be heard,
Some do it with a bitter look,
  Some with a flattering word,
The coward does it with a kiss,
  The brave man with a sword!

Some kill their love when they are young,
  And some when they are old;
Some strangle with the hands of Lust,
  Some with the hands of Gold:
The kindest use a knife, because
  The dead so soon grow cold.

Some love too little, some too long,
  Some sell and others buy;
Some do the deed with many tears
  And some without a sigh:
For each man kills the thing he loves,
  Yet each man does not die. . . .

The Sadder-but-Wiser Girl for Me
(*from* The Music Man)

MEREDITH WILLSON

No bright-eyed, blushing, breathless baby doll baby, no sir,
That kind of child ties knots no sailor ever knew,
I prefer to take a chance
On a more adult romance,
No dewy young miss who keeps resisting
All the time she keeps insisting.
No bright-eyed, wholesome, innocent female, no sir,
Why she's the fisherman; I'm the fish,
You'll see, plop.

I flinch, I shy,
When the lass with the delicate air walks by,
I smile, I grin,
When the gal with a touch of sin walks in,
I hope, and I pray,
For Hester to win just one more 'A',
The sadder-but-wiser girl's the girl for me.

L'ENVOI

The universe resounds with the joyful cry "I am" . . . when children love, they do not give, they only receive; it is a love that creates only a self . . . the aching desire to give, to create life beyond the self, calls boy into man; gratified, this love creates an analogue of heaven on earth . . . to be human is to be in danger, to be terribly vulnerable to the damage that people are capable of inflicting upon one another . . . we are subject to what we are taught to hate . . . knowledge springs not from thinking but from thinking about what happens when we act . . . so your is a my . . . now i love you and you love me . . . there's somebody calling who's we . . . we're anything brighter than even the sun . . . we're wonderful one times one . . . if it were not for the physical side of love we should none of us be here, and the least sophisticated of us knows intuitively much about it . . . but the atmosphere and psychology of passion are other matters, and the trackless maze in which the average reader wanders where his feelings are concerned is none the worse for a night-light or two. . . .

Notes

"I"

In Children's Drawings: "Where was I before I was born?" (pp. 7–11), drawings A–I are the work of males; drawings J–R are the work of females.

1. Michel de Montaigne, "Upon Some Verses of Virgil," *Essays*, III, 5, John Florio, tr. (London: J. M. Dent, 1938), p. 128.

2. Wardell B. Pomeroy, "Homosexuality," *The Same Sex: An Appraisal of Homosexuality*, Ralph W. Weltge, ed. (Philadelphia, Pa.: Pilgrim Press, 1969), p. 4. Within this quotation [a] is cited as Alfred C. Kinsey, et al., *Sexual Behavior in the Human Male* (Philadelphia, Pa.: W. B. Saunders, 1948).

3. Paul Goodman, *Growing Up Absurd* (New York: Random House, 1960), p. 127.

4. Dorothy Parker, "De Profundis," *Not So Deep a Well* (New York: Viking, 1936), p. 46.

5. Montaigne, p. 106.

6. John Keats, "Ode to a Nightingale," Stanza II, lines 11–14.

7. Evelyn M. Duvall, *Love and the Facts of Life* (New York: Association Press, 1963), pp. 54–57.

8. Marlene Dietrich, *Marlene Dietrich's ABC* (Garden City, N.Y.: Doubleday, 1962), p. 102.

9. Erik H. Erikson, *Identity: Youth and Crisis* (New York: Norton, 1968), p. 132.

10. Jessie Bernard, *The Sex Game* (Englewood Cliffs, N.J.: Prentice-Hall, 1968), p. 56.

11. Attributed to La Rochefoucauld, in Irving Singer, *The Nature of Love* (New York: Random House, 1966), p. xii.

12. Singer, pp. xii–xiii.

13. Joseph Fletcher, *Moral Responsibility* (New York: Westminster Press, 1967), pp. 83–84.

14. Fletcher, pp. 89–91.

15. Erikson, pp. 160, 163–164.

16. Morton S. Eisenberg, "Sexuality and Its Implications for Personal Identity and Fulfillment," *Sex Education and the New Morality* (New York: The Child Study Association of America, © 1967), pp. 14–15.

17. Eisenberg, p. 16.

18. Helen F. Southard, "The Issues for Parents," *Sex Education and the New Morality,* p. 73.

19. Bernard, pp. 79–80, 83–84.

20. Rudyard Kipling, "The Female of the Species," *Rudyard Kipling's Verse* (Garden City, N.Y.: Doubleday, 1954), pp. 364–366, lines 16–28, 49–52.

21. Marynia F. Farnham, *The Adolescent* (New York: Harper & Row, 1951), p. 66.

22. Duvall, pp. 228–229.

23. Quoted by Mary S. Calderone, "The Issues for Parents," *Sex Education and the New Morality,* p. 85.

24. Saul Scheidlinger, "The Issues for Parents," *Sex Education and the New Morality,* p. 69.

25. Farnham, p. 57.

26. Farnham, pp. 38, 57.

27. Farnham, p. 27.

28. Farnham, p. 41.

"THEY"

1. Duvall, p. 231.

2. Lester A. Kirkendall and Deryck Calderwood, "The Family, the School, and Peer Groups: Sources of Information about Sex," *The Journal of School Health,* 35 (7), September 1965, p. 290.

3. Dietrich, p. 164.

4. Erikson, p. 132.

5. Duvall, p. 78.

6. Calderone, p. 66.

7. Duvall, p. 78.

8. Duvall, p. 79.

9. Farnham, p. 91.

10. Dietrich, pp. 174–175.

11. Duvall, p. 26.

12. Duvall, p. 27.

13. Goodman, pp. 124, 126–127.

14. Pomeroy, p. 3.

15. Calderone, p. 80.

16. Hugh M. Hefner, "The *Playboy* Philosophy," *Playboy,* Vol. 10, No. 5, May 1963, pp. 72, 168, 169.

17. Hefner, p. 168.

18. Goodman, pp. 124–125.

19. Goodman, p. 125.

20. Dore Schary, "The Arts and the Sexual Image," *Sex Education and the New Morality,* pp. 51. 54.

21. Dietrich, p. 151.

22. A. S. Neill, *Summerhill: A Radical Approach to Child Rearing* (New York: Hart Publishing, 1960), pp. 213–214.

23. Lester A. Kirkendall, "The Search for a Meaningful Sexual Ethic," *Sex Education and the New Morality,* p. 39.

24. Irving Fineman, "Spelling Lesson," unpublished poem.

25. Grace Metalious, *Peyton Place* (New York: Julian Messner, 1956), pp. 368–369.

26. Dietrich, p. 9.

27. John Wilson, *Logic and Sexual Morality* (London: Penguin Books, 1965), p. 217.

28. Calderone, p. 66.

29. Duvall, p. 215.

30. Anne Morrow Lindbergh, *The Steep Ascent* (New York: Harcourt Brace Jovanovich, 1944), p. 61.

31. Henry Drummond, "The Greatest Thing in the World," in *Treasures of the Kingdom,* T. Everett Harré, ed. (New York: Holt, Rinehart and Winston, 1947), p. 6.

32. C. S. Lewis, *The Pilgrim's Regress* (New York: Sheed and Ward, 1944), p. 207.

33. Dietrich, p. 88.

34. W. H. Auden, "Are You There?" *The Collected Poetry of W. H. Auden* (New York: Random House, 1945), p. 35.

35. Ralph Waldo Emerson, "Illusions," *The Portable Emerson* (New York: Viking, 1946), pp. 231–232.

36. Duvall, p. 49.

37. Dietrich, p. 91.

38. Duvall, pp. 25–26.

39. William Shakespeare, *A Midsummer Night's Dream,* Act I, scene i, lines 232–241.

40. Blaise Pascal, "On the Passion of Love," *Miscellaneous Writings of Pascal,* George Pearce, tr., in Walter de la Mare, *Love* (New York: William Morrow, 1946), p. 248.

41. Francis Bacon, "Of Love," *Essays and New Atlantis* (New York: Walter J. Black, 1942), pp. 40–41.

42. Pascal, p. 249.

43. Edna St. Vincent Millay, "Sonnet XXVI," *Collected Sonnets* (New York: Harper & Row, 1941), p. 26.

44. Pascal, p. 249.

45. Karl and Jeanetta Menninger, *Love Against Hate* (New York: Harcourt Brace Jovanovich, 1942), p. 261.

46. Archibald MacLeish, "The Second Love," from "The Woman on the Stair," *Public Speech* in *Collected Poems 1917–1952* (Boston: Houghton Mifflin, 1952), pp. 117–118.

47 Archibald MacLeish, "The Happy Marriage," in *Collected Poems 1917–1952* (Boston: Houghton Mifflin, 1952), p. 8.

48. Arthur Miller, *After The Fall* (New York: Viking, 1964), Act I, pp. 46–47.

49. Fletcher, *Moral Responsibility,* p. 86.

50. MacLeish, pp. 7–8.

51. E. E. Cummings, "NonLecture Three," *i: Six NonLectures* (Cambridge, Mass.: Harvard University Press, 1953), p. 43.

52. Carl Sandburg, "Solo for Saturday Night Guitar," *Honey and Salt* (New York: Harcourt Brace Jovanovich, 1958), p. 84.

53. Miller, p. 95.

54. F. Alexander Magoun, *Love and Marriage* (New York: Harper & Row, 1956), p. 7.

55. Robert O. Johann, *America*, 113 (1965), 404.

56. Lionel Trilling, "The Kinsey Report," *The Liberal Imagination* (New York: Viking, 1950), pp. 226, 231.

57. Fletcher, *Moral Responsibility*, p. 91.

58. Lester A. Kirkendall, "Searching for the Roots of Moral Judgments," an adaptation of his article "Searching for the Roots of Moral Decisions," *The Humanist*, January–February 1967, pp. 20–23.

59. Erikson, pp. 136, 259–260.

60. Fletcher, *Moral Responsibility*, p. 87.

61. *Idem.*

62. Roger L. Shinn, *Tangled World* (New York: Scribner's, 1965), p. 130.

63. Fletcher, *Moral Responsibility*, p. 89.

64. James Ridgeway, "One Million Abortions," *The New Republic*, February 9, 1963. Within this quotation [a] is cited as Calderone, *Western Journal of Surgery, Obstetrics and Gynecology*, March–April, 1964.

65. Shinn, pp. 131–132.

66. Shinn, p. 131.

67. Fletcher, *Moral Responsibility*, p. 88.

68. Kirkendall, "Searching for the Roots of Moral Judgments," postscript.

69. Shinn, p. 130.

70. "Sex and the College Student," Report 60, New York Group for the Advancement of Psychiatry, 1965, p. 40, as cited by Max Levin, "Sex Education and the Physician," *New York State Journal of Medicine*, Vol. 68, No. 13, July 1, 1968.

71. Lester A. Kirkendall, "Sex and Social Policy," *Clinical Pediatrics*, Vol. 3, No. 236 (1964), as cited by Levin, "Sex Education and the Physician."

72. Warren R. Johnson, *Human Sex and Sex Education: Perspectives and Problems* (Philadelphia: Lea & Febiger, 1963), p. 197, as cited by Levin, "Sex Education and the Physician."

73. Dorothy D. Bromley and Florence Britten, as cited by Ira L. Reiss, *The Social Context of Premarital Sexual Permissiveness* (New York: Holt, Rinehard and Winston, 1967), p. 15.

74. Shinn, p. 130.

75. Neill, p. 216.

76. Dietrich, p. 150.

77. Dietrich, p. 129.

78. Havelock Ellis, *Studies in the Psychology of Sex*, in de la Mare, *Love*, pp. 430–431.

79. Fletcher, *Moral Responsibility*, pp. 89–90.

80. Fletcher, p. 90.

81. Fletcher, p. 90.

82. Fletcher, p. 91.

83. E. M. Forster, "Tolerance," *Two Cheers for Democracy* (New York: Harcourt Brace Jovanovich, 1951), p. 45.

84. Shinn, pp. 139–140.

85. Philip Roth, *Portnoy's Complaint* (New York: Random House, 1969), pp. 102–103.

86. Duvall, p. 300.

87. Geoffrey Chaucer, "The Wife of Bath's Tale," *The Canterbury Tales*, lines 1258–1264.

88. Neill, p. 217.

"YOU–I"

1. Attributed to Francis Bacon.
2. Archibald MacLeish, "The Rape of the Swan," in *Actfive and Other Poems,* (New York: Random House, 1948).
3. Edna St. Vincent Millay, "Sonnet XL," *Collected Sonnets* (New York: Harper & Row, 1941), p. 40.
4. William Whitehead, "The Je Ne Sais Quoi," in *Sound and Sense,* Laurence Perrine, ed. (New York: Harcourt Brace Jovanovich, 1963), p. 172.
5. Elizabeth Barrett Browning, "Sonnet XIV," *Sonnets from the Portuguese,* in *The Complete Poetical Works of Elizabeth Barrett Browning* (Boston: Houghton Mifflin, 1900), p. 217.
6. Anon., "Love Not Me for Comely Grace," included by John Wilbye in *Second Set of Madrigals,* 1608.
7. Donald Hall, "Conduct and Work," in *Exiles and Marriages* (New York: Viking, 1955), p. 9.
8. Theodore Spencer, "Escapist's Song," *The Paradox in the Circle* (Norfolk, Conn.: New Directions, 1941), p. 1.
9. Eisenberg, p. 16.
10. Duvall, pp. 318–319.
11. Bernard, pp. 54–55.
12. Southard, *Sex Before 20* (New York: Dutton, 1967), p. 26.
13. Dietrich, p. 103.
14. Bernard, p. 20.
15. Southard, p. 26.
16. Bernard, pp. 194–195.
17. Aldous Huxley, "Fashions in Love," from *Do What You Will* in *Aldous Huxley's Stories, Essays and Poems* (London: J. M. Dent, 1966), p. 295.
18. Alexander Lowen, *Love and Orgasm* (New York: Macmillan, 1967), pp. 13–15, 26.
19. Lawrence Q. Crawley, James L. Malfetti, *et al., Reproduction, Sex, and Preparation for Marriage* (Englewood Cliffs, N.J.: Prentice-Hall, 1964), p. 141.
20. James Jones, *From Here to Eternity* (New York: Scribner's, 1951), p. 95.
21. Southard, *Sex Before 20,* p. 102.
22. Lowen, p. 15.
23. Cited by Crawley, Malfetti, *et al.,* p. 157.
24. Fletcher, *Moral Responsibility,* p. 91.
25. Bernard, p. 305.
26. Montaigne, p. 106.
27. Bernard, p. 88.
28. Bernard, p. 306.
29. Bernard, p. 195.
30. Bernard, p. 194.

"WE"

1. E. E. Cummings, "because it's," *73 Poems* (New York: Harcourt Brace Jovanovich, 1963), p. 10.
2. Erikson, p. 219.
3. Ashley Montagu, "The Pill, The Sexual Revolution, and the Schools," *Phi Delta Kappan* (May 1968), Vol. XLIX, no. 9. p. 484.

4. Dietrich, p. 146.

5. Antoine de St. Exupéry, *The Little Prince (Le Petit Prince)*, Katherine Woods, tr. (New York: Reynal & Hitchcock, 1943), p. 67.

6. Johann, p. 404.

7. Johann, p. 404.

"NIGHT-LIGHTS"

1. John Galsworthy, "Faith of A Novelist," *Candelabra: Selected Essays and Addresses* (New York: Scribner's, 1933), pp. 241–242.

Name Index*

*Italicized numbers indicate the selection itself or quoted passages by the author; all other page references indicate a discussion reference.

Subject Index

Information about sex, sources of, 132, 133–136, 140, 179–182, 548–555
See also Attitudes, sexual
Intercourse, sexual (*see* Sex)
I-orientation, dangers of prolonged, 4, 76–78
  as natural growth stage, 3–76, 86–88, 111–130, 363–369, 372–374, 375–377, 378–391

Jealousy, 241–242, 243
See also Exclusiveness; Possessiveness

Love, 149–150, 226, 230, 244–246, 506, 518, 526, 575–576, 583–586, 587, 588–589
  as an act of will, 250–251, 252–264, 525
  as an art, 246–248
  as bestowal of value, 217–229
  as charity, 539
  as paradox and mystery, 266–267
  as related to sex, 79, 191–193, 194–203, 205–214, 220–229, 252–264, 268–270, 290, 482–484, 485–486, 487–491, 497–498, 514, 517, 518–519, 520, 544, 547, 573–574, 579–580, 590–591
  sources of failure in,
    from fear, 224–225, 229
    from misconceptions about, 246–248, 250–251
    from secrecy, 492–494, 496–497
  tests of, 42–43
  See also Falling in love
Lovers, "vicious" and "virtuous," 306–307
Lust (*see* Sensuality)

Marital relationships (*see* Marriage; Sex)
Marriage, 144–145, 341–356, 409–410, 428–433, 487–491, 492–494, 517, 544, 565–571, 571–572
  choice of partner in, 342–343, 411
  as an "emotion, not a state," 355
  and Eros, 210–214
  friction and failure in, 251, 354, 492–494
  as "politics of love," 343–344
  resistance to, 67, 342, 564
  strategy of love in, 349–352
  "web of bonds" in, 346–348
Masculinity (*see* Sexuality, male)

Mass media as sexual purveyors, 186–190, 208, 269
Masturbation, 33, 34–35, 36–37, 57, 118, 173, 190, 271
Menstruation, 26
Moral absolutism, 276, 302–303, 330
  See also Morality
Moral relativism, 275, 276–277, 293, 295–303, 306–307
  See also Morality; Situation ethics
Morality, 273–340
  and censorship, 179–182, 183–185
  changing concepts of, 190, 268–269, 279–280
  discrepancy between theory and practice in, 273
  fear ethic and love ethic in, 62, 222, 275–276, 278, 295–303, 304
  Puritan, 304, 334–339
  students' queries about, 340
  See also Attitudes, sexual; Chastity; Moral absolutism; Moral relativism; Values, sexual
Mutualism (*see* Symbiosis)
Mutuality, 270, 507–508, 515, 516, 520, 525, 589
  conditions in sexual, 333
  as "interacting oneness," 225–229
  as secret of love, 504–505
  See also We-orientation

Nocturnal emission, 38, 45–46
  See also Ejaculation; Orgasm

Orgasm, 202, 271, 290, 417–418, 421–422, 484, 521–522
  See also Ejaculation; Sex

Parents, children's drawings of, 10–11
  and conflicts with youth, 133–139, 140
  as sex educators, 140
  See also Attitudes, sexual
Petting (*see* Arousal)
Philandering, 486–487, 564
  defined, 374
  See also Flirtation; Promiscuity; Sexuality, adolescent
Possessiveness, 13–21, 257, 259, 536–538, 543–544, 591
  See also Exclusiveness; Symbiosis
Premarital relationships (*see* Sex)
Promiscuity, 78, 532, 556, 579

Symbiosis,
  biological, 254–255
  psychic, 254–255, 536–538, 565–571
  See also Possessiveness

Tenderness and affection, 94–99, 100,
    197–199, 251, 261, 437
  See also We-orientation
"Thrill," 86–92, 363–369, 393
  See also Arousal

Values, sexual, search for, 147–148
  and sex controls, 79
  and virtue, 148
  See also Attitudes, sexual; Love, as
    related to sex; Morality

Venereal disease, treatments for, 278
Virginity (*see* Chastity)
Virility (*see* Sexuality, male)
Vocabulary, sexual, and connotations,
    27–28, 34–35, 286–291

We-orientation, 42–43, 501–527
  as discovery of the "we" of "me," 504,
    526–527
  in Magoun's definition of love, 267
  See also Autonomy; Love, as related to
    sex; Mutuality; Sacrifice; Self-
    realization; Sexuality, mature;
    Tenderness
"Wet dream" (*see* Nocturnal emission)